WOMEN &
CHRISTIAN
ORIGINS

WOMEN & CHRISTIAN ORIGINS

Editors

ROSS SHEPARD KRAEMER

MARY ROSE D'ANGELO

New York ● Oxford

Oxford University Press

1999

Oxford University Press

Oxford   New York
Athens   Auckland   Bangkok   Bogotá   Buenos Aires   Calcutta
Cape Town   Chennai   Dar es Salaam   Delhi   Florence   Hong Kong   Istanbul
Karachi   Kuala Lumpur   Madrid   Melbourne   Mexico City   Mumbai
Nairobi   Paris   São Paulo   Singapore   Taipei   Tokyo   Toronto   Warsaw

and associatd companies in
Berlin   Ibadan

Copyright © 1999 by Oxford University Press, Inc.

Published by Oxford University Press, Inc.
198 Madison Avenue, New York, New York 10016

Library of Congress Cataloging-in-Publication Data
Women and Christian origins : a reader / Ross Shepard Kraemer, Mary
Rose D'Angelo, editors.
p.   cm.
Includes bibliographical references and indexes.
ISBN 0-19-510395-5; ISBN 0-19-510396-3 (pbk.)
1. Women in Christianity—History—Early church, ca. 30–600.
2. Christianity—Origin.   I. Kraemer, Ross Shepard, 1948–
II. D'Angelo, Mary Rose.
BR195.W6W63   1999
270.1′082—dc21   98-5780

1 3 5 7 9 8 6 4 2

Printed in the United States of America
on acid-free paper

the editors and authors
dedicate these essays
to our students

CONTENTS

ABOUT THE CONTRIBUTORS

FRANCINE CARDMAN is Associate Professor of Historical Theology at Weston Jesuit School of Theology in Cambridge, MA. She has written about women and Christianity in late antiquity and translated Augustine's commentary on the Sermon on the Mount in *The Preaching of Augustine* (Fortress, 1973).

ELIZABETH CASTELLI is Assistant Professor of Religion at Barnard College. Her current work is on martyrdom and collective memory among early Christians. She is the author of *Imitating Paul: A Discourse of Power* (Westminster/John Knox, 1991), co-author of *The Postmodern Bible* (Yale University Press, 1995) as a member of the Bible and Culture Collective, and co-editor with Hal Taussig of *Reimagining Christian Origins* (Trinity Press International, 1996). In addition, she has published numerous articles on feminist interpretation of early Christian literature, martyrdom, and asceticism.

CO-EDITOR MARY ROSE D'ANGELO is Associate Professor in the Department of Theology at the University of Notre Dame and formerly Director of the Gender Studies Program. She is the author of numerous articles on women in the origins of Christianity and is currently working on a book on imperial family values, the divine title "father," and early Christian sexual politics.

JUDITH HALLETT is Professor and Chair of Classics at the University of Maryland, College Park, and has published widely in the areas of Latin literature and Roman culture, with a special emphasis on women, sexuality, and the family in Rome of the classical era. Her publications include *Fathers and Daughters in Roman*

Society: Women and the Elite Family (Princeton University Press, 1984), and two co-edited volumes, *Compromising Traditions: the Personal Voice in Classical Scholarship* (Routledge, 1997) and *Roman Sexualities* (Princeton University Press, 1998).

CO-EDITOR ROSS S. KRAEMER is an adjunct faculty member in the department of Religious Studies at the University of Pennsylvania. She is the editor of *Maenads, Martyrs, Matrons, Monastics: A Sourcebook on Women's Religions in the Greco-Roman World* (Fortress Press, 1988) and the author of *Her Share of the Blessings: Women's Religions Among Pagans, Jews and Christians in the Greco-Roman World* (Oxford University Press, 1992) and *When Aseneth Met Joseph: A Late Antique Tale of the Biblical Patriarch and His Egyptian Wife, Revisited* (Oxford University Press, 1998). She is New Testament editor for *Women in Scripture: A Dictionary of Named and Unnamed Women in the Hebrew Bible, Apocryphal/Deuterocanonical Books and New Testament* forthcoming from Houghton Mifflin, and working on a new edition of *Maenads*, to be published by Oxford.

AMY-JILL LEVINE is E. Rhodes and Leona B. Carpenter Professor of New Testament Studies at Vanderbilt University Divinity School and director of the Carpenter Program in Religion, Gender, and Sexuality. Author and editor of several works on formative Judaism, Christian origins, and the "historical Jesus," she is presently completing a volume on representations of women in the Old Testament Apocrypha for Harvard University Press, and is editing, for Sheffield University Press, ten volumes of essays addressing feminist interpretations of early Christian texts.

LYNN LiDONNICI is Assistant Professor of Religion at Vassar College, and the author of *The Epidaurian Miracle Inscriptions: Text, Translation and Commentary* (Scholars Press, 1995).

MARGARET McDONALD is a professor in the Department of Religious Studies, St. Francis Xavier University, Antigonish, Nova Scotia, Canada. Her previous publications include two books: *The Pauline Churches: A Socio-Historical Study of Institutionalization in the Pauline and Deutero-Pauline Writings* (Cambridge University Press, 1988) and *Early Christian Women and Pagan Opinion: The Power of the Hysterical Woman* (Cambridge University Press, 1996).

ANNE McGUIRE is Associate Professor of Religion at Haverford College. She has published several articles on gnostic texts and recently co-edited *The Nag Hammadi Library After Fifty Years* (E. J. Brill, 1997). She is presently working on *Engendering Gnosis*, a study of gnosis and gender imagery in selected Nag Hammadi texts.

GAIL CORRINGTON STREETE is Associate Professor of Religious Studies and chair of the Women's Studies program at Rhodes College, Memphis, TN. She is the author of a number of articles and three books on religion in antiquity and early Christianity. Her latest book is *The Strange Woman: Power and Sex in the Bible* (Westminster/John Knox, 1998).

WOMEN &
CHRISTIAN
ORIGINS

INTRODUCTION

The last twenty years has seen an extraordinary flowering of exciting studies on women, gender, and religion in formative Western antiquity. Yet standard introductions to the New Testament and the origins of Christianity rarely integrate this compelling research. To date, no one has written a comprehensive treatment of women and Christian origins appropriate for a wide audience ranging from undergraduates to general readers to scholars previously unacquainted with this literature. In commissioning the chapters in this volume, we hoped to assemble an anthology that could both serve as a companion to existing textbooks and handbooks and stand on its own as an introduction to the study of women and Christian origins.

Although these chapters represent the diverse stances and scholarship of their authors, all have in common a commitment to the significance of integrating the study of women into the study of Christian origins, as well as a commitment to the importance of recognizing the centrality of ideas about gender in understanding ancient culture and religion. The abundance of recent discussions of "gender" and "sex" by theorists (whether steeped in antiquity or not) suggests that we are far from a sufficient, let alone complete, analysis of the categories and phenomena to which these terms may refer. Nevertheless, the authors of these chapters share the conviction that masculinity and femininity as categories are socially constructed and performative, and that in antiquity, as in modernity, the meanings of these categories and the values attached to them are cultural products and not "given" in any inherent biological nature.

Equally important, all the authors of these chapters agree on the utility of feminist approaches and critique, although as individuals, they may differ in selecting and describing the feminist views they espouse. Throughout the chapters, "androcentrism" refers to language and perspectives that place males at the center of description or analysis. The term "patriarchy" refers not simply to male dominance, but to a social system in which a limited number of privileged males ("fathers") have power over women, children, and less-privileged males (slaves, freedmen, clients, unemancipated sons). All the subjects of the system, both women and men, take their status from their relationship to a "patriarch." The imperial period retained ideological commitment to the ancient ideal of *patria potestas*, the authority of the father over the persons and property in his power, even when such power had been radically curtailed by state authority.

Central to both the chapters and the organization of the book is our belief that questions about early Christian women must be situated within the cultural context of the ancient Mediterranean under Roman domination, a largely Greek-speaking Roman imperial world. We conceive this issue as the evocation of context, not the description of a "background." The actors in early Christianity do not emerge from "Judaism," "Hellenism," or "the Roman empire" to play roles on a Christian stage. Nor should Judaism (or the larger Greco-Roman culture) be assumed to recede into nothing more than a backdrop for a Christian drama. On the one hand, the writers of the Christian texts and the players in these early communities are incomprehensible apart from the cultural assumptions within which they operate. Most conspicuously, these ancient texts are deeply engaged with Jewish scripture and often with relations with contemporary Jews. They are articulated through Greek language and literary and moral categories, and they struggle with and respond to Roman imperial political interests. On the other hand, early Christianity cannot be seen to be the end of Judaism or of Greco-Roman culture, either as their goal or as their termination. Indeed, the same centuries in which early Christianity originated also provide beginning points in the long and complex history of what may be called, for the sake of convenience, "rabbinic" Judaism. Alan Segal's description of Judaism and Christianity as sibling traditions is apt. Approaching this era of Jewish history through the Christian texts inevitably distorts it, not only because of the polemical character of these texts, but also because it tends to obscure the rich development of subsequent Judaism.

The contributions to this volume share certain fundamental assumptions about the study of the New Testament and Christian origins that may be familiar only to readers already acquainted with contemporary critical approaches to early Christianity. All presume that early Christian gospels, whether included in the canon of the New Testament or not, reflect the intentional activity of ancient authors and ancient transmitters of traditions about Jesus and about those who made up the early communities of his followers. All recognize that the fundamental character of these traditions is theological, which means, among other things, that their primary concern is to interpret Jesus called Christ to diverse communities of followers, and they are only incidentally at best interested in what we might understand as "history." All acknowledge that a significant portion of these traditions is unlikely to be historically reliable.

All are in accord that the process by which some, but by no means all, early Christian writings acquired authoritative status and came to be known collectively as the "New Testament" takes place no earlier than the second century CE and is not complete until the fourth century CE at the earliest. Canonical distinctions have little significance for the study of women in early Christian communities: both the study of women and the study of gender require consideration of the broad range of early Christian writings. However, because courses on the origins of Christianity concentrate, often disproportionately, on the writings of the New Testament, chapters in sections 2 and 3 focus particularly on those sources.

Indeed, the process of canonization itself requires feminist scrutiny. Works that authorize the subordination of women to men, such as 1 and 2 Timothy and Titus, ultimately became authoritative and canonical, while works such as the *Acts of (Paul and) Thecla*, which authorize women to teach and lead autonomous lives of Christian piety, were excluded from the canon. Gospels that represent Mary (probably Magdalene) as a principal apostle and recipient of divine revelation and wisdom are excluded from the canon, while gospels that count only males among "the twelve" and minimize the role of Mary Magdalene become authoritative Scripture.

The chapters (especially those by Kraemer, D'Angelo, and Levine) that treat the "synoptic" gospels of Mark, Matthew, and Luke (called synoptic because, when "seen together," it is apparent that strong literary relationships exist between the three) share the prevailing scholarly consensus that the Gospel of Mark was composed prior to both the Gospel of Matthew and the Gospel of Luke, and that the authors of those gospels both knew a form of the Gospel of Mark, though probably not each other. These essays also proceed on the hypothesis that the material common to Matthew and Luke, but lacking in Mark, probably came from a source no longer extant and commonly designated by scholars as "Q" (from the German *Quelle*, meaning source). They also hold to the prevailing scholarly consensus that, despite the identification of these gospels with individual men, we have no reliable historical information about the actual authors of the gospels, whose true identities (including perhaps gender) remain anonymous.

The chapters (by Castelli, MacDonald, Streete, and Cardman) that treat epistles bearing the names of Jesus' early followers, including the self-designated "apostle" Paul, share another prevailing scholarly consensus that not all works written in the name of a particular person may in fact be the work of that individual. The practice of writing in the name of another person often strikes modern readers as deceptive and difficult to accept for authoritative religious texts. Yet ancient works in the name of someone other than the physical author were not necessarily deliberate acts of deceit—on the contrary, the authors of everything from apocalypses and testaments in the names of biblical patriarchs to letters in the names of Paul, Peter, and James may have understood themselves to be divinely authorized agents for persons not available to write in their own names. The issue of "pseudepigraphy" (writings falsely attributed) is a complex one for the study of early Christianity, but it is central to the interpretation of the body of literature claiming the authority of Paul, literature that plays a critical role in ancient Christian debates about the roles and authority of women in early Christian communities.

Further, the contributors to this volume agree that the followers of Jesus of Nazareth, both during his lifetime and subsequently, were diverse not only in terms of their own identities, but also in their beliefs and practices. Early Christian writings manifest multiple and competing views about a range of major issues, from the nature and identity of Jesus Christ, to the form of the resurrection, to ideas about the origins, meaning, and significance of gender and ideas about the appropriate roles for women and men within early Christian communities. In general, the authors refuse to privilege some of these views as normative and "orthodox" (literally, "right-thinking"), while relegating others to the category of deviant, derivative, or "heretical," preferring instead to locate the diversity of early Christian teachings and practices within the complex cultural diversities of various early Christian churches. This more neutral stance on the diversity of early Christianity is particularly important for a volume dedicated to the study of women and Christian origins since, on the one hand, many Christian writers (all male) from the second century on associated "heresy" with women and women with "heresy," while some contemporary Christian feminists (largely, but not exclusively, female) have argued that pristine Christianity was essentially egalitarian, and that Christian hierarchies of gender are secondary (and therefore "heretical").

The organization of the book reflects our original desire to design an anthology that would work well in the kinds of introductory courses we and many of our colleagues regularly teach. The essays are grouped into four divisions, one that focuses on the context(s) in which Christianity emerged, one devoted to Jesus and gospel traditions, one devoted to Paul and the Pauline trajectory, and one that focuses on women and gender in Christian communities through the fourth and even early fifth centuries CE. The first section, "Creating the Context(s)," endeavors to set the study of women and Christian origins within the realities of life under the aegis of the Roman empire. Judith Hallett's chapter, "Women's Lives in the Ancient Mediterranean," surveys a broad range of evidence for women from diverse social and ethnic backgrounds who lived in various regions under Roman domination. She pays particular attention to Roman understandings of gender difference, as well as of gender similarity, laying the groundwork for a fuller understanding of subsequent Christian thought and practice. We chose to begin with this chapter because the vast majority of followers of Jesus, beginning with many of Paul's coworkers, were born and raised in the culture Hallett so richly evokes. Even those persons and communities who saw themselves as separate in many ways from Roman culture (including many Jews) were profoundly affected by the dominant culture in which they lived.

Since it is also true that whatever his stance toward Roman culture, Jesus of Nazareth was a Jew who preached the imminent advent of God's reign to his fellow Jews, the next two chapters, by Ross S. Kraemer, focus specifically on what we know about Jewish women in the first century, particularly in the land of Israel. "Jewish Women and Christian Origins: Some Caveats" warns readers that the study of ancient Jewish women primarily from the vantage point of Christian origins risks not only serious historical distortion, but also the real possibility of furthering Christian anti-Judaism. Kraemer scrutinizes both the methods and the motives of those writers who cast the conditions of Jewish women's lives in the first century CE in the worst possible light in order to portray Jesus and the earliest Christian communities as radically egalitarian. Kraemer shows that, ironically, Jesus' behavior toward women as portrayed in the gospels is actually generally consistent with precisely the rabbinic norms from which he is said to have deviated so radically. In her second essay, intended to be read together with the first, Kraemer surveys the evidence for "Jewish Women and Women's Judaism(s) at the Beginning of Christianity." She concludes that, in many respects, the lives of Jewish women were similar to those of non-Jewish women and were deeply affected by factors of birth, class, demographics, geography, and even diet. She also argues that, while gender may have qualified the ways in which Jewish women and Jewish men responded to encounters with Jesus or with his teachings, on the whole, many of the reasons why Jews in the first century were or were not drawn to the Reign of God movement had little to do with gender difference.

The final chapter of this section returns the focus of our attention to the religious lives of women often designated as "pagan," a term Hallett's chapter has already explicated. In "Women's Religion and Religious Lives in the Greco-Roman City," Lynn R. LiDonnici provides us a detailed and sympathetic representation of the wide range of women's religious lives, both civic and domestic, in the ancient cities of the early Roman empire. From her descriptions, we learn not only the context from which many women came to Christianity, but also the religious possibilities they left to do so, including the worship of goddesses focused on women's lives and concerns. Her work enables us to envision the consequences of all this for developing forms of Christianity, including conflicts over women's cultic leadership and over feminine representations of the divine.

The four chapters of the second section, "Women, Jesus, and Gospels," explore both the dilemmas and the fruits of feminist efforts to use early Christian narratives of the life and teachings of Jesus (that is, gospels) to reconstruct both the presence of women among Jesus' early followers and Jesus' own stance(s) on women and on gender. The first two chapters focus on questions of what lies behind the canonical texts. In "Researching 'Real' Women from the Gospels: The Case of Mary Magdalene," Mary Rose D'Angelo assembles and examines the earliest references to this famous woman. Beginning from Mary's focal role in the *Gospel of Mary*, discovered in Egypt in the late nineteenth century, D'Angelo works through the references to Mary as disciple and witness to the resurrection, dissecting those representations of Mary to explore both this figure's function in the texts and the problems inherent in attempting to recover a historical Mary.

Amy-Jill Levine's chapter, "Women in the Q Communit(ies) and Traditions," focuses more narrowly on these issues in the hypothetical lost sayings source Q.

Viewed by many scholars as among the earliest layers of Jesus traditions available in the gospels, the sayings attributed to Jesus in Q have recently been subjected to intensified scrutiny by feminist scholars seeking to demonstrate the radical egalitarian nature of the earliest Jesus community. While not ruling out the possibility that the community that compiled and revered the sayings in Q began as "a nonhierarchical community in which 'male' and 'female' were equivalent, if not irrelevant categories," Levine demonstrates that even the Q material utilizes androcentric language and cautions that such language, together with Q's use of "images that enforce traditional gender roles for women, and the dismantling and dismissing of the biological family may not spell good news for women outside or even inside the Q group."

The canonical gospels are treated in a pair of chapters by D'Angelo. "(Re)Presentations of Women in the Gospels: John and Mark" delineates the depictions of women in these two relatively independent narratives, inquiring how far these pictures can be assumed to reflect the participation of women in the communities behind the gospels. In "(Re)Presentations of Women in the Gospel of Matthew and Luke-Acts," D'Angelo describes the ways each of these texts combines, revises, and recasts both images of women and gender assumptions from Mark and Q to accommodate and reinforce new social and political contexts.

With the third section, "Mining the Pauline Tradition," we focus on the writings in the name of the self-designated apostle Paul, from those letters he is most likely to have composed himself (Romans, 1 and 2 Corinthians, Galatians, Philippians, 1 Thessalonians, and Philemon), to letters and narratives almost certainly composed by others invoking his name or his authority (including 1 and 2 Timothy, Titus, and the *Acts of [Paul and] Thecla*). In "Reading Real Women through the Undisputed Letters of Paul," Margaret Y. MacDonald analyzes this corpus of seven letters as evidence for those real women Paul encountered in the new churches of the mid–first century and who participated in missionary activity, primarily among non-Jews.

In the middle chapter of this section, Elizabeth A. Castelli excavates the undisputed letters as evidence for Paul's complex views about women and about the significance of gender difference in the community of Christ Jesus. "Paul on Women and Gender" illuminates the tension in Paul's writing and thought between his view of gender difference as inherent in the created order (and therefore immutable) and his belief that the death and resurrection of Jesus inaugurated the dissolution of that divinely given order.

Finally, in "Re-Reading Paul: Early Interpreters of Paul on Women and Gender," Margaret Y. MacDonald surveys early Christian works from the Pastoral Epistles (1 and 2 Timothy and Titus) to the canonical Acts of the Apostles (written by the author of the Gospel according to Luke) to the noncanonical *Acts of (Paul and) Thecla*. MacDonald's chapter demonstrates the needs of Paul's subsequent readers to respond to the tensions inherent in his thought and to the many practical implications of his pronouncements for the lives of later Christian communities.

Three final chapters, grouped under the rubric "Gender, Authority, and Redemption in Early Christian Churches," constitute an attempt to trace the diversity of Christian thought and practice in the areas of gender difference, women's religious leadership and authority, and the use and significance of feminine language for the divine in diverse Christian communities through the fourth century CE. Anne McGuire draws on her many years of reading gnostic Christian texts found near Nag Hammadi, Egypt, to offer lucid interpretations of several important texts that use extensive feminine imagery for the divine. Cautioning that not all of this imagery is positive, McGuire considers the possible relationships between the flourishing of such imagery and the reports of ancient Christian anti-gnostic writers that women held leadership positions in gnostic communities, and that such communities engaged in rituals and practices that undercut gender difference.

In "Women, Ministry and Church Order in Early Christianity," Francine Cardman surveys the evidence for women's leadership, from Paul's recognition of numerous women as his "coworkers" in the mid–first century to vehement responses to women apparently ordained as priests as late as the fifth century CE. Cardman chronicles some of the vigorous debates generated by women's leadership and the increasing resistance women leaders encountered. Drawing on literary references, early Christian council canons, archaeology, and early Christian art, she illuminates women's roles as leaders of house-churches, missionaries, and teachers; as holders of the offices of deacon, deaconess, and probably presbyter (that is, priest); and as members of the orders of widows and virgins.

In the final chapter of the collection, Gail Corrington Streete takes up the subject "Women as Sources of Redemption and Knowledge in Early Christian Tradition." Her work revisits material now familiar from previous chapters, including the worship of goddesses such as Demeter and Isis, women's leadership in early Christian churches, and the prominence of female imagery for the divine in gnostic texts. Streete, however, reads these sources from a slightly different vantage point, considering the ways in which female figures, both human and divine, serve as the means by which others attain redemption, salvation, and/or the crucial knowledge that leads humans to the right relationship with the divine. In focusing on these female figures, Streete illuminates a neglected, rich, and problematic strand within the religious life of the ancient world of which Christianity in its many forms was also a participant.

Feminists who pioneered work in the field of women and Christian origins almost three decades ago were often discouraged from doing so by male teachers and colleagues who insisted that the ancient sources themselves were inhospitable to such inquiry. There was not, they insisted, enough evidence. As the wealth of research in these last three decades has demonstrated, this is simply untrue. Ironically, then, a volume such as this cannot be comprehensive, any more than an introductory course on the study of the New Testament and Christian origins can comprehensively survey early Christian sources. Interested readers will find many useful references for further reading in the bibliography at the conclusion of the book.

The nature of an anthology is such that a complete list of all those persons to whom we are collectively grateful and indebted is far too long. The editors are particularly appreciative of the work of our sister contributors, who labored long and hard to write and hone these pieces. Cynthia Thompson provided the initial stimulus for the book, too long ago. Our editor at Oxford, Cynthia Read, and her assistant, Gene Romanosky, gave us valuable guidance at various stages in the process of producing this book. Deborah Prince compiled the collective bibliography from the citations in the individual essays. Susan Myers compiled the Index of Names.

Philadelphia, Pennsylvania   R. S. K.
Notre Dame, Indiana   M. R. D.
October 1998

I

Creating

the Context(s)

1

⊱—⊹⊱—O—⊰⊹—⊰

WOMEN'S LIVES IN
THE ANCIENT MEDITERRANEAN

Judith P. Hallett

Pagans and Christians

When referring to the Greeks and Romans of the first century BCE through the second and third centuries CE who did not follow the teachings of Jesus Christ, we frequently speak of them as "pagans." The term *pagan* has several meanings, a variety of connotations, and an intriguing history. In the most recent edition of the *American Heritage Dictionary*, the noun pagan is defined as "one who is not a Christian, Moslem, or Jew; a heathen." It is also defined as "a hedonist," that is, "one who pursues or is devoted to pleasure, especially the pleasures of the senses." Other, unabridged dictionaries—such as *Webster's New International*—expand on these brief definitions. They further describe a pagan as "a follower of an ancient polytheistic religion (as in ancient Rome)." So, too, they link paganism with "frank delight in and uninhibited seeking after sensual pleasures and material goods" and with the "joyous outlook of the ancient Greeks." In so doing, they emphasize the association of pagan beliefs with classical antiquity, multiple gods, extravagant pleasure-seeking, and a cheerful approach to life. These dictionaries do not, however, differentiate male from female pagans: a key, albeit implicit, aspect of the category pagan is its equal applicability to both genders.

As these dictionaries also state, the Latin adjective *paganus*, from which we get our word pagan, derives from the noun *pagus*, meaning "country district or community." Such reference works indicate as well that the ancient Romans themselves at times employed the term *paganus* (pagan) to denote a country dweller, a person of civilian status as opposed to a soldier. While *paganus* in this more technical sense can only refer to a male inhabitant of the countryside, several ancient Roman sources use the word *paganus* in a more inclusive fashion when portraying country dwellers as a group happily engaged in worshipping divinities of either gender.

Writing in the late first century BCE, the Latin poet Propertius depicts the Parilia—an annual shepherds' festival that honored a deity of uncertain gender named Pales and marked the birth of Rome—in the days when it was first celebrated. At 4.4.73 ff., Propertius characterizes this occasion as a time when the platters of the country folk (*pagana fercula*) were soaked with rich foods and members of the drunken crowd leaped over burning clusters of hay. A few decades later, at *Fasti* 1.657 ff., the Latin poet Ovid describes another ancient agricultural holiday honoring the goddesses Tellus and Ceres as "the mothers of the crops." In this context, he exhorts the country district (*pagus*) to celebrate the festival, and the farmers themselves to purify the country district and give yearly cake offerings on the country district's (*paganis*) hearths.

By Propertius' and Ovid's day, Rome had conquered the Greek world and enthusiastically embraced Greek culture. Consequently, both the capital city and the vast empire it controlled had acquired a distinctive dual Greco-Roman cultural ambiance. Among the Greek religious traditions that held a strong attraction for the Romans was the practice of engaging in noisy, unrestrained, even intoxicated and sexually provocative, behavior to worship various divinities. Such conduct loomed large in the cults of Dionysos (also known as Bacchus and as Liber to the Romans), god of wine and the irrational; of Demeter (whom the Romans called Ceres), goddess of the crops; and of Cybele, the Great Mother. Yet, we need not search for Greek influences to explain a number of time-honored Roman rituals that Ovid represents as routinely celebrated by the urban, cosmopolitan Romans of his own day, rituals striking for their exuberant exaltation of sensual and sexual delights. These rituals, in which women often played a conspicuous part in worship and in which female divinities were conspicuously worshipped, appear to have roots in Rome's own rustic beginnings. They were, therefore, pagan in their ancient genesis, as well as by our modern definition.

For example, at *Fasti* 3.523 ff., Ovid reports that on the Ides, the fifteenth, of March, the common people of Rome celebrated the feast of a goddess named Anna Perenna. The goddess' name, feminine in grammatical gender, seems to be related to the Latin masculine noun *annus* (year) and the adjective *perennis* (perpetual): it therefore means a female embodiment of "the year which lasts without end." This celebration has been called an "uninhibited day-out in the country for an urban population" by a noted scholar of Roman history and religion, the late H. H. Scullard. And it is thought to reveal its rustic origins by featuring rowdy drinking, boisterous dance, and bawdy song on the banks of the Tiber, as well as the chanting of ribald verses by girls. At *Fasti* 5.183 ff., Ovid also ascribes features suggestive of countryside revelry to the Floralia. A six-day Roman festival held in late April and early May, it honored Flora, an old Italian goddess of flowers and vegetation. Ovid notes the "greater degree of licentiousness and jest" at the Floralia, depicting it as memorable for the wearing of

flowers by drinkers, dancers, and wooers of both genders; for its raunchy enter-
tainments; and for the prominent presence of prostitutes.

Propertius and Ovid resemble other ancient Roman sources of their era by
characterizing ancient Roman religious worship—a pagan phenomenon in both
ancient Roman and modern English senses of the word since most Roman cults
began as countryside celebrations—as joyfully and innocuously hedonistic and
polytheistic. In contrast, early Christian writers stress the intellectually troubling
and morally offensive aspects of paganism. Their aim is to compare pagan attitudes and practices unfavorably with those of Christian devotees, to problematize
if not demonize how pagans think and act. Indeed, Augustine specifically entitled his twenty-two-volume treatise in vindication of Christianity, which he
wrote from 413–427 CE, De Civitate Dei Contra Paganos (About the City of God Against
the Pagans). Augustine objects to much about earlier Greco-Roman religious worship, but finds various hedonistic and polytheistic assumptions and activities
especially objectionable because they are either inconsistent with other pagan
beliefs or shameful according to his moral standards. Furthermore, in singling
out several pagan assumptions and activities for derision, he not only accords
special attention to both female divinities and the life experiences of mortal
women, but also questions the pagan tendency to stress the shared activities and
similar qualities of both genders.

For example, at 7.2 ff., in ridiculing the Romans for their multiplicity of gods
and the trifling tasks assigned to each, Augustine lists some male and female
divinities (a few with Greek pedigrees, but for the most part of Roman extrac-
tion) the Romans connected with human reproductive functions. He cites the
god Janus, who offers access to the male seed; the god Saturn (Greek Cronus),
who bestows the seed itself; the god Liber, who liberates the male from the seed
he expels; the goddess Libera, identified with Venus (Greek Aphrodite), who
liberates the female from the seed she expels; the goddess Mena, who presides
over the menstrual flow along with her stepmother Juno Lucina (Greek Hera).
Augustine then faults the Romans for inconsistency in according all of these
divinities, except Mena, special, "select" status. What is more, he challenges the
low esteem assigned by the Romans to two obscure male deities, Vitumnus and
Sentinus, because the functions of these gods—bestowing, respectively, life (vita)
and feeling (sensus) on the fetus—matter more to him than the functions of those
deities who make pregnancy possible. In posing this challenge to Roman religious thinking, Augustine shifts away from the Romans' own focus on the participation by both sexes in the reproductive act and instead underscores the
importance that he himself accords to woman's unique role as childbearer. Without life and feeling, asks Augustine, what is the entire burden carried in a woman's womb but a most base substance, comparable to mud and dust?

Later, at 7.21, Augustine claims that the impure, pagan soul multiplied the
number of gods because of a belief that Saturn could not by himself do enough
for male seeds. In this connection, Augustine describes rites held in rural areas
of Italy for another god linked with male seed, Liber. Naming Varro, a learned
first century BCE Roman writer, as his authority, he relates that symbols of the
male member were publicly displayed at country crossroads and carried into the

city to appease Liber. As proof, he describes worship of Liber, which lasted for an entire month, in the town of Lavinium. During this period, Augustine maintains, everyone was expected to use the most shameful words until the image of the male organ was carried across the forum and allowed to rest in its own place; furthermore, Augustine states, the most honorable matron of the city was required to place a crown on this most dishonorable portion of the male anatomy. Augustine then emphasizes and strongly criticizes the behavior required of this woman. He asseverates that this disgraceful form of pagan worship forced a matron to do in public what not even a prostitute ought to have been allowed to do in the theater if matrons had been present.

At 7.23 ff., Augustine calls attention to the inconsistency in Varro's assertion that the earth is one goddess, Tellus. He does so by claiming that Varro assigns various functions related to the earth and its products to a number of other male and female divinities. Some of these gods with earthly associations are Greek in origin, others of native Roman provenance: Orcus (Greek Hades), god of the lower world; his wife, Proserpina (Greek Persephone), daughter of Ceres (Greek Demeter); Tellumo, the male counterpart of Tellus; Altor, connected with nourishment (Latin *alere*); and Rusor, so called because all things return again (Latin *rursus*) to the same place. In accounting for Varro's apparent, seemingly self-contradictory, desire to believe in a single earth goddess, Augustine evidently identifies Varro with the "impure pagan soul." To impugn Varro's reasoning even further, he then proceeds to offer a striking analogy for the mental activities of the pagan soul, a comparison that gratuitously demeans one group of women even as it ostensibly redeems them. Just as the most disgraceful women sometimes feel weariness and regret toward the throngs of lovers they have sought out by lust, says Augustine, so the pagan soul, once made disgraceful and prostituted to filthy spirits, sometimes gets the greatest pleasure out of multiplying gods for itself to worship in tainted prostration, yet sometimes also gets disgusted.

There are more discussions of this sort in Augustine's *City of God*, as well as in the writings of other early Christians who also harbored negative feelings about earlier Greek and Roman pagans; these discussions endeavor to prove Christian superiority to paganism generally and often do so through examples from the realm of religion that specifically portray pagan females, divine and mortal, in a less than attractive light. Such discussions have proved to be extremely influential on later Western thinking about the ancient Greeks and Romans. Most obviously, centuries of readers have been taught to accept these negative early Christian assessments of pagans, especially of pagan women, without questioning either the sources or their motives. Furthermore, such readers occupy a vantage point that fosters a trusting attitude toward these sources: the spread and success of Christianity since Augustine's time appear to validate the criticisms Augustine and other early Christian writers make about earlier, pagan, religious practices and attitudes in the ancient Mediterranean, especially in regard to the roles and behavior assigned to Greco-Roman women.

In addition, it is customary even for learned scholars who try to analyze Augustine's and other early Christian interpretations from an objective and de-

tached viewpoint to adopt the emphasis of early Christian writers on the differences between pagan ideas and later Christian notions. These scholars may reject
these unremittingly negative Christian assessments of pagan worship and women
as prejudiced and insufficiently informed. Still, they judge it crucial to contrast
Christian and pagan notions about what constitutes acceptable religious worship
and particularly to contrast Christian and pagan ideas about how to integrate
women into a symbolic system of religious and moral beliefs.

To be sure, some of these Christian-pagan differences are important and easy
to discern. Most obviously, the ancient Greeks, and the Romans who adopted
and adapted many aspects of earlier Greek culture, had not one deity, but many,
among them several female divinities. Various Greco-Roman gods, male and
female, were conceptualized to embody human sexual and sensual qualities.
These gods were worshipped by women and men of diverse backgrounds and
varied social strata through ritual activities that were at times of an uninhibited,
sensual, and even sexual nature. But by the same token, we must not forget that
this ancient Mediterranean pagan world ultimately became a Christian one. For
this reason, we should also reflect on what aspects of pagan Greco-Roman social
life and thought proved most compatible with later Christian attitudes and practices. We need to focus—as these pagan Greeks and Romans themselves so often
did—on similarities, as well as on differences.

Similarities and Differences

This discussion attempts to provide students of early Christianity with some
background information about women in the Greek and Roman world and to
enrich their understanding of the similarities, as well as the differences, between
Greco-Roman attitudes and practices and Christian attitudes and practices involving women. It surveys evidence about women from the geographical region
encompassed by the Roman empire of the first century BCE through the second
and third centuries CE. To place this evidence in a larger historical context,
though, it also examines some texts from earlier eras and those by Greek authors. The women whose images are constructed and whose lives are documented by this evidence represent a range of geographical and ethnic backgrounds, as well as social classes.

Like our introductory consideration of pagan religious practices and attitudes,
however, this discussion primarily draws on the literary testimony of elite Romans residing in the imperial capital city and primarily concerns itself, as they
do, with elite Roman women. It adopts such a focus for two reasons. First, the
evidence these elite sources provide on both the images and lives of women is
plentiful and more likely to be familiar to a general audience. Second, these
literary representations of women by elite Roman authors were used to powerful
effect, to reinforce, and often even to create, assumptions and expectations about
appropriate female behavior in lower social strata and throughout the region
covered by the empire.

But this evidence should not merely illuminate similarities and differences
between pagan and early Christian women and between attitudes toward women

in pagan and early Christian societies. Such evidence should establish, too, that there were important similarities, as well as differences, in the representations of women and men within ancient Greco-Roman society itself: similarities in the ways in which male and female divinities were conceptualized by what we have been calling pagan thinking and similarities in the constructions, the conceptualizations, of male and female gender roles by the ancient Greeks and Romans, especially the latter. Our discussion pays particular heed to these similarities.

This emphasis on these Greek and, particularly, Roman efforts to stress the "Sameness" of men and women—when imagining gods and when defining appropriate human behavior—needs some justification. For one thing, there are more differences than there are similarities in the ways in which male and female gender roles, divine and mortal, were ordinarily conceptualized in Greek, and even in Roman, society. In addition, more scholarly attention is ordinarily given to these differences than to these similarities. Most studies of Roman women during the late republic and early empire, for example, focus on female "Otherness," defining women as a group altogether different from and inferior to men and sharing similarities among themselves that transcend social class.

These differences between Roman males and females were most pronounced in the area of legal and political rights: women could not vote, hold public office, or serve in the Roman military. Unlike other ancient Mediterranean peoples such as the Carthaginians and Egyptians of North Africa, the Romans were never ruled—even in their mythic traditions—by a queen. Authors such as the early imperial historian Tacitus, moreover, recount various efforts to limit Roman women's political influence over the men of their own families. Only after a spirited senatorial debate in the 30s CE were women permitted to accompany husbands on tours abroad when the husbands were chosen to lead armies and govern provinces. While a Roman woman could inherit property in her own right, she needed to be represented by a legal guardian when dealing with and disposing of her material possessions: legislation by the emperor Augustus encouraged child production by exempting a freeborn woman who had given birth to three children (and a freedwoman who had given birth to four) from legal guardianship, but most women did not qualify for this distinction.

Nevertheless, the similarities between Greco-Roman notions of male and female gender roles, as ascribed to gods and as prescribed for humans, are all too often overlooked. What is more, these similarities need to be taken into serious account by those interested in early Christian traditions, which stress commonalities and seek equality between men and women. Such traditions, after all, coexist with the male supremacist tradition represented by Augustine, a powerful tradition that assumes that differences between the sexes are all important.

Recognition of some other kinds of differences must, however, both precede and follow any thinking about these similarities of male and female gender roles within Greco-Roman society itself. First, before speaking about the ancient Mediterranean, about what many would call the classical Greco-Roman world, it is important to acknowledge the diversity of ancient Greek and Roman societies and to realize that the hyphenated term *Greco-Roman society* itself can be extremely misleading. The academic study of ancient Greece all too often promotes the identification of one particular Greek city-state at one particular point in time—namely, Athens in the "classical" period of the fifth and fourth centuries BCE—with Greece as a whole. It is easy to account for the "Athenocentric" perspective taken by this traditional approach to ancient Greece. Abundant, and for the most part laudatory, evidence from and about Athens in this classical era survives. Such evidence takes forms accessible to nonspecialists, as well as to serious scholars. But viewing the accomplishments of this one, democratically governed, society as tantamount to study of the entire "glory that was Greece" entails neglecting, and even ignoring, both earlier and later periods and other places, amply documented societies with different, but effective, political organizations and different, but thriving, cultural environments.

Among these other Greek societies of different times and places and with different political organizations and cultural environments is the world of late Bronze Age civilization in the final centuries of the second millennium BCE: the independent kingdoms on the Greek mainland, islands, and coast of Asia Minor memorably brought to life in Homer's epic poems, which date from the eighth century BCE, centuries after the Bronze Age came to an end. So, too, there is the "archaic" Greece of the seventh and sixth centuries BCE. Immortalized in a body of evocative poetry that includes the lyric verses of Sappho, it was an age notable for colonization in the western Mediterranean and for the sway of tyrants. Vying with Athens at the time of its pan-Hellenic preeminence was the militaristic, yet in its own way culturally vibrant, society of its arch foe, Sparta, which flourished from the seventh through the fourth centuries BCE. Of great historical importance was the affluent, and for the most part despotically ruled, island of Sicily, which attracted and nurtured many leading Greek artists and thinkers during that same span of time. Rome rose to power in the Mediterranean against the backdrop of the geographically far-flung and cosmopolitan Hellenistic empire created by Alexander the Great, which lasted for centuries after Alexander's death in 323 BCE. The Roman empire itself was the larger context that fostered the "university" culture in the city of Athens during the second century CE, an intellectually stimulating milieu that revisited and rearticulated earlier Greek cultural concerns.

In much the same manner, the study of Rome has often concentrated on the early imperial period of the first and second centuries CE. This was the era, of course, when Jesus himself lived and when, as we see in examining texts by authors of this period such as the younger Pliny and Tacitus, Christians were first hunted down and persecuted. By this time, as we observed above, Rome had taken control over what remained of Alexander's empire and had thoroughly absorbed Greek culture along with a huge Greek-speaking population. Consequently, it has recently become popular in some scholarly circles to stress the continuities and similarities between Greece in the second half of the first millennium BCE and Rome in the first centuries of the first millennium CE, that is, to adopt what is called "the ancient Mediterranean model," a construction of the Greco-Roman world that minimizes what was distinctive about Rome itself.

Viewing classical antiquity in this blended, homogenized, and Hellenocentric fashion badly distorts the object of vision. In particular, such a historical perspective seriously shortchanges Rome's important accomplishments in the years between 510 BCE, when Rome legendarily established a republican form of government, and 31 BCE, when Rome became a recognizable empire with Augustus' defeat of Mark Antony and the Egyptian queen, Cleopatra, at the battle of Actium. Such a perspective also fails to take into account Rome's earlier interactions with other cities and peoples of Italy, such as the sophisticated and culturally influential Etruscans to the north. It also runs the risk of ignoring vast regions of Europe and Africa conquered by the Romans and incorporated into their cultural sphere, but virtually untouched by earlier Greeks.

When talking about this pagan Greco-Roman world of the last century BCE and the first three centuries CE, then, we must not lose sight of its complexity and diversity. We need to keep in mind that Greco-Roman society in this period comprised various, individual Greek and Roman societies, some of which had garnered impressive cultural achievements, exercised substantial political power, and commanded wide respect in earlier eras. We should also recognize the varied demographic composition of Greco-Roman society at this time, for the Roman empire was inhabited by countless individuals who differed in vital respects from those we rightly consult as its authoritative spokespeople.

Our literary sources for this period, and indeed for earlier Greco-Roman eras, are with few exceptions male and are very largely urban and elite voices. It is thus hardly surprising that these authors fix their gazes chiefly on the men of various urban elites, on the involvements of such men in political and military affairs, and on the efforts of such men to create and sustain a "high culture" for those able to enjoy considerable leisure, educational opportunities, political power, and social advantages. Nevertheless, we must not replicate the biases of these sources by totally neglecting the information that has managed to survive about women of this same social class and setting and about women and men of other social classes and geographic regions.

Above all, in observing continuities between earlier Greek and later Roman culture, we cannot simply assume that ideas about women expressed in an early and influential Greek source persisted in imperial Roman times without evidence for their currency in contemporary Roman writings. It is, however, often possible to find similarities between ideas about women expressed in early Greek texts and those voiced by Roman sources from the first century BCE and early imperial period. Such similarities are best explained by positing the strong influence of earlier Greek literature and thought on later Roman writing and thinking. Such similarities also show that certain attitudes about women that governed their actual lives, as well as helped to shape their images, persevered throughout classical antiquity. Nonetheless, we need to recognize that these attitudes were not necessarily adopted in all Greco-Roman times and places and quite often acquired different forms in different times and places.

Among these long-lived attitudes was the notion of male-female Sameness: that certain women, specifically those from families possessing power and privilege, shared qualities and traits with men, a notion which in turn facilitated and justified elite women's participation in what were ordinarily deemed to be masculine pursuits. We see this notion first articulated in the portrayal of immortal gods in our earliest surviving ancient Greek literary texts, Homer's *Iliad* and *Odyssey*, which antedate our earliest surviving Latin literary texts by hundreds of years. The Homeric poems characterize divine beings of both genders as engaging, on an apparently equal basis, in various activities which were monopolized on earth by mortal males. By characterizing the family of Olympian gods and goddesses in this manner, Homer launched an influential literary tradition: one in which the Greeks, and eventually the Romans, represent their gods anthropomorphically, as having human form and organizing themselves into a human familial structure, but as endowed with superhuman powers and privileges, and one in which both Greek and Roman authors portray female divinities as behaving in ways contrary to the gender stereotypes routinely applied to mortals.

In the militaristic *Iliad*, one of the ways in which female divinities closely resemble their male counterparts, and sharply differ from mortal women, is by engaging in warfare and taking part in acts of physical aggression. At lines 393 ff. of the *Iliad*'s first book, Homer describes the Greek warrior Achilles as begging his mother, the goddess Thetis, to supplicate Zeus, king of the gods. In reminding her of an episode when she—with the aid of a 100-handed giant—freed Zeus from his shackles, Achilles identifies those who had bound Zeus in chains as Zeus' wife, Hera; brother Poseidon; and daughter Pallas Athene; through such a description, he represents two goddesses and a god as equally responsible for perpetrating an act of brute force. At 8.381–396 of the *Iliad*, Homer portrays the goddesses Hera and Athene as arming for battle; the passage could just as easily describe the efforts of males: Hera harnesses horses, and Athene dons her father Zeus' fighting gear before the two ride off in a chariot through the sky.

At 5.381–394, Homer depicts the goddess Aphrodite as wounded by a mortal in battle and as comforted by examples of two other gods who also had to endure ill-treatment from humans. No gender distinctions are made: the first is a male divinity, Ares, the second a female, Hera. At 21.470–495, the goddess Artemis upbraids her brother Apollo for losing in combat to Poseidon, only to be rebuked and physically assaulted by Hera. Hera taunts Artemis with words that may acknowledge her female gender, but only in the context of predicting that Artemis will be at a great disadvantage when the two engage in masculine-style combat: "It will be hard for you to match your strength with mine, even if you wear a bow, since Zeus has made you a lion among women, and given you leave to kill any at your pleasure."

The *Odyssey* similarly associates its premiere female divinity, Athene, with behavior commonly regarded as the province of both divine and mortal males, albeit behavior that involves the deployment of her mental, rather than her physical, abilities. On several occasions in the *Odyssey*, Athene assumes different human disguises in order to advise and support the poem's hero Odysseus and his son Telemachus. Usually, she is disguised as a male; the importance of one such disguise—that of Mentor, Odysseus' wise and close friend—is underscored by the words that conclude the entire poem: "Pallas Athene . . . who had likened herself in appearance and voice to Mentor." So, too, in the debate among the gods with which the poem opens, Athene acts no differently, and is treated no differently, from the male immortals subject to Zeus when the assembly of gods argue about the relative merits of various suffering mortals. Indeed, Athene convinces Zeus that he has been too harsh with her protégé Odysseus; Zeus, placing the blame for Odysseus' current circumstances on Poseidon, promises that Poseidon will put away his anger, and the other gods will work out Odysseus' homecoming.

This Greek epic tradition—of representing male and female deities as conducting themselves similarly, of portraying goddesses as taking part in conduct ordinarily associated with mortal males rather than with females, and of depicting goddesses as sharing key traits and concerns with the gods to whom they are kindred—exerted an unmistakable impact on later Greek literary texts. Not long after Homer, Hesiod's epic *Theogony* describes the goddess Hecate at lines 411 ff. as wielding power in various areas of masculine activity: war, athletics, seafaring, the administration of justice. We even see this attribution of masculine qualities and behavior to female divinities in the literature of classical Athens, a culture that elaborated a sharper distinction between male and female spheres of behavior than was the case in most other Greek and Roman societies. Aeschylus' *Oresteia*, for example, spotlights the decision of Athene, functioning in a judicial capacity, to exonerate Orestes from the charge of murdering his mother. At *Eumenides* 734 ff., Athene supports the defense proffered by Orestes' attorney (and her own half brother), Apollo, that the mother is merely a nurse of the new-planted seed and not a true parent. Athene cites, as Apollo did, her own, motherless, birth from Zeus' head and proclaims that she "takes the side of the male in all things."

Later Hellenistic poetry, such as the *Voyage of the Argo*, a mythic, Homeric-style epic by Apollonius of Rhodes, also characterizes goddesses as able and willing to perform feats of physical strength ordinarily thought of as masculine behavior. In the epic's second book, Athene extracts the ship *Argo* from treacherous rocks. In the third, Hera tells Aphrodite that she is prepared to fight for the epic's hero, Jason, with all of her physical might. Aphrodite then offers to use physical force to aid Jason in carrying off the golden fleece, although Hera reassures her that force is not needed—merely the services of her son, Eros—to make the king's daughter Medea fall in love with Jason.

We should credit this earlier literary tradition, moreover, with strongly informing Vergil's portrayal of Roman divinities in the *Aeneid*. Written in the early part of Augustus' principate (and still not entirely finished when the poet died in 19 BCE), this epic poem sought, in the Homeric literary fashion, to celebrate Augustus' political accomplishments and aims. It prominently features a mortal female, the Carthaginian queen, Dido, who adopts traditionally male forms of behavior by assuming the political and military leadership of her community. After Dido falls in love with, and is abandoned by, the poem's hero, Aeneas, she takes her own life; some scholars have interpreted her suicidal response to Aeneas' departure as reflecting Vergil's negative assessment, and perhaps even Augustus' own dim view, of women's ability to handle conventionally masculine responsibilities such as involvement in political matters.

It warrants emphasis that Vergil does not represent female divinities as unable to handle the same pressures and duties as their male counterparts. From the start to the finish of the poem, he portrays the goddess Juno as supremely capable of dealing with military and political affairs both divine and mortal: savagely persecuting Aeneas and his Trojan followers and making things difficult for the male and female divinities who support Aeneas' efforts to found a new kingdom in Italy, including her husband, Jupiter, and Aeneas' mother, Venus. At the beginning of *Aeneid* I, Vergil explains Juno's special affection for Carthage by noting that she kept her chariot and armor there, and that she hoped it would become the capital of nations. So, too, Vergil explains her hatred of the Trojans by pointing out that she remembered "the old war that she had long since carried on at Troy." Later in *Aeneid* I, Venus bewails Juno's hatred for her son and, fearing Juno's efforts to detain him at Carthage, soon plots to have Dido fall in love with Aeneas.

Eventually, at 4.90 ff., Juno confronts Venus to sneer at the "glory and spoils" Venus has achieved by rendering Dido lovesick, and he disparages what Venus has wrought as "one woman conquered by the deceit of two gods." In seeking peace through the marriage of Dido and Aeneas, Juno proclaims to Venus, "Let us rule this people—you and I—with equal auspices." Venus immediately asks, "Who is mad enough to shun your terms or would prefer to struggle against you in war?"; she then points out that Jupiter will need to approve Juno's plan, and that Juno will need to persuade her husband to do so. While this plan to have Juno and Venus cogovern Carthage never comes to fruition, Juno does successfully negotiate with Jupiter in the final book of the poem. As a result, there is an end to the fighting between Aeneas' Trojans and the Latin peoples led by Turnus. The Trojan and Latin nations are merged through the marriage of Aeneas and Lavinia, daughter of the Latin king. What is more, as Juno requested, Jupiter allows the native Latins to keep their ancient name, language, and dress rather than take on Trojan speech and customs.

Other Latin literary works, some of them prior to Vergil's *Aeneid*, some written subsequently, also depict female divinities as adopting conduct associated with mortal and immortal males, particularly as performing feats of physical strength and aggression. In poem 63, the mid–first century BCE poet Catullus depicts the goddess Cybele, a divinity of eastern provenance also known as the Great Mother (Magna Mater) as fiercely lashing at a lion yoked to bear her chariot and as threatening madness to her castrated devotee, Attis, for desiring to flee her *imperium* (sphere of power). Two decades after the publication of the *Aeneid*, Ovid not only evoked Vergil's depiction of the power-brokering, battle-waging goddesses Juno and Venus in his *Metamorphoses*, but also provided other striking portraits of goddesses conducting themselves much as gods do; he relates at 6.204 ff. how Apollo and Diana (Greek Artemis) together slew the children of Niobe with their arrows, and he represents Pallas—a Greek name for Athene and the Roman Minerva—at 3.101 ff. as aiding Cadmus in the founding of Thebes by bidding him sow the teeth of the slain dragon and forcing Echion to drop his weapons.

Nevertheless, when Latin literary texts of the first century BCE and early imperial era represent women as sharing qualities and traits with males and portray these women in a positive light for engaging in what were customarily deemed masculine pursuits, these women are far more likely to be mortals, actual historical individuals from powerful and prestigious Roman families. These pursuits, moreover, almost invariably involve mental traits and qualities rather than physical propensities for aggressive and violent action. It merits notice, too, that these well-born mortal women share an important feature with the female deities who are characterized, in epic and in other fictional poetry, as resembling male gods in their involvements in conventionally male activities. Just as these goddesses are depicted as what we would today call "biologically" related to the gods they resemble, as belonging to the same extended divine family, so these actual mortal women are frequently likened to their own blood kinsmen, particularly their fathers. The male familial attributes these women are often thought to manifest and perpetuate are those that secured public recognition among their Roman elite peers for these male kin. And these women are often said to be acting on behalf of their family unit, particularly their family of birth.

For instances of this phenomenon, we may turn to an array of writings from the first century BCE through the second century CE about women from elite families. In a letter to his brother Quintus written during the middle decades of the first century BCE, Cicero—a man renowned in his time and since as a statesman, orator, and political thinker—compliments his daughter Tullia at Ad Quintum Fratrem 1.3.3 by describing her as the image of his own appearance, speech, and mind. Nor did Cicero restrict such compliments to one woman of his blood family. In Brutus, a later essay on oratory, Cicero praises the speaking style of the distinguished orator, Gaius Laelius. He observes that Laelius' daughter has been imbued with her father's elegance in speech; he notes, too, that Laelia's two daughters and granddaughters speak in the same impressive fashion.

Writing in the early first century CE, Valerius Maximus contends at 8.3.3 that a politically influential speech in 42 BCE by the daughter of the oratorical giant Hortensius caused her late father "to live again in the female line and breathe in his daughter's words." Later in that century, in his Consolatio ad Marciam, the younger Seneca comforts an aristocratic female friend, Marcia, on the death of her grown son by citing a series of renowned men she should emulate and by defending his selection of male role models through claiming that women have as much strength, as much propensity for honorable conduct, and as much capacity for enduring strength and sorrow as do men. In this same essay, Seneca also stresses the resemblances between Marcia and her late father, the eminent historian Cremutius Cordus, referring to Marcia's love for books as a benefit inherited from her father.

Half a century later, in his life of Marcus Junius Brutus, who led the conspiracy to slay Julius Caesar in 44 BCE, the Greek author Plutarch provides a moving portrait of Brutus' wife Porcia, daughter of the younger Cato. According to Plutarch, Porcia determined to prove herself a worthy political ally to her husband and cousin—since his mother was also her late father's sister—in the days immediately prior to Caesar's murder. Therefore, Plutarch tells us, she showed her indifference to physical suffering by stabbing herself in the thigh, just as her father had ended his life by stabbing himself after his defeat by Caesar's forces at Utica; in this context, Porcia twice reminded Brutus that she was her father's daughter. Plutarch even concludes another biography, that of the younger Cato himself, by commenting that the younger Cato's daughter did not lack in temperate wisdom and manly courage.

Such notions are also voiced in the letters of the younger Pliny, which date from the late first century and early second century CE, shortly before Plutarch wrote his *Lives*. In 5.26, lamenting the death of Minucia Marcella, thirteen-year-old daughter of his friend Fundanus, Pliny attests to the admiration that he felt for the young woman on a number of grounds. He not only notes the bravery that she displayed in facing her final illness, but also asserts that she was her father's exact living image in appearance and ways, and that she shared her father's devotion to books and learning.

Of interest in this context are 10.96–97, Pliny's correspondence with the emperor Trajan about how he, in his capacity as provincial governor of Bithynia in Asia Minor, is and should be dealing with those accused of and attacked for being Christians. Although Pliny notes that the accused include people of both sexes and different ages, he is only concerned about whether or not he should treat the accused differently on the grounds of age. So, too, Pliny acknowledges that he felt it necessary to use torture to obtain the truth about Christian practices from two Greek-speaking female attendants "who are called ministers." Yet, other than that, neither Pliny nor Trajan distinguishes between the male and female devotees of Christ. Admittedly, Pliny refers to Christian beliefs as "madness," a "fault or mistake," and a "perverse and excessive superstition." Still, one is tempted to connect this disregard for gender difference among the Christians with Pliny's emphasis elsewhere on the similarities between women who have shown courage in difficult circumstances and their male relations.

At *Annales* 1.41 ff., Pliny's friend Tacitus depicts the elder Agrippina, a Roman woman of the early first century CE and the imperial household, as summoning to mind the memory of both her father, Agrippa, and her grandfather, Augustus, when displaying military leadership and bravery. Tacitus relates that Agrippina refused to leave her husband's German military camp and justified her decision by stating that she was descended from the divine Augustus and thus not unworthy of her family in facing dangers. He also portrays her as assuming the official duties of a commander by suppressing mutinous attempts of soldiers to destroy a bridge over the Rhine River and by standing at the bridgehead to praise and thank the remaining legions. Elsewhere in the *Annales*, he characterizes her as mercilessly tortured by the emperor Tiberius—her stepfather and her husband's adopted father, to whom she was related by marriage, but not by blood.

Like Pliny's letters about his and Trajan's treatment of Christians in Asia Minor, Tacitus' report in *Annales* 15.44 ff. about Nero's persecution of early Christians in Rome makes no distinction between Nero's male and female victims. Tacitus, too, evinces little sympathy for Christians and Christian beliefs. He calls Christians "notoriously depraved" and their religion a "deadly superstition;" he refers to their guilt as Christians and to the punishment it deserved. But he does recognize that they were scapegoats on whom Nero pinned the blame for the great fire at Rome; he also attests to the sympathy felt for the Christians after they were dressed in wild animals' skins, torn to pieces by dogs, crucified, or made into torches to be ignited after dark at displays in the Circus Maximus. As we did in the case of the younger Pliny, therefore, we might posit a connection between Tacitus' failure to consider gender differences when relating the plight of the viciously victimized Christians and Tacitus' portrayal of a noble Roman woman, the target of imperial cruelty, as transcending gender stereotypes.

The one Roman female whose literary efforts survive in any quantity also appears to represent herself as acting in ways that her society deemed more appropriate for men and as invoking, as well as resembling, her well-born male blood kin when so doing. In the love poetry of the aristocratic Sulpicia, who—like Vergil—writes in the early part of Augustus' principate, she writes and characterizes herself as behaving in the fashion of male love poets from this same period, such as Propertius and Ovid. She proudly announces her love affair to her readers and, indeed, asks the members of her audience to tell of her erotic joys if they lack joys of their own. She refers to her male beloved by a pseudonym, while having no qualms about disclosing her own identity; she demands freedom from her guardian's supervision so that she can spend her birthday with her lover. Significantly, in 3.16, she contrasts herself to a lowborn rival for her lover's affections by emphasizing that she is "Sulpicia daughter of Servius." While there is some debate as to which of two noblemen named Servius Sulpicius was in fact her father, both possibilities were highly regarded orators with impressive verbal gifts. It has been recently suggested, as well, that Sulpicia's brother also wrote love poems under the pseudonym Lygdamus; these poems survive in the same collection that contains Sulpicia's work.

Significantly, too, in the earliest known document in the Latin language known to have been handwritten by a woman, we also find females of high social station engaging in conduct associated with males and invoking ties of blood kinship (if not ties to male blood kin) in the process. A tablet recently excavated at the Roman fort of Vindolanda in northern England, it is dated to about 100 CE. Its author, an officer's wife, Claudia Severa, invites her friend Sulpicia Lepidina to her forthcoming birthday party in strongly affectionate language. Not only does Claudia call this Sulpicia *anima mea* (my life's breath), darling, and *carissima* (dearest), she also refers to Sulpicia twice as *soror* (sister), although the women's dissimilar names seem to indicate that they were not related (Roman sisters were ordinarily given the feminine form of their father's family name along with an adjective to distinguish among different female siblings; thus, a sister of Claudia Severa, presumably the daughter of a man named Claudius, would also be named Claudia).

Claudia Severa's reference to Sulpicia Lepidina as *anima mea* is striking because earlier Latin literary texts feature this phrase merely as a term of endearment used by men, whether to express affection for women or for others of their own sex. The Augustan poet, Horace, for example, calls his fellow poet Vergil *animae dimidium meae* (half my soul). Another Vindolanda writing tablet, moreover, contains correspondence from one man to another that resembles Claudia Severa's letter in various ways. This tablet contains five words of greeting before quoting a line from book 9 of Vergil's *Aeneid* about *Fama* (Rumor) bringing a woman the news that her son and his male beloved have died together in battle; curiously, Claudia Severa's repeated use of the word *soror* in conjunction with *cara* calls to mind book 4 of Vergil's *Aeneid*, in which Dido addresses her actual sister Anna in similarly affectionate terms (especially after Fama spreads the news of her illicit affair with Aeneas, and Dido resolves to die after he abandons her). Four of these five introductory words also figure among the fifty-odd words in Claudia Severa's letter: *salutem* (greetings), *rogo* (I ask) (found twice in the male-authored tablet), and a reference to the male addressee as *carissim*[*e*]. The fifth word, moreover, is *frater* (brother), the masculine counterpart of *soror*. Presumably, the male author and addressee of this second tablet are not blood kin either, but they employ terms of blood kinship to express their affection in the same manner as Claudia Severa does with Sulpicia Lepidina.

Finally, it bears noting that the one surviving fragment by another female poet named Sulpicia, who dates from approximately the same time as the Vindolanda tablets, also portrays her as writing in the fashion of male literary predecessors. In these two lines, she proclaims her desire for her husband, Calenus, stating, "If, after the bindings of my bed frame have been put back in place, [it] would bring me forth, nude, lying down with Calenus." Scholars have noted that, in this swatch of verse, Sulpicia is appropriating masculine language. Not only is she evoking a passage by the love poet, Propertius, about a torrid erotic encounter he enjoyed with his mistress, but also she is providing physical details of lovemaking far more explicit in nature than any to be found in words of her best-known, and proudly passionate, female literary predecessors: her namesake, the Augustan love poet Sulpicia, and the Greek Sappho, to whom this later Sulpicia is favorably compared by the poet Martial. No less importantly, this Sulpicia also employs language that Propertius uses for the celebration of extramarital love to describe marital passion.

While Martial, our main ancient source on this "second" Sulpicia, says nothing about her male blood relations and merely emphasizes the mutual love she shared with her husband, he does characterize her poetry as equally valuable for young women wishing to please their husbands and husbands wishing to please one wife. What is more, he praises her poetry specifically because it does not treat such mythological topics as Medea's murder of her children, Thyestes' devouring of his sons, Scylla's betrayal of her father, and Byblis' affair with her brother—all tales that involve violations of blood bonds. Sulpicia's respect for the blood ties of others, if not the respect merited by her own activities owing to her blood ties, command Martial's attention.

To be sure, Roman efforts to stress resemblances between females and males are not exclusively limited to portrayals of goddesses and of women from elite families. As we have observed, various Roman religious cults, literally pagan in their rural genesis, emphasized the shared activities and similar qualities of male and female worshippers. Ovid's description, at *Fasti* 2.617 ff., of the Caristia, a celebration by near kinfolk of their family gods, may list different types of evil blood relations, male and female, who do not belong at this event. But he makes no distinction between the ways in which men and women participate in this particular rite. At 4.393 ff., Ovid uses gender-neutral terms when depicting the key activities performed at the games honoring Ceres, an event closely associated with Rome's second-ranked social order, the plebeians.

This deemphasis on gender difference even manifests itself in the younger Pliny and Tacitus' descriptions of early Christian believers, presumably individuals of relatively low social station, in Asia Minor and Rome. We find gender distinctions minimized by other Roman authors when they describe slaves and others of the lower social classes. For example, at 2.10, in a section on the breeding of slaves who tend the herds, a treatise on agriculture by the first century BCE Varro describes the slave women assigned the task of following herding parties to remote areas, preparing food for the herdsmen and making the herdsmen more energetic. Recommending that such women be physically strong and not disgraceful in conduct, Varro claims that, in certain regions—such as Illyricum in the Adriatic—women are not inferior to the men as they are able to perform the men's job of tending the herd, carry firewood and cook the food, or keep the huts in order.

Sandra Joshel's 1991 study of first-century CE Roman occupational inscriptions discusses some tombstone inscriptions of male and female former slaves, who seem to have been married couples, but preferred to identify their bond publicly in terms of their shared work. They are merely described as *brattiaria* and *brattiarius* (female and male goldbeater) in one instance, as *vestiarii* (tailors, both male and female) in another. The epitaph of yet another freedwoman discussed by Joshel mentions that both this woman's husband and her own freedman were goldsmiths, implying the woman's desire to be identified with her husband's occupation, as a supporter if not as a practitioner.

Yet, efforts such as these to cite similarities between men and women from lowly backgrounds and different parts of the Roman empire do not—as did the foregoing descriptions by male authors of elite women in Rome—involve males and females related to one another by blood. They do not represent these women as acting in ways that add luster to the reputation of their blood family and as able to excel in the same pursuits as the men with whom they interacted by virtue of sharing traits and qualities with their male blood kin. As is the case with the three women writers whose texts and contexts we have just examined, they do not even emphasize the respect for blood ties evinced by women who write about their valued emotional relationships with others. If women of less-privileged and less-powerful backgrounds, whether resident in Rome or in other parts of the ancient Mediterranean world, are portrayed as interacting with men who hold politically powerful positions, it is usually as these men's sexual partners, often of the paid variety. Their blood ties and similarities to their male kin are of little, if any, concern to our sources; their involvement in public affairs is of scant interest as well.

This Roman practice of linking elite women who take part in conventionally masculine pursuits with an emphasis on these women's blood relationships seems a phenomenon unto itself and deserves further reflection. Admittedly, there are earlier Greek texts that resemble, and perhaps in some measure exerted an influence on, our Roman sources from the first century BCE and the first few centuries CE by according importance to the bloodline of women with powerful male blood relations. Some of these texts also portray such women as therefore enabled and entitled to engage in conventionally masculine pursuits. At *Odyssey* 7.53–77, for example, Homer has Athene first inform Odysseus that Arete, wife of the Phaeacian king Alcinous, is the daughter of Alcinous' brother Rhexenor, and that both Alcinous and Rhexenor were the sons of Alcinous' royal predecessor, Nausithoos. Athene then tells Odysseus that Arete is revered by her people as if she were a god, lacks nothing of good intelligence, and "dissolves quarrels even among men when she favors them." That Arete, like her husband, descends directly from Phaeacia's earlier king would seem to help account for the public esteem in which she is held, the outstanding mind with which she is attributed, and the weighty public responsibilities she is assigned.

Oedipus at Colonus, the final tragedy by the fifth-century BCE Athenian playwright Sophocles, highlights the "doubled" blood ties that bind the title character to Antigone and Ismene. The play emphasizes that their mother, Jocasta, was also Oedipus' own mother, and thus they are both his daughters and his sisters. At the same time, moreover, Sophocles has Oedipus lament that his male and female children have reversed conventional Greek gender roles. Likening his offspring to the Egyptians (i.e., the men stay indoors working at the looms and the women work outdoors for sustenance and livelihood), Oedipus claims that his sons neglect their proper duties and resemble maidens by staying within the house, while his daughters shoulder his wretched labors in the public domain. Sophocles thus implies that Antigone and Ismene are able to assume the public duty of supporting their politically powerful, albeit exiled and dying, father because they possess a greater share of their father's bloodline than do ordinary daughters.

Arete, Antigone, and Ismene are, however, fictional figures from a past, mythic age, not actual women of Sophocles' time. In this way, they differ sharply from the Roman women—such as Hortensius' daughter, or Porcia, or the elder Agrippina—whom we have seen characterized as similar to males of their blood families. No less noteworthy is that the Athenian state government in Sophocles' day assigned special value to the bloodline of females related to the most privileged and powerful Athenian males—those men born to citizen status. Yet, it did so in a way and for a reason quite different from those operating in the high Roman valuation of elite women's blood ties for Athenian legislation contained various provisions regarding a particular category of women from citizen families: the *epikleros*, a fatherless daughter who also lacked brothers.

To create a kindred male offspring who could inherit her late father's estate by filling the role of a son her father had lost or never had, an *epikleros* was legally required to marry (or at least have a marital partner chosen by) her father's closest male kinsman, ordinarily his brother. Girls as yet unwed when assigned the status of *epikleros* would be married to a close male kinsman of their father (or another male meeting with that kinsman's approval) as soon as they reached marriageable age, in their early teens. But such regulations forced other Athenian women from citizen families to be divorced from their current spouses—even husbands their late fathers had chosen for them—and to abandon the children these marriages had already produced to enter a new union with one of their father's male relations (or someone this kinsman had selected).

That the epiklerate accorded immense importance to a woman's blood ties with her father and her father's male kin is made clear by a comparison between this Athenian institution and its ancient Hebrew counterpart, the levirate. The levirate, from the Latin word *levir* (husband's brother), required a man to marry the widow of his brother. While the goal of the levirate, like that of the epiklerate, was to maintain the brother's family line, it was premised on an altogether different assumption about how best to keep that line alive. The levirate regarded a brother's wife, the woman with whom the dead man would have sired children during his lifetime, as the female family member worthiest of perpetuating the dead man's name and identity. The epiklerate, though, viewed the late man's surviving wife as no longer of procreative use after his death, even if she were of childbearing age with no other marital prospects in sight. Rather, Athenian society thought it preferable that a dead man's line be continued by having his brother or another male kinsman mate with (or at least choose someone to mate with) the dead man's daughter, even if she were already married to someone else and the mother of his children. After all, a daughter would indubitably be kindred by blood to the dead man, and a union between the dead man's daughter and one of his male blood kin would intensify the concentration of their shared bloodline in the son the couple created.

Nevertheless, women of Athenian citizen families are not recognized, in the way that so many elite Roman women are, for behaving publicly in ways that recalled their politically prominent male kin, and they are not characterized by sources at the time as especially well equipped to engage in traditionally masculine activities. The existence of the epiklerate did not translate into a deemphasis on gender difference or into increased public opportunities for women, even as members of politically prominent families in classical Athens. Athenian society merely employed the epiklerate, with its emphasis on the bloodlines of women from citizen households, to assign such women additional procreative responsibilities. Our literary evidence on elite Roman women of this period, then, with its stress on their similarities to men and their familially oriented public activities, as well as on their ties with male blood kindred, shows that the Romans had very different motivations from the classical Athenians for calling attention to the blood ties between elite females and their male blood kin. Roman authors seem eager to acknowledge, to endorse, and to explain such women's public involvements on their family's behalf and at times even to privilege bloodline over gender difference.

Women of lower social strata were obviously affected by, and beneficiaries of, the Roman assumption that men and women had important traits and concerns in common. This assumption enabled such women to practice some of the same business occupations and engage in some of the same ritual activities as men. Furthermore, the failure of our ancient sources to focus on the links between non-elite women and their male blood kin is hardly surprising. After all, what primarily distinguished elite from non-elite Roman women were the advantages accorded to the families of the former as a result of their blood ties. To be regarded as a male or female member of the Roman elite in the first place, one needed to be blessed with blood relatives, particularly those of earlier generations, who had achieved social and political prominence in addition to possessing substantial material wealth.

There are, moreover, other reasons why references to male blood kin loom so large in descriptions of elite Roman women: why male blood kin played key, and indeed controlling, roles in their lives, as well as figuring prominently in elite women's images. The men of their blood families—most notably their fathers, uncles, and brothers—served as their legal guardians before, and at times even after, they were married, arranged their marriages, funded their dowries, "took them in" when they were widowed or divorced, and played an active part in the education and acculturation of their children. By way of contrast, women of lower social station, particularly slaves and ex-slaves, had a difficult time maintaining their ties with parents, siblings, and other blood relations, even with their own children. Being sold into slavery in the first instance, and living at the whim of a master capable of selling them and their families thereafter, separated them from blood kin and limited their opportunities to stay in close contact with members of their blood families. In denying the importance of ties between women and their blood relations, we should note, early Christian sources seek to validate the experiences and circumstances of non-elite Romans and to eliminate social traditions that gave special advantages to women of aristocratic backgrounds.

Elite Roman women's dependence on their male blood kin undoubtedly curtailed their personal autonomy, restricting their opportunities to make decisions for themselves and to act on these decisions. Yet, the elite Roman women's situation appears to be an advantaged one if we compare their circumstances with those of women in lower social strata. For, unlike their less loftily positioned counterparts, women of elite family were able to rely on their male relations for protection and support of different sorts. Somewhat ironically, this state of dependence, this ability to rely on male blood kin for various kinds of support, also allowed elite Roman women a degree of independence in marriage unavailable to females lower on the social scale. Having male blood relations who had selected her husband and subsidized her dowry in the first place, who could intervene with her husband to protect her interests, and who might well be of aid in her child-rearing responsibilities, made it possible for an elite woman to avoid being totally subjected to her husband, to create her own "space" in a difficult marriage, or to exit—temporarily if not permanently—from an unendurable marriage.

A wide range of Latin literary texts from the late first century BCE and early centuries CE—among them the historical writings of Tacitus; the biographies of Plutarch and Suetonius; and the love poetry of Sulpicia, Propertius, and Ovid—provides testimony that elite Roman marriages often ended in divorce, and that elite women, as well as men, often sought erotic satisfaction from partners other than their legitimate spouses. Indeed, the frequency of both divorce and extramarital liaisons on the part of both men and women of the Roman elite strongly supports a key contention of the anthropologist Laura Betzig: marriage in Rome may have been monogamous, but it was a phenomenon altogether separate from erotically pleasurable mating. To be sure, elite Roman men seem to have pursued sexual pleasure outside marriage with greater frequency (and to have attracted less criticism for such conduct) than did elite Roman women. For this reason, Betzig refers to Roman mating as "polygynous," involving multiple female partners. So, too, elite Roman men's extramarital partners were likely to have been women of lower social station, slaves and freedwomen given financial and other forms of remuneration for their sexual services.

But the large-scale involvement of lower class females in the Roman extramarital sexual economy did not necessarily lead women of this group to disparage marriage. Unable to rely on blood relations for financial support, emotional sustenance, and social protection, at least to the extent possible for women of elite families, women of the lower classes could only look to their marital partners, and (if possible) the offspring such unions created, to fill these basic human needs. Inasmuch as marriage was not even permissible in Rome unless both partners were free or freed, it seems to have been particularly valued by men and women of the lower classes, couples in which one or both partners were still slaves. As countless tombstone inscriptions attest, they commemorated and endeavored to exalt their long-standing, but unlegitimated, unions in the language ordinarily used to describe and exalt the marital bond.

As I remarked above, the foregoing examination of evidence for Roman notions of women, and especially of goddesses and elite women, as Same, as sharing traits and activities with men, has been accorded so much space because this evidence has received relatively little notice elsewhere. Let us now turn to some testimony for the Roman emphasis on female Otherness and to the Roman effort to deny and erase differences among women by characterizing all women as a single group different from and inferior to men. This emphasis on how women collectively differ from males is responsible for various gender stereotypes prominent in Roman thinking, stereotypes strongly rooted in earlier Greek thinking. These stereotypes, moreover, persisted and strengthened in the antipagan tradition represented by Augustine and his Christian literary followers.

To postulate that all Roman women constitute a single group requires a certain obliviousness to the abundant testimony about the differences among Roman social classes, which resulted in very different "lifestyles" for the women among them. But the notion of all women as Other, and the importance given to gender as a key conceptual category of group differentiation among the Romans, are not incompatible with other Roman assumptions, even aristocratic ones, about women's place in society. To be sure, women of elite families were often highly educated, were given opportunities to study with the learned men hired to teach their brothers, and even had tutors of their own. Unlike their counterparts in classical Athens, elite Roman women regularly dined and socialized with the men of their families and in this way took part in an array of Roman cultural and intellectual activities. Still, even though these practices—and others that contributed to and resulted from the aforementioned view of elite women as sharing outstanding attributes of their fathers and male blood kin—may have invested such women with an aura of "maleness," viewing and at times treating women as Same should not be confused with notions of gender equality.

Rather, such a conceptualization served as a convenient means of distinguishing elite women from those of lowly backgrounds and, indeed, utilized the category of gender to elevate one particular social class—that in which males and females shared certain outstanding traits—to a separate and superior position. A further and related way of differentiating, and according higher status to, elite Roman women involved the area of gainful labor. Although the wealthier among them had what we would call extensive managerial responsibilities, supervising large household staffs of slaves and ex-slaves in the performance of various specialized tasks, women of this class did not pursue independent occupations that enabled them to make money in their own right. Both literary texts and inscriptions, by way of contrast, document that lower class women worked in a wide range of jobs. We have already discussed evidence for their employment as shepherds, tailors, weavers of gold, and prostitutes; there is also testimony for their employment as, among other things, actresses, dancers, painters, gladiators, musicians, farmers, scribes, midwives, wet nurses, fishmongers, grocers, weavers, hairdressers, and barmaids.

The category of gender, though, was more frequently utilized to elevate another social group—men of all classes—to a separate and superior position. Employing symbolic designations for women as a group, most notably by associating all women with wool—working, was perhaps the most visible way of erasing class distinctions and of positing a domestically defined gender unity among all females. As it happens, the ancient association between women of all classes and wool—working dates to our earliest Greek literary texts and artifacts. Homer's *Iliad* and *Odyssey* represent the wives and lovers of the leading Greek and Trojan warriors as laboring at their looms; these women included Agamemnon's captive slave woman, Chryseis; Menelaus' wife (and Paris' lover), Helen; Hector's wife, Andromache; and Odysseus' wife, Penelope, and lover, Circe. Even though Homer indicates that Helen is of divine descent and identifies Circe as a minor goddess, he does not portray the great Olympian goddesses as involved in wool—working.

In Roman culture, however, wool—working is depicted as absorbing the energies of lofty female divinities, as well as women of every station. Minerva, a native Italian crafts goddess the Romans had merged with the Greek Athene, is explicitly associated with excellence in the working of wool: the sixth book of Ovid's *Metamorphoses* opens with the tale of Arachne's weaving competition with Minerva, after which the goddess destroyed Arachne's flawless tapestry and turned the maiden into a spider. At the time Ovid was writing, it should be noted, the emperor Augustus is said by his biographer, Suetonius, to have made spinning and weaving part of his daughter's and granddaughters' education and to have worn garments woven and sewn for him by his wife, sister, daughter, or granddaughters. At the same time, Roman authors such as Cicero and Ovid emphasize that the representation of wool—working as a quintessentially female pursuit served as a form of distinguishing proper female from proper male behavior: each author characterizes men as effeminate and homosexually passive merely by attributing them with working in wool.

Another way in which the Romans sought to define women as a group distinct and different from men was through the promotion of all-female cults and rituals, which shared the Roman religious calendar with pagan forms of worship that involved both men and women. Our elite male literary sources portray several of these female festivals as activities reserved for women of the upper classes: the worship of Juno Lucina by *matronae* (respectable married women) on March 1, of Venus by elite women on April 1, of the *Bona Dea* (the good goddess) by elite women in both May and December, and of the virgin goddess Vesta and Mater Matuta by *matronae* in June. Archaeological and inscriptional evidence, however, would suggest that some of these celebrations attracted women from lower social strata as well. Other cults for women, such as the Greco-Roman worship of the Egyptian goddess Isis, seem to have involved participation by females of diverse social backgrounds on a more or less equal basis.

So, too, Roman authors of the late republic and early empire represent women as a distinctive group and minimize the distinctions among females of different social backgrounds when writing about societies of other times and places. While ostensibly documenting the conduct of these women elsewhere and "elsewhen," they implicitly criticize and prescribe conduct by Roman women in their own day; in so doing, they tend to generalize about *all* women in these alien societies and thereby deny that women in their own society differ in circumstance and motivation from one another. Tacitus' essay on Germany, for example, does acknowledge that "noble" maidens make the most effective military hostages, but otherwise relies on the general category of "women" to praise German females for their support of males in battle, religious sanctity and prescience, simple dress and tastes, marital fidelity, and suckling of their offspring (and in this indirect way, to fault Roman women for their shortcomings on all of these fronts).

The pagan world of Rome in the last century BCE and first centuries CE, then, was one in which women and their lives were simultaneously likened to and differentiated from males and the existences of men. In likening women to men, Roman society perpetuated and greatly expanded notions that may be traced to earlier forms of Greek thinking, especially Greek conceptualizations of divinity. In stressing the differences between women and men, Romans continued to espouse earlier Greek, particularly Athenian, constructions of gender. Both views of women, as similar and as different, exerted their own, albeit dissimilarly powerful, impacts on later Christian thought and practice.

2

>─┼◆>─●─<◆┼─<

JEWISH WOMEN AND
CHRISTIAN ORIGINS

Some Caveats

Ross S. Kraemer

If writing women's lives is never simple, to write about Jewish women's lives during the years and in the regions where Christianity first emerged is fraught with distinctive perils. In recent years, Christian scholars (especially, though by no means exclusively, some feminist Christian scholars) have had considerable interest in painting a particularly gloomy portrait of Jewish women's participation in Jewish life at the time of Jesus, so that Jesus himself can be seen as a first-century liberator of women. In service both to contemporary Christian theology and to modern debates about issues such as women's ordination to Christian ministerial office, extravagant and derogatory claims have sometimes been made about women in first-century Judaism.

These claims are widespread in both scholarly and popular literature. Their precise contents, together with their role in contemporary debates, are amply illustrated by brief contributions in two recent (1992), well-respected reference works intended for a broad range of readers. One, the work of a male conservative Christian scholar (Ben Witherington III), occurs in the prestigious *Anchor Bible Dictionary.*[1] The other, written by a French feminist scholar (Monique Alexandre), was published in the five-volume *History of Women in the West.*[2] It is noteworthy that in each case, the study of Jewish women is subsumed within discussions of "Women, in the NT" (*ABD*) or "Early Christian Women" (*HWW*), rather than deemed worthy of consideration for its own sake.

Though the *Anchor Bible Dictionary* and the *History of Women in the West* differ in many regards, their coverage of Jewish women at the beginning of Christianity is remarkably similar. Both sketch a monolithic Jewish society in the first century CE that was highly "patriarchal," confining women primarily to the domestic realm, with little access to any public life. Both concur that Jewish women were generally secluded at home: one specifies that Jewish women in Palestine wore veils when they ventured out in public.[3] They agree that menstrual impurity excluded women from synagogue participation and/or from society for lengthy periods of time,[4] that women could not inherit or initiate divorce proceedings and were married off by their fathers at puberty, with little regard for their own wishes. Jewish men, one claims, "maintained a prudent silence" with women.[5]

In the realm of communal religious life, women are similarly envisioned as largely absent. They could not be counted in a *minyan* (the quorum for communal prayer) and were exempt from morning and evening prayers, from the observance of positive precepts, and from pilgrimage to Jerusalem for the three annual festivals of Sukkoth, Pesach, and Shavuoth. Not obligated to attend synagogue, women were physically segregated from men if they did. While in theory, Jewish law permitted women to read the Torah (here meaning the Five Books of Moses) in communal assembly, in practice, they did not out of "respect for the congregation."[6]

Neither author conceals the significance of these data. Witherington moves quickly from a succinct summary of this portrait to a negative comparison of Judaism with Jesus: "there is no evidence that prior to Jesus' ministry Jewish women were ever allowed to be disciples of a great teacher, much less travel with such a teacher, or instruct anyone other than children. In such a restrictive context, Jesus' relationship to women must have seemed radical indeed."[7] Concluding his survey of women in the ministry of Jesus, he proclaims, "Herein we see the liberating effect the teaching and life of Jesus had on women, and the loyalty with which they responded to that life."[8]

Alexandre similarly contrasts her depressing picture of Jewish women with the language and imagery of the gospels, which she terms "a marked change."[9] For Alexandre, as for Witherington, "Jesus' relations with women seem to have been remarkably free, given the reserve that Jewish custom in his day required."[10] The hemorrhaging woman whose bleeding Jesus cures (Mark 5: 25–34//Matt 9:20–22//Luke 8:43–48) is adduced as demonstration of Jesus' rejection of purity regulations, particularly those concerning women with genital bleeding.[11] Gospel narratives that depict women as witnesses to the empty tomb (Mark 16:1–8; Matt 28:1–8; Luke 24:1–11; John 20:1–18) and Mary of Magdala as the first to see the risen Christ (Matt 28:9–10; John 20:11–18) are adduced as evidence of a "break with Jewish custom" about women's ineligibility as witnesses in Jewish courts of law.[12] Women's roles in Christian missionary contexts are presented as equal to those of men, and even Paul himself is read as evidence that "there is no sign that women's tasks were in any way considered inferior to men's."[13]

Negative portraits of Jewish women in the first century are thus contrasted with New Testament narratives to buttress claims of Christian superiority over Judaism. Similar contrasts sometimes serve to support claims that, at its inception, pristine Christianity and Jesus himself were free of any misogyny or gender bias. The subsequent presence of gender restrictions in Christian churches and in the works of (male) Christian writers is then explained in any number of ways, including, although not limited to, corrupting influences from Judaism, as well as from the surrounding Greco-Roman polytheist culture.

Given how useful this portrait of Jewish women proves to be for debates about contemporary Christian concerns, is there any accuracy to it? As I show, this portrait of Jewish women is far from any "simple truth," but at points it bears just enough glimmers of veracity to seem persuasive, and therein lies the most serious problem. Thus, before we can begin to ask what we might more reliably say about Jewish women at the beginnings of Christianity, we need to look more carefully at why the portrait exemplified by Witherington and Alexandre is unreliable and misleading.

Witherington, Alexandre, and many other writers derive most of their evidence for Jewish women's lives in the first century CE from rabbinic Jewish sources. These writings contain teachings and legal opinions attributed to rabbis believed to have lived around the same time (as well as later and sometimes even earlier) as Jesus, together with stories about these men and their circles. But the earliest of these, called the Mishnah, was assembled and edited around the year 200 CE, roughly 170 years after the crucifixion of Jesus. The Babylonian Talmud, containing both Mishnah and extensive commentary, was assembled and disseminated several centuries later still (fifth–sixth centuries CE) by Jews living under Sassanid Persian rule in modern-day Iraq, far from the land of Israel. Other important rabbinic works include the Talmud of the Land of Israel, sometimes called the Jerusalem Talmud (perhaps fifth century CE), and the Tosefta, a kind of compendium of material similar to the Mishnah, comparable in date, often with different readings and rulings.[14] From this complex material (or, often, from secondhand treatments of this material), Witherington, Alexandre, and many others extract sayings, stories, and legal rulings and retroject them onto life in first-century Judea and Galilee.

The use of rabbinic sources in this manner is disturbing for multiple reasons. First, it is by no means certain that the attribution of a given saying, or a certain tale, to a particular rabbi is historically reliable. Nor is it generally possible to verify either the historicity of a particular rabbi or any of the limited (and sometimes conflicting) biographical data scattered throughout rabbinic traditions about various rabbis. Further, and perhaps most importantly, rabbinic literature intentionally transmits multiple voices, whose weight in the tradition is not necessarily equal. Some opinions may be preserved in the tradition precisely in order to be contradicted. The mere presence of an opinion cannot be taken as evidence that it reflects normative views or social practice, let alone both.

While much contemporary critical scholarship, whether Jewish or Christian, is well aware of the many difficulties and dangers inherent in such an approach, it is hardly unique to Christian scholars attempting to contrast Jesus favorably with his Jewish contemporaries. On the contrary, the relatively uncritical use of rabbinic sources as reliable historical evidence for Jews and Judaism in the several centuries before the codification of the Mishnah typified generations of Jewish scholarship and is by no means wholly abandoned. Partly because the Mishnah and the Talmud have a status comparable to that of scripture itself in traditional Judaism, many Jewish scholars treat these sources as reliable portraits of ancient Jewish life and law. This, ironically, is why some Christian scholars have not seen anything problematic in their use of rabbinic sources to demonstrate the inferior treatment of Jewish women—at least some Jewish scholarship seems to endorse and advocate precisely such an approach. But where some Christian scholars have construed gender distinctions in early Judaism as demonstration of a fundamental Jewish misogyny actively opposed by Jesus, certain Jewish scholars consider these same distinctions evidence of great Jewish respect for women and women's divinely ordained roles. Such Jewish and Christian scholarship agrees on the details, but not on their significance.

To be fair, this portrait of Jewish women is not entirely based on later rabbinic sources, though rabbinic sources are offered as substantiation for virtually every detail I have identified above. It is supplemented with misogynistic statements of demonstrably earlier authors such as Jesus ben Sira (a writer of the second century BCE whose *Wisdom* is included in the so-called Apocrypha or Deutero-canonical books). The writings of the Jewish philosopher, Philo of Alexandria (who wrote in the first half of the first century CE), and the Jewish historian and apologist, Josephus (who wrote in the last quarter of the same century), are also frequently utilized selectively and uncritically.

To demonstrate in detail what is wrong with each of the claims enumerated above is far beyond the scope of this intentionally introductory essay. But dissecting just a few examples should be sufficient to alert readers to the potential flaws with the rest.

Particularly instructive is Alexandre's assertion that Jewish men "maintained a prudent silence" with regard to Jewish women. To support this claim, she cites a saying found in the well-known Mishnaic tractate *Pirke Avot* (*Sayings of the Fathers*) 1:5. This particular saying is attributed to Yose ben Yochanan of Jerusalem, thought to have lived no later than the first century CE and perhaps somewhat earlier.

There are essentially three problems with Alexandre's claim. First, *Avot* does not advocate "silence," prudent or otherwise, though it does, as we shall see, favor limited conversation between men and women. Second, the idealized prescription of *Avot* should hardly be confused with social description, whether for the rabbinic circles out of which it comes, the larger Jewish communities around the rabbis of the Mishnaic period, or the Jews of first-century CE Palestine. Finally, ironically, nothing Jesus does in the gospel narratives is inconsistent with the dictum of *Avot*.

As Alexandre's own quotation of the passage demonstrates, *Avot* transmits the saying of Yose ben Yochanan warning against excessive discourse with women:

> Yose ben Yochanan of Jerusalem says . . . "don't talk too much with women." He spoke of a man's wife, all the more so is the rule to be applied to the wife of one's fellow. In this regard did the sages say, "So long as a man talks too much with a woman, (1) he brings trouble on himself, (2) wastes time better spent on studying Torah, and (3) ends up an heir of Gehenna."[15]

The precise nature of such discourse is not apparent in the saying attributed to Yose ben Yochanan, necessitating the explanatory clarifications of the subsequent verses.[16] That it was understood by subsequent rabbinic interpreters to limit, but not exclude, men speaking with women is apparent in a narrative of the Babylonian Talmud. A woman named Beruriah, here said to be the wife of a famous second-century rabbi named Meir, chides Rabbi Yose of Galilee for asking her a question in a less-concise form than he might have.[17] Elsewhere, Beruriah is portrayed in Talmud as a woman learned in Torah, who discourses with men (see next chapter). Partly because the Beruriah traditions are historically dubious, crafting this as an encounter between Rabbi Yose and Beruriah may therefore suggest some polemical tinge. The audience is reminded that women shouldn't talk much to men, and Beruriah, a learned woman said to have given scholarly opinions to men, here affirms the rightness of these practices.

Interestingly, another mishnaic tradition may be adduced as further circumscription of speech between men and certain women, in this case married women. The passage is from the mishnaic tractate on marriage contracts (m. Ketuboth 7.6) and states that if a woman transgresses the law of Moses and Jewish law, she is not entitled to payment of the marriage contract on the termination of the marriage. The text provides three instances of what is meant by the term "Jewish law": "D. And what is the Jewish law? If (1) she goes out with her hair flowing loose, or (2) she spins in the marketplace, or (3) she talks with just anybody."[18]

Yet the precise meaning of this last phrase, kol ʾadam, is again somewhat ambiguous. Another translator gives "if she hold converse with all men," which he further annotates as "loose talk."[19] Tal Ilan, an Israeli feminist historian, translates it as "if she . . . speaks with any man" and suggests that the three instances here share a concern that married women not do in public things that ought to remain within the domestic domain.[20]

But do such concerns and admonitions translate to widespread social practice? Within rabbinic sources themselves, women are portrayed in conversation with respectable rabbinic males. In b. Shabbat 13a-b, we find the story of a widow having a scholar to dinner and engaging in extensive conversation with him. It is, of course, not insignificant that the woman is a widow and thus not (currently) some other man's wife. Though the story may not constitute a window into first-century Jewish life, it does make clear that rabbinic sources themselves provide a complex, and sometimes contradictory, portrait.

The claim that Jesus differed from other Jewish men in his willingness to speak with women is undercut not just by a careful analysis of rabbinic evidence, it fails from the testimony of the New Testament as well. A brief survey of the relevant New Testament passages suggests that Jesus' behavior, as presented there, is generally quite in line with rabbinic representation. (Ironically, of course, Jesus' own behavior might be taken as better evidence for the practices of first-century Jewish men, but that would hardly serve the apologetic interests of the Witheringtons and Alexandres, for whom Jesus' actions are not representative of Jewish men, but rather distinguish him from them.)

Excluding resurrection appearances, Jesus speaks directly to women in twelve episodes in the canonical gospels.[21] Four are unique to Luke; one is unique to

Matthew; three are unique to John. None occur in the Q material, which many scholars consider earlier and potentially more historically plausible than material likely to originate with the gospel authors themselves (see chapter 7). I limit myself to canonical texts simply because the proponents of such arguments rarely consider anything but canonical texts reliable sources for the life and teachings of Jesus.

In almost every instance, Jesus' conversation with women is terse and fits easily within the rabbinic notion of limited speech with women, particularly married women. In all three synoptics (Mark 5:34//Matt 9:22//Luke 8:48), Jesus says to the hemorrhaging woman, "Daughter, your faith has saved you (from your disease)"; each gospel also has Jesus say a few other, somewhat different words. To the widowed mother in Nain (Luke 7:11–17), Luke's Jesus says exactly two words: "Don't cry" (mē klaie)." To the woman who anoints him, Matthew's and Mark's Jesus says nothing, but Luke's Jesus says (Luke 7:50) just what he says to the hemorrhaging woman: "Your faith has saved you: go in peace."[22] To the woman bent over for eighteen years (Luke 13:10–17), Luke's Jesus speaks a mere five words in Greek: "Woman, be released from your ailment."

Even in scenes that may seem to represent significant exchanges between Jesus and women, rarely does he actually speak more than a few words with women. In Luke, Mary of Bethany is depicted as sitting at Jesus' feet and listening to what he is saying, but the only dialogue in this scene takes place between Martha, called her sister,[23] and Jesus. It consists of only one exchange: Martha complains about Mary's failure to participate in the housework, and Jesus responds definitively, praising Mary's choice and ending the dialogue. Similarly, Jesus' encounter with a gentile woman in the vicinity of Tyre (found in Mark and Matthew, but not in Luke, and the subject of considerable feminist exegesis) consists of only a few short lines of dialogue. Even in the raising of Lazarus in John 11:18–45, Jesus only speaks to Martha three times and to Mary once. Only in the encounter between Jesus and the Samaritan woman in John 4:7–30 is Jesus portrayed as engaging in extended discourse with a woman.

Interestingly, of those few narratives where Jesus speaks more than a few words or engages in actual dialogue, two involve non-Jewish women (i.e., the Syro-Phoenician/Canaanite woman, respectively, in Mark 7:24–30//Matt 15:21–28; the Samaritan woman in John 4). Further, not a single woman with whom Jesus speaks in the gospels is explicitly represented as married. No mention of a husband occurs for the distressed gentile mother of the possessed daughter (ancient readers might have taken her to be divorced or a widow). Several other women are either explicitly or implicitly portrayed as unmarried: the Samaritan woman in John 4 (whatever vv. 16–18 really mean) and Mary and Martha of Bethany. In fact, in the entire canonical corpus, apart from his mother, only one woman in the Jesus entourage is explicitly identified in terms of a spouse: Joanna, the wife of Chuza, the "steward" of Herod. This lack of marital identifiers tends to be true for men as well; it might reflect the actual marital status of Jesus' followers or merely the disinterest of the evangelists (or even both).

It is important to recognize that in this analysis, I have deliberately refrained from any critical consideration of the probable authenticity of any of these narratives. Instead, though I have serious doubts that any of these episodes go back to Jesus himself,[24] I have confined myself only to the ways in which Jesus is portrayed within the canonical gospels.

Thus, regardless of the historical reliability of either rabbinic sources or the gospels, nothing Jesus does in the canonical gospels may actually be seen to conflict with these putative rabbinic restrictions. On the contrary, Jesus speaks only to women who are not portrayed as the wives of other men. He also speaks, in one instance in the Gospel of John, to his own mother; interestingly, there is no mention of her husband apart from the birth narratives in Matthew and Luke, and it seems a plausible inference that she, too, may have been widowed, though there are other possibilities.[25] Rarely does Jesus speak more than a few terse words to any woman. In the few instances when he does, the woman is either not Jewish (John 4:7–30) or part of a large crowd (Luke 23:28–31).

Other components of the portrait of Jewish women are similarly vulnerable to a nuanced reading of both rabbinic and early Christian sources. For instance, Tal Ilan points out that while some rabbinic texts evince an ideal that women never venture into the marketplace, other texts simply presume the presence of respectable women in the market as the context for discussion of some other concern. In a passage from the Tosefta tractate *Niddah* (on menstrual impurity) 6.17, it is matter-of-factly suggested that one possible source of blood on a woman's garment might not be menstrual blood, but rather blood from the butchers' market (which would not incur the impurity of menstrual blood). In the Babylonian Talmud *Nedarim* 49b, we find a story of a married couple (a rabbi and his wife), who share an embroidered garment. He wears it to pray; she wears it to market.[26]

Other evidence for the unremarkable presence of Jewish women in public comes from the gospels themselves. Mark, and following him Matthew and Luke, give us the hemorrhaging woman (Mark 5:25–34//Matt 9:20–22//Luke 8:43–48), who comes up to Jesus in public and touches his fringes in hope of a cure. In Mark 6:3 and Matthew 13:56 (though not Luke), the (unnamed) sisters of Jesus appear to be present when Jesus preaches in his hometown synagogue of Nazareth. This is not an unambiguous example—it presumes that those who respond (negatively) to Jesus' preaching in the Nazareth synagogue are doing so while still in the synagogue itself. That the women are present with the speakers and probably in the synagogue itself seems slightly clearer in Mark; the absence of the word "here" in Matthew's formulation mutes the immediate presence of the sisters and may then be read somewhat more generally, as an indication of their presence in the village.

Luke recounts a narrative (Luke 13:10–17) in which, in a synagogue one sabbath, Jesus heals a woman crippled for eighteen years by a demonic spirit. The head of the synagogue protests Jesus' performance of a healing on the sabbath, but neither the woman's presence in the synagogue nor her subsequent praise of God in response to her cure evokes any comment. Matthew 15:37 is explicit (though Mark 8:9 is not) that women are among the crowd gathered to hear Jesus and that is miraculously fed with seven loaves and a few small fish. Luke, too, portrays women present in the crowds attracted to Jesus (e.g., Luke 11:27–28 and 23:27, where women whom Jesus addresses as "Daughters of Jerusalem" are part of the crowd following Jesus on the way to his crucifixion).

In identifying these passages, I am again not arguing for their historical accuracy—here, too, as in the case of the narratives depicting Jesus in conversation with women, there are many reasons to be skeptical about the reliability of these episodes. Whether or not these specific incidents occurred, their recounting in the gospels tells us much about what ancient authors and audiences took as plausible, unremarkable and the givens of ordinary social life, most notably, for our purposes, the presence of Jewish women in a variety of public venues.

By now, it should be sufficiently clear that the stereotypic portraits of Jewish women in the first century CE found in many contemporary treatments are seriously distorted by concerns to present Jesus and the earliest movement around him as free from any trace of misogyny. The more Jewish women are presented as subordinate and disadvantaged by virtue of being Jewish, the more Jesus and earliest Christianity can be presented as liberating. But the representation of Jewish women as subjugated plays a further role in some Christian arguments. As in Witherington's article, it functions not only to construct the presence of Jewish women in the Jesus movement as unusual, but also to explain their presence: Jewish women are understood to be attracted to Jesus and the Jesus movement precisely for its liberating view of women. This, too, is not without some modern resonance: its implicit message is that then, as also now, Jesus liberates women.

This raises, then, a particularly vexing question. Feminist scholarship of the last two decades has demonstrated and emphasized not only the presence of women in early Christian communities, but also their active roles in shaping the identity and fostering the growth of those same communities.[27] Yet, perhaps unconsciously assimilating the Pauline view (Gal 3:28) that in Christ, there is no longer Jew or Gentile, few have thought to discriminate between the presence of Jewish women and that of non-Jewish women. In fact, any essay on Jewish women in the first century as prelude to the study of women in early Christianity must ask more discriminating questions about the roles Jewish women actually played in the Jesus movement and thus how significant the study of Jewish women really is for understanding women in the Jesus movement and in early Christian churches after the death of Jesus.

The entire New Testament identifies something like forty[28] women by name. Of these, three are clearly not members of the Jesus movement: Berenice, Drusilla, and Herodias (all historical figures known independently from Josephus and other ancient sources). Approximately twelve named women are associated with the movement during Jesus' lifetime: these include Johanna; five or perhaps six women named Mary (his mother, Mary of Magdala, Mary of Bethany, Mary the mother of John Mark, Mary the mother of James and Joses, and Mary "of Clopas" [John 19:25]: Mary the mother of James and Joses may be identical either to Mary the mother of Jesus [see Mark 6:3//Matt 13:55] or to Mary "of Clopas," but not to both); Martha of Bethany; Salome; and Susanna. It seems likely, though not certain, that the servant, Rhoda, in the house of Mary, mother of John Mark, should be included in this list. All these women may be counted as Jews, with the possible exception of Rhoda, whose Greek name and servile status might point to her not being Jewish. (To pursue this requires a much more detailed discussion both of names as indicators of identity and of the question of Jewish use of non-Jewish servants and ownership of non-Jewish slaves, none of which is feasible here.) Two other unambiguously Jewish women are mentioned only in the Gospel of Luke: Elizabeth, the mother of John the Baptist, and a woman named Anna, whom Luke portrays as a prophet living in the temple, who prophesies about the baby Jesus (Luke 2:36–38). Despite their place in later Christian tradition, neither of these women can be placed with confidence among the members of the Jesus movement. Anna is said to be eighty-four at the birth of Jesus; to have witnessed him preach publicly, she would have had to have lived to be almost 125 years old. Though Luke portrays Elizabeth as praising Mary, the mother of Jesus, while both women are still pregnant, nothing else in Luke or any of the other gospels presents the mother of the Baptist as a member of the Jesus movement.

In Luke's account of the followers of Jesus who continued the movement after his death, a small number of Jewish women are mentioned who may or may not have been followers of Jesus in his lifetime and who round out my list of about a dozen: the less than exemplary Sapphira, wife of Ananias; the more exemplary widow, Tabitha (also called Dorcas in Greek); and the formidable Priscilla, known also from Paul's letters as Prisca.

Apart from these three, of the named women associated with the Jesus movement in the decades after his death, none is explicitly or demonstrably Jewish. (The single possible exception may be the Mary greeted by Paul in Romans 16: 6. But since her name appears as Maria, rather than as Mariam, the usual Greek transliteration of the Hebrew/Aramaic Miriam, it may be a form of the Latin gentilic Marius.)[29] On the contrary, many of these women appear unlikely to have been born Jews by virtue of their names, their geographic locations, and perhaps also their association with churches affiliated with Paul, the self-described apostle to the Gentiles: Julia, Persis, Tryphaena, and Tryphosa, all known from Romans; and Euodia and Syntyche in Philippians. Some, particularly in Acts, are explicitly identified as non-Jews, such as Damaris, an aristocratic woman converted by Paul in Athens. Lydia, the trader in purple goods, converted by Paul in Philippi, is also described by Luke as non-Jewish by birth, though Luke portrays her as a gentile worshipper of the God of the Jews and sets her encounter with Paul in a Jewish place of worship after a worship service that appears to consist primarily of women.

A similar portrait of unnamed women emerges from these same sources. To the list of demonstrable Jewish followers of Jesus, we could add the woman who anoints Jesus in all four gospels (Mark 14:3–9//Matt 26:6–13//Luke 7:36–50; John 12:1–8). In all three synoptic accounts, unnamed Jewish women are also said to have been present at the crucifixion.[30] The majority of the additional unnamed followers who may reasonably be presumed Jewish come from the writer of Luke-Acts: the unnamed women who, together with Susanna, Johanna, and Mary of Magdala, travel with Jesus and support the movement financially;

the woman who, seeing Jesus on the way to the cross, cries out in praise of the breasts and uterus of Jesus' mother; the women of Jerusalem who lament Jesus on the same occasion; the unnamed women accompanying the male disciples in Jerusalem after the resurrection; the women in Jerusalem persecuted by Saul for their membership in the movement; the "widows" of the "Hebrews," and probably also the "widows" of the "Hellenists," whose inequitable treatment is the subject of an internal dispute Luke relates in Acts 6:1–6.

This brief prosopographic survey suggests that apart from the movement in Jesus' lifetime and community, whose membership was virtually if not entirely Jewish,[31] it becomes increasingly difficult to identify Jewish women as members of early Christian churches. While it is possible that similar patterns hold for the presence of Jewish men in the movement as well, the answers to the broader questions do not change the significance of this observation. That is, the prosopographic data raise significant questions about just how relevant the study of Jewish women in the first century truly is for understanding those women who joined the Jesus movement. It flies in the face of common sense to suggest that it has no relevance: as we have just seen, the first women followers of Jesus were clearly Jewish, and to that extent, it cannot but be helpful to know as much as possible about the realities of such women's lives. Yet it may also be that precisely because we are dealing with the attraction of Jewish women to a new Jewish charismatic leader, and to a movement around that leader that consists virtually, if not entirely, of other Jews and expresses itself wholly within the broader framework of first century Judaism, that their gender matters more than their Jewishness. This is, of course, a very different approach than that represented by the work of Witherington, Alexandre, and others, who view the Jewishness of the women around Jesus as the element of identity that most determined the conditions and experiences of Jewish women's lives. From their perspective, the subordination and disadvantages of Jewish women were more a function of their being Jewish women, than of their being women in a larger Greco-Roman culture characterized by constructions of gender difference and hierarchy shared by almost everyone. That is, for the Witheringtons and Alexandres of the world, what attracted Jewish women to Jesus must be understood in terms of specifically Jewish constructions of gender and their practical manifestations in the lives of Jewish women. But such an assumption seems to me not only unwarranted, but also part and parcel of the arguments they wish to construct.

In fact, careful scrutiny of the Jewish women said to have joined the Jesus movement (in canonical gospel narratives, Luke's portrait of the Jerusalem community in Acts, and the undisputed letters of Paul) suggests a very different conclusion. As we have seen here, the actual number of women represented by the texts as participating in the Jesus movement who are identifiable as Jews is fairly small. As I have pointed out in several earlier studies, these women are almost always represented as anomalous in some respect, often with regard to ancient cultural constructions of gender.[32] That is, they are represented as women old enough to be married, but who do not appear to be so (Mary of Magdala and Mary and Martha of Bethany); as widows or apparently childless;

and as (perhaps) unnamed women whom men pay for sex (if, for instance, Matt 21:31–32 accurately reflects the presence of prostitutes).[33] They are portrayed as possessed by demons (Mary of Magdala) or afflicted with grievous illness (the woman with the twelve-year hemorrhage; the woman bent over) or as mothers of stricken children (the wife of Jairus, the widow of Nain). Those who explicitly have children are disproportionately the mothers of sons, and it sometimes seems that their presence in the movement is a result of their sons' involvement. Whether this portrait is historically reliable, rather than the construction of Christian tradition, is difficult to know.

Though I do not want to downplay the complex reasons women, both Jewish and non-Jewish, may have had for joining the movement centered on Jesus and his teachings, I think it is unwise to ignore the potential implications of these observations. Missing among the women portrayed as Jesus' close disciples and supporters are married women with husbands and children. This may reflect the reality that such women were both less likely to join the movement and perhaps also less likely to be able to do so were they so inclined. Though Jesus resurrects the daughter of Jairus and his unnamed wife, it is only Jairus' belief in Jesus' powers that we see, and we are never told that the mother believes.

Missing also are aristocratic Jewish women comparable in social class and status to the non-Jewish women who populate the pages of Acts. Several Herodian women appear to have had actual opportunities to consider the claims of Jesus' movement, yet none are portrayed as followers. Herodias is explicitly portrayed as an enemy, responsible for the death of John the Baptist; we cannot imagine her to have been sympathetic to Jesus' movement. According to Acts 26, Berenice presided with Agrippa over Paul's hearing and affirmed his innocence, yet apparently was not moved to join the new movement. Drusilla, too, appears on the edges of Acts, but not as a supporter. Prisca/Priscilla, mentioned in both Acts and Romans, may have been a woman of some social status, though hardly in a class with the Herodians.

Ironically, then, it may be more misleading than many scholars have recognized to seek the appeal of the Jesus movement to Jewish women in their circumstances as Jewish women rather than to seek it in either their identity as women (regardless of ethnicity) or their identity as Jews (regardless of gender). Scholars like Witherington locate Jesus' appeal to Jewish women in Jesus' own rejection of those elements of first-century Judaism that are presumed to disadvantage women as a whole (purity restrictions, domestic seclusion, lack of access to Torah study, exclusion from the temple or from synagogue participation or from both) and in his inclusion of women within the redemptive community. But if this is true, why is it that what the Jewish women in the Jesus movement have in common appears to lie elsewhere, in their relative marginality within ancient systems of gender that are by no means unique to Judaism? Why is it, that is, that they are represented as disproportionately unmarried, widowed, childless, possessed, and otherwise physically afflicted? Why are they not rather married women with responsible husbands and healthy children, chafing at their seclusion at home, knocking on the doors of the synagogue or of the study house?

It is important to emphasize that the connection between these representations and any historical reality is far from clear. Indeed, this representation of
Jewish women in the Jesus movement may point to concerns of either the authors of the gospels or other early Christian tradents. Some (if not all) of those
persons might have found it efficacious to represent women in the gospels as
marginalized—a representation that might, for instance, function to minimize
their authority or status. The author of Luke-Acts, for instance, may prefer to
represent women around Jesus as marginalized women to minimize women's
stature within early Christian churches. Other male writers may be less self-
conscious about this and more likely only to notice or only to mention women
when the women are anomalous. The nature of the evidence available to us does
not allow us to resolve these issues. We can only note the ways in which women
are represented and attempt to consider how those constructions might function
and how they might conceivably correspond to social reality.

Nevertheless, to me, all this suggests that to understand why Jewish women
joined the Jesus movement, we must look to the issues that engaged Jews of
both genders in the first century (the oppressive presence of the Romans, the
corruption of the Herodians, the purity and efficacy of the temple) and to the
pressures on women, Jewish and otherwise, to conform to ancient understandings of gender. But appealing as it may be for contemporary Christian purposes,
there seems to be little reason to argue that the particular constructions of gender within Judaism led Jewish women to join the Jesus movement.

How relevant, then, and how problematic is the study of Jewish women for
the origins of Christianity? In an important essay published in 1986, Bernadette
Brooten argued that the reconstruction of Jewish women's history in the Roman
period was an important task for Christian theology.[34] Given the uses to which
Jewish women's history has been put in service of contemporary Christian feminist goals, Brooten is unquestionably correct if good theology is the goal. Yet,
in the desire to combat feminist Christian anti-Judaism, there is always the danger that we may unwittingly allow Christian scholarship and theological concerns to dictate the reconstruction of Jewish women's lives. And as I have argued
here, it may well be that the history of Jewish women in the first century provides only limited understanding of the attraction of the Jesus movement to
women and of the roles, presence, and self-understanding of the women who
joined the movement. With all these caveats in mind, we can turn now, in the
next chapter, to the evidence for Jewish women and their lives as Jews in the
first centuries BCE and CE.

NOTES

1. *The Anchor Bible Dictionary*, ed. David Noel Freedman (New York: Doubleday and Co.,
1992), s.v. "Women, in the New Testament," vol. 6:957–61. The section on Jewish
women is 957. Other Christian Bible dictionary entries in the same vein include Robin
Scroggs, "Woman in the New Testament," *Interpreter's Dictionary of the Bible*, suppl. vol., ed.
Keith Crim (Nashville, TN: Abingdon, 1976) 966–68 and R. B. Edwards, "Woman,"
International Standard Bible Encyclopedia (ISBE), 2nd. edn., ed, G. W. Bromiley (Grand Rapids,

MI: Eerdmans, 1988) vol. 4:1089–97. A similar view of Jewish women in the first century is found in a wide range of Christian scholarship, from Joachim Jeremias, *Jerusalem in the Time of Jesus* (Philadelphia: Fortress, 1969) 359–76; to Leonard Swidler, *Women in Judaism: The Status of Women in Formative Judaism* (Metuchen, NJ: Scarecrow, 1976); to Elisabeth Moltmann-Wendel, *Liberty, Equality, Sisterhood: On the Emancipation of Women in Church and Society* (Philadelphia: Fortress, 1978) 9–21. I am indebted to Kathleen Corley for these references. For an additional critique, see also Amy-Jill Levine, "Second-Temple Judaism, Jesus and Women: Yeast of Eden," *Biblical Interpretation* 2/1 (1994) 8–33.

2. Monique Alexandre, "Early Christian Women," in *A History of Women in the West: Volume 1: From Ancient Goddesses to Christian Saints*, ed. Pauline Schmitt Pantel, trans. Arthur Goldhammer (Cambridge, MA: Belknap Press of Harvard University Press, 1992) 407–44. The section on Jewish women is on 416–19.

3. Alexandre, "Early Christian Women" 416.

4. Witherington ("Women, in the New Testament" 957) claims only that ritual impurity impeded women's synagogue participation; Alexandre extends it to a larger exclusion from social life.

5. Alexandre, "Early Christian Women" 416.

6. Relying here on *b. Meg.* 23a.

7. Witherington, "Women, in the New Testament" 957.

8. Ibid. 958.

9. Alexandre, "Early Christian Women" 419.

10. Ibid. 420.

11. So also Witherington, "Women, in the New Testament" 958. For a very different view of Jesus' adherence to purity regulations, see Paula Fredriksen, "Did Jesus Oppose the Purity Laws?" *Bible Review* (June 1995) 19 ff.

12. Alexandre acknowledges that these reports meet with "masculine incredulity . . . in Mark and Luke," but does not see that the responses to the women undermine her conclusion. In Mark 16:8, the terrified women say nothing to anyone; in Luke 24:11, they tell the male apostles, who do not believe them. The author of the Gospel of John presents no response to Mary's announcement of the risen Christ; only when they see Jesus himself do the male apostles rejoice (John 20:18–20). In the longer ending of Mark, as in the Gospel of John, Jesus appears first to Mary of Magdala, and, as in Luke, a woman is not believed.

13. Alexandre, "Early Christian Women" 423.

14. For good overviews, see the entries in the *ABD* (Gary Porton, "Talmud," 6:310–15; Roger Brooks, "Mishnah," 4:871–73; there is no entry for Tosefta). More detailed and technical discussions may be found in H. L. Strack and G. Stemberger, *Introduction to the Talmud and Midrash*, trans. Markus Bockmuehl (London: T&T Clark, 1991; Minneapolis, MN: Fortress, 1992).

15. Jacob Neusner, *The Mishnah, a New Translation* (New Haven, CT: Yale University Press, 1988). Similar translations are found in other English renderings: "Talk not much with a woman" (R. Travers Herford, *Pirke Aboth: The Ethics of the Talmud: Sayings of the Fathers*, [New York: Jewish Institute of Religion, 1945; reprint, New York: Schocken, 1962]); "talk not much with womankind" (Herbert Danby, *The Mishnah* [Oxford: Oxford University Press, 1933]). The translation of Philip Blackman (*Mishnayoth* [New York: Judaica, 1963; reprint 1990]) construes this passage even more narrowly as concerned with too much "gossip."

16. The explanatory material following the saying of Yose ben Yochanan is generally taken to represent later expansion: see, e.g., Herford, who notes (p. 25) the absence of this material in the version found in a different rabbinic work, *Avot de Rabbi Nathan*; see

especially Tal Ilan, *Jewish Women in Greco-Roman Palestine: an Inquiry into Image and Status*, Texte und Studien zum Antiken Judentum 44 (Tübingen: J. C. B. Mohr [Paul Siebeck], 1995) 126–27, for a view of the expansions as evidence of the concerns of subsequent interpreters.

17. *b. Erub.* 53b, on which see Ilan, *Jewish Women* 127.

18. Neusner, *The Mishnah, a New Translation.*

19. Blackman, *Mishnayoth* 3:161.

20. Ilan, *Jewish Women* 129.

21. To the hemorrhaging woman in Mark 5:34//Matt 9:22//Luke 8:48; to the gentile woman in Mark 7:24–30//Matt 15:21–28 (with no Lukan parallel); to the widow of Nain in Luke 7:11–17; to the woman who anoints Jesus, only in the Lukan version in 7:50; to the sisters Mary and Martha in Luke 10:38–42 and also in John 11:18–45 (I have counted these as two separate instances); to the woman bent over for eighteen years in Luke 13:10–17; to the wailing women on the way to the crucifixion in Luke 23:28–31. In Matthew's version of Jesus' conversation with the sons of Zebedee, their mother initiates the discussion (Matt 20:20–28//Mark 10:35–45, with no Lukan parallel). In addition to the exchange with Mary and Martha, Jesus speaks to women three other times in the Gospel of John: to his mother in 2:3–4, to the Samaritan woman in 4:7–30, and, if the passage is authentic, to the woman accused of adultery in 8:10–11.

22. Cf. Luke 8:48.

23. See D'Angelo, chapter 5, on the possible meanings of this designation.

24. Problems of authenticity are considered further in subsequent essays. But in this vein, it is interesting to note that the members of the self-designated "Jesus Seminar" consider none of these sayings authentic to Jesus. Rather, they are all printed in black, denoting the seminar's consensus that Jesus said none of them, and that each is the work of later tradents or authors (Robert W. Funk, Roy W. Hoover, and the Jesus Seminar, *The Five Gospels: The Search for the Authentic Words of Jesus* [New York: Macmillan, 1993]).

25. See, for instance, Jane C. Schaberg, *The Illegitimacy of Jesus* (New York: Crossroad, 1990).

26. For discussion, see Ilan, *Jewish Women* 129.

27. The best known example of such scholarship is Elisabeth Schüssler Fiorenza, *In Memory of Her: A Feminist Theological Reconstruction of Christian Origins* (New York: Crossroad, 1983); for numerous others, see the comprehensive bibliography at the end of this book.

28. In the forthcoming *Dictionary of Women in Scripture*, ed. Carol Meyers, Toni Craven, and Ross S. Kraemer (Boston: Houghton Mifflin), 42 entries are devoted to named women in the New Testament. These names probably represent between 36 and 38 individual women. For a discussion of the problem, see the introduction to the New Testament forthcoming in the *Dictionary.*

29. See Peter Lampe, "Mary.7" *ABD* 4:582–83.

30. One unnamed woman may also be present in John 19:25, depending on whether the phrase "his mother's sister" modifies "Mary of Clopas" or refers to a fourth woman.

31. Narratives of gentile converts during the lifetime of Jesus are notoriously difficult to assess historically given their legitimizing function in later Christian disputes about the origins and appropriateness of a mission to non-Jews.

32. Ross S. Kraemer, *Ecstatics and Ascetics: Studies in the Functions of Religious Activities for Women in the Greco-Roman World* (Ph.D. dissertation, Princeton University, Princeton, NJ, 1976), 124–33; Kraemer, *Her Share of the Blessings: Women's Religions among Pagans, Jews and Christians in the Greco-Roman World* (New York: Oxford University Press, 1992) 128–56.

33. Kathleen Corley, *Private Women, Public Meals: Social Conflict in the Synoptic Tradition* (Peabody, MA: Hendrickson, 1993).

34. Bernadette Brooten, "Jewish Women's History in the Roman Period, A Task for Christian Theology," in *Christians among Jews and Gentiles: Essays in Honor of Krister Stendahl on His Sixty-Fifth Birthday*, ed. G. W. E. Nickelsburg and George W. MacRae (Philadelphia: Fortress, 1986) 22–30 (*Harvard Theological Review* 79/3–4 [1986]).

3

>─+─◆──0──◆─+─◄

JEWISH WOMEN AND WOMEN'S
JUDAISM(S) AT THE BEGINNING
OF CHRISTIANITY

Ross S. Kraemer

The previous chapter considers some of the dangers of writing about Jewish women and women's Judaisms in the context of the study of women in early Christianity. This chapter, which I hope will not be read independently of the prior one, concerns itself primarily with critical, historical questions; with what we know about Jewish women in the period ca. 100 BCE to 150 CE that is particularly germane to the study of early Christianity in general and to the study of women and Christian origins more specifically.

Our Sources and Their Dilemmas

What we know about Jewish women in the centuries just preceding and follow-ing the emergence of Christianity is limited by the ancient sources that have been preserved and our ability to read them critically. Most of the surviving literary sources shed little light on the lives of Jewish women. Not surprisingly, the Jewish historian Flavius Josephus, whose *Antiquities of the Jews* and *Jewish War* (both written in the last quarter of the first century CE) are our primary sources for much of what we know about Jewish history in the first century, particularly in Judea, tells us little about ordinary Jewish women. He does, however, provide important information about a number of aristocratic women, including Alexan-dra, wife of Alexander Jannaeus, who succeeded her husband as queen and ruled from 76 to 67 BCE,[1] and Helena, queen of Adiabene, a small kingdom northeast of Judea (modern-day Iraq), who became a Jew, as did much of her kingdom.[2] Particularly prominent among the women in Josephus' narratives are the women of the Herodian family that ruled Judea, with Roman acquiescence, from the second half of the first century BCE through the Jewish revolt (66–73 CE).

Interestingly, three of these women appear in the pages of the New Testament as peripheral players in the early Christian drama. Drusilla, the Jewish wife of the Roman governor, Felix, receives brief notice when she accompanies her husband to Jerusalem (Acts 24:24).[3] Her sister, Berenice, co-ruler with their brother, Agrippa II, and ultimately the lover of Titus, the Roman emperor, also appears in Acts 25:13–26:32; she and Agrippa hear the case against Paul and jointly conclude that he has "done nothing to deserve death or imprisonment." Finally, Herodias, aunt to Drusilla, Berenice, and Agrippa, wife of Herod Antipas, and mother of Salome, plays a more infamous role in the gospels, two of which assign her primary blame for the death of John the Baptist. The presentation of these women in Acts and the gospels differs considerably from that in Josephus, raising intriguing questions of historical reconstruction, among others.

Apart from the writings of Josephus, Jewish literature of the period shows little concern for contemporaneous Jewish women. Philo of Alexandria, a prolific Jewish philosopher who wrote during the first half of the first century CE, composed a short treatise on a monastic Jewish community composed of men and women philosophers, called Therapeutics.[4] In its account of the conflict between Antiochus and the Maccabees in the second quarter of the second century BCE, 2 Maccabees relates the torture and martyrdom of a mother and her seven sons. The historicity of the story is impossible to determine; the story is, in any case, refashioned in elaborate philosophical dress by the author of 4 Maccabees.

Though women as actors figure minimally in Jewish historical writing of the period, women appear as a category in several works (often characterized as "wisdom" literature) that prescribe how the righteous man should live and what conduct he should avoid. Several of these books, including the Wisdom of Jesus ben Sira (written in Hebrew in the second century BCE and translated into Greek by the author's grandson) and the *Sentences of Pseudo-Phocylides* (perhaps early first century CE), contain virulent misogynist language and express deep concern for the regulation of women, particularly their sexuality. They are of interest for what they may reveal of ancient male authors' perceptions and of ancient understandings and constructions of gender, but they reveal little about the lives and self-understandings of Jewish women themselves.

Interestingly, women are often the subjects or significant characters in manifestly fictive narratives composed by Jewish authors writing in Greek (or, occasionally, translated into Greek from Hebrew). However, these women are uniformly located in Israel's past, including Esther, in the Greek translation (with fascinating additions) of the Hebrew Esther; Judith and Susanna, in books that also bear their names; Sarah, the heroine, and Edna, her mother, in the book of Tobit; and numerous biblical characters in the anonymous "rewritten Bible" erroneously attributed to Philo of Alexandria and thus commonly known as "Pseudo-Philo." A tale in Greek about the biblical Joseph and his Egyptian wife, Aseneth, is thought by many scholars to have been composed by a Jewish author in this period, a position I no longer share.[5]

Observing this disproportionate presence of women in works of fiction (something that appears to hold true for non-Jewish writings of the period as well), Israeli feminist historian Tal Ilan concludes that, "in the minds of the ancient historians [such as Josephus or Nicolaus of Damascus], real history was enacted in the male realm, while women were confined to the field of fiction."[6] For the purposes of this essay, the fact that ancient Jewish historical narratives are largely disinterested in postbiblical women is more important than explanations for this disinterest, which requires careful analysis that is beyond the scope of this chapter. It is tempting to try to compensate for this inattention to women in historical narratives by reading other works, including both the novellas and the wisdom prescriptions, as reasonably accurate representations of ancient social and historical reality. If we possessed more reliable information about Jewish women during this period, we might better be able to gauge the relationship between the portraits of Jewish women in these works and the lives and experiences of actual Jewish women. Largely lacking such controls, though, we should be extraordinarily cautious about reading this material as "factual" or as trustworthy representations of women's lives.

Beyond this corpus of literary materials, much of it written or translated into Greek by and for Jews whose primary language was Greek (that is, the majority of Jews in the Roman empire), there are also isolated references to Jewish women in the works of non-Jewish, non-Christian authors such as Juvenal, Tacitus, and others. One additional category of ancient literature in Greek is pertinent to the study of Jewish women: early Christian writings themselves, especially those now part of the New Testament. Since Christian apologetic shapes the representation of Jews, both women and men, from a very early date in Christian writing, these texts must be read only with great caution as evidence for women's lives and experiences. Nevertheless, they are a useful source, particularly where the depiction of women appears incidental to the larger interest of the narrative, such as parables of Jesus that depict the ordinary lives of women and men (women grinding grain and sweeping houses; men tending flocks and overseeing estates). Elsewhere, as, for instance, in much of the Lukan narratives, we must be alert to the possibility that representations of women have more to do with the author's construction than with the realities of the first century.[7]

As the previous chapter considered, many contemporary portraits of Jewish women in antiquity have relied heavily not on these sources, but on rabbinic Jewish writings, assembled and edited from about 200 CE to the fifth century CE or even later, both in the land of Israel and in Sassanid Persia (neo-Babylonia). Because some of the traditions and rulings in these sources are attributed to (or associated with) rabbis thought to have lived in the first centuries BCE/CE, traditional Jewish scholarship and much Christian scholarship has relied heavily on these texts for evidence about Jews and Judaism in the formative Christian period. For reasons suggested in the previous chapter, I do not consider these sources to be particularly useful as primary evidence for Jewish women in first-century Judea and Galilee (the major areas of earliest Christian activity).[8]

For all their differences, the sources catalogued so far share one particularly frustrating characteristic: none of them is known to have been authored by a woman. Many are unquestionably the work of male authors. Because many Jewish writings from this period are anonymous or patently pseudonymous, it is not impossible that some mask female authorship. It is, however, almost impossible to move beyond this recognition to more definitive statements.[9] The significance of this is considerable: it means that the only voices we are certain we hear are those of men. Certainly, it is not impossible for male authors to transmit reasonably reliable representations of women's lives and experiences. But ancient male authors often display such hostile attitudes toward women, and such strong assumptions about gender difference, that modern readers may feel quite skeptical. Further, ancient male authors may well have been hampered by a true ignorance of the realities of women's lives. Since many men and women in antiquity spent much of their time in the company of other members of their sex, male authors might have had little opportunity to observe, let alone participate, in women's activities and to obtain insight into their experiences.

Fortunately, however, we are not wholly dependent on literary sources, with all their attendant difficulties, for our knowledge of Jewish women's lives. A variety of archaeological sources from the Greco-Roman period qualifies and enhances what we may learn from literary works. In the first century CE, substantial numbers of Greek-speaking Jews lived both in the hellenistic city of Alexandria and in the outlying Egyptian countryside. The dry climate of Egypt has preserved for us a significant number of documents written on papyrus, a plant with fibers that make a particularly effective writing surface. These papyri, as the documents are called, range from tax registers that list the names and ages of Jewish inhabitants of various villages,[10] to wet-nurse contracts,[11] disputes between neighbors,[12] and slave manumissions.[13]

From the borders of the land of Israel has come the most important papyrus find for the study of Jewish women in the Greco-Roman period. In the late 1950s, Israeli archaeologists excavating a cave associated with Simeon bar Kokhba, leader of the second Jewish revolt against Rome (ca. 132–35 CE), found a set of papyrus documents rolled up in a leather bag. These turned out to contain the personal papers of a Jewish woman named Babatha, who was probably born around the year 100 CE and who may have died in the revolt.[14] (Several skeletons, both male and female, were found in the cave, along with various personal items, such as mirrors, sandals, bowls, etc., and it is not impossible that Babatha is among those dead.) Her archive includes marriage contracts, loan documents, guardianship papers, land registrations, and more. Written in Greek, Aramaic, and the regional language of Nabatean, transacted in diverse legal jurisdictions and involving Jews, Roman citizens (who may or may not have been Jews), and Nabateans, these papyri throw into sharp relief the diverse cultural and legal environments in which Babatha and those around her lived their lives. They offer us the most detailed portrait yet of an actual Jewish woman from Greco-Roman antiquity; and we return to Babatha and her archive below.

Although the preservation of documents on papyri is peculiar to those regions with a conducive climate, such as Egypt and the Dead Sea area, inscriptions on stone, marble, and other durable surfaces also yield important information about Jewish women. Burial inscriptions from Egypt afford some touching glimpses of women's experiences of infant and maternal mortality.[15] Those inscriptions from the city of Rome, from Asia Minor, and from various places across the Mediterranean give us women synagogue officers,[16] women converts to Judaism,[17] bereaved widows, mourned wives, mothers and grandmothers, wealthy independent heads of household,[18] enslaved women, and many more. Ancient donor inscriptions honor the financial contributions of Jewish women to synagogue and communal life;[19] inscribed manumission documents testify to Jewish women's participation, both as owners and as slaves, in the ancient slave economy. Some of these date from the first century CE, though a few are earlier, and many come from the second, third, and even fourth centuries CE. Since many of these inscriptions would have been ordered and paid for by women, their very existence (like that of the papyri) demonstrates women's presence in ancient communal life and occasionally allows us, then, to hear something of real women's voices.[20]

Berenice, Babatha, and Jewish Women's Lives

The surviving sources do not allow us to write a full biography of a single Jewish woman from Greco-Roman antiquity. But what we do know and may reconstruct of the lives of two women in particular, the Herodian Berenice in the first century CE and Babatha of Ma'oza in the early second century CE, affords us an excellent starting point to discuss Jewish women's lives.

Berenice was born around 28 CE, one of the five children of Agrippa I and Cypros. A great-granddaughter of Herod the Great, she ultimately became the lover of a Roman general named Titus, who is perhaps far better known in Jewish history for his role in the destruction of the second temple, and his building of the famous Arch of Titus. It still stands in Rome today in commemoration of his triumph over the Jewish revolt. Titus and Berenice apparently wanted to marry, but when Titus became emperor, marriage to a Herodian Jewish princess was out of the question.

Berenice's complicated, fascinating life may be glimpsed through a fairly wide range of ancient sources. Josephus, while silent on her relationship with Titus, provides the most details; Suetonius, Tacitus, Dio, and several other ancient historians treat her affair with Titus. Two ancient inscriptions shed further light on her life.

None of these sources describes her childhood. At a relatively early age, she was married to a man from an elite Alexandrian Jewish family, Marcus Julius Alexander, the son of Alexander, alabarch of Egypt, and nephew of Philo. When Marcus died, her father, Agrippa, then married her to his brother, Herod of Chalcis, with whom she had two sons. In 50 CE, at 22, she was a widow for the second time.

From a feminist perspective, it is at this point that Berenice's life becomes increasingly fascinating. After Herod's death, Berenice did not immediately remarry. Rather, she ruled as queen with her brother, Agrippa II.[21] An inscription on a statue set up to honor her in Athens testifies to her title as "great" queen during this period. A Latin inscription from Beirut also calls her "queen." The narrative from Acts is set during the reign of Berenice and Agrippa.

According to Josephus, Berenice's relationship with her brother, Agrippa, was rumored to be an incestuous one, though his report is not substantiated in the works of several other writers and may reflect Josephus' own hostility toward Berenice for her support of one of his opponents.[22] In any case, Berenice eventually arranged her own marriage to Polemo, king of Cilicia (a non-Jew who agreed to be circumcised for the occasion). Josephus claims that the marriage failed quickly, when Berenice, motivated by *akolasia* (inappropriate sexual desire),[23] deserted (or, perhaps, divorced) Polemo.

When, precisely, Berenice and Titus met does not appear to be known. Roman historians concur, though, that Titus was deeply in love with her. We do know that after the war, Agrippa and Berenice went to Rome with Titus. One Roman historian, Dio Cassius, says that Berenice acted in all respects as though she were Titus' wife, creating enough tension between Titus and the Roman aristocracy that she was forced to leave Rome.[24] When Titus was proclaimed emperor, she returned to Rome, apparently hoping, finally, to become his legitimate wife, but sufficient pressure was brought to bear on Titus that he dismissed her for good.[25]

We know less of the outlines of Babatha's life, though we know some of the specifics in surprising detail. Babatha was born to a couple named Simon and Miriam, probably around the year 100 CE, in an area known as the Roman province of Arabia, just south of the Dead Sea. Whether she had siblings is unknown. Her parents were financially comfortable, owning land, houses, and orchards in their village. Prior to her father's death, he made a deed of gift to her mother, transferring considerable assets into her control, which later appear in Babatha's possession. As with Berenice, though, we know nothing of the specifics of her childhood except that she was not taught to read and write.

Her first marriage was to man named Jesus (in Greek; Joshua in Aramaic) with whom she had a son, also named Jesus. Whether she had other children is unknown, but it seems unlikely—the existing papyri make no mention of them. Her husband Jesus died while their son was still legally a minor. The boy remained in Babatha's care, but two guardians were appointed to administer Jesus' estate and provide for the son.

Sometime around 125 CE (the precise date is unclear), Babatha remarried a man named Judah, also called Khthousion, who already had a living wife, named Miriam, and a daughter, Shelamzion. Babatha's papyri thus provide the only known documentation of a polygynous Jewish marriage in this period.

They also provide some indication of the tensions and complexity of an ancient blended family. It appears, for example, that Babatha loaned Judah the cash portion of Shelamzion's dowry. Shelamzion's marriage contract was among the papers in Babatha's archive, testimony, perhaps, to a close tie between Babatha and her stepdaughter.

Several years later, Judah died, leaving Babatha and Miriam to wrangle over the effects of the estate. The latest of Babatha's papyri testify to her disputes with her late husband's relatives over assets owed to her.

Not long after, the Bar Kokhba revolt broke out (around 132 CE). En-Gedi, where Babatha lived, was a stronghold of the revolt. Documents and artifacts that pertain to the revolt, including those of Bar Kokhba himself, were found in the same cave as Babatha's papyri. Some scholars have speculated that Babatha, like others caught in the revolt, may have fled to the caves in the Judean desert for refuge and there met their deaths. But if Babatha is not among the cave's dead, it seems likely that she was never able to return to retrieve the personal archive left there, perhaps for safekeeping.

Interestingly, there is even some possibility of a historical connection between Babatha and Berenice. As several papyri in Babatha's archive document, Babatha's stepdaughter, Shelamzion, was engaged in a dispute with two of her cousins, the minor, "orphaned" sons of her father's brother, over property that her father (Babatha's second husband) had deeded to her. One of the guardians representing the boys was a woman named Julia Crispina. Crispina's father's name was Berenicianus, a fairly unusual name for this period, but known to be the name of one of Berenice's sons by her marriage to Herod. Tal Ilan has suggested that Julia Crispina was in fact the granddaughter of Berenice, an identification that is chronologically feasible and supported (though perhaps not conclusively) by additional evidence.[26]

It might be objected that neither Berenice, for reasons that should be obvious, nor Babatha, by virtue of her relative financial affluence and independence, is particularly representative of Jewish women's lives in antiquity. But as we shall see, while Berenice's extreme privilege and political power unquestionably mark the limits of Jewish women's experiences in this period, much about these two women's lives is consistent with what we reconstruct from the more fragmentary sources we possess for other women.

In important respects, the lives of Jewish women appear similar in many ways to those of their non-Jewish sisters. Distinctions such as residence (urban or rural), relative wealth, and, in particular, social status and citizenship were significant factors in determining aspects of women's lives, Jewish and otherwise. This is true both for Jewish women living in the land of Israel and for residents of the many Diaspora communities.

For Jews, as for non-Jews, it mattered whether one was born free or born a slave or whether, having been born into slavery or otherwise enslaved, one was subsequently freed. Our evidence for Jewish participation in the pervasive ancient slave economy comes particularly, though by no means exclusively, from Diaspora sources that reveal Jewish women both as slaves and as slave owners.[27] Even the writings of the New Testament may afford such glimpses: Luke identifies one of the women traveling with and supporting the Jesus movement as Joanna, the wife of Chuza, the *epitropos* (steward) of Herod (Antipas).[28] Persons in such positions were often legally slaves, as were members of their immediate families. In Acts 6:9, Luke also mentions a synagogue known as that of the "freedpersons" (that is, of former slaves) in Jerusalem. Formal citizenship (whether of individual cities or of the empire) was also of considerable importance, though relatively few Jews appear to have been actual Roman citizens; in any case, women's "citizenship" was almost always a function of their relationship to male citizens.

Ordinarily, most women, like most men, received little formal education, and this appears to have been true for Jews as well, despite traditional Jewish representations of Jewish men as highly educated. Unquestionably, factors of social status played a significant role in determining how much formal education one received and of what sort. Philo of Alexandria, for instance, a member of an elite Jewish family, received a classical Greek education, together with extensive studies of Jewish scripture and interpretation, although there is considerable doubt that he knew Hebrew or Aramaic. Philo's description of the Therapeutic society, noted above, presumes that the women, as well as the men, were highly literate and well educated. Papyrus documents, on the other hand, suggest that the formal schooling of many men was limited to reading and writing that is far more basic, and most persons required the services of a literate minority to read and write for them. All the available evidence suggests that fewer women than men, by a significant degree, learned letters. Women of the Herodian household, such as Berenice, were almost certainly well educated, but, despite her relative affluence, business dealings, and litigious life, Babatha was illiterate, as her own papers attest: others sign for her because she is "without letters."[29]

For the overwhelming majority of women in antiquity, becoming an adult, both socially and physiologically, meant having heterosexual intercourse and, consequently, children. For free and freed women, this generally meant entering into a socially validated arrangement, although our modern notions of marriage do not transpose easily to ancient social practices (see, for instance, chapter 1). Many persons entered into licit marriage, although doing so often entailed little more than a (public) agreement to live together and raise children. Many Jews appear to have signed a written "prenuptial" contract called a ketubbah, though it is impossible to know how prevalent this practice was, particularly among the poor. Among Babatha's documents are two such contracts, and we have a few other examples from finds in the Judean desert.[30] A formal divorce document appears also to have been used routinely; a few papyrus examples survive. Interestingly, though, of the Jewish papyri from Egypt, we have only one marriage contract, dated to the early fifth century CE.[31] We also have only one divorce document from Egypt that might be Jewish, and its content is significantly different from those found in the Judean desert and from rabbinic prescriptions of what such documents should contain.[32]

The circumstances of enslaved Jewish women are harder to assess. Under non-Jewish legal systems, slaves could not contract licit marriage with either one another or free persons (see chapter 1). Enslaved Jewish women owned by non-Jews would almost certainly have routinely found themselves required to provide sexual services for their owners and, doubtless, sometimes would have borne children to those owners. We know almost nothing about the domestic arrangements of actual enslaved Jews in this period. An episode from the apologetic autobiography of Josephus, though, may be surprisingly instructive.[33]

Josephus relates that toward the end of the Jewish revolt against Rome, while he was enslaved by Vespasian, the emperor compelled him to marry a virgin, who was also enslaved, having been taken captive by the Romans at Caesarea, where she lived. The marriage terminated shortly thereafter, when Josephus was freed and went to Alexandria (where he married another woman). From Josephus' description, it is by no means clear what were the formalities, if any, of this marriage and its dissolution. Though Josephus uses the Greek verb *gameo* ("to marry"), he says only that subsequently, this woman "left" him (*apolatto*), apparently, once he had been freed. Whether she was also freed is unknown.

Josephus' failure to describe any formalities of divorce is particularly interesting in light of his criticism of Salome (sister of Herod the Great) for instigating the termination of her marriage and giving her husband, Castobarus, a decree of divorce contrary to Jewish law.[34] Significant in itself as evidence of what powerful elite women might be able to do, this passage also demonstrates that Josephus believed that Jewish marriages needed to be terminated by a husband giving his wife a divorce decree (and certainly not vice versa). Thus, it seems quite possible that Josephus, perhaps inadvertently, shows us that enslaved Jews entered into "marriages" not governed by Jewish law, in his case, at the direction of his owner, the Roman emperor.

Though customs seem to have varied widely, most women, including Jewish women, appear to have married or otherwise entered into active sexual and reproductive lives at a fairly early age, anywhere from twelve to eighteen. Their first marriages were typically to older men. Women who did not die early (frequently from childbirth) could routinely expect to be widowed and to enter into additional marriage(s). First marriages were regularly a matter of family arrangements, often negotiated between the couple's fathers or between the bride's father and her future husband. Subsequent marriage arrangements might often involve more active participation by the woman, particularly when her father was no longer alive.

Here, the experiences of both Berenice and Babatha turn out to be more typical than one might think. Berenice's first marriage was, interestingly, as I noted above, to Philo's nephew, Marcus Julius Alexander. Though the exact date of this marriage is unknown, Berenice must have been in her very early teens at the time since she married a second time, at age 16, after Marcus' death left her a widow.[35] No children are known from her marriage to Marcus. Her second marriage, arranged by her father, was to her paternal uncle, Herod, king of Chalcis. It lasted six years, until Herod died in 50 CE, leaving Berenice 22 years old, again a widow, now with two children.

Josephus claims that Berenice remained widowed for a considerable amount of time after Herod's death and was accused of an incestuous relationship with Agrippa. Apparently, though, Berenice eventually arranged and then terminated her next marriage to a non-Jew, Polemo of Cilicia, who agreed to be circumcised for the marriage. To the best of our knowledge, this was the last of her formal marriages, though her most significant historical liaison, with the eventual Roman emperor, Titus, was still to come.

Babatha's marital history lacks the political weight of Berenice's, but is none-theless telling. Her age at her first marriage, to Jesus, son of Jesus, is uncertain. Jesus left Babatha a widow while their son, also called Jesus, was still relatively young. Sometime around 125 CE, Babatha entered into a polygynous marriage with Judah, known as Khthousion. Their marriage contract, written in Aramaic, was among Babatha's papers, but its opening lines are poorly preserved and do not allow us to determine its precise date or whether Babatha's father was a party to the contract. This marriage does not appear to have produced children, and it, too, ended with the husband's death.

The sources that we have suggest that Jews, like their gentile neighbors, placed a heavy cultural and economic premium on virginity at first marriage. Writers like Jesus ben Sira and Pseudo-Phocylides express, in somewhat misogy-nist language, the anxieties of fathers over the preservation of their daughters' virginity.[36] Shelamzion's marriage contract specifies her virginity, and the amount of her dowry is consistent with that status, while the ketubbah of Babatha's second marriage appears consistent with her status as a widow.

Determining the number of children Jewish women are likely to have had is difficult to do on the basis of the available evidence, though much suggests that the number would have been similar to that of non-Jewish women. As with non-Jewish women, many factors would have been relevant here, including eco-nomics, maternal health, knowledge of birth control techniques, and so forth. Jewish women's experience of infant and child mortality is similarly likely to have been consistent with that of non-Jewish women, with perhaps one excep-tion. There is some evidence that Jews were less likely to practice abortion or to expose unwanted children, or both, though the evidence is not unambiguous. It is interesting to note that a number of Herodian marriages, for which economic advantage may be presumed, produced at least five children each (Herod the Great and Mariamme; Aristobulus and Berenice; Phasael and Shelampsio[n]; Agrippa I and Cypros). But so many factors affected fertility rates that it seems injudicious to say more here.

The termination of Jewish marriages through divorce, rather than death, has been the subject of much discussion, particularly in light of sayings of Jesus in several New Testament writings that forbid or greatly restrict divorce.[37] Later rabbinic law is fairly clear that a legitimate divorce required the husband to give his wife a document called a get, which terminated the marriage, triggered any appropriate clauses in the prenuptial ketubbah, and allowed the wife to enter an-other licit Jewish marriage. (Because polygyny was legal, a Jewish man did not need to divorce one wife in order to take another.) Such practice is also attested (if indirectly) by Josephus' castigation of Salome, sister of Herod the Great, for sending her husband, Castobarus, a bill of divorce contrary to Jewish law, as noted above.[38]

Yet, as Bernadette Brooten and others have pointed out,[39] there is evidence that the position implicit in Josephus, and explicit in later rabbinic formulation, was not universal even among Jews living in the land of Israel and writing Jewish marriage contracts. The ketubbah of Shelamzion, found among Babatha's papers, contains an ambiguous clause that may mean that the bride has the right to demand payment of the prenuptial agreement (the *ketubbah*), thus terminating the marriage, whenever she chose.[40] Notice of an actual ancient *get* given by a woman to her husband was reported in the scholarly literature for some time, but it was only recently published (in Hebrew), and debate continues over whether this assessment is correct.[41] A papyrus from a Jewish colony at Elephantine in Egypt also appears to provide the bride the right to initiate the termination of the marriage, though its much earlier date (fifth century BCE) makes its relevance to first century practices questionable.[42] A divorce decree from Egypt, dated 13 BCE, which many scholars consider Jewish by virtue of the names of the couple and the absence of polytheist indicators, differs significantly from the language of a rabbinic *get*.[43] If it is Jewish, it demonstrates a diversity of practice regarding divorce in the Greco-Roman period. Nevertheless, it is likely that many Jews in the first century would have agreed that wives could not unilaterally terminate marriages contracted under Jewish law.

Women in Public

As I pointed out in the previous chapter, much has been made of the relative exclusion of Jewish women from much public life. Here, again, the realities of Jewish women's lives appear to have been more similar to those of non-Jews than different. There is no question, for instance, that in many social circles in antiquity, respectable women were expected to be sheltered from inappropriate public exposure, "shelter" that took a variety of forms. Virgin daughters of elite families were often closely guarded, and respectable married women were routinely accompanied by relatives and servants or slaves, whose presence was expected to safeguard their reputations. Images of such practices may be found in a range of Jewish literary sources. Describing a violation of the temple in second-century BCE Jerusalem, 2 Macc 3:19 mentions briefly that on this occasion, young women normally kept indoors ran to the gates, walls, and windows (of their homes) to observe the horrible happenings. In 4 Macc 18:7, set at a similar time, the mother of the seven martyrs gives a speech that refers to her seclusion as a virgin. Philo of Alexandria writes a carefully structured description of male and female spheres in which public spaces are appropriate for male activities: marketplaces, council halls, law courts, and public assemblies. Domestic spaces, on the other hand, are most suited to women, with the more-interior spaces for virgins and the outer rooms for mature women. Only for purposes of religious devotion should women venture out and only at times when they are least likely to be exposed to public view.[44] Elsewhere, describing the indignation of Alexandrian Jewish men when their houses were searched for weapons, Philo expresses outrage that modest Jewish women were thus subjected to the insult of being exposed to inappropriate male gaze.[45]

Yet such references must be read cautiously. Philo's first description is often presumed to describe social practices peculiar to Jewish life rather than broader Alexandrian norms, but I now think this is unlikely. In both Maccabean texts and Philo's second description, the presence of virtuous women in public, or exposed to outside male gaze, is a literary device that underscores the aberration of the events taking place. This is not to say by any means that some segments of Jewish communities did not limit the presence of women in public. Equally, if not more, important is the evidence from literary, papyrological, and epigraphic sources that testifies to the presence of women in public in many contexts. As I pointed out in the previous chapter, women's presence in the market, in the synagogue, and in other public venues is frequently the backdrop for some rabbinic narrative. The gospels, too, presume the presence of women outside the private domain. A third-century BCE papyrus from Egypt details the dispute of a Jewish woman and a Jewish man. Not only does the complaint indicate that the dispute (involving, among other things, perceived insults and torn cloaks) took place in a public venue, but the woman complainant appears personally in court.[46]

Here, as elsewhere, factors of social class and status are significant. As I have argued elsewhere, true seclusion is likely to have been restricted to families with sufficient economic resources, for whom the seclusion of women functions as a sign of prestige. Poor women, let alone enslaved women, could hardly have participated in such a system. Freed women, who would have continued to have obligations to their former owners, would also have been unlikely to be able to lead lives of complete public absence.

Yet it is also true that women's participation in certain spheres of public life required acknowledgment of widely shared concerns for propriety and family honor, both closely tied to female virginity and chastity. Many papyri testify to Jewish women's involvement in ancient legal disputes aired before non-Jewish courts. Often, though not always, those documents specify that the woman is represented by a legal guardian. This is true, for instance, of most of Babatha's various court documents. Interestingly, though, Babatha appears to have utilized a number of such guardians, particularly after the death of her second husband, which may suggest that the practice was often pro forma (or even useful in enabling women litigants to prevail in their cases). The use of such guardians did not prevent women from appearing in court in person. As Hallett has also discussed in chapter 1, some women were exempt from the requirement to utilize a guardian, and such exemptions may have pertained to certain Jewish women as well.

It is more difficult to assess the participation of women in specifically Jewish courts since much of that evidence comes from rabbinic writings, which have particular difficulties I discussed in the previous chapter. But it is worth noting here that Babatha made extensive use of non-Jewish courts to litigate her various legal disputes, and none appears to have been aired in Jewish courts.

Whatever the protocols of women's presence in public spaces, Jewish women, like non-Jewish women, were frequently actively involved in communal economic life.[47] Babatha, again, provides an excellent example. From her parents, Babatha had apparently acquired a considerable amount of real estate. The legal means by which such transfer occurred is not wholly apparent in the surviving papyri, though we may make some educated guesses. One of the earliest documents in her archive records a deed of gift from her father, Simon, to her mother, Miriam, transferring all his property in the village of Ma'oza, including houses, courtyards, gardens, and so forth. (Babatha's second husband, Judah, makes a similar gift to his daughter, Shelamzion, at the time of her marriage). Some of this property is subsequently enumerated in a registration document filed by Babatha in December 127 CE. The absence of a similar deed of gift from Miriam, while still living, to Babatha may suggest that Babatha inherited the property when her mother died. (That Babatha continued to retain possession of the original deed of transfer between her parents raises questions beyond the scope of this essay.) In addition, Babatha appears to have received assets from her first husband.

The death of her second husband, Judah, appears to have thrown his extended family into protracted legal disputes, giving Babatha's affairs a distinctly modern resonance. Several papyri concern Babatha's disputes with her late husband's relatives over the ownership and disposition of date orchards. They demonstrate not only the legal wranglings over the orchards and the estate, in which Babatha appears to have prevailed, but also her business acumen with regard to the sale of date crops.

One other aspect of Babatha's papyri highlights the occasions on which women's lives were likely to require their participation in more public arenas. Several papyri, spanning a number of years, document Babatha's disputes with the guardians appointed for her son, Jesus, after the death of his father. The very fact that the death of the elder Jesus rendered his son an "orphan" in need of such guardians points to the legal disabilities of widows in the management of their children's affairs. Unlike her disputes with Judah's family, Babatha was not as successful obtaining additional support for the child from his father's estate. Nevertheless, we see in these documents no reticence on Babatha's part to utilize the courts to press her claims on behalf of her child.

Women's Judaism(s)

Modern distinctions of religious life as easily separable from other dimensions of life are highly problematic when applied to Greco-Roman antiquity (not to mention to many other cultures and historical periods as well). Nevertheless, since we have seen that, in many ways, the lives of Jewish women had much in common with the lives of non-Jewish women, it is useful here to ask specific questions about aspects of their lives as Jews.

Temple Cult

Until its destruction by the Romans in 70 CE, the temple in Jerusalem was, at least in theory, the heart of Jewish religious devotion. Jews living in reasonable proximity to the temple could regularly make the prescribed sacrifices and pilgrimage for festivals, particularly Passover. Many Jews living outside the land of Israel sent contributions for the temple's maintenance, though given the realities of travel in the ancient world, few would have had the resources to go up to Jerusalem to make sacrifices in person or to partake of festival celebrations there.

Women's inclusion in the sacrificial system of the temple was fairly limited. Priests were, by definition, men born into priestly families, and no women are known to have served as priests in the temple cult in Jerusalem.[48] As were their male relatives, though, women members of priestly families were entitled to eat certain special offerings.

The sacrificial codes laid out particularly in Exodus, Leviticus, and Numbers, do require women, as well as men, to bring certain offerings to the temple, and there is every reason to think that, on various occasions, women who lived close enough to the temple would have done so. Both the biblical codes and the writings of Josephus indicate that the temple was divided into areas that were progressively more restricted. The outermost courtyard, according to one description by Josephus, was open to anyone, male or female, Jew or non-Jew, with the exception of women rendered ritually impure by menstruation or childbirth. The next courtyard was restricted to Jews of both genders, again excepting women impure for the same reason. The third courtyard was restricted to ritually pure Jewish males, and the fourth to ritually pure priests wearing priestly clothing. The sanctuary itself was limited to high priests in appropriate dress.[49] Elsewhere, in a more detailed description of the temple, Josephus writes that a space was set aside for Jewish women for worship (threskeia). Special gates opened only to this area, and women were not permitted to use other gates.[50] This "women's court" appears to be an innovation of Herod the Great's restoration of the temple.[51]

In this same passage, Josephus remarks that this designated space was available both to women living in the land of Israel and to those from outside. This suggests that Jewish women from diaspora communities did sometimes travel to Jerusalem and worship at the temple. Precisely what Josephus means by the term threskeia (worship) is not specified in this passage, though elsewhere Josephus regularly uses the term either as a synonym for sacrifices or in a context in which temple rituals (including, but perhaps not limited to, sacrifices) are clearly meant.[52] But it seems likely that women, like men, brought the sacrifices required of them for various reasons. Although biblical codes appear to obligate only men to come to the temple for the three festivals of Sukkoth, Pesach, and Shavuoth, and subsequent Jewish law clearly reads them this way, it seems likely that Jewish women also came to the temple to celebrate festivals (almost certainly with other members of their familes). This is also consonant with stories in later rabbinic sources that "remember" women who also went up to Jerusalem for festival celebrations.[53]

Synagogue Life

Despite the centrality of the temple, by the first century CE, if not earlier, synagogues had become important sites of Jewish community and ritual life. This is most apparent in the gospels, which refer to synagogue officials and regularly depict Jews in the land of Israel gathering in synagogues on the sabbath for communal reading and interpretation of Torah. As I noted above in another context, Acts mentions a particular synagogue in Jerusalem, that of the Libertini (freedpersons). That women attended synagogues during the period when Christianity first emerges we have already seen in the previous chapter.

The precise functions of synagogues in this period are difficult to determine with certainty. Even the meaning of the term synagogue raises questions. In some cases, it clearly refers to discrete congregations of Jews (more than ten different synagogues are attested by inscriptions for the city of Rome over several centuries), but in other cases, it may designate the entire Jewish community of a particular town or city, with legal and political ramifications. Even when the first meaning is more likely, it is clear that ancient synagogues were significantly different from contemporary ones. They were led not by rabbis, but by an archisynagogos, literally a head or ruler of the synagogue. One such person is mentioned in the gospels: Jairus, whose afflicted daughter is healed by Jesus. Though the majority of archisynagogoi were undoubtedly men, several women synagogue heads are attested in Jewish inscriptions.[54] Other inscriptions identify women as members of the council of elders (gerousia), the members of which may have functioned similarly to boards of directors in modern synagogues.[55] Still others demonstrate that women were significant financial contributors to synagogues.[56] One important inscription bestows the privilege of sitting in the seat of honor in the synagogue on a woman named Tation in recognition of her great generosity.[57]

So far, all these inscriptions come from outside the land of Israel, and none are earlier than the second century CE. But since there are so few inscriptions altogether, given the size of the Jewish population in antiquity, it would be hasty to conclude that women did not serve in such capacities prior to the second century CE and only did so outside the land of Israel.

Many discussions of Jewish women in Roman-period synagogues have focused on the question of segregated seating, presuming that the customs of much later Jewish communities are likely to have prevailed earlier as well. The evidence for such an assumption is virtually nonexistent. None of the ancient synagogues excavated to date has yielded identifiable "women's sections" in the form of either balconies or separate first-floor areas. On the contrary, many synagogues show no areas that could possibly have served in such capacity. Nor do ancient literary sources, including Josephus, rabbinic sources, and the New Testament, testify to such divisions.

One passage from Philo has sometimes been offered as support for such practices,[58] but when closely examined, it suggests, if anything, precisely the opposite. In his description of the Therapeutic society, Philo relates that during their communal sabbath assembly, the women and the men sit in the same room, separated by a divider that did not extend all the way to the ceiling. This divider serves the function, Philo says, of preserving the modesty of the women, while allowing them to hear everything.[59]

When assessing the significance of this passage, we must first keep in mind that the Therapeutics were a celibate community, whose members regularly live in single cells. That they would choose to sit segregated by gender during their one weekly communal assembly seems highly consonant with their devotion to celibacy. Second, it is important to note that Philo does not call their gathering a synagogue or a *proseuche* (literally, a prayer place), another term that often designates a Jewish place of assembly. Third, and perhaps most important, the very fact that Philo must describe this practice and explain its purpose (to preserve the modesty of the women) suggests that his audience would neither have expected or have understood such practice. Further, Philo does not observe here that this practice is common to Jewish synagogues, and nowhere else in his writings does Philo attest to such practices in Alexandria and Egypt.

As I have argued elsewhere, gender-segregated public seating was by no means unknown in Greco-Roman antiquity and is, in fact, well attested for everything from the theater to Christian churches.[60] Thus, in fact, for Jews to have done so as well would not have been particularly remarkable. But the fact remains that in the absence of better evidence than what we presently have, there is no reason to assume that they did so and considerable reason to think they did not.

Home-Based Observances

Though it is often assumed that ancient Jewish domestic life had much in common with later Jewish practices, we have little reliable information about Jewish women's observance in their homes. For the most part, the sources that survive, whether literary or otherwise, tell us little about women's domestic piety.

Rabbinic sources pay considerable attention to regulations of menstrual purity (*niddah*) and to observance of *kashrut*, the kosher laws regarding acceptable foods and their preparation. They portray the wives of Pharisaic men, for instance, as meticulous observers of *niddah*, who consult a male expert any time they cannot determine the identity of suspicious blood. Interestingly, these same later sources express skepticism about the ritual purity of other Jewish women, such as the wives of Sadducees.[61] It is difficult to know, though, how much their concerns were shared by the larger Jewish populace.

Several passages in the gospels have often been read in the light of assumptions about menstrual purity regulations in the first century. Some interpreters, correctly noting that the woman hemorrhaging for twelve years would have been ritually impure according to biblical prescription (Lev 15:25–30), claim that Jesus' healing her by his physical touch demonstrates his rejection of menstrual impurity.[62] They thus take this passage as implicit testimony to routine first-century acquiesence to these laws.

This reading presents numerous difficulties, not the least of which is the fact that the woman seeks out Jesus' healing touch without his consent or knowledge (after the fact, he asks who has touched him and only finds out when the woman comes before him and acknowledges her actions). Since this healing is not portrayed as volitional on the part of Jesus, it is difficult to claim that it represents his views of ritual purity. Furthermore, this interpretation rests on faulty assumptions about ritual impurity. First, ritual purity is concerned only with whether a person is fit to have physical contact with the temple. As Paula

Fredriksen points out, Jews contracted ritual impurity on a regular, if not a daily, basis, and so long as they did not go to the temple, it was a matter of little, if any, concern. Persons living far from the temple, in the diaspora, for example, could easily have lived their entire lives in a state of ritual impurity. Second, as the text of Leviticus states quite clearly, the ritual impurity contracted by contact with the woman described in the gospels is quite easily remedied. It requires nothing more than bathing, washing one's clothing, and waiting a brief period. "Whoever touches these things shall be unclean, and shall wash his clothes, and bathe in water, and be unclean until evening" (Lev 15:33; see also Lev 19–23). Finally, it is also important to note that the gospel texts do not speak to issues of impurity and are poor evidence for women's adherence to menstrual purity regulations in the first century.

Women's observance of kashrut is similarly difficult to determine. Here, too, later rabbinic traditions envision different standards of observance between the Pharisees and other Jews, and some of these differences may undergird New Testament representations as well. The observation of the kosher laws affected both the purchase of food and its preparation, as well as the maintenance of pots, dishes, and other household implements. Buying food was sometimes, but by no means always, the responsibility of women. In elite households, shopping was often done by men, or by slaves and servants, while elite women stayed home.[63] Food preparation was also often, but not always, the responsibility of women; here, too, it often fell to slaves, including male slaves.

Jewish Women's Alignment with First-Century Jewish Movements or Factions

Discussions of Jews and Judaism as the context for the Jesus movement invariably devote considerable attention to movements or factions within first-century Palestine. The Pharisees and the Sadducees receive the bulk of the attention, partly because they figure so predominantly in the writings of the New Testament as the opponents or competition of Jesus.[64] (Josephus, too, counts them among his four Jewish "philosophies," the others being the Essenes and the Sicarii, a revolutionary faction).

Were women Pharisees or Sadducees, Essenes, or Sicarii? Certainly, we know that Pharisaic and Saducean men had mothers, sisters, wives, and daughters. (Whether Essenes had wives and daughters is a more complicated question to which I will return.) In what ways, if any, might these women have understood themselves to be Pharisees, Sadducees, or perhaps even Essenes or Qumran covenanters? And these factions are by no means the only options for self-identification within the larger umbrella of first-century Judaism(s).

Pharisees

None of the extant sources describes any woman, or women in general, as Pharisees per se. Not surprisingly, the language of ancient writers presumes that

Pharisees are men, albeit men who have wives, daughters, and other female relatives. All the Pharisees Jesus encounters in the gospels are men.

Yet Josephus relates that several prominent Jewish women were strong supporters of the Pharisees. Most significant of these women was Queen Alexandra Salome, who ruled Judea from 76 to 67 BCE after the death of her husband, Alexander Jannaeus (known in rabbinic sources as King Yannai).[65] Josephus also reports that a century later, the unnamed wife of Herod's younger brother, Pheroras, was a financial and political supporter of the Pharisees. Tal Ilan has recently argued that the Pharisees garnered the allegiance of some aristocratic women because the Pharisees were, in reality, an opposition group during the second-temple period, and opposition groups were more likely to attract the patronage of aristocratic women. She writes that "[the Pharisees] accepted [aristocratic women's] support and did not enact detrimental rules again women."[66] I am not wholly persuaded by Ilan's arguments, but in any case, they do little to alter the perception that these divisions were largely, if not entirely, male alliances.

Sadducees

It is even more difficult to determine whether women might have considered themselves Sadducees. Neither Josephus nor any other ancient sources mentions women supporters of the Sadducees, let alone women who might be called Sadducees. Although the Sadducees are strongly associated with the (male) temple priesthood, it is probably unwise and simplistic to presume that this association suffices to account for the lack of any evidence for women Sadducees. Nevertheless, it is probably not irrelevant.

Essenes

Women Essenes are a far more complicated matter (as are the Essenes as a whole). Josephus, Philo, and the Roman Pliny the Elder all describe the Essenes as a voluntary association of men who lived a regimented communal life that emphasized fidelity to the law, ritual purity, ascetic practices, and group loyalty.[67] For Philo, the Essenes (unlike the Therapeutics) are exclusively male. He emphasizes that they abstain from marriage because of the inherently negative characteristics of women, who intentionally divert men from the life of the mind and the life of the Essene community.[68] Pliny states that "no Essene takes a wife,"[69] confirming in this one phrase that Essenes are (solely) men and that they do not marry: Pliny affirms the absence of women.

However, Josephus (who classes the Essenes as the third Jewish "philosophy") claims that while some Essenes do not marry, one branch among them does.[70] But assuming for the moment that Josephus is better informed than either Philo or Pliny, does this mean that women were Essenes? Josephus' language (in contrast to Philo's description of the Therapeutics, for instance) still utilizes a distinction between Essenes (who are men) and their wives, whose identity as Essenes may go no further than their marital roles. Josephus says that the Essenes take wives only for the purposes of procreation. Essene wives were required to demonstrate their potential fertility prior to the marriage, and Essenes abstained from marital intercourse once their wives became pregnant. Nothing in Josephus' description supports the participation of these women in the communal, ritual, or intellectual life of the Essenes.

Prior to the discovery of the Dead Sea Scrolls in Judean desert caves in 1947, it was impossible to go much beyond these basic observations. If, as many scholars believe, those scrolls come from an Essene community living at Qumran, on the shores of the Dead Sea, we now have additional sources for Essenes. Unfortunately, the scrolls do not provide unqualified answers to our questions. Some, such as the *Damascus Document*, and the *Rule of the Congregation*, speak of married members and their children, while the *War Scroll* proscribes the presence of women or children in the camp of the Sons of Light during the eschatological battle to come in the future.[71] Other, more fragmentary texts may allude to the presence and participation of women.[72] Part of the problem with all these documents, though, is that it is difficult to tell how many of them describe actual communities and practices, and how many envision an ideal life that may or may not have ever corresponded to historical reality.

Archaeological evidence from Qumran muddies the waters further. A relatively large main cemetery exists on the site, together with an extension and northern and southern "secondary" cemeteries. Although stones arranged on top of the individual graves indicate that approximately 1200 persons were buried there, only a small number of graves (yielding fifty-one skeletons) have been opened. Nine skeletons have been identified as those of adult women; six more are those of children of both sexes; the remainder, thirty-six, have been identified as male.[73] Statistically, adult female skeletons comprise 18% of the total, and 20% of the adult skeletons. Were this to constitute a representative sample, it would suggest a strong prima facie case (though still not definitive proof) for women members of the community. However, since only 4% of the graves have been opened, it seems far too early to know whether these results are, in fact, representative.

The evidence available at present has been construed in several ways. The skeletons of the women and children come from those areas considered by many scholars as "secondary" and distinct from the main burial site. They consider this separate burial of women evidence that the women were not actual members of the Qumran community. Others find this argument artificial and somewhat tendentious and see no reason not to take the women's skeletons as indicative of women among the community.[74] A fuller excavation of the cemetery would provide a better picture of the gender distribution of those buried there, but this is unlikely in the near future.

The fact remains that while women may have been present at Qumran and (if Qumran was not Essene) in Essene communities by virtue of their marriage to male Essenes, there is virtually no evidence[75] that women joined either Essene communities or the Qumran community on their own or as full participants in the association. Eileen Schuller has pointed out that from a feminist perspective, one might presume women's full membership in the absence of evidence to the contrary.[76] However, the extraordinary concern for ritual purity expressed in numerous scrolls makes me wonder how probable it is that adult, premenopausal women could have been integrated into the life of the association given the relative frequency with which they would have been ritually impure through menstruation or childbirth.[77] The misogynist, gender-specific, and sometimes gender-exclusive language of many of the Qumran scrolls raises serious doubts, still, about how and why women might have joined the association apart from marriage (or, possibly, other family commitments).

Finally, regarding the Essenes, one other point may be worth making. Scholars who have recently focused attention on women Essenes have frequently linked these questions to debates about early Christian women. For Linda Bennett Elder, for instance, and for Kathleen Corley to argue that women were Essenes has positive significance: it demonstrates that women had many options within first-century Jewish life, some of them akin to the alternatives offered by Jesus, the Jesus movement, and later Christianity.[78] Yet it is precisely this usage that should make us cautious. From a feminist perspective (Jewish, Christian, or otherwise), the inclusion of women in a highly androcentric (male-centered) system is not necessarily a matter for rejoicing. Whether that is what we have here remains to be seen, but in the absence of better evidence, it is important to reflect on what scholars have invested in the interpretations we offer.

The Herodian Household

Interestingly, we know a fair amount about the women of the Herodian dynasty in the first century CE, chronicled by Josephus, particularly in Book Eighteen of his *Antiquities of the Jews*. These include not only the women discussed above in this chapter (Drusilla, Berenice, and Herodias), but also several others of considerable interest, including Herodias' daughter, Salome and Cypros, long-suffering wife of the dissolute Agrippa I and mother of Drusilla, Berenice, and their brother, Agrippa II. In some cases, non-Jewish sources supplement our knowledge of these women's lives.

These women have received relatively little scholarly scrutiny in recent years.[79] Some of this may stem from the fact that feminist historiography has focused attention on the lives of ordinary women, considering elite women unrepresentative of most women's experiences. But in significant ways, these women are problematic within both Jewish and Christian tradition, something that may also account for their relative neglect. Berenice's long affair with Titus has hardly endeared her to Jewish historians. Herodias' alleged involvement in the death of John the Baptist (recounted in Matthew and Mark, but not in Josephus) has cast her as an exemplar of female villainy in Christian tradition.[80] Josephus, too, has few kind words for Herodias; he was particularly offended by her marriage to her uncle Herod, apparently because he viewed it as a violation of Jewish law concerning uncle-niece marriages (Lev 18:15) and perhaps also because Herodias, like Salome and perhaps Berenice, may have instigated the termination of her prior marriage.[81]

These few details from the lives of Herodian women highlight their deep involvement in Jewish political life in the first century. All the evidence suggests that Berenice co-ruled with her brother, Agrippa II, and came perilously close to being empress of Rome. Her mother, Cypros, appears to have exercised power more indirectly, but nevertheless quite effectively, repeatedly using her political and social connections to rescue Agrippa I from the consequences of his imprudent actions.[82]

The Herodian women were clearly not representative of the majority of their first-century Jewish sisters. They were Roman citizens, wealthy and educated, deeply involved in imperial Roman intrigue and affairs. They are likely to have had little sympathy for the revolt against Rome or for renewal movements such as that around John the Baptist, Jesus of Nazareth, or Simon bar Giora (see below). Their privilege appears to have afforded them a degree of autonomy that eluded more ordinary Jewish women (and men). Nevertheless, they deserve extensive consideration in any reconstruction of the lives of Jewish women in the first century.

Therapeutics

As I have already indicated, Philo reports that women were an integral part of the monastic, contemplative, mystical Jewish association called the Therapeutae. Like their male counterparts, the Therapeutrides were highly educated, mostly older women, who had severed their familial and social ties to pursue the contemplative life. In contrast to the situation with the Pharisees, Sadducees, and Essenes, there is no doubt in Philo's representation that the women were full members of the society, dedicated to the philosophical life, and fully trained to engage in it.[83] As I noted above, the society made a few concessions to gender difference; women and men sat separately in their communal assemblies, separated by a divider that hindered their sight, but not their hearing, of each other.

In several earlier studies, I have argued that, at least for Philo, the inclusion of women among the Therapeutics was facilitated by the fact that they were of relative old age (probably menopausal), childless, apparently virgins, and probably never married. That is, while possessing the bodies of women, they were, in all significant respects, male. The implications of this, both for the lives of Jewish women in antiquity and for early Christian women, are quite significant, pointing to strong connections between celibacy and autonomy.[84]

Anti-Roman Factions

Josephus narrates at great length the conflict between two prominent anti-Roman Jewish factions: the so-called Zealots and the followers of a man named Simon bar Giora. (This mutual antagonism unquestionably impaired their revolutionary endeavors.) Though Josephus clearly portrays the entire revolt as masculine warfare, he does remark in passing that Simon was early on accompanied by a following of women.[85] He later says that the Zealots managed to capture Simon's wife and her female attendants. Simon responded with such violence that the Zealots eventually returned her.[86] Josephus also remarks that Simon's response had less to do with affection for his wife than with the insult. This may or may not be true (Josephus' contempt for Simon unquestionably colors his representation), but it might also suggest that Simon's unnamed wife was a significant figure in the faction.

Elsewhere, Josephus claims that Simon abandoned the kosher laws and Jewish laws of ritual purity; he is also said to have declared freedom for enslaved persons. Though it may be difficult to know how much of Josephus' portrait is accurate and how much is unsubstantiated hostile polemic, the fact that all these elements (inclusion of women; negation of traditional laws, particularly those concerning food, purity, and sexuality; and obliteration of social distinctions— here, freeing slaves) are characteristic of many millenarian movements[87] may lend credence to the representation of women in at least one revolutionary faction.

Much less is known about any of the other Jewish revolts against Rome, including the uprising in Cyrene and other parts of North Africa around 115– 117 CE and the Bar Kokhba rebellion ca. 132–35 CE. But it is worth noting that Yigal Yadin, the archaeologist who found the Babatha papyri in a cave used by the Bar Kokhba revolt, wondered early on what connection Babatha might have had with the revolt. He attributed the presence of her papers in the cave to the fact that her co-wife, Miriam, appears to have had family ties to the revolt. Given the hostility between Babatha and Miriam after the death of their husband, I am more inclined to think the link might have been with Miriam's daughter, Shelamzion, whose ketubbah is among Babatha's papers. We might also wonder whether Babatha might have been a participant in the revolt or one of those who gave financial and material support to the rebels. It would appear that she had the resources to do so, but the evidence allows us to do nothing more than hypothesize the possibilities.

The Movement around John the Baptist

No women disciples are explicitly associated with early Baptist traditions in Christian sources. According to Matt 21:32, tax collectors and prostitutes were among those who believed John the Baptist. But the saying, which does not appear in any other gospel, may well be the creation of the gospel writer. Further, given the probable competition between John and Jesus, as well as among their subsequent followers, it is difficult to use early Christian sources as reliable evidence for the Baptist movement.[88]

Proto-Rabbinic Circles

No descriptions of proto-rabbinic circles in subsequent rabbinic sources portray women as rabbinic disciples. As numerous studies have pointed out, there is substantial debate in rabbinic sources over whether and under what circumstances women should study or be taught Torah. One passage in particular from the Mishnah, which deals with the treatment of wives accused of adultery, has

often been understood to reflect rabbinic opposition to teaching women anything more than the most minimal grasp of laws relevant to their lives.[89]

In later rabbinic tradition, however, a Jewish woman steeped in rabbinic
knowledge appears in the pages of the Babylonian Talmud. Called Beruriah, she
is said to have been the daughter of R. Hananiah ben Teradion and the wife of
R. Meir, a prominent rabbi thought to have lived in the mid–second century CE.
She was allegedly so wise that she learned 300 *halakhot* (laws or teachings) from
300 scholars in one day.[90] The great medieval Jewish scholar, Rashi, transmits
a terrible story about Beruriah's downfall. At her husband's behest, she was
propositioned by one of his students and, ultimately shamed, took her own
life.[91] Though Beruriah's case is often cited as evidence that it was possible for
Jewish women to be great scholars in the rabbinic period, recent studies are far
more skeptical about the historicity of any of the Beruriah traditions. Instead,
they emphasize the uses to which the Beruriah traditions are put within rabbinic
sources. Daniel Boyarin has suggested that the story of Beruriah and another
story of her unnamed sister are two sides of the same coin that express rabbinic
fears and fantasies about the connections between women's knowledge of Torah
and illicit sexuality.[92]

Conclusions

Taken together, this chapter and chapter 2 yield several important conclusions
relevant for the study of Jewish women and Christian origins.

First, the stereotypes articulated by writers such as Ben Witherington, Monique Alexandre, and far too many others are inaccurate, polemical, and misleading. To the degree that they continue, consciously or unconsciously, to
support and legitimate Christian anti-Judaism, they may ultimately even be dangerous.

Second, Jewish women's lives in the centuries during which Christianity
arose and spread were similar in many ways to those of non-Jewish women.
The lives and opportunities of Jewish and non-Jewish women alike were affected
by factors such as family and social class, free birth and enslavement, diet, demographics, and geography. There is no question that, for the vast majority of
women in Greco-Roman antiquity, gender, qualified by these other factors, imposed all sorts of limitations on their lives. Gender constrained women's participation in public life (social, political, and religious), women's dress when they
went out, women's access to education, women's ability to represent themselves
in diverse legal systems, and so forth. All this was true for most Jewish women
as well. For Jewish women in certain Jewish communities, including later communities that adhered to rabbinic principles, these constraints took particular
forms. They limited women's participation in the temple cult, their access to
higher Jewish learning, and probably their ability to act autonomously with
regard to divorce, property transmission, and so forth. Yet, we have also seen
that in diverse Jewish communities in the Greco-Roman diaspora, Jewish women
were active participants in communal life, contributing financial resources and
serving as synagogue officers and benefactors.

Third, although careful study of Jewish women in the first century or two of the common era is unquestionably important for understanding early Christian women, it is possible to overstate its significance and to misrepresent and misuse the circumstances of Jewish women in order to represent both Jesus and the earliest movement around him as radically and innovatively egalitarian. As is probably also true for Jewish men, the evidence suggests that apart from Jesus' immediate circle, few Jewish women were major players in the Jesus movement (Prisca/Priscilla being the most notable, perhaps). After the mid–first century CE, even fewer Jewish women can be documented, particularly in leadership roles, in most early Christian communities.

The questions of why few Jews joined and remained in the Jesus movement and why Christianity spread largely through its incorporation of non-Jews are not only historically complex, but deeply enmired in the tragic history of Jewish-Christian relations. It is probably not too much of an overstatement to say that until the Shoah (the Holocaust) compelled many Christian theologians to confront the extraordinary ultimate consequences of centuries of Christian anti-Judaism, Christian theology has needed to portray, indeed to construct, Jewish denial of Christian claims in the worst possible terms. For many Christians, beginning in the gospels themselves, Jewish disbelief in the claims of Jesus and his followers has been taken as evidence of the willful sinfulness and blindness of Jews, resulting in deserved divine rejection and punishment.

To broach, then, questions about why Jewish women might not have been particularly interested in the Jesus movement is to come perilously close to encouraging yet another dimension of Christian anti-Judaism. Yet the questions are of historical interest, all the more so given the claims recently made by writers such as Witherington and Alexandre. Contrary to their claims, the message of the Jesus movement may not have been heard by most Jewish women as quite so liberating or appealing. Some of the reasons for this may have been gender specific. Most Jewish women may not have found teachings that encouraged family dissolution and the rejection of marriage and childbearing particularly compelling. But many reasons (and perhaps even those) are likely to have been shared by Jewish men as well. For many, indeed most, Jews living under Roman occupation in the land of Israel in the first century, the Jesus movement may ultimately have offered insufficient or inadequate answers to their most pressing concerns, including the experience and effects of Roman domination. Clearly, some followers of Jesus were able to transform the apparent tragedy of his death into a theology that made his crucifixion evidence of his triumph and divine standing. Most first-century Jews, however, either found the death of Jesus compelling contradiction of any messianic claims or were never aware of, or interested in, such claims in the first place. When Jesus failed to return in glorious form as many of his followers anticipated and as the conditions of Roman domination persisted, many Jews might easily have drawn the conclusion that salvation and redemption were to be sought elsewhere. In any case, it seems clear that the vast majority of first-century Jews in the land of Israel, both women and men, continued to seek answers to the conditions of their lives, and to find meaning, in other forms of Judaism.

NOTES

1. Josephus, *Jewish War* 1§76, 85, 107, 119; Josephus, *Antiquities* 13§320, 405–32; 14§1; 15§179; 20§242; Josephus, *Life* 5.

2. Josephus, *Jewish War* 5§55, 119, 147, 253; 6§355; Josephus, *Antiquities* 20§17–53, 92–96 (also in Ross S. Kraemer, *Maenads, Martyrs, Matrons, Monastics: A Sourcebook on Women's Religions in the Greco-Roman World* [Philadelphia: Fortress, 1988] no. 111).

3. Josephus, *Antiquities* 18§109 ff.

4. Philo, *On the Contemplative Life*; (excerpts in Kraemer, *Maenads* no. 14).

5. The story is commonly known as *Joseph and Aseneth*, though its actual ancient title is unknown, and I currently prefer to call it simply *Aseneth*. An English translation of much of the text is available in Kraemer, *Maenads*, no. 113. Until recently, I considered *Aseneth* important evidence for Jewish women's experiences in this period (see Ross Shepard Kraemer, *Her Share of the Blessings: Women's Religions among Pagans, Jews and Christians in the Greco-Roman World* [New York: Oxford University Press, 1992] 110–13; also Kraemer, "Jewish Women in the Diaspora World of Late Antiquity," in *Jewish Women in Historical Perspective*, ed. Judith Baskin [Detroit, MI: Wayne State University Press, 1991] 53, 55–56), but I no longer hold this view (see now Kraemer, *When Aseneth Met Joseph: A Late Antique Tale of the Biblical Patriarch and his Egyptian Wife, Revisited* [New York: Oxford University Press, 1998]). On Hellenistic Jewish novels, see Larry Wills, *The Jewish Novel in the Ancient World* (Ithaca, NY: Cornell University Press, 1995). On the treatment of biblical women in Ps.-Philo, see Cheryl Anne Brown, *No Longer Be Silent: First Century Jewish Portraits of Biblical Women. Gender and the Biblical Tradition* (Louisville, KY: Westminster, 1992), and Pieter van der Horst, "Portraits of Biblical Women in Pseudo-Philo's Liber Antiquitatum Biblicarum," in *Essays on the Jewish World of Early Christianity* (Göttingen: Vandenhoeck and Ruprecht, 1990) 111–122. Some scholars would also consider the story about the daughters of Job in the pseudepigraphic *Testament of Job* to be another example of Jewish interest in women of the past, but I have reservations about the date and Jewishness of the text.

6. Tal Ilan, *Jewish Women in Greco-Roman Palestine: an Inquiry into Image and Status*. Texte und Studien zum Antiken Judentum 44 (Tübingen: J. C. B. Mohr [Paul Siebeck], 1995) 28.

7. See, e.g., Mary Rose D'Angelo, "Women in Luke-Acts: A Redactional View," *JBL* 109/3 (1990) 441–61; Turid Karlsen Seim, *The Double Message: Patterns of Gender in Luke-Acts* (Nashville, KY.: Abingdon, 1994); Seim, "The Gospel of Luke," in *Searching the Scriptures, Volume 2. A Feminist Commentary*, ed. Elisabeth Schüssler Fiorenza (New York: Crossroad, 1994) 728–62; Jane Schaberg, "Luke," in *The Women's Bible Commentary*, ed. Carol A. Newsom and Sharon H. Ringe (London: SPCK; Louisville, KY: Westminster/John Knox, 1992) 275–92.

8. A valiant effort to use rabbinic literature judiciously as evidence for Jewish women in Greco-Roman Palestine has been made by Tal Ilan, *Jewish Women in Greco-Roman Palestine*. On the whole, I remain unpersuaded that the effort yields much in the way of historical fruit, but Ilan's work is nevertheless extremely important, not the least for her careful and critical analysis of rabbinic texts (see my forthcoming review in the *Journal of the American Society of Oriental Studies*. On rabbinic literature and rabbinic constructions of gender, see also Kraemer, *Her Share of the Blessings* 93–94; Judith Wegner, *Chattel or Person: The Status of Women in the Mishnah* (New York: Oxford University Press, 1988); Daniel Boyarin, *Carnal Israel: Reading Sex in Talmudic Culture* (Berkeley, CA: University of California Press, 1993); Michael L. Satlow, " 'Try to be a Man': The Rabbinic Construction of Masculinity," *HTR*, 89/1 (1996) 19–40.

9. Ross S. Kraemer, "Women's Authorship of Jewish and Christian Literature in the Greco-Roman Period," in *"Women Like This": New Perspectives on Jewish Women in the Greco-Roman*

Period, ed. Amy-Jill Levine. Early Judaism and its Literature 1 (Atlanta, GA: Scholars Press, 1991) 221–42.

10. CIJ/CPJ 421 (Kraemer, *Maenads* no. 48) dated to 73 CE. Jewish inscriptions from Egypt are now also collected in William Horbury and David Noy, *Jewish Inscriptions of Greco-Roman Egypt* (Cambridge: Cambridge University Press, 1992).

11. CPJ 146 (Kraemer, *Maenads* no. 44).

12. CPJ 19 (Kraemer, *Maenads* no. 37) and CPJ 133 (*Maenads* no. 38), both second century BCE.

13. CPJ 473 (Kraemer, *Maenads* no. 49), dated 291 CE.

14. Naphtali Lewis, ed., *The Documents from the Bar Kochba Period in the Cave of Letters: Greek Papyri*. Judean Desert Studies 2 (Jerusalem: Israel Exploration Society, Hebrew University, Shrine of the Book, 1989) esp. 3–5; see also Yigal Yadin, *Bar Kokhba. The Rediscovery of the Legendary Hero of the Second Jewish Revolt against Rome* (New York: Random House, 1971) for description of the find, with illustrations.

15. CIJ/CPJ 1509 (Kraemer, *Maenads* no. 40), 1510 (*Maenads* no. 41), 1513 (*Maenads* no. 42), 1530 (*Maenads* no. 43).

16. CIJ 741 (Kraemer, *Maenads* no. 84), 731c (*Maenads* no. 85), 756 (*Maenads* no. 86); CIJ 400, 581, 590, 597, 692 (all in *Maenads* no. 88; see also *Maenads* no. 89). At least one additional leadership inscription was reported in an obscure Turkish journal published in 1912; a second is also possible.

17. CIJ 462 (Kraemer, *Maenads* no. 115), 523 (*Maenads* no. 116).

18. CIJ 741 (Kraemer, *Maenads* no. 84).

19. CIJ 738 (Kraemer, *Maenads* no. 60; see also *Maenads* no. 65).

20. Many, but by no means all, of these inscriptions are reproduced in Kraemer, *Maenads*.

21. Grace H. Macurdy, *Vassal Queens and Some Contemporary Women in the Roman Empire*, The Johns Hopkins University Studies in Archaeology 22 (Baltimore, MD: Johns Hopkins Press, 1937) 84–91; also, Macurdy's almost identical article, "Julia Berenice," *AJPhil* 56 (1935) 246–53. Macurdy offers evidence that Berenice's title of queen derives from her joint rulership with Agrippa. Tal Ilan asserts without discussion that it derives from her marriage to Herod, King of Chalcis ("Josephus and Nicolaus on Women," in *Geschichte—Tradition—Reflexion: Festschrift für Martin Hengel zum 70. Geburtstag, Band I: Judentum*, ed. Peter Schäfer (Tübingen: J. C. B. Mohr [Paul Siebeck], 1996) 221–62, here 229), but as Macurdy's discussion indicates, the question is quite complex.

22. See Macurdy, "Julia Berenice" 250–51, and *Vassal Queens* 88–89.

23. The term is difficult to translate precisely. It is the opposite of *sophrosyne*, one of the cardinal Greek virtues that, for women, primarily signified sexual chastity.

24. Dio Cassius, *Historia Romana* 66.15.3–5, preserved in Xiphilinus. Text, translation, and commentary in Menahem Stern, *Greek and Latin Authors on Jews and Judaism* (Jerusalem: The Israel Academy of Sciences and Humanities, 1980) no. 433 (2:378–439).

25. Suetonius, *Divus Titus* 7.1. Text, translation, and commentary in Stern, *Greek and Latin Authors* no. 318 (2:126–28).

26. See Tal Ilan, "Julia Crispina, Daughter of Berenicianus, a Herodian Princess in the Babatha Archive: A Case Study in Historical Identification," *Jewish Quarterly Review* 82/3–4 (1992) 361–81. The identification is dismissed rather cavalierly by Jonas Greenfield, "'Because He/She Did Not Know Letters': Remarks on a First Millennium CE Legal Expression," *JANES* 22 (1993) 39–43.

27. CPJ 148 (Kraemer, *Maenads* no. 89) concerning the freedwoman Martha; CPJ 473 manumitting Paramone and her children; CIJ 741 (*Maenads* no. 84) Rufina of Smyrna, head of the synagogue, as slave owner; CIJ 709 and 710 from Delphi, second century

BCE. For a detailed survey and discussion of evidence for Jewish slaves, freedpersons, and slave owners, see Dale B. Martin, "Slavery and the Ancient Jewish Family," in *The Jewish Family in Antiquity*, ed. Shaye J. D. Cohen. Brown Judaic Studies 289 (Atlanta, GA: Scholars Press, 1993) 113–129.

28. Acts 8:3.

29. P. Yadin 15.35.

30. P. Yadin 10 and 18. P. Yadin 31, found in the same cave, but not part of Babatha's archive, is another *ketubbah*. For other references, see Kraemer, "Jewish Women in the Diaspora World" 56–58.

31. See Kraemer, "Jewish Women in the Diaspora World" 67, fn. 51.

32. CPJ 144, dated 13 BCE, in Kraemer, *Maenads* no. 45.

33. Josephus, *Life* 414–415.

34. Josephus, *Antiquities* 15§259–60.

35. Ibid., 19§354.

36. Ps.-Phocylides ll.215–217; ben Sira 7:24, 26:10–12, 42:9–14.

37. See Ilan, *Jewish Women* 141–47.

38. Josephus, *Antiquities* 15§259–60.

39. Bernadette Brooten, "Konnten Frauen in Alten Judentum die Scheidung betreiben? Überlegung zu Mk 10, 11–12 und 1 Kor 7, 10–11," *Evangelische Theologie* 42 (1982) 66–80. See also E. Lipinski, "The Wife's Right to Divorce in the Light of an Ancient Near Eastern Tradition," *The Jewish Law Annual* 4 (1981) 9–27.

40. P. Yadin 18.21–23; 57–59.

41. Initial notice appeared in J. T. Milik, "Le travail d'édition des manuscrits du Désert de Juda," *Volume du congrès Strasbourg 1956*. Supplements to Vetus Testamentum IV (Leiden: E. J. Brill, 1956) 21. The papyrus, designated *Papyrus Se'elim* 13, was published by Ada Yardeni, *Nahal Se'elim Documents* (Jerusalem: Israel Exploration Society and Ben Gurion University in the Negev Press, 1995); Yardeni espouses the view taken by the late Jonas Greenfield that the papyrus is not a *get*, but rather the receipt for a *get* issued to a woman. Tal Ilan, however, argues that the more plausible interpretation is that Milik's initial assessment was correct ("Notes and Observations on a Newly Published Divorce Bill from the Judaean Desert," HTR 89/2 [1996] 195–202, with Aramaic text and English translation).

42. P. Cowley 15, probably Oct. 11, 435 BCE.

43. CPJ 144 (Kraemer, *Maenads* no. 45).

44. Philo, *The Special Laws* 3.169–75.

45. Philo, *Against Flaccus* 89.

46. CPJ 19 (Kraemer, *Maenads* no. 37).

47. See chapter 1, pp. 28, 30, 33–34; see also Sandra Joshel, *Work, Identity and Legal Status at Rome: A Study of the Occupational Inscriptions* (Norman, OK: Oklahoma University Press, 1992).

48. Bernadette Brooten considers the possibility that a small number of women called "priest" in inscriptions may have served priestly functions; see *Women Leaders in the Ancient Synagogue*, Brown Judaic Studies 36 (Chico, CA: Scholars Press, 1982) 73–99. The evaluation of this evidence is extremely difficult.

49. Josephus, *Against Apion* 2§102–4.

50. Josephus, *The Jewish War* 5§198–200.

51. So Susan Grossman, "Women and the Jerusalem Temple," in *Daughters of the King: Women and the Synagogue, A Survey of History, Halachah and Contemporary Realities*, ed. Susan Grossman and Rivka Haut (Philadelphia: Jewish Publication Society, 1992) 15–37, esp. 19.

52. E.g., Josephus, *Jewish War* 2§10, 42, 198; 6§100, 427, 442. The term recurs frequently in Josephus' works.

53. E.g., b. Ned. 36a; see Ilan, Jewish Women 179–80.

54. CIJ 741 (Kraemer, Maenads no. 84), 731c (Maenads no. 85), 756 (Maenads no. 86); all treated in Brooten, Women Leaders 5–33. As noted above, at least one additional such inscription was reported in an obscure Turkish journal published in 1912; a second is also possible.

55. CIJ 400, 581, 590, 597, 692, and others (Kraemer, Maenads nos. 88–89); Brooten, Women Leaders 41–55.

56. E.g. CIJ 738 (Kraemer, Maenads no. 60) and others (Maenads no. 65).

57. CIJ 738 (Kraemer, Maenads no. 60).

58. Monique Alexandre, "Early Christian Women," in A History of Women in the West: Volume 1: From Ancient Goddesses to Christian Saints, ed. Pauline Schmitt Pantel, trans. Arthur Goldhammer (Cambridge, MA: Belknap Press of Harvard University Press, 1992) 418.

59. Philo, On the Contemplative Life 32–33, in Kraemer, Maenads no. 14.

60. Kraemer, Her Share of the Blessings 106–7, 126.

61. Discussion and references in Ilan, Jewish Women 103–4. See also Kraemer, Her Share of the Blessings 102–4.

62. Ilan here specifically notes Leonard Swidler, Women in Judaism: The Status of Women in Formative Judaism (Metuchen, NJ: Scarecrow, 1976) 180–81, and Ben Witherington III, Women in the Ministry of Jesus (Cambridge: Cambridge University Press, 1984) 72–73. The commentary of Mary Ann Tolbert, "Mark," in The Women's Bible Commentary, ed. Carol A. Newsom and Sharon H. Ringe (Louisville, KY: Westminster/John Knox, 1992) 269, clearly understands her state as one of contagious ritual impurity that could infect anyone who came into contact with her. See, however, Shaye J. D. Cohen, "Menstruants and the Sacred in Judaism and Christianity," in Women's History and Ancient History, ed. Sarah B. Pomeroy (Chapel Hill, NC: University of North Carolina Press, 1991) 271–99, who points out that there is likely to have been little interest in the impurity of the woman in these gospel narratives: "For most Jews of the second temple period the locus of God's presence was the temple and the temple mount, and as long as those affected with impurity stayed away from the sacred precincts Jewish society did not care about their impurity. Thus the gospel story about the woman with a twelve-year discharge, clearly a case of zaba, does not give any indication that the woman was impure" (279); see also Amy-Jill Levine, "Discharging Responsibility: Matthean Jesus, Biblical Law and Hemorrhaging Women," in Treasures New and Old: Recent Contributions in Matthean Studies, Society of Biblical Literature Symposium Series 1, ed. David R. Bauer and Mark Allen Powell (Atlanta, GA: Scholars Press, 1996) 379–97.

63. See, e.g., b. Git. 56a. Set against the backdrop of the famine in Jerusalem during the Jewish war, this passage narrates how an aristocratic woman, Martha b. Boethus, repeatedly sent her male servant to the market to purchase food to no avail.

64. There are numerous references to the Sadducees and Pharisees in rabbinic writings, but their historical utility is highly problematic. For a good introduction to the study of these movements, see Lester Grabbe, Judaism from Cyrus to Hadrian. Volume 2: The Roman Period (Minneapolis, MN: Fortress, 1992) 467–87.

65. Josephus, Jewish War 1§110–14; Josephus, Antiquities 13§405–417; both treat Alexandra's relations with the Pharisees. See also Tal Ilan, "The Attraction of Aristocratic Women to Pharisaic Judaism During the Second Temple Period," HTR 88 (1995) 1–33, esp. 11–13.

66. Ilan, "Attraction" 28.

67. Philo, That Every Good Man is Free 75–91; Philo, Hypothetica; Philo, On the Contemplative Life 1; Josephus, Jewish War 2§119–61; Josephus, Antiquities 13§171–2; 18§18–22; Pliny (the Elder), Natural History 5.73.

68. Philo, *Hypothetica* 11.14.

69. Pliny (the Elder), *Natural History* 5.73.

70. Josephus, *Jewish War* 2§160–1.

71. CD 7:6–7; 1QSa 1:4; 1QM 7:4–5. Comprehensive English translations of the scrolls may now be found in Florentino Garcia-Martinez, *The Dead Sea Scrolls Translated: The Qumran Texts in English*, 2nd ed., trans. Wilfred G. E. Watson (Leiden: E. J. Brill, 1994). For a fuller discussion of specific texts, see Eileen M. Schuller, "Women in the Dead Sea Scrolls," in *Methods of Investigation of the Dead Sea Scrolls and the Khirbet Qumran Site: Present Realities and Future Prospects*, ed. Michael O. Wise et al. (New York: New York Academy of Sciences, 1994) 115–31; see also Lawrence Schiffman, "Women in the Scrolls," in his *Reclaiming the Dead Sea Scrolls: The History of Judaism, The Background of Christianity, The Lost Library of Qumran* (Philadelphia: The Jewish Publication Society, 1994) 127–43.

72. E.g., 4Q502, on which see Joseph M. Baumgarten, "4Q502, Marriage or Golden-Age Ritual?" *Journal of Jewish Studies* 34 (1983) 125–35.

73. Linda Bennett Elder, "The Woman Question and Female Ascetics Among Essenes," *Biblical Archaeologist* 57/4 (1994) 220–34, esp. 223–225, relying on the excavations of Steckoll, reported in 1967, and de Vaux, in 1973. Elder also notes that the excavation of a small cemetery at Ain El Ghuweir, several kilometers south of Qumran (which she considers to have possible connections to Qumran), yielded the skeletons of twelve males, seven females, and one child. At a conference in Jerusalem, July 1997, commemorating the fiftieth anniversary of the discovery of the scrolls, questions were raised concerned the adequacy and accuracy of the testing of the skeletons for biological sex.

74. E.g., Elder, "The Woman Question." L. Calista Olds, in Emil Schürer, *The History of the Jews in the Age of Jesus Christ*, A new English version revised and edited by G. Vermes, F. Millar, and M. Goodman (Edinburgh: T & T Clark, Ltd., 1986, 2:578), notes that most of the remains of women and children come from "secondary" sites, and that only one skeleton from the "main" cemetery is female (citing Roland de Vaux, *Archaeology and the Dead Sea Scrolls* [London: The British Academy, by Oxford University Press, 1973]). Olds concludes that "the Dead Sea community . . . included members of both sexes" and thinks that married sectarians outnumbered the celibates (578).

75. Some scholars consider references in a few, fragmentary documents to be suggestive of the participation of women on their own, rather than because of their husbands; see, e.g., Baumgarten, "4Q502."

76. Schuller, "Women and the Dead Sea Scrolls."

77. This is, in fact, a more complex question than it might initially appear. Women in antiquity are likely to have menstruated far less frequently than women in the late twentieth century in the west due to later onset of menses, frequent pregnancy, extended lactation, dietary insufficiencies, and even maternal mortality. Nevertheless, given the intense interest in ritual purity apparent in many scrolls, it seems hard to imagine that Essene men would have easily accommodated women of childbearing age into their communal life. Postmenopausal women, however, might have been a different story (on which, see note 71 above).

78. Elder, "The Woman Question"; Kathleen Corley, "Feminist Myths of Christian Origins, in *Reimagining Christian Origins: A Colloquium Honoring Burton L. Mack*, ed. Elizabeth A. H. Castelli and Hal Taussig (Valley Forge, PA: Trinity Press International, 1996) 51–67, esp. 58. Corley argues this point in far more detail in a manuscript in progress. Injuries sustained in an automobile accident have delayed publication of her work, and I am extremely grateful that she was able to share many of her arguments with me in advance.

79. See, however, the fascinating and little-known study by Grace H. Macurdy, "Royal

Women of Judaea," in her *Vassal Queens* 63–91, and Ilan, "Josephus and Nicolaus on Women."

80. Edith Deen calls her "the most striking example in the NT of how far reaching can be the evil influence of a heartless, determined woman in a high position" (*All the Women of the Bible* [New York: Harper and Row, 1955; reprint San Francisco: HarperSanFrancisco, 1988] 184).

81. Josephus, *Antiquities* 18§136.

82. See, e.g., Josephus, *Antiquities* 18§159–60.

83. Philo, *On the Contemplative Life*, esp. 12, 32, 68–69 (in Kraemer, *Maenads* no. 14).

84. Ross S. Kraemer, "Monastic Jewish Women in Greco-Roman Egypt: Philo and the Therapeutrides," *Signs: Journal of Women in Culture and Society* 14/2 (1989) 342–70; Kraemer, *Her Share of the Blessings* 113–17.

85. "Simon . . . had joined the brigands who had seized [the desert fortress] Masada. At first, they regarded him with suspicion, and permitted him and his following of women access only to the lower part of the fortress, occupying the upper quarters themselves; but afterwards . . . he was allowed to accompany them on their marauding expeditions" (Josephus, *Jewish War* 4§504–506).

86. Josephus, *Jewish War* 4§538–544.

87. On which, see Kenelm Burridge, *New Heaven, New Earth: A Study in Millenarian Activities* (New York: Schocken, 1969); see also John G. Gager, *Kingdom and Community: The Social World of Early Christianity* (Englewood Cliffs, NJ: Prentice-Hall, 1975).

88. For a more positive view of this, see Kathleen Corley, *Private Women, Public Meals: Social Conflict in the Synoptic Tradition* (Peabody, MA: Hendrickson, 1993) 154–58.

89. m. Sota. 3.4. For discussion, see Wegner, *Chattel or Person* 161–62; Daniel Boyarin, *Carnal Israel* 170–80; Kraemer, *Her Share of the Blessings* 97–98.

90. b. *Pesah* 62b.

91. From Rashi's commentary to b. *Avodah Zarah* 18b.

92. Boyarin, *Carnal Israel* 190–96.

4

>-+◦-O-◦+-<

WOMEN'S RELIGIONS
AND RELIGIOUS LIVES IN
THE GRECO-ROMAN CITY

Lynn R. LiDonnici

Introduction: Stories about Women and Women's Stories

The religious landscape of the Greco-Roman city was rich, varied, and exciting.
Almost every aspect of life, from sports to shopping to taking a bath, from eating
to cleaning the house, was made part of a whole system of hopes, practices, and
beliefs that involved divine forces (the gods and goddesses) with the minute
details of everyday activity. Religion was a fully functional dimension of public
life (reflected by rites that all city members were expected to share), as well as
an intellectual space for reflection on the most deeply held personal concerns
(reflected by private, voluntary worships of a staggering variety). Many of these
activities were shared by women and men, but there were some very important
worships that both genders felt it was important to separate. In order to think
about and evaluate the significance of shared and separated worships, and of the
experience of religion that was unique to the women of the ancient city, we
have to begin by considering several factors that have influenced the way wom-
en's stories have been remembered and told.

Until recently, whatever little attention was paid to women and women's
religious activities around the ancient Mediterranean was based largely on surviving representations of women from literature and art. Though useful in their
way (and certainly better than nothing), these studies are flawed by their generally uncritical assumption that such sources accurately portray ancient women.
Two factors are consistently overlooked: (1) literary representations are designed
to amuse (comedy), frighten (tragedy), or prescribe (moral or philosophical

essays) and, therefore, these representations may be extremely distorted (bearing about as much relationship, possibly, as exists between the classic "hooker with a heart of gold" beloved in films and actual streetwalkers); and (2) these representations unanimously (as far as we can tell) demonstrate men's visions of women, presented to exclusively male audiences at theaters and symposia (drinking parties).

The voices of the real women of the ancient world are very hard to find and hard to hear. The last twenty years have seen a widespread revolution in the study of ancient women, based largely on the changeover from reliance on representational sources to documentary evidence: public documents, like inscriptions and tombstones, and private documents like personal letters, contracts, and wills. These new studies have begun to uncover the rich texture of possibility and activity, even within their societal constraints, that some (many?) women were able to enjoy. Three important factors, however, need to be remembered when using this material. First, if we are studying public monuments, and even inscribed tombstones (though to a lesser extent), we are for the most part dealing with wealthier women of middle-to-high social position. The inscriptions bear witness to this since the erection of monuments necessitates "spare cash." Second, when dealing with private correspondence and contracts, again, we find ourselves either studying the literate strata of society[1] or viewing the parties through the filter of a literate scribe. Third, although the literary works described above are problematic as sources for women's actual religious practices, they provide helpful information on male attitudes toward women; in antiquity as today, women may often have internalized these views, influencing new practices or attitudes. Therefore, even modern studies must proceed with caution.

In the particular case of the religious lives of ancient women, we find many more public inscriptions (usually honoring a priestess' term) and archaeological materials (religious objects, representations of rituals in which women participate) than documentary letters or contracts. To this we add fragments of historical writing that describe women's religious activities, always remembering that the historian may be including these stories because they are extraordinary, not usual. Careful analyses of some of the literary portrayals of goddesses and exemplary women can also be helpful for learning about some of the models presented to women, but we need to remember that such models are usually of contrast rather than identity. Most often, myths outline what women may not do. Goddesses are divine and, as such, for Greco-Roman religion, "totally Other." One of the most central religious messages throughout Greco-Roman worship, for both women and men, was this emphasis on the unbridgeable gap between humanity and divinity, and the foolishness—and danger—of forgetting this distance, unless the deities themselves are extending the invitation. This sense of difference means that the gender of a deity is not often a good indicator of the gender of the worshippers or officiants because, although sometimes a given believer may be unconsciously looking for identification with a god, at other times he or she may seek out a symbol that reflects this basic and unchangeable difference.

Women's Religious Lives in the Greco-Roman City

The major element shared by most of the religions of the ancient Mediterranean was the basic assumption of a polytheistic universe. The world was felt to be full of deities, some more familiar and some stranger; some on your side, and some against you. New, unknown, but just as powerful, deities could lie around every bend in the road. The general attitude toward this multiplicity was, essentially, the more the better (though corporate bodies, such as cities, often took the opposite view). This sense of diversity and, often, disagreement between divine forces is an important theological component of such systems, explaining, for example, such things as military defeats and natural disasters sometimes as punishment by a favored god, but sometimes as interference from another god, without reference to the behavior of an individual family or city. This element would disappear if all the gods were envisioned as exactly the same and in perfect agreement. The sense of fracture built into the structure of the universe is expressed symbolically in the broad range of "personalities" and attributes of divine figures, who differ from each other in all the ways that people do, by temperament, gender, ethnicity, appearance, and so on. The use of a particular gender to describe a deity is only one of the significant details we need to take into account in explaining what he or she meant to worshippers.[2]

These divergent personalities were also worshipped in divergent ways, depending on the particular "history" that an individual, a family, or a city had with each figure. The classic formulations of myths with which educated Westerners are most familiar are not usually good indicators of the religious activities and expressions associated with a given god in ancient religion, except for savior-oriented or intercessory religions, which are discussed below.[3] The myths and stories that are important to particular sanctuaries or festivals usually involve the great power of the specific, local image or statue of the deity, which appears in a miraculous manner, saves the city, or averts a plague, for example, rather than involving the independent activities of the figure. Such events introduce new deities or modify worship forms, leading to an even greater sense of diversity among divine powers since no two cities shared exactly the same favored gods and goddesses, no two cities conceptualized even a shared god or goddess in exactly the same manner, and each community conducted religious observance in individual and characteristic ways.

One classic example of this diversity of approach relates to the goddess Aphrodite (Roman Venus). Most poetic and mythological accounts present Aphrodite as the "goddess of love," a sexual powerhouse who subverts both marriage and civilized life. This view was a part of the general discourse of ancient society, in which there were likely to be "wisecracks" about Aphrodite when sexual irregularities were being discussed.[4] But this same "personality" functions elsewhere as a city protectress, with her images rigid and draped and with no element of either her myth-stories or her sexual relationships with other gods relating to the worship; she is, in fact, a protectress of legitimate marriage in these cities.[5] At the same time in other places, guilds of prostitutes adopted her as their patron goddess.[6]

These various formulations of the goddess are clearly in tension, but did not create tension among the various groups in antiquity, who simply approached the relevant aspect of the deity for whatever the need of the moment may have been. To conflate these disparate elements in the attempt to write the "biographies" of given deities robs each of its individuality and creates a distorted view of ancient religious life. In this case, when the prostitutes' devotion is applied to Aphrodite of the city as well, we get false, but persistent, reports that in Corinth (which Aphrodite protected), she was worshipped by "sacred prostitutes" throughout antiquity.[7] When this process is extended even further, conflating all female divine figures into a single Great Goddess, the meanings of these symbols and rituals to their ancient worshippers can become completely lost. This modern search for an all-encompassing and all-powerful feminine divine figure is an understandable and legitimate theological development[8] greatly influenced by Western traditions of monotheism. But this religious impulse is not usually a feature of ancient religious thinking and practice.

Polytheism and diversity of divine beings do help explain the vast differences between the nations of the world and the events that happen to them, but with the passage of time and the great historical developments associated with bringing all of these people into one political and conceptual system (first the Greek empire begun by Alexander and then the Roman empire), religious attitudes underwent certain changes. By the time of the Roman empire, most people agreed that, though the great gods of the Olympian pantheon (Zeus, Hera, Apollo, etc.) existed, they had little concern for the everyday conduct of most peoples' lives. Such deities interacted with human life on a cosmic or political level, if at all. Personal events, such as illness or health, success in business or shipwreck, requited or unrequited love, were not generally thought to be reflective of the divine will or judgments of these increasingly abstract and distant divine beings but, like everything in the world, governed either by chance (Fortuna) or by fate. Even fate, however, was not a reflection of the design for your life laid out by a conscious deity, but rather an unalterable force of nature—also not personalized—that can be neither angered nor pleased by anything humans do. But a lack of interest or confidence in the great Olympian gods (except in political and philosophical contexts) should not suggest a lack of interest in religion or in divine helpers overall. Throughout the centuries of the Greco-Roman period, both women and men were on the lookout for new and effective deities, who did care about the personal events of human life and who would step in and take positive action to help or save their worshippers within the context of a random or fated universe.

The religious expression of these basic assumptions took many forms. They do not form any single, coherent "system," and this makes it impossible to encapsulate them all into a brief overview. I will, however, venture to say that two of the most important mental concerns that underlie most of them are "The gods protect our city (or state, tribe, etc.)" and "What about me?" These two preoccupations concerned almost everyone, in varying proportions that depended on the circumstances of their lives.

The two dimensions of public and private cannot always be neatly separated.

Worships that are public, procultural institutions in one place may be private countercultural expressions in others. The liberator-god Dionysos, for example, also had a political meaning for Macedonians and their later descendants;[9] the countercultural philosopher-mystic Apollonius of Tyana was worshipped after his death as a city protector at Ephesos. In addition, public, procultural deities may be approached in countercultural ways. For example, most forms of sorcery and ritual coercion ("magic") were prohibited in the Greco-Roman cities, but this did not stop individuals from invoking the names of public, procultural deities such as Apollo in their spells.[10] This diversity of approach and ability to choose elements at will always needs to be remembered. It is, however, useful to separate worship practices directed toward public good and private benefit.

Public Worship and the Life of the State

In the ancient world, the concept of the "city" usually expressed more than just a bunch of buildings and a place to live. By the Greco-Roman period, the city represented society, and what was good for the city was also good for the region and the empire and for the family and tribe. In large measure, the city and one's place (and the place of one's family) within it gave people their personal identities relative to other cities and citizens.[11] Individuals, for example, from the city of Ephesos burst with pride when they could see the slogan "First in Asia" on their coins, knowing they were "better" (in regard to imperial favor) than the other cities. But even those in the small city of Magnesia could feel better than someone—their coins read "Fourth in Asia," so at least they could have more pride than cities numbered five and higher.[12] Prestige and power were intimately related concepts, and it is hard to say which was valued more.

While most of the Greco-Roman cities shared several common worships, the specific pantheons of individual cities were unique. Every city had one or more patron deities, and each city's religious landscape grew richer with the passage of time as extraordinary people or events were likely to be remembered with religious celebrations for a very long time. Let us look at, for example, the city of Ephesos.[13] Ephesos' main city protector was the goddess Artemis, worshipped there as a particular manifestation of the goddess embodied in a unique statue, *Artemis of Ephesos*. The myths and rituals surrounding this worship related to the creation of this image and the power of this image, among other things, to protect the city from invasion. These myths bear little or no relationship to the tragic or Homeric Artemis, the "virgin huntress"—indeed, Artemis Ephesia is, like many religious statues, heavily draped and veiled, rigid and unmoving. At home, Artemis of Ephesos was a civic and political goddess, but as Ephesians traveled and even settled elsewhere, they brought this worship with them, so by the Roman period, "Ephesian" Artemis was worshipped in a wide variety of places. Outside Ephesos, this worship was largely personal, its political resonance being tied to the home city, even if the goddess was not. Along with this main deity, Ephesos celebrated important religious activities dedicated to Aphrodite, Apollo, possibly Athena (a city god at Athens, but in Ephesos worshipped as a patron of the arts), Dionysos, the Egyptian gods Isis and Serapis, and so forth. The power of Rome was recognized in the extremely important imperial cult: the tag "First in Asia" probably means it was the first city in the province of Asia to have permission to build a temple for Rome. In addition, great city benefactors were worshipped. The philosopher-mystic Apollonius of Tyana was worshipped at Ephesos for at least 100 years after his death in gratitude for his help in averting a plague. Finally, a simple individual called P. Servilius Isauricus had a temple and a cult. This man was the Roman proconsul of Asia from 46–44 BCE and was a just and generous ruler. This made such an impression (and formed such a contrast to many other Roman officials) that he was worshipped in Ephesos and other Asian cities for several generations. In the past, as today, good rulers are hard to find.

All of these worships had temples, or at least altars, for sacrifice, festivals, games, and processions; some claim that there was a major procession for Artemis of Ephesos as often as every two weeks.[14] Artemis of Ephesos possessed herds, farmland, and fishponds; her temple and images were famous and needed maintenance. The altar of her temple alone was large enough for the simultaneous sacrifice of hundreds of cattle. Who took care of all of this?

One of the most important ways to gain prestige in a city was to hold public religious office and to sponsor important religious functions, festivals, or temples. People took these civic religious responsibilities extremely seriously and desired to perform as many of them as they could, despite the huge expense involved,[15] since each sponsor had to buy the cattle, hire the priests, and provide all of the other elements required for the production of a major event or parade. Here, we see power and prestige in a very close relationship since both would be greatly enhanced by providing a wonderful spectacle; at the same time, one needed both (specifically, money and influence) to be awarded the honor of sponsorship in the first place.[16] Public benefactions of this kind provide for us the greatest amount of source material since one of the "perks" of these prestigious offices was the city's grant to an individual of the right to erect a statue or inscription for himself or herself that commemorated the term of office; many of these statues and inscriptions survive.

The majority of "priestly" offices from the Greco-Roman city were of this kind.[17] They involved responsibility for the upkeep of a particular temple, for the proper conduct of the sacrifices there, for the maintenance and care of the temple's sacred image, and, usually, for processions, festivals, and games (if any) involving that temple. These public priesthoods were for limited periods of time and did not usually involve the officeholder in any kind of personal constriction, such as celibacy or the avoidance of certain foods, and the officeholders lived at home. Although a given priesthood was the responsibility of one individual or family for a given year, the larger festivals involved the entire city, and each person in each particular social role had a part to play. In these cases, the officeholder was the primary producer of the huge festival or procession.

These festivals and processions expressed civic pride and identity, but also reinforced the social structure of the city by assigning specific roles to specific groups (including the relevant deities). For example, even if a man was "in charge" of a given festival, the women of the city would be involved, perhaps by weaving a beautiful garment for the deity's image to wear. The women would feel pride in their accomplishment, but also in their status as members of one of the noble or prominent families from which the group was drawn.[18] In addition, social control might be exercised by the threat of exclusion—"If you do that, we won't let you into the weaving group this year." Since public participation was such an important measure of personal and family prestige, these threats could be extremely serious and powerful checks on individual behavior. Ideally, all citizens were involved together in the correct and beautiful celebration of the festival, which reflected, psychologically, the sense that the world was in order and that the people were safe. Changes and innovations were avoided whenever possible;[19] the message of the public festivals was that things were right as they were, and that they would stay that way as long as all of the members of the cosmos (people and deities) kept to their places.

Substantial evidence exists to indicate that women held many of these public offices and were expected to exercise their public religious duties just as men were.[20] Women's names are recorded in a wide variety of official inscriptions recording—and honoring—their public service and generosity. They maintained temples and sponsored games, processions, and sacrifices. Women are praised in these inscriptions as model citizens of the type "married wealthy woman." At least one woman, Tata of Aphrodisias, earned the title "mother of the city."[21] Tata was a priestess of Hera for life, a much greater—and much more prestigious—office than the temporary appointments. This is a reflection of her prominent family and great resources. Tata is praised for the generosity with which she managed the worship of Hera and of the imperial family, of which she was also priestess; but, just as importantly, she is praised for her own moral qualities: her love of honor and her virtuous and chaste (nonadulterous) lifestyle. These are key elements in the concept of "leadership" for both women and men in the ancient city. Prominence and influence were intimately related to the conduct of private lives, and public figures were expected to lead by example, as well as by action. Another woman, Berenice of Syros[22] is similarly praised for both her public generosity and her private conduct, in the midst of which she has managed to raise her own children. While these public inscriptions are precious records of the lives of real women from antiquity, they should also be read as prescriptions for the behavior of the other women of the city. Just as no one today can avoid seeing the "role models" presented by advertising and the media, no one in an ancient city could go anywhere without encountering several of these honorary statues or inscriptions, which lay out a very clear-cut set of expectations about what a praiseworthy woman should be.[23] Both women and men, especially from upwardly mobile families, took these prescriptions very seriously and attempted to embody them in their lives. This was an important religious act in the context of the ancient city, where "religion" and the ideologies of city, state, and family were so closely related as to be practically indistinguishable categories.

Private Concerns in This Life and the Afterlife

While public and festival religion were geared toward the collective life of city and family, they were not helpful at moments of individual pain, for which sometimes it was temporarily not enough to be reassured that, even though a specific individual may be suffering, the state or the family will live on. Though this is an important idea that has sustained many a soldier, on occasion that soldier might wonder what purpose there might be to his specific life other than the protection of the group. In addition, every city had many people lacking the money or influence that would enable them to participate in the public rituals as anything other than spectators, who may, in fact, have disagreed with the rulers without any realistic chance of ever changing their circumstances. For them, the value of public and festival observances for comfort and self-understanding was minimal.

For some people, whether cut off from power or simply alienated from that power, the limited choices and preset roles they were offered by the city, the family, and public religion were sometimes disappointing on a personal level and were incapable of addressing all the questions they asked about life. What religious options existed for all those people, both women[24] and men, who were not satisfied with things as they were, for whom the boosterism of the public festivals was an empty reinforcement of what they already thought was wrong with their lives? What did people do when, even though they usually supported and enjoyed public religion, they suddenly needed private and personal contact with the powers of the universe to make sense of the world they saw?

Even though many people lived with a sense of fatedness, this did not mean that in antiquity, any more than today, people watched unfazed as the events of their lives unfolded (though the popular version of Stoic philosophy urged exactly this).[25] Rather, emotional and actual control were sought by two major means: (1) to learn what their fate might be, usually through astrology or other modes of divination, in order to plan accordingly and (2) to find an advocate or intercessor to act for them and alter their fortunes. These intercessors, while not usually in overtly hostile relations with the great gods of the city and the empire, were sometimes countercultural figures in the sense that the public and imperial religions urged acceptance of circumstance and performance of duty, while these figures offered the possibility of change. These intercessor figures are most important to bear in mind for understanding the context of the appeal of early Christianity.

In the worship of these figures, we find a major exception to the general rule of the unimportance of myth for religious practice and belief. Each of these worships was centered around a figure with a "life" story that caused them, people felt, to be able to "relate" more directly to the pains of humanity and therefore to help people out of empathy. These myth-stories, therefore, were of great importance and often governed the forms of rituals and celebrations. They could also serve to draw new people into that worship.

Every ancient city had at least one religious complex dedicated to healing.

The most frequently occurring deity is the god Asklepios, usually accompanied by other figures, such as Hygieia (health), his "daughter." Persons who desired healing would approach the god at one of his many temples or shrines. Sometimes, this involved a long pilgrimage, but most often people approached him at a local sanctuary.[26] The "faith" in Asklepios was that, even though the gods were remote and life on earth was governed by fortune and fate, he might choose to intervene in your life and remove whatever illness (usually chronic disabilities or infertility) was troubling you. After healing (or even without a clear-cut healing), worshippers would give votive objects such as inscriptions or figurines to the god, and many of these survive. Such objects tell us a great deal about the private concerns of ordinary citizens, but also what they felt it was appropriate to ask for from an essentially procultural god. For example, while many women asked the god for children, no one asked for the termination of an unwanted pregnancy. While many sought the end of paralysis, no one asked for superior strength, for example, to win victory in games. Yet people desired these things and sought them by religious means, as we know from the surviving descriptions of spells and rituals clearly performed despite being illegal.[27] Asklepios was prepared to intervene only when what you wanted was "proper."

Why would Asklepios—or any intercessory god—do this? The question is answered by myth. Every intercessory god was surrounded by an important central story that emphasized the sufferings or other humanlike experiences of that god, and it was felt that these deities would be more sympathetic to human pain due to their own knowledge of what that pain was like. In one version of his myth, Asklepios was said to have been a human doctor, who was eventually killed by the gods for restoring the dead to life by his medical skill. When later he was restored to life and made into a god, he retained his compassion and continued to help people.[28]

The idea that a god's suffering made him or her a willing advocate or assistant in human trouble was a potent one in popular piety. One figure, Herakles (Latin Hercules), who is usually regarded by us as the emblematic strong man, was actually one of the most frequently invoked intercessors in the Greco-Roman world, though he lacked a widespread, formal salvific "cult." Stories about Herakles do tell of his strength, but most often stress his recurrent bouts of madness (which drove him to murder several sets of wives and children), his many years spent in atonement for these crimes, and finally his agonizing death.[29] These life events allowed ordinary people to relate the great hero to their own problems, causing them to call out "mehercule" ("Herakles, come here!!") many times a day.

By far, the most widely worshipped intercessory figure was the Egyptian goddess, Isis.[30] Like Asklepios and Herakles, Isis' personal story gave believers a sense that she could empathize with their problems. According to Plutarch's account of the myth,[31] Isis became a widow when her brother-husband Osiris was nailed into a sarcophagus and thrown into the Nile by another brother, Typhon. When Isis heard about it, she mourned and wandered all over the world, asking everyone she met if he or she knew where Osiris was. In this way, she not only discovered the sarcophagus, but also gained the bitter knowledge that Osiris had slept with and fathered a child by another sister, Nephthys. Isis found and adopted this child, Anubis, and then recovered the sarcophagus and again mourned over the dead Osiris with her son, Horus. Typhon, meanwhile, managed to steal the body again, and this time dismembered it and strewed the pieces throughout Egypt. Isis again embarked on a long voyage to recover and reassemble the pieces. When she had found all of them except his phallus, she reassembled the body and, by a mighty feat of power, reanimated Osiris enough for him to rule all the dead and to impregnate her with another child, Harpocrates, who was "untimely born" and not completely healthy. This is a long and beautiful narrative that I have had to compress rather ruthlessly, but the main points to consider are Isis' sufferings (multiple losses, multiple betrayals) and her responses to them—loyalty and unswerving devotion. Because all of her long searches were aided by humanity, while other gods were obstructive or even the cause of her pain, in her gratitude and her empathy (having suffered ι e same things), she was felt to be a particularly strong advocate in human concerns; her demonstrably great power made her a favorite helper—a savior—in all kinds of situations.

Isis helped anyone who called upon her, both women and men, in any area of trouble, from childbirth to shipwreck. The details of her myth, however, which touch upon so many elements that are the common experiences of women (marriage, widowhood, motherhood, attachment to first love, adulterous betrayal by a spouse and a sister, fostering of children, a problem pregnancy, rearing of a sick child, care for the dead) make it natural that many women would turn to her and be extremely attracted to this worship. It is, however, difficult to argue that the worship of Isis was exclusively, or even primarily, a religion of women.[32] Many men also responded to the great compassion that the goddess showed, and many women resonated more with other divine figures. At the same time, we must remember that, in a polytheistic society, people worship many gods, some of which may seem contradictory combinations to our minds. One could, so to speak, approach Isis with the Isis-related problems and approach other gods for other needs with little or no tension or conflict. The point is not whether or not the Isis religion was "for" women, but rather, that it was there for women, and many of them participated in it, both privately and in positions of cultic office.

Salvation from the dangers and crises of this life and salvation from death in the afterlife—the attainment of immortality—were separate concepts in the religions of the ancient saviors. Eternal salvation was a function of initiation into one or more religions, usually called *mysteries*, which brought the initiate into an intimate and permanent relationship with a particular deity. By this means, the believer was promised that, when he or she died, that deity would rescue his or her soul from the ordinary, rather miserable place of the dead and transport it to a place of happiness. Anyone could pray to Isis for help in a crisis, but only her initiates would be granted eternal life.

Isis is actually unusual in the sense that she functioned both as a "this-life savior," like Asklepios,[33] and as a grantor of eternal life. The great majority of ancient saviors offered only eternal blessedness and were totally unconcerned with the events of life before death. This disinterest extends to all areas of life: gender, wealth, social status, events that may befall initiates, and behavior while alive. Although there are exceptions, for the most part it was the fact of initiation rather than moral perfection that brought the soul of the dead person to the place of happiness. This fits in well with the overall presumption that the gods, in general (Isis is always an exception), were timeless, infinite powers not involved with human life on earth, which was governed by capricious fortune and blind fate. The gods were impersonal loci of power. If some of the gods, for a variety of reasons, had compassion for humanity, this was usually expressed as a transportation of the soul away from the pain of human life rather than as any attempt to improve it.

One result of this perspective is that we find a much more egalitarian attitude within the mystery religions about who could be admitted. Anyone, woman, man, king, or slave, usually could be initiated if they met the basic requirements and had the necessary cash. This is a reflection of the idea that the gods do not really care enough about the details of human life to have regard for who you are—or were—to observe the petty social distinctions of life on earth. But this disconcern, which seems harsh, cuts both ways: if the gods do not care who we are, then people without "noble families" or wealth are just as acceptable as leaders and worshippers within a religion oriented toward the afterlife rather than this life. Because of this, we do find a greater demographic variety of people involved in mystery religions, and a greater number of socially uninvested or marginal people there as well. This combination often alarmed official bodies, which sometimes tried to block the acceptance of a new worship into a given city. Usually, however, even mysteries that originally met with opposition were eventually incorporated and permitted, to the extent that they did not threaten the social order. Had any of these religions advocated, for example, violent overthrow of the government or slave revolt, it would have been persecuted and stamped out thoroughly. Each mystery that survived contained this element of future blessedness, an extremely useful and meaningful belief for people without much blessedness in their lives here on earth. These religions also sometimes had appeal for members of influential or noble families, and problems sometimes arose in relation to this, as such people were expected to carry out important duties (such as childbearing or fathering and the sponsorship of city temples and festivals) in public life and civic religion. When elite individuals turned away from these responsibilities toward an exclusive attachment to a mystery religion, widespread outrage and persecution of that religion was likely to result. This is extremely important to remember when considering the persecutions of early Christians and the particular route that Christian apologetic literature, such as 1 Timothy 2:8–15, felt it necessary to take.[34]

The most famous of all the initiations into eternal life was the Eleusinian mystery religion. This extremely ancient worship continued to be highly popular throughout the Greco-Roman period and only ceased with the forced closure of all Greco-Roman shrines initiated by the Christian emperor, Theodosius, in 391 CE. The Eleusinian mysteries were, according to the religion's own myth, initiated by the great goddess Demeter in gratitude and pity toward humanity.[35]

Demeter, a goddess of grain (and therefore of human life and civilization), had a daughter, Persephone, by Zeus. This girl (she is often called just "girl" [Korē]) was kidnapped (for marriage) by Hades, lord of the underworld and king of the dead, with Zeus' connivance, but without her mother's knowledge. Demeter began to search the earth for news of Persephone and, disguised as an old woman, landed in the town of Eleusis, where all of the women of the court, particularly the queen, were extremely kind and welcoming to her. Given the job of nursing the baby prince, Demeter set about making the child immortal by holding him over a fire each night. When the queen noticed this and objected, Demeter revealed herself as a goddess and demanded a temple. She then holed herself up in the temple and caused all growth on earth to stop as a means of forcing Zeus to restore Persephone to her. Meanwhile, in the underworld, Persephone had eaten some pomegranate seeds, which meant that she could not return to Demeter permanently, but had to live in the underworld with Hades as her husband for a certain part of the year. With this arrangement, all parties had to be satisfied.

This is the portion of the myth that anyone could know, but it is clear that the mystery initiation contained much more detail, a unique interpretation, as well as whole sequences, probably, that one only learned in the initiation rituals and that then had to be kept secret. It is one of the wonders of antiquity that, with the massive numbers of people who knew these secrets, no serious breach of security made it into the sources that survive for us; for all intents and purposes, the secrets remain closed (though speculation was rife in antiquity—and continues to be today). This should tell us how seriously initiation was taken by the participants: no one wanted to lose out on immortality (or risk premature mortality—the revelation was a crime punishable by death) just for the sake of the "fifteen minutes of fame" they might gain by revealing the secrets. What is important for the present purpose is not the content of the mysteries, but their function in the lives of ordinary believers.[36]

Although the Eleusinian mysteries were open both to women and to men, Demeter and Persephone were particularly favorite goddesses for women. Like Isis, both of the Eleusinian goddesses could be seen to have suffered many of the problems that real women faced on a daily basis and therefore could be approached about these matters. In particular, the myth of Demeter and Persephone can be read as a critique of the realities that marriage posed for Greek women and girls and an attempt to come to terms with them. At marriage, mothers and daughters could well be separated for life unless they happened to live near each other, and the dangers of childbirth created a very real association between marriage and death.[37] But such things were felt to be unalterable, even for the gods. The Eleusinian initiation promised a future beyond the suffering of life, with even, perhaps, a reunion of loved ones with no more threat of separation.

The Eleusinian rituals were celebrated once a year and were extremely elaborate and complex. Many officials were involved, including both priests and priestesses, each of whom was essential for the performance of the initiation. Although the worship did have political overtones for Athenians, people from all around the Mediterranean made the long voyage to Eleusis to participate in what was an intensely personal and rewarding experience for them.

Initiation and Voluntary Associations

In addition to the completely public worships of the Greco-Roman city and the private initiations many people undertook, there were many "clubs" or voluntary associations, each of which had important religious, social, and economic functions.[38] Sources for these clubs pertain to sponsorship or leadership rather than simple membership, so we have more mention of men, but there is also a small, but significant, number of women honored for sponsorship or leadership in a club, which possibly points to a significant membership. Hard and fast "gender-counting" may be ultimately misleading, however, since the clubs sponsored many activities in which the whole family, women included, of the member could usually participate.

These clubs were of many different kinds. There were clubs of people who had been initiated into a particular mystery and wanted to be together even after the experience was over. There were clubs for residents of the same home city now living elsewhere, people who had the same job,[39] people who liked particular sports teams, military veterans of certain campaigns, or people who shared a particular philosophy.[40] The clubs were an extremely important element of daily life for many as they sponsored banquets, particular rituals, and tombs for members and were important sources of hospitality for travelers from "branches" of the clubs in other cities. In a commercially and bureaucratically oriented society such as the Greco-Roman world, in which families were often displaced from home and "on the move" and men often had to spend long periods away from home on commercial ventures or for military service, club membership provided a way for individuals and smaller groups to find community and a way to relate to others and themselves in a context that was less overwhelming than the huge city could often be.

Many of the clubs were oriented around a particular religious perspective or experience. As noted, Eleusinian initiates often joined an Eleusinian club when they returned home. One of the most popular initiations, into the mysteries of Dionysos, created huge numbers of these clubs and was a very important component of many people's spiritual lives.

Unlike the Eleusinian mysteries, which occurred only once a year and in a set location, by the Greco-Roman period, Dionysiac initiation was celebrated in a wide variety of places and so was more available, especially to those with relatively less cash (who could not afford a long pilgrimage to Eleusis in Greece). Because of this, it is important to allow for regional variation in the ways the mysteries were celebrated and the elements of the myth that specific groups thought important. Another consideration is that, like many of the great gods, Dionysos had many public temples and festivals, such as the great theatrical competitions at Athens and elsewhere and popular celebrations of the new wine, in addition to the more private mystery religion. Therefore, we know many different myths about him and even many versions of these myths; but it is not

always easy to determine which of these versions was significant for the mysteries as celebrated in a particular place and which were used in other ways.

One myth of Dionysos that seems to have been used prominently in the
mysteries concerns his "double birth." In this myth, Zagreus, a child of Zeus,
was brutally killed, cooked, and, except for his heart, eaten by a rival group of
gods called the Titans. When Zeus discovered this, he destroyed the Titans with
a thunderbolt and rescued the heart, sewing it up inside his own thigh for it to
grow again into another baby, who, when he was born, became the god Dionysos. At the same time, Zeus took the ashes of the burned-up Titans and out
of them created the human race. Because of this, although people are created
out of base and terrible material, there is a spark of divinity in us by way of the
pieces of Zagreus that were in the stomachs of the Titans when they were killed.
Further episodes of the myth concern the second birth of the god, which was
assisted or celebrated by two "helper-gods" called the Curetes, his growth to
maturity, and, finally, his apotheosis or acceptance by all the other gods.[41] It is
not clear whether this myth was shared by all or most of the Dionysiac initiates,
but it does seem attractive in that it presents a new and much more intimate
relationship between gods and people than is presented in most other worships.
From the perspective of the myth, gods and people share the same substance,
and if the divine element in us is surrounded by awful, evil, Titan matter, it is
there nonetheless and can be activated by ritual, prayer, and initiation. This
activation will, however, become effective only at death, at which time the initiated soul will be taken by Dionysos or the Curetes from the "bad" underworld
and brought to a place of feasting, banqueting, and joyful communication with
the god. In the living world, initiates experienced a foretaste of that future in
the initiation itself and also in the fellowship, festivals, and banquets in which
they participated as members of their local Dionysiac club or association, which
was a new and extended family, a family for eternity.

The myth as I have described it above is remarkably "goddess free." Real
women, however, were extremely important to this worship in a variety of ways.
Ancient literature abounds with examples of women who were particularly attracted to the worship of Dionysos at all levels of society; when Dionysiac worship is depicted in art, the most common symbolic representation is the female
worshipper (the maenad), with her wild hair, leopard skin, ritual wand (thyrsos),
twining ivy, and ecstatic dance postures. Though most of these representations
come from the classical period, long before the Greco-Roman manifestations we
are discussing, the close relationship between women and the worship of Dionysos continued throughout antiquity. Women played a major part, both in the
afterlife-oriented initiations described above and in another form of worship for
the god, the maenadic association (or thiasos).

Sources describe how groups of women gathered, usually every two years,
to travel into the mountains and reenact another myth of Dionysos, one that
centers on the introduction of his worship to Greece. In this myth, which bears
little relation to the Zagreus myth described above, Dionysos is the son of Zeus
and a princess of Thebes, Semele. When Semele became pregnant by Zeus, she
notified her sisters and father, who, perhaps understandably, found it hard to

believe that this particular unwed pregnancy was of divine origin and were made even more angry by what they perceived as Semele's blasphemous lies in naming the great god Zeus as the father. Semele wanted to prove the truth of what she said, so she contrived to force Zeus to grant her a wish, thinking that this would be irrefutable proof for her family. Either on her own, or spurred by a jealous Hera, she asked for the god to reveal himself in his true form. Unfortunately, since his true form was the thunderbolt, Semele was burned to death. Rather than proving Semele's claim, this only convinced the father and sisters even more that she had been lying—the proof now being that Zeus had stricken her down. Zeus removed the baby Dionysos from her body and gave him to various nurses. When he had grown to maturity, however, he returned to Thebes and demanded that he and his mother be worshipped there as gods and for everyone to admit that Semele had been telling the truth. By this time, Thebes was ruled by an arrogant young prince, Pentheus, who refused to acknowledge the god or allow the worship to take place. At this point, the god cast a religious "madness" over the women of Thebes, causing them to leave their homes and band together in his worship, dancing through the mountains, hunting wild animals with their bare hands, and exhibiting many supernatural abilities. Among these women were the original sisters of Semele, including Agave, mother of Pentheus. Dionysos incited Pentheus to spy on the women, but when he was discovered, they, perceiving him to be a wild animal, killed him and tore him limb from limb. Agave returned to Thebes triumphantly bearing his head on a stake, thinking it to be a wild animal's head. At that moment, Dionysos opens everyone's eyes. They all realize he is a great god, and his worship is established in the city of Thebes.[42]

These events continued to be celebrated throughout the Hellenistic and Roman periods. Although it is not completely clear how the rituals were celebrated, we know that the worship was governed by priestesses, who led the worship, brought it into new places (sometimes by official invitation), and controlled the right to establish new thiasoi. Some sources suggest that this worship was originally restricted to women,[43] but by the Greco-Roman period, participants of both genders are attested,[44] though the leaders continued to be priestesses rather than priests. The rituals were celebrated in the mountains during winter. This alone should alert us to their importance for the participants, since winter mountain camping is no "vacation"; at least once, celebrating women were caught and cut off by a storm and needed to be rescued.[45] These rituals appear to reenact the original madness (mania: in Greek, a religious state of mind) visited upon the women of Thebes by the god, but it is important to note that this re-created mania was experienced by the participants as a blessing rather than a punishment. It is not clear whether participation in these thiasoi was also geared toward the attainment of a blissful afterlife. However, since the afterlife initiations described above were open to women, as well as men, it is clear that worshippers of Dionysos expected many women to be present at the eternal banquets, however their initiation was achieved. In leaving their cities and their established roles, women created a space for themselves in which they could interact with their god on a personal, rather than a corporate, level, and also interact with each other and with the male participants as individuals, not as women or as members of families. In the highly stratified and role-dominated society in which they lived, this was a precious and rare opportunity.

Religious Expressions of Women Alone

As we have just seen, the Dionysiac *thiasoi* of the Greco-Roman period were mixed-gender religious groups probably led by women. There were, however, a variety of religions that only women celebrated from which men were completely excluded. As we will see, some of these were procultural, while others contained a firm critique of the world in which the women lived.

Most cities celebrated some kind of festival in which only the married women of the city could participate. One such was the worship of Demeter Thesmophoros, celebrated in Athens and, with variations, in many other cities. This festival, known as the Thesmophoria,[46] was of great importance to the city and the women involved. Once a year, at the time of the fall sowing, the legitimate wives of citizens gathered for a three-day festival. During this time, the political and legal work of the city was suspended, and the women created, in effect, a temporary "city of women." Unlike the Dionysiac *thiasoi*, however, this worship was intensely procultural. Participation was defined by family status, and leadership and importance within the city of women reflected the standing of a woman's family. The women used the language and format of the political life of the city, and the entire festival was governed by tradition and custom. Each year, part of the sacrifice involved the throwing of piglets and various cakes into a crevasse or underground chamber. These things would, naturally, rot during the course of the year, and part of the next year's festival would be to retrieve this material, which was to be dedicated as an offering to Hades and then to be mixed with the seeds about to be planted. The women then observed an ascetic day of fasting and mourning and a final day of feasting, ribald humor, and celebration of the beautiful children, future citizens, that they hoped to bear.

The festival celebrated the linked issues of fertility and civilization, both of which were given to humanity by the goddess Demeter during the course of her search for Persephone. A little reflection will show us how little of civilization as we know it would be possible without agricultural fertility and the surpluses necessary to allow for specialized masons, soldiers, potters, writers, and the like. At the same time, no surplus can be harvested without people or if people are lawless. Demeter's title, *Thesmophoros*, touches upon both of these concepts. The term *thesmoi* refers to laws, but also to the rotted sacrificial material, which "energizes" the seeds and the future crop. In this way, the women prepare a substance by which law itself can be planted in the earth and grown to sustain human civil life.

All of this is very satisfying from the "the gods protect our city" perspective, but the individual soul always cries out, "What about me?" In theory, all of these marriages were stable, and everyone was happy as long as the beautiful children continued to appear. But the experience of three days in the ideal city of women was a far cry from the day-to-day realities of most women's lives, and many found it hard to be satisfied with patriotism when faced with a do-nothing or abusive husband or the nonstop demands of small children, who often behave in a manner far from "beautiful."

In the worship of Adonis, it seems, many women found a meaningful, if bittersweet, response to these unavoidable realities. According to the festival's myth, Adonis was born, the product of father-daughter incest, in some eastern locale. The place is not as important as the fact that he is clearly identified as not being Greek or Roman—he is a foreigner. Growing to the brink of maturity, the beautiful, gentle Adonis becomes the lover of the goddess Aphrodite, but before long, he is killed by a wild boar, usually by being gored in the thigh or genitals. Aphrodite mourns for her young lover and tries to restore him to life, but while he is in the underworld, Persephone, queen of the dead, has also fallen in love with him and is unwilling to let him go. Finally, Zeus orders that Adonis spend a part of the year in the underworld with Persephone and the rest of the time with Aphrodite.[47]

The festival celebrated the cyclic separation and reconciliation of the lovers. Every year, during the hottest and driest part of the summer, women of every social status, age, and class planted small, shallow bowls with various kinds of herbs and grains. These planters were called the "Gardens of Adonis." When the gardens had sprouted, they were taken to the house roofs, and it was there that the women celebrated their festival, which involved a feast, dance, great good humor, and song. The next day, however, the fragile gardens would wither and burn in the sun. The women then grouped together to "bury" both gardens and god in a spring or in the ocean, where they performed many rituals of mourning, such as hair tearing, breast beating, and wailing.

It is said that "the unions of the gods are always fruitful." It is significant, however, that Aphrodite and Adonis had no children together, just as the gardens sprouted and grew but died before they became useful food. Many modern interpreters focus on these rituals for Adonis as a reflection of women's dreams of the perfect lover, one who is (1) foreign and therefore free of the cultural expectations of the women's own society; (2) young and timid, therefore open to sexual instruction from his lover; (3) motherless, therefore thirsty for female nurturance and tenderness; (4) beardless, therefore soft and tender (like another woman); and (5) presumably infertile (since Aphrodite has no child by him), which greatly separates the pleasures of sexuality from their consequences; and so on.[48] This is an extremely attractive interpretation, and one that, I believe, accounts for many of the iconographic and symbolic features of the worship of Adonis as practiced in the Greco-Roman city. On an additional level, however, the ritual also provides a space for women from all walks of life to come together as individuals and to both celebrate and mourn the fragility and brevity of life itself, of interpersonal connections, and of beauty—their own and that of all the natural world. The mourning itself, however, implies the return of Adonis, which will inevitably occur the following year, to renew the world we see. The absence of afterlife components to this worship may account for the prominence of the element of mourning—even if we are reborn into blissful afterlife, our attachment to this world must eventually be broken and ended.

Conclusions

This has been a brief and basic introduction to some of the ways that the people of the ancient city used religion to understand their lives and make them meaningful. We have seen two basic approaches to religion, the collective or political approach and the individual approach. Each "side" of this religious coin had a great impact on the development of early Christianity, though in different ways and at different stages.

We have seen how the mystery or salvation religions addressed many elements of the personal alienation from public and family life and were used to create meaning for the individual life as opposed to the collective institution. Yet, none of these religions was exclusive. One could be initiated into as many or as few of them as he or she liked, and this led to a great openness to religious "news" of all kinds and from all parts of the empire. In addition, the tolerance and flexibility of polytheism meant that it was usually possible, without great mental contortion, to expand upon the basic myths of a given religion to cover new situations. This, combined with the vast stockpile of savior deities who had been born in some extraordinary way, lived, died, and returned to redeem humankind with the promise of eternal life, created an instant connection between the extremely familiar patterns of mystery religion and whatever original Christian message these Greco-Roman people received. Indeed, it is possible to argue that much, if not most, of the symbolism and details of the Jesus story was generated from this preexisting stock of Greco-Roman expectations about what saviors were like.[49]

While this led to ready acceptance of Christianity in some circles, it led to great misunderstandings as well, as when the Jewish Paul and his Greco-Roman audience discovered each other meant totally different things by such basic terms as "chastity," "body," "salvation," and, especially, "resurrection." After the first generation of Paul and eyewitness Jewish-Christian missionaries died, the developing gentile Christian communities borrowed symbols and structures from their Greco-Roman heritage for the organization of their basic institutions. For example, the clubs or voluntary associations provided a model for the formation of the earliest churches, which, like the clubs, sponsored feasts (the Eucharist), rituals (such as baptism), fund-raising (the collection for Jerusalem), tomb space, hospitality for traveling members, and many other things. The cyclic repetitions of death and rebirth of the various salvation gods added a yearly rhythm to the one-time resurrection of Jesus. Traditions about the experiences of saviors appear to have contributed to the great elaboration of the birth story for Jesus and many believe that the symbolism and importance of the Virgin Mary are derived from the worship of the great savior, Isis.

In all of this, women were important participants. If the membership and leadership of the Greco-Roman mysteries were more open and egalitarian than the public cults, the same seems to have been true of some of the early Christian communities, especially in second century Asia.[50] As Greco-Roman women desired to break free of the constraints, not only of their social roles, but also of the fortune and fate that were widely agreed to control the events of human life, it is not surprising that they would respond to a new religion that appeared, at least at first, to offer the ultimate in freedom.

As these early communities grew and developed their own, internal centers of power, such as general overseers of many individual communities (bishops) and even financial aid programs for needy members or foreign churches in distress, they began to borrow the structures of the public religions of the Greco-Roman city. At the end of the first Christian century, we see adoption of terminology, such as deacon, from public political life and the adoption of Greco-Roman social-moral standards, such as proper management of a household, as requirements for religious leadership. At the same time, there continued to be Christians who saw their faith more in terms of the personally oriented mystery model and as a clear call for a countercultural lifestyle, which usually meant celibacy.

At this point, we begin to see Christians in conflict with each other over the "true" Christianity and especially over the role of women and the degree of freedom that they should have. On the one side, we see the social and family concerns of what is usually called proto-orthodoxy (represented by the Pastoral Epistles); on the other side, there is an astounding variety of ascetic and ecstatic (or prophetic) movements, such as Marcionism, various types of "gnosticism," and the "New Prophecy" (Montanism), firmly oriented toward the salvation of the individual soul. In this inter-Christian conflict, we see the preservation and transformation of both sides of the spectrum of Greco-Roman polytheism; to a great extent, these continue to be active modes of religious expression (and conflict) to this day.

NOTES

1. On the issue of women's literacy, see Susan Guettel Cole, "Could Greek Women Read and Write?" *Women's Studies* 8 (1981) 129–55. Reprinted in Helene P. Foley, ed., *Reflections of Women in Antiquity* (New York: Gordon & Breach, 1981) 219–45.

2. To modern English speakers, the assignment of a specific gender to a given being or object carries a great deal of meaning, and we are justified in paying a great deal of attention to its interpretation. It is important to remember that, in the languages of the ancient Mediterranean, "gender" was at the same time a more pervasive concept and a less significant marker. It is easy to forget this and to attach too much significance, for example, to the fact that the great deity Fortuna is depicted as female. The concept of fortune or luck probably came before the goddess; in both Greek and Latin, abstract concepts usually carry feminine grammatical gender—in many cases, due more to the ease of declension than to any deep psychological association. It is a short step from the grammatical gender of the word to the femininity of the actual goddess, when the need arose for a concrete image.

3. This is a very difficult concept for Western readers to absorb, especially since most of us first "meet" these figures in association with literature, myth, or psychology and not in association with worship.

4. For example, sex as "the voyage of Venus," Apuleius, *The Golden Ass*, trans. Jack Lindsay (Bloomington, IN: Indiana University Press, 1960), 57 and *passim*.

5. For example, Aphrodisias and Cyprus.

6. If this satirical source is accurate; Athenaeus, *The Deipnosophists* (Philosophers at Dinner), 13.572e–573a.

7. Consultation of almost any New Testament commentary or dictionary will confirm this. The worship of sexual deities by sexual means was not unknown in the ancient Near East; modern Western value judgments translate this as "prostitution." The likelihood of this practice ever having been celebrated in Greece is remote, however; certainly in historical times, there is no indication of the practice, although Corinth, like many port cities, enjoyed a reputation for licentiousness in the fourth century BCE. An ancient author, Strabo, has probably made his own conflation between myth and city goddess when he mentions sacred prostitution (*Geography* 378), but even Strabo does not suggest this was actually practiced near his own time.

8. The modern construction of the "Great Goddess" comes from two directions: the feminist rejection of traditionally patriarchal religious figures and the psychologizing interpretation of religious phenomena influenced by Freud and Jung. Interest in a "female archetype" in nineteenth- and twentieth-century Western thought has led to a wholesale "telescoping" of troupes of goddesses—and women—into a single Great Goddess, whose many attributes are reflected by the individual personalities, stories, and worships of particular goddesses in antiquity, including Demeter, Isis, and the others. Significantly, it is female figures—goddesses and women—who are usually interpreted (one might even say dismissed) in this depersonalizing manner. Full discussion of this issue is well outside the scope of this study. For an excellent overview, see Nicole Loraux, "What Is a Goddess?" in *A History of Women in the West* 1: *From Ancient Goddesses to Christian Saints*, ed. Pauline Schmitt Pantel, (Cambridge, MA: Harvard University Press, 1992) 11–45.

9. As supposed biological father of Alexander, but also as an important traditional god of Macedonian women; Plutarch, *Life of Alexander* 2–3.

10. Much interesting work has been done on the role of magical practice in Greco-Roman religion; for an excellent collection of essays, see Christopher Faraone and Dirk Obbink, eds., *Magika Hiera: Ancient Greek Magic and Religion* (New York: Oxford University Press, 1991). An English translation of many ancient spells can be found in Hans Dieter Betz, ed., *The Greek Magical Papyri in Translation, Including the Demotic Spells*, 2nd ed. (Chicago: University of Chicago Press, 1992). For excellent methodological perspectives and analysis of the whole problem of the relationship between "magic" and "religion," see John G. Gager, ed., *Curse Tablets and Binding Spells from the Ancient World* (New York: Oxford University Press, 1992) esp. 3–42.

11. Although women were excluded from most formal political offices, they, too, were frequently identified on a similar scale, sometimes through their connection to powerful males. Sometimes women attained their own power and prestige, within social constraints, through family connections and personal wealth. The whole issue of the degree to which women participated in the power relationships of the city is a thorny one, and the evidence for the actual practices of women is often in tension with ideological claims stated in laws or constitutions. For the purposes of this chapter, I am more interested in what women were apparently actually doing, and it often appears that women of prominent families exerted more influence than obscure men.

12. For discussion of these cities and coins, see Simon R. F. Price, *Rituals and Power: The Roman Imperial Cult in Asia Minor* (Cambridge: Cambridge University Press, 1984).

13. For a more detailed discussion of the elements of this section, see the excellent survey by Richard E. Oster, "Ephesus as a Religious Center under the Principate I: Paganism before Constantine," *ANRW* 2.18.3, 1661–1728; see also Steven J. Friesen, *Twice Neokoros: Ephesus, Asia and the Cult of the Flavian Imperial Family* (Leiden: E. J. Brill, 1993).

14. I personally doubt it. See, however, Guy MacLean Rogers, *The Sacred Identity of Ephesos: Foundation Myths of a Roman City* (London: Routledge, 1991) 83.

15. Often, new "priesthoods" were created to divide the responsibilities and reduce the financial burden on any one individual.

16. By the end of the Greco-Roman period, sponsorship of these great events became an important way for wealthy individuals from not-so-powerful families to gain the prestige to go along with their money, as the right to sponsor was extended to wider groups of people, as wealth traveled away from the traditionally noble families and to the merchant families; Rogers, *The Sacred Identity of Ephesos*, is an excellent study of this opening up of benefaction. However, individuals who benefited from this simply moved from being obscure to prestigious; the importance of prestige was not diminished, at least for them.

17. For excellent essays on many topics relating to ancient religious offices of many kinds, see Mary Beard and John North, eds., *Pagan Priests: Religion and Power in the Ancient World* (Ithaca, NY: Cornell University Press, 1990).

18. Sixteen women from noble families were responsible for many activities associated with the worship of Hera at Elis and may even have originally exercised some type of judicial function (Pausanias, *Description of Greece* 1.16.2–8).

19. For a sensitive analysis of the processes of ritual formation in the Greco-Roman world, see Jonathan Z. Smith, "The Bare Facts of Ritual," in *Imagining Religion: From Babylon to Jonestown* (Chicago: University of Chicago Press, 1982) 53–65.

20. The best collection of primary source materials for women's religious lives and leadership roles in the Greco-Roman world is Ross S. Kraemer, ed., *Maenads, Martyrs, Matrons, Monastics: A Sourcebook on Women's Religions in the Greco-Roman World* (Philadelphia: Fortress, 1988).

21. H. W. Pleket, *Epigraphica*, vol. 2: *Texts on the Social History of the Greek World* (Leiden: E. J. Brill, 1969) 18; Kraemer, *Maenads*, no. 81 (p. 216).

22. Pleket, *Epigraphica* 25; Kraemer, *Maenads*, no. 82 (p. 217).

23. The flip side of these positive prescriptions are the negative caricatures of women in the contemporary comedies and satiric poetry of the Greco-Roman period, which also instructed women, but here by negative example.

24. Determining the degree of alienation from established religion felt by all women simply by virtue of their gender is extremely difficult and involves a complicated set of issues that cannot be delved into here; for overall discussion and explanation, see Ross Shepard Kraemer, *Her Share of the Blessings: Women's Religions Among Pagans, Jews and Christians in the Greco-Roman World* (Oxford: Oxford University Press, 1992) throughout, but esp. 3–21, 199–208.

25. See, for example, Cicero, *The Dream of Scipio*, in which submission to duty is envisioned as one of the main natural forces animating and holding together the universe (*On the State* 6).

26. For discussion of the worship of Asklepios and the votive inscriptions found at his major sanctuary, see Lynn LiDonnici, *The Epidaurian Miracle Inscriptions: Text, Translation and Commentary* (Atlanta, GA: Scholars Press, 1995) 1–19.

27. For spells and discussion, see n. 10 above.

28. Although there are several versions of the Asklepios myth, all stress the element of compassion based on experience of suffering. For versions and discussion, see Emma and Ludwig Edelstein, *Asclepius: A Collection and Interpretation of the Testimonies* (Baltimore, MD: Johns Hopkins University Press, 1945) vol. 1, 1–178; vol. 2, 22–53, 65–101.

29. In default of the unfortunately lost *Life of Herakles* by Plutarch, the best source for Herakles' story is Apollodorus, *The Library* 2.61 ff. For discussion, see Nicole Loraux, "Herakles: The Super-Male and the Feminine," in *Before Sexuality: The Construction of Erotic*

Experience in the Ancient Greek World, ed. David Halperin et al. (Princeton, NJ: Princeton University Press, 1990) 21–52.

30. Isis is an extremely ancient goddess in Egypt, where her worship was originally political, intimately connected with the sovereignty and prosperity of the land and the state. Here I consider the popular version of Isis that became prominent all around the Greco-Roman Mediterranean from the second century BCE through Christianization.

31. Plutarch, *On Isis and Osiris* 355–58; Kraemer, *Maenads*, no. 131 (pp. 354–59).

32. For a full discussion of this issue, see Kraemer, *Her Share of the Blessings* 71–79; Sharon Kelly Heyob, *The Cult of Isis among Women in the Graeco-Roman World*, EPRO 51 (Leiden: E. J. Brill, 1975); Sarolta A. Takács, *Isis and Sarapis in the Roman World*, Religions in the Graeco-Roman World (formerly EPRO) 124 (Leiden: E. J. Brill, 1995) 1–26.

33. Asklepios "saved" only in this life—there were no mysteries associated with his worship.

34. For further discussion of these issues, see chapters 9, 10, 11, 13, 14.

35. By "great goddess Demeter," I mean simply that she was a goddess and that she was important.

36. There is an excellent discussion of many elements of the worship in *The Homeric Hymn to Demeter: Translation, Commentary, and Interpretive Essays*, ed. Helene P. Foley (Princeton, NJ: Princeton University Press, 1994) esp. 65–76.

37. See Susan Treggiari, *Roman Marriage: Iusti Coniuges from the Time of Cicero to the Time of Ulpian* (Oxford: Oxford University Press, 1991).

38. Helmut Koester, *Introduction to the New Testament I: History, Culture and Religion of the Hellenistic Age* (Philadelphia: Fortress, 1982) 65–67.

39. In the case of military veterans and holders of the same job, we may find more gender-specific clubs, for example, the prostitutes' guild mentioned above. But as before, where a club sponsors family events, mixed groups should be assumed.

40. In many ways, the synagogue can be understood in terms of these clubs. For women's involvement in the synagogues of this period, see chapter 3.

41. This myth is known from fragmentary literary sources, especially Pindar, frag. 133; Plutarch, *On Isis and Osiris* 35; and Clement of Alexandria, *Exhortation to the Greeks* 2.17–18; and many other passing references and artistic representations. Though these references are fragmentary, their number indicates a fairly widely known myth. There are also several inscriptions on metal, buried with worshippers, that suggest elements of the myth and its relationship to an afterlife. For these and the Dionysiac mysteries overall, see Thomas H. Carpenter and Christopher Faraone, eds., *Masks of Dionysos* (Ithaca, NY: Cornell University Press, 1993) 239–96.

42. This is an extremely bald retelling of a complicated myth, the fullest version of which appears in Euripides' play *The Bacchae*, first performed in 406 BCE. This play has many important details, such as cross-dressing by Pentheus and many reflections of gender, religion, and power, which I do not have space to address here. For full consideration of the issues involved with the interpretation of this play and its influence on Greco-Roman religious practice, see Kraemer, *Her Share of the Blessings* 36–49.

43. Through the Hellenistic period in some places (Kraemer, *Her Share of the Blessings* 41).

44. See discussion of Plutarch, *Alexander* 2.1–5 in Kraemer, *Her Share of the Blessings* 42.

45. Plutarch, *On the First Cold* 18 (953D).

46. For more on the Thesmophoria, see Louise Bruit Zaidman, "Pandora's Daughters and Rituals in Greek Cities," in Pantel, ed., *A History of Women in the West* 1, 338–76, esp. 349–53.

47. Ovid, *Metamorphoses* 10.298–559, 10.708–39; Apollodorus, *The Library* 3.14.4.

48. The symbolism of Adonis provides yet another interesting example of how the ideal man of women differs greatly from the ideal man of men; see Eva C. Keuls, *The Reign of the Phallus: Sexual Politics in Ancient Athens* (Berkeley, CA: University of California Press, 1985) 24.

49. Scholarship on this issue is voluminous; see, most recently, Burton L. Mack, *A Myth of Innocence: Mark and Christian Origins* (Philadelphia: Fortress, 1988), and see also chapter 14.

50. For further discussion, see chapter 13.

II

Women, Jesus,

and Gospels

5

⊱━⬦━●━⬦━⊰

RECONSTRUCTING "REAL" WOMEN FROM GOSPEL LITERATURE

The Case of Mary Magdalene

Mary Rose D'Angelo

Every sober-sided history is at least half sleight-of-hand: the right
hand waving its poor snippets of fact, out in the open for all to
verify, while the left hand busies itself with its own devious agendas,
deep in its hidden pockets.

Margaret Atwood, The Robber Bride[1]

Among the most striking and successful results of feminist reinterpretation
has been the remaking of Mary Magdalene. The image of Mary as a prostitute converted to spiritual devotion to Jesus and expending the years after his
death in mourning and penitential practice provided centuries of pious exhortation and artistic representation. This image appears to have arisen in the sixth
century, when the example of penitent whores became fashionable in the West,
producing legendary lives of Pelagia, Thais and Mary of Egypt.[2] It was instanti-
ated in the Western liturgy for her festival (July 22), whose gospel reading
identified Mary with an unnamed woman sinner "in the city" who expressed
penitence and love by washing Jesus' feet with her tears and wiping them with
her hair (Luke 7:36–50). The opening verse (introit) and the first reading (epistle) caused the saint to speak the lines of a woman of the streets: "The wicked
have waited for me to destroy me. . . . I have seen an end of all consummation"
(Ps 118 [119]:95–96). "I shall arise and go about the city: in the streets and
the broad ways I shall seek him whom my soul loves" (Song of Songs 3:2–5).[3]

Feminist interpretation has debunked the image of the fallen and repentant
Magdalene, substituting the figure of Mary Magdalene as the intrepid and faithful
disciple of Jesus, an apostle with and to the twelve and a witness to the resurrection. Her new image is the result of a confluence of forces. Historical research
called for more stringent and critical attention to the biblical texts; the discovery
of the Nag Hammadi library (1945) provided new sources that spoke of Mary

and provoked interest in other extracanonical sources. But most of all, the feminist search for a usable past made the question important beyond the rather narrow circle of biblical interpreters. The view of Mary as an apostle is in fact based not only on recent rereading of biblical and extrabiblical texts, but also upon a long-standing traditional interpretation of John 20:18 that awarded her the title *apostola apostolorum*, "apostle of apostles," that is, "apostle sent to apostles" or even "supreme apostle." Repeated as late as Thomas Aquinas, the title has recently been revived primarily to refute the bizarre argument that, since Jesus chose only men as "apostles," women should be excluded from the ministerial priesthood.[4]

Mining the gospels for evidence from which to reconstruct "real women" presents all the usual difficulties attending women's history in antiquity, plus the complex problems of research on the historical Jesus. Mark, probably the earliest of the four canonical gospels, was written near or (more likely) after the fall of the temple (70 CE), that is, approximately forty years after the death of Jesus.[5] While some scholars have argued that Mark was written in the Galilee, most locate the text farther away—in Syria or even Rome.[6] Even more significant than the distance in time and (most likely) place is the character of the gospels.

First of all, the interest of authors (and of their written and oral sources) is in Jesus and, in particular, in the need to explain him, his words and his life, and especially to explain the great trauma of his death and the message of his resurrection. In the four canonical gospels, all his words and deeds are remembered for and through this event. Thus all the women in the narratives and all the other men are written into the gospels to support and enhance these explanations.

Further, the image of Jesus himself varies quite strikingly among the gospels. The gospel writers sought to re-present Jesus—to make him newly present and active in the communities for whom they wrote. This is true not only of the four gospels in their final forms, but also of their sources, whether oral or written (like Q, the sayings collection widely believed to be the common source of Matthew and Luke), as well as of the surviving gospels that never attained canonical status (like the *Gospel of Thomas* and the *Gospel of Mary*). Thus the Jesus of the gospels acts in and speaks to and for communities of the late first and early second century. Sayings of Jesus have been revised to suit their needs, and questions or objections that are put to him often articulate the issues the communities understand themselves to be facing.[7] The other figures in the gospels, both the unnamed antagonists and recipients of miracles and the named disciples who figure in individual stories, tend to represent positions within or related to the evangelists' communities. Titles and practices, like disputes, may reflect the practices and decisions of the early Christian churches.

The layers of interpretation and application through which these figures meet the reader do not necessarily mean that there are no recollections of "real women" in the gospels. When specific names like Mary Magdalene are remembered and used, it is likely to be because the names are famous enough to have been known and important to those communities. Both the canonical gospels and other materials that reflect the traditions about Jesus include the names of women as well as men among those who belonged to the circle around him.

The Example of Martha and Mary

A search for the historical Mary Magdalene involves the investigator in the complexities of trying to unearth the personae and lives of specific women from the gospels. Looking briefly at Martha and Mary, who appear only twice in the gospel literature, in Luke 10:38–42 and John 11:1–12:8, offers an example of these complexities. Martha and Mary are usually remembered only as they are depicted in Luke's very short exemplary story. This story pits the two women against each other and shows Jesus affirming the silent Mary who "sat at his feet and listened to his word" against a complaining, bustling Martha, who is busy with the "women's work" of serving a meal. Earlier feminist reinterpretations of the story began from the description of Mary as "sitting at the feet of" Jesus and "listening to his word," that is, being instructed as a disciple (compare Acts 22:3, where Paul's claim to have been brought up "at the feet of Gamaliel" positions him as a disciple of the most famous Pharisaic teacher of his day).[8] They thus reread the story as permitting women to step out of the gender roles assigned to them, but at the cost of denigrating women who engage in the work of sustaining life. More recent feminist commentators attend also to the widespread early Christian use of the word "serving" or "ministry" (diakonia) as a metaphor for community service and leadership.[9] Reading Martha's "serving" as "ministry" revises the picture of Martha, but raises the issue of Luke's attitude toward her. In general, Luke's gospel seeks to include women, but to restrict them to roles acceptable to Roman imperial mores. In Luke 10:38–42, the author uses the final saying of Jesus to prefer the silence of the woman disciple to the activity of the minister.[10]

The stories about Martha and Mary in John 11:1–12:8 present a quite different picture; they show the two women acting in concert on behalf of their brother (11:17–44) and in gratitude for his restoration to them (12:1–8). Differing versions of both stories appear in other sources with unnamed women as their protagonists. John 11:1–44, usually called the resurrection of Lazarus, seems to revise a story of the raising of an unnamed woman's brother; another version is found in the *Secret Gospel of Mark*.[11] In John, the story is elaborated with a dialogue between Jesus and Martha, which makes the miracle a sign of the special Johannine understanding of the resurrection. In the course of the dialogue, Martha makes a confession of faith in Jesus' messiahship (11:20–27) that is sometimes compared to Peter's confession in Mark 8:29.[12] John 12:1–8, the anointing of Jesus, focuses on Mary, the sister of Martha. Stories of unnamed women anointers occur in Mark 14:1–11 and Luke 7:36–50. Thus it seems likely that the author of John has attached the names of famous women to two simple traditional stories, then woven them together into a complex theological drama proffering resurrection and life as the true meaning of Jesus' death.

Is it possible to look behind the two different versions of Martha and Mary? Should one be accepted over the other? The two stories have only minimal common traits. In both, Martha is said to serve or minister (diakonein; Luke 10: 39–40; John 12:1), while Mary is designated as "sister." In both, Martha welcomes Jesus (Luke 10:38; John 11:20); this may imply that she is the owner of the house. This minimal information suggests that behind these stories is the memory of two famous women who formed a missionary partnership, like the pairs in Matt 10:1–4. They were known and remembered as Martha the *diakonos* (minister; cf. Rom 16:1, Phoebe the *diakonos*/minister of the church of Cenchreae) and Mary the sister (*adelphē*), just as Paul signed letters as Paul the *apostolos* with a companion) designated "the brother" (*adelphos*; e.g., Sosthenes 1 Cor 1:1).[13]

It is possible to speculate a bit further about the relationship of the two women. Romans 16 includes male and female pairs which may have been marital pairs (Prisca and Aquila, Junia and Andronicus, Nereas and his "sister") and a pair consisting of two women, Tryphaena and Tryphosa. The title "sister," which applies to Martha as well as Mary, may indicate kin, erotic partners, and Christians in general, as well as specific roles in the mission. Thus in the case of Martha and Mary, sisterhood may represent but a shared commitment to the mission, rather than blood relationship. This shared commitment may also have involved a mutual commitment; if so, they contribute to a sort of prehistory of women's same-sex commitments, a version of Adrienne Rich's "lesbian continuum."[14] The references to Martha welcoming Jesus could also stand for a role in the community; like Prisca and Aquila, Philemon, and Nympha, Martha the *diakonos* may have been the host to a house-church along with "Mary the sister." At any rate, it seems that Martha and Mary were remembered primarily because of the roles they played as "minister" and "sister" in the (postresurrection) early Christian mission.[15] The narratives in which they appear in Luke and John are less insights into the history and character of these particular women than vehicles for the authors' theological concerns and their assumptions or prescriptions about gender.

A similar set of problems and ambiguities must be expected of depictions of Mary Magdalene in the gospels. In her case also, it is necessary to examine the testimony of the different texts and then to attempt to ask what lies behind them. These tasks are complicated by the diverse character of the texts and the experience they represent. Titles and functions which were very fluid in the early period were revised or erased by later use and practice. If *diakonos* was obscured by translation or demoted by later usage, *apostolos* was both inflated and restricted in application, identified with the twelve by tradition (through Luke-Acts) and with the person of Paul by his writings. In earlier sources, the role of the twelve is less clear, the reference of *apostolos* broader, and the participation of women more varied.

The basic meaning of *apostolos* is "emissary, one who is sent," as opposed to disciple, which means "learner" or follower; in Christian contexts "apostle" refers to missionaries. In Paul, whose writings are the earliest in the New Testament, "the twelve" are primarily witnesses to the resurrection (1 Cor 15:5), and "apostles" refers to a wider group among whom he counts himself (1 Cor 9:1, 15:8) and at least one woman (Junia; Rom 16:7). He appears to have regarded the criteria of apostleship as two. The first was to "have seen the Lord," that is, to have experienced a vision of the risen Christ as a call to apostleship (see Gal 1:12–17). The second was to have been the founder of, or among the founding missionaries in, a community (1 Cor 9:1; 3:10; 4:15), apparently by preaching the gospel (1 Cor 1:16–17). Thus inquiring after the role of Mary Magdalene in any given source requires looking into the ways the source understands roles like apostle, minister and disciple.

The sources that mention Mary Magdalene are more varied than those for Mary and Martha and (for the most part) more slender. The best-known group is the narrative and dialogue gospels, which depict Mary as witness to resurrection and offer the basis of the claim that she was apostle of the apostles: the four canonical gospels; the summarizing appendix added by a later author to the gospel of Mark (known as the longer ending of Mark and printed in some versions as Mark 16:9–20); the *Gospel of Peter*; and the *Gospel of Mary*. A second group of dialogue and sayings gospels depicts Mary (with Salome) as a disciple and interlocutor of Jesus; these include the *Gospel of Thomas*, the *Dialogue of the Savior*, *Sophia of Jesus Christ*, *Pistis Sophia*. In a few of the texts, the treatment of Mary has erotic overtones: *Gospel of Philip*, *Gospel of John*, *Gospel of Mary*. In what follows, I first review the picture given by these three sets of sources, then evaluate the claims they make, and finally offer some alternative reconstructions of a Mary Magdalene of history.

Witness and Apostle: Mary Magdalene in the *Gospel of Mary* and the Narrative Gospels

In treating the narrative sources and the *Gospel of Mary*, I abandon the convention of beginning with Mark in order to begin with the *Gospel of Mary*. This is not because I contest the widespread view that Mark is the earliest of the gospels, but rather because the *Gospel of Mary* casts Mary in a central role, refocusing the more familiar gospel narratives and illuminating the ways in which the concerns of authors and communities affect the narratives. While the gospel's date is uncertain, at least some scholars have argued for an origin in the late first or early second century; this would make it contemporary with the canonical gospels. It belongs primarily to the genre of dialogue gospels, that is, gospels consisting of a revelatory dialogue in which Jesus (or "the Savior") instructs the disciples in response to their questions, usually in the setting of an appearance after his death. The protagonist is identified only as Mary in the extant Greek and Coptic fragments of the gospel, but scholars who assume that she is Mary Magdalene are probably correct.

The text falls into two parts; the first part, now largely missing, appears to have consisted of a revelatory dialogue in which at least four disciples participated. It terminates with the Savior's commission to go and preach and his departure. The male disciples are bereft and frightened, and when Mary tries to encourage them, Peter asks her for the revelation that she knows and they do not. She complies, recounting a lengthy vision which is only partly preserved. At the end of her recital, Andrew and Peter object to her revelation. Their objections are preserved in both the earlier Greek fragment and the Coptic translation.

In the Greek version, Andrew complains of its difference from the Savior's thought, while Peter objects to the idea that the Savior spoke to a woman secretly and not openly so all would hear. Levi leaps to her defense, rejecting Peter's question as hostile and the act of an adversary and asserting the authority of her revelation on the grounds that the Savior "knew her completely [and] loved her devotedly."[16]

The Coptic version intensifies the terms of the debate; there, the issues clearly emerge as twofold, the assault on the content of the vision as "strange ideas" and the objection to women as instructors of men: "Are we to turn and listen to her?" Peter asks. In response, Levi affirms that the Savior "loved her more than us."[17] The dialogue closes with Levi's reiteration of the command to preach the gospel, "not be laying down any rules or making laws [that differ from what the Savior said]."[18]

Although the term "apostle" is not applied to any of the disciples in the *Gospel of Mary*, *apostola apostolorum* seems an especially appropriate characterization of Mary's role in that her encouragement and her revelation provide the spur to fulfill the Savior's command by preaching the gospel. In both Greek and Coptic versions, the objections of the male disciples seem to reflect debates in the contexts in which the text was written and used. The issues were twofold: the status and reliability of visionary experience, secret teaching, and prophecy on one hand, and the suitability of women as communal leaders on the other.[19] The figure of Mary is used to defend both women and visionaries. The more stringent objections and the more adamant assertion of Mary's worthiness in the Coptic version suggest more acrimonious disputes at a later date and perhaps also at a different geographical location. But this text also invites reexamination of the other texts in light of the questions that they may address in their own contexts. Especially in John's gospel, which also makes extensive use of the dialogue form, the persons of Mary, Peter, and the beloved disciple seem to be used to address issues in the identity and structure of the community for which it was written.[20] In no case are these the only issues addressed by the narratives, so caution must be used in drawing conclusions about the way in which they reflect conflict, practice, or both in the authors' communities, as well as about the way they reflect the earliest stages of the movement.[21]

Mary Magdalene in John

The Gospel of John is often characterized as the latest and least "historical" of the gospels, but the evidence for this claim is problematic. Most investigators of John have concluded that the gospel went through a lengthy and complex process of writing and editing in a relatively remote and independent community. Some argue that the gospel, at least in the final stages, reflects knowledge of Mark and perhaps also of Matthew and Luke. But it is possible that a first edition of the gospel was completely independent of Mark and originated at about the same time (near or after the fall of the temple in 70 CE).

In John as in Mark, Mary is introduced only at the death of Jesus. In John she accompanies the (unnamed) mother of Jesus, his mother's sister, who may or may not be Mary of Clophas, and the unnamed beloved disciple; she is not named first and is without any identification except her surname (19:25). Perhaps she was too well known to the Johannine community to require further introduction. In her second appearance, she arrives at the tomb alone and, upon finding it empty, runs at once for Simon Peter and the beloved disciple. She voices the natural conclusion that the grave has been robbed (19:2). At her word, they inspect the tomb; on the basis of what they see, the beloved disciple becomes the witness to the true meaning of the empty tomb (8–9).

On their departure, Mary is accorded two apparitions. First she sees two angels in the tomb, who lead her to repeat her interpretation of the empty tomb; then she sees Jesus and, mistaking him for the gardener, reiterates her desire to take care of the missing corpse. Mary is used here to defend the community against the charge of credulity, just as in Luke 24:11 "the apostles" are presented as skeptical toward the women's announcement. Her insistence on the theft of Jesus' body both invites the reader to offer the true interpretation and shows that the disciples, rather than leaping to the conclusion that Jesus had been raised, had to be convinced by overwhelming experiential evidence. She recognizes Jesus when he speaks her name and apparently seeks to embrace him (cf. Matt 28:10–11); Jesus rebuffs her with the words, "Do not touch me, for I have not yet ascended to the father. But go to my brothers and say to them, 'I ascend to my father and your father, to my God and your God.'" The narrator recounts that Mary reported to the disciples, "I have seen the Lord," and that she repeated his message.

This speech is of particular importance in interpreting Mary's role in the tradition. "I have seen the Lord" is the formula Paul uses in basing his claim to apostleship on a vision of the risen Lord (1 Cor 9:1). Like Paul and other apostles, she is sent with a message. Like Paul's apostleship, her experience seems to be prophetic; she is apparently to deliver the message as a prophetic oracle, in the person of Jesus ("the Lord says, 'I ascend to my father and your father to my God and your God'"). Unlike the angel's message in Mark 16:7 and Matt 28:7, hers does not imply future appearances of Jesus. Instead, this oracle explains his departure as an ascension; with or without other appearances, it can in itself serve as the foundational proclamation for the new community. Thus John's Mary fits Paul's criteria for apostleship. But it is very difficult to say what, if anything, this meant to the author of John. Even in its latest stages, the gospel seems to represent a community in which structure was very low. The meaning of leadership and authority in the community are even less definable than in other early Christian texts; the word *apostolos* is used only once, at 13:16 where it delineates the requirement of discipleship. There, *apostolos* applies to all disciples, but more importantly, to the reader and hearers; all are sent, as Jesus is sent.

The disputed question of whether or not John is dependent upon Mark is significant in assessing the gospel's treatment of Mary Magdalene. If so, then the revisions amount to a striking and apparently deliberate reversal of Mark's narrative; where Mark associates Mary and the women with the empty tomb and appears to promise a resurrection vision to Peter and the eleven, John associates Peter with the tomb and Mary with the vision of Jesus. If, as seems more likely, the Gospel of John does not depend upon Mark, it attests an older tradition that depicts Mary as the first to encounter Jesus alive from the dead. The message entrusted to her constitutes an explanation of that experience and of his departure: he ascends "to my father and your father, my God and your God." It is not clear who is meant by "my brothers (and sisters?)"; the words might refer to Jesus' kin, so little favored by the author (2:2, 7:7–15), but verse 18 clearly applies "brothers" to the disciples. The message itself suggests a wider application for "brothers;" Jesus speaks to all who share with him a God and father. This notably Johannine proclamation differs from the more common early Christian explanation "he is risen" that is enshrined in and dramatized by the empty tomb narrative (Mark 16:6). It neither requires nor precludes further appearances, although John 20:19–31 provides two more and the appendix (John 21) a third, all of which are in some way concerned with the commissioning of the other disciples. It is possible that 20:19–31 was added precisely to undercut the impression that the definitive interpretation of Jesus' departure was delivered only through a woman. Even more notably, the appendix to the gospel, which was probably supplied by a later member of the community specifically to define the relative roles of Peter and the beloved disciple, does not mention Mary Magdalene. Further, John 21:14 counts the appearance on the sea of Galilee as "the third time Jesus appeared to his disciples," apparently excluding the appearance to Mary, perhaps because the author of the appendix did not wish to include her in that category.[22]

Thus it seems likely that in John and its revisions, as in the *Gospel of Mary*, the extraordinary vision and revelation given to Mary address the situation of women leaders.[23] Some interpreters make invidious comparisons between the appearances to Mary and those to the male disciples, claiming that she sees Jesus before he is "glorified" or contrasting the command "do not touch me" with the invitation to Thomas to touch his wounds.[24] But the text does not really support either of these conclusions: neither Mary nor Thomas is said actually to touch Jesus in John 20, and the two commands should probably be taken together as evidence of quite different concerns.[25] The appearances in John 20 confer authority on figures who represent positions within the community or perhaps differing communities: Mary, Peter, the beloved disciple and Thomas and perhaps, tangentially, the twelve. In later and gnostic settings, Peter seems to represent the "orthodox" position or community, while Thomas and Mary are the embodiments and patrons of alternative or gnostic communities. In John 20:1–18, Peter is not disparaged, but it is very clear that the beloved disciple and Mary in some way represent an inner circle.[26] Their differing roles in the narrative undoubtedly make distinctions among them, but these distinctions are very difficult to recover. But as will become clear, the appearance of Mary in a text seems to evoke issues of gender and authority within a community.

Mark and the Revisions of Mark by Matthew and Luke

Mary Magdalene appears for the first time in the Gospel of Mark at its denouement, Mark 15:40–41:

There were also women looking on from a distance; among them were Mary
Magdalene, and Mary the mother of James and Joses, and Salome. These used to
follow him and provided for him while he was in Galilee; and there were many
other women who had come up with him to Jerusalem. (NRSV)

Here three women are named as having stood afar and watched the death of
Jesus: Mary Magdalene; Mary, the mother of James and Joses; and Salome. None
of these women has been introduced before in the gospel; in fact, no women
except Jesus' mother and Herodias (6:22) are named until this point. The surname "Magdalene" distinguishes this Mary from her companion of the same
name; it is generally assumed to derive from the name of her place of origin,
identified as a city of Galilee called Magdala.

The second Mary is identified by a relationship to two men, James and Joses;
these men are sometimes identified with the two brothers of Jesus in Mark 6:3,
but the names are too common to make this identification certain.[27] The third
woman, Salome, appears in the canonical gospels only in Mark 15:40 and 16:
1–8; her name is dropped from Matthew and Luke, and she makes no appearance in John. But she does appear in the *Gospel of Thomas*, where she challenges
Jesus and, on the basis of his reply, declares herself his disciple.[28] In later Christian legend, the name Salome was attached to two rather unsavory female characters. One is the daughter of Herod from the lurid tale in Mark 6:22–29. Some
manuscripts of Mark give this figure the name Herodias; others give her no
name at all, identifying her merely as the daughter of Herod and Herodias. Mark
6:22–29 depicts her as the instigator of John the Baptist's death. Later Christians
identified her with a daughter of Herodias (not by Herod) named Salome mentioned by the Jewish historian Josephus.[29] A second Salome appears in the *Protevangelium of James* in the role of doubter of Mary's virginity; she is punished and
converted (19:18–20:12).[30] Thus the name Salome, once attached to a disciple
of Jesus, became identified with either a woman of ill repute or a penitent
doubter.

Of Mary and her two companions, the author relates that they had followed
Jesus in Galilee and had "ministered to" him, and that they had traveled up
from Galilee to Jerusalem with him. The text notes that many unnamed women
also accompanied Jesus up to Jerusalem (15:41). While it is possible that the
author means to distinguish these women's status from that of the named
women, it is more likely that they too are understood as disciples and ministers.
The author singles out and names three women in order to provide specific and
continuous witnesses to the death of Jesus, his burial (15:47), and the empty
tomb (Mark 16:1). Mentioning their ministry in Galilee enhances their testimony by underlining their long association with Jesus.

That these women are disciples is indicated by the word translated "followed"
in the NRSV. The words "follow" and "come after" are technical terms in Mark
(1:16–20, 2:14, 8:34). The women's discipleship is obscured in part by their
late introduction into the story and in part by the conventional view that Jesus
was attended primarily by twelve male disciples (followers) appointed by Jesus
as his apostles (missionaries, emissaries) and understood to be his deputies and
heirs; women entered the picture only as a sort of ladies' auxiliary to Jesus and

the twelve, providing financial and material support for the men. This picture involves several interpretive steps beyond the Gospel of Mark.

Mark does depict a special group of twelve male disciples who function as close companions of Jesus and whose names are listed in 3:16–19: Simon, nick-named Peter; James and John, the sons of Zebedee, nicknamed the sons of thun-der, Andrew, Philip, Bartholomew; Matthew; Thomas; James, son of Alphaeus; Thaddeus; Simon, called the Canaanean; and Judas Iscariot. In Mark 6:7–13, the twelve are sent out "two by two" as Jesus' ambassadors who extend the mission of preaching, exorcism and healing; they provide the reader with models for the early Christian mission. On their return in Mark 6:30, they are identified as "apostles" (missionaries or emissaries; in some manuscripts, this word is used in 6:14). But the twelve are by no means the only companions of Jesus in the gospel. After the selection of the twelve, the author speaks of "those that were around him with [including] the twelve" (4:10) as the recipients of secret teaching; "disciples" in Mark seems to refer to this larger group (4:34; see also 7:2, 15, 17; 8:27, 33–34; 9:29, 31), which also goes on the road with him to Jerusalem and his death (10:10, 13, 24, 46; 11:1). Mark 15:40–41 shows that the author assumes women to have been (and to be) among those addressed in 8:34 and wherever the term "disciples" is used. Mark 3:30–35 also suggests that for this author discipleship includes "sisters." The gospel offers no account of a woman disciple being called that corresponds directly to the call of the first disciples or the appointment of the twelve. But a new invitation to discipleship in 8:34 that is directed to a large crowd (and to the reader and hearers of the gospel) requires the one who wishes to "come after" Jesus to "take up the cross and follow." In the context of this invitation, the appearance of Mary Magdalene and her companions at the cross suggests that Mark makes them exemplary of discipleship.

A second important term in 15:40–41 is hidden by the NRSV translation "provide for him." The Greek word is diēkonoun, which means "wait on table, serve," and, throughout the New Testament, but especially in Mark, "minister." W. D. Davies has argued that the word group diakon- is the Greek equivalent of a Hebrew term used to denote special disciples, who are close personal attendants, apprentices, and heirs of the teacher, like Joshua to Moses. He attributes this meaning to the verb in 15:41 and interprets the words that offer the proof or response to the miraculous cure of Peter's mother-in-law ("she began to serve them") as indicating her new commitment to this role.[31] Thus this second mira-cle can be read as narrating a woman's call at the gospel's very beginning (1:29–31). In secular Greek, the word group had long had wider usage as a meta-phor and model for communal leadership. An extended metaphor in Plato's *Gorgias* treats rulers and statesmen as the servants or ministers of the city.[32] In the late first to early second century, the philosopher and ex-slave Epictetus de-scribed the true Cynic as the diakonos of God.[33] Josephus uses the word to refer to priestly service.[34]

In Mark the noun "servant, minister" applies to the ideal disciple and leader (9:35, 10:43); the verb is used as a metaphor for the redemptive function of Jesus' death (10:45). While the angels who serve/minister to Jesus in the wilderness may feed him (1:13) as the angel fed Elijah (1 Kgs 19:5–6), they are not explicitly said to do so, and they clearly function not as waiters but as attendants to the divine (cf. Heb 1:14).[35] The same is true of Mary and her companions in Mark; it seems that Mark uses the word diakoneō to characterize their relationship to Jesus because, like Martha and Phoebe, Mary Magdalene (as well as the other Mary and Salome) was remembered as a diakonos in the early Christian mission.

The second scene in which Mary appears is the burial of Jesus (15:42–47); only Mary "of Joses" is said to accompany her. Mark ascribes the burial to Joseph of Arimathea, who has no clear connection with Jesus, but is "awaiting God's reign"; that is, Mark sees him as a righteous Jew for whom the burial is a charitable deed. The two women have no role in it and appear still to be watching from afar (15:47).

The final scene of the gospel opens with Mary Magdalene and her two companions buying perfumes when the sabbath had passed "in order to go and anoint him" (16:1). On the way, they voice the obstacle to their enterprise for the benefit of the readers: "who will roll back the stone?" The apparent futility of their task may have been intended to remind the reader that this burial preparation has already been done by the unnamed woman prophet in 14:1–11. Confronted by the empty tomb, they are entrusted by a "youth" with a message for Peter and the other disciples: Jesus precedes them into Galilee. This message can be interpreted as a promise of a resurrection appearance to Peter and the others in the near future in Galilee; Matthew has interpreted it as a climactic appearance to the eleven (28:16–20). Luke rejects the idea of a return to Galilee, but offers a brief reference to a single appearance to Simon (24:34), and narrates appearances to two disciples and to the twelve (24:13–35, 36–52, Acts 1:1–11). But it is by no means certain that Mark 16:7 predicts resurrection appearances; other scholars argue that the vision referred to is the final vision of "the Son of Man coming in the clouds with much power and glory" (13:26).[36] Whether Jesus' disappearance is understood by Mark as the prelude to the comfort of resurrection appearances or to the rigors of the parousia (advent of Jesus as judge), the women are entrusted by Mark's narrative with the definitive interpretation of Jesus' departure—which they do not deliver (16:8). Elizabeth Struthers Malbon concludes that Mark portrays Mary and her companions as "fallible followers," like the men who had fled at Jesus' arrest.[37] This conclusion does not take full account of Mark's revision of the call to discipleship; the invitation to take up the cross and follow (8:34) must be embodied by the women, at least ironically. But the women's failure underlines for the first readers and hearers their own privileged knowledge.

Mary Magdalene, like her two named companions, functions in Mark primarily to provide specific named witnesses who can attest to the death of Jesus and his burial and to connect the empty tomb backward to the burial and forward to the (implied) resurrection appearances. It is possible that communal conflicts over leadership are also reflected in the women's roles in Mark's narrative. Numerous scholars have suggested that Mark's ending seeks to undercut the prestige of the twelve, and that the description of the women as serving or ministering to Jesus, coupled with their appearance at the cross, makes them emblematic of the leadership patterned on Jesus, who came not "to be served (ministered to) but to serve and give his life as a ransom for many" (10:45). But if Mark 16: 1–8 reflects gender conflict, its resolution is ambiguous; the message to the disciples and Peter can be read as either a warning of a coming judgment or a reauthorization. At any rate, Mark set the stage on which Matthew and Luke build: Mary and her companions are associated with the empty tomb and are given a message for the other disciples; Peter and the disciples (or the disciples) are to be the recipients of a vision.

Matthew's revisions of Mark 15:40–41 and 47 are minimal; Matt 27:55 gives specific names only after describing the women's ministry and so includes the unnamed women in the category of disciples. Salome is no longer the third named witness; in her place is the mother of the Zebedees, probably so that she may witness the terrible fulfillment of the prophecy that the places on Jesus' right and left hand are already allotted (20:40; cf. 27:38); she disappears after this scene. Only Mary Magdalene and "the other Mary" appear at the burial (27: 61) and empty tomb (28:1); they provide the two witnesses required by Deut 19:15 (cf. 17:6, cited explicitly in Matt 18:16). In Matthew the purpose of their visit is to visit the tomb; their testimony is enhanced by the presence of the guards and by the spectacular character of the discovery scene: the stone is rolled back before their eyes by an angelic visitor and the earth shakes.

When the overjoyed women run off to tell the disciples (Matt 28:8), they are interrupted by a vision of Jesus (28:9–10). This very brief narrative recounts a resurrection appearance peculiar to Matthew; the speech of the risen Jesus in 28:10 seems to be a condensed version of the speech of the angel (28:5–6; cf. Mark 16:5–7). Thus the scene seems to have been created by Matthew; it may simply be narrative connective tissue, whose purpose is to provide a scene in which Jesus actually does promise to meet the disciples in Galilee (cf. Mark 16: 7). But given the accounts of appearances to Mary in John and Gospel of Mary, it is equally possible that it reflects the author's acquaintance with memories that Mary Magdalene, like other apostles, could claim to have "seen the Lord" (1 Cor 9:1). But "apostle" is not a term of much import in Matthew; this author uses "disciple" both of the eleven in a specialized sense and of the followers in general. In Matthew the location of leadership and authority is not so much resolved as assumed in the final vision in which Jesus, endowed "with all authority in heaven and on earth," sends the eleven to make disciples of all the Gentiles.

The author of Luke revises these three scenes rather significantly. No special mention is made of Mary or any other woman at the cross; instead Luke claims that "all his acquaintances, and the women who had accompanied him from Galilee, stood by from afar to see these things" (23:49). In Luke's picture, all of these women followed Jesus' body to the tomb, saw where Jesus was buried (23:55), then went and prepared ointments before resting on the sabbath. Although no names are mentioned here, Mary Magdalene must be included, for Luke closes the account of the empty tomb with the note that the women re-

ported all this to the eleven, and that these women were Mary Magdalene, Johanna, and "Mary of James" (presumably taken over from Mark 16:1 and mentioned only here in Luke) and "the rest with them" (24:10). A final editorial
comment notes that the apostles refused to believe the women (24:11).[38] That
Luke closes the empty tomb scene with this remark has been seen as denigrating
the women's witness.[39] But the reader knows the women to be right, so that the
remark's main function must be to defend the disciples against the charge of
credulity. Still Luke's revisions do, in fact, work to separate women from the
apostolic witnesses; the women are not sent to the disciples, no message is
committed to them, and it is not clear whether women are included among
those with the eleven who witness the appearance (Luke 24:33).[40] Either the
author or a later hand also made Peter a witness to the empty tomb (24:12; the
verse is suspect because it is missing in a few important manuscripts and appears
to reflect John 20:4–6).

A version of Mark's list of specific women disciples who traveled with Jesus
does appear in Luke, but no longer in the context of Jesus' death; the women
are introduced early in Jesus' career (Luke 8:1–3), apparently as a parallel to the
list of the twelve (Luke 6:12–16).[41] But the women disciples and the twelve are
very differently described. In 6:12–16, Jesus selects the twelve after a night of
prayer, calling them apostles (12–13); Acts explicitly restricts apostleship to men
(1:21). In 8:2, the women are described as women who have been cured from
evil spirits and diseases. Instead of locating them as followers and ministers to
Jesus, Luke designates the women as ministering to "them" (i.e., Jesus and the
twelve, the preachers and healers) "out of their resources." These revisions contrast the women with the twelve on two points: first Luke's text depicts them
not as having been called as disciples, but as beneficiaries who respond out of
gratitude; second, it presents them not as preachers and healers themselves, but
as benefactors and patrons of Jesus and the twelve, ministering out of their
means.[42] As in the lists of Mark and Matthew, Mary Magdalene is mentioned
first, but she is characterized as the one "from whom seven devils went out."
Thus her prominence is both explained and undercut by being attributed to the
severity of her (supposed) former possession. The second of two named
women, Joanna, the wife of Herod's steward Chusa, is of relatively high social
status and so justifies Luke's implication that the women have the means to
support the mission.[43] A third woman, Susanna, is named without further identification. This is Susanna's only appearance in early Christian materials; she may
still have been famous as a disciple of Jesus in Luke's time, or Luke may have
used this fairly common name to evoke the tale of Susanna.

The gender conflicts over leadership in the early second century seem to be
reflected throughout Luke-Acts.[44] The gospel's treatment of Mary Magdalene is no
exception. This gospel writer excludes Mary Magdalene (as well as all other
women) from the status of apostle. The list, with its note that seven devils had
gone out of Mary, immediately follows the story of the sinful woman anointing
Jesus (7:36–50) and probably inspired the traditional identification of Mary Magdalene with this story, eventually earning her the status of repentant prostitute.

The Summary Appendix to Mark and the *Gospel of Peter*

The two other relatively early narrative texts that depict Mary Magdalene are heavily influenced by, if not entirely derived from, the canonical gospels. One of these is the summary appended to the Gospel of Mark in some of the manuscripts (printed as Mark 16:9–20). It appears to have originated in the late second or early third century and combines the memory of a first appearance to Mary (probably dependent on John 20:11–18) with the note identifying her as the one "out of whom seven devils had been cast" (almost certainly dependent on Luke 8:2). When she announces this to "those who were mourning and weeping with him," they do not believe her (cf. Luke 24:11).

The surviving portion of the *Gospel of Peter*, also seen by some scholars as originating in the second century, likewise appears to combine traces of narratives from other gospels in a new way, through the voice of Peter.[45] It does not mention Mary at the cross and tomb, perhaps because its interest has passed from a continuous internal witness to Jesus' death, burial and empty tomb to the guards as external witnesses to these events. Identifying her as "the disciple [*mathētria*, a feminine noun] of the Lord" it relates that she and "her friends" went to the tomb "to weep and beat our breasts." Having voiced the problems that face them in this enterprise, they see the empty tomb and a youth who explains it to them in terms not dissimilar from those in Mark 16:6, adding, "he has returned whence he was sent." No message is given to them, and they flee in fear. This scene follows an extensive and spectacular scenario that proffers the guards at the tomb as external witnesses to its emptiness and the angelic visitation; thus the impact of the scene is considerably less than in the canonical gospels.

Mary as Disciple and Interlocutor of Jesus: Sayings and Dialogue Gospels

In some of the gospel literature that consists of sayings of Jesus strung together or arranged into revelatory dialogues, Mary and, to a lesser degree, Salome appear in the same roles as male disciples and in some cases in a rather more exalted role. Most of these works are gnostic (see chapter 12); in the earliest and most famous of the sayings gospels, the hypothetical Q, Mary plays no role at all—indeed no named disciple plays any role in any reconstruction of that gospel (see chapter 7).[46]

The next earliest is probably the *Gospel of Thomas*, a sayings gospel extant in a handful of Greek fragments and in a complete text in Coptic—albeit with significant differences from the Greek. While not all scholars will concede the gnostic origins of *Thomas*, its use by gnostics and Manicheans is certain. The complexities of gendered imagery in *Thomas* are discussed at length in Anne McGuire's treatment of gnosticism in chapter 12. Here I shall discuss only the role of Mary. The final saying in the gospel, Saying 114, appears, like the *Gospel of Mary*, to raise the question of women's roles in the community. In response to

Peter's demand that she be sent away, Jesus affirms the access of women disciples to "life," promising to lead Mary so that she "becomes male."

Despite Peter's objection in Saying 114, the role of the women disciples in *Thomas* is as prominent as Peter's and rather more exemplary. Both Mary and Salome appear in cryptic exchanges in *Thomas*. Sayings 21 and 22 form a unit that begins when Mary asks Jesus "Whom are your disciples like?"; Jesus responds with two comparisons with children.[47] While Mary's role appears minimal here, she has more impact than at first might appear. Her question reverses Jesus' request in Saying 13: "Compare me to something and tell me what I am like."[48] The disciples' replies reveal the superiority of Thomas, justifying the special role he plays in the transmission of the saving sayings. Jesus' response to Mary's question in 21–22 delivers what may be the single most important pronouncement on gender in the gospel.[49]

If Mary confidently questions Jesus in Saying 21, in Saying 61 Salome issues a challenge to Jesus: "Who are you, man, that you have come upon my couch and eaten from my table as if you were from someone?"[50] His response concedes her perceptiveness: he claims to originate from the whole and to share in the things of his father. This claim draws forth from her the profession and assertion: "I am your disciple." This saying seems to express the desire to share in his knowledge, as Thomas is said to do in Saying 13. Jesus appears to accept this ambition, promising illumination to the one who is whole. Thus the exchanges with the two women interlocutors evoke not only explorations of gender, but also paradigmatic teaching on discipleship and wisdom.

Dialogue of the Savior, another dialogue gospel that features Mary Magdalene as an interlocutor of Jesus, manifests the same dual role. Mary as disciple is as capable as Thomas, Matthew and Peter of representing the disciples; she is able to produce a list of parables analogous to one logion, and she earns the title of a woman "who has understood perfectly." At the same time, her presence and speech evoke the dilemma of gender. She is the one who inquires after, longs for, the destruction of the "works of womanhood."[51] Likewise, in the *Sophia of Jesus Christ*, Mary operates as an interlocutor of Jesus among the male disciples. In the later, massive dialogue *Pistis Sophia*, the male disciples are consistently bested by Mary, who, with Salome, Martha, and the mother of Jesus, dominates the exchanges.[52] The appearance of Martha suggests that the figure is both Mary Magdalene and Mary, the sister of Martha. As in *Gospel of Mary*, gender conflict in *Pistis Sophia* is expressed through Peter's objections, which seem to respond to the very excellence of her understanding.[53]

Erotic Elements in the Treatment of Mary

One of the texts from the Nag Hammadi corpus, *Gospel of Philip*, speaks of Mary Magdalene as "the one who was called his companion."[54] The Greek word for companion has the same connotation as the contemporary use of the English "companion," and even more of the Spanish *companera*: both comrade and sexual partner. The *Gospel of Philip* claims that Jesus loved Mary more than all the disciples, kissing her frequently.[55] Although it may also function as the kiss bestowed by a teacher (rabbi) on the pupil who has shown wisdom, their kiss undoubtedly has erotic overtones. As McGuire explains in chapter 12, in Philip, "the companionship of Mary and Jesus serves as prototype and symbol of the salvific union of female and male"; their kisses symbolize the kiss by which the perfect conceive, producing spiritual utterances.[56] Thus this erotic designation is central to the theology of Philip.

There are erotic overtones in the descriptions of Mary in other gospels as well. In the *Gospel of Mary*, Peter approaches Mary with the acknowledgment that "the Savior loved her more than any other woman"; the contrast with other women introduces an erotic suggestion that is absent from Levi's defense: "the Savior knew her completely and loved her devotedly" (in the Coptic, "loved her more than us").[57] In John 20:17 Jesus seems both to expect and rebuff or postpone an embrace in private from Mary Magdalene. I have argued elsewhere that this rebuke functions primarily to draw attention to the liminal state of Jesus and is analogous to a similar command given by Adam to Eve about his unburied body in *Apocalypse of Moses* 31:3–4. But it cannot be excluded that the danger of a touch between Mary and Jesus involves the sexual connotations of the word "touch"; they are well attested in the period.[58] Other interactions between Jesus and women characters of John also display a dialectic of erotic and ascetic overtones.[59]

Behind the Texts

This review of the early sources' treatment of Mary Magdalene leads to questions of what lies behind them. What do the gospels suggest about the "historical" Mary Magdalene? What was her role in the foundation of the Christian communities? What does it mean to claim she was a witness to the resurrection? Should she be called *apostola apostolorum*? How did she participate in the career of Jesus? Was she in fact his disciple, his companion, or both, faithfully following Jesus to his death?

The more proximate and accessible questions are about Mary's role in the origins of the postresurrection Christian community. In John, Matthew, *Gospel of Mary*, and the summary appendix to Mark, Mary is presented as a witness to a vision of Jesus alive from the dead. In Mark, as well as Matthew and Luke following Mark, in John and *Gospel of Peter*, Mary is presented as first among the witnesses to the empty tomb. What then can be said about the claims that Mary is to be seen as a witness to the resurrection and a disciple? It is sometimes claimed that the stories about the women at the tomb and about Mary as the first visionary must have been true: since women were so ill regarded as witnesses, the authors of the gospels could have had no reason for making up stories that create women witnesses. If they were making up stories, why not make up stories that featured men?

This argument underestimates the complexity and sophistication of both the writers and the tradition that preceded them. In fact, while the authors of the gospels do attempt to deflect doubt, they also acknowledge, and even insist upon it. The narratives make clear that neither the empty tomb nor the visions offer unambiguous proof. One might even argue that the lesser credibility of women witnesses could be used to enhance the verisimilitude of pious fictions because the supposed unreliability of women witnesses could help explain why the stories only became known later. Women's association with mourning rites might have suggested a pretext for their appearance at the tomb.[60] Women watching the cross from afar (or, in John, from beneath it) are more credible because less likely to threaten the Romans as dangerous sympathizers with sedition.

A widespread, though by no means universal, theory among scholars holds that earliest experiences that gave rise to belief in the resurrection were visions of Jesus alive from the dead. The confession "He is risen" thus originated as an explanation of these experiences, an explanation that endowed the fate of Jesus with cosmic significance as the hinge of the ages.[61] It never was the only explanation; the fate of Jesus was also interpreted as exaltation or ascension on high (as in John 20:18). On this theory, the empty tomb stories developed later as a dramatization of "resurrection."

In contrast to this reading of the stories, Elisabeth Schüssler Fiorenza rejects the idea that the visionary experiences preceded the proclamation of the empty tomb, arguing that it is not easy to tell whether the vision stories or the tomb stories are more primitive.[62] While some scholars have assigned the stories about or near the tomb to Jerusalem-based traditions and the appearance stories to Galilee-based traditions, she divides the stories into a "male tradition" of the visions and a "women's tradition" of the empty tomb. She disclaims any attempt to make a positivist argument for the historicity of the empty tomb; instead, she argues for its significance for feminist theology, urging feminists to take a stand in the open space of the empty tomb and the open road to Galilee. In her view, the empty tomb stories do not provide proof of the resurrection, but rather underline the ambiguity of Jesus' fate and call into question any theology of the cross that glorifies suffering and excuses victimization with the promise of resurrection.[63]

Positivist historical claims about any form of witnessing to the resurrection are impossible to establish. But it is worthwhile attempting to sort out the claims made by the various forms of witness and to reckon their relative probability. The visionary experiences, although they are used in the interest of Paul's claims to authority in 1 Cor 15:3–8, should not be dismissed as a male tradition that authorized men only. While 1 Cor 15:5 counts Cephas as the first visionary, the five hundred who are said to have seen the risen Jesus at one time are likely to have consisted of "sisters" as well as "brothers" (1 Cor 15:6; the NRSV makes this explicit) and Paul's claim that Christ was seen by all the apostles (1 Cor 15:7) should include at least Junia (Rom 16:7). In other sources Mary is placed among the very early visionaries, and her announcement is couched in the same terms as Paul's claim to be a visionary and witness to the resurrection. Even in the accounts of the empty tomb, Mary is depicted as a visionary and as the bearer of the definitive interpretation of Jesus' fate. The claim that she was the first of them seems at least as well supported by the texts as the claim that Peter was. Indeed, if Bart Ehrman is right in arguing that the Cephas listed as the first witness in 1 Cor 15:5 is not the Peter of the synoptics but another virtually unknown figure, the evidence for Mary is stronger.[64] Mark 16:7 can be interpreted as singling Peter out among the first visionaries, and Luke 24:34 may or may not claim that Peter saw Jesus before the two disciples on the road to Emmaus. But John 20:14–18 and Matthew 28:9–11 unambiguously place Mary first.

Thus it could well be argued that Mary fits Paul's criteria for apostleship: she "saw the Lord" and was sent with a message that provided the foundation for the community. The earliest sources do not actually associate the title apostle (or the word "sent") with Mary; the closest thing to an early Christian title applied to Mary is the word diakoneō (Mark 15:41; Matt 27:55; Luke 8:2–3); she may have been known as diakonos, like Phoebe and Martha, as well as Paul, Apollos, Timothy, and Tychikos.[65]

The questions about a preresurrection Mary, Mary as an associate of Jesus, are equally complex. The first question is whether such a Mary existed. One of the recent investigations of the history of Jesus has asked the question, "How Many Years Was Easter Sunday?"[66] One possible implication of this question is whether the first visionaries, like Mary and the Cephas of 1 Cor 15:5, need have been disciples of Jesus or whether, like Paul, they might have come to know him only through their revelations.[67] Only in Mark and Mark's interpreters is Mary explicitly introduced as a disciple during the time in Galilee; only in Luke is she introduced before the crucifixion. Dialogue and sayings gospels clearly present Mary as the equal of other disciples, but these generally appear to be set after, rather than before, the resurrection or ascension—it is the Savior, or the "living," transformed Jesus who speaks in these gospels.

But other indications weigh on the side of a (relatively) long association between Mary and Jesus. Mark not only names Mary first among the women disciples at the cross and tomb, but also stresses their participation in the mission in Galilee. John places her among Jesus' intimates, as does Philip, who designates her as one of three women who "always walked with the Lord," as well as his companion. While "walking with the Lord" may simply attest fidelity to a way of life, here the phrase associates Mary with Jesus' mother and his mother's sister. As I mentioned above, Mary's last name is generally understood to derive from her town of origin and often is translated as "of Magdala." "Magdala" is usually identified as Migdal Nunnayya (tower of fish), which, in its turn, is identified with the substantial town with the Greek name Tarichaea on the sea of Galilee, engaged largely in the salting and export of fish.[68] Its location between Nazareth, the apparent place of Jesus' origin, and Caphernaum, the apparent base of the movement, may suggest that the association of Mary and Jesus predated the time in Caphernaum, and that she was among the first members of the movement. On the other hand, designations like "of Magdala" and "of Nazareth" might well be used precisely when one no longer lived there and might apply only to the family's origin. There is no way of establishing the degree of her actual connection with the town.

The question of whether Mary or anyone from within the movement could have witnessed the death of Jesus and followed him to his grave remains an acute one. The gospels' claim that he was buried by the charitable deed of Joseph of Arimathea seems to imply that no one within the movement could have obtained the body or attended the burial. It is also less than likely that the Romans would have allowed any demonstrations of sympathy for a seditious criminal during the execution, even by women.

Considering Mary as an associate of Jesus raises the question of how she understood that association, of why she or any Jewish woman joined the "Jesus movement." As Kraemer makes clear in chapter 2, this is a complex question that has too frequently been addressed by juxtaposing an overly definitive and rather generous reconstruction of Jesus' views on and practice toward women with an equally definitive, but highly pejorative, depiction of Jewish views and practices toward women. Recent social science treatments of the context of Jesus that locate him in a movement within Judaism ought, at least in theory, to make it easier to avoid contrasting Jesus and Jewish practice. But the few social science reconstructions of that movement that attend at all to the question of gender have tended to postulate Jesus' supposedly more inclusive practice or his rejection of purity laws as the attraction of the Jesus movement for women.[69] Nor is it the case that other features of that movement are uniformly described. There are at least two major current lines of approach; one sees those in the movement as practitioners of radical pragmatic wisdom, the other sees them as charismatic and apocalyptic prophets.

Two shifts in rethinking these alternative visions of the movement can assist in retrieving the hopes of a Jewish Mary Magdalene within them. First, the older insight that Jesus preached not himself but God's reign should revise the designation from "Jesus movement" to the "reign-of-God movement" in which Mary has a place as a participant rather than as a follower only. The traditions and the gospels have recast the members of the movement as followers of Jesus, but at least before his martyrdom, Mary may have understood herself to be as much the teacher of Jesus as his disciple. She may have been his elder, and perhaps even his predecessor in preaching God's reign. The shift from the "Jesus movement" to "the reign-of-God movement" helps to enable a second, and essential shift from depicting Jesus in conflict with Jews and Judaism euphemistically designated as "the religious authorities of his day" to relocating the movement as a resistance to Rome—God's reign in conflict with Caesar's. Thus the investigation of Mary's and other Jewish women's concerns in joining the movement shifts. The problematic character of earlier reconstructions might be avoided by revising the question of why women joined the movement from a search for Jesus' uniquely liberating practices or teaching to "the issues that engaged Jews of both genders in the first century (the oppressive presence of the Romans, the corruption of the Herodians, the purity and efficacy of the temple)."[70]

These two shifts suggest revisions of the two prevailing scholarly models for the reconstruction of the historical Jesus or the so-called Jesus movement. One depicts Jesus as a Cynic-like sage, a Jewish peasant philosopher; the other envisages him as an eschatological prophet, or as I would prefer, an apocalyptic revolutionary.

According to one scenario then, Mary Magdalene, in enlisting in the reign-of-God movement, chose to join a Cynic-like movement of wandering sages who drew upon an alternative Jewish wisdom tradition to propose the reign of God as an alternative way of life.[71] Their preaching consisted largely of aphoristic sayings that challenged the investment of those they encountered in property, family, money, honor—things that keep them within the reign of Caesar. Their concern was not with the future, but with offering a different way of life in the present; whether they are seen as revolutionaries or not, they sought to change the lives of their hearers in order to change the social order.[72] In this version of the reign-of-God movement, Mary Magdalene might have been a wandering preacher and sage whose very presence was a challenge both to the safe control of the household head over the women in his care and to the security of women within the household. If Jesus of Nazareth and Mary of Magdala were "companions" as *Gospel of Philip* claims, their arrangement, whether it included sexual partnership or not, might have been a deliberate choice meant to call sexual mores and familial structure into question or might simply have been the social concomitant of poverty and an itinerant life. But Mary may have been a companion of Jesus in the same sense that any of the wandering sages were companions—neither erotic partners nor disciples, but simply fellow travelers on the way. Mary Magdalene the visionary does not easily fit into the picture of a cyniclike movement of sages: her role in the resurrection narratives must be regarded as later legend or as part of the apocalyptic transformation of the movement. She might even be seen as the source of that transformation, the "hysterical woman" who, in the view of a second-century critic of Christianity, produced the resurrection faith.[73]

Other scholars retain the older view that the movement consisted principally of wandering charismatic preachers or prophets, announcing the secret revealed to them: the fulfillment of history and the arrival of God's reign.[74] In this scenario, Mary joined the movement under her experience of the compulsion of the spirit. While wisdom sayings and practice also play a role in most versions of the movement as apocalyptic revolution, its focus would have been on God's act: God's reign standing in judgment against the reign of Ceasar.[75] Changing one's life was not the means of God's reign, but the result; going on the road was a way of going out to meet it. The itinerant practice placed the movement with those who make up God's reign: the poor, hungry and oppressed. Like Jesus, Mary was driven by the spirit onto the road as a prophet of God's reign, with all "who hear the word of God and do it" and, like Jesus, she spoke the words given to her by the divine Wisdom who sent them as prophets and emissaries (Luke 11:49).

In this picture, if Jesus of Nazareth and Mary of Magdala were companions in the sense suggested by Philip, their arrangement, as the social concomitant of poverty and an itinerant life, might have been without significance before the urgency of their expectations. But again, Mary may have been the companion of Jesus in the same sense as any other prophet of the movement. And she may have been his predecessor in the movement, a sister in the spirit subordinated in the narrative as the exodus traditions subordinated Miriam to Moses.[76] Envisioned as prophetic and apocalyptic, the reign-of-God movement readily accommodates a visionary Mary Magdalene. Whether she followed Jesus in the movement or preceded him, once Jesus became the martyr of the movement, the visions that she saw were of him, the spirit in which she prophesied was his, the "word of the lord" she spoke was the word of the lord Jesus. It was perhaps her interpretation of the visions, her proclamation of their meaning, that laid the foundation for the new community.

Conclusion

This survey and interrogation of the sources about Mary Magdalene has helped to clarify the claims made on her behalf and the basis for some of them. It is difficult to argue that much more can be known about any of the male disciples named in the gospels, except perhaps Peter and John, who appear to be briefly mentioned in Galatians (2:7, 9).[77] Carefully examining the evidence broadens and complicates the picture of the ways she was remembered by the earliest communities—in fact broadens and complicates the pictures of those early communities' interests and concerns, of their sexual politics and other agendas, both hidden and overt. But if the investigation multiplies the nuances of reconstructed Mary, it does not increase the security with which a picture of a "real" Mary can be drawn. Whether the feminist historian evokes Mary of Magdala, companion of Jesus, a wandering wise woman, a prophet of God's reign, a visionary and revolutionary, *apostola apostolorum*, *diakonos*, and missionary, any version of Mary Magdalene she constructs is pieced together out of snippets. Nor are they snippets of fact, but rather snippets of the memories and expectations embedded in the distant conversations of long-dead authors with long-dispersed communities. The interpreter selects and arranges, waving these three or four relics out in the open, holding up these two or three iconic narratives, mapping both onto imagined vistas, only dimly aware of the agendas that must always remain even less clear to her than her own.

NOTES

1. New York: Doubleday 1994, 518.

2. For a collection, see Benedicta Ward, *Harlots of the Desert: A Study of Repentance in Early Monastic Sources* (Kalamazoo, MI: Cistercian Publications, 1987). For more critical texts and introductions for some of these figures, see Sebastian P. Brock and Susan Ashbrook Harvey, eds., *Holy Women of the Syrian Orient* (Berkeley, CA: University of California, 1987).

3. These are my own translations of the biblical texts, made from the Latin of the Roman Missal, not from the Hebrew or Greek of the Bible. All other translations of biblical texts in the rest of the essay are my own unless otherwise noted and are made from the original texts.

4. See Carla Ricci, *Mary Magdalene and Many Others: Women Who Followed Jesus* (Minneapolis, MN: Fortress, 1994) 192 and n. 39; see also Raymond E. Brown, "Roles of Women in

the Gospel of John," *Theological Studies* 36 (1975) 688–99, reprinted in *The Community of the Beloved Disciple: The Life, Loves and Hates of an Individual Church in New Testament Times* (New York: Paulist, 1979) 183–89. For a fuller history of the tradition, see Jane C. Schaberg, "Thinking Back through the Magdalene," *Continuum* 1 (1991) 71–90.

5. Paul J. Achtemeier, "Mark, Gospel of," *ABD* 4:543.

6. Ibid.; see also Helmut Koester, *Ancient Christian Gospels* (Philadelphia: Trinity Press International, 1990) 289–92.

7. Mary Rose D'Angelo, "Re-Membering Jesus: Women, Prophecy and Resistance in the Beginnings of Christianity," *Horizons* 19 (1992) 203–5.

8. Constance F. Parvey, "The Theology and Leadership of Women in the New Testament, in *Religion and Sexism*, ed. Rosemary Radford Ruether (New York: Simon and Schuster, 1974) 139–46.

9. Elisabeth Schüssler Fiorenza, "A Feminist Critical Interpretation for Liberation: Martha and Mary: Luke 10:38–42," *Religion and Intellectual Life* 3 (1986) 21–35; Schüssler Fiorenza, *But She Said: Feminist Practices of Biblical Interpretation* (Boston: Beacon, 1992) 52–76, esp. 64–65; Mary Rose D'Angelo, "Women Partners in the New Testament," *JFSR* 6 (1990) 65–86; D'Angelo, "Women in Luke-Acts: A Redactional View," *JBL* 109 (1990) 441–461; Jane Schaberg, "Luke," in *The Women's Bible Commentary*, ed. Carol A. Newsom and Sharon Ringe (Louisville: Westminster/John Knox, 1992) 288–89. Turid Karlsen Seim contests this interpretation of *diakonia* in this context; see "The Gospel of Luke," in *Searching the Scriptures, Volume 2: A Feminist Commentary*, ed. Elisabeth Schüssler Fiorenza (New York: Crossroad, 1994) 745.

10. D'Angelo, "Women in Luke-Acts" 453–54; also D'Angelo, "Women Partners" 81; see Schüssler Fiorenza, *But She Said*; Schüssler Fiorenza, "Martha and Mary" 31.

11. Text available in Robert J. Miller, ed., *The Complete Gospels: Annotated Scholars Version* (Sonoma, CA: Polebridge, 1994) 408–13.

12. Schüssler Fiorenza, "Martha and Mary" 59.

13. D'Angelo, "Women Partners" 72–80.

14. Ibid. 81–84.

15. Ibid. 80.

16. Trans. Karen L. King, "The Gospel of Mary," in Miller, *Complete Gospels* 365.

17. Ibid.

18. Ibid. 366; bracketed material is added in the Coptic version.

19. See also Anne M. McGuire, chapter 12; Karen L. King, "The Gospel of Mary Magdalene," in Schüssler Fiorenza, *Searching the Scriptures* 621–25.

20. Brown, "Community of the Beloved Disciple," passim.

21. Contra John Dominic Crossan, *The Historical Jesus: The Life of a Mediterranean Jewish Peasant* (San Francisco: HarperSanFrancisco, 1992) 395–416.

22. Other possible explanations are that the author is counting only appearances to the group of disciples, or that the count does not refer to John 20 at all, but remains from a collection of appearances in Galilee only, as John 4:54 counts only signs in Galilee. See also Claudia Setzer, "Excellent Women: Female Witness to the Resurrection," *JBL* 116 (1997) 259–72; Setzer seems to attribute the appendix to the author of the gospel (p. 268).

23. Mary Rose D'Angelo, "A Critical Note: John 20:17 and Apocalypse of Moses 31," *JTS* n. s. 41 (1990) 529–36.

24. So, for example, Kathleen Corley, "Jesus, Mary Magdalene and Salome," *The Fourth R* (January–February 1996) 16.

25. See discussion of erotic and ascetic aspects in chapter 8.

26. Cf. Deidre J. Good, "Pistis Sophia," in Schüssler Fiorenza, *Searching the Scriptures*

680–82; Gregory Riley, *Resurrection Reconsidered: Thomas and John in Conflict* (Minneapolis, MN: Fortress, 1995).

27. See David Hagner, "James," *ABD* 3:616–618; Gareth Lee Cockerill, "Joses," *ABD* 3:998; Stanley E. Porter, "Joseph," *ABD* 3:968–69.

28. GThom Saying 61.

29. Josephus, *Antiquities* 18§136. She remains unnamed in Matt 14:3–12 and Justin Martyr, *Dialogue* 49:4–5.

30. Miller, *Complete Gospels* 393–94. See also Corley, "Jesus, Magdalene and Salome" 14.

31. W. D. Davies, *The Setting of the Sermon on the Mount* (Cambridge: Cambridge University Press, 1966) 422–23.

32. See esp. 517b–521b, also *Laws* 955cd; *Republic* 371–372 describes other functions necessary to the city this way.

33. *Discourses* 3.22.69, 24.65, 26.28; 4.7.20.

34. Josephus, *Antiquities* 7§365, 17§140.

35. See also Mary Ann Tolbert, "Mark," in Newsom and Ringe, *Women's Bible Commentary*, 267.

36. This interpretation has been disputed; Willi Marxsen applies this promise to the future appearance of Jesus as son of man in the parousia in *Mark the Evangelist*, trans. James Boyce, Donald Juel, and William Poehlmann with Roy A. Harrisville (Nashville, TN: Abingdon, 1969) 102–16.

37. Elisabeth Struthers Malbon, "Fallible Followers: Women and Men in the Gospel of Mark," in *Semeia* 28 (1983) 29–48.

38. Luke 24:12 is missing in some ancient manuscripts and is likely to have been extrapolated from John 20:4–10.

39. Schüssler Fiorenza, "Word, Spirit and Power: Women in Early Christian Communities," in *Women of Spirit: Female Leadership in the Jewish and Christian Traditions*, ed. Rosemary Radford Ruether and Eleanor McLaughlin (New York: Simon and Schuster, 1979) 52.

40. See also Schaberg, "Luke" 291.

41. See chapter 8.

42. D'Angelo, "Women in Luke-Acts" 449, 452.

43. On Luke and high status women, see D'Angelo, "Women in Luke-Acts" 448.

44. See chapter 8.

45. Translation is in Miller, *Complete Gospels* 399–407.

46. See chapter 7 for a discussion of Q.

47. Pheme Perkins treats 21–24 together as teaching on Jesus' disciples in "Gospel of Thomas," in Schüssler Fiorenza, *Searching the Scriptures* 546–47.

48. Trans. Marvin Meyer in *Q-Thomas Reader*, John S. Kloppenborg, Marvin W. Meyer, Stephen J. Patterson, Michael G. Steinhauser, eds. (Sonoma, CA: Polebridge, 1990) 132.

49. For interpretation, see chapter 12.

50. Trans. Thomas O. Lambdin, in James M. Robinson, ed., *Nag Hammadi Library in English*, 3rd rev. ed. (San Francisco: HarperSanFrancisco, 1988) 133.

51. See chapter 12 for discussion.

52. See Good, "Pistis Sophia" 678–707.

53. Ibid. 684–85.

54. GPhil 59.8–9, trans. Wesley W. Isenberg, in Robinson, *Nag Hammadi Library* 159.

55. GPhil 63.34–35.

56. See chapter 12.

57. Trans. King, "Gospel of Mary" 365.

58. 1 Cor 7:1; Col 2:21; H. G. Liddell, R. Scott, H. S. Jones, and R. McKenzie, *A Greek*

English Lexicon (Oxford: Clarendon, 1968) 231 s.v. ἅπτω 3, 5; Walter Bauer, William F. Arndt, F. Wilbur Gingrich, and Frederick Danker, A Greek-English Lexicon of the New Testament and Other Early Christian Literature (Chicago: University of Chicago Press, 1979), 102 s.v. ἅπτω 2a.

59. See chapter 8.

60. So Corley, "Jesus, Mary Magdalene and Salome" 15–16.

61. Willi Marxsen, The Resurrection of Jesus of Nazareth, trans. Margaret Kohl (Philadelphia: Fortress, 1970) 138–48.

62. Elisabeth Schüssler Fiorenza, Jesus: Miriam's Child, Sophia's Prophet: Critical Issues in Feminist Christology (New York: Continuum, 1994) 125.

63. Ibid. 123–28.

64. Bart D. Ehrman, "Cephas and Peter," JBL 109 (1990) 463–74.

65. Paul uses the word of himself (1 Cor 3:5, 2 Cor 3:6, 6:4, 11:23), Apollos (1 Cor 3:5), and perhaps also Timothy (1 Thess 3:2). Ephesians uses it of Paul (3:7) and Tychikos (6:21); in Colossians, it seems to be a preferred designation of Paul (1:23, 25) and of Epaphras (1:7); 1 Tim 4:6 applies it to Timothy.

66. The question is a chapter title in John Dominic Crossan, Jesus, A Revolutionary Biography (San Francisco: HarperSanFrancisco, 1995) 159–92.

67. This question is not pursued by Crossan.

68. James F. Strange, "Magdala" ABD 4:463–64; on the basis of the town's Aramaic name and economic interests, Kathleen Corley suggests that Mary might have been a fisherwoman ("Jesus, Mary Magdalene and Salome" 14).

69. Elisabeth Schüssler Fiorenza, In Memory of Her: A Feminist Theological Reconstruction of Christian Origins (New York: Crossroad, 1983) 110–59; Crossan, Historical Jesus 265–302.

70. Chapter 2, p. 46.

71. See, for instance, Burton L. Mack, A Myth of Innocence: Mark and Christian Origins (Philadelphia: Fortress, 1988) 25–97; Crossan, Historical Jesus esp. 417–26; Crossan, Revolutionary Biography 193–201.

72. This picture is a summary of some major features of reconstructions by Mack and Crossan.

73. The critic was Celsus, reported by Origen in his refutation of Celsus' True Doctrine; see Margaret Y. MacDonald, Early Christian Women and Pagan Opinion: The Power of the Hysterical Woman (Cambridge: Cambridge University Press, 1996) 1–13.

74. Gerd Theissen, Sociology of Early Palestinian Christianity, trans. John Bowden (Philadelphia: Fortress, 1978) esp. 1–16; Alan Segal, Rebecca's Children: Judaism and Christianity in the Roman World (Cambridge, MA: Harvard University Press, 1986) 68–95; Schüssler Fiorenza, In Memory of Her 99–159; Schüssler Fiorenza, Miriam's Child esp. 141–43; Mary Rose D'Angelo, "Re-Membering Jesus" 199–218; D'Angelo, "The Concrete Foundation of Chistianity: Re-Membering Jesus," in Proceedings of the Catholic Theological Society of America, Baltimore, June 9–12, 1994, Vol 49. ed. Paul Crowley, 13–146.

75. Mary Rose D'Angelo, "Abba and 'Father': Imperial Theology and the Traditions about Jesus," JBL 111 (1992) 627–30; D'Angelo, "The Concrete Foundation" 131–46; D'Angelo, "Re-Membering Jesus" 198–218.

76. See Phyllis Trible, "Bringing Miriam out of the Shadows," Bible Review 5 (1989) 14–25, 34.

77. If Peter and Cephas are the same, then the letters of Paul give more substantial evidence about Peter in 1 Cor 1:10–18, 15:5–8 and Gal 2:11–16.

6

(RE)PRESENTATIONS OF WOMEN IN THE GOSPELS

John and Mark

Mary Rose D'Angelo

What are you looking for?" Jesus asks the first disciples in the Gospel of John (1:38).[1] This is an important query for feminist investigation of the gospels. A wide variety of questions has been put to these texts: whether the gospel writers view women positively or negatively, whether their messages are inclusive or exclusive, whether they challenge or accommodate established gender roles, which gospel is the most or least inclusive, the most or least patriarchal, and even (since these works are all actually anonymous) whether a woman could have been the author of one or more of them. These questions produce very different answers about the same texts. For instance, two social science approaches come to nearly opposite conclusions about the representations of women in Mark and Matthew.

Antoinette Clark Wire's sociological approach asks whether the gospels are congruent with or deviant from their settings in the matter of gender.[2] In Wire's view, the narratives of Mark reflect the tradition of "oral storytellers who show a dependent peoples' searing critique of power"; the gospel includes stories told by women of their healings, although the narrative as it stands is distanced from the women, whom she regards as nonliterate.[3] Wire describes Matthew's community as scribal, drawing an analogy between the practice reflected in Matthew and the living conditions and accommodations of a medieval Chinese culture. The Pharisees and Covenanters of Qumran (that is, the community reflected in the sectarian documents from the Dead Sea) offer her analogous scribal communities from the same milieu as Matthew; Wire sees the women of the Pharisees and the community of Matthew as nonliterate.[4] She concludes that the author of Matthew views women as "'embedded' in male relatives," and that the gospel does not present women as disciples.[5] For Wire, the function of the gospel was primarily to train literate male disciples while holding up women and other marginal people as examples of faith.

Kathleen Corley, on the other hand, uses the methods of social anthropology to locate the three synoptic gospels' views of women in the context of the changing meal practices of antiquity.[6] By comparing the ways in which women appear to be included in meal settings, she attempts to decide which of the gospels and gospel writers shows the most advanced social ideology. She comes to the conclusion that Mark's gospel never shows women eating or reclining with men, and that Mark is not free of "social conservatism," while Matthew does show women reclining with men, and presents women as meeting the criteria for discipleship, and as examples of "true faith and Christian service."[7] For Corley, the Gospel of Matthew is both the "most Jewish" and "most egalitarian" of the three synoptic gospels.[8]

Both of these fascinating and complex endeavors present illuminating perspectives while involving some problematic presuppositions. Yet in some ways, they make their greatest contribution by providing counterweights to each other. Their opposing conclusions derive in part from different assumptions they make about the contexts and in part from their differing choices of entrée into the text. Even so, the conflict raises questions about the very enterprise of asking whether one of these ancient texts is more deviant from the gender prescriptions of its setting, more or most egalitarian, better or best for women. A wide variety of factors enters into the portrayal of women in the gospels. Among them are questions of what genres formed these works, what sources were used and how they have been revised, what new material has been created, what variety of roles is permitted to women, and whether and how women are allowed to speak within the narrative. Nor do representations of women exhaust the operations of gender in the texts; the questions of how leadership is conceived, to whom moral exhortation is addressed, and what christological images come into play and how the christology of the gospel defines discipleship roles must all be considered in discussing gender in gospel literature.

In what follows, I attend both to narratives in which women appear and to explicit teaching about sexuality and gender. My goal is not to decide which of the gospels is most or least inclusive of women, but rather to attempt to trace out the ways that women and gender function in the literary and theological enterprises of the texts. At some points, it will be possible to detect reflections of the history of late first- early second-century readers and writers and the conditions of their lives in the Greek-speaking Roman world.

In this chapter, I have made the somewhat unusual decision to treat John and Mark together and to begin from John. In part, this is because similar approaches must be used in evaluating gender in these two gospels; while it is clear that both Mark and John had access to earlier sources, none of these sources has survived. While it is possible and sometimes necessary to speculate about them, the direct comparisons between Matthew or Luke and Mark as their source are not possible between the Gospels of Mark and John and their sources. Further,

I am inclined to see Mark and John as roughly contemporary. The Gospel of Mark is believed by most scholars to be the earliest of the synoptic gospels and to have provided the outline and much of the narrative material used by both Matthew and Luke. While John was once regarded as the latest of the gospels and as dependent on all the others, these assumptions are now widely contested. The gospel's narrative outline differs radically from Mark's; John includes three Passovers and therefore at least parts of three years, while Mark has only one. The amount of material the two works have in common is very limited and often very differently formulated. Further, John appears to have developed through a relatively long process of revising and editing in a rather idiosyncratic community recently separated from the local Jewish synagogue. The letters called 1, 2 and 3 John are thought to be later productions of the same community. Many scholars envisage a first edition of John that was contemporary with and independent of Mark.[9] Thus it is possible to place at least the first full version of John around the year 80 and to see Mark as from approximately the same date. Beginning with the gospel attributed to John has the salutary effect of dislodging the overly precise gospel narrative pattern that has largely been established by the dramatic skills of the author of Luke.

Since the gospels originated as anonymous works and were later attached to names that would accord the texts apostolic authority, it is a priori possible that one or more was written by a woman.[10] The formal introduction to Luke includes a masculine modifier for the narrator (1:3), thus that author at least assumes a male persona. But there are no explicit clues to the gender of the other three authors, and in speaking of them I avoid the masculine pronoun.[11] From time to time throughout these chapters, I refer to the readers and hearers of the gospels. Like most ancient literature, the gospels were expected to reach the majority of their audience by being read aloud, whether in a communal setting or for a few listeners. Readers and hearers of the gospels would have had differing degrees of literary skill; so, indeed, would the authors. The Greek and narrative patterns of John in particular are very simple and repetitive; this gospel is never far from oral performance.

John

Some of the first attempts to reread the gospels in search of authority for a more inclusive treatment of women turned to the Gospel of John.[12] Women appear relatively frequently and in speaking roles: the mother of Jesus, who is never named (John 2:1–11, 19:25–27), a woman of Samaria (4:1–42), Mary and Martha (11:1–44, 12:1–8) and Mary Magdalene (19:25, 20:1–18). These women are not included in the opening series of call narratives (1:35–51), but neither is Thomas, Judas or Judas Iscariot.

The famous figures Martha and Mary are said to be loved by or friends of Jesus, terms that indicate discipleship in John (11:5; cf. 11:3, 11; 15:13, 14, 15). The community seems to have been very little concerned with structures,

offices, and titles. Both connection and leadership are understood through ancient models of friendship. "The twelve" are referred to only in passing (6:67,
70, 71; 20:24); these few brief references can be attributed to the later layers
of the gospel. There is no list of the twelve, and twelve famous disciples can be
produced only by including Mary Magdalene, Martha, Mary, Lazarus, and the
unnamed beloved disciple. The term "apostle" is used only once, not of a specific disciple, but generically (13:16). Mary Magdalene appears to fit the Pauline
definition of apostle (1 Cor 9:1, 15:3–8); she is accorded the first vision of the
risen lord and delivers an apparently oracular message in his person and words
(20:17–18).[13] This scene reflects the strong prophetic and visionary element
that persists through the stages of communal development from the earliest
levels of the tradition through the letters (see 1 John 4:1–2, 5:6). Like the *Gospel
of Mary*, the last chapter of John and its appendix seem to reflect struggles or
negotiations of authority within the community; the differing positions are represented by Peter, the beloved disciple, Thomas, and Mary Magdalene. The
prominence given to Mary suggests that the authority and leadership of women
are at issue in the community.[14]

One of the letters begins, "The elder to a chosen lady and her children"
(2 John 1). The female figure in this address and the "chosen sister" whose
"children" send a closing greeting (2 John 13) are often explained as feminine
personifications of communities rather than as real women members or leaders
of congregations.[16] But these phrases resemble an attack on a woman prophet
whom the author of Revelation calls "Jezebel" and on her "children" (Rev 2:
20, 2:23). Thus the "chosen ladies" of 2 John may have been women prophets,
while "children" referred to their congregations or disciples, and the "elder"
who wrote the letter was allied with the prophet described as "your chosen
sister."[17]

The Gospel of John includes a number of sayings that begin with the words
"I am." These sayings are likely to have originated as the product of the prophets
of John's community. The prophets of the second-century movement called the
New Prophecy (Montanism) produced similar sayings. Not only Montanus, but
also the two women prophets Priscilla and Maximilla are credited with oracles
in which the spirit that speaks in the prophet identifies itself for the community.
The saying of Maximilla, "I am driven as a wolf from the flock; I am not a wolf;
I am word, power and spirit,"[15] resembles the saying, "I am the good shepherd"
(John 10:11, 14), not only in imagery but also in function. It defends the
prophetic spirit and leadership against the claims of an orthodoxy.

John resembles the gnostic dialogue gospels that present Jesus as the heavenly
visitor.[18] This gospel makes extensive use of dialogue forms and explains Jesus
as everything in the Bible, from the Davidic Messiah to Jacob's ladder, but primarily as the one who comes from God, both as the prophet like Moses and as
bread, light, life, water come from "heaven." Its message is also similar to some
aspects of gnostic thought: what distinguishes both Jesus and the true disciple
is their knowledge of their own origin and destiny (see also chapter 12). They
are like the spirit-wind in that outsiders can know neither where they come
from nor where they are going (3:5–7).

Several types of dialogues appear in John. Chapters 13–16 strongly resemble works like *Dialogue of the Savior* and *Apocryphon of James*, in which the disciples ask questions in turn in order to structure what is basically a revelatory discourse. In another dialogue format, "the Jews" appear as stereotyped hostile questioners; John 6:22–59 and 10:22–39 belong to this category. But there are also dialogues of a more dramatic type peculiar to John. In these, two parties hold the stage and speak: the protagonist, usually (but not always) Jesus, and the interlocutor, the questioner or "straight man." A third, invisible party, the (early Christian) reader and hearers are drawn into the dialogue by the use of irony and double meaning, which invite them to fill in what the interlocutor does not know. The most important of these are the dialogues with Nicodemus (3:1–21), the Samaritan woman at the well (4:1–42), the blind man (9:1–10:21), and Martha or Martha and Mary (11:1–44).

The dialogue with the Samaritan woman provides a relatively easy entrée into the rather peculiar thought world of the gospel and is also an excellent example of the interplay of gender in the text and between the text and its interpreters. With the exception of the early fifth century writer John Chrysostom, most commentators of the past tended to denigrate the woman, reading her history as sinful and her reactions as obtuse.[19] This misreading results not only from misogyny but also from failure to recognize that 2:23–4:42 forms an integrated whole. The dialogues with Nicodemus (3:1–21) and with the woman (4:1–42) illustrate 2:25: Jesus "needed no one to testify to him about the human being for he himself knew what was in the human being."

The dialogue with the woman is set in the context of baptism (1–3), and attention is drawn to the location in Samaria and at Jacob's well (4–6). The time is given as noon (6), but not, as is sometimes suggested, because the woman was shunned as immoral by other women and could not come at the normal hours (morning and evening). Rather the purposes of this comment are dramatic. It contrasts the woman with Nicodemus: whereas he came by night and left in the dark, she comes at the point of fullest possible light (3:1, 4:6–7).[20]

Jesus initiates their first exchange (7–9), accosting the woman with a request for a drink. Her reply calls attention to their ethnic identifications and to her own gender. The gospel writer notes for the reader that the Samaritans and Jews do not have dealings or, perhaps, share utensils (like water jars). With the second exchange (10–12), Jesus offers "living water" and shifts the focus to his own identity; the woman responds to the shift: "Are you greater than our father Jacob?" she asks. Calling Jacob "our father" underlines the common ancestor of Jesus and the woman and points to the separation of the Samaritans and Jews, an issue addressed further on in the dialogue (4:20–24). If later commentators see her question as obtuse, the (first-century Christian) reader cannot help answering her with a resounding "yes!"

In the climactic third exchange (13–15), Jesus presents her with the offer she cannot refuse: water from a source within herself that will enable her never to thirst. Behind this promise is the reformulation of a wisdom motif that is used to explain both Jesus and the spirit in John. This motif portrays Wisdom as that female aspect of the deity that human beings can take into themselves as food and drink so that she becomes part of them—or perhaps they become part of her (Sir 24:19–22; cf. Isa 55:1–4; Prov 9; Ps 34). If for Sirach eating and drinking of wisdom will cause the sage to hunger and thirst continually, for John the one who eats and drinks of Jesus will never hunger or thirst again (John 6:35, 50). In John 7:37–39, "living water" is explicitly identified with the spirit and is said to flow from the breast of the one who believes. In response, the woman asks for this water, "that I may neither thirst nor come here to draw." This clause has frequently been seen as evidence of her incomprehension; most commentators have concluded that she has taken his offer literally. But the rest of the dialogue belies that assessment.

The next set of exchanges (16–20) form the turning point of the dialogue. Jesus orders the woman to bring her husband (or her man; the Greek word $an\bar{e}r$ is used for both). When she responds that she has none, he agrees and announces that she has had five and the one she has now is not hers. This verse has been the subject of a wide variety of exegetical extravaganzas, which have ranged from the allegorical, claiming the five husbands are the five gods supposedly worshipped by the Samaritans, to the misogynist, characterizing the woman as a well-known sinner.[21] It is difficult to specify the meaning of Jesus' comment; multiple husbands in the scriptures either are the result of Levirate marriage (Mark 12:18–27) or depict the woman as victim (Tob 6:10–7:16). A more intriguing possibility is suggested by a wall painting from the House of the Dioscurii in Pompeii, in which a woman in a sun hat offers a drink to a traveler with a staff and a dog. The painting is worn, but the woman appears to be elderly; she sits upon a round object that looks like a well with a water jug beside her.[22] The scene may evoke some well-known comic vignette; perhaps a first-century audience would have taken the five husbands mentioned in John 4: 18 to indicate the woman's age and have assumed that number six was not up to sex or preferred the slave girl.

It is equally possible that Jesus' pronouncement is meant to remain mysterious to the audience; whatever its meanings, the woman hears his words as revelatory. In relating her encounter with Jesus to the other Samaritans, she declares "Come and see a man who told me everything I've ever done" (4:29, 4:39). In response to Jesus' insight, she recognizes him as a prophet (19). One gross misreading claims "She changes the subject away from this embarrassing question."[23] Despite the best efforts of centuries of Christian commentary, the text imputes neither sin nor shame to the woman. She expresses no repentance and Jesus neither forgives her nor warns her against sinning again (as he does the paralytic in 5:14). In the paradigm of Johannine judgment, this woman shows that her works are good by coming to the light (3:19–21).

This exchange foregrounds the importance of prophecy in John 2:23–4:42 (and the gospel as a whole). Jesus' pronouncement and the woman's response both represent one of the most important functions of early Christian prophecy: knowledge of what is in the human heart (John 2:25; see also 1 Cor 14:24–25, 2:10–16; Rev 2:23). His insight reveals to her that he knows all about her (4: 29, 4:37) as his seemingly casual comment illumines Nathanael (1:48–49). Her recognition of him as a prophet manifests her special knowledge as well, and she builds upon it by asking him to perform a second prophetic function, that of advising on dilemmas, especially of right worship (see 1 Macc 4:46). She puts to him the single most important theological question between her own people and his: the question of where to worship, on Mount Gerizim (revered by the Samaritans) or in Jerusalem.[24]

Jesus' response is double. First, he exercises a third function of early Christian prophecy, prediction; he foretells the fall of the temple in Jerusalem with the warning, "the day is coming when you will worship neither on this mountain nor in Jerusalem" (4:21). When Jesus supposedly spoke with these words, the temple on Mt. Gerizim had already been destroyed (128 BCE); by the time the first readers and hearers came upon his prophecy, the temple in Jerusalem also lay in ruins.[25] The second response speaks directly to the readers and hearers as well: it is they who have the prerogative of true spiritual worship (4:23–24). The excellence of this answer leads the woman to propose a further identification of Jesus as the coming Messiah who "will tell us everything" (4:25). And Jesus concedes with the words, "I am [he]"(4:26).

The aftermath of the dialogue underlines its effect. The woman leaves behind her water jug (4:28) for her aspiration of 4:15 is fulfilled; she no longer needs to come and draw water. Instead, without a command or commission from Jesus, she proselytizes her neighbors (4:28–30, 39–42). In this she is contrasted with the disciples, who puzzle over the meaning of Jesus' harvest sayings while she performs them (4:31–38). Raymond Brown concluded that the author portrayed the woman as performing apostolic functions.[26]

Are there literary and theological functions of gender in this dialogue? Does the dialogue function to challenge or to reinforce gender prescriptions? It is clear that gender does play some role; the author causes both the woman (4:8) and the disciples (4:32) to emphasize that there is something unexpected about the interaction between Jesus and this woman. These comments have frequently been used to claim that Jesus or the author rejected Jewish or rabbinic practice in the treatment of women (see chapter 2). But there is no suggestion of conflict with the Jewish community here. The virulently anti-Jewish polemic that characterizes the story of the blind man (9:1–10:21), the bread of life discourse (6:1–72), and passages like 8:30–59 and 10:22–39 is lacking in this passage and in all the passages in which women play a prominent role.[27] This strongly suggests that the community did not experience the role of women within it as a source of tension with the Jewish communities it knew. That the questions are voiced (or not voiced) by the disciples and the woman herself argues that, if there was tension over the participation and leadership of women, it arose from expectations within rather than from extramural disputes.

The community still appears to identify more closely with the woman at the well, who is both a woman and a Samaritan, than with Nicodemus, the Jerusalemite teacher, Pharisee and ruler of the synagogue. Unlike the Pharisees depicted as opponents of the blind man, Nicodemus is not a hostile character, but one whose fear keeps him in the dark until the end of the gospel (7:50–52, 19:

39). But the narrative demonstrates that the learning accessible to this teacher in Israel is less effective than the drink of water the woman gets and the enlightenment that comes to the blind beggar (9:1–10:21).

The stress on the woman's gender (or the beggar's blindness) might be no more than an attempt to show that even the most unlikely candidate can be endowed with spirit and wisdom and become a source of life in her/himself. But throughout the gospel, the best examples of the "autonomy of the believer" are women. Inspired by some mysterious source of knowledge, the Samaritan woman proselytizes her neighbors without any commission from Jesus (4:29–42). Jesus' mother, ignoring his abrupt response to her plea on behalf of the wedding hosts, prepares the stewards for the miracle (2:4–6). Martha pushes Mary to meet Jesus, claiming that he has summoned her, when (as far as reader can tell) this is not true.

When Mary anoints Jesus, her act apparently foresees and foretells his death and may have messianic overtones. Since the scene implies that he reclines on a dining couch, the author's comment that "the house was filled with the perfume of the ointment" (John 12:3) may evoke Song of Songs 1:12: "When the king was on his couch, my nard gave forth its odor."[28] Thus although she anoints his feet rather than his head, her deed has no penitential overtones, but rather seems to effect the same result as the prophetic acts of Samuel, who anointed Saul and David as king. Male disciples also experience revelations: the beloved disciple intuits the meaning of what he saw in the empty tomb, and Nathanael recognizes Jesus on the basis of Jesus' knowledge about him.[29] But they rarely exemplify the spiritual knowledge exhibited by the women.

Erotic touches in the representations of women in John coexist with ascetic and spiritualist tendencies and anxieties about physicality, particularly the physicality of Jesus, that frequently accompany prophecy. Mary, the sister of Martha, is described as anointing Jesus' feet with pure nard and wiping them with her hair. If the scene is prophetic and messianic, it achieves these effects by casting Mary in the role of the woman lover from Song of Songs 1:12. The scene in which Mary Magdalene seeks the body of Jesus (John 20:1–2, 11–15) may echo the woman of Song of Songs seeking her lover (3:1–3). Martha is singled out as loved by Jesus, then Mary and Lazarus added (11:5). So, too, both Lazarus and the unnamed male disciple are described as "the one whom Jesus loved."

At the same time, ascetic concerns surface in the text. Jesus refuses food for the sake of living off the will of God (4:31–34) and never actually gets the drink he asks from the woman; she leaves her jug behind, and so herself never gets the water she came for (4:7, 29). In the resurrection appearances, Jesus rejects a touch or embrace from Mary (20:17), and although he invites a touch from Thomas, it never actually takes place (20:26–29).[30] The author also notes that Jesus came into the disciples' midst while the doors were closed (20:19, 26). The later appendix may imply that Jesus ate bread and fish (21:13) in order to restrict the implications of scenes in which Jesus refuses a touch from Mary or passes through walls. Luke 24:36–43 depicts Jesus as eating bread and fish to prove that he is not a spirit. Thus it appears that, at least at the earlier stages, this community adopted a ploy that is also found in other spiritualist and prophetic movements, like the New Prophecy, Encratite Christianity, and the Shakers: anxieties about the flesh were contained by relegating eros to the spiritual realm, and ascetic practice enabled the fuller exploitation of eros and a relatively wide realm of participation for women.[31] But the identification of women with flesh and sexuality remained, and ascetic ambitions helped to lay the groundwork for future tensions about women's roles.

Thus the Gospel of John offers powerful pictures of women, apparently enabled by the communal prophetic experience that made every believer a source of spirit and life. What little leadership and structure there was seems to have been charismatic and dynamic in character. This did not exclude conflict over communal roles. It is noteworthy that Mary Magdalene does not appear in the appendix (John 21) with Peter and the beloved disciple, and 21:14, in counting the appearance as the third time Jesus appeared to his disciples, seems to exclude Mary either as a visionary or as a disciple.[32] The verse may reflect less participation in leadership among women in the community in its later years, or the desire to restrict women's participation on the part of the author of the appendix or its audience. This communal prophetic experience offers itself through the persona of Wisdom as food and drink. But within the gospel, the female persona of Wisdom who makes this offer disappears entirely behind the male dyad of father and son: in its prologue, the masculine personification of the Word preempts her. And the powerful figures of women in the gospel are presented in erotic and familial categories. In so far as ascetic and spiritualist tendencies liberated women from these categories, they do so only by limiting them as actors in the world.

Mark

Mark is assigned to a variety of dates ranging from 66 CE to the early 80s CE because the prophecies of Mark 13:1–2, 14–20 appear to have been written after the destruction of the temple in 70 CE or at least long enough after the beginning of the Jewish war that its outcome was predictable. There is some evidence the gospel went through more than one edition; until the middle of the twentieth century, most editions of the Bible published a later appendix as Mark 16:9–20, and in the late second century, Clement of Alexandria knew a longer version of Mark.[33] Tradition long associated the gospel with Peter and the city of Rome. While some scholars continue to regard Rome as the likely place of composition, most are skeptical about this location.[34] Arguments have been made for both Galilee and Syria, but the gospel's provenance remains uncertain.[35]

Only three women disciples are named in the Gospel of Mark. Mary Magdalene, Mary the mother of James and Joses and Salome are named to provide continuous witnesses to the death of Jesus, the burial, and the empty tomb (15: 40–41, 47; 16:1–8). While their major function is thus to show that Jesus actually died, that someone knew where he was buried, and that the tomb found empty was the right one, the role of these women is more indicative of the role of women in Mark's community and more central to the theology of the gospel than might at first appear. Mark 15:41 designates them as "following" Jesus, that is, as disciples, and as "ministering to him," that is, as disciples and heirs of his teaching. These terms, especially "minister" (diakoneō) reflect the terminology used by early Christian communities, and the verse as a whole probably reflects the participation of women in the community of Mark, as well as memories of women in the movement during Jesus' lifetime.[36] At the death scene, the three women are accompanied by many others who had come up with him from Galilee (15:41). While this is the first explicit mention of these women, it implies that women were on the road with Jesus throughout his preaching career. In 3:32, the sisters, as well as the mother and brothers, of Jesus seek him out, and Jesus claims the one who does God's will as brother, sister, and mother; this suggests that the author envisages women amidst the crowds that assemble to hear Jesus and probably among his companions (3:32, 35).

The three named women also play important dramatic and theological roles. The Gospel of Mark is dominated by a focus on the cross. Halfway through the gospel, the prediction of Jesus' death is made a test of true understanding of Jesus' messiahship. When Peter fails this test, a new invitation to discipleship requires that the true follower take up the cross and expect to share Jesus' death (8:34–35). After Judas betrays Jesus, Peter denies him, the others flee, and Jesus dies crying out his abandonment by God. The women remain faithful, and two of them follow his corpse to the burial. The last verse of the gospel, 16:8, describes their flight and their silence about the vision and message committed to them. The flight of the male disciples is sometimes seen as evidence of Mark's desire to discredit the twelve, and the flight of the men and the women's silence can be interpreted as parallel failures that function as warnings to the reader.[37] But this warning hardly exhausts the meaning of the scene in 16:1–8. In Mark, Jesus appears for the last time hanging dead on the cross, and the departure of the women closes the gospel; they are the last figures the reader sees. Their flight and silence may have been intended to leave the first readers and hearers with the conviction that they themselves were the true recipients of the message, obligated to proclaim the gospel of God and "the coming of the son of man" (compare Mark 1:14–15; 13:26; 14:9).

Six unnamed women play roles in the narrative: Peter's mother-in-law (1:29–31), Jairus' daughter and the woman with the flow of blood (5:21–43), the so-called Syro-Phoenician woman (7:24–30), the widow who contributes her whole living to the temple treasury and provides Jesus with the occasion to castigate the scribes (12:41–44) and the woman who anoints Jesus (14:1–11). The narrative also offers two female villains, the daughter of Herod and her mother Herodias, depicted as the catalysts for the death of John the Baptist, as well as one woman bit player, the woman servant of the high priest who questions Peter (14:66–70). While it is clear that the names of the three women at the cross and tomb and of Herodias are given because the author wishes to use their fame as testimony to the veracity of the narrative, it is less clear why no other women's names are given. Does the author wish to respect the Greek view that the names of respectable women should not be unnecessarily made public?[38]

Is it the case that the unnamed women function as primarily typical or representative figures, who invite the readers and hearers to locate themselves within the narrative?

Four of the women appear in miracle stories that are juxtaposed with miracles in which a male figure is central. The first of these stories establishes the importance of the miracles in Mark's apocalyptic history.[39] The healing of Peter's mother-in-law, with an exorcism of a demoniac in the synagogue, constitutes the first day of Jesus' ministry (1:21–39). The spiritual power displayed in the exorcism demonstrates the authority of Jesus' teaching (1:22, 27), and the encounter with the demon reveals his mission: he has come to destroy Satan's reign (1:24). The healing story illustrates the effect of that mission for the audience: "he raised her," and "she served/began to minister" (1:31). Together, the two miracles initiate a flood of spiritual deeds at the end of the sabbath; after spending a night in prayer, Jesus concludes from them that he must go on the road to preach (1:38).

Does gender play any role in the narrative? Claiming that in these stories "Jesus shows his willingness to heal women as well as men" misreads the context; it seems more accurate to suggest that the two miracles show Mark's Jesus his power to heal.[40] Pairing of stories of women and men is a compositional technique present also in Q and highly developed by Luke; it may have originated as a catechetical device for engaging the women among the audience.[41] Another possible function of gender here is found in Davies' claim that the woman's "serving" identifies her as a disciple. This suggestion has been developed by some feminist commentators as a testimony to women's ministry and has been challenged by others who see the word as relegating her to female household tasks.[42] These perceptions are not actually mutually exclusive. The woman's literary function must be considered here: the author uses her gender role as a way to introduce Christian terminology into the career of Jesus and to invite the readers and hearers to place themselves within the narrative at its outset; like her, they have been raised by Jesus and minister to him.

Equally important for Mark's readers is the rather startling story of the "Syro-Phoenician woman," who could be better identified as the Greek woman. While this figure has sometimes been described by feminists as representative of the excluded and marginal, "a triple outsider" by gender, ethnicity, and religious-cultural affiliation,[43] for Mark and the first audience of Mark, this woman is very much an insider. She is first identified as "Greek"; this descriptor is usually taken to mean "Gentile" (not Jewish). She was certainly meant to be Gentile, but Mark's audience would likely have been even more struck by the recognition that she was linguistically and culturally Greek, like themselves, as well as Gentile, probably also like many, if not most, of them. She is identified only secondarily as Syro-Phoenician, that is, from the southern part of Syria known as Syria Phoenicia.[44] If Mark was written in Syria, she would have been a triple insider for the audience, winning her petition from Jesus through her "word" or message as the representative of Mark's community in the text. This story of a woman who wins aid by a smart answer is followed immediately by the healing of a man who is deaf and mute, or rather impaired of speech, and who is enabled to speak rightly (7:31–37). This cure takes place in the largely Gentile area called the Decapolis (7:31). The implication seems to be that the Greek woman's struggle with Jesus signaled a change in the scope of his mission.

Was her gender intended to play a role in the story's impact? Corley has seen the introduction to this story as an instance of Mark's need to confine women to household settings. But a more obvious function of the note that "he went into the house, wishing no one to know"(7:24) is simply to emphasize Jesus' reluctance to be known, the "secrecy" motif and concern with inner and outer circles that characterizes the gospel as a whole. Perhaps this instance of secrecy was intended as a discouragement for Gentile favor seekers and prepared the reader for Jesus' rebuff of the mother. The callousness of Jesus' comment violates Christian perceptions about how Jesus ought to have behaved; discomfort with this picture has caused many commentators to deflect attention from the calculated insult by castigating "Jewish exclusivity." This implication is not foreign to Mark; the woman's demand for access for Gentiles like herself follows Mark's critique of the Pharisees' interpretation of the laws by tradition. But for Mark, the emphasis is on the combination of boldness and humility that enables the woman (and the Gentile community) to wrest what she wants from the reluctant Jesus. The woman's verbal assertiveness violates twentieth century views of ancient expectations of women and, in fact, probably challenged such expectations, but since she speaks on behalf of her daughter, her riposte would have met with the same approval as the sayings of the Spartan women that were popular in antiquity.[45] And it should be noted that the content of the riposte is quite submissive; in fact, Ross Kraemer has suggested that the story may focus on a woman in order to make Jesus' rebuff less offensive to ancient ears.[46] One gendered aspect of the text that deserves attention is that the woman's assertiveness is on behalf of her daughter: she undertakes the obligations of the good mother.[47]

The double miracle account of the daughter of Jairus and the woman with the flow of blood (Mark 5:21–43) has become an important locus for feminist interpretation of the Gospel of Mark, and rightly so. This narrative does have at least an implicit focus on gender and furthermore strikingly displays the character of the miraculous for Mark. But the focus of much feminist interpretation has been problematic.[48] A wide variety of commentators remark on the ritual impurity of the woman with the flow of blood, and some applaud Jesus' willingness to incur impurity, both by suffering her touch and by touching the dead girl.[49] These observations are sometimes made the basis for positioning the stories in a larger picture that posits a special Markan inclusivity, or Mark's rejection of Leviticus' purity regulations, and the other stories about women are then fitted into this picture.[50]

But Mark's narrative shows no interest in purity, and for good reason.[51] The stories are set in Galilee, and the ritual purity that would be lost by touching a corpse or touching a menstruant was required only for participation in the temple in Jerusalem. Since purity was easily reacquired by waiting until sunset and bathing, it was of interest only once the fairly arduous trip to Jerusalem had already been made.[52] In the early part of the gospel Jesus is presented as upholding the temple's authority to recognize the cleansing of leprosy (1:44). This is not to say that purity is of no interest in Mark; Mark 7:1–23 complains about the Pharisaic insistence on washing hands before meals and on pure vessels for food. But it is unsurprising that there is no comment on impurity in 5:21–43. Neither the story of the daughter of Jairus nor that of the woman with the flow of blood shows any controversial elements at all. No opponents call attention to the supposed breach of purity, the miracle effects no refutation of such objections, and no scornful or judgmental authorities are put to shame.[53]

Using Antoinette Clark Wire's category of demand story to analyze these intertwined narratives puts the focus on two quite different and central aspects of the stories themselves and of the miraculous in Mark: the activity or perseverance of the inquirer, characterized by Mark as faith, and the transfer of spiritual power, especially by touch.[54] While Wire developed her categories in the hope of interrogating their function for the original tellers, they are also helpful in reading the miracles of Mark. The demand story's major feature (lacking in Wire's other three categories) is a demand (or request) for healing or help.[55] "The demanding party from the first takes an active part in the struggle and overcomes."[56] Wire sees the key to the demand stories' function in their focus on an obstacle: a rebuke or rebuff from the healer or an intensification of the difficulties of the cure, like a crowd that obstructs access. The teller or narrator invites the hearers to identify with the one making the demand. The story of the woman with the flow of blood Wire describes as the "most remarkable" in this respect, noting that the crowd presents an obstacle to the woman in reaching Jesus and an obstacle to Jesus in recognizing the woman. The crowd and the woman together, by delaying Jesus, intensify the obstacles in Jairus' case. The conjunction of the two stories underlines the perseverance of the woman and, less explicitly, of Jairus. The structures of these two stories illustrate the importance of transfer of power and of touch as its means in striking ways. All healings are to some degree manifestations of power (dynamis) overcoming weakness, and touch is a particularly important (though not the only) means of this transfer.[57]

It is precisely touch and the transfer of power that are foregrounded in the unique features of Mark's narrative of the healing of the woman with the flow of blood. The woman is introduced into the narrative of the daughter of Jairus with a long string of participles that recount the unhappy history of her disease; the first finite verb is "she touched" (5:27). The woman herself prescribes this touch as the means of her healing: "'if I touch even his garments I shall be saved'"(5:28). The success of her prescription is immediate: "and at once the spring of her blood was dried up, and she knew in her body that she was healed" (5:29). This first assurance of the healing is immediately reinforced and explicated by the parallel description of Jesus' reaction: "and immediately Jesus, having recognized in himself the power gone out of him, turned and said, 'who touched me?'"(5:30) Jesus' parting commendation of her faith simply concedes to her what she has already taken from him: the power with which to supply her weakness.[58] Wire notes that "her faith has saved her even without [Jesus'] will."[59] This emphasis on the exchange of power and the special knowledge by which Jesus recognizes it disappears in Matthew's revision. In Matthew, "your faith has healed you" is not an acknowledgment of what has already taken place, but rather the formula of healing; the woman is healed only after Jesus utters these words (9:22).

The Life of Sulla by the second-century writer Plutarch relates an anecdote that sheds some light on this narrative. Valeria Messalla, passing Sulla at the games, drew a thread out of his garment and excused herself with the plea that she sought to share a little of his luck.[60] She was entirely successful in this quest, eventually becoming his fourth wife. Plutarch implies that her touch and apology were a calculated ruse by which she effected an introduction to him. But the anecdote underlines the belief that a touch can transfer power, showing that the woman's prescription for her own healing would be entirely comprehensible to the audience of Mark: as Valeria Messalla's touch could draw out Sulla's luck, the woman's touch can draw out of Jesus the power she seeks and needs. The woman's indirect approach to Jesus does not really need to be explained as "timidity" induced by psychological or social constraints. Mark explains it by the overwhelming crowd, but it functions in the narrative to draw attention to the unique knowledge that Jesus has "in himself," creating the pretext on which he makes known his ability to distinguish the one powerful touch from all the others that press upon him.[61] As in the Gospel of John, early Christian prophecy is reflected in the christology of Mark and in this narrative in particular; the exchange of spiritual power in the miracle, the special knowledge both Jesus and the woman experience, and perhaps even the woman's prediction of her cure reflect the community's prophetic and charismatic experience.[62]

The raising of Jairus' daughter likewise manifests the transfer of the ultimate power, life itself, to overcome the ultimate weakness, death, through the touch of Jesus and the supporting presence of the believing disciples and the parents of the child. One of the most intriguing aspects of this miracle is the ambiguity about whether the child is asleep or dead. A similar ambiguity appears, and in fact is underlined, in a story in which the second century philosopher, Apollonius of Tyana, raises a young girl on the brink of her wedding.[63] This ambiguity serves a variety of functions. In both authors, it offers the occasion to present and disarm natural skepticism about the miraculous. In Mark, it also evokes the Christian language that draws together awakening, resurrection, and baptism (Eph 5:14). And it contributes to the larger function of the miraculous in Mark. Miracles in Mark illustrate the conjunction of power and faith, including those miracles that are illustrations of the power of prayer (9:14–31, 11:20–25).[64] The miracles of the woman with the flow of blood and the seemingly dead girl form the climax of a suite of miracles that begins in 4:35 and leads to the summary in Mark 6:1–6. Often characterized as "Jesus' rejection at Nazareth" (on the basis of Luke 4:16–30), Mark 6:1–6 might better be called "Mark's theory of miracles." The claim that Jesus "could do no miracles there because of their lack of faith" (6:5) underlines what Matt 13:58 carefully obscures: the conviction that miracles require faith. The ambiguity of sleep or death does not detract from but evokes the faith the power invites, requiring the reader to choose as the woman did.

Does gender function in these stories? Is it significant that it is two stories about women that are told together and, in fact, interwoven? For an ancient audience, there may have been an inherent connection, or perhaps symmetry, between the two stories in Mark 5:21–43: the two stories record healings or wonders that cure two opposing dangers to which the female body was understood to be subject. The woman with a twelve-year flow of blood suffers from a womb that is inappropriately open. The twelve-year old girl may well represent the young girl who dies because her womb is closed; at twelve, she is just at the age for marriage in Roman law (and in subsequent rabbinic law).[65] Older medical writers saw young girls at this age as threatened by "hysteria," suffocation by a closed womb, and prescribed marriage, sexual intercourse, and childbearing as the remedy. Soranus, the early second-century physician, describes acute "hysteria" as a disease that was deathlike, but not necessarily mortal.[66] While Soranus does not list virginity as one of the causes of hysterical suffocation or recommend marriage as older sources do, an audience without his scientific outlook might well share his view of hysteria's symptoms as deathlike, but not necessarily fatal, while continuing to believe that unmarried girls are particularly vulnerable to its seizures.

Three other stories deploy central women characters as foils for male characters. The villainous Herodias and her daughter who bring about death of John the Baptist are contrasted with the twelve who take up his fate (6:7–31). The widow who gives all she owns (12:41–44) is contrasted with the scribes who devour the households of widows (12:38–40). Most importantly, the woman who anoints Jesus is contrasted with Jesus' betrayers, the Jewish leaders (14: 1–2) and Judas (14:9–11). In anointing Jesus' head, she acts in the role of Samuel anointing Saul and David; as a prophet, she designates him as the messianic (anointed) king. Jesus' defense of her deed identifies it as a work of mercy (burying the dead), similar to but more urgent than feeding the poor, and so changes her prophetic message of his messiahship into a prophecy of his death. The women who go to the tomb to anoint his body set out to do what the readers know has already been done. Mark adds a prophecy of Jesus' own that is fulfilled for and by the reader, who hears her memorialized in the preaching many years and miles away (14:9).

It would be difficult to argue that Mark's representations of women challenge ancient gender roles. In fact, at least some gender stereotypes contribute to the theological or literary functions of many of these characterizations. The malice of Herodias underlines the probity of the "just and holy man" John (Mark 6: 20), the vulnerability of the widow helps make her generosity a foil to the rapacity of scribes (12:38–44), and the powerlessness of the servant girl points out Peter's cowardice (14:66–70). Not only do stereotypes of femininity play a role in the narrative, the author also appears to be concerned with restricting antifamilial, antipatriarchal aspects of the tradition. Mark 10:1–31 has been structured to exclude the idea that one may divorce one's wife or, probably more importantly, one's husband or abandon small children for the sake of God's reign (in Mark, for the sake of Jesus and the gospel). Mark 10:17–31, the story of the rich man and the private teaching to the disciples that completes it, puts forward the demand that one leave all and follow Jesus (10:21, 28); "all" might be "household or brothers or sisters or mother or father or children or fields" (10:2). Luke's version of the saying mentions a wife among these ties that can be left for the gospel (Luke 18:29, compare Luke 14:26, which requires that disciples hate their family members), and this version is sometimes seen as original.[67] But to prepare for the demands of Mark 10:17–31, the author offers a debate on divorce, which opposes it on the grounds of the monogamous creation (10:2–9), coupled with private teaching for the disciples, which equates divorce and remarriage with adultery (10:10–12). The two scenes are followed by a brief anecdote in which Jesus rebukes the disciples for turning away little children brought by their parents, declaring "of such is God's reign" (Mark 10:13–16).[68]

These passages are sometimes interpreted as part of an egalitarian platform; Mark 10:2–9 has been seen as undoing the right of a man to discard a wife, 10:10–12 has been seen as equalizing the status of wife and husband in regard to adultery, and 10:13–16 has been treated as an endorsement of communal child care.[69] But while divorce was and is often deeply and comprehensively damaging for women, so is and was the inability to obtain a divorce. While it is true that both Jewish and Roman law permitted divorce, proscribing divorce could still have had political and apologetic motivations. In the mid–second century, the early Christian writer Justin described one divorce as the catalyst for a persecution of Christians (2 Apology 2). A woman who had converted to Christianity and objected to her husband's sexual practices divorced him. In retaliation, the husband denounced both the woman and the teacher who had instructed her in Christianity; both were arrested. The teacher was executed and further arrests of Christians followed. From the perspective of the Roman empire, early Christianity was an innovation in religion, in itself a bad thing; worse, it was an innovation in Judaism, an Eastern, barbarian and suspect worship. Communities might well feel the need to show that they were by no means a threat to Roman imperial "family values." The equation of remarriage with adultery (Mark 10:10–12) is particularly suggestive in light of the anxiety about adultery that both produced and was increased by the antiadultery law promulgated by Augustus in 18 BCE.[70] That Mark explicitly considers the case of a woman who divorces a husband as well as of a man who divorces a wife has often been interpreted as a reflection of more "liberal" Roman, rather than Jewish, legal practice. This assessment has been questioned as more evidence emerges that Jewish women in antiquity did, in some cases, initiate divorces.[71] More importantly, it responds to the political reality that a woman divorcing an unbelieving husband is as likely, and in fact more likely, to endanger the community.[72]

Both the shared spiritual power offered in the miracles of Mark and the appearance of women as disciples and ministers presumably reflect experience and practice. Mark's community relied on faith that could move mountains, used Aramaic words remembered as efficacious in Jesus' miracles (5:41, 7:35) as words of spiritual power, and was ministered to and administered by women as well as men. The twelve men described in the gospel as an inner circle within the inner circle exemplify leadership and missionary roles, but their main function, both literarily and theologically, is the conflict between their chosen status and their failures. That the twelve are all men and that women disciples are mentioned only at 15:40–41 undoubtedly reflect the androcentric perspective of the gospel.[73] In the apocalyptic context of Mark, the urgencies of the present tribulation (13:7–8,19), of preaching the gospel (13:10), and of testifying before kings and councils (13:9, 11) could supersede the restrictions of gender; for the most part, men and women appear to have done what the spirit gave them to do as well as to have spoken what the spirit gave them to speak without thinking beforehand (13:11). But it does not seem to have eliminated gender assumptions, and when forethought entered, the author, and perhaps the community, seem to have chosen to defend the gospel as supporting the family, at least by prohibiting the dissolution of marriages and by welcoming small children.

Conclusions

It would be difficult to argue that either Mark or John addresses the issue of gender or foregrounds the participation of women in any coherent or comprehensive way. Neither of the authors or the communities behind them appears to have made the status of women any central focus in their concerns. Nor is it the case that either narrative reflects gender practices that were unheard of or even challenging for their time. What is clear is that these two gospels differ in their representation of women and in the workings of gender in their narratives. They differ from each other, from the rethinkings of Mark by Matthew and Luke, and from later attempts to synthesize the gender arrangements of early Christianity. They give the lie to simplistic claims that Jesus was a campaigner against the gender prescriptions of his time on the one hand and, on the other, that Jesus selected twelve male disciples in order to create an all-male ministry.

John and Mark do seem to accept, indeed to assume, the participation of women in communal life in ways that would cause dissension, become marginalized, and eventually be eliminated and to offer at least some vivid and dynamic representations of women. They have two factors in common that seem to enable this. One is the continued importance of prophetic experience; for both communities, leadership appears to have depended on a call based in spiritual experience rather than on appointment. As in both Judaism and Greco-Roman religions, prophecy in early Christianity was accessible to women as well as men, though not necessarily equally or in all settings. Secondly, in both works, the communal life seems to have been identified with the private and voluntary sphere. In John, ancient models of friendship and familial language provided the terminology for association and leadership. Mark also uses the model of an alternative family for the community and locates special teaching for the disciples within the house. While this does not necessarily mean that the setting directly reflected the practice of house churches, this material addresses the readers and hearers, the real insiders. At this early stage these ways of constructing the community enabled women to transfer socially sanctioned realms of activity and forms of authority to the larger communal setting. But ancient constructions of family and friendship also required control of female sexuality and prophetic traditions were strongly allied to suspicions of the flesh. Thus the very factors that empowered women in these contexts also laid the ground for the tensions that were to come.

NOTES

1. This translation and all translations in the chapter are my own unless otherwise acknowledged.

2. Antoinette Wire, "Gender Roles in a Scribal Community," in *Social History of the Matthean Community: Cross Disciplinary Approaches*, ed. David L. Balch (Minneapolis, MN: Fortress, 1991) 87–121.

3. Ibid. 119–20.

4. Ibid. 111–12, 115.

5. Ibid. 103.

6. Kathleen E. Corley, *Private Women, Public Meals: Social Conflict in the Synoptic Tradition* (Peabody, MA: Hendrikson, 1993).

7. Ibid. 106–7, 178.

8. Ibid. 186.

9. For a discussion of theories of dating and stages of development, see Robert Kysar, "John, The Gospel of," *ABD* 3:918–22.

10. On the possibility of women writers behind anonymous early Jewish and Christian texts, see the exchange between Mary R. Lefkowitz and Ross S. Kraemer in the following: Mary R. Lefkowitz, "Did Ancient Women Write Novels?" in *"Women Like This": New Perspectives on Jewish Women in the Greco-Roman World*, ed. Amy-Jill Levine (Early Judaism and its Literature I, Atlanta, GA: Scholars Press, 1991) 199–219; Ross S. Kraemer, "Women's Authorship of Jewish and Christian Literature in the Greco-Roman Period," in Levine, *"Women Like This"* 221–42.

11. In John 19:35 ("the one who has seen has testified"), the third-person singular masculine participle has traditionally been taken as referring to the author, who is identified as the beloved disciple. More recently, the author is distinguished from the beloved disciple, who is understood to be the real or symbolic mediator of the tradition. It is also possible 19:35 refers to the spirit; 1 John 5:6 identifies the spirit as the one who testifies.

12. See Raymond E. Brown, "Roles of Women in the Gospel of John," *Theological Studies* 36 (1975) 688–99, reprinted in Brown, *The Community of the Beloved Disciple: The Life, Loves and Hates of an Individual Church in New Testament Times* (New York: Paulist, 1979); Elisabeth Schüssler Fiorenza, *In Memory of Her: A Feminist Theological Reconstruction of Christian Origins* (New York: Crossroad, 1983) 323–34.

13. See chapter 5.

14. Ibid.

15. Reported in Eusebius, *Ecclesiastical History* 5.16.17.

16. Bultmann not only rejects the idea that it applies to a real woman, but also questions whether it can apply to a real congregation; *The Johannine Epistles*, trans. R. Philip O'Hara with Lane C. McGaughy and Robert W. Funk. Hermeneia (Philadelphia: Fortress, 1973) 107–8.

17. Ross S. Kraemer, *Her Share of the Blessings: Women's Religions among Pagans, Jews and Christians in the Greco-Roman World* (New York: Oxford University Press, 1992) 176.

18. Pheme Perkins, *The Gnostic Dialogue: The Early Church and the Crisis of Gnosticism* (New York: Paulist, 1980); Ruth Majercik, "Dialogue," *ABD* 2:185–88, esp. 188.

19. John Chrysostom, *Homilies 30–35 on the Gospel of John.*

20. Gail R. O'Day marks this contrast on other grounds; "John," in *The Women's Bible Commentary,* ed. Carol A. Newsom and Sharon H. Ringe (Louisville, KY: Westminster/John Knox, 1992) 295.

21. R. Bultmann, *The Gospel of John: A Commentary,* trans. G. R. Beasley-Murray (Philadelphia: Westminster, 1971) 189, n.3; Raymond E. Brown, *The Gospel According to John, Volume 1.* Anchor Bible Commentary, Volume 29 (New York: Doubleday, 1966) 171.

22. For a reproduction see John Bryan Ward-Perkins and Amanda Claridge. *Pompeii A.D. 79: Essay and Catalogue* (New York: Knopf 1978) 24.

23. Theodor Zahn, cited in Bultmann, *Gospel of John* 189, who rejects this reading. Brown retains the reading without attribution John, vol. 1:176, 177.

24. So also O'Day, "John" 296.

25. Josephus, *Jewish War* 1§63; Josephus, *Antiquities of the Jews* 13§255; worship continued after that date and, like the temple, Mount Gerizim was also defended against the Romans in 70 CE, with colossal Samaritan losses (Josephus, *Jewish War* 3.7.32).

26. Brown, *Community* 188–89.

27. On the Jewishness of Martha and Mary in John, see esp. Adele Reinhartz, "From Narrative to History: The Resurrection of Mary and Martha," in Levine, *"Women Like This"* 161–184; Reinhartz, "The Gospel of John" in Elisabeth Schüssler Fiorenza, *Searching the Scriptures: Volume 2, A Feminist Commentary* (New York: Crossroad, 1994) 580–82.

28. It also provides a contrast to 11:39.

29. Even this is not clearly prophetic; it may only mean that he believes Mary's pronouncement.

30. Mary Rose D'Angelo, "A Critical Note: John 20:17 and Apocalypse of Moses 31," *JTS* n. s. 41 (1990) 529–36.

31. Rosemary R. Ruether, *Sexism and God-Talk: Toward a Feminist Theology* (Boston: Beacon, 1983) 130–38.

32. Claudia Setzer, "Excellent Women: Female Witness to the Resurrection" *JBL* 116 (1997) 259–72; Setzer seems to attribute the appendix to the author of the gospel (268). It is also possible that the verse refers to the group appearances only, or that the number reflects an older, unrecoverable source of appearances in Galilee.

33. Helmut Koester, *Ancient Christian Gospels* (Philadelphia: Trinity Press International, 1990) 276–303.

34. Ibid. 274–76.

35. See Koester, *Ancient Christian Gospels* 289–91.

36. See chapter 5.

37. Elisabeth Struthers Malbon, "Fallible Followers: Women and Men in the Gospel of Mark," *Semeia* 28 (1983) 29–48.

38. Plutarch (*The Bravery of Women, Moral Essays* 242E-F) attributes this view to Thucydides, contrasting it with a less stringent opinion on the part of Gorgias and setting the stage for the Roman custom of eulogizing women, as well as men, at least after death.

39. This description of the genre is that of Adela Yarbro Collins, *The Beginning of the Gospel: Probings of Mark in Context* (Minneapolis, MN: Fortress, 1991) 29–48.

40. Corley, *Private Women* 87.

41. Mary Rose D'Angelo, "Women in Luke-Acts: A Redactional View," *JBL* 109/3 (1990) 447–48.

42. W. D. Davies, *The Setting of the Sermon on the Mount* (Cambridge: Cambridge University Press, 1966) 422–23; Corley, *Private Women* 87.

43. Elisabeth Schüssler Fiorenza, *But She Said: Feminist Practices of Biblical Interpretation* (Boston: Beacon, 1992) 12.

44. Septimius Severus eventually made it an independent province.

45. (Pseudo?-) Plutarch, *Sayings of the Spartan Women, Moralia* 240C–42D.

46. Kraemer, *Her Share of the Blessings* 133.

47. See Suzanne Dixon, *The Roman Mother* (Norman, OK: University of Oklahoma Press, 1988) 210–32.

48. For the fuller discussion on which this is based, see Mary Rose D'Angelo, "Gender and Power in the Gospel of Mark: The Daughter of Jairus and the Woman with the Flow of Blood" in *Aspects of the Miraculous in Ancient Judaism and Christianity*, ed. John C. Cavadini (Notre Dame, IN: University of Notre Dame Press, forthcoming). See also chapter 3.

49. E.g., Daniel Harrington, "The Gospel According to Mark," *New Jerome Biblical Commentary*, 41:36, ed. Raymond E. Brown, J. Fitzmyer, and R. Murphy (Englewood Cliffs, NJ: Prentice-Hall, 1988) 608.

50. See Johanna Dewey, "The Gospel of Mark" in Schüssler Fiorenza, *Searching the Scriptures* 483; Marla J. Selvidge, *Woman, Cult and Miracle Recital: A Redactional Critical Investigation on Mark 5:24–34* (Lewisburg, PA: Bucknell University Press, 1990) 83. See also Selvidge, "Mark 5:25–34 and Leviticus 15:19–20: A Reaction to Restrictive Purity Regulations," *JBL* 103 (1984) 619–623; Selvidge's material is reused in a Japanese feminist reading of Mark that seeks to challenge purity restrictions in Japanese religions and popular culture: Hisako Kinukawa, *Women and Jesus in Mark* (Maryknoll, NY: Orbis, 1994).

51. See chapter 3.

52. D'Angelo, "Gender and Power"; Amy-Jill Levine, "Discharging Responsibility: Matthean Jesus, Biblical Law and Hemorrhaging Women," in *Treasures New and Old: New Essays in Matthean Studies*, ed. Mark Allan Powell and David Bauer (Atlanta, GA: Scholars Press, 1996) 388.

53. Johanna Dewey, "Jesus' Healings of Women: Conformity and Non-Conformity to Dominant Cultural Values as Historical Reconstruction," *SBL Seminar Papers* (1993) 187–88.

54. Antoinette Wire, "The Gospel Miracle Stories and Their Tellers," *Semeia* 11 (1978) 83–113.

55. Ibid. 99–108 for the full description of demand stories.

56. Ibid. 100.

57. Gerd Theissen, *The Miracle Stories of the Early Christian Tradition*, trans. Francis McDonagh (Philadelphia: Fortress, 1983) 90–93.

58. See also John Donahue, "Though the story reflects popular belief in the physical power of holy people [cf. Acts 5:15; 19:11–12], the final words of Jesus shift the emphasis to the faith of the woman" in "Mark," *Harper's Bible Commentary*, ed. James L. Mays (San Francisco: Harper & Row, 1988) 991.

59. Wire, "Gospel Miracle Stories" 102.

60. Plutarch, *Sulla* 35.

61. Theissen infers from this anecdote that a woman's touch could have been seen as dangerous and hostile and attributes both Valeria Messalla's excuse and the "timidity" of the woman in Mark to this fear (*Miracle Stories* 134).

62. See also Mary Rose D'Angelo, "Theology in Mark and Q: *Abba* and 'Father' in Context," *HTR* 85 (1992) 156–62.

63. Philostratus, *Life of Apollonius of Tyana* 4.45

64. Sharyn Echols Dowd, *Prayer, Power, and the Problem of Suffering: Mark* 11:22–25 *in the Context of Markan Theology* (Atlanta, GA: Scholars Press, 1988); Collins, *Beginning of the Gospel* 58–72.

65. For a fuller treatment, see D'Angelo, "Gender and Power."

66. Soranus, *Gynecology* 3.26; trans. Owsei Temkin, *Soranus' Gynecology* (Baltimore, MD: Johns Hopkins, 1956) 149.

67. See Gerd Theissen, *Sociology of Early Palestinian Christianity* (Philadelphia: Fortress, 1978) 11.

68. For a more extensive presentation of this argument, see Mary Rose D'Angelo, "Remarriage and the Divorce Sayings Attributed to Jesus," in *Divorce and Remarriage: Religious and Psychological Perspectives*, ed. William P. Roberts (Kansas City, MO: Sheed and Ward, 1990) 78–106, esp. 94–95.

69. Johanna Dewey "The Gospel of Mark" 491; E. Schüssler Fiorenza (*In Memory of Her* 143, 149) credits these ideas to a pre-Markan tradition.

70. *Lex Iulia de adulteriis coercendis*; see discussion in Susan Treggiari, *Roman Marriage: Iusti Coniuges from the Time of Cicero to the time of Ulpian* (Oxford: Oxford University Press, 1991) 277–98, esp. 294.

71. See chapter 3.

72. D'Angelo, "Remarriage and the Divorce Sayings" 99.

73. So Dewey, "Gospel of Mark" 506–8.

7

WOMEN IN THE Q COMMUNIT(IES) AND TRADITIONS

Amy-Jill Levine

As the parentheses in the title suggest, any discussion of Q must be qualified, queried, and questioned. Indeed, to discuss women in the Q communit(ies) and traditions requires several leaps of faith: Q is a hypothetical source, divided into hypothetical literary strata representing equally hypothetical social settings; efforts to reconstruct women's history are hampered by Q's androcentric language, the difficulties of moving from single examples to collective experience, and the frequent silence of the source regarding explicit mention of women.[1] At each step, be the subject "Q" or "women," there is debate over interpretation and emphasis. Surely all this is folly, if not scandal (cf. 1 Cor 1: 23). Nevertheless, "folly" and "scandal" once accompanied women's studies as they made their way into the academy, and from that uneasy birth has come productive, if not necessarily unified, life.

The same holds for research on women in the Q communit(ies). Q's recollection of Sophia traditions, depictions of women in parables, pairing of female and male characters, and reflections on the dismantling of the traditional family portend much for the historian. In Q, women's work is acknowledged (e.g., the parable of the leaven, Matt 13:33//Luke 13:20–21; the reference to women grinding at the mill, Matt 10:41//Luke 17:36), and social divisions are broken down (e.g., the elevation of the humble and the humiliation of the exalted, Matt 23:12 //Luke 8:14). Q thus becomes for many scholars the prime evidence for a Jesus movement that, at its core, was antipatriarchal in both its sociological makeup and its theological focus.[2] For some, Q offers "striking evidence that the sayings source is deliberately addressing women."[3] According to Burton Mack, Q attests a movement whose ethos was "to explore human community based on fictive kinship without regard to standard taboos against association based on class, status, gender, or ethnicity."[4] Alicia Batten attempts to "show how through its language, pairing of men's and women's activities, and testimony to a radical lifestyle entailing the division of families, the sayings source Q provides glimpses of a group of people who offered a more inclusive environment for women."[5] Elisabeth Schüssler Fiorenza finds that:

> Some of the earliest traditions of the Jesus movement understood the mission of Jesus as that of a prophet of Sophia sent to proclaim that the Sophia-G*d of Jesus is the G*d of the poor, the outcasts, and all those suffering from injustice. It is likely that these early Jesus traditions interpreted the Galilean mission of Jesus as that of Divine Sophia because Jesus of Nazareth understood himself as the messenger and child of Sophia.[6]

There is no doubt that women were among the groups that preserved the Q traditions; problems arise, however, both in locating how those women were perceived by the editors responsible for the Q collections, and, even more, in how those women may have perceived their own roles. Depending on the presuppositions, method, and focus of the historical analysis, women in the Q communit(ies) have been located at points ranging from egalitarian participation in a movement catalyzed by the invitation of the Sophia-Christ to an acknowledged but secondary status in a group reflecting and reinforcing gender-based hierarchies.

In terms of presuppositions, the first leap of faith concerns the existence of Q itself since antiquity preserved no such text. Q is a reconstruction based on materials found in the Gospels of Matthew and Luke, but absent from Mark. These first three canonical gospels are usually called the "synoptics" in that they "see together": they repeat a great deal of material, often in the same order and with the same wording. In certain cases, however, Mark and Matthew agree with each other against Luke; in other cases, Mark and Luke agree against Matthew. In still other cases, Matthew and Luke recount sayings and events missing from Mark. To explain these phenomena, some sort of literary relationship among the three needs to be posited. The original suggestion of St. Augustine (ca. 400)—that the order of composition mirrored canonical order, with Mark using Matthew, and Luke using both—does not account for the disagreements among the three in wording and order. Over a millennium later, under the influence of the Enlightenment, a new model was promulgated. Johann J. Griesbach (1745–1812) and his scholarly heirs proposed that Matthew's gospel was written first, that Luke relied on the text of Matthew and supplemented it with independent traditions, and that the Gospel of Mark is a conflation of Matthew and Luke. In this scenario, Q is absent.[7]

Greisbach's theory did not satisfy all those seeking a solution to the synoptic problem. It does not explain Mark's omission of the infancy and resurrection narratives or teaching material such as the "Lord's Prayer"; it cannot clarify why Mark, if an epitome of Matthew and Luke, actually tells longer stories; it fails to account for the higher christologies, and the smoother grammar and syntax of Matthew and Luke, etc. Thus, an alternative to Griesbach was needed. In 1838,

Hermann Christian Weisse developed what has become, today, the more popular solution to the synoptic problem. Weisse argued that Mark was the first written, and that this gospel was used independently by the authors of Matthew and Luke because they change the same texts in different ways. Yet Weisse needed to address the materials shared only by Matthew and Luke; these include such well-known passages as the three temptations (Matt 4:1–11//Luke 4:1–13); the Beatitudes (Matt. 5:3–12//Luke 6:20b-23); the "Lord's Prayer" (Matt 6:7–15// Luke 11:1–4), and the "Golden Rule" (Matt 7:12//Luke 6:31). He proposed the existence of a second "source"; the word for "source" in German is *Quelle*, and the initial "Q" became the means of identifying this lost-but-now-found text.[8]

Q material is conventionally listed according to its placement in Luke's gospel (for the convenience of the reader, this chapter lists examples under discussion by both the Matthean and Lukan references). In general, it consists of between 200 and 235 verses, which include (Luke) 3:7–9, 16b-17; 4:1–13; 6:20b-23, 27–49; 7:1–10, 18–28, 31–35; 9:57–60; 10:2–16, 21–24; 11:2–4, 9–26, 29–35, 39b-52; 12:2–12, 22–31, 33–34, 39–46, 49–59; 13:18–21, 24–30, 34–35; 14:11, 16–24, 26–27, 34–35; 15:4–7; 16:13, 16–18; 17:1–4, 6, 23–30, 34–37; 18:14b; 19:12–26; 22:28–30. These verses reveal the influences of wisdom literature (e.g., the analogy of the faithful individual to a house built on rock, Matt 7:24–27//Luke 6:47–49) and an interest in the figure of Wisdom herself (Greek: *Sophia*; e.g., Matt 11:7–19//Luke 7:24–35), of apocalyptic thinking (e.g., the separation between those who will dine with the patriarchs and those who will be cast out, Matt 8:11–12//Luke 7:28–29; warnings of divisions within households, Matt 10:34–36//Luke 12:51–53), and of the role of John the Baptist (e.g., his preaching, Matt 3:7–10, 11–12 //Luke 3:7–9, 16–17, and his question from prison, Matt 11:2–6//Luke 7:18–23).

This list can only be an approximation of what originally stood in Q. While general themes are easily located, the precise content remains debated. Matthew and Luke each adapted Markan material by supplementing (e.g., the birth and resurrection narratives), condensing (e.g., Mark's twenty-verse account of the Gerasene demoniac [5:1–20] becomes in Luke fourteen verses [Luke 8:26–39] and in Matthew, seven [Matt 8:28–34]), and omitting (e.g., both Matthew and Luke omit Mark's comment that the temple should be called a house of prayer "for all the nations" [Mark 11:17]; this may be because Matthew and Luke, unlike Mark, wrote after the destruction of the Jerusalem Temple in 70 CE). Just as Matthew and Luke differ in their presentation of Marcan material, so they offer distinct versions of Q. Who is blessed: "you poor" (Luke 6:20) or "the poor in spirit "(Matt 5:3)? What are forgiven: sins (Luke 11:4) or debts (Matt 6:12)? Matthew and Luke likely adapted Q to fit the needs of their followers. Alternatively, they may have used different versions of Mark and Q. The question of content has specific bearing on the reconstruction of women in the Q communit(ies). According to Luke 14:26, Q encourages its followers to hate their wives along with the rest of their (biological or legal) family; thus, Q in this version would be fully androcentric in address. Yet the Matthean version, 10:

37, does not mention hating one's wife and therefore may be seen as directly relevant to both men *and women* (Matt 10:37).

Compounding the difficulties in reconstructing Q is the probability that some material is preserved only in one gospel; on occasion, Matthew, but not Luke, records Marcan details; on other occasions, Luke, but not Matthew, preserves the Marcan account. Most likely, neither Luke nor Matthew repeated all the materials found in their copies of Q, either verbatim or in order. For example, the parable of the lost coin, found only in Luke 15:8–10, may be a Q saying originally paired with the parable of the lost sheep (Matt 18:12–14//Luke 15:1–7). If original to Q, the parable may attest to the community's recognition of women as independent householders: they are domestically situated, but they control their own monies. Then again, the example may not indicate the presence of such women in the communities any more than the parable of the lost sheep need indicate the presence of shepherds.

The placement of sayings presents a corollary problem: Q material is distributed throughout Matthew and Luke's gospels: in what order did the sayings first appear? Did the order or context signal specific nuances of interpretation? Increasingly confusing the situation: was Q, as a written document, originally transmitted in Aramaic (possible, although unlikely) or in Greek?[9] Thus, from the leap toward the existence of Q, we must move to a second leap, to the exact contents, wording, order, and even original language of the document.

The third leap concerns Q's date and compositional history. This approach, in turn, holds substantial implications both for the reconstructions of the communities responsible for collating and preserving Q materials and, in particular, for the role of women in these communities.

The attempt to locate literary strata and attendant sociological settings in Q frequently begins with the observation that the material has little christological development. That is, Q emphasizes instructions for its readers rather than Jesus' mighty works (the one miracle account is the healing of the centurion's boy, Matt 8:5–11//Luke 7:1–10), has (apparently) no interest in the passion and resurrection, and little to say on the divinity of Jesus. This relative lack of emphasis on Jesus himself, coupled with the early dating of the sayings collection—it must pre-date Matthew and Luke, and it may predate Mark, who does not use it—has led a number of scholars to conclude that Q may be the best source for locating the concerns of the earliest Jesus movement, if not of Jesus himself.[10] If we can determine what Q looked like, then perhaps, so these scholars suggest, we can learn through our reconstructed source something about the original community and maybe its founder. Given this possibility, analysis of Q becomes more than an intellectual exercise concerning a hypothetical text; it becomes the window to Jesus.

There are, at present, several models of the strata underlying the composition of Q; of these, two appear to present the most plausible scenarios. The first model, associated with the International Q Project of the Institute for Antiquity and Christianity (Claremont, CA), generally views Q as a scribal document, composed in stages, and originating in the lower Galilee among non-elites.[11]

The first stratum, according to this thesis, reflects the interests of individuals who sought not "to transform the world" but to provide a counter to reigning cultural values.[12] In his detailed rhetorical analysis of Q, John Kloppenborg posits that the first literary stratum is marked by a substantial use of imperatives, rhetorical questions, and programmatic statements that resemble the Wisdom materials of Near Eastern and Jewish traditions such as Sirach and Proverbs.[13] This collection of wisdom sayings proclaimed a countercultural and even subversive ethos: don't worry where your next meal is coming from or what you should wear; rest assured that the Deity regards equally both the sinner and the pious (Matt 6:25–34//Luke 12:22–32); "love your enemies" (Matt 5:43–48//Luke 6:27–28, 32–36). As Kloppenborg puts it:

> The intensified wisdom of Q . . . not only disorients the hearer with respect to ordinary existence (e.g., with sayings such as [Q] 9:57–58, 59–60; 12:33–34; 14:26, 27; 16:13; 17:33), but it also reorients toward the new reality of the kingdom (6:20b) and God (6:35, 36; 11:9–13; 12:4–7, 22–31, 33–34). This new reality is radical indeed. Q exhorts its followers to reverse or reject the very systems that make society work: the borrowing and lending of capital, appropriate treatment of the dead, responsible self-provision, self-defense and honor of parents.[14]

Q1 in this reconstruction offers a model of permanent liminality, of an uneasy and critically distant relation to society. For those who would locate Jesus himself within this formulation, the emergent picture is of a wandering teacher and gadfly, much like the Cynics; who, in the words of one popular article on Q, is "a Jesus for the America of the third millennium, a Jesus with little supernatural baggage but much respect for cultural diversity."[15]

Subversive ethics are a challenge to the status quo, and Q's exhortations are, according to this model, no exception. When the countercultural message was rejected, then is set "a man against his father, and a daughter against her mother, and a daughter-in-law against her mother-in-law" (Matt 10:35; cf. Luke 12:53). Thus, Q's message changes from invitation to condemnation and from subversive wisdom to dualistic apocalyptic motifs and forms of ethical exhortations more comparable to Greek non-Jewish sources even as its sociological emphasis shifts from itinerants to a more settled community of householders in greater contact with Gentiles. It is in this second stratum of Q that the materials concerning women are found.

The Jesus implied by this reconstruction is historically problematic: noneschatological and nondualistic, more sage than prophet; more Cynic than Jew involved with Torah and Israel. Equally problematic is the division between wisdom and apocalyptic: as the traditions of Enoch, Daniel, Ezra, and Baruch indicate, to be a sage and a prophet, to offer instruction, and to issue apocalyptic judgment are not mutually exclusive categories. Complicating this discussion are the problematics of determining the system to which Q provides an alternative. Q may well encourage a countercultural ethos, but such a reconstruction of Q's motivations and social location are hampered by the lack of sources for reconstructing life among non-elite Jews in late second-temple Galilee and Judea. Moreover, the polemics of Q at best offer a caricature of the dominant systems. Finally, even the christological beliefs of the Q people cannot be securely determined; as Dale Allison points out: "Surely the failure of Jesus in Q to call himself 'Christ' is a feature of the Jesus tradition in general, not some telling fact about the Q people in particular."[16]

Allison—who originally thought to offer a critique of the theories of the composition of Q—has contributed his own model.[17] Utilizing a composition-history schema of chiastic structures, matching themes, and order as presented by Luke, Allison divides Q into five sections with concomitant sociological backgrounds. Q 3:7–7:35, the preaching of John the Baptist, the temptations, the Sermon on the Plain, the centurion's servant, and the comparison of John and Jesus comprise a first section; the audience appears to be settled and general rather than itinerant and specialized. The second section, Q 9:57–11:13, presents the call stories, missionary instructions, eschatological revelation, the "Lord's Prayer," and teaching on seeking and finding. The materials address a select group: wandering preachers. Section three, Q 11:14–52, offers controversy narratives (Beelzebul, the unclean spirit, the sign of Jonah, light, and the woes against the Pharisees). Here, there is nothing directed to itinerants; rather, like the first section, this third unit presupposes a group already estranged from, if not rejected by, those to whom the message was originally preached. The two units of section four, Q 12:2–12, 22–32, provide consolation for the missionaries and so match the concerns of the second section: the lilies of the field and the birds of the air can only be models for those who forsake their regular work.[18] Finally, Q 12:33–22:30 is a conglomeration of hortatory materials addressing such matters as the delay of the *Parousia* (Jesus' return), the need for reconciliation, the dangers of familial connections, and the final judgment. The audience implied is not that of itinerant radicals, but members of a settled group. According to this model, Q1 (Q 9:57–11:13, 12:2–12, 22–32), addressed to missionaries, is updated by Q2 (Q 12:33–22:30) to include the broader community. The remaining materials, sections one and three, were added at yet a third stage and so comprise Q3. It is in this material that christological concerns become of interest, apologetic interest in the Scriptures emerges, and eschatological concerns are heightened.

Arguments about Q's redactional strata have been critiqued, refined, supported, and even dismissed, yet rarely do either the advocates or the detractors of the thesis comment on women's representations.[19] Nor have many feminist scholars been drawn into the arguments concerning the Q strata. Some ignore the suggestions of strata, and others express their doubts and use them anyway.[20] Nevertheless, the location of references to women—a location that remains consistent in the models proffered by both Kloppenborg and Allison—may hold substantial implications for how the compilers of Q regarded the women within their midst. In both reconstructions, women appear explicitly only in the stages reflecting a settled, noniterant worldview.

Recognition of strata within Q material provides some means of locating the women of the Q communit(ies) in sociological perspective. The shifts in genre, terms, and themes variously located by both Kloppenborg and Allison indicate a transition to an increasingly routinized, institutional community. In the latter stages of Q, the majority of the group members appear to be members of a settled, fictive kinship group.

If the location of Q is the relatively small area of lower Galilee, it is unlikely the Q missionaries traveled without some secure base.[21] Thus, even if the original message of Q addresses wandering missionaries, some settled support system can plausibly be presupposed. Within missionary materials, some domestic support may be seen in Matt 10:11–13//Luke 10: 5–7, "Whatever house you enter, first say 'Peace be to this house!' And if a son of peace is there, your peace shall rest on him; but if not, it shall return to you" (Luke's version). Household bases are also indicated by other Q sayings which imply a less mobile, more settled audience. For example, comments on the division that will arise over the new message are located within the household: the domain of "father against son . . . and daughter-in-law against mother-in-law" (Matt 10:35–36//Luke 12:51–53, see also Matt 10:27//Luke 12:3; Matt 24:45//Luke 12:42).[22] For those inclined to see strata within Q, the emphasis on the settled community marks a second or third layer. In this stratum, women's representations are found, and these representations recognize, even as they reinforce, traditional gender roles.

The move from literary representation to the social setting is particularly difficult for women's history. Secondary sources concerned with women in the early Jesus movement often present extensive discussions of women's social roles in antiquity—constructed from Philo or Sirach, Diogenes Laertius or Plutarch, or even according to contemporary Mediterranean practices—over which Q is mapped.[23] Ironically, the better of such surveys conclude correctly that it is impossible to suggest more than generalizations about women's lives in antiquity. Lacking are clear data on the class of people Q addresses, by whom Q was preserved, and on the social roles of Jewish women in late second temple Galilee or Judea.

Consequently, studies must turn to Q's rhetoric (how Q speaks), contents (what Q says), and composition history (where Q notices women). Throughout, scholars must remain cognizant that the presence of women can be buried beneath androcentric language and plural references. Many Q sayings, for example, are applicable to men and women alike: both mourn, both may be anxious about food and clothes. Such contents are replete with egalitarian potential. Yet, the descriptive language is masculine: according to Matt 6:45a//Luke 6:35c, the desired goal is to become "sons" (huoi) of the Most High, not "children" (tekna); in Matt 10:24–25//Luke 6:40, the model is master and disciple (both masculine singular); Matt 7:21–27//Luke 6:46–49 offers the example of the construction worker, an occupation associated with men.[24] The instructional sayings of Q do not address women directly, but even given this observation, women likely responded apart from any direct call, just as they have to other androcentric voices of liberation, from Amos to Gandhi.[25]

Women may be seen as included, in the eyes of the Q people, within these androcentric sayings, just as today women may choose to see themselves, and may be seen as, included in terms like "mankind." Alternatively, members of the Q community may have found the idea of such gender-based egalitarianism and inclusivity at best surprising. The effort to locate women in the Q group necessarily involves a combination of textual archaeology, hermeneutical imagination, and attention to sayings that have implications for, if not references to, women's lives.

In Kloppenborg's scenario, where Q1 addresses the poor (Luke's version of the first beatitude) and those on the margins of society, Q's relevance to women, who are usually the poorest of the poor and the most marginal of the marginalized, is increased. The itinerant radicals commissioned by Q can be seen as including, if not epitomized by, women; the Q community, set according to some reconstructions in a social context of desperate poverty, is then described as consisting of the "poor, children, and women whose liberating praxis seeks to extend itself to the whole nation."[26]

Deriving women's sociological roles from general references to itinerants, the poor, or the family is itself a plausible, although problematic, move. The problems arise from Q's lack of clarity regarding both the economic conditions of those to whom it is addressed and the distinction it draws between itinerants and householders.

Several Q pronouncements exhort a complete reorientation away from the stable environments of family and home. One is to forego ties to the biological family (Matt 10:37//Luke 14:26), and even to avoid returning home to bury a parent (Matt 8:21–22//Luke 9:59–60). Followers are to take nothing on the road: no sandals, no bag, no food. Resembling that of wandering Cynics, their (self-)impoverishment is more extreme. It is certainly possible that, in the Q community, women were among the itinerants. In antiquity, women traveled for various reasons:[27] trade, pilgrimages, visiting relatives, even engaging in political protest. Women likely followed Jesus from the Galilee to Judea.

Yet Q does not make women's itinerancy explicit. "Women are never acknowledged as independently operative outside of the home—the queen of the South (Q 11:31) being the exception that proves the rule."[28] Further, Mark and Paul do not themselves attest female "itinerant messengers." The women who accompany Jesus are not seen as independent of him, and the women of Romans 16 may be Jews displaced by Claudius' Edict of Expulsion (49 CE). To be on the road is not necessarily to be an "itinerant prophet." Women may have engaged in itinerant missionary work, or they may have remained among those who supported the missionaries (cf. Luke's Mary and Martha).[29]

Women as well as men who remain domiciled would function in the secondary role of helper rather than the primary role as missionary. But even in this reconstruction, such women anchored to traditional domestic roles—whether part of the "Q community" or simply individuals behind the door at which a prophet knocked—go unacknowledged by Q rhetoric. To the contrary, Q men and, especially, the heavenly Father are the principal hosts. It is the Deity who supplies the "daily bread" (Matt 6:11//Luke 11:3), the father who provides egg, fish, and bread (Matt 7:7–11//Luke 11:9–13). As for women itinerants: again, Q offers no clear evidence.

Some feminists have appropriately noted the possible biases of such a reconstruction. The two-tiered model of itinerants and householders is, according to Luise Schottroff, tainted by an androcentric scholarly bias that incorrectly locates "love patriarchalism"—the view that while "in Christ" all are equal, social hier-archies remain in place—at the core of Q; simultaneously, it fails to acknowledge Q's dismantling of oppressive domestic systems in favor of "a new society in the name of Jesus [that is] nonhierarchical, nonpatriarchal."[30] Consequently, those scholars, including feminists, who argue for the possibility of such a gender-based division of roles, who question women's presence in Q's direct address, or who see the economic situation underlying Q as more complex offer a model that has been labeled "not subjected to rigorous questioning."[31] Schottroff argues that neither the model of "itinerant radicals," in which "individual middle-class men leave their families to follow Jesus" and "survive because patriarchal households continue to function within the Christian community," or the model of the "soldier" in which the call into discipleship replaces the family with a superior patriarchal system, "challenges the patriarchal structure of Christian communities or churches, or of society."[32] Appropriately, Schottroff's discussion is located under the subheading "Feminist Reflection on the History of Interpre-tation," and within this frame of discourse, she is correct. It is difficult, however, to take the next step and argue that Q itself must have challenged such patriar-chal structures along gender lines. Indeed, contrary to her claim, most argu-ments concerning women's location within the Q groups are subject to rigorous questioning. Debates emerge when the theological point is equated with histori-cal reconstruction and when this single feminist interpretation is taken to be the only feminist reading.

If Q1 addresses those who are not at the bottom of the socioeconomic scale, those who *choose* a liminal status, those who actually have a "purse, bag, and sandals" to give up, then Q's evidence concerning women needs some recon-figuration. If "it is less that the marginals of society comprise the Q community than that the Q community creates marginals,"[33] women in the Q communi-t(ies), like their male friends and family members, may have been negatively, rather than positively, affected by their affiliation with the Jesus movement. Moreover, the association of women and severe poverty, while cross-culturally indicated, itself risks masking (at least some) women of means who were at-tracted to the Jesus movement. None of this denies that impoverished women were called to the Jesus movement; it simply observes that Q does not take notice of them.

According to Schottroff, the women may have had little choice other than to become itinerants: the breakup of the patriarchal family (so Q 12:51–53 [Matt 10:34–36]) would have rendered them homeless and without support. Schot-troff also locates evidence of such women missionaries in Mark 15:40 and Ro-mans 16.[34]

Matt 10:34–36//Luke 12:51–53 does indicate household dissension, but di-vision need not lead to women's impoverishment, displacement from the home, and subsequent itinerant radicalism.[35] The instructions to provide missionaries with support indicates that at least some within Q's purview had sufficient means (cf. Matt 6:24//Luke16:13): "You cannot serve God and mammon" has no relevance to those lacking money (mammon) in the first place. Exhortation to leave a purse implies there is a purse to leave. As for women in the household, discord could be generated if they welcomed missionaries, preached a counter-cultural ethos, or refused to respect their generational roles. Enmity easily exists under a single roof or in a shared courtyard.

To forego family ties, particularly in a culture where the extended family is the primary social unit, would cause reaction ranging from surprise to revulsion. Yet Q, like many texts reflecting sectarian, reforming, revitalizing, or renewal movements (e.g., the Dead Sea Scrolls), insists that the biological family is not the locus of self-identity or loyalty; rather, these values are found in the fictive kinship group. Q's rhetoric is as extreme as the demand: "Let the dead bury their own dead, but as for you, go and proclaim the basileia of God" (Matt 8: 22 //Luke 9:60); "Whoever comes to me and does not hate father and mother, wife and children, brothers and sisters, yes, and even life itself, cannot be my disciple" (Matt 10:37//Luke 14:26). Luke likely has added "wife" to the list, although it is possible that Matthew omitted it.[36]

Given such exhortations, it follows that, within the household, the family "will be divided, father against son, and son against father, mother against daughter and daughter against mother, mother-in-law against daughter-in-law and daughter-in-law against mother-in-law" (Luke 12:51–53; in Matt 10:34–36, the younger members separate from their elders, but not vice versa). Consistent with Matt 8:22 //Luke 9:60, as well as with Mic 7:6 (cf. Jub 23:19; SibOr 8:84; Mark 13:12), the emphasis here is on intergenerational conflict; this is a standard eschatological motif.[37] Nor is the presence of women surprising: Micah already noted that "the daughter rises up against her mother, the daughter-in-law against her mother-in-law." Also consistent throughout these sayings is the presupposition of the patrilocal family. The system that is disrupted is one based on the power of the father over the household and of the older generation over the younger. While such division may be interpreted as "freeing" the younger generation "from the direct control and domination of their fathers,"[38] it can also be read as "disinheriting" the younger by the elder or removing the support of the elder by the younger. Whether the lines are read positively or negatively, however, they do not address gender roles. As Batten observes, correctly, "Nowhere does patriarchy [here referring to gender roles] appear to be an explicit issue."[39]

Q's depictions of stable households are similarly dismissive of the biological family. Luke's text, 17:27, notes that "they were eating and drinking, and [the men] marrying and [the women] being given in marriage, until the day Noah entered the ark, and the flood came and destroyed all of them" (Matt 24:28, using only the active form of "to marry," obscures the parallel between the man who marries and the woman who is given in marriage). In both Lucan and Matthean versions, there is necessary concern for women: men cannot, in this culture, marry without one. Yet the logion is androcentric: the woman is the object of the man's action, although independent women such as widows, emancipated daughters, and divorcees could conceivably give themselves in marriage.[40]

Schottroff suggests that Matt 24:28//Luke 17:27 locates the offense of Noah's generation in "the persistence of an intact patriarchal household." It is this "rigid arrangement" that "ought to have been shattered by Jesus' message, had it been heard."[41] The ethos of Q does consistently attempt to undermine conventional behavior, but the direction of that undermining need not be on the "patriarchal household" per se. What may be perceived as a critique of patriarchal domestic arrangements may not have been intended or originally interpreted in this manner.

Arland Jacobson's observations are pertinent:

> It seems clear that the Q group was a potential menace to the patriarchal household. But there is only scant evidence that the patriarchal household was rejected because it was patriarchal; rather, it appears that the patriarchal household was simply eclipsed by more urgent matters. There are, to be sure, a few hints of an anti-patriarchal spirit (evidence noted above that the Q group consisted of both women and men), but no explicit critique in language such as Mark 3:31–35 or Matt 23:9. If we knew how the Q group organized itself, whether along the lines of a fictive or ritual family which was non-patriarchal, we would have a good basis for deciding the attitude of the Q group to the patriarchal household. But aside from the apparent fact that G-d functioned as the fictive father for the group, little else can be discerned from the texts; and G-d as fictive father *could* be anti-patriarchal but need not be.[42]

Whether such domestic dissension would have been liberating for women depends on the social situation of the individual involved. One can speculate on the problems familial breakups cause: parents abandoning young sons and daughters, or children abandoning elderly mothers and fathers.

Such abandoning, however, may not have extended to the dismissal of the marriage bond. Matt 19:9//Luke 16:18 proclaims: "Anyone who divorces his wife and marries another commits adultery, and whoever marries a woman divorced from her husband commits adultery" (cf. Mark 10:11–12).[43] Kloppenborg observes that the saying "reverses the logic of divorce, a mechanism designed to protect the honour of males, and insists that honour is also gynecocentric."[44] However, given that a major concern of Q is precisely to call into question social honor, such emphasis here would be anomalous at best. Kloppenborg's point is hermeneutically encouraging, but not historically convincing.[45]

For both utilitarian and ideological reasons, the saying may be less about divorce than remarriage and, in particular, the concern that group members not enter into a new, private familial relationship. Because the saying is followed in Luke closely by exhortations to avoid occasions for stumbling (Matt 18:6–7// Luke 17:1–3a, cf. Mark 9:42), the forbidding of remarriage may have also been intended to decrease negative reaction from outsiders: divorce and remarriage— including the divorcing of a "nonbeliever" in order to marry a member of the new movement—then, as now, can easily create scandal. Divorce may also have been of issue for those who chose the itinerant life. Finally, avoiding marriage would be consistent with Q's disinterest in the biological family.[46]

The "father" according to Q is the one in Heaven; it is he who takes the major role of providing for the needs of his children (Q 11:2–3, 13; 12:22–31). The fictive family preserves domestic systems, but reorients them away from the biological. Traditional marriages, and so procreation, are not Q desiderata. Matt 11:25//Luke 10:21 identifies the hearers of the instructions as "babies" (nēpioi). The image is a powerful one, especially for men who have forsaken domestic responsibilities, and the ability to distinguish themselves by means of biological and generational ties, to become part of the Basileia.[47]

The image is also powerful in its implied displacement of the biological family. For Q, procreation and children function figuratively, but not literally or practically. That is, images of children are illustrations of adult behavior. Q does not refer to actual pregnancy or childbirth, and its language removes women from their maternal role without providing any concurrent indication of liberation. The ideal parents in Q are "Abraham our father" and Wisdom as mother, and even Abraham's role as progenitor is eclipsed: "God is able from these stones to raise up children to Abraham" (Matt 3:9//Luke 3:8). The only productive "mother" is Wisdom (Matt 11:19//Luke 7:35; Lukan version: "Wisdom is vindicated by her children"), and she replaces the human mother ("woman") of John the Baptist (Matt 11:18–19//Luke 7:33–35). Moreover, she is removed from her position of authority and patronage (cf. Wis 10:14b) and placed in a position dependent on her (male) children, Jesus and John. Jesus himself also is depicted as assuming, if not coopting, maternal roles; he "would have gathered your children together as a hen gathers her brood under her wings" (Matt 23: 37–39//Luke 13:34–35).[48]

Wisdom had a rich, complex history in Judaism long before the time of Q. A feminine noun (Sophia in Greek, Hochma in Hebrew), Wisdom represented not only a manifestation of transcendent Divinity, but also a figure of desire for and a teacher of men. Occasionally depicted as rejected by those to whom she had come (Prov 1:20–33, 8:22–36; 1 Enoch 42), she is appropriately invoked by Q, whose messengers were also rejected. In Q, Sophia sends her prophets, notably, but not only, Jesus and John the Baptist; they are rejected and killed (cf. Q 7: 31–35, 11:49–51).[49] Jesus, along with John, is thus not Sophia, but her envoy and defender (Q 7:35).

Although Jesus' identification as Wisdom's envoy may celebrate the feminine nature of the Divinity, it may conversely be a masculinization of Sophia. Christopher Tuckett even wonders whether any gendered language is appropriate in this context since Sophia's appearances in Proverbs, Sirach, and elsewhere frequently do not contain explicitly gendered references and because Q demonstrates no embarrassment over the connection of Jesus to (female) Wisdom.[50]

If the community that preserved and compiled the Q sayings associated Jesus with an explicitly gendered Sophia tradition, then masculinization of that tradition occurred at some point. Jesus states: "I thank you, Father, Lord of heaven and earth, because you have hidden these things from the wise and the intelligent and have revealed them to infants; yes, Father, for such was your gracious will. All things have been handed over to me by my Father, and no one knows who the Son is except the Father, or who the Father is except the Son and anyone to whom the Son chooses to reveal him" (Matt 11:25–26//Luke 10:21–22). The masculine depiction incorporates and thereby erases Sophia, the embodiment and distributor of Wisdom. Schüssler Fiorenza appeals to the theory of redactional strata: "The Q people (men?) who articulated this saying replaced the inclusive sophialogy of the earliest Jesus traditions with an exclusive understanding of revelation."[51] That Sophia is replaced is clear; that there was an originary inclusive sophialogy, while plausible, is less certain.

Schüssler Fiorenza's observation is of particular note in that it matches (unintentionally?) the theory of Q strata. In Kloppenborg's model, Q's female characters, including Sophia, appear in the second layer, Q2. According to Allison, the Sophia materials appear not in the earliest layer of Q, but in Q3, the final layer,[52] and the other references to women again appear in the later materials. The references to these figures can, consequently, be contextualized in light of the hypotheses concerning the group's changing fortunes and self-perception. In this scenario, the authors of Q notice women only when the community is faced with external pressure and is consequently forced to redefine its mission. The later stratum's location of women within the domestic sphere—baking bread, grinding grain, negotiating with relatives—may be indicative not of an egalitarian ethos, but of a renewed patriarchalism or even of patriarchalism that was never absent. Thus, the move to define Q according to redactional layers places women (back) into the domestic sphere, if they were ever, in the Q communities, removed from it.

The various composition histories of Q locate women's explicit representations within a social context of a settled community. Itinerants may still be spreading the good news, but the emphasis of the document has shifted to those believers who find that their relatives, friends, and neighbors do not share their views. At this stage, dualistic language emerges, apocalyptic scenarios are celebrated, and women are, finally, depicted in parables and paired sayings. The setting that emerges is one of women in traditional arrangements.

Parables combine old ingredients in new ways and thereby attempt to question or redefine social tastes in worldviews, personal interactions, economic concerns, etc. For example, the well-known "Good Samaritan" (Luke 10:29–37) forces a redefinition of "neighbor" in light of ethnic loyalties and prejudices. As with all food for thought, parables are open to multiple interpretations drawn both from readers' differing social locations and from reconstructions of the original audiences of the parables. These observations hold true for the parable of the leaven both in its modern interpretations and in its ancient context.

Matt 13:33//Luke 13:21 compares the *basileia* to "yeast that a woman took and hid in three measures of flour until all of it was leavened." For Schottroff, this entirely positive and affirming image "intends to call attention to the work of women."[53] Enhancing this positive image, she offers sympathetic, even romanticized, connections between the parable and descriptions of both bread making and her grandmother's cookbooks.[54]

However, the parable is open as well to much less positive readings. First, it focuses not on the woman per se but on the leaven, just as in the paired parable of the mustard seed the focus is on the seed, not on the (male) sower.[55] Second, within the symbolic vocabulary of both formative Judaism and the early Church, yeast has negative connotations. Arnal suggests that the "proverbial noxiousness" of both the mustard seed and the leaven signals the "inversionary and countercultural ethos of Q."[56] "The woman's 'hiding' (kryptō) rather than kneading leaven suggest that her manual labour is underhanded, and the process she cooks up is one of decay."[57] In contrast are Q's positive, paternal images: it is the father who provides the daily bread (Matt 6:11//Luke 11:3).[58] The parable does recognize women's labors, but the impact of the saying may be at the expense of the woman herself: she is associated with negative symbols, however redefined they may be, and located only within the domestic, rather than missionary, role.

Although the parable of the lost coin (Luke 15:8–10) is absent from Matthew, biblical scholarship often treats it as original to Q.[59] Like its pair, the parable of the lost sheep (Matt 18:12–14//Luke 15:4–7), the "lost coin" has as its central figure a human character in a traditional location: the male shepherd outside with his sheep; the woman householder inside with her broom. These paired characters are all depicted in traditional gender roles. More, their descriptions are distinct. The men and women are not associated with each other as husband and wife, parent or child, brother or sister.[60] Such may well have been the social roles of members of the Q groups: gender-determined quotidian activity combined with a deemphasis on biologically based familial structures. Such a conclusion is tentative at best: there is no necessary correspondence between depictions in parables and actions of the people who told the stories. That is, occupations may be conventional tropes: the rhetoric is effective because it is recognized by its audience, not because its audience participates in the activities described.

The same observation extends to the analysis of the paired characters. In Q, two men reclining to dine are matched with two women grinding meal (Matt 10:40–41//Luke 17:35); a man who loses a sheep resembles a woman who has lost a coin (Matt 18:12–14 [just sheep]//Luke 15:4–7, 8–10); the man who plants a mustard seed is paired with the woman who hides yeast in dough (Matt 13:31–33//Luke 13:18–21). From scriptural legend, the "queen of the South" along with the "men from Nineveh" arise to condemn the present generation (Matt 12:41–42//Luke 11:31–33). In sayings on family construction, there are [men] who marry and [women] who are given in marriage (Matt 24:38//Luke 17:27); Q proclamations will cause the hating of father and mother, sons and daughters (Matt 10:37–38//Luke 14:26–27). "Prostitutes" may also have appeared alongside the "tax collectors" in the Q version of what is presently Luke 7:29 (cf. Matt 21:31–32).[61] To these examples perhaps should also be added Matt 6:25–34//Luke 12:22–32; even the (feminine) lilies of the field, which do not spin, are seen in comparison to the (masculine) ravens, who neither "sow nor reap [and] have neither storehouse nor barn."

These pairs may indicate "a deliberate attempt to address both men and women."[62] For Schottroff, the explanation for women's presence, even given Q's androcentric perspective, "lies in the experiences of equality within the hard daily lives of an impoverished population. . . . The Jesus movement's hopes for the coming of the reign of Gd, and attempts to live in just relationships, enhanced (to a limited degree) men's ability to see women's labor as hard work and to recognize that it was equal in value to that of men."[63] Luz, as noted above, sees the "lilies" of the field as representing women, even as the birds represent men.[64]

Conversely, William E. Arnal suggests that "the phenomenon is more indicative of a penchant for legal and regulatory formulation than it is of an interest in the deliberate critique of patriarchy."[65] Similar to the representations of Sophia, the paired figures are a common trope in the contemporary literature. Arnal further observes that the gendered pairs appear in discussions concerning group affiliation: women as well as men are thus seen by Q as both insiders and outsiders. But the pairs describe rather than prescribe: "in no instances of direct exhortation is any effort made to pair examples by gender."[66]

In all these cases, the work is of equal value; in all these cases, the work has no value in Q's system. Grinding is neither rewarded nor punished; the act of baking is subordinate to the process created by the yeast; both spinning and sowing are equal, and finally irrelevant, in the Q economy of salvation. Indeed, for Q, even food preparation is of little import; one's focus is to be on the *basileia*, and of the rest, the heavenly father will provide. Nor can those lilies, that also bend in the wind, bear the weighty thesis that they indicate women's participation in missionary activities: while the metaphor is feminine, the application may not be to real women. Women may have been among the missionaries; the point is simply that, if they were, the composers of Q do not notice them. Finally, if Matt 24:40–41//Luke 17:34–35, which pairs dining men and grinding women, has any social implications, then the saying may be read as dismissing, rather than enforcing, egalitarian meal practices.[67]

Women belong to Q: they are represented in Q's sayings, and they lived in Q's communities. Yet their specific and most likely quite diverse roles, let alone how they viewed themselves, in those communities are at best difficult to reconstruct. Even granting that Q may tell us more of what Jesus said than what was said about him and in his name, it is still a major leap to move from the text to the community behind it. There is no surety that the Q material was the only text read by those who preserved it; the very existence of the Gospels of Matthew and Mark indicates that Q was not the only document preserved by at least two different church groups. It may be no more appropriate to reconstruct a community on the basis of Q alone than it would be to reconstruct a community on the basis of Sirach or John's Apocalypse.[68] Nor is there surety that Q is descriptive, as opposed to prescriptive or metaphorical. The quest for women in the Q communit(ies) is therefore more secure when Q materials can be matched with data from Mark, Paul, John, or even cross-cultural studies of nascent religious movements. It is on the basis of such a triangulation of internal content, extratextual parallels, and theoretical comparisons that the search for the women of the early Jesus communit(ies) is most productively located.[69]

Although the language of Q is androcentric, women may have perceived themselves as included within it. Even if the expressions intended a male response, women were not precluded from appropriating good news for their own situations.[70]

Perhaps, like other revitalization groups, Q did begin as a nonhierarchical community in which "male" and "female" were equivalent, if not irrelevant, categories. On the other hand, the combination of androcentric language, images that enforce traditional gender roles for women, and the dismantling and dismissing of the biological family may not spell good news for women outside or even inside the Q group. To establish order internally, and to decrease hostility from the outside, the group may have done what other sectarian or revitalization movements do: regulate its women. And yet, what may appear patriarchal or oppressive to the modern reader may not have so appeared to the women within Q.[71]

Even if some analyses of Q do not lead to the conclusion that the women of the groups lived within an egalitarian ethos, the hermeneutical appropriation of the Q materials can lead to such a community today. By calling into question patriarchal domestic arrangements, insisting that men and women have equal access to salvation, providing hope in a world free from economic exploitation, social oppression, and personal anxiety, Q continues to inspire. And thus, as is always the case with scripture, the words take on meaning beyond their historical contexts.[72]

NOTES

1. See the very helpful summary of the scholarship on "women and Q" by William E. Arnal, "Gendered Couplets in Q and Legal Formulations: From Rhetoric to Social History," JBL 116 (1997) 75–94. I thank Professor Arnal for sharing his manuscript with me.

2. "Patriarchy" here refers to a class system in which power is held by a limited number of privileged individuals, usually male. The model of the Roman household, in which the patresfamiliae (family heads) control all women, children, slaves, and property, provides an accurate example. Because patriarchy is based in class rather than gender constructions (although the two often substantially overlap), to be antipatriarchal is not necessarily equivalent to being concerned explicitly with women's roles and rights; in turn, a woman of sufficient economic means can function as a patriarch.

3. Alicia Batten, "More Queries for Q: Women and Christian Origins," Biblical Theology Bulletin 24.2 (1994) 44.

4. Burton Mack, The Lost Gospel. The Book of Q and Christian Origins (San Francisco: HarperSanFrancisco, 1993) 9.

5. Batten, "More Queries" 49.

6. Elisabeth Schüssler Fiorenza, Jesus: Miriam's Child, Sophia's Prophet: Critical Issues in Feminist Christology (New York: Continuum, 1994) 140 (in the section "The Sayings Source Q").

7. This theory is known as the "Griesbach" hypothesis or the "Griesbach-Farmer" hypothesis. William R. Farmer has been the most influential modern proponent of this model. See his The Synoptic Problem: A Critical Analysis (New York: Macmillan, 1964). On the implications of source criticism for the reconstruction of women's roles in the Jesus movement, see Farmer, The Gospel of Jesus. The Pastoral Relevance of the Synoptic Problem (Louisville, KY: Westminster/John Knox, 1994).

8. Alternative solutions to the synoptic problem also do not require a Q. Some scholars argue that all three evangelists wrote independently; others that Luke had access to both Mark and Matthew. See E. P. Sanders and Margaret Davies, Studying the Synoptic Gospels (Philadelphia: Trinity Press International, 1989).

9. Heinz O. Guenther, "The Sayings Gospel Q and the Quest for Aramaic Sources: Rethinking Christian Origins," Semeia 55 (1992) 41–75, and cf. the summaries and evalu-

ations in Dale C. Allison, Jr., *The Jesus Tradition in Q* (Philadelphia: Trinity Press International, 1997) 47–49, with the argument that the materials concerning itinerants were originally composed in Aramaic. I thank Professor Allison for sharing his manuscript with me.

10. For example, Mack, *Lost Gospel.*

11. So several articles on Q's social context in John S. Kloppenborg (ed.), *Conflict and Invention: Literary, Rhetorical and Social Studies on the Sayings Gospel Q* (Valley Forge, PA: Trinity Press International, 1995); Leif E. Vaage, *Galilean Upstarts. Jesus' First Followers According to Q* (Valley Forge, PA: Trinity Press International, 1994). On the relationship among genre, social setting, and theology, cf. Kloppenborg's introduction in Kloppenborg (ed.), *The Shape of Q: Signal Essays on the Sayings Gospel* (Minneapolis, MN: Augsburg/Fortress, 1994). Kloppenborg himself ("Literary Convention, Self-Evidence and the Social History of the Q People," *Semeia* 55 [1992] 85) finds the "more likely setting for [stage 1 of Q to be] among those who might anachronistically be called the 'petit bourgeois' in the lower administrative sector of the cities and villages." See also William E. Arnal, "The Rhetoric of Marginality: Apocalypticism, Gnosticism, and Sayings Gospels," HTR 88/4 (1995) 482–89 on Q as a Galilean scribal document.

12. Mack, *Lost Gospel,* 5, cf. 9.

13. John S. Kloppenborg, *The Formation of Q: Trajectories in Ancient Wisdom Collections* (Philadelphia: Fortress, 1987).

14. Ibid. 318, and Amy-Jill Levine, "Who's Catering the Q Affair? Feminist Observations on Q Paraenesis" *Semeia* 50 (1990) 147.

15. Charlotte Allen, "The Search for a No-Frills Jesus," *Atlantic Monthly* 278.6 (December 1996) 51.

16. Allison, *Jesus Tradition,* 43 n. 186; in Mark, Jesus explicitly calls himself "Christ" once (9:41), in Matthew once (23:10), and in Luke not at all.

17. Allison, *Jesus Tradition,* 1–66. The opening pages comment on Kloppenborg's model and survey other compositional histories of Q. Allison himself follows Dieter Zeller, "Redactional Processes and Changing Settings in the Q-Material," in Kloppenborg, *Shape of Q,* 129.

18. Allison, 22, noting, inter alia, Ulrich Luz, *Matthew in History: Interpretation, Influence, and Effects* (Minneapolis, MN: Fortress, 1994) 29, on "men and women who have left their ordinary work for the sake of the kingdom of God."

19. See Christopher M. Tuckett, "Q (Gospel Source)," *ANRW* 5:567–62, and contrast Tuckett's contribution on Sophia, below note 50; Kloppenborg, *Conflict and Invention;* In *The Gospel Behind the Gospels: Current Studies in Q,* Ronald A. Piper, ed., Supplements to *Novum Testamentum* 75 (Leiden: E. J. Brill, 1995), only the last two articles (see note 22) mention women's history and gender roles, and only the penultimate, Luise Schottroff's "Itinerant Prophetesses: A Feminist Analysis of the Sayings Source Q," addresses the questions directly.

20. Luise Schottroff, "The Sayings Source Q," in Elisabeth Schüssler Fiorenza (ed.), *Searching the Scriptures, Volume 2, A Feminist Commentary* (New York: Crossroad, 1994) 511, states: "[T]he isolation of different strata of tradition within Q (Q1 and Q2) does not strike me as persuasive; however, I will take it into account when it has consequences for the content of individual sayings."

21. Kloppenborg, "Literary Convention" 89–90, and following him, Kathleen E. Corley, "Women and Gender in Q," Unpublished essay ms. 4–5. I thank Professor Corley for sharing her essay with me.

22. See Arland Dean Jacobson, "Divided Families and Christian Origins," in Piper, *Gospel Behind the Gospels* 375.

23. See Amy-Jill Levine, "Second-Temple Judaism, Jesus and Women: Yeast of Eden," *Biblical Interpretation* 2/1 (1994) 8–33, passim, for references.

24. See Levine, "Who's Catering?" 151. Schottroff is consistently helpful on Q's androcentrism. (See notes 19, 20 above, 51 below.)

25. Ibid. 145–61.

26. Schottroff, "Sayings Source Q" 528. On 530, she elaborates: "I understand the Jesus movement . . . even at the time the Sayings Source was composed, as a Jewish liberation movement within a people oppressed by the Pax Romana, and emanating primarily from those suffering the oppression: the poor (women and men), the sick, the prostitutes, the tax collectors of both genders, fisher folk (male and female), the day laborers, both men and women." Less clear are the specifics on precisely how "liberation" is accomplished or from what, specifically, the adherents of Q are liberated. Mack, *Lost Gospel* 121, notes in Q the "hint of fascination with what might be called an egalitarian view of social roles and rankings," but he has little to say about gender roles. Mack reads Q, especially Q1, not as a "liberation movement," but as a Cyniclike social experiment "for individuals to live against the stream, not a program offered for the reforms of society's ills" (46). James M. Robinson reads "The Jesus of Q as a Liberation Theologian" (in Piper, *Gospel Behind the Gospels* 259–74), but ignores gender issues.

27. Detailed discussion, including cross-cultural examples, in Corley, "Women and Gender," ms. 6. Stephen J. Patterson, *The Gospel of Thomas and Jesus*. Foundations and Facets Reference Series (Sonoma, CA: Polebridge, 1993) 155, posits a connection to the Gospel of Thomas, a Coptic collection of Jesus' sayings that shares material and possible form with Q. Drawing upon Saying 114, which reads in part, "For every female who makes herself male will enter heaven's kingdom," Patterson proposes that female missionaries disguised themselves as men to prevent attack on the road. The saying, however, need not refer to physical disguise or to missionary activity.

28. Schottroff, "Itinerant Prophetesses" 347.

29. Members of the Q Project and scholars associated with Claremont typically follow, yet modify in varying ways, Gerd Theissen's thesis that the Q community comprised both itinerant radicals and settled sympathizers (Gerd Theissen, "Wanderradikalismus: Literatur-soziologische Aspekte der Überlieferung von Worten Jesu im Urchristentun," *ZTK* 70 [1973] 245–71, cf. his *Sociology of Early Palestinian Christianity* [Philadelphia: Fortress, 1978]). For summaries and critiques, see esp. Patterson, *Gospel of Thomas* 158–214; R. Conrad Douglas, "'Love Your Enemies,' Rhetoric, Tradents, and Ethos," in Kloppenborg, *Conflict and Invention*, 119–22; Arnal, "Rhetoric of Marginality," 480–82 (disagreeing with the itinerancy hypotheses for both Q and Gospel of Thomas). See also Risto Uro, *Sheep among the Wolves: A Study of the Mission Instructions of Q* (Helsinki: Suomalainen Tiedeakatemia, 1987). On recent questioning by Kloppenborg, John Horsley, Vaage, and Piper of the focus on itinerancy, see Ronald A. Piper, "In Quest of Q: The Direction of Q Studies," in Piper, *Gospel Behind the Gospels*, 17–18. For a feminist approach, see Levine, "Who's Catering?"

30. Schottroff, "Sayings Source Q" 514.

31. Ibid. 515.

32. Ibid. 514.

33. Levine, "Who's Catering" 148.

34. Arguments in Schottroff, "Itinerant Prophetesses" 354–55.

35. Jacobson, "Divided Families" 364; see also Arnal, "Rhetoric of Marginality."

36. See Elisabeth Schüssler Fiorenza, *In Memory of Her: A Feminist Theological Reconstruction of Christian Origins* (New York: Crossroad, 1983) 145–74, and following her, Levine, "Who's

Catering" 152. The reference to "wife" is absent from Matt 10:37, but Luke 18:29b adds the same reference to Mark 10:29b. A reference to wives would be generically expected, given analogies to 1 Cor 7:29, as well as Cynic statements advising separation of husbands from wives. The rhetoric of Q 9:60 is androcentric.

37. See also b. Sanh. 97a; m. Sota 9:16; 4 Ezra (Armenian) 5:9. How much Q 12:51–53 reflects reality, and how much it can be explained as a literary tradition that begins with the end of Malachi (which seems to foretell the undoing of Mic 7:6) remains open to debate. I thank Dale Allison for these observations.

38. Batten, "More Queries" 49. Corley, "Women and Gender," ms. 4, suggests that familial disruption is not caused by gender conflict, but by generation conflict centered specifically on the denial of burial rites to family members (so Q 9:59–60).

39. Batten, "More Queries" 47. Jacobson argues that Q should be seen as standing against the biological family, rather than against patriarchy per se (see "Divided Families" 361–80).

40. Contra Batten, "More Queries" 48.

41. Schottroff, "Itinerant Prophetesses" 349.

42. Jacobson, "Divided Families" 374–75. Jacobson's point, while cautious, might be even more so: the presence of women is not necessarily indicative of an antipatriarchal ethos. Patriarchal structures by no means exclude women; the issue is the gender construction within the system.

43. James M. Robinson, "International Q Project Work Session, 17 November 1989," JBL 109 (1990) 501. See also John S. Kloppenborg, "Jesus and the Parables of Jesus in Q," in Piper, Gospel Behind the Gospels 315–16, with additional references and discussion; Jacobson, "Divided Families" 369–73.

44. Kloppenborg, "Jesus and the Parables" 315.

45. See Mary Rose D'Angelo, "Remarriage and the Divorce Sayings Attributed to Jesus," in William P. Roberts (ed.), Divorce and Remarriage: Religious and Psychological Perspectives (Kansas City, MO: Sheed and Ward, 1990) 78–106. I thank Prof. D'Angelo for this reference.

46. See Jacobson, "Divided Families" 371, who also observes (372 n. 33, against Kloppenborg) that the "association of remarriage with adultery was neither innovative nor intended to protect the honour of women."

47. On the relationship among metaphors of infants/children, language of status reversal, and the anthropological phenomenon of liminality, see Levine, "Who's Catering?" esp. 153–55.

48. For discussion of Q's metaphoric depictions of parental concerns, see Levine, "Yeast of Eden" 31–32.

49. See Patrick J. Hartin, "Yet Wisdom Is Justified by Her Children (Q 7:35): A Rhetorical and Compositional Analysis of Divine Sophia in Q," in Kloppenborg, Conflict and Invention 151–64. For summaries of the Jesus/Sophia materials and commentaries (again omitting reference to gender or women), see Edward P. Meadors, Jesus: The Messianic Herald of Salvation. WUNT 2.72 (Tübingen: J. C. B. Mohr [Paul Siebeck], 1995).

50. Christopher M. Tuckett, "Feminine Wisdom in Q?" in George J. Brooke (ed.), Women in the Biblical Tradition. Studies in Women and Religion 31 (Lewiston, NY: Edwin Mellen, 1992) 112–28. The same question can be put in the modern idiom. In the same note (citing my "Who's Catering?" 155, on the masculinization of Sophia), Tuckett speaks of "Levine . . . he." My gender/sex may be irrelevant to, or masked by, Tuckett, but they may be of no small concern to others, including myself. The appropriateness of emphasizing gendered language varies among present-day scholars, and it may have varied as well among members of the Q groups.

51. Schüssler Fiorenza, *Jesus* 14. Luise Schottroff, *Lydia's Impatient Sisters: A Feminist Social History of Early Christianity*, trans. Barbara and Martin Rumscheidt (Louisville, KY: Westminster/John Knox, 1995) 137, finds feminist implications in the saying: "Those not of age are the poor who cannot talk well and have no formal education. There were hardly any chances for girls of the poverty-stricken majority of Palestine's population to become educated; nor is there yet much chance for girls in the two-thirds world." Whether Jesus (if the statement is authentic) or the authors of Q were as perceptive and inclusive as Schottroff is a separate question, as Schüssler Fiorenza's observation might suggest. For an alternative perspective to that of Schüssler Fiorenza on the Sophia traditions in Q, see also Schottroff's contribution in "Sayings Source Q" 525–32; she concludes that "wisdom traditions are not relevant for the Sayings Source."

52. Allison, *Jesus Tradition*, ms. 101 and n. 274.

53. Schottroff, "Sayings Source Q" 522; Schottroff, "Itinerant Prophetesses" 351 ("The parable of the leaven most obviously shatters the laws of patriarchal perceptions of women's labor since it equates a woman's labor with G-d's activities"). Schottroff's "Itinerant Prophetesses" first called attention to "A Woman's Labor and Its Theological Implications" 350–53, in discussion of the paired parables. See also her extensive, often inspired, theological discussion in *Lydia's Sisters* 86–90.

54. Schottroff, "Sayings Source Q" 521. In the same kitchen is John Dominic Crossan, *In Parables: The Challenge of the Historical Jesus* (San Francisco: Harper and Row, 1973) 38, he observes that, while the parable of the lost sheep can be related to Jesus as the Good Shepherd, the parable of the leaven never leads to the proclamation of Jesus as "the good housewife." Citation in Arnal, "Gendered Couplets," n. 42.

55. On the assimilation of the structure of the mustard seed parable, in which the "person" (*anthrōpos*) has no "proper function" to the parable of the leaven, see Kloppenborg, "Jesus and the Parables" 306–11.

56. Arnal, "Gendered Couplets" 9–10. Vaage, *Galilean Upstarts*, 65, sees the mustard seed and the leaven as elements of "uncertain social value in classical antiquity." On the negative, threatening ("a little too much beyond human control"), and wry (rye?) aspects of both the leaven and the mustard seed, see also Wendy Cotter's "Prestige, Protection and Promise: A Proposal for the Apologetics of Q2" in Piper, *Gospel Behind the Gospels* 122.

57. Levine, "Who's Catering?" following B. B. Scott, quoted in Batten, "More Queries" 48. See also Patterson, *Gospel of Thomas* 240; Arland Dean Jacobson, *The First Gospel: An Introduction to Q* (Sonoma, CA: Polebridge, 1992) 204–5, esp. n. 40. My "Yeast of Eden" 24–25 suggests: "A helpful modern hermeneutical shift would be to associate yeast with the infection of that name and thereby regain the connotations of women's dis-ease." The negative images, in connection with women, appear as well in the Gospel of Thomas: "The Kingdom is like a certain woman who was carrying a jar full of meal. While she was walking on the road, still some distance from home, the handle of the jar broke, and the meal emptied out behind her on the road. She did not realize it; she had noticed no accident. When she reached her house, she set the jar down and found it empty." See discussion and connection with Q in Levine, "Yeast of Eden" 25.

58. Levine, "Yeast of Eden" 26.

59. David Catchpole, *The Quest for Q* (Edinburgh: T&T Clark, 1993) 191–92, argues that "it is easy to see why Matthew would have dropped the parable of the lost coin. . . . The image of the housewife would hardly appeal to this evangelist when depicting concerned church leaders. Matthew was no instinctive sympathizer with the ordination of women!" (exclamation point his). Catchpole does not, however, explain what the image would have to do with the question of "ordination" or attempt the reverse of his argu-

ment: Q's image or its retention in Luke does concern women's ordination. On including the parable in Q, see Kloppenborg, "Jesus and the Parables" 311–17; Jacobson, *First Gospel* 227.

60. Then again, the juxtaposition of the two parables may have suggested to Q hearers that the man and woman were married or members of the same (temporarily ill-fortuned) household.

61. See Corley, "Women and Gender" ms. 20–35, esp. note 59. See also William Arnal's "Reconstruction of Q 7:29–30," paper presented to the International Q Project, Claremont, CA, May 1994, which Corley follows. The reconstruction, including "prostitutes," was rejected by the majority of members.

62. Batten, "More Queries" 48; Corley, "Women and Gender" ms. 4. The point is also made by those supporting Matthean priority (Farmer, *Gospel of Jesus* 76).

63. Schottroff, "Sayings Source Q" 523.

64. See n. 18 above.

65. Arnal, "Gendered Couplets" 2, who offers several examples from contemporaneous literature of forensically based pairs.

66. Ibid. 12.

67. On relating the saying to dining rather than to "two men on a bed," see John Kloppenborg, "Symbolic Eschatology and the Apocalypticism of Q," HTR 80 (1987) 287–306, esp. 302 n. 57. I thank Kathleen Corley for this reference. See also Corley's *Private Women, Public Meals: Social Conflict in the Synoptic Tradition* (Peabody, MA: Hendrickson, 1993) 117–18. In GThom. 61, the reference to the dining couch is explicit.

68. See the sage comments of Allison, *The Jesus Tradition* 43–46.

69. For comparative models using different databases from within the canon, as well as from Greek, Roman, and Jewish outside sources, see inter alia, Schottroff, *Lydia's Sisters*; Schüssler Fiorenza, *Jesus*; Batten, "More Queries"; and Arnal, "Gendered Couplets."

70. Cf. Levine, "Yeast of Eden" 13.

71. Ibid. 32.

72. With thanks to Dale C. Allison, Jr., Mary Rose D'Angelo, William E. Arnal, Kathleen Corley, Jay Geller, Deirdre Good, Ross Kraemer, and Adele Reinhartz for critical comments on earlier drafts of this chapter.

8

> ⊱—◂◆▸—○—◂◆▸—◅

(RE)PRESENTATIONS OF WOMEN
IN THE GOSPEL OF
MATTHEW AND LUKE-ACTS

Mary Rose D'Angelo

Re-presentations is a particularly apt description of the Gospels of Matthew and Luke; these works in some sense present Jesus again by rethinking Mark's narrative so as to integrate the sayings of Q. Both provide (independent) stories about the birth and childhood of Jesus that supply Jesus with the father he lacks in Mark (6:3–4) and bring the narratives closer to ancient biographies. Both aim at cleaner narrative and more elegant diction. Both texts use language and forms that associate them with the Bible, offering themselves as an extension or completion of the sacred writings. For both, interpretation of the Bible is central, but they use very different exegetical techniques to identify and explain Jesus and the early Christian community. Both carefully supply resurrection appearances and commands to the disciples that provide for the continuance, transformation, and growth of the community. In the case of Luke, this effort produced a second volume, the Acts of the Apostles. And each has been read both as the most inclusive and as the most repressive of the gospels for women.

Since both authors reuse material on women and gender from Mark and Q, one entrée into their representations of women is to examine the ways these authors revise the stories about women from Mark and the gendered sayings from Q. But this approach must be used with caution and attention to context; their revisions respond to a wide variety of factors that include, but are not limited to, the gender prescriptions and assumptions that characterized the community. For instance, both Matthew 12:41–42 and Luke 11:31–32 use a saying from Q that contrasts the wickedness of "this generation" to the Ninevites, who repented at the preaching of Jonah, and the queen of the South, who came from the ends of the earth to hear Solomon. They use the examples in reverse order, but this reversal probably corresponds not to the respective genders of the queen of the South and Jonah, but to the authors' preferences in christology. In Matthew, the comparison with the queen is climactic because Matthew prefers Wisdom christology; Matthew's genealogy identifies Jesus as a descendent of David through Solomon (1:7). In Luke, the climactic comparison is with Jonah because Luke prefers a prophet christology; Luke's genealogy identifies Jesus as a descendent of David through Nathan (3:31).

Similar problems arise with the attempt to interpret the omission of stories or sayings that refer to women. Mark's generous widow (Mark 12:41–44) does not appear in Matthew. But any conclusions about gender implications have to take into account Matthew's interest in joining the tirade against the Pharisees from Q (Matthew 23) to a revised version of Mark 13 that predicts the Jewish war, the fall of the temple, and the coming judgment (Matt 24:1–26:1). The Gospel of Luke does not reuse Mark's story of the Greek (Syro-Phoenician) woman. But is the story omitted because the author is hostile to uppity women or wishes to restrict the gentile mission to the male apostles Peter and Paul?[1] In fact, the story of the Greek woman falls into the so-called "great omission," the lengthy section of Mark (6:45–8:26) entirely absent from Luke. If the author knew and omitted the whole section, the omission of this story need not result from Luke's views on gender, but from other concerns.[2] Further, it is possible there was no deliberate omission; Luke may have used an edition of Mark that did not include this section at all.[3]

Matthew

Matthew is widely believed to have been written at the end of the first century in Syria.[4] Much attention has been devoted to its "Jewish background," and Kathleen Corley's claim that Matthew is "most Jewish" and "most egalitarian" was made as a salutary antidote to the tendency among feminists and other scholars to explain away reflections of patriarchy, misogyny, or both in early Christian texts as an inheritance from Judaism.[5] Indeed, Judaism is so widely taken to be the context of Matthew that one scholar refers to "Matthew's Christian Jewish community."[6] Such characterizations are based on the centrality of legal and exegetical traditions to the gospel. The phrase "a scribe discipled to God's reign" in Matthew 13:52 appears to be an apt description of Matthew and, in fact, of the communal life reflected in the gospel. The forms of scriptural interpretation the gospel uses and the legal and pious observances it commends resemble traditions from either of the two forms of ancient Judaism most familiar to Christian interpreters, that is, either the texts of Qumran (the Dead Sea Scrolls) or rabbinic Judaism, whose emergence appears to have been roughly contemporaneous with the writing of Matthew.[7] The only evidence that some rabbinic practices and opinions were extant in the nineties of the common era is the appearance of similar traditions in Matthew, for the surviving major sources of rabbinic Judaism began to be compiled only in the third century CE. While analogies between Matthew's community and Jewish communities like

Qumran and the rabbinic groups are real and important, claiming that Matthew is "most Jewish" underestimates the possibility that the other gospels reflect or react to forms of Judaism that did not survive beyond the first or second century. It also obscures other problematic indicators of the gospel's context and concerns.

Matthew indulges in an anti-Jewish polemic that has contributed heavily to the history of Christian anti-Judaism. A particularly virulent and lengthy revision of Q's tirade against the Pharisees prefaces and justifies the predictions of the fall of the temple (23:1–26:1). This gospel's version of the Roman trial depicts Pilate as washing his hands of the blood of Jesus (and absolving the Roman government of the responsibility for Jesus' death), while the Jews accept blood guilt for Jesus' death on themselves and their children (27:24–25). The final commission to the eleven commanding them to make disciples of all the Gentiles may imply the mission to Jews is over (28:19); it certainly assumes a significant and growing gentile element in the community.[8]

In the Gospel of Matthew, the material from Mark and Q (as well as other unknown sources) was reorganized and integrated into tightly constructed units composing a "messianic biography" that gives a narrative explanation of Jesus as son of David and son of God (1:1, 15).[9] Particularly noteworthy are five sermons or blocks of teaching, which have sometimes been interpreted as an attempt to model the book on the Pentateuch (the first five books of the Bible): the Sermon on Mount (5:1–7:28), a missionary instruction (9:34–11:1), a parables discourse (13:1–53), a "church order" (17:24–19:1), and a tirade against the Pharisees that leads into an apocalyptic speech (23:1–26:1).[10] These sermons, which bear some resemblance to the type of ancient collections called "words of the wise," by no means exhaust the teaching of Jesus in Matthew. And in Matthew disciples are primarily learners or students; the invitation to discipleship is "learn of me" (11:29).

The importance of teaching in Matthew raises the question of whether women are treated as disciples in Matthew. Matthew's frequent references to the "twelve (or eleven) disciples" have been read by some interpreters as excluding women from discipleship.[11] The best starting point for considering this question appears to be the women at the cross.

> There were there many women watching from afar who had followed Jesus from Galilee ministering to him; among whom were Mary Magdalene, and Mary the mother of James and Joseph and the mother of the sons of Zebedee. (27:55–56)[12]

As in Mark, three women are named as witnesses to the death of Jesus. In Matthew, not only the three named women, but also the great crowd of women, are explicitly said to have 'followed Jesus from Galilee.' With the latter phrase, the author elides Mark's note that the women had been followers of Jesus in Galilee, and it is possible to see this revision as changing their role from long-term disciples to mere companions on the journey. But the use of the word "ministering" in conjunction with "followed" makes any demotion unlikely. Two of the named women, Mary Magdalene and Mary, the mother of James and Joses, provide the two witnesses Matthew deems necessary (18:16; Deut 19:15) to connect the death of Jesus, the place where he was buried, and the empty tomb (27:55–6, 61; 28:1–8). At the tomb, the two women prove absolutely faithful, comprehending, and obedient; they withstand the spectacular descent of the angel and delight in his message, while the guards Matthew has introduced into the scene are comatose with fear. The two women also become the first to see the risen Jesus in a new very brief narrative (Matt 28:9–10) in which they are given a message for the disciples.

The woman who anoints Jesus (Matt 26:2–16//Mark 14:1–11) remains a prophet who both designates Jesus as Messiah and predicts his death by preparing him for burial. Kathleen Corley notes that in Matthew the woman seems to be among the diners.[13] She is contrasted not only with the pusillanimous high priests (Matt 26:2–5) and the mercenary Judas (26:14–16), but also with the disciples, who are the ones who object to her "waste" of the ointment. The women at the tomb do not go to anoint Jesus, so Mark's ironic connection between the witnesses and this woman, who has already accomplished this task, is lost in Matthew. The wife of Pilate is also given a bit part in the passion narrative; she is the medium through whom a dream warns Pilate of Jesus' innocence (27:19). On the whole, the role of the women in these scenes seems to have been enhanced rather than diminished; if anything, Matthew is more conscious of the role of women as witnesses than Mark is.

Other issues in the treatment of women in Matthew surround the "mother of the Zebedees" who replaces Salome at the cross. This figure was introduced into the narrative to put forward the request Mark assigns to her two sons, the request for places on his right and left hand in his reign (Matt 20:20–23; compare Mark 10:35–40). By responding that those places are for the ones for whom they have been prepared by God (20:23), Jesus points forward to the two brigands who would be crucified on his right and left (27:38). Thus the author creates a new dramatic irony by making the mother of the sons of Zebedee a witness to this fulfillment of Jesus' prophecy. She disappears after the scene at the cross; it is hard not to conclude that, like Judas, she has learned her lesson. And the characterization of the mother has misogynist overtones. In making the request, she performs the legitimate maternal role of brokering the status and future of her sons.[14] But the author uses her to remove the taint of misunderstanding and ambition from her two sons and at the same time evokes a stereotype of women as liable to cause competition and dissension among men that was a widespread feature of philosophical and literary debates about marriage.[15]

Whereas the first "teaching" of Jesus' ministry in Mark turns out to be an exorcism in the synagogue (Mark 1:21–28), Matthew's author supplanted this narrative with three chapters of practical wisdom, the Sermon on the Mount (5–7). Miracles come second in Matthew's narrative, organized into a suite of ten miracles interspersed with calls and teaching on discipleship (8:1–9:34). With the missionary sermon (9:35–11:1), these miracles provide the "deeds of the Messiah" (11:2–6) that identify Jesus as the "one to come." The cure of Peter's mother-in-law (8:14–15//Mark 1:29–31) is presented with two other miracles that illustrate Matthew's claim that Jesus' cures fulfill Isaiah 53:4 (Matt

8:17). As in Mark, she demonstrates and responds to her cure by "serving/ministering." In Matthew, her cure, with the many cures summarized in 8:16, leads to the emergence of new disciples and teaching on the cost of discipleship (Matt 8:18–22).

The double miracle of Jairus' daughter and the woman with the flow of blood (Matt 9:18–26//Mark 5:21–43) are also set into the context of discipleship; they immediately follow the call of the disciple named Matthew and the controversy stories that defend the practices of Jesus' disciples (Matt 9:9–17//Mark 2:13–22). Both miracle accounts are drastically shortened; the author generally tends to shorten and streamline the narratives of Mark. Miracles in particular are likely to be shorn of any detail that might associate them with magic and are focused more strongly around Jesus. In Matthew's narrative, the woman (described as bleeding) no longer cures herself, as she does in Mark; Jesus' commendation of her faith is no longer an acknowledgment of what has already happened, but the word that effects the healing. So, too, the emphasis on the crowd as an obstacle and the exchange of power and knowledge between Jesus and the woman disappear. Faith is no longer a prerequisite of Jesus' spiritual power as in Mark 6:5, but rather Jesus exercises that power to reward faith (Matt 13:58). The raising of Jairus' daughter is also modified. The girl's age is dropped, so that the symmetry between the woman's twelve years of illness and the girl's twelve years of life disappears. The Aramaic command and its translation have also been dropped, perhaps because the foreign language had magical overtones.[16]

Matthew's version of these two miracles has also been interpreted as a liberation of women from the restrictions of the Levitical purity code, and Amy-Jill Levine has addressed the highly problematic aspects of this interpretation.[17] She notes that the woman is not described as having a flow of blood, but simply as bleeding, and points out that it is by no means certain that the bleeding in question is uterine bleeding.[18] Dropping the note of the child's age also changes Mark's picture of a young girl dying on the brink of marriage. If this reading is correct, then the connection of the two women through twin perils to the female body disappears. Levine suggests a different juxtaposition: the bleeding woman reflects the saving blood of Jesus and the risen girl, an image of his resurrection.[19]

The Greek and Syro-Phoenician woman of Mark 7:24–30 emerges in Matthew 15:21–28 as a "Canaanite." This highly anachronistic characterization increases her foreignness; neither her language nor her place of origin connects her with the readers. Lest anyone miss the implication that "Canaanite" equals "Gentile," Matthew adds to Jesus' rude rebuff the explanatory words "I was sent only to the lost sheep of Israel" (compare Matt 10:6). By causing this gentile woman to address Jesus as "son of David," the author suggests that it is not only her persistence, but also the content of her faith in Jesus as the Messiah of the Jews that wins her case. In Matthew the exchange with this woman effects a unique grant to the Gentiles rather than a shift in Jesus' consciousness as in Mark; the succeeding cures appear to be set in Jewish territory (15:29–31). Thus it appears that, by comparison with Mark, Matthew has reduced not only the active participation of the woman with the flow of blood in her own cure, but also the narrative importance of the gentile woman.

Does this diminution mean that Matthew specifically wishes to reduce the activity of women in the narrative? This does not seem to be the case. For one thing, miracles involving men are equally drastically revised (see Matt 8: 28–32//Mark 5:1–20). For another, Matthew also introduces women into narratives in Mark. Kathleen Corley points out that Matthew explicitly includes women and children in the narratives of the feeding of the five and four thousand in the wilderness (14:15–21, 15:32–38). Corley interprets this note as an indication that Matthew has transformed Mark's version of the feeding story from a male-only symposium to a family meal. Presumably, the author of Matthew either assumed that Mark's reference to five thousand men (andres, Mark 6: 44) implied the presence of many more women and children or else sought to inflate the miracle. She argues that women are consistently present in the meals narrated in Matthew, and that this reflects the practice, including the eucharistic practice, of Matthew's community. Corley also notes that in Matthew Herodias and her daughter appear to be present at Herod's banquet. This suggests that women are accustomed to dining with men in Matthew's social context. At the same time, she observes that in Matthew the hostility toward John is Herod's rather than Herodias' (14:4 as opposed to Mark 6:19).[20]

One explanation for a diminished role of women in miracles may be that, since the gospel's christology is higher, miraculous power resides in Jesus, and the participants in miracles are less active. This could be read in conjunction with the references to "the twelve disciples" to suggest that the prophetic spirit is restricted in Matthew, so that communal authority is less egalitarian. In fact the picture is more complex. The function of miracles in Matthew is different than in Mark, where the miracles are central to the message, offering spiritual power to the reader. In Matthew, miracles function to identify Jesus as the Messiah and fulfiller of the scriptures. The prophetic experience of power and spirit resides in the process of teaching and learning, of making decisions about communal practice of God's will and word, particularly through the interpretation of scripture. The continuing presence of Jesus as the teacher of the community "wherever two or three are gathered" guaranteed this enterprise (18:18–20). The final words of the gospel are the promise, "I am with you always, until the completion of the age" (28:20). This promise is enabled through the Wisdom christology that has developed in part from sayings found in Q. In Matthew 11 the author weaves together a sequence of sayings to answer the question: "Are you the one who is to come, or shall we look for another?" The author claims that the messianic works that Jesus does (11:2–6) are the deeds of Wisdom, the divine female persona: "Wisdom is justified by all her works"(11:19). The invitation of Wisdom herself is placed on Jesus lips to complete his identification with her:

> Come to me all you who labor and are heavily burdened and I will give you rest. Take my yoke on you and learn from me, for I am meek and humble of heart and you will find rest for your souls. For my yoke is kindly and my burden is light.

This invitation draws on a number of speeches of Wisdom (Prov 8:1–9:6; Sir 24:19–23; 51:23–28; Isa 55:1–3). A shorter version is attributed to Jesus in the *Gospel of Thomas*, Saying 90: "Come to me, for my yoke is easy and my lordship is gentle, and you will find rest for yourselves."[21] But the author of Matthew, by joining Wisdom's invitation directly to the sayings that speak of the reciprocal knowledge of father and son, provides an explanation for the title "son of God." For Matthew "son of God" identifies Jesus not merely as the pious martyr of Wisdom 2 or as the messianic king of 2 Sam 7:14, but as Wisdom herself, God's image and God's offspring (Wis 7:24–26). Thus within the gospel the female persona of Wisdom virtually disappears behind the male person of Jesus. In Matt 23:34–35, Jesus articulates the divine plan by saying "on this account, lo, I (Jesus) send you prophets and sages and scribes." In Luke's version (and probably Q's), divine Wisdom is the speaker: "On this account also the Wisdom of God said 'lo, I shall send them prophets and emissaries'" (Luke 11:49–51). Wisdom's female persona may reemerge briefly here when Jesus compares himself to a hen gathering her chicks (Matt 23:36). The comparison between God's reign and the leaven a woman hides in dough may also involve a residual image of Wisdom who sets a table (13:33). The parable of the foolish and wise virgins in the last sermon of Jesus in Matthew draws upon two central wisdom traditions, the choice between the wise and foolish ways (Psalm 1; Matt 7:13–28; Didache 1–6) and the antithesis between woman Wisdom and foolish woman (Proverbs 7–9).[22]

The greatest number of new references to women in Matthew are those in the genealogy and the five brief stories about the birth and early childhood of Jesus that open the gospel. Both the genealogy and the stories are forms of scriptural interpretation; their main purpose is to identify Jesus as the Messiah, the legitimate descendent and heir of David. The genealogy traces the ancestry of Jesus through three times fourteen generations from father to son; it includes the names of four women: Tamar (Gen 38), Rahab (Joshua 2), Ruth, and the wife of Uriah (Bathsheba; 2 Samuel 11–12). The key is Tamar; when her father-in-law Judah accused her of adultery, she produced the tokens to show the child was his. Knowing that she had deceived him in order to force him to fulfill the law by giving children to his deceased sons through her, Judah declared: "She is more righteous than I" (Gen 38:26). All four of the women are in some degree suspect, but each ultimately proves righteous and a worthy mother to the lineage. It may also be the case that the four women are meant to indicate the inclusion of Gentiles in the messianic line, but the ultimate point of including the four seems to be to defend Mary, mysteriously pregnant before cohabiting with her spouse (1:18–25). Mary herself figures in the background of the five tales of Jesus' birth, each built around a dream, a citation of scripture, and a synonym for Messiah or an explanation of Jesus' messiahship. But Joseph is the protagonist, perhaps also to defend Mary from the charge of being a loose woman and Jesus from the charge of illegitimacy.[23]

The bulk of teaching in Matthew addresses practice; the material that most directly addresses gender is the divorce sayings. Wire takes the androcentric articulation of the divorce prohibitions as evidence that teaching in Matthew was directed toward the literate male disciples and not toward the women.[24] In fact, androcentric language in teaching and exhortation does not necessarily imply a male audience or even a male author. Many centuries later, Julian of Norwich and Teresa of Avila both tend to speak of the Christian with the masculine pronoun or the collective "man," even when referring to their own experience. But as Wire notes, more than androcentric language is involved.[25] Several aspects of Matthew's versions raise important issues about the construction of gender within the gospel.

Prohibitions of divorce appear twice in the gospel, once in the Sermon on the Mount (5:29–32) and once immediately following the church order (19: 2–12). The latter is directly based on Mark 10:2–12, which the author reorganizes by combining Mark's debate with the Pharisees (Mark 10:2–9) and the private teaching (Mark 10:10–12) that follows into a single public discourse. In the new debate, the question becomes whether a man may divorce his wife for every reason or only for impurity (a point of debate also attributed to the Pharisees in rabbinic sources). An exception for *porneia* (illicit sex) is added to the proscription of remarriage by a man (Matt 19:9). The proscription of remarriage by a woman who has divorced (Mark 10:12) disappears. Matthew then adds an entirely new section in which the disciples complain that, if that is the case of a man with a woman, it would be better not to marry—an opinion that Jesus commends, suggesting that those who are able to accept the counsel should make themselves "eunuchs for God's reign" (10–12).[26]

The revisions in Matt 19:2–9 are usually seen as aimed at a Jewish context. The prohibition of divorce and remarriage to a woman is assumed to have been dropped because Jewish women were unable to divorce anyway. *Porneia* is frequently interpreted as those sexual relations between kin forbidden by Leviticus. As is widely noted, one of the texts from Qumran does list forbidden relations as fornication, along with polygamy and sex with a menstruating woman (Damascus Document 5:8–9), and Paul applies the word to such relations (1 Cor 5:1). But it is by no means clear that these observations explain Matthew's version of the passage. For one thing, the view that Jewish women never initiated divorce is mistaken.[27] And while *porneia* can refer to forbidden relations, it is used more broadly both at Qumran and by Paul.[28]

While Matthew's revisions undoubtedly take some account of contemporary Jewish practice, they are formed primarily by the situation and concerns of early Christianity. Hermas, an early second century Christian prophet, recounts a visionary question-and-answer session that touches on divorce and remarriage. His formulation uses *porneia* to refer to the wife's adultery: if the husband knows her sin, and the wife does not repent, but persists in her fornication, he becomes liable for her sin and the sharer of her adultery.[29] Matthew appears to share this conviction, commending Joseph's decision to divorce the mysteriously pregnant Mary privately (Matt 1:19). This view was fostered not only by Jewish practice, but also by Roman law. Augustus' marriage legislation made adultery a matter of criminal law; men who did not divorce a wife accused of adultery could be prosecuted under a charge of pimping.[30] Thus an early Christian writer who forbids divorce and remarriage as Matthew does might find it necessary to add the exception of adultery in order to make clear that Christian practice does not fly in the face of the moral standard enshrined in the law by tolerating adultery.[31]

Matt 19:10–12, like Mark 10:10–12, is a special teaching addressed to the disciples. But this teaching, unlike Mark's, is not private, and it changes the context of the divorce question, showing that for Matthew the issue in questions of divorce and remarriage is sexual purity as a spiritual practice whose ultimate demand, for those who can manage, is to become "a eunuch for God's reign" (Matt 19:10–12). Matthew combines the "antifamilial" sayings from Q and sets them into the missionary discourse (Matt 10:34–37//Luke 12:51–53, 14:25–27, 17:33); perhaps the author sees the invitation to "make oneself a eunuch for the reign of God" as an extension of the disruption the reign causes in familial bonds.

Another application of the divorce sayings appears in Matt 5:27–32, within the Sermon on the Mount. In Matt 5:21–48, Jesus proposes a series of interpretations of the law as a way of "being perfect as your heavenly father is perfect" (5:48). In Matt 5:29–32, sayings of Jesus are presented as instruction for spiritual practice of the commandment, "You shall not commit adultery" (5:27, Exod 20:14). The first saying, found only in Matthew, extends the commandment by equating a lustful gaze with adultery (28). Verses 30–31 revise Mark 9:43–47, a set of three sayings commanding that one sacrifice one's right hand, foot, or eye rather than "stumble" (apostasize). In Mark (and in Matt 18:7–10, where the verses also appear), the sayings constitute an exhortation to martyrdom. But in Matthew 5:30–31, the concern is sexual; the hand and eye ("touching" and "looking") are the occasion of sexual sin. In 5:32, Matthew introduces the stipulation of a deed of divorce from Deut 24:1, interpreting it as a casuistic law that protects and explains the command against adultery by ensuring that no one can marry a woman who is still another man's wife. The sermon supplants it with two new commandments, one charging a divorcing husband with causing a woman's adultery and the other equating marriage to a divorced woman with adultery (5:32).[32]

Taken together, Matt 19:1–12 and 5:27–32 testify to the emergence of a Christian practice of sexual discipline regulating both the structures of marriage and the thoughts of the heart and culminating in rejection of sex "for those who can take it" (19:12). Although specifically Christian, this discipline builds on the teaching of Genesis and Deuteronomy, and the "exception" for adultery accommodates the Roman legal requirement that an adulterous wife be divorced. The practice is articulated in terms of the proper use of women by men. Women too are bound by it, but are not directly addressed. This does not mean that either this discipline or any of the rest of the prescriptions and decisions addressed to men throughout Matthew are not learned and practiced by women. But it does mean that women practitioners must either accommodate the teaching for themselves or themselves to the teaching.

Women are also perceived as sexual actors: prostitutes and tax collectors are said to have believed John and are preceding the high priests and elders into God's reign (Matt 21:31–32). Corley has taken this saying as an indication of

Matthew's more progressive gender ideology, which allows the community to risk the stigma of associating with loose women.[33] The first function of the saying in context is to shame the high priests and elders. But in the context of sexual practice in Matthew, the community may not so much signal its acceptance of former prostitutes as boast about its ability to transform them.

Thus Matthew seems to accept the continued communal and prophetic activity of women, as Mark and John do. But also as in Mark and John, anxiety about the flesh intervenes. Matthew's increasing concern with moral and ascetic practice causes women to be perceived as temptations, occasions when a man may give way to lust (Matt 5:28) or to greed and ambition (20:20). The Wisdom christology of Matthew is likewise two-edged; while its insistence on the continuing presence of Jesus endows the community with the capacity to rethink and remake its practice, it also effaces the female persona of Wisdom behind the male person of Jesus.

Luke-Acts

Luke-Acts is a two-volume historical work. In a formal dedicatory introduction, the author describes himself as following (*parēkolouthēkoti*, a masculine participle) other writers and reworking material from sources and witnesses into a narrative that shows the surety of Christian instruction (1:1–4). Some portions of Acts were written in the first person plural, and tradition ascribes the work to Luke, the companion of Paul, but few contemporary scholars believe that the author was an eyewitness to any parts of the narrative. Dates assigned to Luke-Acts range from 90 to about 145 CE. A number of factors in Luke-Acts accord particularly well with a date in the early second century: the style of scriptural quotation, the author's interest in martyrdom, the concern with distinguishing Christians from Jews, the use of the word "Christian," and the character of struggles over gender reflected in the texts all fit best into that period. The gospel could not have been written after 145 CE, as Marcion, a second-century Christian leader who rejected any continuity with Judaism and the Hebrew Bible, possessed a version of the gospel by about that date. Marcion's edition appears to have been both expurgated and originally shorter than the canonical edition. There is yet a third version, the so-called "Western" text of Luke-Acts, which is longer, particularly in Acts.[34] Thus Luke also underwent a process of development and editing. While Acts presupposes Luke, it is not certain that the author projected a second volume while writing the gospel.[35]

The gospel offers a real date for the year of John's appearance and Jesus' ministry (3:1) and is concerned to present its narrative on a world stage (Acts 26:26). The author's cultural attention to the Roman world and frequent references to "cities" (as opposed to villages) suggest that his mental landscape is the cities of Asia Minor and Greece that appear in Acts. The two books are driven by a theory of history that divides it into three periods: the period of the law and prophets through John the Baptist, the center of history in the year of Jesus' ministry, and the era of the church, which begins with the Pentecost story in

Acts 2, but is already envisaged in Luke 24:49.[36] This pattern tends to place Jesus definitively in the past in a way that the other gospels do not. Mark points forward to the appearance of Jesus (16:7), Matthew closes with Jesus insisting on his continued presence (28:20), and John treats ascension as a prelude to Jesus' appearances (20:17). But in Acts 1:3–14, the ascension story explicitly puts an end to resurrection appearances. Luke's Jesus is described in retrospect as "a man, a prophet mighty in word and work" (Luke 24:19), and one whom God "anointed with holy spirit who went about doing good and freeing all those downtrodden by the devil" (Acts 10:38).

The author of Luke-Acts appears to have deliberately multiplied representations of women within the narrative; there are significantly more women in Luke than in Mark and Q together, and stories about women are particularly striking in the gospel's special material. A number of these stories have played an important role in popular Christian feminist interpretation of the Bible. Among them are the cure of the bent-over woman (Luke 13:10–17), the story of Mary and Martha (Luke 10:38–42), and the infancy narratives (Luke 1–2). In the last (unlike Matthew's infancy stories), Mary is the protagonist; the other figures are related to Jesus through her, and the dilemmas and choices are hers. The story of the woman who had been bent over by "a spirit of weakness for eighteen years" (13:10) and became able to stand up straight had obvious appeal to the wide range of women struggling with the centuries of humiliations and restrictions imposed upon women by Christian denominations, as well as by the patriarchal social order. And the story is central to Luke's christology; it is articulated in terms of the prophetic message of release-forgiveness (*aphesis*) announced in Jesus' opening sermon (4:18–19); the woman was "bound" by Satan, and Jesus "freed her from her bond on the sabbath day" (13:17). The story of Martha and Mary played a role in arguments for the inclusion of women in discipleship; its ambiguities are discussed in chapter 5.

Unlike the other three canonical gospels, Luke-Acts uses gender as a central category. This has sometimes caused Luke to be read as the gospel for women.[37] But a number of feminist scholars have observed that Luke's writings also restrict or denigrate the participation of women.[38] Luke-Acts is less a compilation of good news for women than, in the words of Turid Karlsen Seim, a "double message."[39]

The centrality of gender in Luke-Acts emerges most notably in the pairing of stories about women with stories about men. There are two types of paired stories in Luke. The first is a unit of two brief stories with an identical point or similar function, one story about a male figure and one about a female figure.[40] This technique does not originate with Luke; some pairs of this type are taken over from Q, while others are from Mark. But in many cases, the story about the man comes from Mark or Q, while the one about the woman is special to Luke; one example is the man who had a hundred sheep (Luke 15:1–7//Matt 18:10–14) supplemented in Luke by the woman who had ten coins (Luke 14:8–10). Frequently, the story about the woman displays interests characteristic of the author: the cure of the centurion's servant focuses on the centurion's recognition of Jesus as one under authority, whose mighty deed attests both power and obedience (Luke 7:1–10//Matt 8:5–13). The raising of the widow's son follows this story in Luke and defines its christology in a Lukan vein: Jesus is a great prophet (7:16//Luke 4:19); his deed recalls Elijah and Elisha (Luke 4: 25–27), both of whom also raised a woman's only son (1 Kgs 17:17–24; 2 Kgs 4:18–37). In some cases, both members of the pair are special to Luke and display characteristic Lukan themes. Among these are the two annunciations, to Zachariah and to Mary (Luke 1:5–38); the two prophets who greet the child in the temple (2:25–29); the examples of the widow and the judge and the Pharisee and the publican (18:1–17); Peter's cure of lame Aeneas and his raising of Tabitha (Acts 9:32–43).

The second type might be termed "architectural" pairs: two similar stories are told in different contexts to bind the narrative together and to manifest the coherence of "God's plan and work."[41] As a list of the twelve male disciples precedes the sermon on the plain (Luke 6:12–19), so a list of named women disciples precedes the parables sermon (8:1–3).

Lukan pairs of one or the other type can be detected in almost every chapter of the gospel:

two annunciations: to Zachariah and to Mary	1:5–23
	1:26–38
two songs: of Mary and of Zachariah	1:46–56
	1:67–79
two prophets: Simeon and Anna	2:25–35, 36–38
two miracles: for gentile widow and male leper	4:25–27
two first miracles: for possessed man and Peter's mother-in-law	4:31–39 (Mark 1:21–31)
two lists of named disciples: men apostles	6:12–19 (Mark 3:12–19)
and women ministers	8:1–3
two rescues from death: the centurion's servant	7:1–10 (Matt 8:5–13)
the widow's son	7:11–17
two penitents: the paralytic	5:19–26 (Mark 2:1–12)
the penitent woman	7:35–50 (Mark 14:1–11?)
three miracles: the Gerasene demoniac, the daughter of Jairus, the hemorrhaging woman	8:26–56 (Mark 5:1–43)
three questions about discipleship: the scribe	10:25–37 (Mark 12:28–34)
Martha	10:38–42
the disciples	11:1–13
two gentile accusers of Israel: the Ninevites and the queen of the south	11:29–36 (Matt 12:38–42)
two "releases": the bent-over woman and the dropsical man	13:10–17 14:1–6 (Mark 3:1–6?)
two hider parables: man (?) planting mustard	13:18–19

woman hiding leaven	13:20–21
	(Matt 13:31–33)
two finder parables: man with sheep	15:1–7
	(Matt 18:12–14)
woman with coin	15:8–10
two taken: men (?) sleeping, women grinding	17:32–35
	(Matt 24:40–41)
two examples of prayer: widow, Pharisee and publican	8:9–17
two attitudes to worship: scribes and widow	20:45–21:4
	(Mark 12:37–44)
two sets of followers: Simon and women	23:26–32
	(Mark 15:21)
two groups of watchers: women and all his acquaintances	23:49
	(Mark 15:40–41)
two groups of resurrection witnesses	24
	(Mark 16:1–8)

It should be noted that, while the stories about women usually have been added by the author, not every story about a man is doubled with a story about a woman; men still outnumber women in the gospel.[42] And in some cases, men are introduced to the narrative: men are added to the group of women watching at the cross (23:49).

Although the appearances of women are significantly fewer in Acts than in Luke, Acts also includes a number of references to women paired with men. But the pairs in the two works differ significantly. In Luke, the pairs consist of a variety of paired stories that form a single unit or a sequence and architectural pairs of stories, while in Acts most (though not all) of the references to women consist not of paired stories, but of either the names of couples or the merismus: "both men and women"

two groups waiting	1:13–14
menservants and maidservants, sons and daughters	2:17–18
Ananias and Sapphira	5:1–11
a crowd of both men and women added	5:14
Paul as persecutor of both men and women	8:3
both men and women added	8:12
Paul as persecutor of both men and women	9:2
Peter cures lame man and Tabitha	9:32–43
worshipping women and first men of the city	13:50
Paul driven from Lystra by cure of lame man	14:5–18
Paul driven from Philippi by cure of mantic girl	16:16–40
Lydia baptized with all her household	16:15
jailer baptized with all his household	16:32–34
a great crowd of worshipping Greeks and not a few of the first women were persuaded	17:4
not a few respectable Greek women and men	17:12
Dionysus and Damaris converted at Athens	17:34
Paul received by Priscilla and Aquila	18:1–4

four prophesying daughters of Philip and Agabus, the prophet from Judea	21:8–14
Paul as persecutor of both men and women	22:4
Felix arrives with Drusilla	24:24
Agrippa and Bernike	25:13, 23, 26:30

The architectural pairs of women and men clearly serve the literary plan of the work. The two lists of disciples offer a good example; Luke uses them to create two parallel sections in the ministry of Jesus in Galilee and Judea. These sections consist of a suite of miracles and debates followed by a disciple list and a discourse; in each case the discourse closes with a reference to hearing and doing the word:

Lukan Parallel Sections

4:31–5:16 cures, call of Peter	7:1–17 2 rescues from death: centurion's servant, gentile benefactor widow's son, "great prophet"
5:17–6:11 debates, call of Levi	7:18–50 2 debates: question of John, benefactions of Jesus—"a prophet and more" deed of woman, "if he were a prophet"
6:12–19 list of twelve	8:1–3 list of women disciples, women benefactors
6:20–49 sermon	8:4–21 parables discourse: mother and brother and *sister*
sermon closing:	
6:47–49 hearing and doing word	8:21 hearing and doing word

The first section, 4:31–6:49, consists primarily of narrative from Mark followed by a sermon from Q; in the second, 7:1–8:21, partially narrative material from Q alternates with narratives about women that are special to Luke and is followed by an abbreviated version of the parables sermon from Mark. The stories about women manifest Luke's christological concerns. The raising of the widow's son casts Jesus into the heroic mold of Elijah and Elisha, and the crowd's response acclaims him as a prophet (7:16). The story of the repentant woman both demonstrates Jesus' prophetic knowledge of the human heart and proclaims his prophetic message of forgiveness of debts and release from bondage (7:39; cf. 4:18–19; Acts 10:38).[43]

While there is no doubt that this deployment of gender is intentional, it is less clear what the author's intentions are. Closer examination of 8:1–3 underlines the problems:

After that he was journeying from city to village preaching and proclaiming the reign of God and the twelve were with him, and some women who had been cured from evil spirits and diseases: Mary, called Magdalene, from whom seven devils had gone out, and Johanna wife of Chuza the steward of Herod, and Susanna, and many other women, who used to minister to them from their resources.

These verses revise Mark 15:40–41, the list of women disciples at the cross. As I suggested above, the list has been brought forward to parallel the list of male disciples in Luke 6:12–16. This highlights the notable contrast between the treatment of these women and both Mark's view of them and the treatment of the male disciples. In Luke 6:12–16, the twelve were explicitly called, given the title "apostles," and associated with Jesus' ministry. In 8:1–3 the women are said to be with Jesus not as result of a special call, but out of gratitude for cures; they are not described as following (disciples), as the women in Mark 15:40–41 are, and they share in Jesus' ministry not by preaching and healing as the twelve do in 9:1–6, but by ministering to them (Jesus and the twelve) "out of their resources," that is, by supporting them, acting as benefactors to the preachers and healers.[44]

The same distinction between women and men appears in Acts 1:12–26. After a list of the remaining eleven (1:13–14), the author mentions the presence of women. The only named woman is Mary, the mother of Jesus; the women disciples named in 8:1–3 and 24:10 are not mentioned, though their presence must be assumed. These verses provide the introduction to the selection of Barnabas to replace Judas Iscariot in his "ministry and apostleship" (1:17, 25). The requirements for this role are defined here as including maleness (Acts 1:21; see above chapter 5).[45] Only after this distinction is made is the spirit poured out on "all your sons and daughters," all God's men slaves and women slaves (2:17–18).

Similarly, widows in Luke-Acts are distanced from a ministerial role. Acts speaks of widows as a group in 6:1–7 and 9:36–42; in both cases, widows are the recipients of charity. In Acts 6:1–7, the author narrates the creation of a separate ministry of the table distinct from the apostles' ministry of the word and the appointment of seven men to fill it. It is occasioned by dissension over the portions given to the widows of the Hellenists (probably the Greek-speaking community in Jerusalem), but the widows do not participate in the ministry; they are its objects. So, too, in 9:36–39, the widows, who might be considered to be the companions and associates of the disciple Dorcas, are actually described as the recipients of her alms in the form of garments she made (9:36–39).[46]

In the gospel also, widows appear as emblems of vulnerability, and in one case, as contentious. Only one context in Mark mentions widows; in Mark 12:38–44, the accusation that scribes eat up houses of widows is contrasted with the widow who gives her whole living to the temple treasury. This contrast is adopted by Luke (20:45–21:4) and supplemented with a number of other examples: the widow of Sarepta (4:25–26); the widow of Nain (7:12); the troublesome widow and unjust judge (18:3–5); and Anna, the widow and prophetess in the temple (2:36–38). Luke's picture must be considered in light of 1 Tim 5:3–16, which explicitly restricts widows to forms of service that do not include preaching, teaching, or going about from house to house and also restricts those who may be assisted as widows by requiring that they be once married, beyond the age of childbearing, celibate, and destitute.[47] For 1 Timothy, the widow's main task is to spend her days and nights in prayer (1 Tim 5:5).

Anna, Luke's ideal widow, offers both commonalities and points of contrast with 1 Timothy. A virgin until her marriage, Anna was married properly (though briefly) and once only and spends her time in the temple, worshipping God through fasting and praying. Luke does not share 1 Timothy's demand that young widows remarry, but approves Anna's early ascetic commitment. Though she has been stable rather than going from place to place, Anna's sphere is the public domain of the temple, and she is a prophet from Luke's era of the law and the prophets.[48] Thus, while Luke seems to treat widows as a distinct group, they are not allowed to take on the contours of a Christian ministry and function primarily as ascetics and exemplars of vulnerability and endurance. In antiquity, widows with either property or family might well have a relative degree of autonomy; this social reality may have instigated Luke, as well as 1 Timothy and later church orders, to restrict or deny their ministerial role in the community.[49]

The question of prophecy raises further issues; the quotation of Joel that explains the outpouring of the spirit leads one to expect women prophets ("your daughters, God's maidservants") to figure prominently in Luke's narrative, particularly within the era of the church:

> and it will be in those days, says God,
> I will pour out my spirit upon all flesh,
> and your sons and your daughters will prophesy,
> and your youths will see visions
> and your elders dream dreams
> even upon my men slaves and women slaves
> in those days I will pour out my spirit
> and they will prophesy.
> (Acts 2:17–18, Joel 2:29–30)

But this does not prove to be the case. Mary and Elizabeth both are given long and powerful prophetic utterances, but they are not explicitly said to prophesy and are distanced from the reader by the formal and archaic character of their speech and also by Luke's historical scheme: they belong to the period of the law and the prophets. So does Anna, who seems to have been modeled on Judith. Even so, although the reader is told that she spoke about the child Jesus to everyone entering and leaving the temple, Luke gives Anna no prophetic speeches. In Acts, the only Christian example of prophetic women is the four virgin daughters of Philip (Acts 21:8–9), but they are not permitted to speak. The prophecy of Paul's arrest in the succeeding verses is awarded to Agabus, the male prophet who is paired with them (21:10–14).[50] When the mantic servant girl in Acts 16:16–18 proclaims Paul's and Silas' mission, her words are not from the holy spirit, but from the demon from whom Paul frees her (Acts 16:16–18).

Within Jesus' ministry, women are no longer presented as prophets, but rather stories about women serve the portrait of Jesus as prophet. The woman who pronounces a blessing on Jesus' mother in Luke 11:27–28 could be seen as speaking prophetically, but her prophecy is corrected by Jesus' response.[51] Martha likewise speaks only to be corrected by Jesus; Mary, the sister of Martha (10:38–40), and the repentant woman (7:36–50), who are both approved and defended by Jesus, are themselves silent.

Most notably, the woman prophet who anoints Jesus in Mark, Matthew, and John disappears from the narrative. The only anointing in Luke is done by the repentant woman, who is identified not as a prophet, but as a sinner (7:37). She weeps and washes and kisses his feet, as well as anointing and wiping them with her hair (7:38). Jesus interprets her gesture as expressing love and penitence; she neither announces Jesus' messiahship nor predicts his death, but gives Jesus the opportunity to display his own prophetic knowledge of her heart and his host's (7:39–47) and to proclaim his message of release-forgiveness (aphesis 7:48–50; 4:18–19). In part this distancing of women from prophecy is due to Luke's christology and salvation history; references to the spirit and to prophecy, so frequent in Luke 1–4 and in Acts, disappear almost entirely after the sermon in the synagogue at Nazareth. Since Jesus is anointed with the spirit (4:18–19; Acts 10:37–38), his deeds are its manifestation, and it is wholly identified with his activity. But the twelve and the seventy (two) are able to share in his prophetic ministry of preaching and healing (9:1–2), and when a man responds to Jesus with a beatitude, his words are supplemented rather than corrected (14:15–24).[52]

Thus Luke's multiplication of representations of women is accompanied by a corresponding limitation of their roles. Luke is concerned not with changing the status of women, but with the appropriate deployment of gender. The strategies that Luke uses to define the right roles of women also contribute to a construction of manliness. One indication of this is Luke's use of the word anēr, andros (man) as specifically male, as hero or as husband. Most of the other uses in the New Testament connote husband, or at least sexual partner. The speeches in Acts continually open with the address "men, Israelites," (or "men, brethren," or "men, Athenians").[53] The address does not so much exclude women from its audiences as construct these audiences (the audiences within the narrative, but also the readers and hearers) as solemn civic assemblies.[54] The public aspect of the community corresponds to Luke's heroic christology. Luke is virtually alone in the New Testament in defining Jesus as anēr (Luke 24:19; Acts 2:22),[55] specifically as "a man, a prophet" (anēr prophētēs), a compilation that probably reflects the language and the heroic prophets of the Deuteronomic history. The word anēr is used throughout Luke-Acts for heavenly figures[56] and the heroic martyrs Paul and Stephen.[57] The gospel, too, depicts Jesus as the heroic example of martyrdom by the courage and magnanimity with which he faces his death (Luke 23:33–48). In ancient martyr literature, women can also exemplify "manliness" (andreia, courage).[58] But no women are praised for manly virtue in Luke-Acts.

Three interrelated concerns are among those that guide Luke's deployment of gender: the public character of the work, the desire to tame and limit prophecy, and the character of Luke's interest in asceticism. The first then, is the public character of the two-volume work, its conception as history set in real time on a world stage. Seim contextualizes Luke's interest in gender in terms of the Attic conviction that "the world of men is one, the world of women another."[59] While this apothegm captures Luke's careful division and presentation of male and female roles in the community, the cultural and political context of Luke-Acts is Roman rather than Attic.[60] The dual nature of Luke's treatment of women corresponds to the increasing Roman interest in signaling public meanings through appropriations of the domestic world, that is, to the political use of "family values" begun by Augustus.[61] In the late first and early second century, public functions of the women of the imperial family appear to have increased; the imperial women accompanied Trajan, Hadrian, and the Antonines on campaigns,[62] as Drusilla and Bernike do Felix and Agrippa in Acts (Acts 24:24, 25:13, 23).[63] The increasing appearance of *merismoi* and couples in Acts (except for Agrippa and Bernike, marital pairs) probably relates to the heightened prestige and public function of marriage in the late first century and early second century.[64]

A second concern is the desire to tame and limit prophecy. Luke appears to have chosen prophecy as the central explanation for Jesus (and, in fact, for the apostles and ministers) because it is a Biblical role that translates with relative ease into the god-inspired man of Greek and Roman religion and philosophy. But it leaves Jesus and the early Christians open to the charge laid against Paul and Silas in the Roman colony, Philippi: "They are Jews, and proclaim customs which we are not permitted to receive or do, being Romans" (Acts 16:20–21). The author of Luke-Acts transforms glossolalia from unintelligible to universally intelligible language in Acts 2:5–12.[65] More importantly, the author restricts the apostolic role by cutting off the revelatory appearances of Jesus with the ascension story (1:1–26) and awarding a quasi appearance to Paul (9:1–10). Peter and Paul are carefully distinguished from a number of Jewish and Samaritan magicians over whom they conspicuously triumph: Simon Magus (8:9–25), the Jew Bar Jesus (13:6–12), and the seven sons of the Jewish high priest Sceva (19:11–20). Luke is clearly addressing the antique prejudice that equates Jews and other "orientals" with magic.[66] Antique prejudice also associated women with magic and with flirtations with oriental religions; at least one Roman author saw a woman prophet as the prototypical purveyor of Judaism to women:

> No sooner has he pushed off than a palsied Jewess
> Parking her haybox outside, comes round soliciting alms
> In a breathy whisper. She knows and can interpret
> The Laws of Jerusalem: a high priestess under the trees,
> A faithful mediator of heaven on earth. She too
> Fills her palm, but more sparingly: Jews will sell you
> Whatever dreams you like for a few small coppers.[67]

If this conjunction of Judaism, women, and prophecy in Juvenal's mind was shared by others of the imperial ruling class (or by the popular mind), it is not surprising that the author of Luke-Acts sought to minimize the undoubted participation of women in early Christian prophecy, as well as to dissociate Christianity from Judaism.[68]

A third factor in this deployment of gender is the character of Luke's interest in asceticism. Sexual asceticism was by no means always hostile to women, as the story of Thecla shows (see chapters 11, 13, and 14). In fact renunciation of sexuality could allow for a more egalitarian leadership. Luke-Acts provides Anna as an exemplar of female asceticism, and presumably the virgin daughters of Philip are also to be seen as practictioners of asceticism.[69] Luke's revisions of the question about the woman married successively to seven brothers have frequently been interpreted as an endorsement of celibacy (20:20–23).[70] Further, Luke retains the prohibition of remarriage while eliminating prohibition of divorce (16:18). The wording of the saying assumes that only the behavior of the man is at issue, and even this saying functions primarily on the metaphorical level in Luke.[71] While a husband may leave a wife for God's reign, the reverse is not stated, despite alternatives of leaving both parents and children, sisters and brothers (Luke 14:26, 18:29). As I suggested above, the prospect of a wife leaving a husband was seen as an assault on good order and particularly dangerous to a community under suspicion of un-Roman activities.[72] Of particular interest is the relation between two sayings in Luke and *Gospel of Thomas*, Saying 79:

> A woman from the crowd said to him, "Blessed are the womb that bore you and the breasts that nourished you."
>
> He said to [her], "Blessed are those who have heard the word of the father and have truly kept it. For there will be days when you will say, 'Blessed are the womb which have not conceived and the breasts which have not given milk.' "[73]

In Luke, the exchange of beatitudes appears separately (11:27–28), and the prediction that quotes a third beatitude is a prophecy of the revolt and fall of Jerusalem made to the women who weep for Jesus on the way to the cross (23:29). The conjunction of the sayings in *Thomas* constitutes an endorsement of celibacy for women. Seim suggests that it is addressed to the women of Jerusalem who weep over Jesus specifically to contrast them with the women followers of Jesus who are without children.[74] But it may be that Luke was inspired to reset the beatitude on the childless as a woe on Jerusalem by the need to avoid an explicit endorsement for celibacy for women. While sexual asceticism among women could enable their participation in prophecy and communal leadership, when asceticism was encouraged for men and discouraged for women, the anti-marriage tradition's misogynist arguments could emerge in the rationale for male celibacy. This never quite happens in Luke. But Luke's version of the banquet parable suggests that marrying a wife may hold a man back from the reign of God (14:20). When Ananias and Sapphira "lie to the holy spirit" by holding back part of the price of a field they sold, they do it jointly as a couple (Acts 5:1–10). The story may reflect Luke's concurrence in the view that marriage involves a man with material distractions from the world of the spirit.

The common factor in all of this is that the author includes women to display the good order in the private sphere that the Christians foster, and that makes them the best possible contributors to the public matter (*res publica*), potential citizens of Rome like Paul—even if, like Paul, they are so desperately misunderstood. This is not to say that the gospel reflects the reluctant concession of a persecuted minority to the demands of a more rigid culture. Luke invites the Christian readers to exactly what he believes to be genuine good order—to what is safe not only because it is acceptable to Roman order, but also because it constitutes a kind of moral high ground. The Christians' women are omnipresent, but properly behaved. Male and female roles are clearly and appropriately delineated. Women exhibit the excellence of the community by receiving the gift of prophecy, but they do nothing obtrusive with it. They are chaste, and even celibate, but their chastity does not threaten marriage (as Thecla's does) or remove them from the proper role of women within the well-ordered family. And all of this good order is due to the ordered dispensation of the spirit of God in the laying on of the apostles' hands.

Conclusion

The double message in Luke becomes conspicuous precisely because Luke has found it necessary to address gender directly. But a double message inheres in all of the gospel literature. In all four of the canonical gospels (as in Mary and in Thomas), women have some access to the spirit of prophecy. In all of the gospels, anxiety about sexuality and sexual propriety emerges as an obstacle to women's ability to exercise the authority that attends it. Femaleness in antiquity is defined by sexual contact. In John, Mark, and Matthew, the participation of women in communal prophecy is assumed; where issues of sexuality or gender are addressed at all, they are articulated in terms of infringements of propriety or holiness. The exception may be the final chapters of John, which seem to reflect struggles over communal leadership. But if Mary's gender is part of the struggle, this issue is never made explicit. In Luke-Acts, Mary, and Thomas, the issue is addressed directly, and with strikingly different results. For Luke-Acts, women remain women; their role in the community deserves careful attention for the proper participation of women attests the good order and restraint of the Christians. For Mary, women's leadership, however problematic, rests directly on the revelations of the savior; no other consideration can intervene. For Thomas, femaleness remains an inhibition, but one that can, and must, be overcome: Mary becomes male. These varying positions by no means disappeared; they were espoused, rejected, combined, modified, and recombined in the long history of Christian attempts to accommodate its necessary and internal "others" and the concomitant history of women's attempts to accommodate or resist in return.

In retrospect, I want to return to a question I raised briefly above, the question of whether any of the four canonical gospels could have been the work of a woman. This is ultimately an unanswerable question; even the assumption of a male persona by Luke does not exclude the possibility that this Anonymous was a woman. Like Kraemer, I do not believe that a woman's authorship would necessarily be detectable by traces in the text, or that androcentric perspectives in a text exclude the possibility that a woman authored it.[75] Obviously, to be able to show that a woman wrote one of these works would offer the reassurance that women did, indeed, write early Christian books and, even, the central scripture of early Christianity. But would it make any difference to the interpretation of the texts? On the whole, I have been inclined to argue that it would make very little difference: the worldview they enshrine is that of the early Christian communities. Allowing the texts to have women authors would only show what must already be assumed: that women, if they welcomed the participation that was permitted them, also in large part accepted the propriety of limitations that gender placed upon them—and taught it to their daughters. This would be most striking in the case of Luke's double message. But recently, my imagination has been stirred by Crossan's suggestion that the woman author of Mark may have enshrined her signature in the promise that the prophet who anointed Jesus will be remembered wherever the gospel is preached.[76]

I do not, of course, wish to argue that the gospel was written by this woman prophet—or by any eyewitness to Jesus. But it has caused me to rethink the question, especially in the case of Mark and John. Mark ends with the silent women running from the empty tomb, and anonymous women figures, especially the Greek woman, offer themselves as ways for the audience to place themselves within the narrative. It is possible to postulate an early version of John ending with the figure of Mary Magdalene, charged with the message of Jesus' ascension, in which the voices of the Samaritan woman, of Martha and Mary, and of the mother of Jesus were even more prominent. To imagine a woman author of these works does not change the gendered arrangements they reflect. But it does cast the stories about women as signatures, as ways in which the writer declares herself within the narrative, placing a particular emphasis upon women of the final scenes. And this is a speculation that points the twentieth-century reader to what these gospels certainly had: women readers and women hearers for whom the gender of Mary Magdalene could be good news.

NOTES

1. Elisabeth Schüssler Fiorenza, But She Said: Feminist Practices of Biblical Interpretation (Boston: Beacon) 97–98.

2. Franz Neirynck, "Synoptic Problem," in New Jerome Biblical Commentary ed. Raymond E. Brown, Joseph A. Fitzmyer, and Roland E. Murphy (Englewood Cliffs, NJ: Prentice-Hall, 1988) 587–95, esp. 589.

3. Helmut Koester, Ancient Christian Gospels (Philadelphia: Trinity Press International, 1990) 284–86.

4. See the discussion by John Meier, "Matthew, Gospel of," ABD 4:624–25; Jack Dean Kingsbury, "Matthew, Gospel According to," in HarperCollins Bible Dictionary, ed. Paul J. Achtemeier (San Francisco: HarperSanFrancisco, 1996) 661.

5. Kathleen E. Corley, Private Women, Public Meals: Social Conflict in the Synoptic Tradition (Peabody, MA: Hendrickson, 1993) 185–186; see chapter 3.

6. Anthony Saldarini, Matthew's Jewish Christian Community (Chicago: University of Chicago, 1994); see also Saldarini, "The Gospel of Matthew and Jewish-Christian Conflict," in Social History of the Matthean Community: Cross Disciplinary Approaches, ed. David L. Balch (Minneapolis, MN: Fortress, 1991) 38–61.

7. See Alan Segal, *Rebecca's Children: Judaism and Christianity in the Roman World* (Cambridge, MA: Harvard University Press, 1986); see also Segal, "Matthew's Jewish Voice," in Balch, *Social History* 3–37.

8. Saldarini (note 6 above) and Segal (note 7 above) address these tensions in their discussions; Corley (note 5 above) is less attentive to the problem. For a summary of relatively recent opinions on the issue, see John Meier, "Matthew" 624–27.

9. The phrase is that of Wayne Meeks, *The Moral World of the First Christians* (Library of Early Christianity 6; Philadelphia: Westminster, 1986) 136.

10. W. D. Davies, *The Setting of the Sermon on the Mount* (Cambridge: Cambridge University Press, 1966) 14–15. The exact beginnings and endings of some sermons are my own revisions of the standard views.

11. Antoinette Wire, "Gender Roles in a Scribal Community," in Balch, *Social History* 113.

12. This translation and all translations in the essay are my own unless otherwise noted.

13. Corley, *Private Women* 171.

14. See Suzanne Dixon, *The Roman Mother* (Norman, OK: University of Oklahoma Press, 1988) 168–70.

15. Susan Treggiari: *Roman Marriage. Iusti Coniuges from the Time of Cicero to the Time of Ulpian* (Oxford: Clarendon, 1991) 183–210.

16. John Hull, *Hellenistic Magic and the Synoptic Tradition* (Studies in Biblical Theology, Second Series, 28 London: SCM, 1974) 73–86; Mary Rose D'Angelo, "Theology in Mark and Q: Abba and 'Father' in Context," HTR 85 (1992) 156–62.

17. Amy-Jill Levine, "Discharging Responsibility: Matthean Jesus, Biblical Law and Hemorrhaging Women," in *Treasures New and Old: New Essays in Matthean Studies*, ed. Mark Allan Powell and David Bauer (Atlanta, GA: Scholars Press, 1996) 379–97. See also chapter 6 and D'Angelo, "Gender and Power in the Gospel of Mark: The Daughter of Jairus and the Woman with the Flow of Blood," in *Aspects of the Miraculous in Ancient Judaism and Christianity* ed. John C. Cavadini (Notre Dame, IN: University of Notre Dame Press, forthcoming).

18. Amy-Jill Levine, "Discharging Responsibility" 384–85.

19. Ibid. 396–97.

20. Corley, *Private Women* 160–64.

21. Trans. Marvin Meyer, *Q-Thomas Reader*, John S. Kloppenborg, M. Meyer, S. J. Patterson, and M. G. Steinhauser, eds. (Sonoma, CA: Polebridge, 1990) 150.

22. For a discussion of Wisdom christology in Matthew, see Celia Deutsch, "Wisdom in Matthew: Transformation of a Symbol," NovT 32 (1990) 13–47; also Deutsch, *Hidden Wisdom and the Easy Yoke: Wisdom, Torah and Discipleship in Matthew* 11.25–30 (Sheffield, UK: JSOT, 1987); Deutsch, *Lady Wisdom, Jesus and the Sages: Metaphor and Social Context in Matthew's Gospel* (Valley Forge, PA: Trinity Press International, 1996).

23. Similarly, Corley, *Private Women* 147–51.

24. Wire, "Gender Roles" 105.

25. Ibid.

26. Mary Rose D'Angelo, "Remarriage and the Divorce Sayings Attributed to Jesus," in *Divorce and Remarriage: Religious and Psychological Perspectives*, ed. William P. Roberts (Kansas City, MO: Sheed and Ward, 1990) 83–84.

27. See Kraemer chapters 2 and 3.

28. D'Angelo, "Remarriage and the Divorce Sayings" 96–97.

29. *Shepherd of Hermas, Mandate* 4.4; see D'Angelo, "Remarriage and the Divorce Sayings" 98.

30. Treggiari, *Roman Marriage* 288.

31. See also Corley, *Private Women* 158.

32. D'Angelo, "Remarriage and the Divorce Sayings" 96.

33. Corley, *Private Women* 152–158.

34. R. M. Grant, "Marcion, Gospel of," *ABD* 4:516–20.

35. Richard Pervo and Mikael Parson, *Rethinking the Unity of Luke and Acts* (Minneapolis, MN: Fortress, 1993).

36. This is a modified version of the schema described by Hans Conzelmann in *The Theology of St. Luke*, trans. Geoffrey Buswell (New York: Harper and Row, 1961) 150.

37. Constance F. Parvey, "The Theology and Leadership of Women in the New Testament," in *Religion and Sexism*, ed. Rosemary Radford Ruether (New York: Simon and Schuster, 1974) 139–46; Eugene H. Maly, "Women and the Gospel of Luke," *Biblical Theology Bulletin* 10 (1980) 99–104 and the literature cited therein; also Celeste J. Rossmiller, "Prophets and Disciples in Luke's Infancy Narrative," *Bible Today* 22/6 (1984) 361–65; Rosalie Ryan, "The Women from Galilee and Discipleship in Luke," *Biblical Theology Bulletin* 15 (1985) 56–59; Quentin Quesnell, "The Women at Luke's Supper," in *Political Issues in Luke-Acts*, ed. R. J. Cassidy and P. J. Scharper (Maryknoll, NY: Orbis, 1983) 59–79; E. Jane Via, "Women, the Discipleship of Service and the Early Christian Ritual Meal in the Gospel of Luke," *St. Luke's Journal of Theology* 29 (1985) 37–60; Via, "Women in the Gospel of Luke," in *Women in the World's Religions: Past and Present*, ed. Ursula King (New York: Paragon House, 1987) 38–55.

38. For earlier critical views of Luke, see Elizabeth Tetlow, *Women and Ministry in the New Testament* (New York: Paulist, 1980) 101; Elisabeth Schüssler Fiorenza, "Word, Spirit and Power: Women in Early Christian Communities," in *Women of Spirit: Female Leadership in the Jewish and Christian Traditions*, ed. Rosemary Radford Ruether and Eleanor McLaughlin (New York: Simon and Schuster, 1979) 52, n. 114; Schüssler Fiorenza, *In Memory of Her: A Feminist Theological Reconstruction of Christian Origins* (New York: Crossroad, 1983) 161; and Schüssler Fiorenza, "A Feminist Critical Interpretation for Liberation: Martha and Mary: Luke 10:38–42," *Religion and Intellectual Life* 3 (1986) 21–35.

39. From the title of Turid Karlsen Seim's book, *The Double Message: Patterns of Gender in Luke-Acts* (Nashville, TN: Abingdon, 1994); see also Seim's commentary in Elisabeth Schüssler Fiorenza, *Searching the Scriptures: Volume 2, A Feminist Commentary* (New York: Crossroad, 1994). A very similar stance is taken by my article, "Women in Luke-Acts: A Redactional View," *JBL* 109 (1990) 441–61.

40. This technique was first discussed by Parvey ("Theology and Leadership of Women" 139–40). She points out that the pairing technique was noted by Jeremias in The Parables of Jesus (note 39).

41. On the technique, see Charles Talbert, *Literary Patterns, Theological Themes and the Genre of Luke-Acts* (Missoula, MT: Society of Biblical Literature; distributed by Scholars Press, 1974). Cf. Acts 5:38–39, with 2:23, 13:36, 20:27.

42. Jane C. Schaberg, "Luke," in *The Women's Bible Commentary*, ed. Carol A. Newsom and Sharon H. Ringe (Louisville, KY: Westminster/John Knox, 1992) 275–92.

43. For a more extensive discussion of the pairs and their function, see D'Angelo, "Women in Luke-Acts" 443–48.

44. On benefaction in Luke, see D'Angelo, "Women in Luke-Acts" 449.

45. See, similarly, Seim, *Double Message* 111–12.

46. Seim, *Double Message* 229–48; see also Clarice Martin, "The Acts of the Apostles," in Schüssler Fiorenza, *Searching the Scriptures* 780–82.

47. See chapter 11, also chapter 13 below.

48. Seim, *Double Message* 221–48.

49. See chapter 13.

50. See also Martin, "Acts of the Apostles" 786–87; Ivoni Richter Reimer, *Women in the Acts of the Apostles: A Feminist Liberation Perspective* (Minneapolis, MN: Fortress, 1995) 248–49, argues against "competition" between Agabus and the four woman.

51. Mary Rose D'Angelo, "Blessed the One Who Reads and Those Who Hear: The Beatitudes in Their Biblical Contexts," in *New Perspectives on the Beatitudes*, ed. Francis A. Eigo (Proceedings of the Theology Institute of Villanova University; Villanova, PA, 1995) 56–61, 76–78.

52. D'Angelo, "Blessed the One Who Reads" 77.

53. Acts 1:16, compare 1:11, 2:14, 22, 29, 37; 3:12; 5:35; 7:2, 26; 14:15; 15:7, 13; 17:22, 19:25, 35; 21:28; 22:1 23:1, 6; 25:24; 27;10, 21, 25, 26; 28:17.

54. D'Angelo, "Women in Luke-Acts" 449–450.

55. Anēr appears in John 1:30 (the Baptist prophecy), also Eph 4:13.

56. Luke 9:30, 32; 24:4; 1:10; Acts 10:30; 16:9; cf. 10:19.

57. Acts 6:5; 21:11; 22:3; 23:27, 30; 25:1, 17.

58. See the apostrophe to the mother in 4 Macc 15:30: "O more noble than males for restraint and more manly than men for endurance!" See Elizabeth Castelli, "Virginity and Its Meaning for Women's Sexuality in Early Christianity," *JFSR* 2 (1986) 74–78; Mary Rose D'Angelo, "Beyond Father and Son," in *Justice as Mission: An Agenda for the Church* ed. T. Brown and C. Lind (Burlington, Ontario, Canada: Trinity, 1985) 109, 115, nn. 10–11.

59. Seim, *Double Message* 24.

60. It might be even better to say that it is both Roman and atticizing; as Judith Perkins (*The Suffering Self: Pain and Narrative Representation in the Early Christian Era* [New York: Routledge, 1995] 47–50, 66–68) points out, the second century saw a revival of interest in at least the forms of citizenship in the Greek cities; but, in the case of Luke, interest in patriotism for Athens (Acts 17) and Ephesus (Acts 19:21–40) is explicitly subordinated to the attractions of Roman citizenship (Acts 16:19–40, 22:22–29) 150.

61. Treggiari, *Roman Marriage* 291–98; Karl Galinsky, *Augustan Culture: An Interpretive Introduction* (Princeton, NJ: Princeton University Press, 1996) 128–40.

62. J. V. P. D. Balsdon (*Roman Women, Their History and Habits* [New York: Barnes and Noble, 1983; first published New York: John C. Day, 1962] 63) regards this as a significant change over earlier imperial practice. He discusses it under "female emancipation.". But it actually manifests the new importance of marriage described by Peter Brown ("Late Antiquity: The 'Wellborn' Few," in *A History of Private Life, Volume 1, From Pagan Rome to Byzantium*, ed. Paul Veyne [Cambridge, MA: Belknap, 1987] 247–48), but attributed to the age of the Antonines.

63. The mention of women of social prestige or relatively high status (see also Acts 17:4 and 11–12 and Johanna in Luke 8:2) may serve pedagogical purposes by adding a touch of worldly glamour (as the *Romance of Joseph and Aseneth*, the *Acts of [Paul and] Thecla*, and the story of *Cyprian and Justina* do for later Christianity).

64. See Peter Brown, "Late Antiquity."

65. See Krister Stendahl, *Paul among Jews and Gentiles* (Philadelphia: Fortress, 1976) 116–18; Hans Conzelmann, *Acts of the Apostles: A Commentary on the Acts of the Apostles*. ed. Eldon Jay Epp with Christopher R. Matthews, trans. James Limburg, A. Thomas Kraabel, and Donald H. Juel, Hermeneia (Philadelphia: Fortress, 1987) 15–16.

66. B. A. Mastin, "Scaeva the High Priest," *JTS* 27 (1976) 405–12.

67. *Satire* 6.541–548; trans. Peter Green, *The Sixteen Satires* (Harmondsworth, UK: Penguin, 1969) 147–48.

68. D'Angelo, "Women in Luke-Acts" 451–53, 457–60.

69. Seim, *Double Message* 229–48.

70. Ibid. 208–9.

71. D'Angelo, "Remarriage and the Divorce Sayings" 97–98.

72. See chapter 6.

73. Trans. Thomas O. Lambdin, *Nag Hammadi Library in English*, 3rd rev. edition; ed. James M. Robinson (San Francisco: HarperSanFransisco, 1988) 135.

74. Seim, *Double Message* 204–8.

75. Ross S. Kraemer, "Women's Authorship of Jewish and Christian Literature in the Greco-Roman Period," in *"Women Like This' "*: *New Perspectives on Jewish Women in the Greco-Roman Period*. ed. Amy-Jill Levine, *Early Judaism and its Literature* I (Atlanta, GA: Scholars Press, 1991) 235.

76. John Dominic Crossan, *The Historical Jesus: The Life of a Mediterranean Jewish Peasant* (San Francisco: HarperSanFrancisco, 1991) 416.

III

Mining the

Pauline

Tradition

9

>-+-◆>-O-◆+-◄

READING REAL WOMEN
THROUGH THE UNDISPUTED
LETTERS OF PAUL

Margaret Y. MacDonald

In a programmatic essay published in 1985, Bernadette Brooten called for an approach to the history of early Christian women that seeks to bring women to the center. Instead of concentrating primarily on male attitudes toward women as has been done in the past, the focus should shift to reconstructing the lives of the women themselves. Every effort should be made to hear their voices, to witness their behavior. In essence, early Christian women need to be brought back to life. Perhaps nowhere have Brooten's insights yielded more promising results than in the reconstruction of women in the Pauline mission.[1]

Until quite recently, the dominant understanding of "Paul and women" was shaped almost exclusively by the well-known texts that call for women to have their heads covered (1 Cor 11:2–16) and to be silent in church (1 Cor 14: 33b–36; 1 Tim 2:8–15). The fact that the references to specific women are often found in texts that traditionally have held little theological interest, such as final greetings (e.g., Romans 16), only compounded the problem of an incomplete vision of women in Pauline Christianity. However, the effort in feminist scholarship to move beyond an understanding of male attitudes toward women in order to grasp the actual circumstances of women's lives has led to scholars mining the much less well known references to Phoebe, Prisca, and other women of the Pauline mission for information. Since the brief references sometimes point to a surprising openness to women leaders and missionary workers, they have played an important part in transforming the dominant image of the women in Pauline communities as always veiled and silenced.

The following letters contain specific references to women. They fall into the group of Pauline works often labeled by scholars as the undisputed letters of

Paul. That Paul was the author of following documents is generally not contested: Romans, 1 and 2 Corinthians, Galatians, Philippians, 1 Thessalonians, and Philemon. In addition to these undisputed letters, Pauline literature contains works that were attributed to Paul, but that are often understood as having been composed by one (or more) of his followers or disciples to keep his teaching alive after his death. The Pastoral Epistles (1 Timothy, 2 Timothy, and Titus), for example, fall into this category (see chapter 11). In this chapter, I aim to reconstruct the lives of all the women in Paul's circle about whom we have any significant information based on those undisputed letters that name women.

1 Corinthians

Chloe

Chloe is mentioned in conjunction with the very circumstances that led to the composition of 1 Corinthians. Paul wrote 1 Corinthians from Ephesus (1 Cor 16:8) around 54 CE. Among the factors that led him to write the letter was a report made by "Chloe's people" that there were divisions in the Corinthian community (1 Cor 1:11). This is the only mention of Chloe, but the very phrase "Chloe's people" offers a clue as to her status in society at large and possibly also in the Corinthian community. This expression refers to the members of Chloe's household. It may mean members of Chloe's immediate family, but most likely refers also to the members of the kind of extended household that was typical of the ancient world. Chloe's people may have included her slaves, freedpersons (slaves who continued to have obligations to their former owner after they had been freed), or dependent workers.[2] The fact that the people who gave the report are identified in deference to Chloe (literally, the ones belonging to Chloe) suggests that she was the head of this household. Women were sometimes responsible for the management of households of considerable means in antiquity. In particular, wealthy widows frequently exerted independent control over their own affairs. There are suggestions in early Christian literature that well-to-do women were attracted to the movement, and their entry into the group was prized by its leaders (e.g., Acts 17:4, 12). They might have offered their houses for meetings (e.g., Nympha, in Col 4:15) or, as in the case of Chloe, sponsored important travel. As a prominent member of the Corinthian community, Chloe may have sent a delegation to warn Paul of the quarreling that was taking place there. It should be noted, however, that we cannot be absolutely certain that Chloe herself was a believer. There are indications in the New Testament that subordinate members of the household sometimes joined early Christian groups independently (and perhaps without the knowledge) of the heads of households (e.g., 1 Tim 6:1–2; 1 Pet 3:1–2). Chloe's people may have formed a significant contingent in the community as members of the household of a nonbelieving woman of high standing who was known to all in Corinth.

The reference to Chloe's people in 1 Cor 1:11 introduces us immediately to the reality of social stratification in the Corinthian community: membership included people of higher and lower social status. Chloe most likely owned slaves. Assuming she was a believer, it is also important to note her capacity to sponsor emissaries to visit Paul. Chloe's people, however, were representatives of lower strata. Yet it is important to realize that the evaluation of the social status of people in the ancient world is a complicated issue. Social position was determined by a variety of factors: the status of one's family, ones' finances, one's sex, and birth into freedom or slavery all played a part in determining one's status location. 1 Cor 1:11 has been compared to Phil 4:22, where Paul states that members of the "household of Caesar" send their greetings to the Philippians (see also similar references to the household of Aristobulus and the household of Narcissus in Rom 16:10–11). These individuals were the slaves and freedpersons who made up the emperor's household staff or the imperial bureaucracy. Although they were restricted by the structures of the institution of slavery, they had a considerably more comfortable existence than the freeborn poor. In other words, their lives reflected elements of higher and lower social status. It is evident that Chloe was in control of a number of resources and could probably exercise her influence in various ways, but as a woman in ancient society, she nevertheless remained subject to the pervasive ideology which called women to be subject to men and limited the scope of her activities. Scholars have suggested that individuals such as freedpersons and women who displayed status inconsistency (indicators of higher status combined with features of lower status) were particularly attracted to Pauline Christianity with its paradoxical beliefs, such as the "crucified Messiah," which celebrated the ambiguities of their existence.[3]

Chloe's people need no introduction among the Corinthians. The most likely explanation is that they were part of the community there and had simply traveled to Ephesus to give Paul the news. That Chloe lived in Ephesus and that her people had recently returned from a visit to Corinth are also plausible. It is also possible, however, that Chloe's people stopped to give their report "en route" to another destination, perhaps even to conduct other business. Chloe may have instructed her delegation to stop in Corinth on their way to foster her business enterprises in another center. 1 Cor 1:11 offers one of several indications in the undisputed letters of the centrality of travel to the life of the Pauline mission. As a missionary leader, Paul's primary interest lay in starting up small communities of believers and then moving on to the next center, maintaining contact with his many communities by means of letters, occasional visits, and news reports circulated by traveling believers. But from these tiny cells emanated the potential for expansion across countless arteries, by road and sea. The first two centuries of the common era in the Roman empire were a period of an abundance of exchange between populations. Although it could sometimes be perilous, physical mobility was common, as is frequently revealed by Paul's letters (e.g., 2 Cor 11:25–26). Paul himself combined travel as an artisan with travel for missionary purposes. As discussed further below, his fellow workers, including a significant number of women, seem also to have combined business travel with travel for the sake of the gospel.

Prisca

In the closing remarks of 1 Corinthians, Paul sends greetings to the community from Prisca together with her partner, Aquila, and the church in their house (1 Cor 16:19). Of all the missionary partners in the New Testament, we possess the most information about Prisca and Aquila. Paul also refers to the church that meets in the house of Prisca and Aquila in Romans 16:3–5. Their influence in the Pauline mission was apparently so great that the later author of 2 Timothy chose to recognize their contribution (2 Tim 4:19).[4] In addition to the Pauline correspondence, the Acts of the Apostles furnishes us with considerable detail (Acts 18; Priscilla is another version of the name Prisca). As illustrated in chapter 11 (on the first interpreters of Paul on women and gender), comparison of the texts in Paul's letters concerning Prisca and Aquila with the material in Acts is instructive for two reasons. First, it may provide additional information about the nature of their mission. Second, it may also offer important evidence concerning how Paul's involvement with women leaders was interpreted in subsequent generations.

Traditionally, Prisca and Aquila have been judged to be a married couple. It is important to note that they are explicitly identified as such only in Acts. When evaluating the evidence in the undisputed letters, it is important not to jump to conclusions about the exact nature of their partnership. Scholars have presented alternate ways of understanding the missionary pairings, pointing out that legal marriage was only possible between certain categories of people in the Roman empire. Stable, ongoing family relationships were by no means guaranteed for the slaves and freedpersons included among the early Christian constituency.[5] Moreover, how one understands the references to Prisca and Aquila in part depends on how one reads 1 Cor 9:5, where Paul speaks of the right of an apostle to be accompanied by "a sister as wife" (cf. Rom 16:15). Although Paul does not seem to have been involved in such a partnership himself, the references to Prisca and Aquila, and to other partners discussed below, offer evidence that these teams were vital to the successful expansion of the mission. Some important considerations have been raised, however, concerning the meaning of the Greek phrase that has been translated as a "sister as wife." References to brothers and sisters in Paul's letters can be used simply to denote membership in the movement. But like the term "brother" (adelphos), the term "sister" (adelphē) can serve as one in a series of fluid titles (including such terms as "coworker" [synergos] and "deacon" [diakonos]) that denote leadership roles. Thus, in referring to "a sister as wife," Paul is probably referring to full missionary partnership and not only to a helpmate in the husband's mission as has traditionally been assumed.[6] Moreover, certainty about the erotic or legal nature of the relationships referred to in 1 Cor 9:5 is precluded by the fluidity of the term usually translated as wife (gynē); it may simply mean woman.

One important church author, Clement of Alexandria, writing at the end of the second century CE, interpreted 1 Cor 9:5 as a reference to spiritual marriages: marriages in which the woman acted as helpmate, but in which there were no sexual relations. Spiritual marriages did, indeed, occur in early Christianity and may be the topic of concern in 1 Cor 7:36–8 (cf. 1 Cor 7:5), but doubt has also been expressed about whether they existed as early as when Paul wrote 1 Corinthians. In addition, Clement stated that these wives acted as coministers only in the sense that they ministered to women; only women could penetrate to women's quarters in houses without scandal being aroused.[7] Clement's comments need to be examined critically. As is the case with the other missionary pairings of men and women mentioned in Paul's letters, there is no indication whatsoever of the female partner having a different or diminished role in relation to the male partner. Both Prisca and Aquila are called Paul's coworkers (synergos; Rom 16:3). Both play a vital role in the expansion of the mission. The language that Paul uses to greet them in Rom 16:3–5, including the reference to them having risked their necks on his behalf and on behalf of others, is the language of the perils of mission.

Clement's comments cannot be relied on for an accurate depiction of the realities of first century communities, but nevertheless, they may introduce us to some of the values that also characterized the social world in which Prisca moved and suggest some of the challenges and opportunities she may have encountered as a woman leader. As early Christianity spread throughout the cities of the Roman empire, its household-based activities and support of women's initiative came increasingly to be judged as scandalous.[8] By the fourth century CE, the ministry to women in pagan households was understood as a special duty of the deaconess, as it would have been too dangerous to send a male official.[9] As I discuss below, there is New Testament evidence to suggest that women who joined the ranks of believers without their husbands were causing problems in the community's relationship to the broader society, even at a very early stage (1 Pet 3:1–6; cf. 1 Cor 7:12–16). Traveling with a woman partner might significantly increase the opportunities to preach the gospel to women. Traveling with a male partner could no doubt offer the woman missionary protection and other logistic advantages. It has even been suggested that the missionary pairings of men and women in the Pauline mission were inspired by the necessity of giving the appearance of marriage in a world of male power and violence.[10]

Though scholars debate the reliability of many details in Acts, its author portrays Priscilla and Aquila as Jews who shared Paul's trade as a leather worker (18:2–3), and it would have been quite natural for them to live and work together. Historians of early Christianity are gaining a greater appreciation of how the simple arrangements of everyday life in the house and workshop may have been extremely important for the expansion of the movement. The fact that the pair are associated with three different cities in the New Testament offers further confirmation of travel being a typical feature of life in the Pauline communities that undoubtedly led to opportunities to spread teachings (see previous discussion of Chloe). The Acts of the Apostles seems to assume the following chronology of events. Having been exiled from Rome, the couple opened their home to Paul in Corinth (Acts 18:2–3). After spending a significant period of time in Corinth, Paul left for Ephesus accompanied by Priscilla and Aquila. In Ephesus, the pair instructed a Jew named Apollos, who, in turn, left for Corinth (Acts 18:18–19:1; see chapter 11). It was while they were in Ephesus that they sent greetings to Corinth (1 Cor 16:8, 19). They seem eventually to have left Ephesus, for they appear again in Rome (Rom 16:3–5; but see discussion of scholarly debate concerning the origins of Romans 16 below).[11]

Two factors should lead us to pay special attention to Prisca's role in her missionary partnership with Aquila. First, Rom 16:3 and Acts 18:18, 26 list Prisca's name first; this is probably a sign that she was of higher status than Aquila since the usual practice in antiquity was to mention the man's name first. Second, in both Rom 16:3–5 and 1 Cor 16:19, Paul refers to the church (*ekklesia*) that meets in the house of Prisca and Aquila. On both symbolic and practical levels, the household was a very important model for the establishment of communities. The household served as the meeting place for the group, and Paul's letters are replete with familial language used to address community members and to speak of the multifaceted relations among community, Paul, God, and Christ. Moreover, studies of the social status of the early Christians have revealed that the capacity to offer one's house as a meeting place was a factor that affected one's capacity to become a leader.[12] This link between leadership and household probably had a special significance for the roles of women. The fact that the group functioned practically in much the same way as an extended household (the domain traditionally associated with women) has led to a good deal of speculation about how this facilitated the involvement of women in Pauline Christianity. The household base of the movement may have enabled women to turn community leadership into an extension of their roles as household managers. Taken together, the facts that Prisca may have been perceived as having a higher social status than Aquila and that much of her leadership would have been exercised in a household setting means that there is good reason to believe that her influence in Pauline Christianity extended even beyond that of her partner.

Philippians: Euodia and Syntyche

Missionary couples in the Pauline churches were not always a man and a woman. Women sometimes worked together as missionary partners.[13] Phil 4:2–3 offers a window into the importance of the roles of female missionary partners in the Philippian community, but probably also to the expansion of the broader Pauline mission (cf. Rom 16:12). Euodia and Syntyche are urged "to be of the same mind in the Lord." Most commentators have seen here a reference to a conflict between the two women, but it is also possible that the conflict is between the apostle and the two women. In either case, Paul calls on a third party to mediate (Phil 4:3). Settlement of the dispute that involves these two women is vital because they have struggled beside Paul in the work of the gospel, together with Clement and his other coworkers.

We do not know the details of the dispute involving these two women, but the fact that Paul's response is so strong in Phil 4:2–3 and that the need to encourage unity appears consistently as a community concern (e.g., Phil 1:27) suggests that the issues were central to the purpose of the letter.[14] Philippians was written while Paul was in prison, probably either in Ephesus (55–56 CE) or Rome (58–60 CE). In this letter, Paul's reliance on coworkers stands out especially clearly; leadership was exercised within a communal framework. When a missionary team experiences difficulty, the community is called on to offer support.

With Euodia and Syntyche, we encounter indisputable evidence of women acting as leaders without male counterparts. It is also important to note that the manner in which Paul describes these women as participating with him in the work of the gospel implies that they were involved in the evangelizing of nonbelievers. They may have sometimes acted out their leadership in an established "house-church" community, but their ministry extended into the world outside. In the discussion of Prisca above, we saw how the household setting of early Christianity may have facilitated women's leadership. The information revealed about Euodia and Syntyche in Phil 4:2–3 indicates that the domestic character of early Christianity cannot completely explain the nature of women's involvement in the Pauline churches. By being involved in the evangelizing of nonbelievers, Euodia and Syntyche were engaging in activities that extended beyond a local house-church in an effort to expand the network of such household cells throughout the Greco-Roman world. They were actively involved in a mission that sought to win both Jew and Gentile—a mission that was pushing outward toward the west in the hope of transforming the world (cf. Rom 15:19, 15:23–24). Moreover, Euodia and Syntyche were part of a movement that seems to have combined aspects of the life of public institutions with aspects of the domestic realm. The Greek term *ekklesia*, typically used to designate the community in Paul's letters means gathering and is usually translated as "church." In both Jewish usage and elsewhere, it refers to a formal assembly of citizens; the term clearly has "public" connotations.[15] In Pauline Christianity, the *ekklesia* met in individual houses, and the household served as a model for the organization of the *ekklesia*, but the church also had a public dimension. As discussed further in chapter 11 on the early interpreters of Paul on women and gender, this fusing of domestic and public spheres probably was an important factor in the mounting tension between Pauline Christianity and society at large and probably also contributed eventually to efforts to reduce the public visibility of women in the Pauline mission.

In addition to Euodia and Syntyche, we know of a third New Testament woman, Lydia, who clearly also played an important part in the life of the Philippian church (Acts 16; see chapter 11). It has sometimes been suggested that the nature of the involvement of women in the Philippian church was related to the general prominence of women at Philippi (a city of Macedonia). Valerie Abrahamsen, for example, has drawn attention to the participation and leadership of women in goddess cults of Diana and Isis at Philippi.[16] She has suggested that pagan women who joined early Christian groups may have brought the expectation of leadership with them into the new organization. In attempting to reconstruct the lives of early Christian women, scholars are increasingly paying close attention to the situation in particular geographic locations. Such a geographic focus can be especially helpful in drawing attention to points of contact between the lives of early Christian women and the lives of women in other communities found in the same ancient city or region.

Philemon: Apphia

The letter of Paul to Philemon is a short letter that he wrote while in prison (see previous discussion of Philippians) to a leading member of a house-church community (possibly in Colossae; cf. Col 4:9). Apphia is mentioned in the greeting (Phlm 2). Because her name follows that of Philemon, it has been traditionally assumed that she is Philemon's wife, but this is by no means certain. Not only are Philemon and Apphia greeted separately, Apphia is one of three individuals (Philemon, Apphia, and Archippus) singled out in the letter in a way that suggests that each was prominent in the community. Paul bestows honor on each with a different title. Apphia is called sister (*adelphē*). As we have seen, this is a term that could be applied to a female member of a missionary partnership (cf. 1 Cor 9:5; Rom 15:16). Paul also calls Phoebe, a leader in the church at Cenchreae, "sister." The fact that the masculine equivalent of the term is a frequent designation for Paul's very important missionary collaborator, Timothy, leaves little doubt about the respect bestowed by the title (e.g., Phlm 1; 2 Cor 1:1; 1 Thess 3:2).

Apphia is evidently a leader. She may indeed be a member of the household of Philemon where the community meets, but the nature of the greeting suggests greater independence. Both Apphia and Archippus may be prominent members of the community whom Paul includes in the greeting to add weight to his argument. In this letter, Paul deals with the delicate case of the return of Philemon's runaway slave, who has become Christian. Although his language may seem somewhat indirect to modern readers, the main thrust of the argument is clear: Onesimus' life as a believer should result in a changed relationship with his former master (Phlm 11–16, 21). With a house large enough to hold meetings and as an owner of slaves, Philemon is obviously considerably well to do. In singling out Apphia, Paul's strategy may have been to ensure that a woman of similar (or even greater?) means was aware of his instructions. Like Philemon, and possibly Archippus, Apphia may have been a patron of the community.[17] She may have bestowed her generosity on the community in various ways, but in turn would have expected loyalty and respect from community members (on women patrons, see discussion of Phoebe below). Her influence in the community may have rivaled Philemon's own, and reference to her in the letter may have been an indirect reminder to Philemon of the potentially serious consequences of rejecting Paul's appeal.

Romans

The sixteenth chapter of Paul's letter to the Romans might well be our most precious source for recovering the lives of real women in the undisputed letters of Paul. For textual reasons and evidence related to the manuscript tradition, however, Romans 16 has sometimes been considered to have originated as a separate letter (perhaps intended for Ephesus), which later became inserted within the main body of Romans. However, the text fits well with the situation of the letter to the Romans—a letter composed while Paul was in Corinth (cf. Rom 16:23; 1 Cor 1:14). Paul tells us in the letter that he has never been to the church in Rome (Rom 15:22), but he may well be convinced that the people he greets in the community, whom he clearly knows, will encourage acceptance of his teaching. Romans 16:1–16 reveals the importance of geographical mobility (for purposes of both trade and religious conviction) to the expansion of the Pauline mission. Many of the people Paul greets here probably migrated from eastern cities to Rome.[18] The language used in Romans 16 reveals the importance of Paul's coworkers, both men and women, to the expansion of his mission. The text is full of verbs that speak of risk and labor; these individuals clearly participated in many precarious activities for the sake of the gospel.

Ten women appear in Romans 16: Phoebe, Prisca, Mary, Junia, Tryphaena, Tryphosa, Persis, the unnamed mother of Rufus, Julia, and the unnamed "sister" of Nereus. Some of these women are involved in missionary partnerships. Tryphaena and Tryphosa, whom Paul greets as "workers in the Lord," are women missionary partners (Rom 16:12). Four male-female pairs include Prisca and Aquila (Rom 16:3), Andronicus and Junia (16:7), Philologus and Julia, and Nereus and his "sister" (Rom 16:15). The fact that Paul greets "Rufus and his mother and mine" in Rom 16:13 suggests that male-female missionary pairs were not always composed of a husband and wife. In addition to missionary partnerships, Romans 16 offers evidence of women working for the sake of the gospel without specific partners (although it is unlikely that they would have traveled alone). Phoebe is the most obvious example of such a woman (Rom 16:1–2), but Mary and Persis may also fall into this category.[19] About some of the women mentioned in Romans 16, we know virtually nothing, but we are fortunate to be able to recover significant information about Prisca (discussed above), Phoebe, and Junia.

Phoebe

In Rom 16:1–2, Paul commends Phoebe, who is clearly traveling to Rome, perhaps bearing Paul's letter to the Romans. It was quite common for ancient letters to include praise of their bearers, and sometimes letters were written for the sole purpose of commending their bearers. Paul's instructions concerning Phoebe in Rom 16:1–2 appear to reflect this conventional practice (cf. 1 Cor 16:15–18). It is impossible to be certain whether this commendation is made only to guarantee that the Romans offer her the best kind of hospitality or whether Paul intends that she might play a specific role in the life of the Roman community, such as being an interpreter of his teaching. Paul's description of Phoebe, however, implies that she played an important part in the development of the Pauline mission. It has even been suggested that Phoebe was viewed by Paul as a central player in his plans for a Spanish mission (Rom 15:23–24).[20]

Paul calls Phoebe "our sister" (see previous discussion of Apphia) and explains that she is a "deacon" of the church at Cenchreae, Corinth's seaport to the East.[21] The term "deacon" (diakonos, in Greek) here is the same term that was used to refer to the male office holders who participated in the formal organization that emerged in some branches of early Christianity at the beginning of the second century. This threefold organizational framework included the offices of bishop, presbyter, and deacon. We have evidence to suggest that there were women deacons in the second century. 1 Timothy 3:11, for example, might be a reference to women deacons. Most scholars believe that the slave women whom the Roman governor of Bithynia, Pliny the Younger, had interrogated and tortured were deacons (the Latin term is ministra, which probably corresponds to deacons).[22] During the course of the third and fourth centuries CE, the office of the diaconate for women seems to have evolved into an office designed specifically for women, but it was not until about the beginning of fourth century that a special feminine form of this word came into use to refer to the office of the deaconess—an office reserved especially for women and that seems to have been devoted especially to ministry among women: caring for the poor and sick, and assisting at the baptisms of women. Paul writes to the Romans before such established offices came into being and when titles were used in a more fluid way than in subsequent generations. Therefore, it is not at all clear what is meant by the designation of Phoebe as deacon. In fact, the Greek term might also be translated as "helper" or "one who serves." What is clear, however, is that deacon is an important designation in the Pauline mission. Paul uses the same Greek term to refer to leaders in the community of Philippi who may have included both men and women (Phil 1:1). When Paul applies it to himself and to his coworkers, the preaching of the gospel is central (e.g., 1 Cor 3:5; 2 Cor 3:6; 11:23; cf. Rom 11:13; 1 Cor 16:15; 2 Cor 5:18; 6:3). By calling Phoebe a deacon of the ekklesia at Cenchreae, Paul clearly wishes to communicate the importance of her role. In fact, according to Elisabeth Schüssler Fiorenza, the evidence leads to the conclusion that "Phoebe is recommended as an official teacher and missionary in the church of Cenchreae."[23]

In Rom 16:1–2, Phoebe is also called a "benefactor" (prostatis) of many community members and of Paul himself. This text reflects the importance of benefaction as a social structure in antiquity and in early Christianity. In Greco-Roman society, it was common for people from more elite social groups to act as benefactors or patrons to those of lower social status, their clients. The support received by the clients was not limited to financial support in a strict sense, but also included broadly defined social and economic resources. In turn, the clients would honor their patron and be subject to her or his authority. Because Paul recommends her, and she appears to be dependent on him for access to the Roman community, there is a sense in which Paul acts as Phoebe's benefactor. But she also is a benefactor in her own right, and Paul acknowledges that she has also been his benefactor. The relationship between Phoebe and Paul has been described as one of mutual patronage.[24] Phoebe is dependent on Paul in order to extend her influence in the community, but Paul has probably also been dependent on her sphere of influence in order to expand his mission in Cenchreae or elsewhere. Perhaps Phoebe acted as host to the community, offering her home for meetings and offering hospitality to traveling Christians. She may also have introduced Paul to others who became community benefactors. In keeping with the dynamics of the institution of patronage, Phoebe's role crossed the divide between public and private in Greco-Roman society.

Scholars have generally viewed Phoebe as a wealthy, independent woman, who may even have moved in more elite circles than Paul. She probably combined travel for business purposes with travel for church purposes. Lydia, the seller of purple-dyed goods (purple fabrics were a sign of wealth in the ancient Mediterranean world), who is mentioned in Acts 16, is often compared to Phoebe. The acquisition of Lydia's patronage functions as a means of securing protection and a household base for Paul's teaching and mission in Philippi (see chapter 11). Women like Phoebe and Lydia who are singled out for mention in the New Testament as independently offering services to believers, acting as heads of households, or both, have often been viewed as autonomous women, either divorcées or widows in control of significant material resources.

Junia

Andronicus and Junia are greeted by Paul in Rom 16:7. He calls them his relatives, which may mean that they actually were members of his family, or were, like him, Jews.[25] They are described by Paul as having been in prison with him and as having been members of the church before Paul. Most significantly, however, they are said to be prominent among the apostles. Junia has received considerable attention of late because, until very recently, she was understood to have been a man: the Greek text was read as "Junias" (a male name). This supposedly masculine name never occurs in ancient literature, and the earliest Christian interpreters of New Testament texts (commonly known as the Church Fathers) took the name to be feminine. From the Reformation period onward, the main motivation that shaped the decision to understand Rom 16:7 as a reference to two men was that a woman could not have been granted the title "apostle."[26] Junia is not the only New Testament woman who has been the subject of "recasting" as a man. It is now widely recognized that the attempt to masculinize Nympha, which appears in several ancient versions of the text (and is reflected in some modern translations), is rooted in the scandal created by the existence of a woman leader of a house-church (Col 4:15).

In the case of Junia, the significance of her being called apostle along with her partner Andronicus needs to be considered carefully. The popular understanding of the term apostle as referring exclusively to the twelve disciples of Jesus (based largely on the use of the term in Luke's gospel) does not do justice to the complexity of the New Testament evidence. In Pauline Christianity, the term apostle (in Greek, *apostolos*, literally an emissary) has quite a broad application. In Paul's letters, apostleship is based on witnessing resurrection appearances of Jesus Christ and receiving a commission (1 Cor 15:5–9). Paul sometimes uses apostle to refer to itinerant preachers of the gospel who also performed signs and wonders, their apostleship being especially evident in the fruits of their missionary work (2 Cor 11:4–6, 13; 12:11–12). However, Paul also refers to the apostles of the churches in the sense of people who act as official messengers or emissaries of the churches (2 Cor 8:23).[27] The language of Rom 16: 1–16 suggests that Andronicus and Junia were apostles who acted as comissionaries with Paul. Some have proposed that Andronicus and Junia may have been prominent among the apostles in the sense that they were valued by apostles, but without actually being apostles themselves. Although this interpretation is possible based on the Greek text, the most straightforward reading is to understand Paul as calling both Andronicus and Junia apostles. Moreover, there is no reason based on the text to diminish the role of the woman apostle in relation to that of her partner. Finally, it is important to realize that, although Paul's use of the term apostle is broad, we should not underestimate the importance he attached to the designation. He could defend his own apostleship vigorously and call others false apostles vehemently.

Having come to end of our survey of the specific references to women in the undisputed letters of Paul, some conclusions about the real women of the earliest Christian mission are in order. Women were prominent members of the community and acted as leaders. They hosted meetings and acted as patrons. Their friendship must often have been prized and their influence sometimes feared. Working alone or with partners, they were missionaries. Their activities contributed to the expansion of the movement. No doubt they were often publicly visible in the exercise of various leadership roles. They were honored with such titles as coworker, sister, deacon, and apostle. In short, the references to specific women in Paul's letters indicate that women's leadership in this early period was neither different from that of men nor of lesser value to the community than the contributions of men.

The evidence seems especially striking when one compares it to subsequent early Christian texts where women leaders are much less apparent and arguments against women's leadership become explicit (see chapter 11). How does the evidence for the leadership of women in the undisputed letters of Paul compare to what can be known about the leadership of women in Jewish communities, as well as other Greek and Roman communities, in the Roman imperial world? Scholars such Ross S. Kraemer and Bernadette Brooten have illustrated that the appearance of women in leadership roles in early Christianity should not be seen as unique, but rather as in keeping with the roles women assumed in other communities.[28] In fact, in aiming to reconstruct the situation of women in the Pauline mission, scholars are increasingly operating within the broad framework of women's history in the first century. In the process, they are illustrating how the use of traditional labels for religious allegiances in antiquity, such as pagan, Jewish, and Christian, as though they were mutually exclusive can prove to be misleading. Pointing out that both Junia and Prisca were first-century Jewish women, Brooten has argued that these women should be located in the continuum of Jewish women's history. According to Brooten, a study of Junia and Prisca in their historical contexts should mean asking such questions as: "What are the sources for first-century Jewish women in Rome? What do we know about women and the Roman penal code? What do we know about Jewish women's education and about non-Jewish Roman women's education in this period?"[29] No doubt this type of investigation will continue to shed light on the brief references, often made only in passing, to women in Paul's letters.

Other Indications of Women's Lives and Leadership

In general, when scholars engage in the process of reconstructing the lives of women in Pauline Christianity, they deal with two kinds of texts. Most obviously, scholars turn to the references to specific women discussed above. But studying the Pauline tradition for what it reveals about the actual circumstances of women also involves analysis of Paul's pronouncements on sexuality and gender where he sometimes refers to women's activities and circumstances (e.g., 1 Cor 7; 11:2–16; 14:33b–36; see also chapter 10). I analyze Paul's pronouncements thoroughly in chapter 11 (and see also chapter 10). In keeping with the aim of this chapter, we leave aside many complicated issues raised by Paul's position and try understand as best we can what women were actually doing. Throughout our study, we aim to see through Paul's teachings on how women *should* behave in order to catch a glimpse of how women *actually* behaved.

1 Corinthians 7

A notable feature of the lives of women in Pauline Christianity was the choice made by some in favor of celibacy. Throughout 1 Corinthians 7, Paul communicates his preference for celibacy when the believer is gifted to remain unmarried and when the circumstances allow for it. Although marriage was generally viewed in the Greco-Roman world as being essential to the welfare of individuals and the state, the goal of remaining unmarried, understood to be grounded in religious and/or philosophical reasons, by no means originated with Pauline Christianity. Philosophers in Greco-Roman society debated whether marriage was compatible with philosophical life. The most striking parallel to the encouragement of celibacy for both women and men in 1 Corinthians 7 comes from the writings of the Jewish philosopher, Philo of Alexandria (late first century BCE to mid–first century CE), who described an ascetic community, known as the Therapeutic Society, living on the shores of Lake Mareotis near Alexandria, comprised of both women and men. Philo draws attention to the admirable behavior of the women in the group, most of whom are "aged virgins." Their continence is explained by Philo in terms of their philosophical interests; their chastity is rooted in their "ardent yearning for wisdom."[30] Likewise, by the second century, Christians could be admired by pagan observers for remaining unmarried. Galen of Pergamum (who died at the end of that century) identified the restraint in cohabitation demonstrated by the early Christian women and men he encountered as a sign that they had attained "a pitch not inferior to that of genuine philosophers."[31] There is a clear connection in these texts between celibacy and the pursuit of knowledge; however, given the grave dangers for women associated with pregnancy and childbirth in the ancient world, coupled with the high risks of infant mortality, it is tempting to conclude that physical benefits also contributed to celibacy's appeal.

What is particularly striking about the advice Paul gives in 1 Corinthians 7 and its implications for women is that it is so unqualified. Paul does not imply that only those with philosophical talent should remain unmarried. He extends his preference for celibacy to include unmarried men and women, apparently young and old, irrespective of educational background. While, as noted above, a positive valuation of the nonmarried state is by no means unique to early Christianity, there is much to suggest that in the urban world of Greco-Roman society, such encouragement would at least cause controversy. By the first century CE, the authorities in the Roman empire were articulating concerns about the reluctance of some citizens to marry and about the necessity to produce children for the general stability of society and to fill army legions with soldiers. Delays in marriage and efforts to reduce pregnancies were probably sometimes inspired by the desire to preserve family wealth by limiting the numbers of possible descendants who could inherit legacies. In light of fears about falling birth rates, there were expressions of concern about the disintegration of the family and calls for mothers to exercise their traditional roles; these expressions call to mind the sentiments that are sometimes vocalized in the modern world.[32] Moreover, the Roman state took direct measures, in the form of legislation, to discourage inclinations to remain unmarried, childless, or both. With respect to women, the laws promulgated by the Emperor Augustus and his successors made marriage mandatory between 20 and 50 years of age. Divorcées and widows were required to remarry after brief periods which ranged from six months to two years. Unmarried and childless women experienced restrictions on inheritance and were denied certain privileges of legal independence. In contrast, freeborn women who had three children and freedwomen who had four children were rewarded with the privilege of being able to conduct their legal affairs without a male guardian.[33]

Historians have expressed some doubts about the extent to which the Augustan marriage laws were effective in various parts of the empire among people at various echelons of society. At the very least, they reflect the unease among government officials about the deterioration of the household and point to tensions that were ready to erupt given the presence of a perceived social irritant. We can, in fact, see evidence of these tensions erupting in a series of works that date from the second and third centuries CE. Known as the *Apocryphal Acts of the Apostles*, these contain an intriguing version of the Pauline tradition, *The Acts of (Paul and) Thecla*. These apocryphal works relate several stories in which women are inspired by the message announced by apostles to forego marriage or even to dissolve existing marriages (see chapter 11). Although they have a legendary quality, they are generally understood as reflecting elements of the societal clash that occurred when early Christian women challenged the arrangements of non-believing households.

In the end, it is impossible to be sure how the celibacy of early Christian women would have been perceived in Greco-Roman society. The fact that chastity and self-control were sometimes held in great esteem suggests that celibacy may have drawn in church members. In a society in which marriage was the usual fate of daughters and a woman's sexual morality was viewed as a telling sign of the health of household, city, and state, a woman's celibacy could no doubt seem strange enough to elicit suspicion. It is particularly interesting to note, therefore, that there are indications throughout 1 Corinthians 7 that the celibacy of women had a special importance for members of the Corinthian community. As in 1 Cor 11:2–11, throughout 1 Corinthians 7, Paul makes several parallel statements, directed at men and women that may represent an attempt to draw women into the discussion. When Paul speaks of marriage and celibacy, he frequently refers to celibate women as "virgins" in a manner suggesting that this label had become an important designation in the Corinthian community, particularly among those who adhered to strongly ascetic teaching (1 Cor 7:28, 34, 36, 37, 38; cf. 7:25).[34]

The troublesome text, 1 Cor 7:36–38, which concerns the man who feels that he is not behaving properly toward his virgin, is especially important to consider. Virtually every word in this phrase is ambiguous and difficult to translate. The case probably refers to an engaged couple, where the man is concerned about his treatment of his fiancée, but could also refer to a father's treatment of an unmarried daughter or to a spiritual marriage (a couple living together without sex—see previous discussion of 1 Corinthians). The man's belief that the woman's virginity should be maintained may have been challenged by a mix of pressures that ranged from social respectability, to family obligations, to fear of immorality. Paul's reference to the man's hesitancy to go through with the marriage offers a window into the encounter between the priorities of the community and societal values. Moreover, it is important to recognize that 1 Cor 7:36–38 has real implications for the lives of women. The text implies that the virgin may need to sacrifice her desire to remain a virgin if her partner is in danger of losing control. In fact, 1 Corinthians 7 contains evidence that encouragement to remain unmarried was coming from the women of the community. Female initiative is strongly suggested by the teaching directed at a second group of women, without male counterparts, who are exhorted in 1 Corinthians 7. In 1 Cor 7:39–40, Paul instructs the widows. Perhaps responding to those who would ban second marriages altogether, Paul argues that while he feels that a widow will be happier if she remains unmarried, she is free to marry if she wishes. He ends his exhortation with a retort that implies that he expects to be contradicted by some community members and perhaps also asserts his own prophetic authority: "I think that I too have the Spirit of God!"

With respect to women's initiative, it is also interesting to consider 1 Cor 7: 10–11. In this text, Paul applies a command of the Lord against divorce equally to believing men and women, but admits parenthetically that sometimes women do separate from their husbands (no such admission is made with respect to men). This "command of the Lord" may refer to the teachings of the Jesus of history, but may also refer to the teachings of the risen Lord, who is understood to be present in the community and to speak through its prophets (on prophets, see treatment of 1 Cor 11:2–16 below).[35] Given the previous discussion, a possible explanation might be that women sometimes separated from their husbands to pursue a celibate way of life, and Paul is acknowledging this reality. Whatever the precise circumstances, however, Paul's advice is clear: a woman who separates from her husband is to remain unmarried or else be reconciled to her husband. The fact that this advice is directed specifically only at the woman suggests to modern interpreters that Paul has a specific case in mind.

In his teaching concerning marriages between believers and unbelievers, Paul balances instructions to men with instructions to women (1 Cor 7:12–16). There are important reasons, however, for paying close attention to the circumstances of women involved in such mixed marriages. During this earliest period, the fact that some people are entering the community without their spouses is causing problems. Paul states that these marriages should be preserved because of their potential for making the children "holy" and because of the possibility that the nonbelieving spouse might also be saved. Nevertheless, he accepts divorce if the nonbelieving partner refuses to go on living with the believer. God has, after all, called believers to peace. What this implies is that marriages between believers and nonbelievers have been subject to conflict, and some believing partners have probably been abandoned. Later evidence suggests strongly that more women were involved in such difficult circumstances than men.[36] Given the usual marriage arrangements in Greco-Roman society, it would be far more likely that women would naturally accompany their husbands into the group than the reverse. It is interesting to reflect on the significance of the acceptance of women into the movement without their spouses, given that the faithfulness of a woman to her husband's religion was one of the virtues expected of wives.[37] Joining strange, foreign religions (including Judaism, devotion to the Greek deity Dionysos, and worship of the Egyptian goddess Isis) was seen as a sign of a woman's duplicity and immorality. Paul, however, sees such mixed marriages as a source for winning new members.

Thus, 1 Corinthians 7 introduces us to various categories of women living in various circumstances. Celibate women were of special concern in the community. They included women of various ages, who are described with the somewhat fluid labels of unmarried women, virgins, and widows. There seem also to have been divorcées in the community, as well as married women, including women who were married to unbelievers. The slaves instructed in 1 Cor 7:21–3 must have included women. Although Paul does not mention them specifically in 1 Corinthians 7, later evidence from Pauline literature suggests that some of the slave women in the community were part of nonbelieving households (cf. 1 Tim 6:1–2). It is interesting to compare our findings with the results of my survey of the references to specific women in the undisputed letters of Paul. We are reminded that the women who are singled out for mention either alone or as members of missionary partnerships probably had many different backgrounds and were living in various situations.

1 Corinthians 11:2–11

In this text, Paul aims to curtail the efforts of women who pray or prophesy with their heads uncovered. To prophesy in the early church was to engage in some type of inspired teaching—to communicate God's will directly in the midst of the assembly. Although it is not at all clear that these church leaders had completely distinct responsibilities, in 1 Cor 12:28 Paul declares that "God has appointed in the church first apostles, second prophets, third teachers." In 1 Cor 14:1, prophecy is singled out as the most important spiritual gift. The New Testament refers to specific women who were prophets. Philip is described in Acts 21:9 as having four virgin daughters who had the gift of prophecy. As is implied by the terrifying depictions of the suffering that will befall the woman known as "Jezebel" of the church at Thyatira, female prophets could also be feared by some in early Christian groups (Rev 2:19–23). 1 Corinthians 11:2–11 raises many complicated issues concerning Paul's position that must be left aside here. In the end, however, 1 Cor 11:2–11 communicates a basic fact that is enormously important for our reconstruction of the lives of women: there were Corinthian women prophets. There were women whose inspired speech was thought to convey experiences of the divine to the community.

Scholars have debated whether the issue at stake in Paul's response to the Corinthian women prophets involves veiling or hairstyles. What is clear, however, is that some type of removal of head covering is involved. It was probably common for respectable women (Jewish and otherwise) of Paul's day to cover their heads when they were in public view.[38] Loosened hair could be perceived as a sign of an adulteress (Num 5:18), and the release of women's hair might have been part of some foreign religious rituals that Paul did not want associated with the Corinthian community.[39] Why would women seek to uncover their heads in the midst of prophecy? The fact that Paul addresses the consequences of the reversal of patterns of dress and behavior for men and women in 1 Cor 11:2–11 may offer the clue to the puzzle. Although it is not all certain what exactly Paul meant in Gal 3:28 when he proclaimed that in Christ there is no male and female, the abolition of the distinction between the sexes was clearly an important means of speaking about the nature of salvation in some circles. In the second and third centuries CE, among some strongly ascetic and gnostic early Christian groups, salvation could be depicted as the transcendence of sexual differentiation—even as a return to a state of androgynous perfection when creation was both male and female (cf. Gen 1:26–27) (on "gnosticism," see chapter 12). The women who prophesied in Corinth may well have been acting out the notion of unity that they believed Paul himself had taught them, even though he disagreed with the way they acted out its implications. Moreover, some scholars believe that the asceticism which seems to have been strongly embraced by the women of Corinth was inspired by an understanding of salvation that sought to eliminate the distinction between the sexes. The avoidance of sex would be a potent sign that members of the community had been transformed into a new creation.[40]

In her important study of this text, Antoinette Clark Wire has suggested that the women's behavior may also have been perceived as scandalous for reasons of physical space. The women who uncovered their heads may have brought behavior that they practiced in their own homes into the more public arena of the house-church.[41] In addition to 1 Cor 11:2–11, there are other indications in Pauline literature that women's worship was a particularly sensitive issue (1 Cor 14:33b–36; 1 Tim 2:8–15). This sensitivity was no doubt related to cultural ideals in the ancient Mediterranean world where men were associated with the public sphere and women were associated with the home; physical location and degree of visibility were central means of defining virtue and vice. Illegitimate religious groups were accused of encouraging immoral mingling of women and men. By the second century, early Christians were accused of such things.[42]

1 Corinthians 14:33b–36

1 Corinthians 14:33b–36 includes the bold proclamation: "It is shameful for a woman to speak in church!" The uncompromising tone of this text, coupled with the difficulty of harmonizing the text with the acceptance in 1 Cor 11: 2–11 of prayer and prophecy (oral practices in early Christianity) for women, has led some commentators to conclude that 1 Cor 14:33b–36 and 1 Cor 11: 2–11 are actually contradictory. There have been several solutions proposed as explanations for the discrepancy, including the theory that Paul was calling for married women to be silent in 1 Cor 14:33b–36, while allowing celibate women to prophesy, and the theory that the gathering in 1 Cor 14:33b–36 is a gathering of the whole assembly in Corinth as opposed to a more private house-church meeting, as in 1 Cor 11:2–11. None of these solutions has found unanimous support among interpreters. Especially because the verses in 1 Cor 14: 33b–36 seem out of place where they stand (some ancient manuscripts may reflect an attempt to correct this by placing them after 14:40), a significant number of scholars believe that 1 Cor 14:33b–36 represents the work of an interpolator who sought to bring Paul's teaching in harmony with the more restrictive teaching in the Pastoral Epistles, where women are categorically prohibited from teaching and must keep silent (1 Tim 2:12). If this is the case, 1 Cor 14:33b–36, 1 Tim 2:8–15, and 1 Tim 5:3–16 should probably be read in light of a growing preoccupation in some groups with the control of women's speech in the form of teaching, prophecy, and even daily communications between women as early Christianity moved into the second century CE (see chapter 11).

Whether or not one concludes that 1 Cor 14:33b–36 was originally part of 1 Corinthians, in moving from the references to specific women in the undisputed letters of Paul to his pronouncements on gender and sexuality, we encounter ambivalence concerning women's leadership and contributions to early Christian groups. This ambivalence might be partly attributed to the general suspicion of the illegitimate religious activities of women in Greco-Roman society. It is also in keeping with the tendency for women sometimes to be admired in antiquity for their religious talents. When early Christian groups penetrated the cities of the Roman empire, they no doubt encountered various preconceptions as to what their women had to offer. One story told in an early Christian text, dating from early second-century Rome and written in a prophetic style, illustrates the point. In the work known as The Shepherd of Hermas, Hermas concludes that an ancient lady seen in a vision bearing a book of "revelations" is the Sybil, a prophetess of obscure origin known to us from several Jewish and pagan sources. However, Hermas stands corrected; the lady turns out to be the church personified.[43] Hermas' mistaken assumption and the explanation offered perhaps grow out of a desire to respond to the impression of a prominence of female prophets and teachers in early Christian groups.

Because the Shepherd of Hermas communicates its message by means oi ı series of visions and revelations, it is impossible to draw definite historical conclusions. It has been demonstrated, however, that careful analysis of the text, including its use of gender categories, can shed light on the dynamics of a house-church community.[44] In the account concerning the ancient lady, in fact, there is an especially strong indication that the extensive use of female images and references to women characters in the work are tied to the activities of real women. The Greek term for ancient lady is presbytera, the female equivalent of the term used to describe the elders/presbyters (presbyteros), who are depicted as in charge of the church. This terminology was widely associated with leadership at the beginning of the second century CE, including religious offices in Pauline circles (e.g., 1 Tim 5:1; Tit 1:5–9).[45] Particularly intriguing is the reference to a woman named Grapte that sounds very much like a reference to a real historical figure. Hermas is to deliver one book to the elders of the local church himself, but also is to send one book to Clement and one to Grapte. Grapte is, in turn, to instruct the orphans and widows. These believing women and children may well have lived together, forming a type of house-church. With this window into Grapte's world, we anticipate chapter 11 on the early interpreters of Paul on women and gender, in which we encounter further evidence of women living together and teaching one another.[46]

Conclusion

In reconstructing the lives of women in the Pauline mission, scholars have shifted their focus away from Paul's attitude to women toward the actual circumstances of women's lives. The references to such women as Prisca, Phoebe, Euodia, and Syntyche in Paul's undisputed letters have been judged especially important. Scholars have carefully analyzed the brief texts in which their memory is preserved, paying close attention to the titles used to describe them and the roles they are said to play alone or in missionary partnerships. It is important to recognize, however, that in addition to the references to specific women in the undisputed letters, there are also indirect indications of women's lives in the form of pronouncements on women and gender (e.g., 1 Cor 7; 11:2–16). These texts not only offer additional information about women's leadership and about the many different circumstances of their lives, but also suggest occasions when women's choices may have been restricted.

In an effort to recover real women, scholars have set out to understand all the relevant texts within the framework of the particular interests of individual letters. Frequently, the attempt to bring women back to life has led historians beyond the New Testament writings to consider the setting of women's lives in Greco-Roman society. The comparison of women of the Pauline mission to Jewish women and women belonging to other Greek and Roman communities in the Roman imperial world has proved to be especially instructive. Perhaps the most important conclusion that has resulted from the reconstructions of the many women coworkers who participated in the Pauline mission is that women's leadership was neither different nor diminished in relation to that of men. Comparative studies have illustrated, however, that the appearance of women in leadership roles should not be seen as unique in ancient society. Rather, early Christian women acted in ways that were in keeping with the leadership of women in other communities in the Roman imperial world.

NOTES

1. Bernadette J. Brooten, "Early Christian Women and Their Cultural Context: Issues of Method in Historical Reconstruction," in *Feminist Perspectives on Biblical Scholarship*, ed. Adela Yarbro Collins (Chico, CA: Scholars Press, 1985) 65–91.

2. On Chloe, see Gerd Theissen, "Social Stratification in the Corinthian Community," in *The Social Setting of Pauline Christianity* (Philadelphia: Fortress, 1982) 92–94.

3. See Wayne Meeks, *The First Urban Christians: The Social World of the Apostle Paul* (New Haven, CT: Yale University Press, 1983) 51–73, 164–92. On social status, see also Theissen, "Social Stratification."

4. The Pastorals are thought to have been composed anywhere between the late first and the mid–second centuries CE. I favor a date in the early second century.

5. See Ross Shepard Kraemer, *Her Share of the Blessings: Women's Religions among Pagans, Jews and Christians in the Greco-Roman World* (New York: Oxford University Press, 1992) 136–38.

6. See Mary Rose D'Angelo, "Women Partners in the New Testament," JFSR 6 (1990) 73–74, 78–81; Elisabeth Schüssler Fiorenza, In Memory of Her: A Feminist Theological Reconstruction of Christian Origins (New York: Crossroad, 1983) 168–73.

7. See Clement of Alexandria, Stromateis 3.6.53.3.

8. See Margaret Y. MacDonald, Early Christian Women and Pagan Opinion: The Power of the Hysterical Woman (Cambridge: Cambridge University Press, 1996).

9. See The Constitutions of the Holy Apostles 3.15.

10. See discussion of 1 Cor 9:5 in John Dominic Crossan, The Historical Jesus: The Life of a Mediterranean Jewish Peasant (San Francisco: HarperSanFrancisco, 1991) 335.

11. See Antoinette Wire, "1 Corinthians," in Searching the Scriptures: Volume 2, A Feminist Commentary, ed. Elisabeth Schüssler Fiorenza (New York: Crossroad, 1994) 193–94.

12. See Theissen, "Social Stratification" 83–87.

13. See D'Angelo, "Women Partners" 65–86.

14. In "A Rhetorical Analysis of Philippians 4.2–3: Euodia and Syntyche Reconsidered" (paper presented at the annual meeting of the Canadian Society of Biblical Studies, Université du Québec à Montréal, 31 May–2 June 1995), Caroline F. Whelan-Donaghey has suggested that the problems involving these two women may have been the main inspiration for the letter.

15. See Wendy Cotter, "Women's Authority Roles in Paul's Churches: Counter-cultural or Conventional?" NovT 36 (1994) 369–70.

16. Valerie Abrahamsen, "Women at Philippi: The Pagan and the Christian Evidence," JFSR 3 (1987) 17–30.

17. Pheme Perkins, "Philemon," in The Women's Bible Commentary, ed. Carol A. Newsom and Sharon H. Ringe (Louisville, KY: Westminster/John Knox, 1992) 362–63.

18. Meeks, First Urban Christians 16–17.

19. D'Angelo, "Women Partners" 73–74.

20. Robert Jewett, "Paul, Phoebe and the Spanish Mission," in The Social World of Formative Christianity and Judaism: Essays in Tribute to Howard Clark Kee, ed. J. Neusner et al. (Philadelphia: Fortress, 1988) 142–61.

21. On Phoebe, see Caroline F. Whelan, "Amica Pauli: The Role of Phoebe in the Early Church," JSNT 49 (1993) 67–85.

22. See Pliny, Letter 10.96.

23. Schüssler Fiorenza, In Memory of Her 171.

24. Whelan, "Amica Pauli" 81.

25. See Meeks, First Urban Christians 216, n. 29.

26. See Bernadette Brooten, "Junia . . . Outstanding among the Apostles (Rom 16:7)," in Women Priests: A Catholic Commentary on the Vatican Declaration, ed. Leonard and Arlene Swidler (New York: Paulist, 1977) 141–44.

27. See Elisabeth Schüssler Fiorenza, "The Apostleship of Women in Early Christianity" in Swidler and Swidler, Women Priests 135–40; Meeks, First Urban Christians 131–33.

28. Kraemer, Her Share of the Blessings esp. 191–98. See also Bernadette J. Brooten, Women Leaders in the Ancient Synagogue. Brown Judaic Studies 36 (Chico, CA: Scholars Press, 1982).

29. Brooten, "Early Christian Women" 81.

30. See Philo, On the Contemplative Life 68–69, in Ross S. Kraemer (ed.), Maenads, Martyrs, Matrons, Monastics: A Sourcebook on Women's Religions in the Greco-Roman World (Philadelphia: Fortress, 1988) 27.

31. Galen's description of Christian continence comes from an Arabic source translated and edited by Richard Walzer, Galen on Jews and Christians (London: Oxford University Press, 1949) 15.

32. See MacDonald, Early Christian Women 166–70.

33. For the details of the Augustan legislation, see Jane F. Gardner, Women in Roman Law and Society (Bloomington, IN: Indiana University Press, 1986) 77–78.

34. See Margaret Y. MacDonald, "Women Holy in Body and Spirit: The Social Setting of 1 Corinthians 7," NTS 36 (1990) 161–81.

35. Mary Rose D'Angelo, "Remarriage and the Divorce Sayings Attributed to Jesus," in Divorce and Remarriage: Religious and Psychological Perspectives, ed. William P. Roberts (Kansas City, MO: Sheed and Ward, 1990) 87–88.

36. See, for example, 1 Pet 3:1–6; Justin, Apology 2.2.

37. See, for example Plutarch, Moralia [Advice to Bride and Groom], 140 D.

38. See Kraemer, Her Share of the Blessings 146.

39. See Schüssler Fiorenza, In Memory of Her 227–28.

40. See Dennis R. MacDonald, *There Is No Male and Female: The Fate of a Dominical Saying in Paul and Gnosticism* (Philadelphia: Fortress, 1987).

41. Antoinette Clark Wire, *The Corinthian Women Prophets: A Reconstruction through Paul's Rhetoric* (Minneapolis, MN: Fortress, 1990) 183.

42. See, for example, the comments of Marcus Cornelius Fronto recorded in *Octavius* 8–9, in *The Octavius of Marcus Minucius Felix*, trans. G. Clarke (New York: Newman, 1974).

43. *Hermas, Vision* 2.4.1.

44. Steve Young, "Being a Man": The Pursuit of Manliness in the *Shepherd of Hermas*," JECS 2 (1994) 3:237–55.

45. Schüssler Fiorenza, *In Memory of Her* 289–90.

46. *Hermas, Vision* 2.4.2–3.

10

PAUL ON WOMEN AND GENDER

Elizabeth A. Castelli

> How then can [women] be excluded from the priesthood since they
> were thought fit by the founder of the religion and by one of his
> apostles to preach? That was the question, and the Commission [of
> the Archbishops of Canterbury and York in 1935] solved it by ap-
> pealing not to the mind of the founder, but to the mind of the
> Church. That, of course, involved a distinction. For the mind of the
> Church had to be interpreted by another mind, and that mind was
> St. Paul's mind; and St. Paul, in interpreting the other mind, changed
> his own mind.
>
> Virginia Woolf, *Three Guineas*[1]

One of the more remarkable survivals from early Christianity is the collection
of letters written by a first-century hellenized Jewish man turned Christian
missionary and leader, the "apostle" Paul. The seven letters whose authorship is
undisputed by scholars—Romans, 1 and 2 Corinthians, Galatians, Philippians, 1
Thessalonians, and Philemon—offer historians an unparalleled body of literature
produced by a first-century Christian hand. These same letters offer contemporary readers of the text a complex and often confounding set of interpretive
challenges. No challenge is more trenchant than the one raised by the claims
made about women and gender in these texts, as Virginia Woolf's provocative
characterization makes clear. Not only are the ideologies of sex and gender derived from Paul's letters ambiguous, but the directives about practical questions
of leadership and religious office in the letters have inspired strongly felt, if also
conflicting, interpretations. Historically, Paul has occupied a privileged place as
a persistent, if often uncomfortable, authority on matters of doctrine and practice among Christians in a range of institutional locations. Questions of sexuality
and gender are often referred to him, no less so than questions of women's
liturgical and leadership roles in congregations and religious communities. This
chapter seeks to present a survey of the ongoing attempts by feminist scholars
to meet the challenges these texts raise.[2]

Paul's biography has been the subject of many scholarly investigations as
writers have combed through the sparse evidence preserved in his own letters
and have evaluated the usefulness of often-contested external evidence, searching
for details to flesh out a portrait of the enigmatic first-century Christian leader.
Paul himself offers his readers few details, and perhaps the biographical approach

is not the most useful one in reading these ancient texts. It might be more important and more fruitful to situate the texts within their own cultural milieu and their social function as missionary letters.

Paul is clearly a hellenized Jewish writer: he writes in Greek; he cites the Greek translation of the Hebrew Bible when he quotes scripture; and he routinely borrows from a range of interpretive and rhetorical practices that would be available to him from first-century Judaism, as well as Greco-Roman, philosophical and rhetorical schools. Working within a context where different cultures' values, practices, and languages met, clashed, and blended, Paul writes in the style of a cultural craftsman—making use of the tools that lie closest to hand. At times, he will interpret the Hebrew scriptures using the Jewish exegetical approach called *midrash*—using exact quotations from the scriptures to elaborate his own arguments, often interpreting the scripture in question in a nontraditional way. (His use of the Abraham story and the quotation from Gen 15:6 in Rom 4:3 and Gal 3:6 are clear examples of this approach.) At other times, he will appropriate forms of argument whose roots are clearly planted in the soil of Greek and Roman rhetoric and philosophy. His letters are occasional pieces, situational and partial. They do not present a coherent, systematic explication of his theological project. Rather, they are letters written to address particular circumstances and local conditions. As such, their later use by Christian communities as systematic and normative texts strains against the texts' own contingent histories.

It is also the case that the Pauline corpus has been read through the contemporary concerns and lenses of a wide range of communities, religious or otherwise. Hence, Paul's brief references to virginity and marriage have become cornerstones in the foundations of the towering edifices of institutional asceticism, as well as the basis for theologies of marriage.[3] Paul's resistance to the religious leadership of the women prophets in mid-first-century Corinth has been appropriated in other institutional locations where the male leadership of the church has questioned the legitimacy of women's claim to religious experience and to church leadership.[4] Paul's enigmatic references to homoeroticism have fueled the fires of homophobic intolerance and have produced complex counter-readings of the ideology of sexual difference at the heart of such texts.[5] Paul's often peculiar claims about women for a time fueled a complex debate as to whether, indeed, Paul was a feminist.[6]

The point is that Paul's texts have taken on a rich life of their own, being reread and rewritten in a range of contexts that must have been quite unimagined by their author. Although some will argue that "texts must speak for themselves," I argue here that texts, in fact, never do (only) that—that they also speak for others, they speak for history and ideology, and (according to some ingenious feminist interpreters) they can also speak for some of the silenced women of history. If texts spoke simply for themselves, any act of interpretation would be superfluous. These particular texts continue to be read 2000 years after they were written, not because of some historical accident, but rather because of their critical position in the history of the dominant religious tradition in the

West. Therefore, it is worth considering what these texts "speak" beyond "themselves."

Shadows and Echoes of Women's Histories

One of the most critical projects of feminist scholarship as it has been pursued over the last twenty-five years or so has been to reconstruct women's history or, in the words of Joan Kelly, "to restore women to history and to restore our history to women."[7] Feminist biblical interpreters and historians have contributed their part of the larger revisioning project by combing the material remnants of early Christianity for evidence of women's participation in the early Christian movement. Paul's letters have played an important role in this reconstructive project.

Methodologically, Paul's letters present significant difficulties as sources for historical reconstruction. First, these letters are situational and contingent; that is, they were written to particular communities, with those communities' peculiar circumstances in mind. To what degree can we generalize about "early Christianity" from these particular examples? Moreover, Paul's letters are, after all, Paul's letters. They represent his perspective and point of view, not those of all early Christians. To what degree can we grasp an adequate image of the historical circumstances of the first century from this highly perspectival group of texts? Finally, Paul's discussion of women—either in specific or in general—is sporadic and tantalizing, but poor on details. How do historians cope with the difficulties presented by such limited evidence?

With these concerns, there also exists the methodological difficulty of accounting for the blending of theology and history in much of the writing about the New Testament in general and about Paul in particular. Different scholars have approached this methodological problem in different ways. Elisabeth Schüssler Fiorenza, for example, has argued throughout her work that the work of historical reconstruction is a theological project, as can be seen in the subtitle of her groundbreaking feminist historical reconstruction of Christian origins, In Memory of Her,[8] as well as in her more recent assertion that the feminist biblical interpreter is a "feminist theological subject."[9] Others, like Ross Shepard Kraemer, have situated their work explicitly outside the theological realm, pointing out that theology can have a tendentious effect on historical writing.[10] Bernadette Brooten has probably put the history-theology problematic in relation to Paul's writings most succinctly in her insistence that ideology, theology, and material claims are inseparably bound with one another and cannot be easily distinguished.[11]

When scholars have turned their attention to the task of historical reconstruction, theologically inflected or not, one fairly obvious strategy in reconstructing the history of early Christian women has been to examine the information made available about particular women actually named in the biblical texts. If this recuperative project is ultimately only the first step in the ongoing feminist negotiation with early Christian texts, it is nevertheless a critical one. Looking at Paul's letters from this vantage point, it becomes clear that the greetings that appear at the end of some of Paul's letters mention numerous women who were active in Christian communities in the mid–first century. These cursory references have become the ground for extensive historical reconstruction and re-imagination (see also chapter 9).

Romans 16 is probably the most fruitful ground on this account, as well as some of the most contentious in the history of translation and interpretation.[12] This chapter begins as a letter of recommendation for Phoebe, who is called by Paul the *diakonos* of the churches in Cenchreae and the *prostatis* of many and of Paul himself (Rom 16:1–2). Translators routinely render the Greek term *diakonos* as "minister" in English when the Greek term refers to one of the many Christian men who taught, preached, rendered a variety of spiritual services to newly formed Christian communities, and possessed an ample amount of authority and leadership status within such communities. These same translators, however, appear rather less sanguine about according to Phoebe the same role that Paul assigns to Timothy, for example, in 1 Thess 3:2. Rendering her title as "deaconess" (though the Greek term does not have a feminine ending) or "deacon" rather than "minister" transforms Phoebe from a leader of and minister to the churches of Cenchreae into a second-level functionary. (Why she would be carrying a letter of recommendation from Paul—a letter that would have been carried by a missionary as an introduction to communities not yet encountered—if she were not a person of considerable importance within the earliest Christian movements is not addressed by those who reduce her circumstances via translation.) Phoebe's second title, *prostatis*, is less clear: attested only here in the New Testament, this feminine form of the noun *prostatēs* suggests a public role of patronage and protection. Translators obscure this public role by rendering the word "helper" (RSV). They do a bit better when they translate the term as "benefactor" (NRSV) as long as one emphasizes when reading this word the significance of the term within ancient systems of patronage. If so, then one would highlight the likely financial sponsorship involved in Phoebe's role as a benefactor to the Christian communities, a sponsorship that would require a significant level of both economic means and social independence.

Phoebe is by no means the only woman mentioned in this chapter of Romans. Paul includes greetings to various other women who played important roles in the work of the early church. Among these, Prisca is named with Aquila (presented in Acts 18 as her husband) as a coworker of Paul. The Greek term used here is *synergos*, which Paul uses elsewhere in relation to both centrally important colleagues like Timothy (Rom 16:21; 1 Thess 3:2) and Apollos (1 Cor 3:9) and less well known participants in the work of the early Christian mission (Rom 16:9; Phil 2:25; Phlm 1:24). Although it is not entirely clear what it would mean for anyone to be a *synergos*, it is clear that it is a position to which Paul accords a significant amount of importance and respect. When Paul speaks, for example, of Apollos in 1 Corinthians 3, he uses the notion of *synergos* to emphasize the shared characteristics of his own and Apollos' contributions to the missionary work in which they are both engaged. Prisca's presence among those who are called *synergoi* allows us to conclude that some women participated centrally in the framing and enactment of early Christian missionary activity. That Paul simply calls Prisca a *synergos* without any further comment suggests that her presence is, in important respects, unremarkable.

If the text were only to identify these two women, we might be tempted to conclude that Phoebe and Prisca are singled out as relative exceptions. But Paul continues in the rest of Romans 16 to pass along greetings to numerous other women: Mary, "who has worked hard among you" (16:6); Tryphaena and Tryphosa, "those workers in the Lord" (16:12); the "beloved" Persis (16:12); and Julia and Nereus' sister (16:15). While the last three women who are named are not assigned particular roles, the first three are all described through the use of the verb, *kopiaō*, which likely possesses a near-technical sense that refers to missionary work. Although such evidence is far from complete, it all points in a similar direction—toward the significant and sustained presence of women in the ranks of early Christian missionary work.

Romans 16 does not stop at the point of alerting careful readers to the reality that there were numerous women in the early Christian movement who labored as ministers, patronesses, and coworkers with Paul. It goes on to offer a tantalizing (if unique) reference to Junia, who is called, along with her companion Andronicus, an apostle. As Bernadette Brooten has shown, this passage—unremarkable in earlier centuries—became a troubling translational problem for later interpreters. The circular argument ran like this: the text refers to "Junia . . . outstanding among the apostles," but women (it is assumed) could not be apostles, so therefore Junia cannot possibly be a woman. Therefore, they solved the problem by changing the ordinary and well-attested name, "Junia," into the nowhere-attested masculine name, "Junias."[13]

A handful of verses with references to a small group of women, some of whom are named nowhere else in early Christian literature, hardly constitutes a major archive of historical information to be mined by eager scholars who want to reconstruct women's history from it. Indeed, these scanty references raise many more questions than they answer: If women were part of the leadership of the early Christian movements, as Paul's greetings would seem to suggest, how did they experience this level of participation? What did it mean in terms of their relationships with their natal families or with the families they formed when (or if) they married? Are the women who are named without reference to male relatives living independently by choice or by circumstance? Would they do so whether or not they were part of Christian communities? What does it mean that Tryphaena and Tryphosa are named together, like Andronicus and Junia or Prisca and Aquila?[14] What is the economic status of these women? Since Paul argues vociferously at one point for the importance of Christian leaders supporting themselves through work, how would these women have done so? What trades would they have plied? Why are children never mentioned in relation to any of these women?

It is unlikely that we will ever find answers to many of these questions as the sources do not offer insight into such particularities. What is important about raising these questions is that they force us to confront the limited nature of our sources and the imaginative demands that historical reconstruction can make on those who read with these questions in mind. Moreover, as with so much of women's history, the resounding silence that answers back to the questions we pose is itself part of the story of women's past, and it is a silence that insists on being continually acknowledged.

While some scholars have reconstructed early Christian women's history from explicit references to particular women in Paul's letters, others have attempted to reconstruct the past through recourse to the presence of unnamed but critical players in the letters themselves. The most significant of such reconstructions may be found in Antoinette Clark Wire's important rhetorical reading of 1 Corinthians, *The Corinthian Women Prophets: A Reconstruction through Paul's Rhetoric.* In this book, Wire begins with the recognition that we have no direct access to the women of the early Christian community in Corinth since no written sources, if they ever existed, still survive. Unwilling to allow that material silence to have the last word, Wire undertakes to reconstruct the theological positions and the religious lives of the prophetic women of Corinth. Undergirding her work is the operative premise that no argument is ever one-sided. Moreover, she asserts that no argument is made unless there is some compelling reason for it—that is, arguments point to the circumstances that produce them, and furthermore, strong arguments presuppose strong counterarguments. Therefore, it is possible to reconstruct the counterarguments and whole social and political backgrounds from the arguments for which one has direct evidence.

Reading Paul's arguments with the Christian community in Corinth over questions of sexual practice, religious observance, and the relative relationship of religious experience and religious authority, Wire offers a full-bodied rendering of the situation in Corinth—one in which Paul's fretful concern about authority and order is matched (and perhaps exceeded) by the ecstatic, ascetic, and inspirited life of prayer and prophecy embodied by the Corinthian women prophets. In 1 Cor 11:2–16, for example, Wire sees a Christian theology that is a vibrant alternative to Paul's theology. In her view, the Corinthian women embrace a particular notion of new creation in Christ that rejects conventional honor-shame distinctions, notions of idolatry, and religious and sexual practice. Wire's project demonstrates the possibility that a tendentious and polemical text can nevertheless offer significant pieces of evidence for a historical reconstruction.

Sexuality, Ideology, and Gender Trouble

The rhetorical reading of Paul's corpus can offer historical remnants and elements crucial to a retelling of the historical narrative of early Christian women's lives, as Antoinette Clark Wire's work ably demonstrates. Whereas Wire emphasizes what might be known about the historical circumstances that produced Paul's rhetoric, other feminist scholars have focused on what constructions of sex and gender are promoted by Paul's letters. Galatians, Romans, and 1 Corinthians are the most critical texts for this discussion.

1 Corinthians 7 offers a complex reading by Paul of the nature and meaning of sexual relations within the context of marriage. Because the text addresses the specific question of women in the context of marriage, it has been the subject of much debate and interpretation among feminist and other scholars. The questions that the text engages are several: Under what circumstances is marriage desirable? What is the status of the spouse's body in marriage? What are the relative merits of celibacy, marriage, and widowhood? What is the status of marriage between a Christian and a non-Christian?

The passage's opening has been the subject of significant debate. According to the NRSV, 1 Cor 7:1 reads: "Now concerning the matters about which you wrote: 'It is well for a man not to touch a woman.'" The earlier RSV translation of the same passage is: "Now concerning the matters about which you wrote. It is well for a man not to touch a woman." At issue, first, is whether it is the Corinthian community or Paul who has uttered the statement: It is well for a man not to touch a woman. Moreover, one might well ask what such a statement means in historical context: Is this a text that underwrites a stringently ascetical position? Is it an ethical norm or a practical proscription? Does it have a theological impetus? Is it a sentence that means the same thing to both men and women?

Paul occupies an uncomfortable middle ground in the midst of the debate over the status of marriage in Corinth. Whether he wrote the sentence under debate above or is simply responding to it as a slogan of his correspondents, he goes on to say that each man and woman should have their own spouse *dia tas porneias* (on account of "immoralities"), by which Paul means any sexual activity with a partner who is forbidden to one (cf. 1 Cor 5:1–11). He then goes on to assert that husbands and wives should give each other their conjugal rights (lit., their due or their obligation) because neither has authority (*exousia*) over his or her own body, but the husband has authority over the wife's body, while the wife has authority over the husband's body. Expressing a wish that all could be as he himself is, Paul acknowledges that people have different gifts from God, by which he implies that not all have the gift of celibacy. The passage continues to elaborate on the theme that marriage is good, but celibacy is better, and rationalizes the argument by pointing out that marriage diverts the attention of the believer away from the things of God.

A tremendous volume of ink has been spilled over analyses of this passage. Paul has been characterized on its basis as a radical apocalypticist (why marry when history will soon come to an end, rendering moot the need for procreation and reproduction?), a radical egalitarian (wives and husbands are equally bound in their obligations and the constitution of mutual authority over the other), and a radical misogynist (condemning women to submit their bodies to the authority of potentially abusive husbands). Whether any one of these characterizations is fully adequate, it remains the case that Paul, in this passage, seems to express the view that sexual expression is a matter of last resort—not a good in itself, but a bulwark against evil: "To the unmarried and the widows I say that it is well for them to remain unmarried as I am. But if they are not practicing self-control, they should marry. For it is better to marry than to be aflame with passion" (1 Cor 7:8–9). Moreover, Paul apparently does not discern any particular difference in the social circumstances, physical conditions, or meanings derived from the experiences of marriage or sexual relations on the part of men and women. One might pose the following question, as many interpreters have: does the syntactical parallelism of 1 Cor 7:3–4 ("The husband should give to his wife her conjugal rights, and likewise the wife to her husband. For the wife does not have authority over her own body, but the husband does; likewise the husband does not have authority over his own body, but the wife does") mirror social experience? That is, does the delivery of one's physical obligation to one's partner mean the same thing for women and men? Do the pervasive gender differences in social status, access to redress, and potential for violence make a difference in how verse 4 might be read? As Sheila Briggs has put it in another context: "In a patriarchal society the call for self-sacrifice toward others can take on gender-specific forms in which mutual giving way to one another is transformed into women's subordination to men."[15] Furthermore, how might the call to celibacy be experienced differently among men and women?

The problematic of sameness and difference that this text raises makes a second appearance in 1 Corinthians in chapter 11, where Paul worries about the dress of women in the context of worship. "I want you to understand," he writes, "that Christ is the head of every man, and the husband is the head of his wife, and God is the head of Christ. Any man who prays or prophesies with something on his head disgraces his head, but any woman who prays or prophesies with her head unveiled disgraces her head" (1 Cor 11:3–5). The verb that the NRSV translates here as "to disgrace" in Greek is *kataischynō*, which, by a more literal translation, would be rendered "to dishonor" or "to bring shame upon." That men and women bring shame upon themselves through nonidentical behavior—that is, men are shamed by covering their heads, but women are shamed by not covering their heads—suggests that Paul's potential egalitarianism (as it is discerned by some in chapter 7) is not as thoroughgoing as it might at first appear. Indeed, as the argument continues in 1 Corinthians 11, it becomes clearer that Paul is quite concerned with the careful maintenance of gender differences in appearance (justified in part by the curious argument that "nature" affirms the conventional practice of men wearing their hair short and women wearing their hair long) not simply because he thinks it is a good idea, but because he thinks that the created order demands it.[16] He closes the argument with the observation that "if anyone is disposed to be contentious, we have no such custom nor do the churches of God" (1 Cor 11:16)—in other words, no one else suffers women to pray with their heads uncovered, and therefore such a practice is not recognized.

A historian would be quick to observe that this text must indicate that women were, in fact, in Corinth praying and prophesying with their heads uncovered—otherwise, Paul would not need to make such a strong, if occasionally obscure, set of arguments against the practice. But in addition to this historical observation is the recognition that Paul is also concerned here with a particular set of ideological constructions: gender differences are borne by the physical body.

They can be read by observers, they matter, and they function as signs that stand for deeper ethical essences. To blur the lines between male and female—to imagine women prophesying with their heads uncovered or to wear their hair short while men are prophesying with their heads covered or are wearing their hair long—violates some more essential set of differentiations, crosses the line from honor to shame, and challenges the authority that has been established through Paul's theological rendering of the order of creation.

Bernadette Brooten has elegantly traced the connections between Paul's view of the nature of women in this passage in 1 Corinthians and his assertions concerning homoeroticism in the opening chapter of his letter to the Romans. The only completely unambiguous passage in the New Testament on homoeroticism, as well as the only biblical passage that has anything to say about *female* homoeroticism, Rom 1:18–32 provides another occasion for readers to evaluate Paul's ideology of gender.

The passage itself occurs in the broader context of a discussion of idolatry, which claims that human beings are punished by God because "they exchanged the truth about God for a lie and worshipped and served the creature rather than the creator" (Rom 1:25). Paul's characterization of idolatry is no innovation: biblical proscriptions against idolatry would render this characterization ordinary, a cliché even. What is a bit unexpected is what comes next in the passage: "For this reason [i.e., because of idolatry], God gave them up to degrading passions. Their women exchanged natural intercourse for unnatural, and in the same way also the men, giving up natural intercourse with women, were consumed with passion for one another" (italics added; Rom 1:26–27).

Brooten connects this passage with 1 Cor 11:2–16, in part, because the appeal to nature appears in both and because both describe practices that blur gender differences as being disgraceful (*atimia*; more literally, dishonorable). Moreover, like 1 Cor 11:2–16, Rom 1:18–32 interweaves its indictment of a particular human practice with theological propositions. Both texts argue that the human behavior in question—whether it be abandoning conventionally gender-linked appearance and dress (in general or in certain contexts) or engaging in certain apparently non-normative sexual practices—is a violation of a worldly order that is grounded in a cosmically, divinely willed order. Gender differences, according to these texts, are not the mere fruits of social conventions, but are God given and divinely warranted.

Paul's response to the problem of gender trouble may have been time bound, as some commentators have suggested; it is undoubtedly linked to the responses of others writing at the same time and in related cultural circumstances as both Brooten and Margaret Davies have demonstrated. What sets Paul's ideas apart is their ongoing cultural reception and authority; the fact that his constructions of sexuality and gender continue to operate as a foundation for the formulation of judgments on social relations and identities in the contemporary setting. For those interpreters who dismiss Paul's positions on these matters as mere reflections of his own time and circumstances easily excised from a more universal and timeless message, the ongoing cultural impact of Paul's arguments is, at the very least, confounding. For those who accept the view of interpreters like

Brooten, who argue that Paul's ideology of sexuality and gender is thoroughly interwoven with and, indeed, inseparable from his theology, the project of engaging Paul's arguments becomes rather more urgent.

Paul's Rhetoric of "Women" and "Gender"

Probably the most frequently quoted passage of Paul's letters in relation to questions of gender and women is the baptismal formula that appears in the middle of the letter to the churches in Galatia: "There is no longer Jew or Greek, there is no longer slave or free, there is no longer male and female; for all of you are one in Christ Jesus" (Gal 3:28).[17] Placing this formula and its usage within ancient Christian ritual practice and within Greco-Roman cultural context, Wayne Meeks has argued that these words function in essence as a speech-act or, in his words, a "performative utterance:" They enact a new reality through the very process of being spoken.[18] The question that such a formula raises, especially in light of the other passages discussed in this chapter, is what the lived reality being enacted really looks like.

Paul's use of this baptismal formula takes place within the broader context of his angry letter addressed to the churches in Galatia, a letter whose immediate goal is to interrupt the adoption by those churches of observances inscribed in Jewish law. The mode of argument within this text is relentlessly dualistic and oppositional. Paul presents a series of binary oppositions whose repetition and amplification work rhetorically to persuade his readers to adopt his view of things and to reject alternative views. Slave and free, law and promise, flesh and spirit echo as irreconcilably separate in Paul's argument against the adequacy of the law for providing a framework for life in the new Christian creation.

The baptismal formula that Paul quotes resounds increasingly paradoxically in the broader context of this letter. What does it mean to invoke such a formula (which on its face seems to imply a radical dissolution of socially constructed differences) when the rest of the argument in whose service the formula is invoked is predicated on precisely the same oppositions one claims to be undoing through ritual? Moreover, how is one to read this formula within the broader context of Paul's collected writings, where, as we have just seen, gender difference bears the inscription of divine authority? How is one to think the complex relationship between sameness and difference that pulses through the writings of Paul?

Some of this ambiguity emerges quite clearly in a text that appears in the following chapter in Galatians. Since Paul argues against the law as a useful framework for Christian life, it is ironic to see him turning to the Torah for examples to undergird his argument that the law is not adequate. In doing so, Paul approaches familiar territory by taking up the story of Sarah and Hagar in the Abraham cycle.[19] Not addressing the particularities of the narratives, but drawing on Sarah and Hagar as rhetorical figures, Paul proceeds to construct an allegory:

For it is written that Abraham had two sons, one by a slave woman and the other by a free woman. One, the child of the slave, was born according to the flesh; the other, the child of the free woman, was born through the promise. Now this is an allegory: these women are two covenants. One woman, in fact, is Hagar, from Mount Sinai, bearing children for slavery . . . and corresponds to the present Jerusalem, for she is in slavery with her children. But the other woman corresponds to the Jerusalem above; she is free, and she is our mother. (Gal 4:22–26)

In this passage, the difference that Paul sees inscribed indelibly and irreducibly on his subjects is not that of gender, but that of social status and class. Categories of difference are here not rendered immaterial and meaningless, but rather come to stand for the radical differences between those who are born into slavery (life under the law) and those who are born into freedom (life under the promise). These are differences not only at the level of theological significance, but also at the level of essential nature. It is troubling that Paul derives his figurative imagery in this passage from the economic institution of slavery and from women's own particular relationship to that institution.[20] It is also clear that the very notion of difference works in the passage as a conceptual problem for Paul, something that his argument requires, and yet that his philosophical framework cannot sustain. Moreover, the logic of the passage requires that difference remain such a foundational contradiction for Paul's argument. As Hagar and Sarah are abstracted from their points of narrative origin into rhetorical figures of a theological allegory, the heady expectation that "there is no longer slave or free" dims and grows more remote and utopian.

Paul's argument concerning the law turns to the Jewish practice of circumcision as the focal expression of religious identity and difference. It is clear that Paul chooses circumcision as a synecdoche (an abbreviated reference to a small part of something to signify the entire thing) for the law as a whole because it allows him to make connections with ideas about covenant and identity and because it is probably the most important of the several ways by which Jewish identity and difference were signaled in ancient societies—along with the observance of dietary laws, sabbath-keeping, and separation. Circumcision is different from these other practices because, although it functions as an ongoing and abiding sign, it takes place only once in a life cycle, and it is practiced only on male bodies. It may be that the attention to circumcision in Paul's discussion is focused by the concerns of the community to which he writes—circumcision is controversial in the community, so he writes about it instead of about other things. It is also the case that circumcision intersects with ideas that concern gender and generation in ways that the other identifying practices of Jewish women and men in antiquity did not. Although scholars debate the meanings that accrue to circumcision, it remains a ritual of marking the male body as a sign of belonging to a particular group.

In the history of feminist interpretation of Paul, one more critical topic needs to be addressed: the prevalent tendency of many Christian interpreters to caricature purity ideas and practices (particularly those pertaining to women) in order to create a negative backdrop against which to project a utopian and preconceived notion of "Christian freedom."[21] In this context, it is important to keep in mind that our evidence about how ancient Jewish women understood and observed the law (both as an abstract, ideological framework and as a practical guide for the transformation of everyday life into an expression of holiness) is both fragmentary and ambiguous (see also chapters 2 and 3). Nevertheless, the tendentious view that Jewish women experienced singularly oppressive treatment within the context of their religious lives and fled this oppression, escaping into an egalitarian Christian context, must certainly be rejected as a simplistic and inadequate rendering of the historical record, however fragmentary and open to multiple readings it may be. Gender ideologies and their enactments in the lives of historical women and men across the board in the ancient world were infinitely more complex than such caricatures can begin to allow. This is true for early Christianity and Judaism alike.

Women's Leadership in the Church, or Using Paul to Think With

Thus far, this chapter has dealt with a range of topics that concern women and gender in the Pauline corpus, questions of historical reconstruction, rhetorical interpretation, and ideological constructions. All of these concerns come together in one of the most contentious and debated passages in the writings of Paul, the passage that asserts:

> As in all the churches of the saints, women should be silent in the churches. For they are not permitted to speak, but should be subordinate, as the law also says. If there is anything they desire to know, let them ask their husbands at home. For it is shameful for a woman to speak in church. (1 Cor 14:33b–35)

Interpreters, particularly those who hope to find scriptural warrants for women's full participation within the religious life of Christian churches, have long struggled with this particular passage. Some point to the apparent contradiction between this passage and the testimony of 1 Cor 11:2–16, which, although portraying Paul's displeasure with the gender-blurring practices of the Corinthian women, assumes without comment that women are praying and prophesying in worship. These interpreters argue that the passage must represent a later scribal or editorial interpolation (addition) into the text. Others, such as Antoinette Wire, argue for the authenticity of the passage and interpret its rhetoric within the broader context of Paul's argument about prophetic speech in the letter. Still others attempt to rationalize the two passages through reference to different classes of women or to different kinds of gatherings for worship. Some will raise the broader question of how Paul could possibly take such a position when there is the evidence, in Romans 16 and elsewhere, that Paul worked in close association with a number of women and perhaps maintained strong personal friendships with these women.[22]

One of the most ingenious accountings for this text may be found in a nineteenth-century autobiography written by an African American woman, who herself felt a deep call to undertake a life of preaching and ministry. Describing her own struggle to come to terms with the apparent contradictions she saw between her religious feeling, on the one hand, and the scriptures on the other, she wrote:

> It is true, that in the ordinary course of Church arrangement and order, the Apostle Paul laid it down as a rule, that females should not speak in the church, nor be suffered to teach; but the Scriptures make it evident that this rule was not intended to limit the extraordinary directions of the Holy Ghost, in reference to female Evangelists, or oracular sisters; nor to be rigidly observed in peculiar circumstances.[23]

In a remarkable hermeneutical turn, Mrs. Zilpha Elaw saw clearly the problem presented by the biblical text and circumvented it by claiming to stand outside its purview—indeed, by asserting that the text itself authorized precisely the claim to stand outside.

What all of these assessments of Paul's position on the question of women's role in worship have in common is the attribution to Paul of a thoroughgoing authority to pronounce on such matters. Indeed, it is precisely in the context of such contentious passages that the whole question of scriptural authority is raised with considerable urgency. What Paul says on such questions, even if contradictory or convoluted (as Virginia Woolf has characterized it), has frequently taken on a foundational kind of authority for Christian churches across the centuries. Consequently, the interpretation of these statements becomes a practice of significant institutional and political import.

The continual recourse to Paul's (and more generally, the Bible's) authority theologically and culturally invites further theoretical interrogation and elaboration. It is one thing for Christian communities to make the letters of Paul normative for their own communal organization, division of labor, and liturgical practice. It is another thing altogether when these same texts are used within secular contexts to underwrite the authority of political or social claims, as occurs increasingly frequently in American civil discourse. Whether one agrees with a particular view expressed by Paul or any other biblical writer, one must ask what is at stake when that view is deployed in a nonreligious context to support a particular stance. Feminist or otherwise, professional interpreters and ordinary readers of the Bible alike continue to undertake to understand what the intersecting lines among history, theology, ethics, and ideology in a set of texts produced almost 2000 years ago might have to tell them about the past and the present. Being able to assess critically this process of using Paul to think with will be crucial to the ongoing project (feminist or otherwise) of engaging with these rich and complex texts without necessarily capitulating to their own rhetorical operations, which insist that they should or will have the last word.

NOTES

1. Virginia Woolf, *Three Guineas* (New York: Harcourt, Brace and World, 1938) 122.

2. For detailed feminist readings of these texts, see Elisabeth Schüssler Fiorenza, ed., *Searching the Scriptures: Volume 2, A Feminist Commentary* (New York: Crossroad, 1994): Antoi-

nette Wire, "1 Corinthians" 153–95; Shelly Matthews, "2 Corinthians" 196–217; Sheila Briggs, "Galatians" 218–36; Carolyn Osiek, "Philippians" 237–49; Lone Fatum, "1 Thessalonians" 250–62; Elizabeth A. Castelli, "Romans" 272–300; S. C. Winter, "Philemon" 301–12.

3. See pertinent essays in Richard Valantasis and Vincent L. Wimbush, *Asceticism* (New York: Oxford University Press, 1995).

4. See esp. Antoinette Clark Wire, *The Corinthian Women Prophets: A Reconstruction through Paul's Rhetoric* (Minneapolis, MN: Fortress, 1990).

5. Bernadette J. Brooten, "Paul's Views on the Nature of Women and Female Homoeroticism," in *Immaculate and Powerful: The Female in Sacred Image and Social Reality*, ed. Clarissa W. Atkinson, Constance H. Buchanan, and Margaret R. Miles (Boston: Beacon, 1985) 61–87; John Boswell, *Christianity, Homosexuality, and Social Tolerance: Gay People in Western Europe from the Beginning of the Christian Era to the Fourteenth Century* (Chicago: University of Chicago Press, 1980) 335–53; Robert Goss, *Jesus Acted Up: A Gay and Lesbian Manifesto* (San Francisco: HarperSanFrancisco, 1993) 87–111. See now Margaret Davies, "New Testament Ethics and Ours: Homosexuality and Sexuality in Romans 1:26–27," *Biblical Interpretation* 3 (1995) 315–31; Dale B. Martin, "Heterosexism and the Interpretation of Romans 1:18–32," *Biblical Interpretation* 3 (1995) 332–55; and Bernadette J. Brooten, *Love between Women: Early Christian Responses to Female Homoeroticism* (Chicago: University of Chicago Press, 1996).

6. See the literature cited in Bernadette Brooten, "Early Christian Women and Their Cultural Context: Issues of Method in Historical Reconstruction," in *Feminist Perspectives on Biblical Scholarship*, ed. Adela Yarbro Collins (Chico, CA: Scholars Press, 1985) 69, n. 6.

7. Joan Kelly, "The Social Relation of the Sexes: Methodological Implications of Women's History," in Kelly, *Women, History, and Theory: The Essays of Joan Kelly* (Chicago: University of Chicago Press, 1984) 1.

8. Elisabeth Schüssler Fiorenza, *In Memory of Her: A Feminist Theological Reconstruction of Christian Origins* (New York: Crossroad, 1983).

9. Elisabeth Schüssler Fiorenza, *But She Said: Feminist Practices of Biblical Interpretation* (Boston: Beacon, 1992) 160.

10. Ross Shepard Kraemer, *Her Share of the Blessings: Women's Religions among Pagans, Jews, and Christians in the Greco-Roman World* (New York: Oxford University Press, 1992) 133.

11. Brooten, "Early Christian Women" 91. For a lengthier discussion of these issues, see my "Heteroglossia, Hermeneutics, and History: A Review Essay of Recent Feminist Studies of Early Christianity," *JFSR* 10:2 (1994) 73–98, esp. 79–85.

12. For more extensive discussion of this text, see Elisabeth Schüssler Fiorenza, "Missionaries, Apostles, Coworkers: Romans 16 and the Reconstruction of Women's Early Christian History," *Word and World* 6 (1986) 420–33; Schüssler Fiorenza, "The 'Quilting' of Women's History: Phoebe of Cenchreae," in *Embodied Love: Sensuality and Relationship as Feminist Values*, ed. Paula M. Cooey, Sharon A. Farmer, and Mary Ellen Ross (San Francisco: Harper & Row, 1987) 35–49; Castelli, "Romans" 277–80.

13. Bernadette J. Brooten, "Junia . . . Outstanding among the Apostles (Romans 16: 7)," in *Women Priests: A Catholic Commentary on the Vatican Declaration*, ed. Leonard S. Swidler and Arlene Swidler (New York: Paulist, 1977) 141–44.

14. This question is addressed creatively and with insight by Mary Rose D'Angelo, "Women Partners in the New Testament," *JFSR* 6/1 (1990) 65–86.

15. Briggs, "Galatians" 230.

16. See Brooten, "Paul's Views" for an extended discussion of this argument. See also Wire, *Corinthian Women Prophets* 220–23, for a summary of the scholarship on this passage.

17. See Briggs, "Galatians" 218–36.

18. Wayne Meeks, "The Image of the Androgyne: Some Uses of a Symbol in Earliest Christianity," *History of Religions* 13 (1974) 165–208, esp. 181–82.

19. See my essay, "Allegories of Hagar: Reading Galatians 4.21–31 with Postmodern Feminist Eyes," in *The New Literary Criticism and the New Testament*, ed. Edgar V. McKnight and Elizabeth Struthers Malbon (Journal for the Study of the New Testament Supplements [JSNTS] 109; Sheffield: Sheffield Academic, 1994) 228–50.

20. See Briggs, "Galatians" 224, on this question.

21. For a concise collection and evaluation of this idea in scholarship, see Kathleen Corley, "Feminist Myths of Christian Origins," in *Reimagining Christian Origins. A Colloquium Honoring Burton L. Mack*, ed. Elizabeth A. Castelli and Hal Taussig (Valley Forge, PA: Trinity Press International, 1996) 51–67.

22. Elizabeth A. Clark has discussed this same kind of paradox in the lives and ideas of other early Christian men. See her "Friendship between the Sexes: Classical Theory and Christian Practice," in *Jerome, Chrysostom, and Friends: Essays and Translations* (New York: Edwin Mellen, 1979) 35–106; and Clark, "Theory and Practice in Late Ancient Asceticism: Jerome, Chrysostom, and Augustine," *JFSR* 5/2 (1989) 25–46.

23. Zilpha Elaw, *Memoirs of the Life, Religious Experience, Ministerial Travels and Labours of Mrs. Zilpha Elaw, an American Female of Colour; Together with Some Account of the Great Religious Revivals in America [Written by Herself]*, in *Sisters of the Spirit: Three Black Women's Autobiographies of the Late Nineteenth Century*, ed. William L. Andrews (Bloomington, IN: Indiana University Press, 1986) 124.

11

>─◄◆─○─◆►─◄

REREADING PAUL

Early Interpreters of Paul on Women and Gender

Margaret Y. MacDonald

As it expanded and moved into the second century CE, the form known as "Pauline" Christianity underwent an institutionalization that has been understood as having important consequences for the lives of women. The literature it produced includes New Testament writings that date from the middle of the first century CE to the first half of the second century CE. Among these are several of Paul's letters to communities located in various cities around the eastern Mediterranean, but also documents attributed to Paul, often understood as having been composed by one of his students or disciples to keep his teaching alive in the generations that followed his death (a practice that was not without precedent in the ancient world). These so-called deutero-Pauline works include Colossians, Ephesians, 1 Timothy, 2 Timothy, and Titus, and perhaps also 2 Thessalonians, but the authorship of this document is heavily debated.

Pauline literature is interesting to study because it offers a large body of writings that come from the same author (or, in the case of deutero-Pauline works, from a tradition that developed from the same author) and thus offers significant evidence concerning a fascinating branch of early Christianity. The value of Pauline works for reconstructing Christian origins is also related to the fact that they reflect community life during a relatively long period of about 100 years and, hence, can be analyzed with the hope of understanding the nature of group development over time. Sometimes drawing on sociological theory, New Testament scholars have set out to understand the institutionalization of church communities—the development of set rules of behavior, belief codes, patterns of worships, structures of government, offices, and so on.[1] The Pauline writings are particularly well suited for attempting such an investigation.

An important change in the circumstances of women has sometimes been linked to the death of the apostle Paul and the attempt to secure the continuation of the type of Christian commitment that grew under his leadership by means of deutero-Pauline authorship. Sociologists have noted that new religious groups often begin with quite informal structures of authority and are sometimes heavily dependent on the guidance of a particular leader. When that leader dies and the group is faced with problems of governance, which might be worsened by other problems such as rapid expansion and disagreements over what might be the true teaching, more clearly defined rules and structures begin to demarcate what is acceptable in community life. Something like this might have been at work in Pauline Christianity.

Paul's letters exhibit somewhat fluid leadership roles. Numerous women are listed as among Paul's collaborators. They are given titles such as "deacon" (Rom 16:1) and "coworker" (Rom 16:3), and there are no indications that, in their leadership roles, these women occupied positions subordinate to their male counterparts (see chapter 9). Moreover, Paul's undisputed letters contain no unequivocal statements that women should obey men. In fact, there are indications that the usual understanding of the hierarchical relations between men and women has been transformed in anticipation of the reign of God (e.g., 1 Cor 7: 3–4; Gal 3:28). But in the deutero-Pauline writings of Colossians, Ephesians, 1 Timothy, 2 Timothy, and Titus, the number of women who are singled out for mention drops off noticeably. Most significantly, in these works, the treatment of the marriage relationship in light of the relationships of children to parents and slaves to masters leaves little doubt about the acceptance of hierarchical patterns (Col 3:18–4:1; Eph 5:21–6:9; 1 Tim 2:8–15, 3:4, 6:1–2; Tit 2:2–10). Paul's openness to celibacy for women of various ages and in various circumstances (1 Cor 7) receives important qualification in 1 Timothy. Because of various problems in the author's community, young widows are instructed to marry, bear children, and manage their households—that is, to assume the life of the traditional matron (1 Tim 5:14).

A similar attempt to define and restrict the roles of women can be detected in the interpretation of Paul on women and gender reflected in the Acts of the Apostles. The Acts of the Apostles, the second volume of a two-part work by the same author who composed the Gospel of Luke, narrates the spread of Christianity from Jerusalem to Rome. Acts is not a work of Pauline theology in the same sense as the deutero-Pauline works; its major themes are consistent with those found in the Gospel of Luke. Moreover, scholars debate to what extent Acts offers a historically reliable account of Christian origins. Paul's missionary activities dominate the second half of the book. Yet, Paul is never presented as writing letters, and the author does not even seem to be aware of the existence of Paul's correspondence. Nevertheless, Acts might be described as one form of the Pauline heritage—offering insight into how Paul's contribution was presented to a later audience.[2] There is some information about Paul's missionary activities in Acts that is consistent with what we know from his letters. In both his letters and in Acts, the support of women is integral to the expansion of Paul's mission. The author of Acts interprets the involvement of women in the birth of Christianity in a particular light. In her important study, Mary Rose D'Angelo has demonstrated how the presentation of women in Luke-Acts has been influenced by the desire to respond to accusations against the new movement concerning women's leadership, especially their prophetic roles. The involvement of women would have been seen as a sign of the group's foreign and suspicious character and would have raised fears about social disorder (Judaism and other religions from the eastern Mediterranean were depicted in this way in the Roman world). In response, the author of Acts sought to demonstrate Christianity's respectability.[3] We discover subtle traces of this agenda at work when we consider the presentation of Paul's dealings with women in Acts.

Despite the points of contact between the interpretations of Paul on women and gender in Acts and the deutero-Pauline literature, it is important not to view development in Pauline Christianity as monolithic. Increasingly, the second century *Acts of (Paul and) Thecla* is viewed as a product of the Pauline tradition that has points of contact with the Pastoral Epistles of 1 Timothy, 2 Timothy, and Titus, but represents an alternate interpretation. The practice of women remaining unmarried is clearly viewed with suspicion in the Pastoral Epistles, and strong efforts are made to encourage the adoption of traditional gender roles. In contrast, the story of Paul and Thecla reflects a belief system in which Paul's preference for celibacy has become the conviction that celibacy is fundamental to one's acceptance of the gospel, and a celibate woman is depicted as having a prominent leadership role. It is useful to think in terms of several trajectories of the Pauline tradition emanating from the teaching and leadership of the apostle that would have had varying consequences for the lives of early Christian women.

In this chapter, I explore several forms of the Pauline legacy. First, it is necessary to consider the following words of caution. Even in documents in which one encounters gender hierarchy and apparently silenced women, it is important not to jump to immediate conclusions about the nature of community life. The writings of Ignatius of Antioch that come from the early second century, and are therefore perhaps contemporary with, or even somewhat earlier than, the Pastoral Epistles, exhibit a hierarchical understanding of household life and are the first clear witnesses to the emergence of the system in which the bishop stands above the other leaders, the presbyters and deacons.[4] Like the Pastorals, Ignatius' letters are indebted to their Pauline legacy, yet unlike the Pastorals, they nevertheless single out women for the important contribution they make to community life in much the same way as the undisputed letters of Paul. They serve as a reminder that the presence of traditional ideologies might not always mean that women were without influence.[5]

Acts

Although in this chapter our study is confined to how the author of Acts presents Paul's dealings with women, it is important to recognize that this aspect of the Lukan treatment of women is in keeping with the whole. In Acts, women are in the background, not the foreground. They are clearly part of the story, but details are offered in passing and sometimes with such brevity that it would seem that the author was reluctant to mention them at all. We are presented with tantalizing details that often raise more questions than they answer.

We are told, for example, of Paul's visit with Philip, who had "four unmarried daughters who had the gift of prophecy" (Acts 21:9). The reputation of these women may have been so great that they could not go unmentioned, but no further information about them is provided. In contrast to the situation when it is men who prophesy, we are not informed as to the content of the prophecy (Acts 21:4; 10–11; cf. Acts 2:17–18). The author of Acts clearly does not want to emphasize women's prophetic activities.[6]

There is one type of women's contribution to the development of early Christianity, however, of which the author of Acts definitely approves: benefaction. (Benefaction was an important social structure in Greco-Roman society by which people of higher social status offered support in various forms to those of lower social status—their clients. In return, clients bestowed honor on their patrons and were subject to their authority.) That Paul wins the support in Greece of "not a few of the leading women"—by which he means women of high social standing—is highlighted by the author of Acts (Acts 17:4, 12; cf. Acts 17:34). As will be made clear by the discussion of Lydia that follows, to be able to provide resources such as housing for the benefit of the community represents the ideal woman's contribution.[7] My study of the women in the undisputed letters of Paul also revealed the importance of women patrons for Paul's mission, but in Acts, one detects a subtle attempt to play down leadership functions that may have sprung out of, or even gone beyond the boundaries of, the role of female patron. Phoebe, for example, is acknowledged as a patron (*prostatis*), but is also called minister or deacon (*diakonos*) in Rom 16:1–2, and there is good reason to believe that the designation "deacon" was used in conjunction with Phoebe's role as a missionary leader (see chapter 9). In Acts, it is only men who participate in "ministry" (*diakonia*; Acts 6:1, 4; 11:29; 12:25).[8]

Lydia and Other Women at Philippi

The story of Paul's activities in Philippi begins with a reference to an intriguing setting: Paul addresses a sabbath gathering composed exclusively of women (Acts 16:13). The frequency of Paul's encounter with women in Philippi (a city of Macedonia) may reflect the fact that women in this city had more prominent roles than in other parts of the Greco-Roman world (chapter 9). Paul's audience at Philippi includes Lydia, a gentile woman who, while not Jewish, nevertheless worships the God of Israel. (Evidence for Gentiles practicing Judaism comes to us from divers ancient sources. Luke's description of such persons as "fearing God" suggests a technical terminology, though scholars continue to debate this.)

Lydia is described as a seller of purple-dyed goods (purple fabrics were a sign of wealth and rank in the ancient Mediterranean world). The fact that Paul encountered her in Philippi although she was originally from Thyatira (in Asia Minor) is probably an indication that her role as a merchant of purple goods required her to travel. Because she traded in luxury goods, Lydia was probably quite well to do. She is presented in Acts 16 as Paul's first convert in Philippi. In keeping with the male-female parallelism that runs throughout Luke-Acts, Lydia's conversion mirrors that of Cornelius (also a prosperous "God fearer;" Acts 10:1–11:18). That she is presented as in control of her own resources suggests that she may have been a widow. We are told that she and her household (probably an extended household including children, but also slaves and clients) were baptized, and that Paul and his entourage went to her house to stay (Acts 16:14–15).

Lydia's home is depicted as housing community gatherings (Acts 16:40), but any leadership role she may have had in a house-church is never made explicit. We hear nothing of a teaching role or of participation in missionary activities. Rather, securing Lydia's patronage means securing a base for Paul's teaching and mission. For the author of Acts, Lydia no doubt serves as a fine example of the women of high standing who were drawn to early Christianity and who benefited the community in various ways by acting as patrons.

The account of Paul's stay in Philippi also includes the story of his encounter with "a slave-girl who had a spirit of divination and brought her owners a great deal of money by fortune-telling" (Acts 16:16). As she follows Paul, the spirit causes the woman to announce the identity of Paul and his entourage and to proclaim the goal of their mission: "These men are slaves of the Most High God, who proclaim to you a way of salvation" (Acts 16:17). We are told that this recurring scene eventually annoys Paul, and he orders the spirit to come out of her in the name of Jesus Christ. Having had her "prophetic" voice silenced, we hear nothing more about the woman. But the scene sets in motion a series of events that may shed light on how women were implicated in charges that Christianity led to social disruption.

Her owners had made the woman the center of a lucrative business. Her exorcism meant the end of this business opportunity, and consequently Paul and Silas were accused of causing a disturbance in the city and generally of advocating "un-Roman activities" (Acts 16:16–21).[9] The author of Acts is clearly not interested in the fate of the slave woman and may even believe that such women are a source of aggravation and a cause of trouble for the early Christian community. However, in the author's view, Paul's innocence is beyond question; he is punished for freeing a woman from enslavement by a spirit.

The scene offers an opportunity to communicate the message that early Christians are not rabble-rousers. On the contrary, they are respectable persons and even include some who hold the relatively rare privilege of formal Roman citizenship (Acts 16:37–39; cf. Acts 22:25–29).

Priscilla

In addition to the information contained in Acts, reference is made to the contribution of Priscilla and Aquila in the undisputed letters of Paul (1 Cor 16:19; Rom 16:3–5; here, Priscilla is called Prisca) and in 2 Timothy 4:19 (see chapter 9). In this chapter, I concentrate on the distinctive information provided about

Priscilla in Acts and seek to take account of any significant departure from the undisputed letters of Paul.

Acts offers many biographical details about the couple that are not mentioned by Paul, including their identity as Jews, their expulsion from Rome, and their involvement in the same tent-making craft as Paul (Acts 18:2–3). In addition, when the material from Acts is considered alongside Paul's references to this missionary couple, we arrive at the probable association of Priscilla and Aquila with believers in three different cities: Rome, Ephesus, and Corinth (18:1–3; 18:18–19:1).

As in Rom 16:3, Acts 18:18, 26 list Priscilla's name first; this is probably a sign that she was of higher status than her partner. Moreover, in keeping with the evidence in Paul's letters, there is no indication whatsoever in Acts of Priscilla having a different or diminished role in relation to her partner. In fact, while in Ephesus, both Priscilla and Aquila are said to have taught Apollos, an eloquent Jew who was very knowledgeable about the scriptures. Although Apollos already had some familiarity with the Christian message, Priscilla and Aquila are said to have taken Apollos aside and "explained the Way of God to him more accurately" (Acts 18:24–26). This is an important text, for it offers indisputable evidence of a woman acting as a teacher. Even if we are to understand Priscilla and Aquila's taking of Apollos aside as bringing him into their home for some private teaching (cf. 1 Cor 16:19), we should not underestimate the significance of the act. The home was the basic cell of organization in the Pauline mission; it was the arena of celebration, teaching, and probably often also of conversion (cf. Acts 16:14–15, 40).

Given the tendency in Acts to play down the leadership roles of women, the presentation of Priscilla stands out as especially remarkable.[10] The prominence of Priscilla in Acts should probably be taken as confirmation of the importance of her leadership during Paul's day; she was so well known as a teacher and missionary leader that her role could not be circumscribed. In one respect, however, one senses the author's attempt to recount the tradition with as much decorum as possible. In contrast to the references to the missionary pair in Paul's letters, in Acts, Priscilla and Aquila are explicitly presented as husband and wife (see chapter 9).

Colossians and Ephesians

It is useful to consider Colossians and Ephesians together because these documents are very similar. The close connection is probably the result of the dependence of Ephesians on Colossians.[11] Despite the presence of some significant differences in content, these works display a similar worldview—one that favors unity, integration, and cosmic harmony. Both documents extol the supremacy of Christ, who fills the universe with his body (e.g., Col 1:19–20; Eph 1:22–23). Moreover, these works include ideas and reflect historical developments that have led many scholars to believe that they must be deutero-Pauline. Colossians is probably the earliest deutero-Pauline writing, composed within a decade of

Paul's death. The period 90–100 CE is plausible for the composition of Ephesians. It should be acknowledged, however, that a significant number of scholars think that Paul composed Colossians. The vast majority of scholars understand Ephesians to be deutero-Pauline.

With the exception of Nympha, who has a church in her house (Col 4:15), no references are made to specific women in Colossians and Ephesians. Nevertheless, these documents offer evidence of a significant development in Pauline Christianity that has real consequences for the lives of women: wifely submission is explicitly stated as a community ideal. Colossians and Ephesians embrace traditional household ethics in the form of household codes (a pattern of ethical teaching concerned with the relationship between husbands and wives, masters and slaves, and parents and children; Col 3:18–4:1; Eph 5:21–6:9). Household code material is also found at various junctures in the Pastoral Epistles and in 1 Peter (1 Tim 2:8–15, 3:4, 6:1–2; Tit 2:1–10; 1 Pet 2:13–3:7). Scholars have noted significant convergence between these codes and the traditional ethics of Greco-Roman society.[12]

In seeking to understand the emergence of household codes in early Christian literature, scholars have sought to explore the nature of the relationship between early Christian groups and society at large. It has been noted that as Christian groups approached the end of the first century CE, they exhibited increasing concern about hostile treatment at the hands of outsiders. This concern is probably reflected in Col 4:5–6, where community members are instructed to conduct themselves wisely toward outsiders. Composed probably in the last few decades of the first century CE and drawing its origins from circles that have much in common with Pauline Christianity, 1 Peter reflects great concern about relations with outsiders. For example, the circumstances of a woman with a nonbelieving mate are depicted in a manner that offers a window into mounting tension in the household. In the midst of household code teaching, the author of 1 Peter exhorts the wives of husbands "who do not obey the word" to accept the authority of their husbands so that they may be won over "without a word" by their wives' "pure and reverent conduct" (1 Pet 3:1–2). That the exhortation to wives in 1 Pet 3:1–6 culminates in the instruction that the women should let nothing terrify them strongly suggests that they have been suffering—perhaps even suffering violence (1 Pet 3:6). In a situation where a woman might be haunted by fears, she is instructed to keep silent; she is to be encouraged by the hope that this model behavior might one day convince her husband (cf. 1 Pet 3:1–6).[13]

1 Peter 3:1–6 suggests that early Christians were being accused of disrupting households. Indeed, in about the middle of the second century CE, an intellectual named Celsus produced a detailed critique of early Christianity along those lines. Religion, which should be properly linked to affairs of the city and state (the male domain), had become, according to Celsus, a private affair among the early Christians. He spoke of the secret tactics of the early Christians—their efforts to dupe women and children and to teach them to be disrespectful of authority. He characterized the hub of Christian activity as domestic settings: the women's quarters of private dwellings and the shops where women worked.[14]

Celsus' comments are clearly intended to mock the early Christians, and they have much in common with other criticisms of early Christianity and other religions, such as Judaism and the Dionysos and Isis cults; these groups were considered to be foreign and suspicious. They were censured for the disruptive effect they had on society and for causing women, who were understood as more gullible with respect to "strange" religions, to behave in immoral ways. Because the critique of illegitimate or "other" religious groups in the Greco-Roman world often employed stereotypes, it is impossible to be certain that Celsus' comments offer an accurate picture of the way early Christians behaved. Yet, when Celsus' comments are placed side by side with references to women in early Christian texts, the result is an important confirmation of female visibility. Moreover, from the perspective of outsiders, the activities of women could be an important indicator of the suspicious nature of early Christian groups.

Although they come from a later period, there is good reason to believe that the kind of accusations made by Celsus were already directed against some Christians much earlier. It has frequently been suggested that the greater correspondence between the ethical exhortations concerning household relations and the ethics of Greco-Roman society that emerges in deutero-Pauline literature was the result of an attempt to offer an apologetic response to those who critiqued Christians for the effect they had on the household and on the behavior of women. In other words, the Christian home could be the subject of public scrutiny, but it could also serve as part of a defensive strategy adopted in various church circles. The author of 1 Timothy comes closest to making this challenge and response explicit in the statement that young widows should give up their celibate life with all its potential for movement between houses; they should marry and manage their household in order that the adversary might have no occasion to revile them (1 Tim 5:14).

At this point, a few remarks about the specific content of the household codes of both Colossians and Ephesians are in order. The household code is introduced into Pauline Christianity via Colossians (Col 3:18–4:1); it is the most succinct example of such teaching in all of the New Testament. In addition to the need to lessen tensions between the community and society, it is possible that the problem of false teaching may have been related to the tightening of authority structures in the form of the household code. The false teaching troubling the community is strongly ascetic; it involves fasting and participation in certain rites (e.g., Col 2:16, 18, 20–3). However, there is no explicit evidence that the avoidance of marriage was an aspect of the teaching that the author of Colossians sought to combat. If this were the case, the importance given to marriage in the code—a clear departure from Paul's preference for celibacy in 1 Corinthians 7—would be more readily understandable. The longest exhortation in the code concerns slaves and suggests that perhaps their participation in the community was raising concerns (Col 3:22–25). The insistence that they remain subservient to their masters is unequivocal.

Like Ephesians, Colossians emphasizes Christ's dominion over the universe and describes salvation in terms of a heavenly enthronement that believers are already experiencing (e.g., Col 2:12; 3:1–3; cf. Eph 2:5–6). The attention of the believer is directed away from the earthly realm toward the heavenly realm. There are aspects of symbolism in Colossians that imply a critique of the ultimate importance and validity of earthly institutions. When these symbols are considered in conjunction with the household code, the potential for empowerment is lost. Mary Rose D'Angelo has suggested that the imagery in Colossians may, in fact, have "encouraged double consciousness in women and slaves, demanding that they deny their subjected status in the religious realm while submitting to it in the social world."[15] It is clear, however, that women's influence continues to be felt in the community despite the proclamation of hierarchical household rules. A church meets in the house of Nympha (Col 4:15). Her memory has been preserved despite attempts to masculinize her in the manuscript tradition (see discussion of Junia in chapter 9).[16]

The household code of Eph 5:21–6:9 devotes greatest attention to the relationship between husband and wife; marriage serves as a metaphor for the relationship between Christ and the church (Eph 5:22–33). The metaphor draws its origins from the use of marriage as a metaphor for God's relationship with Israel found throughout the book of Hosea and elsewhere in the Hebrew Bible (e.g., Ezek 16:8–14). The exhortation concerning marriage brings together scriptural allusions, traditional values, and central beliefs. In fact, the Ephesian household code seems particularly well suited to encouraging church members to become integrated within Greco-Roman society. In using Christian marriage as a means of articulating the identity of the group, the author of Ephesians is in keeping with tendencies in Greco-Roman society to see the married couple as an expression of the ideal harmony of society.[17]

The use of Genesis in some ancient texts to refer to a sexless state for humanity at the beginning of time[18] and the use of marriage as an image for heavenly unification in gnostic literature[19] have led to many questions about the background of Eph 5:22–33. In particular, it has been suggested that the reference to Gen 2:24 in Eph 5:31, the reference to a great mystery in Eph 5:32,[20] and the high esteem for marriage in general should be given special attention; they should be taken as signs of an attempt to respond to an alternate understanding of sexual relations or perhaps even to the devaluation of sexual relations altogether, which may have been present in the community.[21] Early Christian literature contains examples of the use of the marriage metaphor that are much more conducive to asceticism than the usage in Ephesians.[22] Moreover, virgins are sometimes called the brides of Christ in later Christian literature.[23]

Yet arguments that see an attempt to respond to such tendencies in Ephesians must remain tentative. The author of Ephesians mentions opponents (Eph 5: 6–14), but says nothing explicitly about those who reject marriage. What is plain, however, is that marriage lived out according to traditional patterns is viewed as central to participation in divine fullness. The image of the pure bride is infused with the symbols of baptismal purification—"the washing of water by the word" (Eph 5:26–7). The sanctification of marriage is further reinforced by the interplay between allusions to baptism and allusions to the Jewish practice of purifying the bride with water in preparation for marriage (Ezek 16:9).[24]

Despite the fact that the household code is introduced with a general call for believers to be subject to one another (Eph 5:21), with respect to actual social relations, Eph 5:22–33 is unambiguous: wives are the ones who are subordinate in the marital relationship. The hierarchical relationship is legitimated with the strongest possible language. Just as the church is subject to Christ, so also wives should be subject to their husbands (Eph 5:24). Feminist interpreters have frequently noted the problematic nature of the use of marriage as a metaphor for the relationship between divinity and humanity. The problem lies in the fact that it is the husband who is seen to represent God or Christ and the woman who is the reflection of the human community. When the metaphorical nature of the language is forgotten, there is potential for enormous abuse.[25] The association of Christ with husband comes to be understood as a description of social reality and ultimately provides justification for male impunity in the face of female fallibility. Despite the highly problematic nature of the metaphor, however, it is important to understand the implications of depicting the church as a pure bride (Eph 5:27) in a first-century Mediterranean context. This notion reflects deeply rooted values in the Mediterranean world that associate a woman's purity and circumspect behavior with the preservation of the reputation of the house or village. Rather than seeing the obedient and cleansed wife simply as a static image of a pure church, recent anthropological discussion invites exploration of how the use of women's bodies to define household or group identity or both functions in the maintenance of boundaries and the mediation between realms.[26]

For example, on the basis of her investigations in rural Greece, anthropologist Jill Dubisch offers the following illustration of how concern for the maintenance of a woman's body reflects a larger preoccupation with the identity of the family:

> The natural impulses of sexuality must be transformed through marriage and controlled through a woman's dropi, or sense of "shame," so that they are channeled into a culturally circumscribed and acceptable act that ensures family continuity. Illicit sexual penetration is a violation of the family; it is like gossip, "matter out of place," dirt, and, like all dirt, polluting. Through a woman's sexual orifice, dishonor can occur. Through her mouth, gossip and the revelation of family secrets can run uncontrolled. A woman's body thus becomes the symbol of family integrity and purity and, more generally, of society as a whole.[27]

Such anthropological observations invite further reflection about the use of the female body as a symbol for church identity and about how such symbolism may be related to the lives of real women like Nympha who opened their houses to church meetings (Col 4:15). Yet, it is clear that to depict the ekklesia as woman is to draw on female identity as a means of communicating the nature of the transition from the outside world into the community of believers and, ultimately, of the nature of the journey from the earthly to the heavenly realm.

The Pastoral Epistles

Most scholars believe that the Pastoral Epistles (1 Timothy, 2 Timothy, and Titus) were composed about the beginning of the second century CE (although some

would place them closer to the mid-second century CE). When aiming to reconstruct the situation of women reflected in these epistles, it is essential to keep
in mind the changed situation created by the passing of time and the death of
Paul. In many respects, the community life and worldview reflected in these
works are closer to such early Christian writings as letters of Ignatius of Antioch
or 1 Clement than they are to Paul's undisputed letters. 1 Timothy, 2 Timothy,
and Titus have come to be known as the Pastoral Epistles because they are so
obviously concerned with "tending the existing flock" rather than the expansion
of the mission.[28] They are interested primarily in the management of the community and in the resolution of internal problems. One of the major priorities
of the Pastoral Epistles is the management of women's behavior. In general, the
Pastoral Epistles offer abundant material for illustrating that New Testament texts
should be read with an understanding of the cultural values of Greco-Roman
society; they reflect common stereotypes about the nature of the female character, such as the tendency for women to gossip (1 Tim 5:13) or their inclination
for being easily duped (2 Tim 3:6).

1 Timothy 2:8–15 contains probably the most well known New Testament
restrictions of women's behavior. In this text, women are prohibited from teaching or leading prayer in public. They are called to emulate societal ideals of
feminine modesty and virtue. Their subjection to the authority of men is justified by means of an appeal to the creation accounts in Genesis 1–3. The author
stresses that Adam was formed first, then Eve. The author then offers a tendentious interpretation of Genesis: "Adam was not deceived, but the woman was
deceived and became a transgressor" (1 Tim 2:14). A woman will be saved
through her bearing of children and, by implication, her fulfillment of other
domestic responsibilities (1 Tim 2:15). Even though Paul restricts women's activities in 1 Cor 11:2–11 by making reference to Genesis, nowhere in the undisputed letters do we find such a blatant justification of women's inferiority. Even
the route to salvation for women in this text, unlike any other in the New
Testament, is seen to be a different one from that of men.[29] The response is so
strong and represents such a departure from Paul's preference of celibacy for
both men and women in 1 Corinthians 7 that one suspects that much is at stake.
My analysis of 1 Tim 5:3–16, the instructions concerning widows, will indeed
confirm that women in the community are engaging in activities that the author
feels must be stopped.

Like 1 Corinthians 7, 1 Tim 5:3–16 reflects the lives of women in a variety
of circumstances. When the author of 1 Timothy speaks of honoring widows
who are real widows, the protection of widows who require the community's
material support is probably intended (1 Tim 5:3). There is a good deal of
evidence in various early Christian sources about the importance of caring for
widows as a community priority (e.g., Acts 6:1). But most likely to prevent
communities from becoming overly burdened, 1 Tim 5:3–8 aims to ensure that
only women who are truly widows who are alone receive support; the children
and grandchildren of widows are to care for these women if possible. An intriguing reference to the real widows enables us to catch a glimpse of women
living in a variety of circumstances: "If any believing woman has relatives who

are really widows, let her assist them; let the church not be burdened, so that it can assist those who are real widows" (1 Tim 5.16). A literal translation of the Greek text might be rendered as follows: "If any believing woman has widows." It is probably best to think of the support of women extending beyond relatives when it came to caring for other women. One early Christian source contemporary with 1 Timothy refers to "the virgins called widows" in a manner that implies that celibate women of various ages sometimes lived together in a house, in contrast to the usual family arrangements.[30] The Acts of the Apostles tell the story of a woman called Tabitha (Aramaic; Dorcas in Greek) who apparently acted as the patron of a group of needy widows in the community (Acts 9:36–42). Because widows in Greco-Roman society were sometimes in charge of households and in control of considerable resources, there is good reason to believe that 1 Tim 5:16 refers to the situation of a widow of some means caring for poorer women in her own household.

1 Timothy 5:9 calls for a widow to be "put on the list if she is not less than sixty years old and has been married only once." Early Christian literature confirms that widows occupied a formal office by the second century CE; the enrollment referred to here probably applies to such an office. In fact, the Pastoral Epistles display considerable interest in defining who is eligible for offices and what kind of qualities they should display (e.g., 1 Tim 3:1–7); 1 Tim 5:3–16 probably reflects this interest with respect to the roles of women. However, in this text, emphasis is clearly placed on restriction. It is intriguing that, in antiquity, only women who would have been considered very elderly are described as eligible. Yet, in supporting the celibacy of this group of elderly women, the author's position is consistent with Augustan marriage laws, which made marriage mandatory for elite women between twenty and fifty years of age. The legislation was designed to discourage any inclinations to remain unmarried, childless, or both, and this also seems to have been the intention of the author of 1 Timothy (see chapter 9). The reference to the woman being "married only once" is probably a reflection of the preference in early Christianity for officeholders only ever to have had one spouse, that is, in the case of widows, never to have remarried after the death of the first husband. It may also reflect the ideals of ancient society more generally: Roman funerary inscriptions reveal the special esteem granted to women who had been married only once. Moreover, in this text, we also hear of some widows having "violated their first pledge" (1 Tim 5:12), which probably refers to the breaking of a pledge to remain unmarried that was attached to the office.

The major difficulty in using 1 Tim 5:3–16 to reconstruct women's leadership is that there is no direct information provided as to the nature of the responsibilities attached to the office of widow. We know from other sources that prayer on behalf of other members of the community was a special responsibility attached to the office of widow.[31] Continuing in supplications and prayers night and day is described as the priority of the real widows (1 Tim 5:5). While the categories of "real widow" and "enrolled widow" do not necessarily refer to the same women, there is no reason to doubt that some of these needy women participated in the office of widow. 1 Timothy 5:10 calls for women to be chosen for the list who have a past characterized by such model home-based activities as caring for children, showing hospitality, and caring for the sick and needy; it seems reasonable to conclude that women would continue to provide such services once they were enrolled. In addition, Tit 2:3–5 calls for older women to teach younger women to be model wives, mothers, and household managers, and this duty may have been undertaken by both older married women and widows.

In evaluating the evidence for the office of widow in early Christianity, it is important to recognize that widows were not merely passive recipients of community support; they were leaders who offered important services. Prayer that intercedes for others has an active dimension.[32] Moreover, in learning about the widows in early Christianity, it is important not to assume that their way of life was diametrically opposed to that of married women, even though the widows might well have been free to assume certain duties that were impossible for married women. It is interesting to note that widows and orphans are listed together in early Christian literature. In the second century work, *The Shepherd of Hermas*, widows and orphans are described in a way that suggests that they form a group, perhaps living together in the same house.[33] One of the earliest references to early Christians by a non-Christian mentions widows accompanied by children. Writing in the middle of the second century CE, Lucian of Samosata described the imprisonment of a Christian and noted that "from the very break of day aged widows and orphan children could be seen waiting near the prison."[34] As in most societies, in early Christian groups, where there are women (even celibate women), there are often children.

Young widows are a subject of great concern in 1 Tim 5:11–15. They are to be refused enrollment into the office of widow. Various reasons are given for this: young widows eventually break their promise to remain unmarried; they tend to be idle; they run from house to house, acting as gossips and busybodies; and they say things that they should not say. Much of what the author says about the delinquent widows corresponds to stereotypical notions about female vice. In an effort to curtail their activities, the author instructs that they should marry, bear children, and manage their households—they should take up traditional wifely duties and become faithful representatives of the community's virtue. Such a recommendation is designed to "give the adversary no occasion to revile us" (1 Tim 5:14). The position adopted by the author of this Pastoral is clearly much more restrictive than that adopted by Paul in 1 Cor 7:39–40, where the apostle expresses his preference that all widows remain unmarried if possible, regardless of age.

The reference to reviling may offer a clue as to why things have changed. The activity of the widows is apparently understood by the author of the Pastoral Epistles as one of the reasons why the community has been experiencing slander. The desire of young women to remain unmarried and their active movements from house to house have apparently contributed to the community being viewed as suspicious. As the early Christian groups moved into the second century CE, hostile reactions of outsiders increasingly tended to ignite into physical violence.

Dennis R. MacDonald has shed light on the worldview that likely inspired the young widows of the Pastoral Epistles. His thesis is based on the relationship between the Pastoral Epistles and the The Acts of (Paul and) Thecla—documents that probably originated in second-century Asia Minor. With respect to the Pastoral Epistles, MacDonald has drawn attention especially to the problem with false teaching that involves injunctions against marriage (1 Tim 4:3), the description of the false teachers as intent on capturing women (2 Tim 3:6), and the warning to have nothing to do with "old wives tales" (1 Tim 4:7). He has suggested that the Pastoral Epistles were actually written in response to the kind of teaching one finds in The Acts of (Paul and) Thecla.[35] In this apocryphal work, the heroine, Thecla, becomes attracted to a version of Pauline teaching where marital sexuality (and, indeed, sexuality of any kind) is seen as incompatible with Christianity; she refuses to marry her nonbelieving fiancé and gains support from women.

Reflection on the relationship between the Pastoral Epistles and The Acts of (Paul and) Thecla leads to the realization that there were various permutations of Pauline teaching in the second century CE. 1 Timothy 5:3–16 is a very good text for illustrating that the author of the Pastoral Epistles represents one perspective on women in competition with others. The author of 1 Timothy in no way sees the movement of the young widows from house to house as "pastoral" in intent, but did the widows themselves understand the purpose of their visits as the circulation of the true teaching from Paul? Did they seek to pass on teaching that was faithful to the type of instruction one finds in 1 Corinthians 7 about the superiority of celibacy? 1 Timothy 5:3–16 is designed to stop the young widows from speaking, but a feminist reconstruction of the lives of these women calls for the recovery of their silenced voices.

The Acts of (Paul and) Thecla

In the second-century Acts of (Paul and) Thecla, Thecla acts with such independence that she gradually distances herself from her mentor and teacher, Paul, and becomes an "evangelist" in her own right. Despite its dubious historicity, this text offers remarkable insight into the social tensions experienced by women who joined early Christian groups.[36] The Acts of (Paul and) Thecla has a legendlike quality, and some aspects of the story approach the fantastic: Thecla escapes as if by magic from various life-threatening situations, and the support she receives from women even extends to female animals, including a lioness brought in to kill her, which instead chooses to lick her feet (ch. 28).

Many scholars have come to believe that the account nevertheless reflects some of the experiences of second-century women who rejected marriage on the basis of their understanding of Paul's message and who found themselves in violent confrontation with society. The Acts of (Paul and) Thecla may be understood as a depiction of how early Christian women came to threaten the traditional Greco-Roman household understood as a reflection of the state. It should be noted, however, that some recent comparisons of The Acts of (Paul and) Thecla (and other works belonging to the collection generally known as *The Apocryphal Acts of the Apostles*) to the ancient novel have resulted in quite different conclusions.[37] Rather than offering an open window onto women's experiences, the account has been understood to reflect conflicts, mainly between men, conerning authority and social order. Kate Cooper, for example, has recently argued that the heroine's continence functions "as a narrative device to propel the conflict between the apostle and a symbolic representation of the ruling class of the cities he visits."[38]

For those who are interested in the history of early Christian women and gender constructs in the ancient world, *The Acts of (Paul and) Thecla* is undoubtedly a precious source. Debates about its meaning and purpose are bound to continue for many years among scholars adopting both literary and historical approaches. In this chapter, however, it is helpful to concentrate on the basic content of the work and its presentation of Thecla and other female characters.

Thecla is described in the account as a virgin. She is depicted moving in wealthy circles in the city of Iconium (Asia Minor). Thecla's activities are inspired by Paul's teaching: "to fear one single God only and live a pure life" (ch. 9). In this work, marriage is understood as incompatible with the gospel. Thecla refuses to go through with her marriage to the similarly wealthy Thamyris, and her actions are interpreted by nonbelieving members of her family as a rejection of her predetermined role as a wife, mother, and mistress of maidservants (ch. 10). As the tale unfolds, we witness how family hostility can turn into societal violence, for on several occasions people try to kill Thecla. Thecla receives support from women who cheer for her and denounce her persecution as unjust (chs. 27–28, 32–33, 35, 38).

The influence of one woman, Tryphaena, in Thecla's life is particularly significant. This wealthy woman, whose own daughter has died, offers shelter to Thecla (chs. 27–29). Since no mention is made of her husband, she may well be a widow. Tryphaena's actions are in keeping with the practices of wealthy women supporting celibate women discussed above (cf. 1 Tim 5:3–16). Her house eventually serves as a base for Thecla's ministry (chs. 39–40). Thecla becomes a teacher, and we are told that "after enlightening many with the word of God, she slept a fine sleep" (ch. 43).

Even if Thecla's life is purely fictional, it remains significant that in second-century Pauline circles, a woman could be depicted as a teacher and evangelist in her own right. (It should be noted that Thecla's life story inspired the cult of St. Thecla, which enjoyed considerable popularity for several centuries.) Moreover, her story sheds light on how women who chose to remain unmarried or who dissolved engagements and marriages to nonbelievers may have contributed to growing hostility between early Christian groups and Greco-Roman society. It is interesting to note how little the negative reactions seem to focus on the essence of the religious beliefs. For example, at the beginning of the story, we hear how Thecla sat at the window listening to Paul. Thecla's mother attributes her interest in the apostle to a kind of bewitchment and sees her behavior as a type of infidelity:

Indeed, for three days and three nights Thecla has not risen from the window either to eat or to drink but, gazing intently as if on some delightful sight, she so devotes herself to a strange man who teaches deceptive and ambiguous words that I wonder how one so modest in her virginity can be so severely troubled. (ch. 8)

Despite Thecla's own determination to remain unmarried, suspicion of shamelessness and sexual immorality follow her throughout the account. In her refusal to marry, she interrupts the usual fate of virgin daughters. In a society in which the modest behavior of women was vital to household honor and communal identity, the reaction is one of outrage. While in discussing Thecla we may not be dealing with a real historical person like Phoebe (Rom 16:1–2), Thecla's story offers perhaps the best illustration of the necessity of studying the values and institutions of Greco-Roman society for reconstructing the lives of women in the Pauline mission.

Conclusion

The early interpreters of Paul on women and gender include the authors of deutero-Pauline works, Acts, and the *Acts of (Paul and) Thecla*. While deutero-Pauline writings and Acts reflect a similar attempt to define and restrict the roles of women, *The Acts of (Paul and) Thecla* reminds us that development in Pauline Christianity should not be viewed as monolithic. In contrast to the other works discussed in this chapter, *The Acts of (Paul and) Thecla* often depicts believers who show little regard for social respectability and boldly portrays a woman's initiative and leadership. There is debate among scholars concerning the extent to which the account reflects the lives of real women. Many see this work as offering insight into the experiences of women who were attracted to a strongly ascetic version of Pauline Christianity and consequently engendered the wrath of their households.

Although it is most clearly obvious in *The Acts of (Paul and) Thecla*, all the writings discussed in this chapter reflect mounting tension between early Christianity and society. Acts responds to this tension by stressing the involvement of women of high standing in the group and by highlighting the conventional contributions of well-to-do patrons like Lydia. The authors of Colossians and Ephesians probably adopted the traditional ethics of the household codes as a defensive strategy in light of the perception that Christians contributed to social disruption. There is good reason to believe that the restrictions placed on celibate women in the Pastoral Epistles and the general encouragement that believing women should emulate virtuous Roman matrons were inspired by the same motives. The evidence considered here concerning the leadership of such women as Nympha, Priscilla, and the widows of 1 Timothy makes it clear that the sometimes blatant attempts to silence women and to circumvent their activities in these documents by no means completely eradicates all traces of their memory. It is important to remember that the presence of traditional ideologies in early Christian documents should not lead to the immediate conclusion that women were without influence and power.

NOTES

1. See Margaret Y. MacDonald, *The Pauline Churches: A Socio-historical Study of Institutionalization in the Pauline and Deutero-Pauline Writings* (Cambridge: Cambridge University Press, 1988).

2. On the Pauline legacy in Luke-Acts see, for example, Raymond E. Brown, *The Churches the Apostles Left Behind* (New York: Paulist, 1984) 61–74.

3. Mary Rose D'Angelo, "Women in Luke-Acts: A Redactional View," *JBL* 109/3 (1990) 441–61.

4. See Ignatius, *Letter to Polycarp* 4.1–5.2.

5. Ibid. 8.2–3; Ignatius, *Letter to the Smyrnaeans* 13.1–2.

6. See D'Angelo, "Women in Luke-Acts" 453.

7. See Gail R. O'Day, "Acts," in *The Women's Bible Commentary* ed. Carol A. Newsom and Sharon H. Ringe (Louisville, KY: Westminster/John Knox, 1992) 310.

8. See D'Angelo, "Women in Luke-Acts" 455.

9. Ibid. 458–59.

10. See Clarice J. Martin, "The Acts of the Apostles," in *Searching the Scriptures: Volume 2, A Feminist Commentary* ed. Elisabeth Schüssler Fiorenza (New York: Crossroad, 1994) 785–86.

11. For discussion of the relation between Colossians and Ephesians, see Paul J. Kobelski, "The Letter to the Ephesians," in *The New Jerome Biblical Commentary*, ed. Raymond E. Brown, J. Fitzmyer, and R. Murphy (Englewood Cliffs, NJ: Prentice-Hall, 1990) 884.

12. On these codes, see David L. Balch, "Household Codes," in *Greco-Roman Literature and the New Testament: Selected Forms and Genres*, ed. David E. Aune (Atlanta, GA: Scholars Press, 1988) 25–50.

13. See Margaret Y. MacDonald, *Early Christian Women and Pagan Opinion: The Power of the Hysterical Woman* (Cambridge: Cambridge University Press, 1996) 195–204.

14. For Celsus' text, see Henry Chadwick, *Origen, Contra Celsum* (Cambridge: Cambridge University Press, 1953). See esp. *C. Cels.* 3.55. This and other relevant texts are cited together in MacDonald, *Early Christian Women* 94–120.

15. Mary Rose D'Angelo, "Colossians," in Schüssler Fiorenza, *Searching the Scriptures* 320.

16. For a full explanation of the case, see Elisabeth Schüssler Fiorenza, *In Memory of Her: A Feminist Theological Reconstruction of Christian Origins* (New York: Crossroad, 1983) 51.

17. Peter Brown, *The Body and Society: Men, Women, and Sexual Renunciation in Early Christianity* (New York: Columbia University Press, 1988) 57–58.

18. See discussion in Robin Lane Fox, *Pagans and Christians* (New York: Alfred A. Knopf) 366.

19. See Schüssler Fiorenza, *In Memory of Her* 274–75.

20. On the significance of the concept of "mystery" in Ephesians, see Sarah J. Tanzer, "Ephesians," in Schüssler Fiorenza, *Searching the Scriptures* 339–40.

21. See, for example, Walter F. Taylor and John H. P. Reumann, *Ephesians, Colossians* (Minneapolis, MN: Augsburg, 1985) 24, 80–81.

22. See, for example, 2 *Clement* 14.1–15.1. On asceticism in 2 Clement, see Dennis R. MacDonald, *There Is No Male and Female: The Fate of a Dominical Saying in Paul and Gnosticism* (Philadelphia: Fortress, 1987) 42–43.

23. On the virgin brides of Christ, see Fox, *Pagans and Christians* 371.

24. See Tanzer, "Ephesians" 336.

25. E. Elizabeth Johnson, "Ephesians," in Newsom and Ringe, *Women's Bible Commentary* 341.

26. See, for example, Jill Dubisch, "Culture Enters through the Kitchen: Woman, Culture and Social Boundaries in Rural Greece," in *Gender and Power in Rural Greece*, ed. Jill Dubisch (Princeton, NJ: Princeton University Press, 1986) 207–8. See also MacDonald, *Early Christian Women* 240–43.

27. Dubisch, "Culture Enters" 210–11.

28. Brown, *The Churches the Apostles Left Behind* 31.

29. See Joanna Dewey, "1 Timothy," in Newsom and Ringe, *Women's Bible Commentary* 355–56.

30. Ignatius, *Letter to the Smyrnaeans* 13.1.

31. See Polycarp, *Letter to the Philippians* 4.3.

32. See B. Bowman Thurston, *The Widows: A Women's Ministry in the Early Church* (Minneapolis, MN: Fortress, 1989).

33. Hermas, *Vision* 2.4.3.

34. Lucian, *The Passing of Peregrinus* 12–13; trans. A. M. Harmon, Loeb Classical Library (LCL), 1936.

35. See Dennis R. MacDonald, *The Legend and the Apostle: The Battle for Paul in Story and Canon* (Philadelphia: Westminster, 1983).

36. All references are to the translation found in Ross S. Kraemer (ed.), *Maenads, Martyrs, Matrons, Monastics: A Sourcebook on Women's Religions in the Greco-Roman World* (Philadelphia: Fortress, 1988) 280–88.

37. See Judith Perkins, *The Suffering Self: Pain and Narrative Representation in the Early Christian Era* (New York: Routledge, 1995) 15–40, 124–41; Kate Cooper, *The Virgin and the Bride: Idealized Womanhood in Late Antiquity* (Cambridge, MA: Harvard University Press, 1996) 45–67.

38. Cooper, *The Virgin and the Bride* 54.

IV

Gender, Authority,
and Redemption in
Early Christian Churches

12

WOMEN, GENDER, AND GNOSIS IN
GNOSTIC TEXTS AND TRADITIONS

Anne McGuire

Introduction

Female characters figure so prominently in gnostic texts and traditions that many
have asked whether women played similarly significant roles in ancient gnostic
communities. Unfortunately, the relation between the mythic worlds of Sophia,
Barbelo, Eve, and Norea and the social worlds of real "gnostic" women is not
clear,[1] and the task of reconstructing the social roles of women in "gnosticism"
remains one of the most challenging in the study of ancient Mediterranean
religions. Difficulties arise in part from the problem of defining "gnosticism"
and related terms, but even more serious problems of evaluation, interpretation,
and analysis face those who would evaluate, interpret, and analyze the evidence
for this complex and esoteric religious phenomenon of the ancient world.

The evidence for "gnosticism" consists principally of two types: (1) the detailed, but highly polemical reports from the antiheretical writers of the early
Christian church; and (2) primary sources, such as the writings of the Nag
Hammadi library,[2] which are attributed to ancient "gnostics" or associated with
"gnostic" themes. Before the discovery of the Nag Hammadi library in 1945,
our knowledge of gnostic traditions derived almost exclusively from the reports
of the antiheretical writers of the early Christian church. These writers, including Irenaeus, Tertullian, Hippolytus, Clement, and Epiphanius, provide relatively
systematic accounts of "gnostic" teaching, the names of individual "gnostic"
teachers, schools, and sects, as well as occasional reports of social organization
and ritual practice. Even more important, their writings preserve the names and

roles of specific women in "gnostic" schools, sects, or communities.[3] Nonetheless, the value of these sources has diminished in recent years as scholars have recognized the distorting effects of their authors' polemical concerns and as the writings of the Nag Hammadi library have become available.

Since the discovery at Nag Hammadi, it has become increasingly clear that the term "gnosticism" is a modern scholarly construct that derives not so much from the self-designation of those who called themselves "gnostics" or "knowing ones" (gnōstikoi), though some individuals and communities undoubtedly did,[4] but rather from the antiheretical writers' efforts to identify and expose their opponents under the pejorative term "falsely so-called gnosis" (1 Tim 6: 22).[5] Traditional definitions, it has been pointed out, often retain or reflect the antiheretical strategies of unifying several varieties of thought and practice into a single system or school of Christian heresy and of attributing to all the same stereotyped set of negative characteristics, including conceptual error or falsehood, immorality, and behavioral extremes.

In recent years, several serious challenges to traditional definitions of "gnosticism" as a single religion or heresy have emerged. Some scholars have chosen to abandon the category altogether as hopelessly outdated and distorting.[6] Still, a majority of scholars has chosen to retain the category, redefining "gnosticism" with more neutral language, with a clearer distinction of its major varieties, such as "Sethian" and "Valentinian," and with a far broader scope than the single Christian heresy of the antiheretical writers. Among those who take such an approach, "gnosticism" is often defined as a single religious movement that flourished from the second to fourth centuries CE in Jewish, Christian, and pagan forms. While the origins and historical development of the varieties of "gnosticism" continue to be debated, there is general agreement among those who use the term that the varieties of "gnosticism" shared two essential features: (1) an emphasis on the salvific power of gnōsis, that is, a personal or experiential knowledge of the divine, the self, and all that exists ("gnosis"); and (2) radical dualism, that is, a worldview that distinguishes sharply between the superior realm of the divine and the inferior realm of the cosmos and its creator.

Still another option is to retain the categories "gnosticism," "gnostic," and "gnosis," but to reconceive them not as terms that identify a single religion of antiquity, but rather as heuristic devices that highlight a shared pattern of thought, in this case, a shared emphasis on the saving significance of religious knowledge or "gnosis," which appeared across a broad range of ancient religious traditions and phenomena. Given the wide range of such traditions and the differing conceptions of gnosis among them, individual texts and traditions are selected and examined not as products of a single religious movement called "gnosticism," but as expressions of a distinctively "gnostic," that is, "gnosis-centered," pattern of religious thought, which appeared across religious traditions and in many distinct varieties.

The discovery of the Nag Hammadi texts has similarly heightened awareness of the difficulties involved in reconstructing social roles from "gnostic" patterns of thought. It has led to the emergence of at least three distinct positions on the relation between gender imagery and the social roles of women in "gnostic" communities.[7] Elaine Pagels' *The Gnostic Gospels*,[8] originally published in 1979, first called attention to the preponderance of positive female imagery in gnostic texts and argued that such imagery may correlate directly with prominent social roles for women in gnostic communities. A sharply different view emerged in the work of Frederik Wisse,[9] Elisabeth Schüssler Fiorenza,[10] and Daniel L. Hoffman,[11] among others. These scholars, noting many negative references to "femaleness" in gnostic sources, argue that these images betray the devaluation and subordination of women and the female gender in gnostic thought and social practice alike. Despite their very different conclusions, these first two positions appear to proceed from a similar position on the relation between imagery and social practice. In their view, there is a direct correlation between gnostic images of the female and the social status of women in gnostic communities. In addition, even as both positions take account of diversity in form and practice, they both reflect a generalizing conception of "gnosticism" as a single religious movement with a fairly unified body of imagery, thought, and practice.

A third position on the relation between religious imagery and social practice has appeared more recently in the work of several scholars, who seek a more nuanced approach to the analysis of gendered imagery and the roles of women in gnostic texts and traditions.[12] Central to this approach is the notion that the relation between gendered imagery and social roles is varied and complex and depends on several factors, including variations in literary form and the social location of authors and readers. Recognizing that gendered imagery and social roles may have a direct correlation, an inverse relation, or no apparent relation at all,[13] this approach seeks to ground its interpretation in the analysis of varying patterns within and among texts and in the relations between texts and their readers.[14]

As an interpreter sympathetic to this third approach, my contribution to this volume seeks primarily to illustrate the varied representations of women and gender in a selection of individual texts. The survey begins with the external reports of the antiheretical writers of the early church and moves to the central task of analyzing a selection of primary sources. In each case, the central task is to analyze the ways in which each of these texts represents the "female" as a social and symbolic category. The analysis is organized around three distinct types of gender imagery in gnostic sources: (1) the gendered depiction of characters (divine and human) in mythic narratives; (2) direct statements about gender (male and female relations, differences, social roles) in narrative and nonnarrative sources; and (3) more abstract references to "femaleness" and "maleness" as categories of existence in narrative and nonnarrative sources. Each text is analyzed independently and internally, with a particular focus on the interrelation of gender imagery, religious reflection, and ideological construction of the female. The results of this analysis may well contribute to our understanding of the social impact of female imagery in gnostic texts and traditions, but its primary concern is to suggest a broader range of interpretive possibilities than a strictly social-historical approach focused on the "positive" or "negative" charge of female imagery would allow.[15]

Women and Gender in Antiheretical Sources

Almost all of the evidence describing women's roles in gnostic communities or schools comes from the reports of Christian antiheretical writers, who were concerned primarily to expose and undermine the teaching and practice of their gnostic opponents. In the course of describing such practice, these writers refer to a small number of women by name and describe the behavior of many un-named women among "gnostic" schools and sects. These accounts are designed to illustrate both the multiplicity of "gnostic" teachers and schools and their adherence to shared heretical themes. As a result, they tend to follow the same formulas, emphasizing recurring patterns in the behavior and thought of their opponents.[16]

References to Historical Women in Antiheretical Sources

While Irenaeus and other antiheretical writers report in detail on a wide variety of "gnostic" teachings, they provide potentially more valuable evidence in occasional references to specific women. Some of these represent legendary or mythicized women, but together these references provide evidence of the names and activities by which various historical women were remembered and revered in "gnostic" traditions and communities. Among the most prominent of these are references to the following four women:

Helena, a former prostitute from Tyre who was said to have accompanied Simon Magus during the time of the emperor Claudius (41–54 CE).[17] According to Justin and Irenaeus, Simon claimed that Helena represented the "Mother of All" and the "First Thought" (Ennoia, f.) begotten by him, and that Helen/Ennoia had descended and created the angels and powers who created the world. These powers took Helena captive in the body, and Simon delivered her. Origen preserves a tradition that Celsus "knows of some also who are Simonians, who reverence as teacher Helena or Helenus and are called Helenians."[18] While these reports may not tell us much about the historical Helena, they do suggest that second-century followers of Simon looked back to the relations of Simon and Helena as earthly manifestations of a familiar mythic pattern. As Simon rescues Helena from prostitution, so the divine male principle redeems the divine First Thought, now descended into captivity as the female soul.

Marcellina, a Carpocratian teacher, who, according to Irenaeus, "came to Rome in the time of Anicetus" (154–166) and "led multitudes astray."[19] According to Irenaeus, "they" (the followers of Marcellina or Carpocrates?) "call themselves gnostics and possess images." Origen writes: "Celsus knows also of Marcellians who follow Marcellina, and Harpocratians who follow Salome, and others who follow Mariamme, and others who follow Martha."[20] Since Salome, Mariamme, and Martha appear in other early Christian literature, including the canonical gospels,[21] it is possible that Marcellina, like the female disciples of Jesus, was revered not merely as a teacher of Carpocratian gnosis, but as an authoritative source of apostolic tradition.[22]

Philumena, a prophetess associated with Apelles, a disciple of Marcion. According to Hippolytus, Apelles wrote "revelations" of a prophetess, Philumena.[23]

Flora, a disciple of Ptolemy, a leading teacher of the Italian or Western branch of the Valentinian school.[24] Ptolemy's Letter to Flora, an introductory lesson on the character of the law and the Valentinian reading of scripture, was addressed to her.[25] In *Panarion* 33.7.8–9, Ptolemy urges Flora to learn and assures her: "You shall learn since you are adjudged worthy of the apostolic tradition."

References to these four women provide relatively meager evidence for the activities of women in "gnostic" communities. They tell us only that women were active as members of several "gnostic" schools, and that some were regarded as teachers and prophetesses and may have inspired some of their male colleagues to write (Apelles, Ptolemy). We have no evidence that these women were themselves active as writers, ministers, or leaders, except for Marcellina, who was regarded in her own right as a teacher of the Carpocratians, or of her own group of Marcellians, in Rome. Yet the sources describe each of them, including Marcellina, in relation to a male figure, who appears in these sources to have taken a more active role in leadership, teaching, and writing. Whether this male prominence reflects the assumptions of the antiheretical writers, the actual relationships of these individuals, or both is unclear.

Divine Female Figures in Irenaeus, Adversus Haereses 1.1–8

Antiheretical accounts of "gnostic" teaching tend to follow a pattern of elements established by the reports of Irenaeus of Lyons: (1) the depiction of the divine realm as a fullness of male and female spiritual beings; and (2) mythic narratives of creation and redemption, which often focus on the highly ambivalent figure of Sophia, or Wisdom (Greek, f.: Sophia), the divine female who sets in motion the processes of world creation and plays a crucial role in the redemption of humankind. Irenaeus' account of the teachings of the Valentinian teacher Ptolemy in *Adversus Haereses* 1.1–8 provides a particularly detailed example of these patterns.[26]

In Irenaeus' account of the teachings of Ptolemy, Sophia is the last or "youngest" of thirty aeons, organized in fifteen male-female pairs or syzygies.[27] Though narratives of Sophia's actions vary greatly among the sources,[28] it is she whose actions comprise the central events in the drama of creation. In one strand of Irenaeus' account (*Haer* 1.2.2),[29] Sophia suffers passion apart from the embrace of her male consort, Desired, as she seeks to know the first male principle, the "Father" or "Depth," who can be known, according to the myth, only by the second male principle, "Mind." In her misguided and passionate search, Sophia is restrained by a power called Boundary or Limit (*Horos*), which preserves the ineffability of the Father by holding back Sophia and restoring her to herself (1.2.3–4). The Boundary separates the "formless, weak, and female fruit" of Sophia (her thinking and passions) (1.2.5),[30] and establishes them outside the divine realm. Sophia's thinking, called "Achamoth," is given "a fragrance of incorruptibility" by the Anointed (Christ) and the Holy Spirit, but as she searches for "the Light that had left her" (the Anointed), she again experiences passions: grief, fear, uncertainty, lack of gnosis, and "turning back (or conversion) toward the one who had made her alive" (1.4.1). The distraught Achamoth, or lower Sophia, is visited by yet another male figure, "the Savior," who cures her of her passions by turning them from "incorporeal passions" into "incorporeal matter" (1.4.5). The lower Sophia becomes "pregnant with the contemplation of the lights," or angels, that accompanied the Savior, and produces "a spiritual offspring" after their image (1.4.5). From the lower Sophia emerge the three types of substance that constitute the world: (1) the material (hylikos) essence, which derives from her passions; (2) the ensouled or animate (psychikos), deriving from her turning back, but "tainted with passion"; and (3) the spiritual (pneumatikos) essence, which derives from her own conception (1.5.1). According to Irenaeus, the Valentinians derive their understanding of the cosmos and its creator from this mythic account. The cosmos and its matter are formed of the hylic or material substance; the creator (Demiurge) is formed of psychic or ensouled essence; and human beings are composite beings, formed by the creator of hylic matter and soul (psyche), but containing within the superior element of spirit.

Sophia thus appears in Irenaeus' account as a highly ambivalent figure. On the positive side, Sophia (higher and lower) functions as mother and source of the spiritual essence and as a mediator or link between the divine and cosmic realms. On the negative side, her inappropriate emotions or "passions," which are weak and "female" because they lack "male" form, are responsible for generating the cosmos and its creator; bringing into existence all that is nondivine or nonspiritual; and dispersing spiritual elements in the nonspiritual cosmic realms below. Yet the same female figure(s) also work toward the perfection and redemption of the spiritual elements dispersed below. Sophia's redemptive roles, however, pale in comparison to those of the male figures who come to redeem her, the creator, and humankind alike. These include the Boundary or Limit, the Anointed, Jesus, and the Savior, who becomes Achamoth's "bridegroom" in the final, eschatological redemption (1.7.1).[31]

Even while idealizing the union of male-female pairs, the gendered metaphors of Irenaeus' account point neither to a gender balance nor to an equalizing of male and female. Rather, they provide graphic depiction of the calamitous consequences of independent female activity and the benefits of restoring the rebellious female to her proper place. At almost every crucial redemptive moment, the mythic narrative reinforces ancient Mediterranean ideologies of gender relations by idealizing redemption and marriage alike as coming about through the hierarchical union of a superior, perfect, and dominant male and an inferior, imperfect, and subordinate female. In the end, the independent and rebellious Sophia-Achamoth is redeemed and restored precisely by returning to her proper place as subordinate female bride.[32]

Antiheretical Reports about Sexual Behavior and Attitudes

In his account of Marcus, a Valentinian teacher or "magician" who came to the Rhone Valley before 180 CE, Irenaeus provides the most detailed account of the behavior of women in relation to a specific male "gnostic" teacher. According to Irenaeus, Marcus induced "a great number of men and not a few women" to join him as one possessed of "the greatest knowledge and perfection." Marcus deceived these followers, including several "silly" and "deluded" women, Irenaeus reports, into believing they had received through him the gift of prophecy and divine Grace (Greek, *Charis*, f.).[33] Irenaeus describes Marcus' followers as women of great wealth and claims that they practiced a ritual "bridal chamber" in which they received Charis from Marcus as a bride receives her bridegroom. In this way, Irenaeus portrays Marcus as a charlatan who seduced women into believing they received the divine "seed of Charis" through his semen:[34]

> He is especially concerned about women, and those who are well-dressed and clothed in purple and of great wealth, whom he often attempts to seduce. Flatteringly he says to them: "I want you to partake of my Grace (*Charis*), because the Father of all sees your angel in his presence. . . . It behooves us to be united. First receive Grace from me and through me. Adorn yourself as a bride awaiting her bridegroom that you may be what I am, and I may be what you are. Put the "seed" of light in your bridal chamber. Take from me the bridegroom. Receive him and be received in him. Look, Grace is descending upon you. Open your mouth and prophesy." . . . From now on she considers herself a prophetess and thanks Marcus for having given her of his Charis. She tries to reward him not only by the gift of her possessions—in this manner he has amassed a fortune—but by sharing her body, desiring to unite herself with him in every way so that she may become one with him.[35]

In this and other carefully crafted reports,[36] Irenaeus draws on two powerful ideological images:[37] the heretical male teacher as seductive charlatan and the heretical woman as deluded fool, weak and vulnerable to seduction, easily duped into giving her possessions and body to the deceiving male.

While such seduction and ritualized sexual behavior may or may not have occurred, it is quite likely in any case that Irenaeus interpreted his opponents' use of sexual metaphor ("planting seeds," "becoming pregnant," "giving birth") literally and put this literal misinterpretation to powerful polemical use. Even more effectively, while showing how Marcus manipulated the Pauline image of bridegroom and bride (for Christ and the church; 2 Cor 11) to apply to himself and his female followers, Irenaeus instead applies to Marcus and his followers the roles Paul deliberately contrasts with bridegroom and bride: deceiving serpent and deceived Eve:[38] "For as the serpent beguiled Eve, by promising her what he had not himself, so also do these men, by pretending [to possess] superior knowledge, and [to be acquainted with] ineffable mysteries . . . plunge those that believe them into death, rendering them apostates from Him who made them."[39] Here, Irenaeus uses his rhetorical powers to discredit Marcus as the seductive heretic-serpent and his female followers as uncommonly foolish "Eve's." Yet in addition to its polemical punch, Irenaeus' report provides valuable evidence that in the social world of the late-second-century Rhone Valley, a teacher named Marcus appealed to women of wealth, encouraged these women to prophesy, and led them to understand their gift of prophecy and salvation as mediated through him, their teacher and 'bridegroom.' Bishop Irenaeus, by contrast, wrote to convince his readers to perceive this bogus 'bridegroom' as a 'serpent,'[40] leading his female followers astray into spiritual, economic, and sexual exploitation.

Additional information about the roles of women in "heretical" or "gnostic" communities may be gathered from several other heresiological works, including Tertullian's On the Prescription against Heretics, written some twenty years after Irenaeus' work.[41] Like Irenaeus, Tertullian uses the strategy of intertextuality to endow his anti-gnostic polemic with the authority of the apostle Paul, in this case, the Paul of the Pastoral Letters. Criticizing women who would "usurp the power to teach" and "baptize" by appealing to the example of Thecla in the apocryphal Acts of (Paul and) Thecla,[42] Tertullian discredits the authority of both the writing and Thecla herself. He reminds his readers that the presbyter who composed "the writings which wrongly go under Paul's name [and] claim Thecla's example as a license for women's teaching and baptizing" was removed from office. To drive home his point, he contrasts the apocryphal work's empowering message to women with the silencing message of the Pastorals' Paul (1 Tim 2): "For how credible would it seem, that he [Paul] who has not permitted a woman even to learn with over-boldness, should give a female the power of teaching and of baptizing! 'Let them be silent,' he says, 'and at home consult their own husbands.' "[43]

Similarly, with his account of the conduct of heretics (De Praes 41–44), Tertullian criticizes his opponents for failing to maintain proper role distinctions. He focuses particularly on the boldness of women:

> All are puffed up, all offer you knowledge. Their catechumens are perfect before they are fully taught. The very women of these heretics, how wanton they are! For they are bold enough to teach, to dispute, to enact exorcisms, to undertake cures—it may be even to baptize.[44]

While some have read this passage as evidence that women served as "bishops" or "priests" in some "gnostic" groups, the text states only that within communities that may not have recognized the church offices of bishop, deacon, or priest or that sought to blur such distinctions, women engaged in various activities that other communities, including Tertullian's model of the true "church," were increasingly seeking to deny them.[45] If these communities recognized an alternate system of church office or no offices at all, it is unlikely that their activities (teaching, disputing, exorcising, curing, and baptizing) were linked to an office such as bishop or priest. Although the women Tertullian describes engaged in ritual and teaching activities, it does not appear likely that they held official titles, such as bishop, priest, deacon, or presbyter.

While Irenaeus and Tertullian attack their "gnostic" opponents by highlighting the foolish or inappropriate behavior of women among them, Clement of Alexandria and Epiphanius of Salamis provide more detailed reports on their opponents' perspectives on sexuality and marriage. From their accounts, modern scholarship has inherited the stereotype of two types of "gnostic" attitudes toward sex:[46] libertinism and asceticism. Between these two extremes, the Valentinians are often depicted as moderates who "approve of marriage" as a reflection of the union of male and female emanations in the divine realm.[47] On one side of them, Clement reports, are "libertines" like the Carpocratians, who "think that wives should be common property,"[48] and meet for communal "love feasts," having "intercourse where they will and with whomever they will."[49] As with Irenaeus' charges against Marcus, it is possible that Clement's report is based on a literal misreading of metaphorical language. But it is not unlikely that Clement has transformed a pagan polemic against Christian immorality into a Christian polemic against gnostic immorality.[50]

On the other side of the moderate Valentinians, however, Clement describes several of his "gnostic" opponents as ascetics who "reject marriage and the begetting of children."[51] Yet in contrast to the increasingly positive evaluation of asceticism in Christian circles, Clement depicts "gnostic" asceticism negatively, as grounded in radically heretical anticosmic attitudes and in a saying of Jesus found in the apocryphal *Gospel according to the Egyptians*:[52] "When Salome asked the Lord, 'How long shall death hold sway?' he answered: 'As long as you women bear children.'"[53] In another passage, Clement cites a saying of Jesus that even more strongly betrays the negative valuation of sexual reproduction and symbolizes it as among "the works of the female": "They say that the Savior himself said, 'I came to destroy the works of the female.'" Clement adds that in this passage "female" means desire and "works" refers to birth and corruption.[54]

Another saying attributed to a dialogue between Jesus and Salome betrays no clear sign of this negative symbolization of the female, but does describe a sex- and gender-free salvific state:[55]

> On this account he says: "When Salome asked when she would know the answer to her questions, the Lord said, 'When you trample on the robe of shame, and when the two shall be one, and the male with the female, and there is neither male nor female.'"[56]

Here, it is not the category of "the female" itself that will be destroyed, but rather shame and the distinctions of two genders that will be overcome or dissolved in a new redemptive state.

Even more than Clement, Epiphanius of Salamis[57] sought to demonstrate the immorality of his opponents' sexual behavior. To that end, he describes in detail the ritual practices of the Borborians or Koddians, also known as Phibionites and Stratiotics, who "have their women in common,"[58] and perform a love feast involving ritual intercourse and the consumption of semen and blood. According to Epiphanius, after sexual intercourse, these "gnostics" offer up the male semen to God as a gift, "the body of Christ," and then consume it. They do the same, he reports, with menstrual blood, which they claim is the "blood of Christ."[59] They also "have sex with each other," not for the purposes of reproduction, but only for their own pleasure.[60]

They derive warrant for these practices, Epiphanius claims, from a story in the *Greater Questions of Mary*, an otherwise unknown apocryphal work, in which Jesus himself has sexual intercourse and consumes his emission:

> For in the so-called Greater Questions of Mary, they suggest that he revealed it to her after taking her aside on the mountain, praying, producing a woman from his

side, beginning to have intercourse with her, and then partaking of his emission, if you please, to show that "Thus we must do, that we may live."[61]

Since this account, like those of Irenaeus, Tertullian, and Clement, serves polemical purposes and may reflect a literal (mis)reading of sexual metaphor, its historical accuracy is questionable. Nonetheless, it is quite possible, as Jorunn Jacobsen Buckley has argued, that the story of Jesus' mountaintop liaison in the *Greater Questions of Mary* was used to undergird a ritual ideology that stressed the necessity of creating, collecting, and transmitting upward the Christ-energy that was trapped in the Phibionites' own bodies.[62] By ingesting female blood and male semen, rather than the "unnecessarily mediated substances" of bread and wine, these "gnostics" may have understood themselves to be expressing and recreating their spiritual affinity with Christ precisely by reenacting his paradigmatic and salvific release of captured light.[63]

The reports of the antiheretical writers hint powerfully at the wide and rich range of "gnostic" representations of women and the female gender, attitudes toward sexuality, and metaphorical associations between the domains of gender and sexuality and those of theoretical religious reflection. Yet, because of their polemical tendency to exaggerate and misread their opponents, the antiheretical sources can only be used as an opening to some of the features of gnostic texts and traditions. To construct a more persuasive account of women and gender in gnostic texts and traditions, a representative selection of primary sources must be considered and analyzed closely.

Women, Gender, and Gnosis in the Primary Sources

The primary sources for gnostic texts and traditions include epigraphical evidence, or inscriptions; fragments and excerpts from ancient "gnostic" writers quoted in the works of other writers;[64] and, most important, original literary compositions, such as those preserved in the Nag Hammadi library and other ancient codices.[65] The corpus of original gnostic compositions currently available for study includes many genres of religious literature, from mythic accounts of creation and redemption, to collections of Jesus' sayings, narrative accounts of Jesus and his disciples, and revelatory discourses written in the name of the divine. The survey below focuses briefly on one piece of epigraphical evidence and, in much greater detail, on three representative gnostic compositions from the Nag Hammadi library.

Epigraphical Evidence: The Flavia Sophē Inscription

One of the most extraordinary pieces of evidence for the association of actual women with gnostic traditions is not textual, but epigraphical. The tomb inscription of a woman named Flavia Sophē, which dates from third-century Rome, exhibits several features that might well be identified as gnostic in character. The words of the inscription memorialize Flavia Sophē as a woman who yearned for the divine light and was anointed with holy oil so that she might receive a visionary experience of the divine, enter the "bridal chamber," and be joined to the bosom of the Father:

> You, who did yearn for the paternal Light,
> Sister, spouse, my Sophē,
> Anointed in the baths of Christ with everlasting, holy oil,
> Hasten to gaze at the divine features of the aeons,
> The great Angel of the great council (i.e., the Redeemer),
> The true Son;
> You entered the bridal chamber and deathless ascended
> To the bosom of the Father.[66]

This inscription provides invaluable evidence for the spirituality and hopes of a third-century Christian woman in Rome and suggests some of the reasons why such a woman would be attracted to the religious rituals and claims of gnostic traditions. It shows clearly that Flavia Sophē had participated in the redemptive rituals of baptism and anointing, and that she was expected to achieve the visionary experience of gazing at the divine aeons, the great Angel, and the true Son, entering the redemptive bridal chamber and becoming joined to the bosom of the Father. It is even possible that Flavia Sophē, like others before and after her, was understood to have achieved this visionary experience of entering the bridal chamber and ascending to the divine already in this life. One feature of the inscription that stands out is the masculine language used to represent the divine. The only divine figures the inscription mentions by name are male (Christ, the great Angel, the true Son, the Father), but it is quite possible that the "aeons" upon whose "divine features" the inscription hastens Flavia Sophē to gaze were male and female beings, as in the depictions of the divine world in Irenaeus and in several Nag Hammadi texts (*Apocryphon of John, Hypostasis of the Archons* etc.).

Literary Evidence: Gnosis, Women, and Gender in Nag Hammadi Texts

As with the antiheretical sources, women and gender appear in original gnostic compositions in a variety of ways. The female characters in these texts can usefully be divided into three categories: (1) divine beings, such as Barbelo, Sophia, and her daughter, Zoe; (2) mythic women of primordial times, such as Eve and her daughter, Norea; and (3) legendary women of more recent historical times, such as Jesus' disciples Mary Magdalene, Salome, and Martha. The texts' representations of gender include relatively straightforward statements about females, males, or both; symbolic references to the categories of "femaleness" and "maleness"; and more subtle figurative uses of imagery, as in gendered metaphors of kinship, sexual reproduction, birth, marriage, prostitution, and rape.

This discussion of women and gender in gnostic texts addresses three very distinctive genres or types of religious literature: (1) a mythic account of creation and redemption in one of the best examples of gnostic rewriting of Genesis, *The Hypostasis of the Archons* (HypArch); (2) accounts of Jesus and his disciples, especially Mary Magdalene, with particular focus on *The Gospel of Thomas* (GThom); and (3) an aretalogy, or revelation discourse, in the voice of the female deity,

Thunder, Perfect Mind. These texts represent very different religious perspectives and literary genres, but they share two important characteristics: they place central emphasis on the saving significance of gnosis, and they represent female characters (divine and human) and employ the categories of male and female in interesting and challenging ways.

Gender, Gnosis, and Spirit: Creation and Redemption in the Hypostasis of the Archons   In its present form, *The Hypostasis of the Archons* (HypArch) or *The Reality of the Rulers* is a composite of two genres: a narrative of creation—from the origins of the cosmos through the creation of the first humans and their children: Cain, Abel, Seth, and Norea. The second is a revelation or apocalypse to Norea, which includes a dialogue between Norea and the angelic Illuminator Eleleth. These are introduced by a brief letter in which the narrator informs an unnamed recipient of his purpose in writing: to provide an account of "the reality or nature (*hypostasis*) of the authorities" about whom the "great apostle" (Paul) wrote as the "authorities of darkness" (Eph 6:12) and "the authorities of the cosmos and the spiritual forces of evil."[67]

The narrative portions of *HypArch* offer a retelling of the early chapters of Genesis as a story of confrontation and subversion. At the center of the drama is the conflict between two distinct and opposed modes of power: the Archons or Rulers of this world and the divine. Human beings enter the narrative as composite creatures, caught between these two opposed forces, archontic and divine. The narrative begins abruptly with a pointed characterization of the chief Ruler:

> Their chief is blind; [because of his] power and his ignorance [and his] arrogance he said, "It is I who am god; there is none [apart from me]." When he said this, he sinned against [the Entirety]. And this utterance got up to Incorruptibility; and a Voice came forth from Incorruptibility, saying, "You are mistaken, Samael," which is "god of the blind."

The Ruler's claim to be the only God appears immediately to identify him with the God of biblical tradition.[68] In the inverted world of *HypArch*, however, Ialdabaoth (alternately named Samael and Sakla) only thinks he is the only God. He is not the only God; he is not even a real God. He is merely the chief Ruler and Creator, without gnosis (ignorant) of the true God. His vain and arrogant claim elicits a voice of rebuke from Incorruptibility that exposes his error and reidentifies him as Samael, "god of the blind."

This episode introduces two patterns that recur throughout the text: (1) a narrative pattern in which vain and arrogant claims evoke a divine rebuke, and (2) a pattern of representation in which the identity of each character is explicitly gendered. The Rulers are depicted as androgynous, a monstrous mixing of male and female, and divine beings and humans appear as either female or male. The complex intersection of gender imagery and religious perspectives becomes even clearer in three crucial episodes: the origin of the Rulers; the creation of the first humans, with its disturbing account of the rape and abandonment of the bodily "Eve;" and Norea's struggle against the Rulers, with its account of rape resisted and overcome.

The origin of the Rulers is narrated late in the text, in response to Norea's request for instruction from Eleleth.[69] Eleleth reveals that the Rulers are a product of the divine, the imperfect result of Sophia's misguided effort to create alone. Eleleth offers a highly condensed account of Sophia's action and its consequences:

> Within limitless aeons dwells Incorruptibility. Sophia, who is called Pistis (Faith), wished to create something, alone without her consort; and her product became a celestial image. A veil exists between the things above and the aeons below; and shadow came into being beneath the veil; and that shadow became matter; and that shadow was cast apart. And that which she had made became a product in the matter, like a miscarried fetus. And it took (its) pattern from the shadow, and became an arrogant beast resembling a lion. It was androgynous (oy-hoyt-shime) as I have already said, because it was from matter that it came forth.[70]

Sophia appears in HypArch as a decidedly ambiguous character. Although all things may take place according to "the will of the Father,"[71] Sophia's desire to create without her male consort has disastrous results. Her product is grossly deficient, lacking the generative principle of form that can come only from the male.[72] Ialdabaoth possesses only the formless, material principles of body and matter from the female, his mother Sophia.

Sophia's independent act also brings into being a shadow beneath the veil that serves as a boundary around the previously limitless divine realms. Prefiguring the fate of Adam and Eve,[73] Sophia's product is expelled from the divine and enters this shadowy realm of matter "like a miscarried or aborted fetus." He becomes an arrogant, androgynous beast, more closely aligned with the lower elements of matter and the passions than with the higher elements of Spirit and Wisdom from his mother. Sophia's product becomes the first of many Rulers of this world and sets in motion a chain of disturbing events.

In Eleleth's narration, the chief Ruler also claims to be the only God and is rebuked by a voice from above. In response, Ialdabaoth puts forth the challenge: "If any other thing exists before me, let it become visible to me!" Sophia, in turn, responds to the challenge by "stretching forth her finger" and introducing Light into matter.[74] The chief Ruler proceeds to make himself a vast realm after the pattern of the divine realms, complete with seven offspring of his own. But in contrast to the beings of the divine realms, these offspring are "androgynous just like their father."[75] In their presence, he claims once again to be "the god of the Entirety," and this brings forth yet another rebuke from above, this time from Zoe, spiritual daughter of Sophia. Zoe's response moves beyond verbal correction to the creation of a fiery angel as Zoe breathes into his face: "Her breath became a fiery angel" and "that angel bound Ialdabaoth and cast him down into Tartaros, below the abyss."[76] Seeing the power of that angel, Sabaoth, one of his offspring, repents and is raised by Sophia and Zoe to the seventh heaven, where he reigns as God of the forces.[77] Ialdabaoth's envy at seeing his offspring's splendor engenders envy, death, and further offspring, until "all the heavens of chaos became full of their multitudes." Even this, the narrator insists, took place "by the will of the Father" so that "the sum of chaos might be attained."[78]

The conclusion of Eleleth's narration leads Norea to question her own origin and the future of her "offspring." Eleleth assures her that Norea and her offspring "belong to the primeval Father," that they possess "the Spirit of Truth," and that "all who have gained gnosis with this way exist immortal in the midst of dying humankind."[79] In three generations, Eleleth promises, when "the True Human Being (Anthropos)" comes to teach and anoint them, "all the children of Light" will be freed from error and gain gnosis of "the Truth, their root, the Father of the entirety, and the Holy Spirit."[80]

Eleleth's promise rests in part on a distinction between the divine parentage of Norea and her offspring and the archontic parentage of the Rulers and chaos. To understand Eleleth's characterization of Norea, her offspring, and all who gain gnosis as immortal "in the midst of dying humankind," the attentive reader must recall the events of the second crucial episode in the narrative: the creation of Adam and Eve and the rape of Eve.

Immediately after the vain claim with which the text abruptly opens,[81] the Voice from above projects an image of incorruptibility in the waters and thereupon sets in motion the creation of the first human beings. Upon seeing the image in the waters, "the authorities of darkness became enamored" of the female image and conspired to capture her by means of a "male counterpart" that they would create for her. The Rulers, however, fail to understand their utter inability to grasp the divine—for they are made only of matter and soul (*psychikos*), while it/she (the image) is made of Spirit (*pneumatikē*).[82] Nonetheless, the plot proceeds according to the plan of the Father from above, and the Rulers create as their "male counterpart" a composite being. Formed from soil, after the body of the Rulers and after the image in the waters, their creature is animate or *psychikos*, from the soul (*psychē*) or breath infused by the Rulers. But it is only the Spirit that brings him Life. When the Spirit "came to dwell within him," the first human creature became "a living soul."

Soon after placing him in the garden, the Rulers conspire, bring ignorance and forgetfulness upon Adam, and open "his side like a living woman." When they build up his side with flesh in her place, Adam came to be "entirely of soul." The Rulers have extracted from Adam the Spirit, who now appears before him as "the spiritual woman" (*pneumatikē shime*). She awakens Adam from sleep. He, in turn, addresses her: "It is you who have given me life; you will be called 'Mother of the Living.'—For it is she who is my Mother. It is She who is the Physician and the Woman and She who has given birth." Adam's praise of the Spiritual Woman is immediately interrupted as the Rulers, aroused once again by the female Spirit, draw near and conspire. This time their conspiracy takes the form of attempted rape.

And when they [the Authorities] saw his [Adam's] female counterpart speaking with him, they became agitated with great agitation; and they became enamored of her. They said to one another, "Come, let us sow our seed in her," and they pursued her. And she laughed at them for their senselessness and their blindness. And in their clutches, she became a tree, and she left her shadow resembling herself before them; and they defiled [it] foully.[83]

The victim of this rape is neither the intended target (the Spiritual Woman) nor the heroine of the story. The female Spirit evades the Rulers' attempts to grasp and dominate by metamorphizing into a tree and laughing at them. From the perspective of the text, this is a moment of victory and mockery, for the rape victim is "only" the bodily Eve, a shadowy reflection of the Spiritual Woman who departs and laughs. From a more critical, contemporary perspective, however, as Karen King has perceived, this is a scene of victory and horror: victory for the disembodied Spirit, but horror for the bodily Eve.[84] Even as the narrative condemns rape and allows the female Spirit to escape, "the victory of the Spiritual Woman is traded against the division of her self, against the denial of her material body, the carnal Eve."[85]

This dissociation of Spirit and body, King points out, is not unlike the dissociation of mind and body that functions as a survival mechanism among victims of incest and rape. While such dissociation can be effective at maintaining some sense of self, King writes: "Ultimately it is an extremely painful solution to violence, insofar as it abandons the body as one's self."[86] This is precisely what HypArch asks its readers to do: dissociate the "defiled body" of Eve from the "real Mother" of humankind, the female Spirit that escapes the body and becomes a tree. The negative effects of dissociation become even clearer in the account of struggle between Norea, spiritual daughter of Eve, and the Rulers.

Following Cain's murder of Abel, the births of Norea and her brother, Seth, mark a decisive improvement in the situation of humankind. Two epithets associated with Norea—"an assistance for many generations" and "the virgin whom the Forces did not defile"—link her immediately to the spiritual realm. At the same time, they set her apart from her mother, Eve. The account of Norea's struggle against the Rulers discloses the character of Norea's virginal power as it recalls the rape of Eve and adds to her abandonment.

> The Rulers went to meet her [Norea], wishing to lead her astray. Their supreme chief said to her, "Your mother Eve came to us." But Norea turned to them and said to them, "It is you who are the Rulers of Darkness; You are accursed. And you did not know my mother; instead it was your female counterpart that you knew. For I am not your descendant; rather it is from the world above that I am come." The arrogant Ruler turned with all his power . . . and . . . he said to her presumptuously, "You must render service to us, [as did] your mother Eve." But Norea turned, in the power of [. . .], and cried out in a great voice to the Holy One, the God of the Entirety, "Rescue me from the Rulers of Unrighteousness and save me from their clutches—at once!"[87]

Here, as in previous episodes, a powerful spiritual female challenges the Rulers and overturns their efforts to grasp the female Spirit by speaking out in a powerful voice.

On an explicit level, Norea's words unmask the Rulers' claims, expose their ignorance of the Spirit, and nullify their efforts to extend "sexual service" from mother to daughter. Norea challenges any kinship claims the Rulers might make since they are from below and she is from above and, at the same time, negates her kinship with the bodily Eve. Norea disavows the raped woman, her bodily mother, and recognizes the Spirit alone as her true mother. In so doing, Norea, like the narrative itself, "turns its back on the victimized woman—and both the Spiritual Woman and Norea have traded their purity and spiritual power against this discourse" of division.[88] Though embodied, Norea dissociates herself from the body of Eve and so from her own body. Her real identity resides not in the body, but in the female Spirit that gave her spiritual birth. This spiritual mother dwells in her, yet is fully separable from her body, as from the woman who gave her physical birth.

In a previous essay, I interpreted Norea as a powerful female model of re-demptive subversion. In her resistance to the androgynous Archons who would rape her, Norea represents the subversion of all Powers that falsely claim to rule the cosmos, the social order, and the body.[89] Viewed from a more critical per-spective, however, Norea participates in just such a system of power: an ideolog-ical system in which true identity and value reside only in the spiritual. In siding exclusively with the Reality of the Spirit against the False Reality (*hypostasis*) of the Rulers, *HypArch* encourages its readers to subvert oppressive powers, yet de-nies the value and reality of embodied life. Norea's bodily mother is abandoned by the Spirit, by her own daughter, and by a narrative that oppressively ignores the defiled woman's pain as it denies her identity as "Mother" of Norea or of humankind. Eleleth's promise of redemption for Norea and her "spiritual chil-dren" reinforces this ideological framework. They are "from the Primeval Fa-ther," and when the True Human Being comes, the spiritual seed (*sperma*) sown in Norea and her offspring will become known and will "free them from the bondage of the Authorities' error." All the children of the light will gain gnosis of "the Truth and their Root," that is, the divine spiritual element within them.

For ancient Christian readers, the True Human Being Jesus had come, taught, and anointed. As a result, some of them may have rediscovered themselves as children of Norea, spiritual seeds of light, and possessors of salvific gnosis. From a more critical perspective, however, such readers may be understood as sharing the ideological perspectives of the text. Their anointing may empower them to resist the oppressive Rulers of this world, but it also leads them to dissociate their true selves from their bodies and to distinguish the Spiritual Woman, "Mother of the Living," from the "carnal Eve," "Mother of the Embodied."

The imagery of gender in *HypArch* intersects with the category of gnosis in highly complex ways and must be understood within the context of the text's overarching dualisms (Spirit-Flesh, Entirety-Cosmos, living-dying, gnosis-igno-rance, redeemed-unredeemed) and its tripartite division of Spirit-Psyche-Flesh. These create an ideological system of hierarchical values in which one pole is esteemed, while the other is demeaned.

The narrative uses sexual metaphor to represent both redemptive and nonre-demptive states. Metaphors of virginity, conception, and birth, for example, en-noble the categories of the female and the Spirit, while metaphors of sexual desire and rape criticize the Archontic and the androgynous. As Norea's meta-phorical virginity represents the spiritual power to resist and subvert available to all who have gnosis, the Archons' desire to rape represents the lust for domi-nance, power, and control of the Spirit.

HypArch also uses gender simply to distinguish characters as female, male, and androgynous. Of these, only the category of the androgynous is clustered in a single realm. Female and male intersect and cross the boundaries of Entirety and Cosmos, divine and human, redeemed and unredeemed. The hierarchical distinction of these categories, however, creates other boundaries that are less flexible and more difficult to cross. The distinction between spiritual women of gnosis and carnal women of ignorance, for example, does allow women more than a single value or place, but it decisively grants spiritual women, as well as the spiitual elements of a particular woman, a far higher status than women of the flesh or the fleshly elements of the same woman. Even if persons or elements in the latter group are capable of moving higher,[90] they remain devalued and demeaned as long as they remain in the ignorant and unredeemed category of the flesh.

Women, Gender, and Gnosis in Accounts of Jesus and His Disciples   Stories about Jesus and collections of his sayings provided a powerful and flexible medium in early Christianity for ideas about Jesus' significance and a wide range of other reli-gious and social issues. Gnostic traditions about Jesus include many distinct literary genres and religious perspectives. Among the many representations of women, gender, and gnosis in these traditions, none are more significant than those involving Mary Magdalene. Mary Magdalene appears in a variety of roles in gnostic traditions, but the most important appear in *The Gospel of Mary* (GMary),[91] *The Gospel of Philip* (GPhil),[92] the *Dialogue of the Savior* (DialSav),[93] and *The Gospel of Thomas*. In some of these texts, Mary appears with other female disciples, such as Salome,[94] but more often, she appears as the sole female disciple amidst a group of male disciples. In many, Mary is depicted as especially beloved by Jesus or as having a special relationship with him. This pattern is not found in all the texts in which she appears. Indeed, portrayals of Mary Magdalene in gnostic sources vary so much that generalizations "do not do justice to the great variety characterizing the portraits and the use of Mary Magdalene in all of these texts."[95]

Authority, Apostleship, and Revelation in The Gospel of Mary   In its depiction of Mary Magdalene, *The Gospel of Mary* addresses two issues widely debated in the early church: (1) the validity of teaching delivered in private, visions, or appearances, and (2) the leadership and authority of women.[96] Mary is depicted in GMary as an ideal disciple who understands Jesus and his words and plays a leading role among the disciples after he goes. When Mary receives a vision of Jesus, he commends her "for not wavering at seeing me."[97] After Jesus departs, the disci-ples begin weeping and ask themselves how they will preach the gospel of the Kingdom of the Son of Man.[98] Mary emerges here as the comforter and instruc-tor of the male disciples. She exhorts them: "Do not weep . . . for his grace will be entirely with you and will protect you. But rather let us praise his greatness, for he has prepared us and made us into human beings (anthrōpoi)."[99] Here, Mary shows herself to be an unwavering leader who understands that the disciples must turn toward their nongendered nature as anthropoi in order to gain salvation.[100]

Peter initially appears to acknowledge Mary's wisdom, but ultimately he and the other disciples fall short of the religious ideals of the Savior. The crucial portion of the narrative is set in motion when Peter acknowledges: "Sister, we know the savior loved you more than the rest of women;" he asks Mary to share with him and the other disciples "the words of the Savior that you know."[101] Mary then begins to reveal and reflect on the "hidden" things that she has received through her visionary experience of the Savior.

On hearing Mary's revelations, the disciples become contentious. Andrew, for one, cannot believe the Savior said the things Mary reports "because those opinions seem to be so different from his thought." As Karen King has noted, Andrew's objection to Mary's teaching echoes a much debated problem in early Christian circles: how can the validity of such teaching be determined? For Andrew, Mary's words did not seem to conform to the teachings that he knew and used as a standard for the truth. But Mary's teaching concords perfectly with that given by the Savior himself in the first part of the text. GMary clearly affirms the truth and authority of Mary's teaching and thus implicitly affirms the validity of Mary and of visionary revelations.[102]

Peter also expresses skepticism and doubt about Mary's teaching, but not principally on the grounds of its visionary character. The narrative depicts Peter as addressing the entire group with his doubts about the secret character of the teachings. As he expresses these doubts, he also reveals a specific concern about the gender of their carrier: "Has the Savior spoken to a woman and not openly so that we would all hear? Surely he did not wish to indicate that she is more worthy than we are?"[103] Although Peter does express doubt about the secret, seemingly exclusionary, character of the Savior's revelation, Peter's doubts are more clearly directed to Mary's gender and her status relative to the male disciples than they are to their content.[104] In response, Mary challenges Peter to declare, before all the disciples, if he thinks she made it all up. Levi comes to Mary's defense:

> If the Savior considered her to be worthy, who are you to disregard her? For he knew her completely and loved her devotedly. Instead, we should be ashamed and, once we clothe ourselves with perfect humanity, we should do what we were commanded . . . and announce the good new as the Savior ordered, not laying down any rules or making laws.

While Peter and Andrew express doubt concerning Mary's teaching, the narrative itself casts doubt on the witness of Andrew and Peter, and identifies the true apostolic witness with Mary Magdalene and Levi. King summarizes the relevance of the narrative to the nongendered issue of "the reliability of apostolic testimony" and the gendered issue of "the authority of women":

The prominence of Mary Magdalene gives one example of the leadership roles of women in early Christianity, roles that came to be increasingly challenged. . . . Peter was willing to admit the Savior loved Mary "more than all other women," but he balks at the idea that the Savior may have preferred her, a woman, to the male disciples. Yet Levi states explicitly that this is the case. . . . In every way, the text affirms that her leadership of the other disciples is based upon superior spiritual understanding. Peter, however, cannot see past the superficial sexual differentiation of the flesh to Mary's true spiritual power. He again shows his ignorance of the Savior's true teaching, while the *Gospel of Mary* unreservedly supports the leadership of spiritually advanced women.[105]

Peter's deficiencies are based in part on his inability to overcome his competitive feelings of jealousy in response to the favor shown Mary. Even more important, Peter's question about the Savior's choice of a woman over the male disciples illustrates his inability to move beyond gender bias, as it exposes his failure to understand the Savior's teaching that gender differentiation is insignificant in the true identity of an anthropos. The authority of Mary, in contrast, is grounded in her nonwavering character, her visionary experience, and her spiritual insight into the significance of becoming human beings (*anthrōpoi*) and thus transcending the petty differences of social status and gender differentiation.

Union as an Image of Salvation: The Gospel of Philip   There is no narrative or dialogue comparable to GMary, and no explicit discussion of the authority of women, revelation, or revelation-receiving women in *The Gospel of Philip*. Instead, Mary Magdalene appears in GPhil as the female part of a symbol of salvific union. In one passage that depicts the special relationship of Mary and Jesus, Mary is one of "three who always walked with the Lord: Mary his mother, her sister and the Magdalene, the one who was called his companion (*tef-koinōnos*). For Mary is his sister and she is his mother and she is his companion (*tef-hotre*)."[106]

In a second passage, which describes Mary as "companion," it is said that Jesus loved Mary "more than [all] the disciples [and used to] kiss her [often] on her [. . .]."[107] Their kiss may have been understood to express love, but even more important, it provided a mythic foundation for the ritual kiss in the religious life of the community: "For it is by a kiss that the perfect conceive and give birth. For this reason we also kiss one another. We receive conception from the grace which is in one another."[108] In this way, the kiss of Mary Magdalene and Jesus establishes a paradigm and originating moment for spiritual conception through the mouth, that is, for the production of spiritual utterance: prophecy, poetry, song, and other manifestations of the divine *Logos* in language and sound.[109]

The kiss of Jesus and Mary Magdalene leads the rest of the disciples to recognize that Mary was not only loved more than all women, as the GMary claims, but that she was loved more than the other disciples as well.

They [the rest of the disciples] said to him [Jesus]: "Why do you love her more than all of us?" The savior answered and said to them, "Why do I not love you like her? When a blind man and one who sees are both together in darkness, they are no different from one another, but when the light comes, then he who sees will see the light, and he who is blind will remain in darkness."[110]

In reply to the disciples, Jesus poses a question that turns the disciples away from their concern about Mary and toward themselves. The juxtaposition of this question with the saying contrasting the blind man and the person of sight, however, at the same time offers an answer to the disciples' question. It suggests strongly that Jesus loves Mary precisely because she has seen the light, while the jealous disciples remain in darkness.

Even more important, the companionship of Mary and Jesus serves as prototype and symbol of the salvific union of female and male. Behind this image of salvation as union lies a mythic narrative that consists of three stages: primordial union, separation, and reunification.[111] The first stage, based on a rereading of Gen 2–3, involves the separation of Eve from Adam, of female from male:

> If the woman had not separated from the man, she would not die with the man. His separation became the beginning of death. Because of this Christ came to repair the separation which was from the beginning and again unite the two and to give life to those who died as a result of the separation and unite them.[112]

Within the mythic context of the separation of Eve from Adam, the relationship of Mary and Jesus represents a reunification of the separated female and male.[113] As with the iconic or imaged "bridal chamber,"[114] the companionship and kiss of Mary Magdalene and Jesus symbolizes the salvific moment when female and male are reunited and bring forth spiritual fruit. As female "companion" to Jesus, Mary Magdalene plays a role in GPhil that is at once symbolic and salvific.

Discipleship and Destroying the "Works of Womanhood": The Dialogue of the Savior   The *Dialogue of the Savior* provides another depiction of Mary in conversation with Jesus and other disciples, but in this case, the disciples are not contending for authority, and Mary does not take on a highly symbolic role. Instead, Mary is depicted, along with Judas and Matthew, as a representative of all the disciples. All three are depicted in a positive light. One of Mary's utterances earns her praise, revealing her "as a woman who had understood completely."[115] Another of her sayings leads Jesus to declare that she has "made clear the abundance of the revealer."[116]

Later in the same dialogue, however, Mary becomes involved in a discussion that appears to devalue the category of the female or "womanhood." Judas asks Jesus how the disciples should pray. Jesus replies: "Pray in the place where there is no woman." Matthew interprets this to mean: "Destroy the works of womanhood, not because there is any other [manner of birth], but because they will cease [giving birth]."[117] In the analysis of Antti Marjanen, the text communicates a double message to its female readers with its "contradictory . . . use of gendered language."

> On the one hand, they heard about Mary Magdalene, a prominent woman, who together with her two male colleagues played the most important part in a dia-

logue between Jesus and his disciples. . . . On the other hand, . . . the text used metaphorical language which clearly and in an unqualified way devalued women.[118]

While the text does communicate a complex and mixed message, its negative evaluation of "the works of womanhood" does not necessarily devalue women as a group. Central to the encratic or ascetic perspective that this and many other texts of gnostic tradition reflect[119] is a negative attitude toward sexual intercourse, reproduction, and childbirth.[120] Thus, I would argue that it is not "women," but what the symbolic "works of womanhood" represent, namely, sexual intercourse, reproduction, and childbirth, that are devalued by this text.[121] The symbolic association of the category of the female ("femaleness" or "womanhood") with the negative pole of sexuality and reproduction does not necessarily devalue women, lead to a negative attitude toward women, or exclude women from leadership, as some have implied. Such an association may, of course, lead in that direction and has frequently been used to justify such devaluation and exclusionary practice.[122] Individual women, however, can become free of such devaluation and exclusion, as the example of Mary Magdalene makes clear. Even groups that question women's authority as a matter of course may nonetheless value and legitimate the authority of a woman who exemplifies religious ideals, as Mary Magdalene clearly did within several varieties of Christianity in the ancient world.

Gender, Gnosis, and Redemptive Transformation: Mary Magdalene in The Gospel of Thomas   In the collection of Jesus' sayings known as *The Gospel of Thomas*, Logion 114, Jesus tells Peter that he will lead Mary and "make her male."[123] Many of the sayings in the GThom parallel sayings of Jesus found in the New Testament gospels, especially those usually attributed to the sayings source Q.[124] Mary Magdalene and other women figure significantly in only a few sayings in the GThom, but the gospel's complex use of gender symbolism has become the center of much discussion and debate.[125] To understand its significance, it is important to consider Logion 114 and other sayings within the context of the gospel as a whole and its multiple images of salvation.

Unlike the canonical gospels, which blend Jesus' sayings into a narrative account, the GThom is a collection of sayings with no narrative or historical frame. As a result, the significance of Jesus resides not in the events of his life, death, or resurrection, but rather in the meaning (*hermēneia*) of his sayings.[126] Finding the *hermēneia* of Jesus' utterances and overcoming the state of "death" are two of many images the GThom employs to describe the experience of salvation. Others include "entering the Kingdom," "making an image in place of an image," and "entering/seeing the Light."[127] The gospel also uses two highly gendered images of salvation, which have differences that have generated much debate. One speaks of salvation as transcending male and female altogether ("making the two one"), the other of an ascent to maleness ("making Mary male").

The first of these gendered images is presented in Logion 22, in which Jesus compares nursing infants to those who enter the Kingdom. In response to his disciples' question whether they too must become "little ones," Jesus replies that they will enter the Kingdom when a series of transformations and substitutions have taken place:

> Jesus said to them, "When you make the two one and when you make the inside like the outside and the outside like the inside, and the above like the below, and when you make the male (*hooyt*) and the female (*shime*) into a single one, so that the male will not be male nor the female be female, when you make eyes in place of an eye, and a hand in place of a hand, and a foot in place of a foot, an image (*eikōn*) in place of an image, then you will enter the Kingdom."

With each of these images, something new comes into being, replacing something that was: duality becomes unity, as two become one; opposing spatial categories undergo a transformative exchange (inside like outside, outside like inside, above like below); the two genders become a single one; new "body parts" (eyes, hand, foot) replace old; and a new image is made in place of another image. When "the male and the female" are made into "a single one," this saying suggests, the distinction of the two genders is transformed, but not abandoned. There is still a "male" and a "female," but they are not male and female as they once were: the (new) male will not be male in the old sense and the (new) female will not be female in the old sense. Yet, in contrast to the different states of the old male and female, the new male and female become one and the same. The old, untransformed states give way to a new identity, a new way of being human, for female and male alike. The new redeemed male and female are one and the same as the two become one.

The gospel's second gendered image of salvation emerges in the final saying of the GThom, Logion 114. There, salvation is represented not as a process of male and female becoming a single one, but as a process of the female becoming male. Jesus' saying is enclosed here within a brief narrative in which Peter declares that Mary Magdalene should leave the circle of disciples because "women are not worthy of Life." As in GMary and the synoptic gospels,[128] Peter stands in need of correction, and Jesus' teaching provides it.

> Simon Peter said to them, "Mary should leave us, for women (*shiome*) are not worthy of Life." Jesus said: "Look, I will lead her to make her male (*hooyt*), in order that she too may become a Living Spirit, resembling you males/men (*hooyt*). For every women/female (*shime*) who makes herself male (*hooyt*) will enter the Kingdom of Heaven."[129]

Against Peter's view that "women" or "females" are not worthy of Life, Jesus' response overturns Peter's misconception. He does not argue that Mary and other women are in fact worthy, however, but claims that he can make this female or woman (*shime*) male (*hooyt*) so that she can "become a Living Spirit, resembling you males (*hooyt*)."

The goal may be described here in the gender-neutral terms of becoming "a Living Spirit" and "entering the Kingdom;" Jesus declares that every woman/female (*shime*) must make herself male (*hooyt*) in order to enter the salvific state. The saying thus aligns the categories of Life, Spirit, and entering the Kingdom with that of the male. Only by making herself male, it would appear, will Mary become worthy of the spiritual state of Life in the Kingdom.

The imagery of Logion 114 appears to put forward the asymmetrical view that only women require salvific transformation. This stands in striking contrast to Logion 22, in which male and female achieve the salvific state along parallel lines. Their juxtaposition raises two questions: Are the images of transformation in Logia 22 and 114 essentially different, or do they represent two symbolic expressions of the same thing? Did Peter and the other male disciples undergo a transformation to become "Living Spirits," or were they already "worthy of Life"?

Many scholars have addressed the apparent tension and have adopted one of at least four distinct positions. Some have assigned Logion 114 to a later source,[130] and argued that Logia 22 and 114 do not agree because they come from different editors or layers of the tradition. A second strategy seeks to erase the imbalance and argue that both male and female undergo transformation to become "spiritual males."[131] Peter and the other male disciples have also been transformed from nonspiritual men (hooyt) to spiritual men or males (hooyt). This solution provides a plausible blending of Logia 22 and 114 for the transformation of men, but leaves in place very different accounts of the transformation women undergo. Both men and women must be spiritually transformed, according to this reading, but only women must undergo a second, more radical change in gender identity. The spiritual male that Mary becomes is not literally a man, of course; she needs no sex-change operation. What Mary needs, however, is a radical shift in gendered identity. Here, the asymmetry remains because women must experience both a transformation from nonspiritual to spiritual and a symbolic change in gender identity, from female/woman to male.[132]

A third strategy seeks to relate Logion 114 to some of the same symbols of gender outlined above, as well as to those that symbolize higher and lower elements of the soul as male and female, respectively. Marvin Meyer[133] and Elizabeth Castelli,[134] for example, find an important interpretive clue in Philo of Alexandria's symbolization of male and female as "superior and inferior states," respectively, or elements of the soul that "have been divided and separated." In Philo's language, the goal is to bring together those elements "not that the masculine may be made womanish, and relaxed by softness, but that the female element, the senses, may be made manly."[135]

> For progress is indeed nothing else than the giving up of the female by changing into the male, since the female is material, passive, corporeal, and sense-perceptible, while the male is active, rational, incorporeal, and more akin to mind and thought.[136]

In Castelli's reading, Mary becomes worthy of Life only by transcending the female parts of her self—material, passive, corporeal, and sense perceptible—and allowing the superior male elements—active, rational, incorporeal—to reign.

Within Philo's conception, however, men, as well as women, possess the female elements of the soul. Yet the GThom says nothing about Peter or the other male disciples giving up their female elements to become fully male. Castelli's analysis of the conditions under which "Mary" and other early Christian women were included among the worthy is illuminating,[137] but the argument may move too quickly to link Thomas' categories of male and female to higher and lower elements of the human person or his or her soul as in Philo, or even to the same conception of femaleness as in the *DialSav* and other ascetic texts.[138]

An alternative to these approaches seeks to relate the language of both logia to other sayings in the text and to the traditions of Genesis interpretation on which they draw.[139] Within the immediate context of Logion 114, Jesus' words come as a direct challenge to Peter's claim that Mary should leave "because women are not worthy of Life." Peter's ideology of exclusion is grounded not in the perception that Mary's soul, or part of it, is female, but rather in the misguided view that women like Mary are not worthy of Life, perhaps because they lack something that he and the male disciples have. The phrases "worthy of Life" and "Living Spirit" bring the reader into two of the gospel's central dualisms: Life and Death[140] and Spirit and Flesh.[141] These dualisms, like those of Light and Darkness[142] and Kingdom and Cosmos, represent two hierarchically ordered realms or states of existence and two ways of being human. These dualisms, however, do not correspond directly to the categories of male and female in the GThom as a whole. Most of these opposed categories appear without gendered imagery.[143] Among those dualistic symbols that use gendered imagery, such as Logion 101, both genders are associated with the negative pole of Death and the positive pole of Life:

> Jesus said: "Whoever does not hate his fa[ther] and his mother as I do cannot be a disciple to me, and whoever does [not] love his Father and his Mother as I do cannot be a disciple to me. For my mother [. . .], but my true [Moth]er gave me Life."

This saying echoes the radical Q sayings about hating one's parents[144] and instructs its readers to distinguish their biological parents from their true Father and Mother. Contrary to conventional pieties, one's biological parents are to be hated because they bring merely the bodily life that is Death. Only one's spiritual parents, the "Living Father" and "true Mother," are to be loved, for they alone give the true Life that comes from the Spirit.

The text's dualism of Life and Death may help to illuminate Logia 22 and 114 as two distinct images for the state of Life, but it leaves unanswered the question of why the state of salvation is gendered as male in Logion 114, and why Mary, of all the disciples, is singled out as the one in need of transformation. One intriguing suggestion comes from those who place the GThom within the context of Genesis interpretation, particularly of an Adamic typology, which developed in relation either to baptismal practice (Davies) or visionary mysticism (DeConick). This typology was based on a three-stage myth of creation and redemption:[145] (1) a state of perfection in which the Spirit/primordial Adam existed as Light in perfect unity with the divine; (2) a moment of corruption or loss in which the Light Adam is cast into darkness/the body/the Cosmos; (3) a salvific restoration or return to the beginning in which the primordial human being of Gen 1:26–27 is recovered, and the individual redemptively transformed.

Within this mythic framework, the GThom may be said to reflect the notion that ritual initiation or visionary ascent effects a restoration of the primordial human being, the "Adam of great power and wealth" (Logion 85). This Adam represents primordial human nature before it became subject to death. Recovering this "Adam before Adam" is compared to several things: standing at the beginning and knowing the end (Logion 18); "images of yourselves that came into being before you" (Logion 84); and, most strikingly, "the one who came into being before coming into being" (Logion 19). Paradoxically, the newly redeemed human being is identical to the original and oldest Adam, the primordial self, with "the face he had before the world was made."[146] That face is not literally a physical, fleshly face, but figuratively a metaphor for an uncreated, divine self, the face in place of a face from Logion 22.

In light of this pre-Adamic typology, Logia 22 and 114 may reflect two distinct representations of this primordial and salvific human state. The image of Logion 22 implies a transformation of self and of humankind from duality to unity; from a created face, eye, or hand to an uncreated or precreated image of Light. Neither old nor new state is symbolized as male or female. Rather, each gender has corresponding old and new states. Logion 114, in contrast, represents the restored self as symbolically male. Although neither Adam nor *anthrōpos* is gender-specific in its original sense, Logion 114 appears to reflect an interpretation of the primordial human being (generic ʾ*adam*, *anthrōpos*, *rōme*) of Gen 1: 26–27 in the gender-specific, masculine sense of primordial Man (gender-specific ʾ*ish*, *anēr*, hooyt), the male Living Spirit that was in the beginning.[147] By this reading, both Peter and Mary, like all children of the created Adam and Eve, must put on this new Man which is, at the same time, their oldest and best Self.

This Self is ultimately the same for all, but women require a more radical transformation because the redeemed human being is imaged as male. Although the Peter of Logion 114 blunders by reading Mary's womanhood as a sign of her unworthiness, it is not her womanhood, but her nonredeemed state as a created female that has kept her outside of salvific Life. Similarly, Peter and other readers mistake the physical and social reality of men as one with the symbolic category of the primordial, redeemed Male. Just like Mary, the male disciples, too, must undergo a transformation from nonredeemed created selves to the redeemed state of Living Spirits. The end, however, is the same for all. Those who are transformed achieve the redeemed state of Living Spirits, identical to that of the Primordial Man. The difference is that Mary and women who enter that state undergo a more radical shift from created female selves to precreated spiritual male selves.

Misinterpretations like Peter's have legitimated the exclusion of women from leadership throughout the history of Christianity. What is curious is that the same interpretive maneuver that links the primordial, redeemed human being of Genesis 1 to the symbolic category of male serves to undercut Peter's exclusionary ideology in Logion 114. Jesus transforms Mary and "makes her male" in order to show that women, as well as men, are "worthy of Life," the state of the Primordial Man and of entering the elite circle of the redeemed. But Mary's sense of herself will no longer be that of the woman Mary, female daughter of Eve, but rather of a "Spiritual Male" who has recaptured the primordial Adamic Self and thus has earned a "place" in the Kingdom of the Living Father.

By concluding with Logion 114, the GThom puts an androcentric seal on its multifaceted images of redemption through the Living Jesus. As a result, even as this gospel affirms the inclusion of women like Mary, its representation of the human ideal as male nonetheless devalues the symbolic category of the female, as well as the embodied, sexual identities of all persons. Not only among the literal-minded Peters of the world, but even among those who read symbolically, the GThom may well have legitimated asymmetrical gender roles as it supported ascetic lifestyles for those who found in it a spiritual home.

Gender, Gnosis, and the Revelatory Voice of the Divine: Thunder, Perfect Mind   Thunder, Perfect Mind[148] (Thund) offers a radically different example of gender imagery in gnostic traditions. Thund belongs to the genre of revelation discourse and presents the revelation of a mysterious female divinity whose name may be found in the title of the work. As name and title, "Thunder" (Brontē, f.) may well be related to biblical conceptions of the thundering voice of the divine (e.g., Exod 19:19; Job 40:9; Rev 6:1). Thund's sophisticated reworking of images and ideas from other traditions, especially those associated with hellenistic Jewish Wisdom, the goddess Isis, Middle Platonism, and other gnostic traditions, helps mark this poem as the product of a syncretistic and revisionary imagination.[149]

The opening lines reveal a literary pattern that recurs throughout the text: the divine voice begins with first-person statements of identity and shifts to second-person address. Here, the speaker identifies herself in terms of her origin and destination and then admonishes her audience to use their faculties of sight, hearing, and speech to enter into relation with her.

> It is from the Power that I was sent,
> And it is to those who reflect upon me that I have come,
> And I was found among those who seek after me.
> Look at me, you who reflect upon me; And you hearers, hear me!

Even as the divine voice invites all who "hear" to enter into a "knowing" relation with her, the rhetorical features of the text reconstruct the reader's conception of the speaker and her relation to those who hear her. The alternating structure of first- and second-person address, for example, works both to differentiate and to connect the "I" who speaks and the "you" she addresses. While the first lines suggest a sharp boundary between those who know and those who remain ignorant, other statements point to the paradoxical and liminal character of the speaker. The initial series of self-predications, or "I am" statements, use the language of paradox and kinship to describe the speaker as one who exists "betwixt and between" antithetical categories and as one who exists in relation.

> I am the first and the last.
> I am the honored and the scorned,
> I am the harlot and the holy one.

I am the wife and the virgin.
I am the m[oth]er and the daughter.
I am the members of my mother.
I am the barren one and the one with many children.
I am she whose marriage is multiple, and I have not taken a husband.
I am the midwife and she who does not give birth.
I am the comforting of my labor pains.
I am the bride and the bridegroom.

This passage recalls the imagery of a wide range of divine figures, including Isis, Sophia, Jesus, and Barbelo/Protennoia. But the text's interweaving of paradox and kinship with the imagery of gender resonates beyond such allusions and discloses the complex identity of the speaker and her metaphorical association with the antithetical roles assigned to women in patriarchal culture.[150]

As "the harlot and the holy one," the speaker is linked metaphorically with a pair of female roles that frequently serve to divide and reduce women to the polar opposites of harlot (pornē) and holy one (semnē). The juxtaposition of this statement to the previous reference to "the honored and the scorned" appears even more to reinforce the oppressive polarization of scorned harlots and honored holy ones. Yet, by including negative and positive poles within the divine, Thund pushes beyond the literal sense and valuation of both polarities and links the speaker directly to the conflicting, though sometimes overlapping, roles of women. In this way, the text opens new possibilities for the ideological critique and reinterpretation of such polarities, the identities they shape, and the values they ascribe to the female gender in its divine and human manifestations.

The following lines move from sharply antithetical polarities to the relational language of gender, kinship, and childbirth. As "wife and virgin, and "mother and daughter," the speaker identifies herself with the most basic kinship roles by which women are related to one another and to others. The juxtaposition of these with the claim to be "the members of my mother" points to the unity and multiplicity within the speaker's identity as "Mother" and especially as "daughter(s)" or "children" to her own mother. Insofar as the reference to members echoes the Pauline image of the body and its members (1 Cor 12:12–26) as a metaphor for the church, so this line identifies the speaker not only with the divine Mother, but with her dispersed human members.

The relation of the speaker to the roles of women becomes even clearer with the metaphors of sexual relations and reproduction. The paradoxical pairing of such identities as "the barren one and the one with many children," however, undermines the polarity that defines and values women by their reproductive capacity or incapacity, their fertility or infertility, and revalues both by placing them together within the divine. The association between the speaker and reproduction becomes even more complex, however, as the mother with many children identifies herself as "the midwife," "she who does not give birth," and "the comforting of my labor pains." Echoing simultaneously the curse on Eve (Gen 3:16) and the image of Isis as protector of women in pregnancy and childbirth, these statements identify the speaker with both the divine power of healing and the experience of women in childbirth and infertility.

The paradoxical joining of conventionally opposed categories breaks down their restrictive functions in several ways: (1) they include polarity, particularity, and multiplicity within the identity of the divine; (2) they cross boundaries that often work to separate and divide women; and (3) they question, displace, or even nullify such basic cultural categories as the distinction between the maternal and the virginal, unity and multiplicity, immanence and transcendence, and even the divine and the human.

While this first set of gendered metaphors associates the speaker almost exclusively with female roles, the last of the statements quoted above places both female and male characteristics within the speaker's identity. With its allusion to the bridegroom-bride metaphor for the relation of God and Israel or Christ and the church, this self-predication associates the speaker simultaneously with the "divine" and "male" role of bridegroom, traditionally played by God or Christ (or even Marcus), and the traditional "human" and "female" role of the bride, played by Israel or the church. The speaker thus claims an identity that is simultaneously male and female, singular and collective, divine and human.

From this assertion of female-male union, the text moves to a series of paradoxical statements about the speaker's relation to various male figures:

It is my husband who begot me.
I am the mother of my father and the sister of my husband.
And he is my offspring.
I am the servant of him who prepared me and I am the lord of my offspring.
But he is the one who be[got me] before time on a day of birth and he is my
　　offspring in time, and my power is from him.
I am the staff of his power in his youth and he is the rod of my old age.
And whatever he wills happens to me.

The roles of husband, father, and offspring may belong to different male figures, or they may refer to the same figure at different "moments" or in distinct manifestations in time. In this series, the text reinscribes conventional patterns of gender relations, with the image of a superior male power empowering a subordinate female figure to realize his will, articulate his thought, and utter his name in the world. She may be "the staff of his power," but ultimately the power appears to be his. Against this image, however, the paradoxical mixing of gender and kinship relations, together with other statements that reverse the relation of female and male, undermine a rigid stratification of male dominance and female subordination and set in its place a more dynamic structure of reciprocity and exchange. The multiplicity and paradox of these images of the speaker destabilize the reader's conception of "her" gendered identity and point to her transcendence of the categories of female and male. They suggest that the various self-descriptions of the divine point to, but cannot exhaust, the mysterious identity of the divine or her "members." The figure who speaks in Thund to this point is a single, yet multifaceted, character who exists in the dynamic interrelationship of various female and male roles, yet associates herself particularly with the roles and experiences of women.

In many other passages, the speaker challenges her audience to recognize the antithetical character of their own responses to her and to relate these to her identity and their own. In several statements, Brontë speaks poignantly as the subject and object of conflicting responses. She is the object not only of honor, exaltation, and love, but also of derision, disgrace, and hatred. "I am the disgraced and the exalted one; give heed to my poverty and my wealth. Do not be haughty to me when I am discarded upon the earth . . . and do not look upon me on the garbage heap and go and leave me discarded." She is "hated everywhere and . . . loved everywhere."[151] Insofar as these opposed responses, and the pain that accompanies them, constitute her very identity, she is the subject who experiences, and exists within, the poles of negative and positive human attitudes and response. On the negative side of derision and disgrace, she has solidarity with the vulnerable, the oppressed, and the outcast. On the positive side, she is also "the exalted one," who speaks in the future tense of being found "among those that are to come" and "in the kingdoms." In the present voice of the text, however, her existence is characterized by the dualities of poverty and wealth, weakness and power, fear and pride, silence and speech. She urges her audience to recognize their own complicity in these dualities and to change their vision, attitudes, and relation to her and her "members," recognizing them even in those things or persons that are in disgrace and pain, in shamelessness and shame.

In one of the text's most striking passages, the speaker declares her relation to multiple categories of being, including angels, gods, the spirits of all human beings, and women: "But I am the [perfect] mind and the repose. . . . I am the gnosis of my seeking, and the finding of those who seek after me. . . . And it is with me that the spirits of all humans exist, and it is within me that women exist." In these parallel statements, the text invites all its hearers, both male and female, to perceive their "spirits" as dwelling with the divine, but it leads women to understand themselves as dwelling within the divine. At the same time, the speaker's claim to be "an alien and a citizen" places her simultaneously inside and outside the boundaries of divine and human "society." Insider and outsider, the speaking voice of Thund is both a liminal figure and a figure of liminality itself. She exists at the threshold of, or betwixt and between, the known and unknown, the visible and invisible, the immanent and transcendent, the accepted and rejected. At the same time, she manifests herself in the violation and crossing of boundaries: "[I am] restraint and unrestraint. I am the union and the dissolution. . . . I am the judgment and the acquittal." In attaching no specific objects to these terms, the text remains ambiguous and invites the interpretive claim that the speaker manifests herself in "the union and the dissolution" of polarities, including the duality of divine speaker and human audience, the "I" and "you" of the text.

The dissolution of this duality is supported further by statements that place the linguistic faculties of speaking, hearing, and writing not only within the divine, but also within her hearers:

> Hear me, you listeners, and be taught my utterances, you who know me!
> I am the hearing that is acceptable in every matter;

> I am the utterance that cannot be restrained.
> I am the name of the sound and the sound of the name.
> I am the sign of writing and the manifestation of difference.[152]

As "hearing," these lines suggest, the divine is available to all. As silence or singular utterance, she cannot be grasped or reduced to a singular word, conception, or interpretation. She is, rather, a "mute who does not speak," yet whose "multitude of words" is manifold in number and in polysemic significance. Together, these and other passages link the speaker to the linguistic and intellective faculties. They point suggestively toward the identity of the speaker with the poetic language of the text and with its "hearing" or interpretation as well. The divine is present and active, the text implies, not only in its revelatory utterances, but also in its hearing among those the text addresses, the human audience she calls.

With the speaker's claim to be "the name of the sound and the sound of the name,"[153] the text focuses attention on the reflexive identity of the speaker as divine name and as the thundering sound that utters that name. By juxtaposing this self-description with the claim to be "the sign of writing and the manifestation of difference," the text extends the media of divine manifestation to the activities of reading, writing, and differentiating. In identifying the divine as the "sign (sēmeion) of writing," the text identifies the divine not only with the hidden significance of writing in general, but also, more particularly, with the hidden significance of this text, the revelation discourse of Thunder, Perfect Mind. Finally, as "the manifestation of difference," the text suggests that the speaker's significance is manifested in the differentiation of features, the distinction of categories, the processes of separation and dissolution, and the multiplicity of expression and interpretation.

If the members listen and respond as she commands, the divine voice asserts, they will discover in the text and in themselves both the one who "cries out" and the one who "listens."[154] When she exhorts her hearers to "give heed . . . For I am the one who alone exists," Thund introduces a strikingly new perspective on the identity of the speaker that serves both to solve and to dis-solve the mystery of the speaker's identity. The "one" who speaks in Thund, these lines suggest, is the unity that encompasses all duality and multiplicity, including those of her utterances and her members. Indeed, she is "the one who alone exists," and knowing or "gnostic" readers discover her within themselves as they discover themselves within the divine.

This redemptive moment comes, the concluding lines suggest, when those who have embraced the "many pleasant aspects" of sin, unrestrained acts, and passions "become sober and go up to the place of rest." There, the speaker claims, "they will find me" and "live" and "not die again."[155] Within the symbolic world of the text, this redemptive "place" or state is available already to those who understand the mysterious utterances of the text. For, in understanding the discourse with gnosis, they operate with the divine faculties of hearing, seeing, and knowing, which are simultaneously grounded in the divine and manifested in themselves. Such knowing readers understand the speaker's claim

to be "the union and the dissolution" as they realize the conjunction and dissolution of the central duality of the text: the distinction between the divine "I"
who speaks and the human "you" she calls. When such members of the audience hear the divine voice, they become sober, discover the divine faculties
within, and transport themselves "upward" to the "place of rest" as restored
members of the divine. The symbolic world and rhetorical features of the text
thus work together to break down and dissolve the boundaries separating the I
and you of the text as the divine voice shares her faculties and empowers her
members to speak her/their name and to discover her/themselves.

Within a religious setting, recitation of Thunder, Perfect Mind may have had the
effect not only of invoking divine presence, but also of communicating a distinctive ideology of gnosis and a radically new understanding of both the divine
and the human self. Without denying or negating the particularity and multiplicity of images and categories, Thund leads its readers to discover in the text and
in themselves the one who is "honored and scorned," "she who cries out," and
"she who listens." In realizing their shared identity with the divine, female and
male readers alike might come to a new understanding of the categories of
difference that shape their understanding of themselves and the world, including
those of strong-weak, inside-outside, transcendent-immanent, divine-human,
and male-female. In perceiving the conjunction and dissolution of such categories within the divine, they not only reconceive the divine, but also reconstitute
their member-ship within her complex and multifaceted identity.

More than any texts of gnostic tradition, Thunder, Perfect Mind, uses the imagery
of gender, paradox, and language to communicate a distinctive conception of
the divine and her members. Through its complex literary form and rhetorical
devices, Thund effects a new understanding of the identity of the divine with her
human hearers as it places the "divine" powers of language and interpretation
within them. With these powers, they, in turn, come to understand themselves
in the divine "place of rest," joined to "the one who alone exists," the divine
female voice of revelation and redemption in Thunder, Perfect Mind.

Summary and Conclusions

Gnostic texts and traditions use images of gender extensively, even extravagantly,
as they present their varied and complex religious perspectives. It is possible that
some of the authors and readers of these texts chose images of gender because
they were engaged in a process of contesting, revising categories of gender and
the social roles of women and men. But even more important, they chose images
of male and female because these provided a particularly apt and rich set of
metaphors for reflection on a variety of issues, particularly those involving
differentiation, unity, or both. Although no single pattern exists among the
sources, all of the texts surveyed use the female gender as a symbolic category
to reflect on a variety of topics, especially categories of difference. These range
from the social categories of social class, kinship, ethnicity, and gender to the
more abstract philosophical and religious categories of space and time, being
and becoming, creation and redemption, and Spirit, Soul, and Matter.

As male and female represent two forms of a single species, metaphors of gender allow the transfer of meaning from the social domain of gender difference to other domains—conceptual, spiritual, experiential—which might also concern reflection on difference, unity, and relation: the relation of two or more entities to one another and to others, the relation of different manifestations of one and the same thing to each other and to the thing from which they arise. These texts show clearly that gender imagery was used to represent a variety of more abstract issues in religious speculation, including the relation of duality or multiplicity to unity and of the many to the one.

This survey just begins to touch upon the variety and richness in the representation of women and gender in gnostic traditions. I hope it has demonstrated that those who would unify these texts and traditions under a single category (like "gnosticism"), under a singular attitude toward women, or under a single use of gender run the risk of ignoring the diversity of these texts. At the same time, they fail to understand the complex ways these texts served their ancient readers, particularly in legitimating particular conceptions of gnosis as the key to the meaning of scripture, experience, and salvation. We contemporary readers can begin both to understand these uses and to subject them to critique as we bring new modes of reading that are both more critical and more sensitive to their riches than were those of the antiheretical writers of the early church.

NOTES

1. In this chapter, I use the terms "gnosis," "gnostic," and "gnosticism" (with quotation marks) to refer to the traditional conception of a unified phenomenon, religion, or movement; I use the terms "gnosis," "gnostic" (without quotation marks), and the like to refer to the broader conceptions of experiential religious knowledge, a pattern of thought centered on such knowledge, or both.

2. See John D. Turner and Anne McGuire, eds., *The Nag Hammadi Library after Fifty Years: Proceedings of the 1995 Society of Biblical Literature Commemoration.* Nag Hammadi and Manichaean Studies (NHMS) 44 (Leiden: E. J. Brill, 1997) for essays on the discovery and the first fifty years of scholarship. On the problem of classifying the texts, see especially Louis Painchaud and A. Pasquier, eds., *Les Textes de Nag Hammadi et le Problème de leur Classification,* Bibliothèque copte de Nag Hammadi (BCNH) Section Études 3 (Quebec: University of Laval Press: Louvain-Paris: Peters). In addition, I have created a World Wide Web site with several links to Internet resources: http://www.haverford.edu/relg/mcguire/gnosisnet. html.

3. In addition to the Christian heresiologists, there exist contemporary reports in rabbinic writings and pagan sources (e.g., Plotinus, *Enneads* 2.9, "Against the Gnostics"). These supply relatively little social information about women and gender and carry interpretive problems similar to those of the heresiological sources.

4. Morton Smith, "The History of the Term Gnostikos," in *The Rediscovery of Gnosticism, Volume 2: Sethian Gnosticism,* ed. Bentley Layton (Leiden: E. J. Brill, 1980) 796–807. See also Layton, "Prolegomena to the Study of Ancient Gnosticism," in *The Social World of the First Christians: Essays in Honor of Wayne A. Meeks,* ed. L. Michael White and O. Larry Yarbrough (Minneapolis, MN: Augsburg/Fortress, 1995) 335, who proposes to make the self-designation of some as "Gnostikoi" the starting point for the category of "Gnosticism."

5. Irenaeus, *Against the Heresies* (hereafter cited as *Haer*), written around 180 CE, was

originally entitled *Refutation and Overthrow of Falsely So-Called Gnosis*. For a readable and recent English translation, see Dominic J. Unger, ed. and trans., *St. Irenaeus of Lyons, Against the Heresies. Ancient Christian Writers* 55 (New York: Paulist, 1992).

6. See esp. Michael A. Williams, *Rethinking "Gnosticism": An Argument for Dismantling a Dubious Category* (Princeton, NJ: Princeton University Press, 1996) and Karen L. King, "Is There Such a Thing as Gnosticism?" unpublished paper presented at the Annual Meeting of the Society of Biblical Literature, Washington, D.C., 1993, and in her forthcoming book, *The Origins of Gnosticism* (Princeton, NJ: Princeton University Press).

7. See esp. Karen L. King, ed., *Images of the Feminine in Gnosticism* (Philadelphia: Fortress, 1988) (hereafter, IFIG). In addition, "Diotima: Materials for the Study of Women and Gender in the Ancient World," includes many relevant resources, including a bibliography on gender and gnosticism; it is available at http://www.uky.edu/ArtsSciences/Classics/biblio/gnosticism.html.

8. Elaine H. Pagels, *The Gnostic Gospels* (New York: Random House, 1979; New York: Vintage Books, 1989) 59–60, suggests that the evidence "clearly indicates a correlation between religious theory and social practice." In gnostic communities, "women were considered equal to men; some were revered as prophets; others acted as teachers, traveling evangelists, healers, priests, perhaps even bishops." At the same time, Pagels notes, this "general observation" is "not universally applicable." In her more recent "Pursuing the Spiritual Eve: Imagery and Hermeneutics in the *Hypostasis of the Archons* and the *Gospel of Philip*," in King, IFIG 187–88, Pagels acknowledges the difficulty of moving from symbolism to sociology.

9. Frederik Wisse, "Flee Femininity: Antifeminity in Gnostic Texts and the Question of Social Milieu," in IFIG 305–6: "The meaning of femininity in the passages under discussion appears to focus on sexuality and birth. . . . The obvious link between antifemininity and gnostic literature should caution interpreters against drawing inferences concerning the role of women in gnosticism from the positive role of hypostatized female beings in the pleroma."

10. Elisabeth Schüssler Fiorenza, *In Memory of Her: A Feminist Theological Reconstruction of Christian Origins* (New York: Crossroad, 1983) 274: "Gnosticism employed the categories of 'male' and 'female' not to designate real women and men, but to name cosmic religious principles or archetypes. Salvation in the radically dualistic gnostic systems requires the annihilation and destruction of the female or the 'feminist principle.'" "In gnostic systems, the female principle is secondary, since it stands for the part of the divine that became involved in the created world and history. Gnostic dualism thus shares in the patriarchal paradigm of Western culture" (278–79).

11. Daniel L. Hoffman, *The Status of Women and Gnosticism in Irenaeus and Tertullian*. Studies in Women and Religion 36 (Lewiston, NY: Edwin Mellen, 1995) 3–4: "Gnostics for the most part neither honored femininity in theory, nor treated women equally with men in practice, based on available evidence." It is "unlikely that gnostic women acted as priests or bishops or that they enjoyed a remarkably high status in general in gnostic groups." "The presence of negative female motifs and uncertainty involved in attempting to relate female deities or accounts of prototypical women like Mary or Helena to actual gnostic communities make positive conclusions about the status of women in real gnostic groups based on this evidence very speculative" (211).

12. See esp. the work of Jorunn Jacobsen Buckley, Karen L. King, and Michael A. Williams, esp. Buckley, *Female Fault and Fulfillment* (Chapel Hill, NC: University of North Carolina Press, 1986); King, "Editor's Foreword," in King, IFIG xi–xviii; King, *Reimagining "Gnosticism;"* and Williams, "Variety in Gnostic Perspectives on Gender," in King, IFIG 2–22.

13. Williams, "Variety," notes his indebtedness on this point to Caroline Bynum, "Introduction: The Complexity of Symbols," in *Gender and Religion: On the Complexity of Symbols*, ed. Steven Harrell, Caroline Bynum, and Paula Richman (Boston: Beacon, 1986) 1–20. In addition, Ingvild Gilhus, "Gnosticism—A Study in Liminal Symbolism," *Numen* 31 (1984) 120, adapts Victor Turner's concept of liminality to explain the tension between positive roles for women and negative symbolic value attached to female nature and female sexuality. "In a liminal community—at least ideally—the sex-distinctions are wiped out and transcended. Women are admitted on the condition that their sexual natures are repressed and in this way neutralized."

14. For an illuminating discussion of the relevance of "intertextuality" and ideological analysis for the study of ancient religious texts, see Elizabeth A. Clark, "Ideology, History, and the Construction of 'Woman' in Late Ancient Christianity," *JECS* 2 (1994) 155–84, esp. 164–65, in which she cites Daniel Boyarin, *Intertextuality and the Reading of Midrash* (Bloomington, IN: Indiana University Press, 1990) and other relevant works.

15. Williams, "Variety" 21–22: "The examples provided are sufficient to demonstrate the complete inadequacy of applying only one or two unilinear gauges, such as the amount of female imagery or whether the female imagery tends to be 'positive' or 'negative.' . . . More 'positive' or 'negative' gender roles appearing in the imagery of a text may or may not directly reflect an author's notion of the proper patterns of socialization for men and women."

16. Irenaeus, *Haer* 1.23–30 illustrates well the style of heresiological summaries of "gnostic" teaching.

17. Justin, *Apology* 1.26.1–3; Irenaeus, *Haer* 1.23.2–24.4; Tertullian, *de Anima* 34; Hippolytus, *Refutatio omnium haeresium (Refutation of all Heresies)* 6.19; Epiphanius, *Panarion (Pan.)*. 21–22. Madeleine Scopello, "Jewish and Greek Heroines in the Nag Hammadi Library," in King, IFIG 89–90, notes intriguing parallels between Irenaeus' account of Helena's fate and that ascribed to the soul in The Exegesis on the Soul and Authoritative Teaching from Nag Hammadi. "Gnosticism seems to have had cultivated women in its circles. The role of *hetairai* ('courtesans') probably influenced gnostic writers, surely the first of them, Simon the Magician, in the composition of their myths. . . . Women were probably attracted too by a mythology where feminine figures played such an important role." For a contrasting position, see Hoffman, *Status* 89–92.

18. Origen, *ConCels* 5.62, in Henry Chadwick, ed., *Origen. Contra Celsum*, Translated with an Introduction and Notes by Henry Chadwick (Cambridge: Cambridge University Press, 1980; first published by Cambridge University Press, 1953) 312. In the same paragraph, Origen goes on to report that Celsus "knows also of Marcellians who follow Marcellina, and Harpocratians who follow Salome, and others who follow Mariamme, and others who follow Martha."

19. Irenaeus, *Haer* 1.25.6. Epiphanius, *Pan.* 27.6.1 and 8, writes: "I have now heard in some connection of a dupe of theirs, a Marcellina, who corrupted many people in the time of Anicetus, Bishop of Rome. . . . During Anicetus' episcopate, then, Marcellina appeared at Rome, spewing forth the corruption of Carpocrates' teaching, and destroyed many there by her corruption of them. And that made a beginning of the so-called gnostics." Marcellina appears also in Origen, *ConCels* 5.62, and Augustine, *Haer* 7.

20. Origen, *ConCels* 5.62. Chadwick cites several other references to these figures on 312 nn. 8, 9.

21. In Mark, Salome is described as one of the women who followed Jesus in Galilee and witnessed the crucifixion (15:40) and as one of the women (with Mary Magdalene and Mary, the mother of James) at the empty tomb (16:1). Mariamme may be a reference to Mary Magdalene, referred to as Mariam in the *DialSav*. In *Pistis Sophia*, Salome; Martha;

Mary, the mother of Jesus; and Mary Magdalene appear together in dialogue with Jesus. Salome also appears in *The Gospel of Thomas* (hereafter, GThom), Logion 61, and in *The Gospel according to the Egyptians*. According to Hippolytus, *Ref.* 5.7.1 and 10.9.3, "the Ophites held that their doctrines were taught to Mariamme by James the Lord's brother." Chadwick, *Contra Celsum*, adds: "Her connexion with them appears in the Acts of Philip (M. R. James, *Apocryphal N.T.* p. 446) where Philip and Mariamme go to the land of the Ophites."

22. Origen's report may indicate that the followers of Marcellina represented a distinct group, while the "Harpocratians" were divided into different strands, each following the teachings of an individual woman disciple of the first generation. The juxtaposition of female teachers, however, also suggests that Marcellina's followers claimed that she preserved teachings handed down from Salome, Mariamme, and Martha, revered women disciples of the first generation.

23. See Hippolytus, *Ref.* 7.38.2 (GCS 26.224).

24. Hippolytus, *Ref.* 6.35.5–7.

25. Epiphanius, *Pan.* 33.3–7. In *Pan.* 33.3.1, Ptolemy addresses her as "my good sister Flora."

26. For the entire account of *Haer* 1.1–8, see Unger, *St. Irenaeus* 23–45. For an abbreviated translation with detailed introduction and notes, see Bentley Layton, "Ptolemy's Version of the Gnostic Myth," in *The Gnostic Scriptures* (New York: Doubleday, 1987) 276–302. According to Irenaeus, this version of Valentinian teaching used metaphors of insemination and birth to describe the emanation of thirty divine aeons in male-female pairs or syzygies, from the initial Tetrad of "Profundity (m. Bythos) and Silence (f. Sigē), Mind (m. Nous) and Truth (f. Alētheia)."

27. Irenaeus, *Haer* 1.1.1–3.

28. There are significant variants included even in Irenaeus, *Haer* 1.1–8. See G. C. Stead, "The Valentinian Myth of Sophia," JTS 20 (1969) 75–104, for a detailed analysis of variations among the antiheretical accounts of the Sophia myth. See also George W. MacRae, "The Jewish Background of the Gnostic Sophia Myth," NovT 12 (1970) 86–101. Variant accounts of the Sophia myth also appear in several Nag Hammadi texts, including *The Apocryphon of John* and *The Hypostasis of the Archons*.

29. In other strands, it is Sophia's desire to create something alone, apart from her male consort, that brings the Demiurge and his cosmos into being.

30. Irenaeus, *Haer* 1.2.4: "For, thinking and its consequent passion were separated from her; she remained inside the fullness; but her thinking and the passion were bounded apart by the boundary, were fenced off with a palisade, and existed outside the fullness. This (thinking) was a spiritual essence, since it was a natural impulse to action on the part of an aeon. Yet it was without form and imageless because she had not comprehended anything. And—they say—for this reason it was a weak and female fruit" (in Layton, *Gnostic Scriptures* 285).

31. Irenaeus, *Haer* 1.7.1: "When all the seed has grown to maturity, Achamoth their mother will—they say—leave the place of the midpoint, enter the fullness, and receive as her bridegroom the savior, who derives from all (the aeons), so that a pair is produced consisting of the savior and Sophia who is Achamoth: they are the bridegroom and bride, and the entire fullness is the bridal chamber. And the spirituals are supposed to put off their souls; become intellectual spirits; unrestrainably and invisibly enter the fullness; and become brides of the angels that are with the savior" (in Layton, *Gnostic Scriptures* 294–95).

32. For further analysis of images of Sophia in gnostic sources, see Deidre J. Good, *Reconstructing the Tradition of Sophia* (Atlanta, GA: Scholars Press, 1987); Karen L. King, "Sophia and Christ in the *Apocryphon of John*," in King, IFIG 158–76; Williams, "Variety;" and

Buckley, *Female Fault and Fulfillment* esp. 39–48 (*The Apocryphon of John*), 61–70 (*Excerpts from Theodotus*), 116–20 (*The Gospel of Philip*), 126–36 (conclusions).

33. Irenaeus, *Haer* 1.13.2. As the women drank from the cups, Marcus invoked the presence of Charis with these words: "May that Charis who is before all things, and who transcends all knowledge and speech, fill your inner human being, and multiply in you her own knowledge, by sowing the grain of mustard seed in you as in good soil."

34. J. J. Buckley, "Libertines or Not: Fruit, Bread, Semen and Other Body Fluids in Gnosticism," *JECS* 2 (1994) 17–18, analyses the pattern in Irenaeus' report of "spiritual impregnation" and bodily seduction: "One notes the sequence: 1) Marcos' seducing the women by words, 2) the Charis/spouse as a sort of spiritual seed impregnating the woman, who, 3) gives birth to the word. The woman imitates her initiator, who in turn acts as the male spouse. Spiritual seduction precedes the bodily one."

35. Irenaeus, *Haer* 1.13.3.

36. Ibid. 1.13.5, narrates Marcus' seduction of the wife of a deacon in his own church: "This Marcus compounds philters and love-potions, in order to insult the persons of some of these women . . . A sad example of this occurred in the case of a certain Asiatic, one of our deacons, who had received him (Marcus) into his house. His wife, a woman of remarkable beauty, fell a victim both in mind and body to this magician, and, for a long time, traveled about with him. At last, when, with no small difficulty, the brethren had converted her, she spent her whole time in the exercise of public confession, weeping over and lamenting the defilement which she had received from this magician."

37. For lucid discussion of ideological and rhetorical strategies in the construction of "woman" and "heretic" in early Christian literature, see Clark, "Ideology, History, and the Construction of 'Woman,'" and Virginia Burrus, "The Heretical Woman as Symbol in Alexander, Athanasius, Epiphanius, and Jerome," *HTR* 84 (1991) 229–48.

38. In 2 Cor 11:2–3, Paul represents the members of the church, men and women alike, as "chaste virgin" brides of Christ and as vulnerable to deception, like Eve: "I feel a divine jealousy for you, for I promised you in marriage to one husband, to present you as a chaste virgin to Christ. But I am afraid that as the serpent deceived Eve by its cunning, your thoughts will be led astray from a sincere and pure devotion to Christ."

39. Irenaeus, *Haer* 4. Pref.4.

40. Tertullian of Carthage, *On Baptism* (*De Bapt*) 1.2, uses the image of the serpent to attack a female leader of the "Cainite" heresy, describing her as "a viper of the Cainite heresy, lately conversant in this quarter," who "has carried away a great number with her most venomous doctrine, making it her first aim to destroy baptism."

41. Tertullian probably wrote *On the Prescription of the Heretics* (*De Praescriptione haereticorum*, hereafter, *De Praes*) around 200 CE and certainly before his conversion to Montanism in 207. See J. Quasten, *Patrology, Volume 2* (Westminster, MD: Newman) 269–73, for further discussion.

42. Tertullian, *De Bapt* 17.5. On the figure of Thecla in *The Acts of (Paul and) Thecla*, see Sheila E. McGinn, "The Acts of Thecla," in *Searching the Scriptures, Volume 2: Feminist Commentary*, ed. Elisabeth Schüssler Fiorenza (New York: Crossroad, 1994) 800–28, esp. 803.

43. Tertullian, *De Bapt* 17.5.

44. Tertullian, *De Praes* 41.2–6: "To begin with, it is doubtful who is a catechumen, and who a believer; they have all access alike, they hear alike, they pray alike—even heathens, if any such happen to come among them. . . . All are puffed up, all offer you knowledge. Their catechumens are perfect before they are full-taught. The very women of these heretics, how wanton they are! For they are bold enough to teach, to dispute, to enact exorcisms, to undertake cures—it may be even to baptize. Their ordinations are

carelessly administered, capricious, changeable. At one time they put novices in office; at another time, men who are bound to some secular employment; at another, persons who have apostatized from us, to bind them by vainglory, since they cannot by the truth. . . . And so it comes to pass that today one man is their bishop, tomorrow another; today he is a deacon who tomorrow is a reader; today he is a presbyter who tomorrow is a layman. For even on laymen do they impose the functions of priesthood."

45. On the gradual exclusion of women from church office, see, for example, Karen Jo Torjesen, *When Women Were Priests* (San Francisco: HarperSanFrancisco, 1993).

46. For a useful discussion of the appeal of both ascetic and libertine options for women, see James E. Goehring, "Libertine or Liberated: Women in the So-Called Libertine Gnostic Communities," in King, *IFIG* esp. 329–44. For a thorough discussion of the categories of "libertine" and "ascetic" forms of "Gnosticism," see Williams, *Rethinking "Gnosticism,"* chapters 3–4. Buckley, "Libertines or Not" 15–16, adopts a similar position.

47. Clement of Alexandria, *Stromateis* (*Strom*) 3.1, reports that the Valentinians "hold that the union of man and woman is derived from the divine emanation in heaven above" and "approve of marriage."

48. Clement, *Strom* 3.5–6, attributes their view that women or wives are to be held in common to a radicalized conception of "no distinctions," as in Gal 3:28. In *Strom* 3.10, he attributes it to Epiphanes' misreading of Plato's *Republic* (457D).

49. Clement, *Strom* 3.6–10: "They gather together for feasts. . . . men and women together. After they have sated their appetites, then they overturn the lamps and so extinguish the light that the same of their adulterous 'righteousness' is hidden, and they have intercourse where they will and with whom they will. After they have practiced community of use in this love-feast, they demand by daylight of whatever women they wish that they will be obedient to the law of Carpocrates."

50. On the stereotyped charges of sexual promiscuity, cannibalism, and incest leveled against early Christians and Christian heretics, see Stephen Benko, "Pagan Criticism of Christianity during the First Two Centuries AD," in *ANRW* 2.23.2, 1054–1118, esp. 1081–89, and Robert L. Wilken, *The Christians as the Romans Saw Them* (New Haven, CT: Yale University Press, 1984) 16–21. On the methodological difficulties of interpreting the evidence with its "rhetoric of opposition," see Goehring, "Libertine or Liberated" 332–34.

51. Clement, *Strom* 3.45.

52. Clement cites the work by name in *Strom* 3.63, but there makes clear that he refers to it also at 3.45.

53. Clement, *Strom* 3.45. See also 3.63, 3.66, 3.92, and *ExcTheod* 67.

54. Clement, *Strom* 3.63.

55. Ibid. 3.92. It is not clear that this account of a dialogue between Jesus and Salome comes from the same source as that presented in *Strom* 3.45 (*The Gospel according to the Egyptians*), though it is often assumed that it does.

56. Ibid. The language of this passage is remarkably close to that of *GThom* 22, discussed in this chapter.

57. Epiphanius was Bishop of Salamis in Cyprus from 367 CE and wrote the *Panarion* ca. 375. For English translation, see Frank Williams, *The Panarion of Epiphanius of Salamis, Book I (Sects 1–46)*. NHMS 35. (Leiden: E. J. Brill, 1987).

58. Epiphanius, *Pan* 26.4.1.

59. Ibid. 26.4.3–5.

60. Ibid. 26.5.2. "But though they copulate they forbid procreation. Their eager pursuit of seduction is for enjoyment, not procreation."

61. Ibid. 26.8.1–2.

62. Buckley, "Libertines or Not" 19–20.

63. Buckley, "Libertines or Not" 18, argues that the internal logic of the practice rests on a mythic account of the divine Barbelo's seduction of the Archons to make them release captured light: "Their sacramental theology emphasizes the female blood and the male semen, the two components of Christ's body, to be naturally produced in the Phibionites' own bodies. . . . Direct products of the human body, semen and blood express and recreate the believers' affinity with Christ."

64. Clement of Alexandria, for example, preserves the most important fragments of Valentinus, as well as the Valentinian "Excerpts of Theodotus." See Layton, *Gnostic Scriptures* 229–49, for the fragments of Valentinus; see Robert P. Casey, *The Excerpta ex Theodoto of Clement of Alexandria* (London: Christophers, 1934) for English translation of the ExcTheod, and Werner Förster, *Gnosis: A Selection of Gnostic Texts, Volume 1*, ed. R. McL. Wilson (Oxford: Oxford University Press, 1972) 222–33 for a portion of ExcTheod.

65. James M. Robinson, ed. *The Nag Hammadi Library in English*, 3rd rev. ed. (San Francisco: HarperSanFrancisco, 1988) (hereafter NHLE). For critical editions and commentaries, see especially the volumes published in the Nag Hammadi and Manichaean Studies series (NHMS) published by E. J. Brill. Other important codices include the Berlin Codex (BG 8502). For anthologies of various primary sources, see, for example, Layton, *The Gnostic Scriptures*; Förster, *Gnosis*, 2 vols.; and for a selection of texts on gnostic images of "the Feminine Divine," see Ross S. Kraemer, ed., *Maenads, Martyrs, Matrons, Monastics: A Sourcebook on Women's Religions in the Greco-Roman World* (Philadelphia: Fortress, 1988) esp. 371–92.

66. An English translation appears in Kurt Rudolph, *Gnosis: The Nature and History of Gnosticism* (San Francisco: Harper and Row, 1983) 212, and in Giovanni Filoramo, *A History of Gnosticism*, trans. Anthony Alcock (Oxford: Basil Blackwell, 1990) 176. The full text can be found in A. Ferrua, "Questioni di Epigrafia Eretica Romana," *Rivista di archeologia cristiana* 21 (1944–45) 185–86. See also Gilles Quispel, "L'Inscription de Flavia Sophē," in *Gnostic Studies, Vol. 1* (Istanbul: Netherlands Historical and Archaeological Institute in the Near East, 1974) 58 ff. and M. Guarducci, "Valentiniani a Roma," *Deutsches Archäologisches Institut. Römische Abteilung. Mitteilungen* 80 (1973) 169–86, plates 47–52.

67. HypArch 86.25–27: "[I have] sent (you) this because you inquire about the reality [of the] authorities." For full English translations, see Bentley Layton, "The Reality of the Rulers," in Robinson, NHLE 161–69, and also Layton, *Gnostic Scriptures* 65–76. Consistent with conventions for citing texts from Nag Hammadi, material in square brackets indicates a lacuna in the ancient manuscript. Material in parenthesis has been supplied either by me or by the modern editors to clarify interpretive matters. Unless otherwise noted, translations of Nag Hammadi texts are my own.

68. See Nils A. Dahl, "The Arrogant Archon and the Lewd Sophia: Jewish Tradition in Gnostic Revolt," in Layton, *The Rediscovery of Gnosticism* 689–712, for further analysis of the vain claim of the chief Ruler and its allusions to Isaiah 45:2 and 46:9.

69. HypArch 93.32–94.2: "But I (Norea) said: 'Lord, teach me about the power of these authorities—how did they come into being and from what reality (*hypostasis*) and of what matter, and who created them and their power?'" Norea's question recalls the question of the unnamed recipient ("you have inquired about the reality (*hypostasis*) of the Rulers") and thus sets up a parallel between the narrator-reader relation and the Eleleth-Norea relation. This parallel implicitly links the role of the narrator to that of Eleleth as it connects the text's reader to the implied recipient and to Norea herself.

70. HypArch 94.2–19.

71. Ibid. 96.11–15: "It was by the will of the Father of the entirety that they all come into being." For similar assurances from the narrator, see 87.20–23 and 88.10–11.

72. On ancient reproductive theory, see, for example, Richard Smith, "Sex Education in Gnostic Schools," in King, IFIG 345–60.

73. G. MacRae, "The Jewish Background," argues that the Sophia myth is directly related to the story of Eve in Gen 2–3.

74. HypArch 94.19–33.

75. Ibid. 94.34–95.4.

76. Ibid. 95.4–12.

77. For further analysis, see Francis Fallon, *The Enthronement of Sabaoth: Jewish Elements in Gnostic Creations Myths*, NHMS 10 (Leiden: E. J. Brill, 1978).

78. HypArch 96.3–16.

79. Ibid. 96.19–26.

80. Ibid. 96.27–97.20.

81. Ibid. 87.11–91.10.

82. 1 Cor 2:14–16: that which is of *psyche*/soul (*psychikos*) cannot grasp the things of the spirit (*ta pneumatika*).

83. HypArch 89.17–27.

84. Karen L. King, "The Book of Norea, Daughter of Eve," in Schüssler Fiorenza, *Searching the Scriptures* 70.

85. Ibid.

86. Ibid.

87. HypArch 92.18–93.2.

88. King, "Book of Norea" 70–71.

89. Anne McGuire, "Virginity and Subversion: Norea against the Powers in the Hypostasis of the Archons," in King, IFIG 239–58.

90. See, for example, M. Williams, "Deterministic Elitism? or Inclusive Theories of Conversion?" in Williams, *Rethinking "Gnosticism"* 191–212; and Anne McGuire, "Conversion and Gnosis in the Gospel of Truth," *NovT* 28 (1986) 338–55. In the majority of "gnostic" texts, even those with apparently deterministic worldviews, persons without gnosis may well be considered capable of transformation and redemption.

91. *The Gospel of Mary* (hereafter GMary), trans. K. L. King; Robert J. Miller, ed., *The Complete Gospels: Annotated Scholars Version*, 3rd edn. (San Francisco: HarperSanFrancisco, 1994) 357–66; see also "The Gospel of Mary," in Douglas M. Parrott, ed., NHLE, trans. G. W. MacRae and R. McL. Wilson, 523–27.

92. W. W. Isenberg, trans., "The Gospel of Philip" (hereafter GPhil) 63.34–64.9 and 59.6–11; and Layton, *Gnostic Scriptures* 325–53.

93. S. Emmel, trans. "The Dialogue of the Savior" (hereafter DialSav) 139.8–13, 140.14–19, 144.16–21, in Robinson, NHLE 244–255.

94. *The First Apocalypse of James* (hereafter 1ApocJas) (V,3) 40.25–26: "The Lord said, 'James, I praise you . . . Cast away from yourself all lawlessness. And beware lest they envy you. When you speak these words of this perception, encourage these four: Salome and Mariam and Martha and Arsinoe.'" The names of Salome and Mary also appear in GThom, but not in the same logia.

95. Antti Marjanen, "Mary Magdalene in the Dialogue of the Savior," in *AAR/SBL Abstracts 1996* (Atlanta, GA: Scholars Press, 1996) 266. For a fuller treatment, see Marjanen, *The Woman Jesus Loved: Mary Magdalene in the Nag Hammadi Library and Related Documents*. NHMS 40 (Leiden: E. J. Brill, 1996). I am grateful to the author for sharing with me the manuscript of his Ph.D. dissertation of the same title (University of Helsinki, 1995) before publication.

96. K. L. King, "The Gospel of Mary," in Miller, *The Complete Gospels* 357–58.

97. GMary 10.9–16.

98. Ibid. 8.7–10. Karen L. King, "The Gospel of Mary Magdalene," in Schüssler Fiorenza, *Searching the Scriptures* 610, views their weeping as indicative of their failure to attain the kind of inward peace Mary has attained.

99. GMary 9.15–20. For further discussion of the nongendered significance of *anthrōpoi*, see K. L. King, "Prophetic Power and Women's Authority: The Case of the Gospel of Mary (Magdalen)," in *Women Preachers and Prophets Through Two Millennia of Christianity*, ed. Beverly Mayne Kienzle and Pamela J. Walker (Berkeley, CA: University of California Press) 21–41. I am grateful to the author for sharing the manuscript with me before publication.

100. King, "The Gospel of Mary Magdalene" 610. I am also indebted in this section to M. Greenblatt, "Mary Magdalen: Gnostic Icon of Salvation," and K. Cuffari, "Confrontation of Cosmic and Social Systems of Authority: The Female Character as Textual Tool," unpublished term papers, Religion 222 (Gnosticism), Haverford College, Haverford, PA, December 1996. Citing King, "Prophetic Power," Greenblatt writes: "Differences in gender and sexualities belong to the external, material world Christ warned the disciples against. Gender is of little significance since it exists solely on material bodies that will cease to exist" (5).

101. GMary 6.1–5.

102. King, "Gospel of Mary" 358.

103. GMary 10.3–6.

104. King, "The Gospel of Mary Magdalene" 616.

105. King, "Gospel of Mary" 358.

106. GPhil 59.6–11, my own translation. Contrast with W. W. Isenberg, trans., "The Gospel according to Philip," in *Nag Hammadi Codices* II,2–7, ed. B. Layton (Leiden: E. J. Brill, 1989) 159: "His sister and his mother and his companion were each a Mary."

107. GPhil 63.34–64.9.

108. Ibid. 58.30–59.6.

109. See Patricia Cox Miller, "In Praise of Nonsense," in *Classical Mediterranean Spirituality*, ed. A. H. Armstrong (New York: Crossroad, 1986) 481–505, for an insightful study of theories of language and divine speech in late antiquity.

110. GPhil 63.37–64.10.

111. Elaine Pagels, "Adam and Eve, Christ and the Church: A Survey of Second Century Controversies Concerning Marriage," in *New Testament and Gnosis*, ed. A. Logan and A. Wedderbrun (Edinburgh: T&T Clark, 1983) 146–75; and Pagels, "The 'Mystery of Marriage' in the *Gospel of Philip* Revisited," in *The Future of Early Christianity: Essays in Honor of Helmut Koester*, ed. Birger A. Pearson (Minneapolis, MN: Fortress, 1991) 442–54.

112. GPhil 70.9–17. See also GPhil 68.22–26: "When Eve was still in Adam death did not exist. When she was separated from him death came into being. If he enters again and attains his former self, death will be no more."

113. Their companionship may also parallel the union of Light with Holy Spirit and of angels with images. GPhil 58.10–14: "He said on that day in the thanksgiving, 'You who have joined (*hotr*) the perfect Light with the Holy Spirit, unite the angels also with us, as images.'"

114. "Bridal chamber" appears as a central symbol throughout GPhil; in GPhil 65.11–12, it is modified by *eikonikos* (iconic, imaged, or mirrored), the adjective formed from the Greek noun *eikōn* (image).

115. DialSav 139.8–13.

116. Ibid. 140.14–19.

117. Ibid. 144.16–21.

118. Marjanen, *The Woman Jesus Loved* 64–79, here 79.

119. This includes passages from *1ApocJas*, *Zostrianos*, and *The Book of Thomas the Contender*, all of which are analyzed by Marjanen, *The Woman Jesus Loved*, 76–79, and by Wisse, "Flee Femininity." Rather than assuming that all of these texts use the category of "femaleness" in the same way, it is crucial to examine the significance and social implications of femaleness within each context separately. See also the passage from *The Gospel of the Egyptians* quoted by Clement of Alexandria, *Strom* 3.45 and 3.63, and discussed in this chapter.

120. Marjanen, *The Woman Jesus Loved* 76–77.

121. Gilhus, "Gnosticism—A Study in Liminal Symbolism" 111, links femaleness to bodily symbolism in "gnostic religion" generally: "Gnostic religion implements bodily symbolism of a special kind. It uses symbolism which connects a negative evaluation of the female physiological processes to a negative evaluation of theology, cosmology, society, and material existence. This symbolism concentrates on the female reproductive organs and their discharges—children."

122. See esp. Wisse, "Flee Femininity," for the interpretation that antifemininity is linked to a negative attitude toward women and to the social milieu of asceticism.

123. For English translations, see "The Gospel of Thomas" (II,2) (GThom), trans. T. O. Lambdin, in Robinson, NHLE 124–38; Marvin Meyer, ed. and trans., *The Gospel of Thomas: The Hidden Sayings of Jesus* (San Francisco: HarperSanFrancisco, 1992); Layton, *The Gnostic Scriptures* 376–99. Most scholars date the original Greek version (of which we have three papyrus fragments from Oxyrhyncus) to the period between 100 and 180 CE, though some date it as early as the canonical gospels, i.e., between 70 and 100 CE. This gospel's place of origin cannot be known for certain, but many believe it reflects the cultural environment of Edessa, Syria.

124. See, for example, J. Kloppenborg, M. Meyer, S. J. Patterson, M. G. Steinhauser, *The Q-Thomas Reader* (Sonoma, CA: Polebridge, 1990). For the large and growing bibliography on the relation of GThom and Q, see esp. Ron Cameron, "The Gospel of Thomas: A Forschungsbericht and Analysis," in *ANRW* 2.25.6, 4195–4251, and more recent entries in the annual supplements of "Nag Hammadi Bibliography," *NovT*, edited by D. Scholer.

125. Among the most interesting contributions to the debate are those contributed by M. Meyer, J. Buckley, E. Castelli, and A. DeConick.

126. The opening words of the gospel claim that finding the secret meaning of Jesus' words brings salvation: "These are the hidden sayings that the Living Jesus spoke and Didymos Judas Thomas wrote down. And he said: 'Whoever finds the interpretation (*hermeneia*) of these sayings will not experience death.'"

127. On light imagery in GThom, see esp. April DeConick, *Seek to See Him: Ascent and Vision Mysticism in the Gospel of Thomas* (Leiden: E. J. Brill, 1996).

128. See esp. Mark 8–10.

129. GThom 114. I deliberately translate the same Coptic word, *shime* or *shiome*, as "woman" in the words attributed to Peter and as "female" or "woman" in the words attributed to Jesus. While Peter clearly uses the term in the literal sense, there is ambiguity in Jesus' use of both *shime* and *hooyt*. When Jesus addresses the other disciples as "you males/men," the term carries both literal and symbolic senses.

130. Meyer, *The Gospel of Thomas*.

131. Attempts to harmonize the two sayings may too hastily ignore these tensions and seek to "make the two one."

132. Jorunn Jacobsen Buckley, "An Interpretation of Logion 114 in the Gospel of Thomas," *NovT* 27 (1985) 245–72, argues that women need an extra initiation ritual to

bring them to the intermediary state of "maleness" that men occupy by reason of their sex. In her view, both men and women-become-males must then make the final transition to the status of "living spirits."

133. Marvin Meyer, "Making Mary Male: The Categories of 'Male' and 'Female' in the Gospel of Thomas," NTS 31 (1985) 554–70.

134. E. Castelli, "'I Will Make Mary Male': Pieties of the Body and Gender Transformation of Christian Women in Late Antiquity," in Body Guards: The Cultural Politics of Gender Ambiguity, ed. Julia Epstein and Kristina Staub (London: Routledge, 1991) 29–49.

135. Philo of Alexandria, Questions and Answers in Genesis II:49 (cited by Castelli, p. 32).

136. Philo, Questions and Answers in Exodus I:8, cited by Castelli, p. 32.

137. Castelli, "'I Will Make Mary Male'" 33; GThom 114 reinscribes "the traditional gender hierarchies of male over female, masculine over feminine," even as it opens the religious community to women and "reveals the tenuousness and malleability of the naturalized categories of male and female." In this way, "the double insistence . . . that Mary should remain among the disciples at the same time as she must be made male— points to the paradoxical ideological conditions that helped to shape the lives of early Christian women."

138. In the view of Williams, "Variety" 19–20, interpretation of this passage has too hastily treated the exchange as sheerly allegorical in intent, as if it were an allusion to the transformation of the femaleness of any human, man or woman, into maleness. "The logion simply does not say that there is something female about every human which must be transformed into male . . . Log. 114 suggests that proper socialization involved asymmetrical requirements for men and women." Williams cites P. Perkins, "Pronouncement Stories in the Gospel of Thomas," Semeia 20 (1981) 130 who suggests that this saying may represent a community rule that "justifies the inclusion of women in the community against orthodox slander that these so-called ascetics were really sexual libertines." Even so, Williams points out, the saying would still be calling attention to females as the sex for which special comment is required.

139. So esp. Stephen Davies, The Gospel of Thomas and Christian Wisdom (New York: Seabury, 1983) and A. DeConick, Seek to See Him.

140. Logia 111 and 59 contrast the realms of Death and Life and suggest that one who lives from or looks to the Living One will not see death and becomes superior to the world.

141. Logion 29, for example, illustrates the opposition between Flesh and Spirit as Jesus declares his amazement that the great wealth of Spirit has come to dwell in the poverty of the body.

142. Logia 24 and 61 show that the dualism of Light and Darkness corresponds to two types of people: those who are "undivided," having made the two one, are filled with Light and shine upon the Cosmos; those, on the other hand, who exist in duality are dominated by darkness.

143. Some logia, however, represent either or both poles in images of female or male. A number of sayings, for example, symbolize the positively valued pole as male and the negatively valued pole as female. In Logion 15, for example, Jesus says: "When you see one who was not born of woman, fall on your faces and worship. That is your Father." But there are also a number of sayings that associate the category of male with the negative pole or female with the positive pole of the Spirit.

144. Matt 10:37–38, Luke 14:26–27, and GThom 55: "Whoever does not hate his father and his mother cannot be a disciple to me."

145. Davies, The Gospel of Thomas 119: The imagery of becoming "little children" "is also part of a general Adamic typology, for the little child, the baptized person, was

thought to be as innocent and sinless as Adam and Eve were before the fall." Such innocence has not to do only with sexuality, but also with ignorance of the distinction between good and evil.

146. Harold Bloom, "'Whoever Discovers the Interpretation of These Sayings . . . ':
A Reading," in Meyer, *The Gospel of Thomas* 121, appropriates a trope from W. B. Yeats to
describe this pre-Adamic self and conclude his reading of GThom: "Like William Blake,
like Jakob Böhme, this Jesus is looking for the face he had before the world was made."

147. As with traditional Christian representations of God as literally neither male nor
female, yet most frequently addressed as "Father," so the primordial Human of GThom
114 is not literally male, but is symbolically of the male gender. This human being, a
restoration of the primordial Human Being, is neither male nor female in a literal sense,
but is male in a figurative sense.

148. *Thunder, Perfect Mind* (VI,2) (hereafter *Thund*), trans. G. W. MacRae, in Robinson,
NHLE 295–303, and Layton, *Gnostic Scriptures* 77–85, survives only in the Coptic version
found at Nag Hammadi. The author, date, and place of composition are unknown, but
Thund was probably composed in Greek well before 350 CE, the approximate date of the
Coptic manuscript.

149. For a more detailed version of my reading of the text, see Anne McGuire,
"Thunder, Perfect Mind (NHC VI,2)," in *Reader's Guide to the Nag Hammadi Library*, ed. Karen
L. King and Charles Hedrick (Sonoma, CA: Polebridge, forthcoming), and also McGuire,
"Thunder, Perfect Mind," in Schüssler Fiorenza, *Searching the Scriptures* 39–54. For further
research, see the excellent edition, translation, and commentary by Paul-Hubert Poirier,
Le Tonnerre, Intellect Parfait (NH VI,2), (Quebec: University of Laval Press; Louvain: Peeters,
1996). In addition, see my translation and notes to the text at the Diotima web site:
http://www.uky.edu/ArtsSciences/Classics/thunder.html.

150. For a powerful contemporary use of much of this passage in the work of an
African American filmmaker, see the opening scene of Julie Dash, *Daughters of the Dust*,
American Playhouse Theatrical Films in association with WMG, New York: Kino Video,
1992.

151. *Thund*, 16.9–11.

152. Ibid. 20.26–35.

153. Toni Morrison chose a quotation from this section as the epigraph to her novel
Jazz (New York: Knopf, 1992).

154. *Thund*, 21.13–20.

155. Ibid. 21.20–32.

13

WOMEN, MINISTRY, AND CHURCH
ORDER IN EARLY CHRISTIANITY

Francine Cardman

Recognized by Paul as "coworkers,"[1] women were apostles, missionaries, and leaders of house-churches in the early decades after the death and resurrection of Jesus. But as Christianity made its way through the Greco-Roman world, women's leadership and ministry were increasingly pushed to the margins of evolving church structures. The process of institutionalization of the churches was already under way by the end of the first century CE; by the end of the fourth, it was essentially complete. As Christian churches assumed their place among the social, political, and religious institutions of late antiquity, they began to take on the values of their culture, particularly in regard to gender roles and the ordering of family and society. Although excluded from the established structures of ministry by the beginning of the fifth century, women continued to exercise some forms of leadership in the churches and to engage from time to time in ministries forbidden to them. As a result, bishops and councils continued to issue protests and formal prohibitions of women's ministries well into the sixth century and beyond.

The history of women's leadership in the early Christian missionary movement and within local church communities, especially those with a strong charismatic element, has been carefully documented and vigorously debated by feminist scholars over the past two decades.[2] Interpretive differences about the sources and significance of women's leadership remain. Was the Christian message fundamentally egalitarian and antipatriarchal, so that the communities were discipleships of equals, or did they maintain social and sexual inequities? Did women exercise forms of religious leadership new to the ancient world, or did they simply function as patrons in a recognizably Greco-Roman mode? Was women's acceptance of chastity a source of autonomy, or did it ultimately reinforce gender hierarchy? Despite such debate, scholars generally agree that women played a more publicly prominent role in the earliest Christian communities than they did in later centuries. Accounting for this disparity does not require theories of a fall from an original state of ministerial equality between women and men, but it does demand analysis of the arguments and an unmasking of the issues of power in the process by which women were excluded from public leadership and restricted in their ministries in early Christianity.

By examining significant texts from the first five centuries and considering evidence from the earliest Christian art and inscriptions, it is possible to trace the forces that marginalized women's leadership and ministry in the early churches. Three kinds of texts are relevant to this study: (1) first- and second-century texts that claim the authority of Paul (the Pastoral Epistles and the *Acts of (Paul and) Thecla*); (2) third- and fourth-century church orders that claim the authority of the twelve or of the apostles in general (the *Apostolic Tradition* of Hippolytus, the Syriac *Didascalia*, and the *Apostolic Constitutions*); (3) fourth- and fifth-century decisions of church councils and a letter of Pope Gelasius I. These works originate in a context of conflicting and changing claims to leadership and authority in the Christian communities, issues that led in time to the institutionalization of ministry. Inscriptions and some early Christian art add to the complexity of the picture and raise questions about the continuation of women's ministry in some parts of the church later in this period. Taken together, these sources allow us to delineate the process by which women were excluded from the official structures of ministry during the first five centuries CE.

The *Acts of (Paul and) Thecla*

The story of Thecla in the extracanonical *Acts of Thecla*[3] offers a window to the world of early Christian women (see chapters 11 and 14).[4] Throughout this riveting narrative of conflict and conviction, Thecla acts compellingly on her own behalf, defending her chastity, enduring torture, and defying authority, so that the Roman governors who had condemned her finally marvel at her power, and Paul himself is astonished at her survival. By baptizing herself, she becomes the spiritual equal of Paul; by instructing and presumably baptizing Tryphaena and her female servants who had sheltered her in Antioch, Thecla establishes herself as a missionary preacher independent of Paul's subsequent commission to "go and teach the word of God" (41). Holding to her belief in "continence and the resurrection" (1), Thecla resists the social and political powers of her day and overcomes Paul's objections to her ministry. Her story casts light on the ambiguities of women's exercise of authority in the early Christian communities.

Thecla's figure loomed large in the imagination of Christians, particularly in Asia Minor, where the drama occurred, and perhaps especially among women.[5] Like Thecla, other Christian women in this era experienced chastity as a source of power and agency, as well as of fear and danger. In his *Second Apology*, for instance, Justin Martyr reports that a man denounced his Christian wife to the

Roman authorities when she sought to divorce him for his sexual and other excesses.[6] Women martyrs, especially virgins, were regularly threatened with sexual assault and abuse by the Roman officials who interrogated and condemned them.[7] Yet, even with its dangers, chastity offered a way for Thecla and other early Christian women to assert some measure of autonomy and to distance themselves from male control, if only for a time.

It is likely that Thecla represents not one historical woman, but many women of the first and early second centuries who publicly preached and baptized, claiming the authority of Paul for their ministries. Toward the end of the second century, Tertullian protested against one such unnamed woman, who had assumed the right to teach and then asserted the right to baptize as well. In his treatise On Baptism, he rejects her claims and denounces "certain Acts of Paul . . . [that] claim the example of Thecla for allowing women to teach and baptize."[8] Quoting 1 Cor 14:35, "Let them keep silence and ask their husbands at home," Tertullian asks incredulously: "How could we believe that Paul should give a female power to teach and to baptize, when he did not allow a woman even to learn by her own right?" Tertullian's argument suggests that the continuing memory of Thecla challenged the developing structures of ministry in the churches. It is not difficult to imagine women telling and retelling the story of Thecla to authorize their own ministries: Thecla's bold act of self-baptism was warrant for their ministry of baptism, her preaching license for theirs. The heady mix of imagination, desire, and power in the Acts of Thecla could reassert itself in every telling of the story, empowering women to follow Thecla's example.

For the original storytellers and their audiences, Thecla was a compelling figure, clothed with power from God, zealous to preach the word, a formidable adversary, and an influential teacher. But as Tertullian's reaction demonstrates, this depiction of Thecla could also evoke powerful disapproval. Like all representations, especially heroic ones, the image of Thecla is susceptible to manipulation by its interpreters. Once valorized and cut loose from its original context, the image can be transformed to serve new interests. This is precisely what happens to the figure of Thecla. Despite the narrative's focus on her miraculous deliverance from death, successive generations of Christians commemorated her as a martyr; they honored her as a virgin, although the Acts of Thecla portray her as a preacher and teacher. Thus reduced to more familiar proportions, the transformed image of Thecla furthered the exclusion of women from ministry by erasing the memory of her as a woman who had preached and baptized.

The Pastoral Epistles

Appearing at about the same time and in the same context as the Acts of Thecla, the Pastoral Epistles (1 Timothy, 2 Timothy, and Titus) address many of the same issues as the Acts of Thecla. In effect, the Pastoral Epistles represent the other side of Thecla's story.[9] Written in the name of Paul, the letters seek to secure order in the churches to which Timothy and Titus belong and to guard "sound" teaching by limiting the influence of women, discrediting false teachers, curtailing claims to charismatic authority, and establishing a formal structure of ministry.[10] In their articulation of the requirements of pastoral office, the letters promote the authority of duly appointed leaders and set the terms for much of the later debate about women's ministry in early Christianity.

The Pastoral Epistles model the churches' ministries on the patriarchal order of the Roman household, expanding the household codes of Ephesians and Colossians and applying them to the "household of God" (1 Tim 3:15).[11] The terminology and structure of office in the letters is somewhat fluid: the writer refers to bishops and deacons (1 Timothy) and to bishops and elders (Titus). Although it is not possible to make precise distinctions among these offices, many scholars suggest that the bishop (*episkopos*, overseer) may have been chosen from among the elders (*presbyteroi*, later translated as priests), who perhaps functioned as a supervisory council, with the deacons (*diakonoi*, servants or ministers) acting as their agents.[12] The Pastoral Epistles dictate the necessary qualifications for each office: bishop (1 Tim 3:1–7; Tit 1:7–9); deacons (1 Tim 3:8–13); elders or presbyters (Tit 1:5–6; cf. the passing reference to "elders who rule well" in 1 Tim 5:17). The most important requirements are that a man be "the husband of one wife" (i.e., not remarried after the death of his wife) and that he manage his household well, particularly his children. All the recognized offices seem to be filled by men.

This may not be the case in regard to the elders. Although Titus 1:5–6 describes the elder as the husband of one wife, 1 Tim 5:17 does not specify gender when it speaks of the "double honor" due to the "elders who rule well." The lack of gender specifiers in this verse allows the possibility of female elders at the time of the Pastorals, but the letter writer may have tried to obscure them in the text.[13] If women were elders, they could not have escaped the effects of the restrictive household codes or of the writer's efforts to silence women (1 Tim 2:11–13).[14] They would have been early casualties of the Pastoral Epistles' campaign against false teachers (see chapters 11 and 14).

There may also have been women deacons in this period. At the end of his letter to the Romans, Paul sends greetings to various coworkers and urges his readers to support the work of Phoebe, whom he identifies as a deacon: "I commend to you our sister Phoebe, deacon [*diakonos*] of the church at Cenchreae . . . " (Rom 16:1).[15] Women deacons may be alluded to in 1 Timothy, though this is far from certain. An injunction to women appears among the requirements for male deacons: "Women likewise must be serious, no slanderers, but temperate, faithful in all things" (3:11). The directive interrupts the flow of the paragraph, and the next verse returns to the subject of male deacons. It is commonly assumed that the wives of deacons are meant here, although some scholars argue that the reference is to women in general, while others consider them to be deacons or holders of some sort of office.[16] Brief references in 1 Tim 3:11 and Rom 16:1 offer an intriguing glimpse of the role of women leaders in the Pauline churches and suggest that women's ministries may have been rendered invisible, or even eliminated, in the churches of the Pastoral Epistles.

When the distinct office of deaconess emerged toward the end of the third century, it offered women considerably less opportunity for leadership than Phoebe had in the first.

Widows are the only women about whom the Pastorals speak at any length. Their origins as a distinct group in the churches are obscure, but the complaint about neglect of the "Hellenist widows" in Acts 6:1–6 suggests that widows were recognized as deserving of the churches' support from the beginnings of the Christian movement.[17] References to widows in the letters of Ignatius of Antioch (died ca. 112) and Polycarp of Smyrna (died ca. 155) suggest that the group identified as "the widows" evolved from women supported by the churches after their husbands' deaths to women distinguished by their pledge of celibacy. The circle of widows would then have included young women as well as old, virgins as well as once-married women.[18]

By the time of the Pastoral Epistles, the widows had become the object of "apostolic" efforts to limit their numbers and influence. 1 Timothy 5:3–16 issues directives about the character, conduct, and responsibilities of women who are enrolled as widows. These regulations address two pressing issues: the number of widows relying on the church's financial support and the disruptive behavior of younger widows.[19] Only widows who are without other family to support them are to be maintained by the church. To be enrolled among the widows, a woman must be not less than sixty years old, married only once, and "well attested for her good deeds, as one who has brought up children, shown hospitality, washed the feet of the saints, relieved the afflicted, and devoted herself to doing good in every way" (5:10). In return for the community's economic support, widows are to remain celibate and engage in a ministry of prayer: "The real widow, left alone, has set her hope on God and continues in supplication night and day" (5:5).

In a dialectic that will resound through the centuries, the author of 1 Timothy draws a sharp distinction between "real widows" and those who are not truly widows. "False" widows are to be found especially among the younger women, who do not meet the age requirement and could be supported instead by their families or by marrying again. Once wrongly enrolled as widows, however, these young women are led astray by their "sensual desires" and want to marry again (5:11). They also "learn to be idlers, gadding about from house to house, and not only idlers but gossips and busybodies, saying what they should not" (5:13). Perhaps, in addition to gossiping, the false widows are guilty of spreading the false teachings opposed by the Pastorals. The charge of "gadding about" may not simply be an attack on the frivolity of false widows, but rather a negative depiction of widows making pastoral visits.[20] To prevent any problems, the letter writer wants younger widows to "marry, bear children, and manage their households" (5:14).[21]

The Pastorals tend to transmute charisms into duties. Women recognized as widows may therefore originally have been charismatic individuals with the gift of prophecy, as well as of prayer.[22] Released from the obligations of marriage, widows made their prophetic gifts more fully available to the community, which reciprocated with material support. Prophecy could become a source of discord,

however, whenever it conflicted with other voices of authority in the community. So, too, could the relative freedom of the widows. As recipients of the
community's charity, widows were expected to be obedient to its leaders. Yet,
conflicts between widows and male officeholders are implicit in 1 Tim 5:3–16
and probably also in 1 Tim 2:11–13. Despite attempts to limit their influence,
the widows remained a difficult group to control, which prompted renewed
efforts to restrain them in the third and fourth centuries.

Between the time of the Pastorals and the end of the second century, the
rapidly evolving Christian movement began to develop a more complex infra-
structure to meet the needs of expansion and to establish authoritative teachers.
Early in the century, Ignatius of Antioch championed the authority of the
bishop, presbyters, and deacons, comparing them to God the Father, the apostles, and Jesus Christ, respectively.[23] Irenaeus, bishop of Lyon (ca. 180), argued
in *Against Heresies* that bishops are the successors of the apostles and that, unlike
gnostic teachers, they hand on the apostolic tradition in the churches.[24] By the
end of the century, leadership in many of the churches had coalesced around
the "apostolic" offices of bishop, presbyter, and deacon. Bishops and their male
clergy became increasingly powerful in this structure, overshadowing the ministries of women and pushing them to the periphery of Christian communities.
The authority of the apostles soon surpassed the memory of Thecla as a means
of legitimating ministry.

The *Apostolic Tradition* of Hippolytus

The Pastoral Epistles and the *Didache*, a text from approximately the same period,
are often considered prototypes of early Christian writings known as church
orders.[25] Written or compiled for the most part in the third and fourth centuries,
church orders appealed to the authority of the apostles, particularly the Twelve,
rather than to Paul, whose memory both the Pastorals and the *Acts of Thecla*
evoked. They constitute a peculiar genre that liturgical scholar Paul Bradshaw
terms "living literature," texts that change in form and content as they are transmitted, copied, and incorporated into later documents.[26] Church orders are not
simply descriptive texts, but often are prescriptive, meant to establish new practices or shore up declining ones rather than to report on existing customs and
discipline. Conversely, prohibitions of particular practices may attest to their existence rather than to the success of church orders in outlawing them. Texts of
this sort cannot be taken at face value, but require critical reading and an eye
for the reality behind the dictum.

Early in the third century, the Roman presbyter Hippolytus produced the
Apostolic Tradition, a church order that claims to present "the Tradition which is
[proper for] the churches" (i.2).[27] He compiled the text at a time of factional
disputes about trinitarian theology and penitential discipline in the Roman
church, conflicts in which he figured prominently.[28] By producing the treatise,
Hippolytus also entered into controversy about liturgical practice. His declared
purpose was to ensure that believers "may hold fast to that tradition which has

continued until now" and avoid the error of recent inventions (i.3). Claiming to hold the true tradition in the face of innovation, Hippolytus could as easily be attempting to justify a new practice as defending an old one. In his case, extravagant invention can be ruled out for the practical reason that it would not readily be believed by his audience. But that is not to say that the *Apostolic Tradition* is an accurate description of the practice of the Roman church in his day.

In its present form, the *Apostolic Tradition* consists of three parts that address matters relating to the clergy, the laity, and to everyday Christian life. Part I concerns the selection, ordination, and duties of the clergy. It includes ordination prayers for each office and preserves an early eucharistic prayer and a description of the liturgy. The attention given to the ranking and responsibilities of the clergy in this section suggests that status and power were points of contention in the Roman church at that time. Conflict between Hippolytus the presbyter and Callistus the archdeacon may account for the emphatic subordination of deacons to presbyters in the *Apostolic Tradition* (viii–ix).[29]

Most importantly, the treatise seeks to establish a hierarchical distinction between those offices that require ordination (*cheirotonein*, to lay on hands) and those that may be filled by appointment (*kathistasthai*). Ordination is conferred by the laying on of hands by the bishop and by prayer invoking the Holy Spirit. Appointment is made through some public act of selection and recognition (e.g., the bishop hands the book to one who is appointed as reader). Bishops, presbyters, and deacons are ordained by laying on of hands; all others are appointed to their positions. The interesting exceptions to this rule are the confessors, who suffered imprisonment for their faith during a time of persecution, but were not martyred. If chosen to become deacons or presbyters, they do not require ordination because their confession of faith is considered sufficient to have elevated them to the presbyterate without laying on of hands; should a confessor be elected bishop, however, he is ordained to that office (x).

In this articulation of ministerial order, the prerogatives of maleness and ordination marginalize women and reduce their opportunities for community leadership. Two groups of women, however, remain visible and require Hippolytus' attention. Set apart from other women in the church, virgins and widows are anomalies in the structure of ministry put forward in the *Apostolic Tradition*. They are considered with the clergy in Part I of the treatise because of their distinction from other members of the church, but their roles are not defined, and the differences between them unremarked. Only in Part III, in a chapter on fasting, are their responsibilities noted: "Widows and virgins shall fast often and pray on behalf of the church" (xxv.1). These are not distinct duties, however, for prayer and fasting are also responsibilities of the clergy and the laity. If virgins and widows exercised any other specific ministries at that time, Hippolytus makes no mention of them. Rather, his aim is to establish the fact that these women are not ordained to their positions as widows or virgins.

Widows are appointed but not ordained: "When a widow is appointed (*kathistasthai*) she is not ordained (*cheirotonein*) but she shall be chosen by name" (xi.1). Women who have long been widows may be appointed, but recent widows should go through a time of testing to determine whether they will refrain from remarriage or not. The widows described by Hippolytus are recognizable descendants of those in the Pastoral Epistles. They seem to have presented the same sort of difficulties for the clergy in Rome as the earlier widows did for the author of the Pastorals. That may account for the repetition of the injunction against ordaining widows, which appears twice more in this brief section (xi.4–5) of the *Apostolic Tradition*.

> But let the widow be instituted by word only . . . But she shall not be ordained because she does not offer the oblation nor has she a <liturgical> ministry [*leitourgia*].
> But ordination is for the clergy on account of their <liturgical> ministry. But the widow is appointed for prayer, and this is <a function> of all <Christians>.[30]

The adamant reiteration signals the importance of the issue for Hippolytus, as well as the likelihood that widows were being ordained in the Roman church at the time, a practice that he was determined to halt. Hippolytus employs a circular argument to exclude women from public ministry: women do not perform liturgical ministry because they are not ordained; therefore they do not need to be ordained (indeed, may not be) since ordination is for liturgical ministry, which they do not do. In turn, the argument defines the nature of clerical office: ordination is for the clergy because of their liturgical ministry.

Virgins are neither appointed nor ordained, but simply recognized: "a virgin does not have an imposition of hands, for personal choice alone is that which makes a virgin" (xiii). The text is directed toward female virgins, although two textual variants also mention male virgins.[31] Virgins have no public ministry as such, but they are acknowledged for their voluntary separation (i.e., differentiation) from other lay people. The origins of a distinct group of virgins within the church are unknown, but initially they may have been associated with the widows, who were expected to be celibate once appointed. Perhaps, in time, virgins achieved recognition in their own right for undertaking a life of celibacy, or perhaps they were separated from the enrolled widows as a consequence of the growing disapproval of younger widows. Hippolytus' regulation about the status of the virgins reinforces their separation from the widows while also increasing their distance from the ordained clergy.

The *Apostolic Tradition* contains none of the ambiguities about women's role that can be found in the Pastoral Epistles. Hippolytus does not know of women deacons or an office of deaconess in Rome. His sharp delineation of offices that require ordination from those that need only appointment or acknowledgment enhances the status of the ordained, male clergy and devalues or denies the unordained ministry of women. In his refusal of ordination and liturgical leadership to women, Hippolytus is not far from the position of Tertullian, his near contemporary from Carthage. Tertullian's view is both more complicated and more provocative: although he acknowledged women prophets and accepted their prophecies once he had associated himself with the New Prophecy (Montanists), he nevertheless was adamant that women were not permitted to speak in church, to teach, to baptize, to make the offering, or to claim for themselves any function of men, especially priestly office.[32]

Hippolytus' view of clerical order did not immediately win the day in Rome, and the complicated history of its text limited the influence of the *Apostolic Tradition* primarily to the Egyptian and Syrian churches, where it was incorporated into fourth- and fifth-century church orders. The *Apostolic Tradition* did not directly influence the development of ministerial structures and liturgy in the West. Nevertheless, its "rediscovery" at the end of the nineteenth century brought it to the forefront of contemporary liturgical scholarship and lent retrospective authority to developments that it had only anticipated.[33]

Didascalia Apostolorum

As church orders appealed to apostolic authority rather than the authority of Paul or the memory of Thecla, they began to change the patterns of power and the nature of leadership in the churches. These shifts are evident in the church order known as the *Didascalia* or the *Teachings of the Apostles*. Allegedly written by the apostles at the time of the so-called council of Jerusalem depicted in Acts 15, the *Didascalia* reflects the pastoral situation of the churches in Syria or Palestine at sometime during the third century.[34] It is more a general treatise on church life than a formal church order. Its contents can be broadly categorized as covering the organization and exercise of ministry and leadership in the church, the conduct and responsibilities of the laity, and the need to avoid heresy and to observe other doctrinal and disciplinary precepts.

The *Didascalia* urges the establishment of an episcopal structure of ministry in the churches for which it was written. To this end, it delineates the role and responsibilities of the bishop and stresses his authority over the other ministers, whom he appoints, as well as over the laity. Nearly one-third of the text is devoted to the requirements of church office, the character of officeholders, and the prerogatives of the bishop. There are detailed directives about the conduct of widows and careful descriptions of the duties of deacons and deaconesses, but little is said about presbyters, who are mentioned only in passing. The relative unimportance of the presbyters in the *Didascalia* implies that their role was not yet clearly defined. Deacons and bishops are frequently mentioned together in the text, and deacons have a more prominent liturgical role than the presbyters. The undeveloped state of the office of presbyter argues for an early date for the *Didascalia*. Its efforts to circumscribe the role of the widows suggest that it was written during a time of change and conflict over their place in the evolving structures of ministry.[35]

In promoting episcopal authority, the *Didascalia* places the bishop at the apex of the local church structure and declares that he occupies the place of Almighty God for the congregation. The bishop is physician, father and mother, priest, prophet, king, mediator, preacher of the word, high priest, and Levite, minister of the Lord for the church community. To him falls the burden of caring for all: forgiving sins, healing, teaching, and providing for the community's needy from the donations made to him. In turn, the bishop is entitled to material support, respect, and obedience from the laity.[36] All liturgical and pastoral ministries are organized around the bishop. The other ministers are appointed by him and subject to his authority. Deacons serve the bishop and are his representatives to and from the community. At the bishop's direction, deaconesses assist the deacons in ministry to women. Presbyters are the bishop's counselors; he is appointed to episcopal office from among them. Widows receive assistance from the bishop's distribution of alms, and they pray for their benefactors and for the church as a whole. Lay people honor the bishop and clergy and are responsible for their support.

The reality of church life, however, did not conform to the *Didascalia's* orderly vision. Nowhere is it less accurate than in regard to the widows. Despite the efforts of the Pastoral Epistles to restrain them, the widows remained a disruptive force in the evolution of ministerial structures.[37] The *Didascalia* follows 1 Timothy in attempting to bring the widows into line with its view of church order. It prefers older widows to younger ones, but lowers the minimum age for enrollment from sixty to fifty, influenced, perhaps, by Roman marriage law, which set fifty as the age at which widows were free from the requirement of remarrying within a year of the death of their husband.[38] Although Roman widows no longer derived social benefit from remarrying after fifty, Christian widows benefited from not remarrying and being enrolled in the order of widows instead.

Making use of standard gender stereotypes, the *Didascalia* draws telling portraits of the "good" and the "bad" widow. The sharp antithesis is intended to galvanize support for imposing strict restraints on the widows' activities. The good widow is meek, quiet, gentle, constant in prayer, and remains at home; she is tranquil, modest, unperturbed, reverent, silent, thankful, and does not find fault; she is obedient to the bishop and deacons who are his assistants (XV.iii.5–8). She knows her place and stays in it. In contrast, the bad widow is a gadabout, chatterer, and murmurer who stirs up quarrels; she is bold and shameless, talkative, impatient, and always running after gifts;[39] she is greedy for gain, serves mammon, and neglects good works; she is distracted in prayer and without discipline, envious of other widows, critical of the bishop's distribution, and she reveals the names of benefactors; she runs around asking questions (XV.iii.6, XV.iii.7, XV.iii.10). In short, she is out of control.

In responding to the heightened discrepancy between true and false widows created by its own rhetoric, the *Didascalia* redefines the role and greatly reduces the influence of the widows by placing them firmly under the authority of the bishop. The widows' ministry is defined as prayer for the church and its benefactors, from whose charity they have received material support: "For a widow should have no other care save to be praying for those who give, and for the whole church" (XV.iii.5). Circumscribing the widows' role in this way ensures that the bishop will retain control over the system of donations and distributions and thus over both benefactors and beneficiaries. To reinforce these restrictions, the *Didascalia* advances the virtues of obedience, stability, and silence as particularly appropriate for widows to cultivate.

Obedience requires the widows "to reverence and respect and fear the bishop as God" (XV.iii.8). They are to do only what the bishop and deacons ask them to do and are not to undertake any ministry or receive any donations without permission. By forbidding the widows to accept donations, the *Didascalia* prevents them from establishing close relationships with benefactors. Keeping widows and benefactors apart serves a dual purpose: it avoids sexual scandal when the benefactors are male, and it deprives the widows of the power implicit in their providing the donor the opportunity to exercise charity. The power denied the widows thus accrues to the bishop through his control of donations.

The widows' obedience is further embodied in stability. Remaining at home, they represent no challenge to the bishop's authority or his oversight of charitable and pastoral ministries. Restricted from other activities, they have increased time for prayer. As a symbol of their stability, the *Didascalia* likens the widows to the altar of God and exhorts them to keep to their homes: "For the altar of God never strays or runs about anywhere, but is fixed in one place" (XV.iii.6).[40] The symbolism of the altar has important cultic references that reinforce its message of social control. Its primary significance derives from the function of the altar as a place of sacrifice or offering. Widows are associated with the altar because they are recipients of the offerings that are placed there to be distributed by the bishop and deacons to those in need. The secondary meaning of the symbol relates to the altar of incense and the offering of prayer. Because of their ministry of prayer, the widows are like the altar from which prayer and incense rise to God (cf. Ps 141:2). If they run about seeking gain and talking idly, they become distracted in prayer, and their prayers are not heard; they do not "conform to the altar of Christ" (iii.7). The true widow, however, like the altar, remains fixed in place. As access to the altar is controlled by the bishop and presbyters, so too, is access to the widows; in turn, their access to the community is also controlled.

Silence supports stability and is another expression of the widows' obedience. The silence of the widows envisioned by the *Didascalia* is motivated in part by disdain for the stereotypical figure of the garrulous woman and in part by fear of her disruptive presence. Instructions on the conduct of widows begin by urging them to be silent: " . . . and let [them] not be talkative or clamorous, or forward in tongue, or quarrelsome" (XV.iii.5). A dialectic between silence and speech runs through these directives. Good widows are quiet; bad widows talk too much. Good widows speak only to bless; bad widows stir up envy, criticize both the donors and the distributors of gifts, and even utter curses (XV.iii.10). Good widows pray "for those who give and for the whole church" in the silence and privacy of their homes (XV.iii.5). Bad widows talk in church, chatter rather than pray, and reveal the names of donors (iii.7, iii.10). Perhaps the worst faults of such widows are that they "run about asking questions" (iii.10) and they "wish to be wiser and to know better, not only than the men, but even than the presbyters and bishops" (iii.8).[41]

Further reasons for women's silence reach back to the original mission of the apostles. The *Didascalia* argues that Jesus appointed the Twelve to teach, but did not send the "women disciples" Mary Magdalene and the other Marys along with them: "For if it were required that women should teach, our Master himself would have commanded these to give instruction with us" (iii.6).[42] Thus, the church has appointed women to the ministry of prayer, but not of teaching, and it is neither right nor necessary for women to teach. If questions about the faith are put to them, good widows respond only to the most fundamental points about "righteousness and faith in God" and "in refutation of idols and concerning the unity of God," otherwise sending inquirers "to the rulers." Bad widows, however, speak on topics beyond their ability, such as the incarnation and passion of Christ. Because they lack "knowledge of doctrine" and cannot speak fittingly, and especially because they are women, they cause the Gentiles to "mock and scoff" at the word of God. Widows who discredit the gospel by scandalizing inquirers in this fashion "shall incur a heavy judgment for sin." The prominence given to the problem of women teaching suggests that it was a rather common practice that the proponents of the *Didascalia* were eager to halt.[43] Removing widows from the ministry of teaching deprives women of its inherent authority and contributes to the ongoing consolidation of power in the bishop and his delegates.

The ministry of baptism is likewise forbidden to women and reserved to the bishop and his delegates. "That a woman should baptize, or that one should be baptized by a woman, we do not counsel . . . " (XV.iii.9). Compared to Tertullian's sharp denunciation of women with the temerity to baptize, the advisory tone of "we do not counsel" is noteworthy. Yet, the seeming mildness of the advice is belied by the strength of the reasons adduced against the practice: it is a "transgression of the commandment, and a great peril to her who baptizes and him who is baptized" (iii.9). For women to baptize goes beyond "the law of the gospel," a claim that is bolstered by appeal to the example of Jesus, who would have been baptized by his mother, Mary, had this been lawful, but instead was baptized by John. As in the case of women teaching, the articulation of an explicit policy prohibiting women from baptizing presupposes that they were doing so publicly and with enough frequency to warrant attention. The *Didascalia* does not specify which women were performing baptisms, but the fact that the issue is taken up in the chapter on widows suggests that they were the chief offenders. The brief argument is preceded by a long section on the necessity of the widows' obedience to the bishop and deacon and followed by a longer one on the problem of envy among the widows.[44]

The *Didascalia* also restricts women's participation in ministries of prayer and healing by prohibiting widows from fasting with, praying over, or laying hands on anyone without the command of the bishop or deacon. Nor are they to pray or communicate with anyone who has been expelled from the church. These prohibitions limit the widows' influence and personal authority by preventing them from offering benefactions to other members of the congregation. These restrictions actually protect the bishop's authority, but the the *Didascalia* presents them as being for the widows' own good: acting without the bishop's approval and lacking knowledge of the character of those with whom they pray, the widows endanger themselves, for they will be held accountable for those persons' sins (XV.iii.8).

The difficulty of assimilating the widows into the new structures of ministry is evident throughout the *Didascalia*. Nowhere is it more obvious than in the effort to prevent women from teaching and baptizing. Women disturb the churches' order and transgress the boundaries of approved ministry when they teach or baptize. They constitute a challenge to the authority not only of the bishop, but also of all men. The *Didascalia* aims to put the widows in their place by appealing to what Jesus did not do—he did not send women when he sent the men to teach and baptize—and to what he would have done if he had wanted to: he would have been baptized by his mother, Mary, and would have sent Mary Magdalene and the other Marys to teach. Arguments from inaction or lack of intention are curiously effective since they can neither be proven nor refuted. Jesus' presumed intentions thus weigh heavily against the widows. The *Didascalia* also uses the image of the faithful and obedient Mary to deny women the right to teach and baptize. This is very different from the function of Mary in many gnostic texts, in which she authorizes the ministry of women (see chapters 5, 12, 14). Whether she represents Mary, the mother of Jesus, who did not baptize; Mary Magdalene, who did not preach; or the other Marys, who did nothing untoward, the figure of Mary in the *Didascalia* counters the image of Thecla, who did teach and baptize. The good widow models herself on Mary rather than Thecla and remains quietly in her place—at home praying.

In contrast to its treatment of the widows, the *Didascalia* approves of the public ministry of deaconesses. It is not possible to determine where and how the role of deaconess developed during the second and third centuries, but by the time of the *Didascalia* it was a recognized office, at least in the eastern churches.[45] One of the motivations for promoting the ministry of deaconesses may well have been to counter the influence of the widows. The *Didascalia* draws on 1 Timothy in instructing the bishop to appoint deacons to assist him in the work of salvation: "a man for the performance of most things that are required, but a woman for the ministry of women" (XVI.iii.12). The deacon's role is primary, that of the deaconess is derivative. Deaconesses are needed in the baptism of women, to anoint the women with oil once they have come up from the water, since "it is not fitting that women should be seen by men."[46] This does not mean, however, that women are authorized to perform baptisms. Rather, the *Didascalia* is explicit that, although the deaconess anoints the women, it is the bishop, presbyter, or deacon who baptizes: "let a man pronounce over them the invocation of the divine Names in the water." Deaconesses are also needed to instruct newly baptized women and to visit the sick among Christian women who live in "heathen" households. They thus have an approved, but circumscribed and subordinate, role in teaching and baptizing, ministries that the *Didascalia* forbids to widows.

The deaconesses are well integrated into the ministerial hierarchy, where they are easily subject to episcopal control. This confers on them a degree of respectability unavailable to the widows. The *Didascalia* can therefore declare that " . . . the ministry of a woman deacon is especially needful and important" (XVI.iii.12). In the case of the deaconesses, the example of Jesus validates, rather than repudiates, their ministry: "For our Lord and Saviour was also ministered unto by women ministers, *Mary Magdalene, and Mary the daughter of James and mother of Jose, and the mother of the sons of Zebedee* [Matt 27:56], with other women beside" (iii.12). At the same time, associating the deaconesses with the women who served Jesus subtly reinforces their subordinate status since deacons represent Jesus Christ and the bishop represents God in the typology of the *Didascalia*.

That same typology is the basis for an extended analogy that defines the place of the ministers in the church community and their relationship to each other. The analogy also alludes to the position of the ministers during the liturgy.

> . . . but let him [the bishop] be honored by you as God, for the bishop *sits* for you in the place of God Almighty. But the deacon *stands* in the place of Christ; and do you love him. And the deaconess shall be honored by you in the place of the Holy Spirit; and the presbyters shall be to you in the likeness of the Apostles; and the orphans and widows shall be reckoned by you in the likeness of the *altar* (IX.ii.26, emphasis added).

The analogy conveys a profound sense of divine order, which is embodied in the church's ministers. Trinitarian references emphasize the authority of the bishop, deacons, and, somewhat surprisingly, the deaconesses, who seem to outrank the presbyters (in the sense that the Holy Spirit can be said to outrank the apostles). Liturgical allusions intensify the aura of mystery around these officeholders and recall their deployment before the congregation during the eucharist: the bishop seated on his *cathedra*, the deacons standing around him, the deaconesses and presbyters arrayed nearby, and, in their midst, the altar to which the faithful bring their offerings. Only the widows do not fit easily into this picture. Unlike the other ministers, they have no active liturgical role or obvious authority in the community. They represent an honored but inanimate object—the altar—and together with the orphans are recipients of the bishop's distribution to the needy. The widows thus appear to be different from and dependent on the other ministers, a view that is consonant with the way they are portrayed throughout the *Didascalia*.

The hierarchical arrangements implicit in the analogy become explicit when it is used to legitimate a system of allotments for support of the clergy. The *Didascalia* requires that, when the needy are invited to a supper,[47] a portion of what is served is to be set aside for the bishop, even if he is not present, and for the deacons as well; portions are given to the other clergy if the benefactor so desires. The requisite amount for each officeholder is calculated from the widow's single portion: two portions go to the deacons "in honor of Christ;" two to presbyters[48] if the giver wishes, "for they ought to be honored as the Apostles;" if there is a lector, the same as for the presbyters; for the bishop, two times two portions "for the glory of the Almighty" (IX.ii.28). The deaconesses are notably absent from this distribution, which suggests that, in this matter at least, they are not to be counted among the clergy. No honorific explanation is offered for the widow's portion, perhaps because the care of widows and orphans was already a self-evident duty in the early Christian communities. Support of the bishop and clergy, however, may have been a newer obligation that required powerful justification. In providing the necessary rationale, the *Didascalia* relegates widows and deaconesses to the margins of the ministerial hierarchy or even puts them outside it.

Women occupy an anomalous position in the church order promoted by the *Didascalia*. Widows and deaconesses are distinguished from the laity, yet subordinated to the male clergy. Deaconesses are structurally related to the other clergy, but widows are not. The ministry of the deaconesses is public and approved, while that of the widows is private and, in many instances, problematic. The decided difference between the *Didascalia*'s treatment of widows and of deaconesses sets the two groups of women at odds with each other and creates tensions that can be exploited by those in power. By stressing the episcopal organization of ministry and the deaconesses' subordination to the bishop and deacons, the *Didascalia* favors the deaconesses over widows or virgins, a move that ultimately contributes to the marginalization of women in ministry since the deaconesses' role is so restricted.

The *Didascalia* both legitimates and limits the ministry of women. As the episcopal structure of ministry was established throughout churches in the late second and third centuries, the scope of women's ministry was progressively restricted. The widows' charismatic ministry was eclipsed and, to some extent, displaced by the hierarchically ordered ministry of the deaconesses, and both were subject to clerical control. Once Thecla was an icon of women's leadership in the Christian movement; now, the stolid altar and the silent Marys who served Jesus symbolize women's place in the churches' ministry.

The *Apostolic Constitutions*

Dating to the late fourth century and originating in Syria, the *Apostolic Constitutions* purports to be the work of the apostles, who handed down to succeeding generations eight books of directives and eighty-five canons about Christian life and church order.[49] It reflects the hierarchical development and institutional concerns of the post-Constantinian church while drawing heavily on earlier church orders. The first six books are based on the *Didascalia*, the seventh on the *Didache*, and the eighth on Hippolytus' *Apostolic Tradition*. The *Apostolic Constitutions* carries forward the clericalization of ministry evident in the *Didascalia* and continues to restrict the ministries of women.

The *Apostolic Constitutions* differs from earlier church orders in making its distrust of women explicit. Early in Book I, which is concerned with the laity, there is a devastating portrait of the "bad woman" who ensnares men with her wiles (I.ii.7) and is contentious and talkative in addition to being sexually dangerous (I.iii.10). Juxtaposed to this depiction is an idealized image of the virtuous wife drawn from Proverbs 31: she is quiet and obedient, subject to the headship of her husband, whom she fears and reverences after God the Father and Jesus Christ (I.iii.8).[50] The paradoxical conjunction of women's weak character and their dangerous powers is not uncommon in works of this period, but here this fundamental ambivalence reinforces the exclusion of women from ordained ministry.

The treatment of widows in the *Apostolic Constitutions* follows a now-familiar pattern. True widows are set against false as their character and conduct are

scrutinized. Widows are criticized for their garrulousness and greed. The flight-
iness of widows who run about on their own is contrasted with the stability of
the altar of God. Their role is more limited than in the *Didascalia* and their status
is diminished.[51] Perhaps to reduce the number of troublesome widows or simply
to lower their total number, the *Apostolic Constitutions* increases the age required
for appointment to sixty, as in 1 Timothy. Widows are to be obedient to the
bishop, presbyters, and deacons—and also to the deaconesses. In a telling reminder, they are urged not to usurp authority (III.i.7).

The *Apostolic Constitutions* prohibits widows from teaching and baptizing. Following the *Didascalia*, it appeals to the example of Jesus, who did not send women
with the apostles to teach or to baptize. But it goes further and introduces a
new scriptural argument based on Paul's assertion that "the head of a woman is
her husband"' (1 Cor 11:3). Women should not teach because "it is not reasonable that the rest of the body should govern the head" (III.i.6). Male headship
is also the reason why women should not baptize, and now the argument extends explicitly to issues of priesthood and authority as well: "For if the 'man
be the head of the woman,' and he be originally ordained for the priesthood, it
is not just to abrogate the order of the creation, and leave the principal to come
to the extreme part of the body" (III.i. 9). The argument ties male priesthood
and women's inferiority to men to God's intention in creation. Women do not
simply represent the lower part of the body, they *are* body: "the woman is the
body of the man, taken from his side, and subject to him, from whom she was
separated for the procreation of children." Since the time of Eve, man rules over
woman "for the principal part of woman is the man, as being her head." The
conclusion is inevitable: "For if in the foregoing constitution we have not permitted them to teach, how will anyone allow them, contrary to nature, to perform the office of a priest?"

More is at stake here than the control of unruly widows. Ultimately, the
argument is about the nature of ministry, of women and men, even of God.
This is evident in the almost seamless way in which the argument slips from
the practice of women baptizing to the headship of men over women and the
maleness of priesthood. The shift disguises the fact that there is no necessary
connection between being able to administer baptism and being ordained, or
even between priesthood and dominance. By the late fourth century, however,
the role of presbyters (priests) had become more important and better defined
than in the *Didascalia*, and these connections were taken for granted. By defining
ministry as priesthood and limiting priesthood to males, the *Apostolic Constitutions*
excludes women from ministry. When it organizes ministry into a hierarchy of
offices derived from the bishop, it preempts any claims of charismatic authority
by women or unordained men.

The argument against ordaining women priests rests on a further assumption
about the nature of priesthood that associates women priests with pagan error:
"For this is one of the ignorant practices of the Gentile atheism, to ordain
women priests to the female deities, not one of the constitutions of Christ"
(III.i.9). The underlying premise of the argument—that women priests, because
they are female, serve female gods—can be seen clearly in Epiphanius' fourth-

century report that women in Arabia "prepare a kind of cake in the name of the ever-virgin, assemble together, and . . . in her name they function as priests for women."[52] With Epiphanius, Christians in this period believed that women priests were one of the proofs of the falsity of "pagan" religions. The *Apostolic Constitutions* takes for granted the male gendering of the Christian God, as well as the maleness of "his" priests. Gender itself, then, whether of priests or of God, is not the problem; female gender is. The specter of pagan goddesses and female priests looms large over women's ministries and works hand in hand with the assertion of male headship to limit the roles of women in the churches.

Despite its fear of women priests, the *Apostolic Constitutions* recognizes the need for women to perform the ministry of deaconess. As in the *Didascalia*, their role is narrowly defined. A deaconess is needed "for the ministrations toward women," anointing women in baptism because "there is no necessity that the women should be seen by the men," and for visiting women in their homes when it is not possible to send a man (a deacon) "on account of the imaginations of the bad" (III.ii.15). The deaconess also keeps the doors on the women's side of the church (II.vii.52). A deaconess is to accompany women whenever they speak with the bishop or deacon (II.iv.26). And it is a deaconess, rather than the bishop or deacon as in the *Didascalia*, who makes the distribution of charity to the widows, perhaps also out of a concern for appearances (III.1.14).[53] The need to maintain "decency" and avoid any hint of impropriety in the churches' life shapes the office of deaconess.[54] Like the widows, they are prohibited from teaching or baptizing.

Deaconesses are clearly distinguished from widows and other lay people by their liturgical and pastoral responsibilities. They are considered clergy in the *Apostolic Constitutions*, which uses the typology of office from the *Didascalia* to describe their role: the bishop is compared to God, the deacon to Christ, the deaconess to the Holy Spirit, and the presbyters to the apostles. Deaconesses are counted among the clergy in sharing the unconsecrated loaves of bread remaining after the liturgy (VIII.iii.31), but are not mentioned in the instructions for distributing food from a banquet to the clergy (II.iv.28).[55] An explicit directive subordinates the deaconess to the deacon: just as the Comforter says or does nothing without Christ, so the deaconess should say or do nothing without the deacon (II.iv.26). The diminished role of the deaconess is apparent in the arrangement of the clergy at the liturgy: the bishop sits on his throne in the middle of the assembly with the presbyters seated on either side of him and the deacons standing nearby; the deaconesses stand at the women's doors and supervise their side of the church, as do the porters on the men's side (II.vii.57).

Yet, like the other clergy, deaconesses are ordained to their office by laying on of hands and prayer by the bishop.[56] The bishop is instructed early in the *Apostolic Constitutions* to "ordain fellow workers" to assist him in ministry; along with deacons, he is to "ordain also a deaconess who is faithful and holy . . . " (III.ii.15). The ordination prayers prescribed for each office construct a public understanding of that ministry. Each begins by invoking God and acknowledging divine providence, then looks for antecedents or types of the office in Israelite religion, and finally asks for the appropriate gifts of the Spirit to make the person worthy of the office.[57] The ordination prayer for the deaconess addresses God as "the Father of our Lord Jesus Christ, the Creator of man and of woman" (VIII.-iii.28), as if to lend legitimacy to the woman being ordained by reminding the congregation that women, too, were divinely created. There is no parallel to this in the prayer for the ordination of a deacon. As examples of women with spiritual gifts, the prayer cites Miriam (Ex 15:20–21), Deborah (Judg 4–5), Anna (either 1 Sam 1:1–2:10 or Luke 2:36–38), and Hulda (2 Kgs 22:14–20). The association of deaconesses with women who are usually regarded as prophets is surprising in light of the limited functions of deaconesses. This may be an echo of earlier efforts to wrest the gift of prophecy from charismatic widows and domesticate it within the carefully structured office of the deaconess. Epiphanius, for instance, condemns the Montanists for ordaining women bishops and presbyters, noting that: "They appeal to the sister of Moses as a prophetess and as support for their practice of appointing women to the clergy."[58] The ordination prayer touches more directly on the deaconesses' role as doorkeepers when it refers to the Israelite women appointed to be keepers of the gates in the tabernacle of testimony and in the temple.

The apologetic undertone of the prayer sounds again in the observation that God "didst not disdain that [his] only begotten Son should be born of a woman." It reaches a startling culmination with the petition for the Spirit's gifts: " . . . do Thou now also look down on this Thy servant . . . and grant her Thy Holy Spirit, and 'cleanse her from all filthiness of flesh and spirit' . . ." (VIII.-iii.28). There is nothing comparable to this petition for cleansing in the ordination prayers for the deacon or any other of the male clergy; those prayers ask only for blameless discharge of the duties of office. Uncleanness of flesh or spirit is thus a peculiarly female liability. It can be overcome to some degree by the gift of the Holy Spirit in ordination, but must be kept under control by the deaconess' obedience to the bishop and other clergy who have authority over her.

There is a keen sense of hierarchical position and prerogative in the *Apostolic Constitutions*. Laity are not to perform any office of a priest; presbyters cannot ordain; only the bishop and presbyters can baptize; no other clergy are to do the work of the deacon.[59] Among the clergy, the order of precedence can be articulated with precision in terms of who blesses and who receives blessing. Further distinctions regarding who lays on hands, offers the eucharist, baptizes, deprives of office, or separates (excommunicates) follow from the order of blessing and receiving blessing. The deaconess occupies the lowest rung of this hierarchical ladder, alongside subdeacons, readers, and singers. "A deaconess does not bless, nor perform anything belonging to the presbyters or deacons . . ." (VIII.iii.28). Neither the deaconess nor the others of her rank may separate any of the clergy or laity, "for they are the ministers of the deacon" (VIII.iii.28). This system of precedence is considered "good and acceptable in the sight of God . . . for the Church is the school, not of confusion, but of good order" (VIII.iv.31).

Good order in the churches requires that women exercise a specific, but limited, ministry as ordained deaconesses, while restricting the role the widows play in the churches' life. The ambivalence toward women that pervades the *Apostolic Constitutions* is reflected in the scathing portrayal of false widows and in the ordination prayer for deaconesses. Joined to the notion of male headship, this view of women undermines their authority and their ability to be accepted as ministers and leaders in the church, even when they are necessary for maintaining decorum in certain liturgical and pastoral functions that involve women.

Canons and Decrees about Women Ministers

Among the disciplinary canons (rulings) adopted by the Council of Nicaea in 325 was a decree about receiving back into the church schismatic clergy from among the followers of Paul of Samosata, who had been deposed as bishop of Antioch in 259. It decreed that any Paulianists returning to the church should be rebaptized, and that any clergy among them who were found blameless could "be rebaptized and ordained by a bishop of the Catholic church;" deaconesses and other clergy were to be treated similarly.

> Likewise in the case of their deaconesses, and generally in the case of those who have been enrolled among their clergy [*en kanoni exetazomenon*] let the same form be observed. And we mean by deaconesses those who have assumed the habit [or, enrolled in these ranks: *en to schemati ezetastheison*] but who, since they have no imposition of hands [*cheirothesian tina*] to be numbered only among the laity.[60]

The meaning of the provision for the deaconesses has been debated by scholars. Some take it to mean that deaconesses are deprived of their ordination once they enter the Catholic church; others argue that the canon recognizes that deaconesses (and other clergy below the rank of deacon) were not ordained among the Paulianists, but it permits them to continue in their duties as deaconesses in the Catholic church if they are found worthy.[61] The practice of not ordaining those below the rank of deacon would accord with the directives of the *Apostolic Tradition* in regard to these offices, as well as with its insistence that widows are appointed, not ordained; there are no deaconesses in that church order. In the *Didascalia*, which originated in Syria in the late third century (i.e., around the same time and in the same area as Paul of Samosata), deaconesses are appointed to their office, not ordained. It seems likely, therefore, that deaconesses were not ordained in the Paulianist churches either then or at the time of the Council of Nicaea. But by the end of the fourth century, as the *Apostolic Constitutions* shows, deaconesses were being ordained in Syria and perhaps also in other eastern churches.

An ambiguous canon about women who were leaders or prominent in the church community is included in a collection of canons attributed to the Council of Laodicea from sometime in the mid-fourth century. Canon 11 declares: "So-called senior women [*presbytidas*] or female presidents [*prokathemenas*] are not to be appointed [*kathistasthai*] in the church."[62] The meaning of the terms "senior women" and "female presidents" is much debated. Scholars claim that *presbytis* refers to deaconesses, and that the canon forbids their ordination; or that the canon refers to deaconesses who are senior by age or rank; or that it refers to widows who ranked above other widows by their appointment, and that the canon sought to reduce their status.[63] Canon 45 of Laodicea also addresses the status of women: "Women should not have access to the altar;" it may apply to the "senior women" or "female presidents" of canon 11.[64] There is also the possibility, though it cannot be proven, that these canons refer to actual instances of women, perhaps appointed from among the deaconesses, who functioned as presbyters.

Canon 15 from the Council of Chalcedon in 451 explicitly refers to the ordination of deaconesses and regulates the age at which they may be ordained:

> A woman shall not receive the laying on of hands [me cheirotoneisthai] as a deaconess under forty years of age, and then only after searching examination. And if, after she has had hands laid on her [cheirotonian] and has continued for a time to minister, she should despise the grace of God and give herself in marriage, she shall be anathematized and the man united to her.[65]

The ordination of deaconesses is a recognized practice in this canon, as in the *Apostolic Constitutions.* The age of forty required for a woman to be ordained deaconess is lower than the age for enrolling widows prescribed in 1 Timothy (sixty) or the *Didascalia* (fifty); the *Apostolic Constitutions* specifies sixty as the age for a widow to be enrolled, but says nothing about the age for ordaining deaconesses. There was imperial interest in these requirements, as witnessed by the decree of the emperor Theodosius I in 390, which declared that widows must be sixty to be enrolled as deaconesses or to dispose of their property. Similarly, in 458, the western emperor Majorian set forty as the age at which virgins could be solemnly consecrated and when widows without children no longer were required to marry.[66] Later canons in regard to deaconesses and civil legislation that pertained to the clergy (including, at times, deaconesses) offer a fascinating glimpse of the intersection of ecclesiastical and secular interests at a time when increasing numbers of women and men entered monastic life or ordained ministry, thereby removing themselves—and their fortunes—from the institutions of civil society.[67]

In the west, there is only isolated evidence of the presence of deaconesses before the end of the fifth century. A council at Nîmes in Gaul in 396 noted with disapproval the apparent existence of ordained women and moved to prevent such a thing from happening again:

> It has been reported (suggestum est) by certain ones that, contrary to apostolic discipline and unknown until today, women seem to have been, one knows not where, admitted to the Levitical ministry. Since it is improper, the ecclesiastical rule does not permit this innovation. Made contrary to reason, an ordination of this type must be annulled, and care taken that no one in the future shows a similar audacity.[68]

Gryson points out that the term "deaconess" is not used in the canon, and that the council seems to have little information about the practice it was opposing, so that it is not possible to know exactly the kind of ministry exercised by these women. Latin writers at this time had begun to take notice of the office of deaconess, which makes it reasonable to think the council was reacting to reports of deaconesses.[69]

There can be no doubt that canon 25 of the first Council of Orange in 441 knew of the existence of deaconesses since it expressly prohibited their ordination: "Deaconesses are absolutely not to be ordained; and if there are still any of them, let them bow their head under the benediction which is given the congregation."[70] At the very least, these deaconesses seem to have been associating themselves with the clergy, who offer blessings, rather than with the laity, who are blessed. Recalling that Ambrosiaster considers the Cataphrygians (i.e., Montanists) to have instituted the office of deaconess, Martimort makes the intriguing suggestion that Montanist deaconesses are the subjects of both canon 2 of Nîmes and canon 25 of Orange.[71]

These western developments are the context for the letter that Pope Gelasius I sent to the bishops of southern Italy and Sicily in 494, decrying the fact that some bishops allowed women to minister at the altar:

> Nevertheless, we have heard to our annoyance that divine affairs have come to such a low state that women are encouraged to officiate at the sacred altars, and to take part in all matters imputed to the offices of the male sex, to which they do not belong.[72]

There is some question whether the women whose altar service so offends Gelasius were ordained deaconesses (already forbidden by the first Council of Orange and probably also the Council of Nîmes) or presbyters—women priests. That they are said to take part in all the functions of male ministers suggests that the women were ordained as priests.[73] Even if ordaining women presbyters was an aberration restricted solely to southern Italy and Sicily, it was sufficient to alarm Gelasius, whose decree found its way into later canon collections.[74]

Early Christian Art and Archaeology

Images and inscriptions from ancient Christian art and Jewish and Christian archaeology have become a focal point of research and debate on the ministry of women in the early church. Bernadette Brooten has exhaustively examined Jewish inscriptions from the Roman and Byzantine period that commemorate women and attribute to them titles of leadership in the synagogue. She concludes that the titles head of the synagogue (archisynagogos), mother of the synagogue (mater synagogae), leader (archegos), elder (presbytera), and perhaps even priest (hiereia/hierissa) were functional rather than honorific.[75] Her investigation is significant for interpreting inscriptions and titles that relate to the ministry of women in the early church. If her argument is correct, it demonstrates that, in the Jewish context in which Christianity arose, it was not unthinkable for women to hold religious offices; consequently, it would not have been unthinkable for Christians, either, especially those who had come to Christianity from Judaism. Brooten's findings would then argue for taking presbytera (1 Tim 3:11) as meaning a woman elder and understanding Phoebe the diakonos (Rom 16:1) as having the same function as male deacons in Paul's time.

A number of ancient Christian inscriptions ascribe titles of office to the women they commemorate. One that is of particular interest is an epitaph from fourth century Jerusalem: "Here lies the servant and bride of Christ/Sophia the deacon, the second Phoebe."[76] With its direct reference to Rom 16:1, the epitaph both defines Phoebe's office and honors Sophia by association with her. A sixth-century epitaph from Cappadocia is noteworthy for its scriptural reference: "Here lies Maria the deacon, of pious and blessed memory, who in accordance with the statement of the apostle reared children, practiced hospitality, washed the feet of the saints, distributed her bread to the afflicted. Remember her, Lord, when you come into your kingdom."[77] The qualities attributed to Maria are those required of a widow in 1 Tim 5:10.

There are also inscriptions to women elders or presbyters. Ross Kraemer cites brief two epitaphs, one of uncertain date to "Kale, the elder" and one from third century Asia Minor to "Ammion the elder."[78] Giorgio Otranto reports an epitaph to "Leta the presbyter," from the catacomb of Tropaea in southern Italy, and an inscription on a sarcophagus from Salona in Dalmatia, dated 425, record-ing the purchase of a cemetery plot by Theodosius from "the presbyter Flavia Vitalia." He also notes a fragment of a sarcophagus cover from fifth- or sixth-century Salona with an inscription reconstructed as including the word (sace)rdo-tae, priest.[79] It is difficult to know with any certainty what these titles mean in regard to any of the women, but it is worth considering that they mean what they say.

Titles of office also appear in Christian art. In the Zeno chapel of the ninth-century church of Santa Prassede in Rome, there is a mosaic that depicts four women side by side, three with round halos and, on the left, the fourth with a square halo, indicating that she was alive at the time the mosaic was made. An inscription runs along the left side of the halo and across its top, identifying her as Theodora Episcopa (Theodora, Bishop), which some scholars take to mean that she was a bishop.[80] But the meaning of the inscription is problematic, not only because there are few similar inscriptions, but because of the chapel's his-tory. The church was built by Pope Paschal I around 820, who also had the chapel built and decorated in the style of a mausoleum in honor of his mother, Theodora.[81] Although it has been customary to dismiss such titles by taking them to mean the wife or, sometimes, mother of the officeholder, here it is probably not obfuscation, but accurate interpretation, to understand Theodora as the mother of a bishop—in this case, the bishop of Rome.

In the Capella Greca of the Catacomb of Priscilla, usually dated to the first half of the third century, there is a fresco commonly identified as a eucharistic meal.[82] Known as Fractio Panis, the breaking of bread, the fresco depicts seven figures seated around a table, the central figure breaking a loaf of bread, while some figures have their right arms extended, and the figure on the left end has both hands outstretched. Some of the figures seem to be women, perhaps even all of them are. The fresco poses this question: does a picture of seven women breaking bread together mean that there were women priests who celebrated eucharist in the early church? Arguments in the affirmative suffer from anachro-nism, assuming a more developed practice and theology of both priesthood (ordination) and eucharist than were the case in the early third century. They also sidestep the difficulty of discerning whether a meal scene in the context of the catacombs indicates an agape meal (love feast), a eucharist, or a funeral banquet (refrigerium).[83]

Titles in inscriptions and frescoes, as well as depictions of meal scenes in catacomb art offer fragmentary and highly ambiguous evidence about women's leadership in the early Christian churches. Nevertheless, they constitute part of the context in which to interpret the repeated declarations of church orders and canons that women could not be priests.

Conclusion

The evidence of texts, inscriptions, and art from the first five centuries CE discloses three patterns of argument in Christian texts by which women were restricted from public leadership and formal ministry in the early churches. The first derives from the Christian scriptures that were taking form in the first and early second centuries; it appears in the Pastoral Epistles, the Didascalia, and the Apostolic Constitutions. This argument relies on the example of Jesus, who is thought to have intended to exclude women from teaching or baptizing, and on the prescriptions for women's silence in 1 Tim 2:11–14 and 1 Cor 14:34–35. The second pattern restricts women from ministry by developing the concept of ordination and laying on hands; it argues that ordination is reserved exclusively for liturgical ministry and is the prerogative of men. The Apostolic Tradition of Hippolytus explicitly uses this argument. A third pattern, apparent in all these texts, genders ministries and ranks them so that women are excluded from the ordained ministries and restricted to roles (such as widow and deaconess) that can be controlled by the male clergy and regulated by the patriarchal household codes. The scant evidence presently available from early Christian inscriptions and art perhaps implies the success of these arguments, but the repeated prohibitions of women's ministries in later canons and decrees suggest that the arguments were not as successful as they might once have seemed.

NOTES

1. In Rom 16, Paul sends greetings to many in Rome, including "Prisca and Aquila, who work with me in Jesus Christ" (v.3), "Andronicus and Junia . . . prominent among the apostles" (v.7), and "those workers in the Lord, Tryphaena and Tryphosa" (v.12). For women missionary pairs, see Mary Rose D'Angelo, "Women Partners in the New Testament," JFSR 6/1 (1990) 65–86; for Junia, see Bernadette Brooten, "Junia . . . Outstanding among the Apostles (Rom 16:7)," in Women Priests: A Catholic Commentary on the Vatican Declaration, ed. Leonard Swidler and Arlene Swidler (New York: Paulist, 1977) 141–44.

2. The publication of Elisabeth Schüssler Fiorenza's In Memory of Her: A Feminist Theological Reconstruction of Christian Origins in 1983 (New York: Crossroad) marked a new stage in feminist biblical scholarship, which had been gaining momentum since the mid-1970s. See Ross S. Kraemer, Her Share of the Blessings: Women's Religions among Pagans, Jews and Christians

in the Greco-Roman World (New York: Oxford University Press, 1992) 128–56, for a concise view of developments in the understanding of women's leadership in earliest Christianity.

3. English translation by Robert McL. Wilson in Wilhelm Schneemelcher, ed., New Testament Apocrypha, Vol. 2 (Cambridge: James Clarke and Co. Ltd.; Louisville, KY: Westminster/John Knox, 1991) 239–46. Thecla's story is sometimes also called the Acts of Paul and Thecla; it is found with other apocryphal works relating to Paul that are collected as the Acts of Paul.

4. See Kraemer, Her Share of the Blessings 150–56, for discussion of the Acts of Thecla and other stories of women in the Apocryphal Acts. For the relation of the Aprocryphal Acts to the Pastoral Epistles, see Dennis R. MacDonald, The Legend and the Apostle: The Battle for Paul in Story and Canon (Philadelphia: Westminster, 1983) esp. 54–77. For the written form of Thecla, see Willy Rordorf, "Tradition and Composition in the Acts of Thecla: The State of the Question," Semeia 38 (1986) 43–52, and MacDonald, Legend and the Apostle 14, who puts it between 150 and 195.

5. For Thecla's cult, see MacDonald, Legend and the Apostle 90–96; MacDonald and Andrew D. Scrimgeour, "Pseudo-Chrysostom's Panegyric to Thecla: The Heroine of the Acts of Paul in Homily and Art," Semeia 38 (1986), 151–59; and Léonie Hayne, "Thecla and the Church Fathers," Vigiliae Christianae 48 (1994) 209–18.

6. Justin Martyr, Second Apology 2, in First and Second Apologies of Justin Martyr, ed. and trans. Leslie W. Barnard (New York: Paulist, 1997) 73–75.

7. For accounts of women martyrs, see Francine Cardman, "Acts of the Women Martyrs," Anglican Theological Review 70 (1988) 144–50. Cf. Thecla's prayer, in which she asks that Tryphaena be rewarded for preserving her "pure" while she awaits the day of combat with the wild beasts (Thecla 31).

8. Tertullian, On Baptism 17, in Tertullian's Homily on Baptism, text and commentary by Ernest Evans (London: SPCK, 1964). See MacDonald, Legend and the Apostle 17–18; also Stevan Davies, The Revolt of the Widows: The Social World of the Apocryphal Acts (Carbondale, IL: Southern Illinois University Press, 1980) 10. In "Women, Tertullian and the Acts of Paul," Semeia 38 (1986), 139, Davies argues that it is not the Acts of Paul (or the Acts of Thecla) to which Tertullian refers, but "probably a lost pseudepigraphal Pauline letter," although that does not alter the effect of Thecla's story on other women.

9. For the relationship of the Pastoral Epistles and the extracanonical Acts of the Apostles, particularly in regard to women's chastity and ministry, see MacDonald, Legend and the Apostle 54–77, and Davies, Revolt of the Widows 70–94. See also chapter 11.

10. For questions of authorship and context, see the commentary of Martin Dibelius and Hans Conzelmann, The Pastoral Epistles, Hermeneia (Philadelphia: Fortress, 1972); see also the recent and concise work of Jouette Bassler, 1 Timothy, 2 Timothy, Titus. Abingdon New Testament Commentaries (Nashville, TN: Abingdon, 1996).

11. Eph 5:22–6:9 and Col 3:18–4:1; cf. 1 Tim 3:1–13, 5:1–22, 6:1–2; 2 Tim 2: 2–10, 3:1–2. See Dibelius and Conzelmann, Pastoral Epistles 39–41, on the ideal of Christian citizenship and 50–54 on the household codes; Bassler, 1 Timothy 31, 63–72. See also Karen Jo Torjesen, When Women Were Priests (San Francisco: HarperSanFrancisco, 1993) 53–87, on household management and women's authority.

12. On these terms, see Dibelius and Conzelmann, Pastoral Epistles 50–59, 77–79. See also Eric G. Jay, "From Presbyter-Bishops to Bishops and Presbyters: Christian Ministry in the Second Century: A Survey," The Second Century 1 (1981) 125–62; Frances M. Young, "On EPISKOPOS and PRESBYTEROS, JTS, n.s. 45 (1994) 142–48.

13. Bernadette Brooten, Women Leaders in the Ancient Synagogue. Brown Judaic Studies 36 (Chico, CA: Scholars Press, 1982) 41–55, analyzes inscriptions that recognize women as elders (presbytera) and other leaders of the synagogue; the Jewish origins of the office of

elder would therefore not tell against the possibility of women elders in the Christian church.

14. See also 1 Cor 14:34–35, which many scholars consider an interpolation. But cf. 1 Cor 11:2–16, in which Paul argues that women must be veiled when they pray or prophesy, but does not object to their praying or prophesying as such; see Mary Rose D'Angelo, "Veils, Virgins and the Tongues of Men and Angels: Women's Heads as Sexual Members in Ancient Christianity," in *Off with Her Head! The Denial of Women's Identity in Myth, Religion and Culture*, ed. Howard Eilberg Schwartz and Wendy Doniger (Berkeley, CA: University of California Press, 1995) 131–64.

15. Paul uses *diakonos* to mean "minister" or "servant" in Rom 15:8; 2 Cor 3:6, 6:4, 11:15, 11:23; Gal 2:17. A well-attested textual variant of 1 Thess 3:2 refers to Timothy as *diakonos* where the received text reads *synergos* (coworker). Whatever the precise nature of the role, Phoebe is *diakonos* in the same sense as Timothy is. The RSV translates *diakonos* in Rom 16:1 as "deaconess," with a note that it might simply mean "helper;" the NRSV translates it as "deacon," with a note that it might also mean "minister." On Rom 16:1, see Elizabeth Castelli, "Romans," in *Searching the Scriptures: Volume 2, A Feminist Commentary*, ed. Elisabeth Schüssler Fiorenza (New York: Crossroad, 1994) 276–80 and n. 13 on minister as the preferable translation. Mary Rose D'Angelo takes *diakonos* to mean that Phoebe was a minister, not a servant and probably not a deacon (D'Angelo, "Diakonia," in *Dictionary of Feminist Theologies*, ed. Letty M. Russell and Shannon Clarkson [Louisville, KY: Westminster/John Knox, 1996] 66–67). See also J. G. Davies, "Deacons, Deaconesses and the Minor Orders in the Patristic Period," *Journal of Ecclesiastical History* 14 (1963) 1–2.

16. The NRSV notes that women (*gynaikas*) may also mean "their wives" or "women deacons." Bassler, 1 Timothy 70, considers it impossible to resolve the question; Davies, "Deacons" 1–2, thinks the verse applies to women in general; Roger Gryson, *The Ministry of Women in the Early Church* (Collegeville, MN: Liturgical Press, 1976; English translation of 1972 French original) 8, argues that these women are a new category of minister and have some kind of public function, a view also held by scholars cited in his n. 72.

17. Early Christian writings refer repeatedly to the duty of caring for the poor, particularly widows, orphans, and strangers, in keeping with biblical injunctions and Jewish practice; see Justo Gonzalez, *Faith and Wealth: A History of Early Christian Ideas on the Origin, Significance and Use of Money* (San Francisco: Harper & Row, 1990) 92–105. The story in Acts 6 is traditionally taken as the institution of the office of deacon, but the seven are not deacons as that office developed in the second and third centuries. The function of "serving tables" (*diakonein*) may also include financial administration of the community.

18. Ignatius, *Smyrnaeans* 13.1, *Polycarp* 4.1; Polycarp, *Philadelphians* 4.3; in Cyril Richardson, ed., *Early Christian Fathers* (New York: Macmillan, 1970) 116, 119, 133. Ignatius is roughly contemporary with the Pastoral Epistles. See Bassler, 1 Timothy 93–94, for change in the meaning of "widow;" Gryson, Ministry of Women 13, on the category including both widows and virgins; see also Davies, Revolt of the Widows 70–73.

19. See Bassler, 1 Timothy 92–98, on the issues raised by the widows; see also her article, "The Widows' Tale: A Fresh Look at 1 Tim 5:3–16," JBL 103/1 (1984) 23–41.

20. Dibelius and Conzelmann, *Pastoral Epistles* 75, believe the women are making "pastoral house calls," a duty of widows and a possible source of danger for younger widows; Bassler, 1 Timothy 98, considers the visits an aberration rather than a duty.

21. This echoes the concluding words of the prohibition on women teaching: "Yet she will be saved through childbearing" (1 Tim 2:15); cf. the true widow who has brought up children (5:10).

22. Charlotte Methuen, "Widows, Bishops and the Struggle for Authority in the *Didascalia Apostolorum*," *Journal of Ecclesiastical History* 46 (1995) 203, cites Hans Achelis, *Die syrische*

Didaskalia Texte und Untersuchungen (Leipzig, 1904) 275, who contends that the widows are "spirit-filled prophetesses." Celibacy was a common characteristic of prophets in the Greco-Roman world, a fact that supports the likelihood of charismatic gifts among the widows.

23. Ignatius, Magnesians 6.1, Trallians 3.1, Smyrnaeans 8.1, where the bishop is compared to Jesus Christ and the deacons to God's law; also Philadelphians 7.1–2, where Ignatius claims God's voice spoke through him saying, "Pay heed to the bishop, the presbytery, and the deacons" (in Richardson, Early Christian Fathers 110).

24. Irenaeus, Against Heresies III.1.1–III.5.2. Complete English translation in Alexander Roberts and James Donaldson, eds. and trans., Ante-Nicene Fathers, Vol. 1, The Apostolic Fathers—Justin Martyr—Irenaeus (Grand Rapids, MI: Eerdmans, 1981; reprint of the 1885 Edinburgh T&T Clark edition) 309–567. More recent English translation of Book I by Dominic J. Unger, St. Irenaeus of Lyons. Against the Heresies, Volume 55, Ancient Christian Writers (New York: Paulist, 1992); and selections from Books I, III, V in Richardson, Early Christian Fathers 358–97.

25. The Didache is not considered here since it does not mention the ministry of women. For English translation, see Richardson, Early Christian Fathers 171–79. Dates from ca. 70–110 to 150 and after are proposed; Henry Chadwick considers the earlier range of dates more likely, in The Early Church. The Pelican History of the Church, Vol. 1 (Harmondsworth: Penguin Books, 1967) 46–47.

26. Paul F. Bradshaw, The Search for the Origins of Christian Worship (New York: Oxford University Press, 1992) 101–2; the entire chapter on "Ancient Church Orders: A Continuing Enigma" is useful.

27. English translation, with extensive introduction, in Gregory Dix and Henry Chadwick, eds., The Treatise on the Apostolic Tradition of St. Hippolytus of Rome, 2nd rev. ed., reissued with additional corrections (London: Alban, 1992). All quotations are from this edition. Latin text and French translation in Bernard Botte, La Tradition Apostolique, Sources Chrétiennes 11 bis, 2e éd. rev. (Paris: Editions de Cerf, 1984). Dix dates it to the second decade of the third century, perhaps ca. 215, in Dix and Chadwick, Apostolic Tradition xxxv–xxxvii, but Paul F. Bradshaw argues that the date could be as much as a century later ("Redating the Apostolic Tradition: Some Preliminary Steps," in Rule of Prayer, Rule of Faith: Essays in Honor of Aidan Kavanagh, O.S.B. [Collegeville, MN: Liturgical Press, 1996] 3–17).

28. Surprisingly little is known with certainty about Hippolytus. For an introduction, see Dix and Chadwick, Apostolic Tradition xii–xxxv and Chadwick's preface to the second revised edition (1992), d–i.

29. See Dix and Chadwick, Apostolic Tradition xiv–xviii.

30. For English translation, see Dix and Chadwick, Apostolic Tradition 20–21.

31. See the textual variants of chapter xiii from the Testament of Our Lord and the Canons of Hippolytus, later works that draw on the Apostolic Tradition (Dix, Apostolic Tradition 21).

32. Women reported their prophecies to the community leaders after the church service. Tertullian rails against women speaking in On the Veiling of Virgins 9; English translation in Alexander Roberts and James Donaldson, eds., Ante-Nicene Fathers, Vol. 4 (Grand Rapids, MI: Eerdmans, 1982 reprint of the 1885 Edinburgh edition), Latin text ed. E. Dekkers, in CCL Vol. II, part II, 1209–26. See Ross S. Kraemer, Maenads, Martyrs, Matrons, Monastics: A Sourcebook on Women's Religions in the Greco-Roman World (Philadelphia: Fortress, 1988) 224, n. 101, for Tertullian's report on Montanist woman's visions in On the Soul 9.

33. For the discovery of the document and the history of the text, see Botte, La Tradition Apostolique 11–13, 17–24; also see Bradshaw, Search 80–110, esp. 89–92, for questions of authorship and the complex textual tradition. The recovery of the Apostolic Tradition has greatly influenced twentieth-century liturgical renewal, e.g., both the Roman Catholic

Eucharistic Prayer 2 and Eucharistic Prayer D of the *Book of Common Prayer* of the Episcopal Church in the United States follow Hippolytus closely.

34. English translation, R. Hugh Connolly, *Didascalia Apostolorum* (Oxford: Clarendon, 1929), from the Syriac version and the Verona Latin fragments. Quotations from the text are Connolly's translation; citations follow his numbering by chapter (uppercase Roman numerals) and subsections (lowercase Roman and Arabic numerals), e.g., IX.ii.26. A more recent translation is from the critical edition of Arthur Vööbus, *The Didascalia Apostolorum in Syriac*, Corpus Scriptorum Christianorum Orientalium, Scriptores Syri, Vols. 176 and 180 (Louvain, Belgium: CSCO, 1979); Syriac text in Vols. 175 and 179. There is general agreement about the origins of the *Didascalia* in Syria or Palestine, but much debate about whether it belongs early or late in the third century. Connolly, lxxxvii–xci, locates the original version between Antioch and Edessa and tends to favor an earlier date, perhaps before 250; Vööbus, 25–28, dates the Syriac version only generally to the fourth century.

35. See Charlotte Methuen's incisive analysis, "Widows" 197–213.

36. The character and role of the bishop, IV–VIII; support of the bishop by offerings of laity, IX; descriptions of the bishop in IV.ii.6, V.ii.11, VI.ii.13, VII.ii.18, VII.ii.20, VIII.ii.25, VIII.ii.26, IX.ii.28, IX.ii.29, IX.ii.30, IX.ii.33, IX.ii.34.

37. Lack of effect of the Pastoral Epistles on church order may argue for a relatively early date for the *Didascalia* or a relatively late date for the Syrian church's adoption of the episcopal ordering of ministry promoted by the Pastorals.

38. For the Julio-Papian laws on remarriage after divorce or widowhood, see Jane F. Gardner, *Women in Roman Law and Society* (Bloomington, IN: Indiana University Press, 1986) 50–54. I owe this insight to Mary Rose D'Angelo.

39. In a pun, the *Didascalia* remarks of widows who seek financial gain: "they are no widows [*cheras*] but wallets [*peras*]" (XV.iii.7).

40. The symbolism of the widow as altar appears in Polycarp's letter to the Philippians 4.3. See Carolyn Osiek, "The Widow as Altar: The Rise and Fall of a Symbol," *The Second Century* 3 (1983) 159–69, for the use of this symbol in early Christian literature; see also Methuen, "Widows" 201–2.

41. Cf. 2 Tim 3:6–7.

42. The gnostic *Gospel of Mary*, however, portrays Mary Magdalene as teaching matters Jesus had revealed to her secretly in a vision; Peter is rebuked by Levi for doubting her authority and complaining that Jesus loved her more than the male disciples. Translation by Karen L. King, George W. MacRae, R. McL. Wilson, and Douglass Parrott, in James M. Robinson, ed., *The Nag Hammadi Library in English*, 3rd rev. ed. (San Francisco: HarperSanFrancisco, 1990) 523–27.

43. The question occupies two long paragraphs at the beginning of the chapter on the deportment of widows (XV.iii.5–6). Widows also are forbidden "to speak with anyone by way of making an answer" without permission of the bishop or deacon in XV.iii.8. Methuen, "Widows" 200, 213, also takes these prohibitions as evidence that women were engaging in such activities.

44. Cf. the apparent envy of the Hellenist and Hebrew widows in Acts 6; also see the *First Letter of Clement* 3.2–6.4 for the consequence of envy and rivalry (in Richardson, *Early Christian Fathers* 44–46).

45. The *Apostolic Tradition*, ca. 215, does not mention deaconesses. Aimé Georges Martimort, *Deaconesses: An Historical Study* (San Francisco: Ignatius, 1986; English translation of 1982 French original) 187–96, contends there were no deaconesses in the western church before 500 CE; Gryson, *Ministry of Women* 105–7, notes that some women may

have been ordained deaconesses at the time of their consecration as widows, a practice forbidden in canons from western regional councils.

46. Baptism was by immersion, and the candidates were naked in the water, hence the concern to avoid any scandal. The *Didascalia* concedes that, when there is no woman, especially a deaconess, present, it is necessary for the man performing the baptism to anoint the women. See the rubrics for baptism in Hippolytus, *Apostolic Tradition* xxi.3: "And they shall put off their clothes."

47. Vööbus translates the Syriac as "agape" here, *Didascalia*, Vol. 176, 101; Connolly notes that the Syriac word was used especially in reference to funeral feasts and mentions a charity supper for widows in the *Apostolic Tradition* (III.xxvii) (*Didascalia Apostolorum* notes on p. 89).

48. Cf. 1 Tim 5:17, in which the "elders (*presbyteroi*) who rule well" are "considered worthy of double honor."

49. All quotations are from the English translation by James Donaldson, *Ante-Nicene Fathers*, Vol. 7 (Grand Rapids, MI: Eerdmans, 1982 reprint of 1926 American edition) 391–505. Greek and Latin text in F. X. Funk, *Didascalia et Constitutiones Apostolorum* (Munich: Paderborn, 1905). A date ca. 375–385 is generally proposed; see Bradshaw, *Search* 93–95.

50. Cf. the portrayal of woman Wisdom in Proverbs 8 and 9; also see the foolish woman in Prov 9:13–18 and the adulterous woman in Prov 30:20.

51. See Gryson, *Ministry of Women* 59–60: there is no reference to prayer, fasting and laying on hands over the sick, or power to bless; widows are never mentioned with the bishop, presbyters, or deacons. They recover some status, however, by being associated with the virgins, who were highly regarded in the late fourth century.

52. Epiphanius, *Medicine Box* 78.23, in Kraemer, *Maenads* 50.

53. It is surprising that this function is not mentioned explicitly in III.ii.15 as part of the deaconess' ministry or in the brief description in VIII.iii.28; lack of comment on this new responsibility suggests that it was already common by the time the *Apostolic Constitutions* was written.

54. See III.ii.16, " . . . and let a deacon receive the man, and a deaconess the woman, that so the conferring of this inviolable seal *may take place with a becoming decency*" (italics added); VIII.iii.28, a deaconess "only is to keep the doors, and to minister to the presbyters in the baptizing of women, *on account of decency*" (italics added). Concern for propriety may also have been the reason for having the deaconesses make the distribution to the widows.

55. Perhaps deaconesses are included among the "elder women" who receive a single portion.

56. VIII.ii.4 and iii.27 for the bishop; VIII.iii.16–26 for the others. Virgins are mentioned only here and in IV.ii.14: "Concerning virgins we have received no commandment; but we leave it to the power of those that are willing, as a vow. . . . " See Gryson, *Ministry of Women* 58–59.

57. The bishop is compared to the priests of Israel, including Abel, Seth, Noah, Melchisedek, Abraham, Moses, Aaron, and Samuel (VIII.ii.5); the presbyter to the elders chosen by Moses (iii.16); the deacon is an interesting exception, being compared to Stephen, the first martyr (iii.18); the deaconess is compared to Miriam, Deborah, Anna, and Huldah (iii.20); the subdeacon is compared to those who were keepers of the holy vessels in the tabernacle of testimony (iii.21); and the readers are compared to Esdras, who read the laws to the people (iii.22).

58. Epiphanius, *Medicine Box* 49.2, in Kraemer, *Maenads* 226.

59. III.i.10, III.i.11, VIII.iii.28.

60. English translation of canon 19 from Gryson, *Ministry of Women* 48; the bracketed alternative "in these ranks" is from Martimort, *Deaconesses* 102. Greek text in William Bright, *The Canons of the First Four General Councils* (Oxford: Clarendon , 1892) xv.

61. Both Gryson, *Ministry of Women* 48–49, and Martimort, *Deaconesses* 101–4, take the latter view, which seems to make the most sense of the text; see n. 25 (p. 140) of Gryson, on those who think the canon deprives deaconesses of ordination.

62. English translation in Charles Hefele, *A History of the Councils of the Church*, Vol. 2 (Edinburgh: T&T Clark, 1876) 305; see Gryson, *Ministry of Women* 53.

63. Gryson, *Ministry of Women* 53–54, evaluates these views; see also Martimort, *Deaconesses* 104–5, and Hefele, *History of the Councils* 305–7.

64. Gryson, *Ministry of Women* 54.

65. Translation from Gryson, *Ministry of Women* 63; Greek text in Bright, *Canons* xliii.

66. Martimort, *Deaconesses* 107–112, for Theodosian Code and later *Novellae* of Justinian; Gryson, *Ministry of Women* 64, for Majorian.

67. For some of the legislation from the sixth century onward, see Gryson, *Ministry of Women* 71–74, 106–8, and Martimort, *Deaconesses* 109–12, 197–216.

68. Canon 2, English translation in Gryson, *Ministry of Women* 101; also Martimort, *Deaconesses* 193, with Latin text.

69. Gryson, *Ministry of Women* 101–2, and see 95–96, 98–99.

70. English translation in Gryson, *Ministry of Women* 102; also Martimort, *Deaconesses* 193, with Latin text.

71. Martimort, *Deaconesses* 195–96, see 191.

72. English translation of Gelasius I, *Epistle* 14.26, in Mary Ann Rossi, "Priesthood, Precedent, and Prejudice: On Recovering the Women Priests of Early Christianity," *JFSR* 7 (1991) 81; cf. translation and Latin text in Martimort, *Deaconesses* 196. Latin text of the letter in A. Thiel, *Epistulae Romanorum pontificum genuinae* (New York: Georg Olms Verlag, 1974; first ed. Braunsberg: Eduard Peter, 1867) 360–79, and for 14.26, 376–78.

73. This is the position of Giorgio Otranto, "Notes on the Female Priesthood in Antiquity," translated in Rossi, "Priesthood, Precedent, and Prejudice." Martimort, *Deaconesses* 196–200, associates them with widows who received a diaconal blessing; Gryson, *Ministry of Women* 105, simply asks whether they were deaconesses and finds the evidence insufficient to decide.

74. See Martimort, *Deaconesses* 196, for the decree's place in canon collections.

75. Brooten, *Women Leaders* 149–51; Brooten examines nineteen inscriptions that attribute titles to women and forty-three that name women donors; see n. 14 above and her "Inscriptional Evidence for Women as Leaders in the Ancient Synagogue," in *SBL Seminar Papers 1981*, ed. Kent Harold Richards (Chico, CA: Scholars Press, 1981) 1–17, n. 20. See also the preliminary work of Dorothy Irvin, "The Ministry of Women in the Early Church: The Archaeological Evidence," *Duke Divinity School Review* 45/2 (1980) 76–86, and a similar presentation in "Archaeology Supports Women's Ordination," *The Witness* 63/2 (1980) 4–8.

76. Kraemer, *Maenads*, 221, no. 50.

77. Ibid. 223, no. 100.

78. Ibid. 221, nos. 93, 94.

79. Otranto, "Notes" 86–88.

80. Irvin, "Ministry of Women" 79–81, first called attention to the mosaic in relation to the question of women's ordination; the image of the four women is used on the dustjacket of Karen Jo Torjesen's book, *When Women Were Priests*, and she begins the first chapter with a description of the mosaic. Both Irvin and Torjesen believe Theodora was a bishop.

81. For the architectural history of S. Prassede, see Richard Krautheimer, *Rome: Profile of a City, 312–1308* (Princeton, NJ: Princeton University Press, 1980) 123–34, esp. 128 ff. for the Zeno chapel. Krautheimer does not comment on the meaning of the inscription, but simply notes that "the chapel is associated with the memory of the pope's mother, Theodora Episcopa" (130).

82. André Grabar, *The Beginnings of Christian Art: 200–395* (London: Thames and Hudson, 1967) 98–99, dating; 112, illustration. But John Beckwith, *Early Christian and Byzantine Art*, 2nd ed., The Pelican History of Art (Harmondsworth: Penguin Books, 1979) 21, dates the Capella Greca paintings to the end of the second century.

83. Irvin, "Ministry of Women" 81–84 (in which the image is printed in reverse), considers the scene a "eucharistic vigil" and the women as concelebrants of the eucharist. K. M. Irwin offers a strong critique of Irvin in "Archaeology Does Not Support Women's Ordination; A Response to Dorothy Irvin," *Journal of Women and Religion* 3/2 (1984) 32–42. Torjesen, *When Women Were Priests* 52, places the fresco at the start of a chapter on "Household Management and Women's Authority," noting only that it is a picture of a woman breaking bread, and that most of the surrounding figures are women.

14

>-+◦-○-◦-+-<

WOMEN AS SOURCES OF
REDEMPTION AND KNOWLEDGE
IN EARLY CHRISTIAN TRADITIONS

Gail Corrington Streete

Introduction: Redemption and Knowledge of the Divine

Christianity developed within a matrix of religious traditions, nearly all of which
promised what they defined as salvation.[1] For Judaism and the other Greco-
Roman religious traditions that influenced formative Christianity in the period
from the first through the fourth and early fifth centuries of the Common Era,
the term "salvation" could be understood as embracing three general categories.
In the first, salvation denoted safety, rescue, or being made secure by a powerful
force that overcame other powerful and hostile forces rendering one's existence
in this world and the next powerless and helpless. Salvation could also mean
"salvage," the restoration of the person or the world to some original but lost
perfection or, at the very least, the removal of the restrictions of suffering, limit
and death that hedged about the human situation. This restoration could be
accomplished through powerful outside intervention or through the acquisition
of divine secret knowledge. Third, salvation could be understood as redemption,
in its root meaning of "payback" or "buying back" to cancel out a debt, to
make restitution for something owed or taken, or to ransom a person who had
been sold into slavery to another. In Judaism, for example, the paradigmatic
redemptive act was that of God's deliverance of the Israelites from slavery in
Egypt.[2] God might also on occasion "raise up" a human deliverer to perform
the work of redemption, as in the book of Judges.

However it was understood, the experience of salvation within the religious traditions inherited by Christianity involved a *personal* agent, an "extraordinary personality," whether divine or human, who would exercise his or her considerable power on one's behalf.[3] A savior or redeemer might even go so far as to bestow that power upon a deserving or favored believer. That power sometimes took the form of imparting an intimate and secret knowledge of the workings of the cosmos that led to union of the believer with the divine. The experience of salvation thus involved a special bond of identification, participation, or imitation between the savior and the saved, one in which the gender of either might have considerable significance.

For emerging Christianity, in which the primary model of the redeemer was Jesus, a historical male, the relationship was particularly complex and frequently a source of considerable conflict. In the religious traditions out of which early Christianity emerged and on which it drew, female figures, whether goddesses, actual humans, or idealized versions of "the feminine," were often envisioned as agents of redemption and knowledge. Some Christian circles of the first to early fifth centuries had little difficulty with female imagery or female aspects of the divine, having languages in which the Holy Spirit and divine Wisdom were both feminine nouns and "inherited religious thought patterns" in which female deities like the Syrian Goddess, Cybele, and Isis were prominent.[4] Although this vision of the divine did not necessarily ensure that real women had roles of authority in these congregations, Elaine Pagels asserts that, for gnostic Christian congregations at least, there was indeed a "correlation between religious theory and social practice."[5] Other Christian congregations excluded women from positions of authority and instruction, and for these the male gender of their savior was important and served as a justification for that exclusion. The second-century *Apostolic Tradition* (18.3), for example, portrayed Christ as deliberately choosing males over females to be priests because of female "weakness," and the indignant Irenaeus of Lyons excoriated those teachers who invited women to pray to the feminine Grace, Wisdom and Silence as divine beings thereupon receiving prophetic and priestly authority (*Against Heresies* I.3–5). As might be expected, these differences in perception of the nature of a being powerful enough to accomplish human redemption were reflected in differences in perception of the nature of the redeemed and the means of redemption. Controversies over aspects of Jesus' life, his birth and death, his humanity and divinity, reflected conflicting attitudes toward human embodiment, including issues of sexuality, physicality, and gender. Women in Christian congregations—as leaders, prophets, authorities, and mediators of redemption and knowledge—were often the focal point for these controversies.

What follows attempts to answer four general questions about the roles of women as sources or communicators of redeeming power and knowledge in early Christian circles. First, what models of redeemer and revealer existed in the traditions from which early Christianity drew? Second, what role did embodiment, gender, and sexuality play in each? Third, how were they applicable to Christian ideas of the savior? Finally, how and why did Christians accept or reject female models of redeemer or revealer?

Redemption through Eternal Benefit:
Isis, Mithras, and the Mysteries

Among the religions of the Greco-Roman world that offered salvation were those known as the "mystery religions" (see also chapter 4). These religions were centered around divine personalities who had the power to transform life and to overcome death and who could communicate to their human adherents the ability to do the same. This knowledge was disclosed only to initiates (mystai), hence the name "mystery." Despite the element of secrecy, however, it is known that the mysteries included both public ceremonies and private rituals through which initiates participated in the person, and therefore the power, of the deity over life and death through recitation and reenactment of his or her myth, through the sharing of a sacred meal, and through a symbolic personal death and rebirth.

The central figures of these mystery religions, while not exclusively so, were often female, perhaps because of their connection to the cycles of reproduction. The oldest Greek mysteries centered around the myths of the mother-goddess Demeter and her daughter, Persephone, the maiden (Kore). These mysteries, however, were performed outside Athens at Eleusis and open only to those initiates who spoke Greek. The later Greco-Roman world, with its mixture of cultural and religious traditions, included more universalizing mysteries like those of Isis, Cybele, Mithras, and the Syrian goddess. With the sole exception of the religion of Mithras, the Persian hero-god, these religions numbered many women among their adherents, along with other non-elites like slaves, freedpersons, and foreigners, whose presence made them a frequent object of derision or suspicion by elite male Greek and Roman authors and of persecution by Roman authorities.[6]

The religion of Isis in particular attracted and included men and women of all ethnic groups and social classes among religious officials, as well as among initiates. Found throughout the empire in the early centuries of the Common Era, it proved perhaps even more than Mithraism to be a serious rival to Christianity, especially in Egypt, its place of origin.[7] In the iconography, liturgy and literature of the Isis religion, the goddess is celebrated as the loving and devoted spouse who rescues her slain husband Osiris and raises him from the dead and the loving mother who saves her son, Horus, from attacks by his father's killer, the monstrous Typhon or Seth.[8] In an aretalogy, or litany of praises, from Kyme, dated from the second to third century CE, Isis is also celebrated as the one who provides order to the universe, conquers the constraining force of Fate and institutes justice. She protects women in all phases of their lives and, as guardian of marriage, "compels" spousal and filial affection for women.[9] In another aretalogy (Papyrus Oxyrhyncus [P. Oxy]. 11.1380), Isis is invoked as the universal goddess of many names who "makes the power of women equal to that of men." The second-century novelist Apuleius of Madaura calls Isis "mother" and "holy and eternal savior" (sospitatrix) of the human race (Metamorphoses 11.15–35). It is not only literary works that reveal the extent of the worship of Isis among women. Terra-cotta and bronze figurines representing Isis or possibly themselves are dedicated to the goddess by women in gratitude for helping them through the difficult processes of menarche (the onset of menstruation) and childbirth. Lamps, mirrors, and amulets depicting Isis nursing the infant Horus and funerary monuments that feature the deceased woman wearing Isis' distinctive dress testify to the goddess' human image and her importance to women. Such material remains are evidence that women identified with a savior who embodied and exalted the female functions of giving and sustaining life.

Isis, however, was not a deity worshiped by Christians. Or was she? What impact might Isis have had on ideas of the Christian savior, if any? These are questions to which the answers are by no means certain. A funerary monument or stele from Christian Egypt (500–700 CE) is particularly intriguing in this regard. This representation (Staatliche Museum Berlin, Inv. No. 14726) shows a woman seated on a chair between two pillars, nursing a child. We do not know who either figure commemorates. The female figure, of more interest to commentators than the child, has been taken to represent the deceased herself, the goddess Isis with the infant Horus, a Greek nursing deity (to protect the infant soul, represented by the child, in the next life), Mary nursing the infant Jesus, or perhaps a conflation of all of these.[10] The fact that there are crosses engraved in the spaces above the woman's head on both the left and right encourages an identification of the figure with Mary. In the funerary stele, we perhaps have an early representation of this process, which may have been encouraged by the actions of Cyril, the fifth-century Christian bishop of Alexandria, who attempted to obliterate Isis worship by destroying her temples and replacing her cult with that of the Christian saints Cyril and John.[11] Perhaps Christian women in Egypt simply substituted the more acceptable Mary for Isis rather than adopt protective saints of another gender. It has also been suggested that the iconography of Isis was applied to that of the Christian mother Mary, and some of the earliest representations of Mary with Jesus, though rare, do indeed show her seated on a thronelike chair, presenting her infant to the world, just as Isis presented Horus.[12] Epiphanius accuses certain Christian women in Arabia of going so far as to worship Mary as redeemer rather than Jesus, offering her the cakes of the "queen of heaven," a title also given to Isis (Medicine Box 88; Diodorus Siculus 1.14).

These data, scarce as they are, indicate a fundamental problem for women in a monotheistic religion of salvation like Christianity that personalizes the savior as the sole incarnation of the deity. In that case, bodies do matter. Jesus as a historical figure was undeniably male, and in many cases is portrayed as an incarnation of a father god. He is thus envisioned primarily as the son of his heavenly father, not of his earthly mother (cf. Luke 2:41–52). As a savior-figure, therefore, Jesus resembles Isis much less than he does the male savior, Mithras, the "unconquered sun" of the mysteries. Like Isis, Mithras appeared in many incarnations and with many attributes throughout the Roman Empire, but was most often portrayed as a deity of light emerging from or overcoming darkness. Like other mysteries, those of Mithras included a ritual reenactment of a myth, his slaying of the primeval bull that perhaps ensured the return of light and life. They also included a sacred meal shared by initiates, progress through seven progressively higher levels of knowledge, and the assurance of rebirth and recreation through participation in the mysteries. In the Mithras liturgy from the *Great Paris Magical Papyrus* (PGM 4.475–829), the initiate declares that, despite his previous birth from the womb of a human mother, he is "reborn" into immortality by the power of the god.

Mithraism was not a religion that appealed to or even admitted women. Like the worship of Isis, however, that of Mithras proved a rival, perhaps even a more serious one, to the worship of Christ. Firmicus Maternus, in his Christian polemic against the mysteries, *On the Error of the Pagan Religions* (ca. 350), charges Mithraism with misusing Christian symbols to "adulterate the faith and transfer this holy and worshipful mystery to pagan doing" (20.1). Christian writers, however, had themselves been adopting the language of the mysteries to speak of their religion since the first century. Paul, for example, speaks of himself as a proclaimer of the "mystery of God" (1 Cor 2:1; cf. 15:51), imparter of God's secret and hidden wisdom to "initiates" (1 Cor 2:6–7), and a "steward of God's mysteries" (1 Cor 4:1). In his second-century *Exhortation to the Greeks*, Clement of Alexandria urged them to abandon the pagan mysteries of Demeter and Dionysos and the "hallucinations" of the oracles in order to be initiated in the "truly sacred mysteries" of the "pure light" to be assured of immortality through union with the savior, the dying and rising Christ (12.118–120). Although some of the Christian bishops may have denounced and suppressed Mithraism after Christianity became the state religion in the fourth century, the mingling continued. In the late fourth century, the celebration of Christ's birth was fixed on December 25, which was also the date of the birth of Mithras.

While Mithras, rather than Isis, may have contributed significantly to the image of the redeemer in Christianity, Isis' role as *sospitatrix* (savior, preserver), also drawn from the Greco-Roman world, may have provided the model for another kind of "savior." Women who could be considered "saviors" were those women who exemplified what men considered feminine virtue, that is, the often-sacrificial commitment to save and protect the men of their families and of their cities. Aretaphila of Cyrene (first century BCE) was praised by Plutarch (*Moral Essays* 257 D–E) for having endured torture in her successful effort to rid the city of Cyrene of its tyrant. The citizens of Cyrene hailed her as "hero" and invited her to participate, though a woman, in their government, but she declined the honor to remain at home in the women's quarters. Aurelia Leite gave funds to build a gymnasium at Paros (which, as a woman, she could not enter); the dedicatory inscription which celebrates her as one who "loved wisdom, her husband, her native city," sounds like the description of the ideal wife of Prov 31:10–31.[13]

Such women are also seen in the pages of the New Testament as "benefactors," patrons and supporters, providing out of their own inherited, earned, or family funds for the needs of the fledgling Christian movement. Luke mentions women who apparently accompanied Jesus and "the twelve" male disciples on the road, providing for them "out of their own resources," women who included Mary of Magdala; Joanna, the wife of Chuza, Herod's steward; Susanna; and "many others" (8:1–3). (Nevertheless, since Jesus has himself provided these women with valuable services, healing them of "demons" and illnesses [8:2], it is not clear who is the benefactor of whom; see also chapters 5 and 8) In the book of Acts, Luke mentions the businesswoman Lydia of Thyatira as a prominent convert who offers Paul and Silas her house in Philippi, which becomes a place of refuge after they are released from prison (Acts 16:14–15, 40). Conversely, Acts also mentions powerful "devout women of high standing" in Pisidian Antioch, who form part of the group that drives Paul and Barnabas out of the region (Acts 13:50). In Romans, Paul praises Phoebe, deacon of Cenchreae, as "benefactor of many and of myself" (16:1–2) and "the mother of Rufus—a mother to me also" (Rom 16:13). Prominent women in the Gospel of John are Martha and Mary of Bethany, which is referred to as "the village of Mary and Martha" (John 11:1). It is in their house that Martha prepares and serves a festal dinner to celebrate the raising of their brother, Lazarus (cf. Luke 10:38–42), while Mary spends a laborer's yearly salary on ointment for Jesus' feet in an extravagant act of devotion (John 12:1–8).

Women are also known from later Christian writings as sponsors of house-churches, study circles, and monasteries and as supporters of the often-embattled male clergy, to whom the women acted as advisors, advocates, and comforters. Olympias of Constantinople supported the church there for twenty years and was praised by her frequent correspondent, John Chrysostom (ca. 347–407), for her support of him. Macrina (ca. 327–379) is praised by her brother, Gregory of Nyssa, as "father, teacher, paedagogue, mother and counsellor" of their younger brother (Life of Macrina 14.10). Melania the elder (ca. 342–410) supported Rufinus of Aquileia with her influence and authority and with her considerable wealth founded a double monastery in Jerusalem with him. Marcella of Rome (ca. 325–410) maintained a household on the Aventine that helped to support the controversial Jerome, who praised her as "the glory of the ladies of Rome," who also included the noble and ascetic Paula and her daughters, Blesilla and Eustochium, whom Jerome also praised as exemplars of learning and virtue (e.g., Letter 108.26). As Peter Brown notes, these women were important: "The Christian clergy . . . welcomed women as patrons and even offered women roles in which they could act as collaborators."[14]

Were women like these truly regarded as "redeemers" (sospitatrices)? Even in the most flowery dedications to female benefactors, none is ever addressed by the title soteira (savior) or sospitatrix (rescuer), but by the term euergetēs, literally, "worker of good," a title also applied to men who have performed some extraordinary service. These women do indeed perform the function of benefiting or helping men, a function for which Isis and other saving goddesses are celebrated. In this sense, Christian women who are benefactors also mirror the functions of the life-sustaining figure of Wisdom, our next subject of consideration.

Redemption through Wisdom:
Wise Women, Prophets and Sibyls

Judaism, the religious tradition from which Christianity first emerged and drew most heavily, possessed a female personification of the divine that blended ancient Near Eastern wisdom traditions, like collections of sayings of the wise, with Greek philosophical speculation. The figure of Isis may also have had some impact upon the portrayal of Wisdom (Hebrew *Hokhmah*; Greek *Sophia*) in some texts, for example, the Wisdom of Solomon, which dates from about 100 BCE.[15] Wisdom, as a fully developed female personage connected with the God of Israel, first appears in the postexilic Book of Proverbs, where she is described in chapter 8 as present with God at the creation, taking particular delight in the created world and especially in humankind. Throughout the first nine chapters of Proverbs, the figure of Wisdom as woman is developed as a mediator between the transcendent and distant male deity and the world of human social interaction. She represents the saving knowledge that can preserve the foolish youth from the lures of Folly, which is also personified as a woman, the seductive adulteress whose acquaintance leads to disgrace and death (Prov 7:6–27; 9: 13–18). As Claudia Camp has demonstrated, moreover, the figure of Wisdom owes much to the tradition of wise women in Israel, those whose beneficial activities and wise counsel save their cities and build up their households.[16] It is this kind of saving advice that is transmitted by the figure of Wisdom in Proverbs. On several occasions, a son is urged to listen to his mother's instruction, as well as to that of his father and his teacher (Prov 1:20–21; 8:1–3, 14–16), and the advice in Prov 31:1–9 is a "mother's Torah," supposedly given to King Lemuel by his mother.[17] The figure of Wisdom is also embodied in the good wife, the "woman of worth" in Proverbs 31:10–31, who "opens her mouth with wisdom" and does "good, not harm" to her husband "all the days of his life." She is a steadfast lover who guards her beloved and gives him life (Prov 4: 3–13) and the faithful spouse whose love keeps a man away from the seductive wiles of the "loose" woman, Folly (Prov 7:4–5).

Other Jewish Wisdom texts of the Hellenistic and Roman periods preserve the feminine imagery for Wisdom already familiar from Proverbs. In the writings of Jesus ben Sira of the second century BCE, Wisdom is the creation of God, bestowed like a bride on those who fear him (Sir 1:10), the beautiful spouse (14:23–24; 15:2b; 51:20–21), mother (4:11; 15:2b), and the embodiment of God's teaching (15:1; 24:23). While ben Sira advises young men to get and keep good wives in much the same way that they pursue Wisdom, as a "good possession" (36:29), he also regards women in general as the cause of sin and death (25:24) and as responsible for evil (25:13, 19). The first-century BCE Wisdom of Solomon portrays Wisdom as the desirable and wise spouse, to be preferred to "sceptres and thrones," but also as an agent in creation, an "emanation of the glory of the Almighty" and the savior of humanity, of Israel in particular (10:1–11:16). In other Jewish writings from this period, wise and chaste women bring about the defeat of enemies and the salvation of their people. In the Book of Judith (second century BCE), a virtuous Jewish widow beguiles and defeats a gentile enemy, while the male elders of her city appear helpless. In the Greek additions to the postexilic Book of Esther (second century BCE to first century CE), the sagacious heroine, despite extreme personal peril and a capricious royal fool for a husband, prevents the slaughter of Jews living in a hostile gentile land.

Because these texts formed part of the scriptural heritage of Greek-speaking Jews, they also became scripture for early Christians, who read sacred texts in Greek. There are three other texts, however, that may also have contributed to the Christian conceptualization of wise and redeeming women. One is *On the Contemplative Life* by Philo of Alexandria (ca. 20 BCE to 50 CE), which praises the Therapeutrides, the "elderly virgins" of Lake Mareotis. Living in celibate companionship with celibate males, they devoted themselves to study that was often ecstatic, having retained their virginity out of their "zealous desire for Wisdom" to "contemplate the teachings of Wisdom" and to bear spiritual off-spring from the mind (*Contemplative Life* 68). In a completely different Wisdom text, the romance of *Joseph and Aseneth*, the heroine Aseneth, virgin daughter of a pagan priest, is transformed by her own virtue and with angelic assistance into the embodiment of Wisdom, fit companion for Joseph, the prototypical Wise Man.[18] Aseneth becomes a "City of Refuge," a shelter for those rescued by Re-pentance (Metanoia), a wise divine virgin who, like Wisdom, intercedes before God on their behalf. An angelic visitor reveals the secrets of God to Aseneth, including the secret of immortality (16.7). Both the heavenly female figure of Metanoia and that of Aseneth herself are sources of saving wisdom and are drawn with distinct references to the figure of Wisdom in Proverbs.[19] Yet it must be remembered that both are also idealizations. Metanoia is a heavenly virgin, the daughter of God (cf. Prov 8:30). Aseneth's wisdom, like her virginity, is in the end devoted to her husband, Joseph, just as the wise wife of Proverbs 31 "does her husband good." Wisdom, even when given to women, ultimately ends up the possession of the man who chooses them.

The *Testament of Job*, thought by many scholars to be the product of Greco-Roman Jewish authorship (first century BCE or CE) also presents us with a picture of women who are the possessors of a mystical wisdom. Job's three virgin daughters, Hemera, Kasia, and the oddly named Amaltheia's Horn, receive from their father three multicolored "cords" or sashes—an inheritance that is better than the one he gives their seven brothers. These magical cords give the women the ability to know "heavenly things," to have the strength given to their father by God, and to speak ecstatically, composing hymns of praise (*T. Job* 46–50). Unfortunately, we are not told by the text what happens to the daughters and are referred to other texts for their hymns. The *Testament of Job* is nonetheless extraordinary since it stands alone amongst other pseudepigraphical "testa-ments" that convey the idea that women are sexual beings whose only power over men is seduction and whose intercourse with angels is adulterous and evil (*T. Reuben* 5.1; 5–6, for example). As Rebecca Lesses points out, works like *On the Contemplative Life* and the *Testament of Job* celebrate women as spiritual beings capable of mystic insight and wisdom rather than beings limited by their sexuality, and form a minor, but distinctive, strain in formative Judaism.[20]

In general, however, the dominant personification of feminine Wisdom in texts like Proverbs, ben Sirach, Wisdom of Solomon, and even to a degree in *Joseph and Aseneth*, is the male projection of an archetypal "good" woman, that is, an idealized constellation of women whose activities and counsel are dedicated to and possessed in a very literal sense by men: daughters, lovers, and wives.

The way of Wisdom leads to life and companionship with God, but she is a companion of males, not the embodiment of females, except as pure virgin daughters, industrious wives, and careful mothers who build up their houses and keep their husbands and sons from straying after sexually independent women. Nor do they stray themselves. The wisdom and knowledge of such women is of the practical and nurturant variety, confined to domestic fidelity. Wisdom as Torah is also a possession of men, the male sages, who embrace the wisdom embodied in the commandments and themselves become living Torahs.[21]

In the pagan religions of the Greco-Roman world, women were also known as conduits to divine knowledge. Among these, the Pythia, or prophetess, of Apollo at Delphi and the Sibyl, also a prophetess of Apollo, at Cumae (Kyme) were perhaps the most famous, but there were also the Libyan, Erythrean, and Phrygian Sibyls. Although, according to Amy-Jill Levine, the original term *Sibyl* designated a single itinerant prophet,[22] it was applied to women associated with certain cult sites who prophesied under the inspiration that came from ecstasy or trance-possession by a god, usually Apollo. Their vocation was to provide access to the intentions of divine powers through prophecy and divination rather than through the regular routes of priestly liturgy and sacrifice. Even among priestesses who conducted worship of goddesses, lifelong celibacy was unusual, but apparently the Sibyls were unmarried, presumably to enable the god to "enter" and "master" them in order to direct their speech.[23] The Cumean Sibyl is Aeneas' guide to the future in the sixth chapter of Vergil's *Aeneid* because she alone knows how he can find what he needs to know and from whom he needs to know it amongst the gods and spirits in the Underworld, and how he can return, still living, to the world above. She is also credited by Roman belief with books of oracles, the Sibylline prophecies, consulted in times of national crisis to conduct Roman domestic and foreign policy. Other collections of oracles are credited to a Jewish Sibyl, supposedly the daughter-in-law of Noah, also known as the Hebrew Chaldean or Persian Sibyl; these oracles eventually formed a twelve-volume work later edited by Christian authors.

Were the Sibyls actual women? We have no reason to doubt that some were, given the abundance of evidence. Were the Sibyls responsible for the texts attributed to them? This is a question that we are more likely to answer in the negative. We have no way of knowing whether any "Sibyl" was ultimately responsible for the composition of the Roman pagan oracles, which were rewritten after the originals were destroyed in a fire in 83 BCE and heavily edited during the reign of Augustus (27 BCE to 14 CE).[24]

In any event, their use by the senatorial, and later the imperial, government as a means of social control makes them suspect. The same difficulties apply to the Jewish-Christian *Sibylline Oracles* that apply to the Wisdom texts, namely, the presence of an idealized female figure who is represented as revealing heavenly things to human inquirers. Even though this figure may not be wholly a literary creation, she is an "extraordinary" woman who also represents the interests of men. Other women in the *Sibylline Oracles*, for example, often function as symbols of evil, apostasy, and disaster, translated into the language of sexual "crimes" like adultery and harlotry.[25]

Moreover, the type of prophecy practiced by the Sibyls in the Greco-Roman world was attributed to ecstatic trance ("standing out of oneself"), likened to raving or madness (*mania*) or, more commonly, to possession (*katochē*) by a god.[26] Most commonly, madness was associated with the Maenads, the "god-crazed" followers of Dionysos, but a similar *enthousiasmos*, or "getting the god within," was attributed to the prophetic trances of the Pythia at Delphi and the Sibyl at Cumae and was often described in terms of sexual penetration (Strabo, *Geography* 9.3.5). The first-century Roman poet Lucan describes the Pythia as being forced on one occasion to prophesy unwillingly, as if she were sexually forced by the god Apollo (*Bellum civile* 5.166–67); the epic poet, Vergil, attributes the Cumaean Sibyl's prophetic powers to her spiritual rape by the god after she denied him sexual favors (*Aeneid* 6.77–82) The Christian writer, John Chrysostom (347–407), in *Epistle to the Corinthians Homily* 29.1, declared that the Pythia's inspiration was caused by an evil spirit that entered her through the genitals as she sat on her prophetic tripod. Ecstatic inspiration also proved to be a controversial means of empowerment for Christian women prophets, as discussed below.[27]

The portrait of Jesus as the primary communicator of redemption and divine knowledge within Christianity is drawn in part from that of Wisdom, as a figure who descends to earth in order to call the wise, to reveal to them intimate knowledge of God and in effect to make them God's own children. In the Jewish Wisdom texts, Wisdom is envisioned as feminine, both by grammatical gender and by personification, and is embodied in human women. What connection, therefore, could be made between the historical male person of Jesus and this mythic female personification of God?

There are three ways in which the mythology of Wisdom applied to the person of Jesus as revealer of divine knowledge in early Christianity. In the first, Jesus is the messenger of heavenly (feminine) Wisdom. This role is epitomized by a saying from the hypothetical sayings collection Q, a source used by Luke and Matthew and believed to be a very early layer of the Jesus tradition, in which Jesus quotes "the Wisdom (Sophia) of God" as sending "prophets and envoys" whose deaths will serve as a judgment on "this generation" (Luke 11: 49–51; Q 11:49–52; see chapter 7). Others theorize that the Jesus of Q is a rabbinic or a Cynic sage, one who, in the first case, has embraced Wisdom, one who in the second has been sent as an *apostolos* or envoy by her.[28] According to these views, Jesus is not the sole embodiment or sole prophet of Wisdom.

At some point, however, fairly early in the first century, Jesus himself was envisioned as divine Wisdom. Paul, writing in the mid-fifties, tells the Corinthian congregation that "Christ [is] the power of God and the wisdom of God" (1 Cor 1:24) and that "Christ Jesus . . . became for us wisdom from God, and righteousness and holiness and redemption" (1 Cor 1:30). In Phil 2:6–11, Paul refers to what may be an early Christian hymn, in which Christ is preexistent, like Wisdom, with God, and, like Wisdom, descends to earth. In Col 1:15–20, the identification of Christ with Wisdom is explicit: Christ Jesus is the one who is the "firstborn" of all creation; through him, the rest was made. In the first lines of the Gospel of John, written in the late first century, Jesus appears as the preexistent divine Logos, active and creative reason and word, who descends to earth in human form, calls to "his own," and gives those who receive him the power to become "the children of God" (John 1:1–18). Here Jesus, the historical male, has become the incarnation of a divine male, the Logos, who reveals to those who can receive him the glory of the father God. For Matthew's gospel, Jesus is Wisdom as Torah, the embodiment of the commandments of God (cf. Sir 24:23–24). In the noncanonical *Gospel of Thomas*, parts of which may date from the middle to the late first century, Jesus is identified with Wisdom, who comes into the world (*Gospel of Thomas* 28). The historical male Jesus thus becomes a male personification of God that has parallels with, but takes over from, the female personification of God's Wisdom.

The third way in which Jesus was envisioned as the mediator of divine knowledge is related to a dualistic understanding of God, Wisdom, and humanity. This conception emerges most strongly in the form of Christianity that is described as "gnostic," since it promises its participants *gnosis*, "acquaintance" with or "knowledge" of self, world, and the divine. This knowledge is achieved, as in Wisdom teaching, by close association with a divine figure who appears on earth to impart the truth to those who are able to hear it. Within Christian gnostic traditions, both Wisdom as female Sophia and Wisdom as male Logos or the Savior (Christ) have important roles to play since the godhead and source of all spirit is itself both male and female. Wisdom as a female divine figure and women as teachers of redemptive *gnosis* are also prominent. Jesus as the Christ or Savior is often portrayed as the counterpart, consort, or completion of the feminine Sophia. While it is dangerous to oversimplify the complex play of gender roles and gendered images in gnostic literature, it would be safe to say that male and female together represent complementary poles of divine, as well as human, existence. Neither the divinity, the savior, nor the spirit itself is complete without both. The female, however, is more often portrayed as "incomplete" in gnostic thought than is the male.

Redeemers and Redeemed:
Wisdom and Her Female Emissaries

The basic myth upon which many gnostic texts appear to be based is one that assumes a descent or fall from an original completeness and perfection. Even though many gnostic texts, like *On the Origin of the World*, the *Secret Book of John*, and the *Hypostasis of the Archons*, are interpretive retellings of the first three or four chapters of Genesis, they do not assign responsibility for this fall to human disobedience, but rather to divine error. Their version of the creation of the cosmos, which explains the origin of human limit and the necessity for a savior, usually ascribes the primal error to heavenly Sophia (Wisdom). She desires to conceive and create a being by herself, without a male partner (consort) and without the consent of the "All," the "One,"—the original divine parental unity, the Mother-Father. Because Sophia is incomplete without a male half, her creation, the male deity of Genesis, is himself incomplete, part spiritual and part material. Imitating his "mother," he fashions a material world and beings of matter in which the divine spirit is trapped. Aghast at her mistake, Sophia devotes her divine energies to remedying her error. She appears in various manifestations, as Eve (also called Zoe or "Life"); as Eve's daughter, the virgin Norea; and even as the wise serpent who knows that the fruit of the Tree of Knowledge is beneficial. Like Wisdom in Proverbs, gnostic Sophia constantly summons those who would be truly wise to shake off their material delusions (described as "drunkenness" and "sleep") and to know themselves as spiritual beings. Other gnostic female revealers are the divine virgin Hypsiphrone in the fragmentary work of that title and the angelic Youel, revealer of the divine powers, in *Allogenes*.

Sometimes this "redeemed redeemer" Sophia is split into two, the "higher" or heavenly Sophia, representing the spirit, and the "lower" or material Sophia, representing the spirit fallen into the body. Both are female, however, and in the gnostic Wisdom hymn, *Thunder, Perfect Mind*, they also represent the paradoxical union of opposites that symbolizes completion and perfection. The speaker, who is both Intellect and the individual spirit, is mystically transformed into the divine likeness[29] and declares that "she" is "whore and holy one," mother and daughter, barren and fertile, woman and maiden, bride and bridegroom (13.15–27). Like Wisdom in Proverbs and the Wisdom of Solomon, she calls, invites, seduces, and transforms those who listen. "Sent by the power," she and her messengers are scorned and despised, but listeners ignore her to their peril (13.2; 14.34; 15.31). Like Isis, she has many manifestations: "Sophia" among the Greeks, "Gnosis" among the non-Greeks, and Isis in Egypt (16.3–4, 7). Since the object of the gnostic seeker is to become divine by transcending the limitations of the world and its false categories, including those of sex and gender, "Perfect Mind," like Wisdom, is a saving agent who enables humanity to be restored to its originally "perfect" state, to the divine likeness that knows no boundaries.

In some Christian gnostic texts or gnostic texts like *Eugnostos the Blessed* (*The Sophia of Jesus Christ*) that have been revised in Christian interests, the figure of Sophia becomes submerged in that of the male figure of Christ. Nevertheless, even in these texts, women disciples function as revealers of saving wisdom, equal to male disciples like Thomas and John and often superior to disciples like Peter. Among these, Mary of Magdala is chief, although Martha of Bethany (and possibly her sister, Mary) and Salome also are mentioned. The *Gospel of Mary* features Mary of Magdala as the beloved disciple, and perhaps even the female spiritual consort and counterpart of Christ, whom the Savior "loved more than any other" and to whom he imparted intimate saving knowledge[30] Even in the *Dialogue of the Savior*, in which Jesus declares he has come to "destroy the works of femaleness" and therefore of material imperfection, Mary, "as a woman who knew the All" (139.9–14), is one of his three dialogue partners. That such women continued to be revered within gnostic Christianity as sources of saving revelation is shown by the example of Marcellina, a prominent teacher among the Carpocratian sect, who was nonetheless charged by the orthodox bishop Irenaeus of Lyons with deviation from the "true succession" of knowledge, communicated by Jesus to male apostles, because she considered herself to be a transmitter of secret teaching received from Mary of Magdala, Martha, and Salome (*Against Heresies* I.25.6).

Mary of Magdala, "Apostle to the Apostles"

Of all the women who accompany Jesus in the canonical gospels, the most prominent was Mary of Magdala. Named as one of his companions in Luke 8: 2, she is in all four canonical gospels the one constant among the named women who witness Jesus' crucifixion and the empty tomb. In the Gospel of John, she is the first to whom the risen Christ appears and the first "witness" to that appearance as she tells the disciples what she has seen and heard (John 20: 11–18). A similar resurrection appearance occurs in the longer ending of the Gospel of Mark (Mark 16:9–11), but in this case Mary's story is not believed by the others. (Curiously, the appearance to Mary is not listed in the series of resurrection appearances by Paul in 1 Cor 15:3–8.) In the noncanonical *Gospel of Peter*, dating in its present form perhaps from the middle of the second century CE but containing traditions that may be older, Mary is actually called "a woman disciple of the Lord" (*GosPet* 12.50, see chapter 5).

Mary's prominence in gnostic Christian texts as a companion and revealer of Jesus and his teaching has already been mentioned, but she was also praised by those Christian ecclesiastical authorities who vehemently opposed gnosticism. For example, the theologian Jerome, an opponent of women's leadership and the "wrong doctrine" (heterodoxy) that often supported it, praised his learned patrician Roman supporters Marcella, Sophronia, Paula, and Eustochium by comparing them to Jesus' female followers and especially to Mary Magdalene. In *Letter* 127: To Principia, 412 CE, he writes:

> The unbelieving reader may perhaps laugh at me for dwelling so long on the praises of mere women; yet if he will but remember how holy women followed our Lord and Saviour and ministered to Him of their substance, and how the three Marys [Mary, Jesus' mother; Mary Magdalene; and Mary of Bethany] stood before the cross, and especially how Mary Magdalen [sic]—called the "tower" from the earnestness and glow of her faith—was privileged to see the rising Christ first of all before the very apostles, he will convict himself of pride sooner than me of folly.[31]

Both Jerome's praise of Mary and his distinction of her from "the apostles" are telling. He sought to praise her as an example of female faith and fidelity, but carefully avoided anything that could serve as a warrant for apostolic leadership or clerical privilege for women. Indeed, Jerome claimed, in a letter to Marcella, that the seven demons cast out of Mary by Jesus (Luke 8:2; Mark 16:9) were the demons of sin (*Letter* 59.4). By this claim, Jerome forms a link in a chain of popular belief, clerical misogyny, and the conflation of legends that, by the early sixth century, transformed Mary of Magdala from the wise companion of Christ to the "woman who was a sinner," who wiped Jesus' feet with her hair (Luke 7:37–50), to the prototypical repentant "harlot saint." In this view, which to this day has influenced readings of the New Testament, Mary's wisdom is submerged by her alleged sexual transgressions and can only be elevated by the power of Jesus to forgive.

Possessors of Wisdom or Possessed by Demons?

The taint of female sexual transgression was also used by male clerical opponents to bring Christian women prophets into disrepute, in the same way as women's prophecy in the Greco-Roman world had been connected with sexual madness and demonic possession. Ecstatic prophecy or "speaking in tongues" as a sign of the presence of God's or Christ's spirit seems, however, to have been a common and desired feature of some early Christian congregations (Acts 2:1–13; 10:44–46; 1 Cor 12:10; 13:1; 14:1–32). On the other hand, Paul and Silas cast out, as if it were an evil spirit, the *pneuma pythona* or "prophetic spirit" from a slave girl in Philippi even though it appears to have told the truth about their preaching the "way of salvation" (Acts 16:16–18). Paul's exhortation to the Corinthian women to cover their heads "because of the angels" while praying and prophesying (1 Cor 11:3–16) is an indication that such prophecy by women was problematic, possibly because it had the sexual and demonic overtones previously mentioned.[32] A probable editorial interpolation in the same letter, in a passage on ecstatic prophecy, says that women (probably married women in this case) must be silent in worship and ask their husbands (literally, men) at home what they want to know for women's speech in the congregation is "shameful" (1 Cor 14:34–35). The pseudonymous first letter to Timothy mentions public prayer as desirable for men, but enjoins silence on their wives, giving as his rather specious reason the belief that Adam was not deceived, but Eve was (1 Tim 2:8–15; see also chapters 9 and 11).

The same passage forbids women to teach men or have any authority over them. The author of 1 Timothy also warns against a "falsely so-called *gnosis*" (6:20), connects the pursuit and transmission of such knowledge with young independent "widows," and urges them to remarry and to raise children in order to be saved (1 Tim 5:9–16). According to the author, the widows have allowed their "sensual desires" to alienate them from Christ, and they use their freedom to travel from house to house as "gossips and busybodies, chattering things they ought not to" (5:13). Some have already "turned back to Satan" (15), by which term the author probably means an alternative form of Christianity. The author of 2 Timothy also warns against "little women" who can be swayed "by all kinds of desires" and who crave endless instruction from teachers who invade their households and "captivate" them with false doctrine (2 Tim 3:6–8). It was perhaps independent and "uncontrollable" women like these that so alarmed bishops like Irenaeus, who warned that Christian women were being "seduced" by gnostic teachers like the Valentinians, whose theology was rife with divine female figures and whose liturgies were shared by men and women in nonhierarchical rotation (Irenaeus, *Against Heresies* I.25.6).

As women became associated with "false teaching" and "false knowledge" in some Christian circles, so the association of women with prophecy became dangerous in the eyes of their male coreligionists, perhaps even earlier than the second century. In the late first-century Book of Revelation, the one complaint that the "angel of the church in Thyatira" has against that congregation is that "you tolerate that woman Jezebel who calls herself a prophet" (Rev 2:19–23). The author portrays this woman not only in terms reminiscent of the paradigmatic idolatrous queen of 1 Kgs 16:31 and 2 Kgs 9:22 and 30, but also as an adulteress who will be struck dead along with her incestuous lovers (Rev 2:21). Once again, a female prophet is associated by a male writer with sexual immorality, with "possession" by a demonic and deviant spirit.

As a mark of charismatic authority, moreover, prophecy is not readily susceptible to control by institutions, and those Christian authorities of the second century and later who would be "in control" of the churches necessarily found prophecy suspect, especially when it was associated with women. At the beginning of the third century, an influential group of revivalist Christians in Phrygia and other parts of Asia Minor, practicing the "New Prophecy," laid claim to an "outpouring of the spirit" that signified the end of the present age (Acts 2: 17–21; Joel 2:28–32). Ironically, the New Prophetic movement is better known as Montanism, after the name of its only prominent male prophet. Also ironically, the sayings and visions of its more prominent female prophets, Quintilla, Maximilla and Priscilla, are known only through the writings of their detractors, Christian bishops like Hippolytus, Eusebius and Epiphanius, who were horrified by the female leadership of the movement. Maximilla is supposed to have called herself the last prophet before the "completion" or the end of the present age, the one through whom Christ spoke (Epiphanius, *Medicine Box* 48.2.4, 12.4). She also supposedly revealed that she embodied divine "Word and Spirit and Power" (Eusebius, *Ecclesiastical History* V.16.17). Priscilla claimed that a vision of a female Christ, "radiantly robed," had "implanted wisdom" into her, showing her that Pepuza in Phrygia was the site where the new Jerusalem would descend (Epiphanius, *Medicine Box* 49.1.3.). Hippolytus of Rome (ca. 170–206 CE) concedes that those who followed Maximilla, Priscilla, and Montanus acknowledged certain tenets of the Christian faith consistent with his own, primarily the scriptures and the gospels, but that the ascetic "novelties" of fasting and strange foods "introduced by women" made the New Prophecy suspect (*Refutation of All Heresies* VIII.12). Writing more harshly a century later, Epiphanius, bishop of Salamis (fourth century CE) also concedes that, unlike other groups he also considers heretics, adherents of the New Prophecy do not deny the authority of either Old or New Testament and accept the resurrection of the dead. On the other hand, they employ "useless testimonies," such as giving Eve credit for "special grace" since she ate the fruit of the tree of knowledge first, and they acknowledge Miriam, Moses' sister (Exod 15:20–21; Num 26:59; Mic 6:4), and the four daughters of Philip (Acts 21:8–9) as prophets in support of their claim that women should be prophets, bishops, presbyters, and holders of other clerical office. This feminine delusion, says Epiphanius, belongs to "deranged minds" and is "full of madness." As proof of his contention, he cites the teaching of

Paul in 1 Cor 11:11 and that of the author of 1 Timothy, whom he also believes to be Paul, that women should not teach or hold authority over men because Eve was the first deceived (*Medicine Box* 49.1–3; 1 Tim 2:12–15). These two opposing strains of Christianity in the second to the fourth centuries (the New Prophecy and its followers and those bishops and their followers who called themselves orthodox) both claimed scriptural warrant for their beliefs. The first held that scriptural precedent validates both the charismatic gift of prophecy and clerical leadership for women, while the other found scriptural counterexamples to close both prophetic and institutional power to women. The latter voice was the one that prevailed.

Redemption through Holy Power: Divine Men and Divine Women

There are redeeming figures who also possess divine power in the Greco-Roman world other than those associated with wisdom and prophecy. Unlike deities and the figure of Wisdom, who are heavenly beings with human faces, these may perhaps be deemed human beings with a divine face. That these figures are mainly men is indicated by their collective designation, *theioi andres* or "divine men." Often itinerant wanderers, the *theioi andres* attracted and impressed crowds with their possession of superhuman power through miracles, "signs," and "wonders." Their admirers and adherents believed that deities themselves had bestowed their own power and wisdom upon the *theioi andres* as a sign of approbation of their life and message. Their detractors accused them of being magicians who used sorcery to delude and defraud the innocent. Laudatory biographies like Philostratus' *Life of Apollonius of Tyana*, a second-century CE work about a first-century Pythagorean, hailed miracles, healings, and resurrections that were perceived as the "salvation of humankind" and "prophetic wisdom" (Philostratus, *Life of Apollonius of Tyana* 3.42.5–6, 3.44). Satirists like the second-century Lucian of Samosata, on the other hand, charged wonder-workers like Peregrinus Proteus, sometime Cynic philosopher and later teacher of "the amazing wisdom of the Christians," with charlatanry and the deception of fools (Lucian, *On the Death of Peregrinus* 11.1–2, 13.2). Jewish writers of the first century and later, like Josephus, Philo, and Artapanus, also tended to cast their "men of God," heroes like Moses and Joseph, in the mold of divine men, wonder-working prophets, and sages. Numerous legends surrounding the "man of deed" ('*ish ma'aseh*), the wise man and miracle-worker Hanina ben Dosa (ca. 70 BCE) found their way into the Mishnah (early third century) (m. *Sota* 9.15) and into the later Palestinian and Babylonian Talmuds. As has been pointed out by many scholars of the New Testament, the portrait of Jesus in the gospels as charismatic sage and miracle-worker owes much to the grasp of this image on both the popular and literary mind.[33] The ability of Jesus' followers to work miracles, frequently better than those of their opponents, who are portrayed as magicians and sorcerers, through the "power from on high" that they received from Jesus is also a theme in the canonical Acts of the Apostles.[34]

Miracle-working as a sign of divine power sanctioning the apostles' message and manner of life appears throughout the noncanonical Acts of the Apostles (second to fourth centuries). In the apostles of the apocryphal Acts, the model of the Greco-Roman divine man is conflated with that of the ascetic holy man, who derives his power largely from his celibate devotion to God.[35] Moreover, many of these apocryphal Acts include prominent female characters, whose conversion to Christianity is always accompanied by a conversion to a celibate lifestyle. Like the male apostles, they reject or forsake marriage or live in a marriage that eschews "filthy intercourse" (Acts of Thomas 12–13). Some remove themselves quite literally from the domestic sphere, leaving home and pursuing an itinerant life that is often dangerous. As a result of their conversion, the women are persecuted by their families, often their husbands or fiancés, and male civic authorities; sometimes, as in the Acts of (Paul and) Thecla, they are shunned by male apostles like Paul until they "prove" the strength of their resolve to pursue "the virgin life" (Acts of [Paul and] Thecla 25).

That this life is praiseworthy in the Christian circles within which the apocryphal Acts were generated and transmitted is indicated by the fact that the women who choose it, like their male counterparts, have the ability to perform miracles of healing, exorcism, and even resurrection from the dead, all parts of the standard repertoire of the theios anēr. Moreover, the divine power that approves of their choice gives them strength and guards them from the assaults of their enemies. As in the case of the "divine men," the miracles also point to the possession and transmission of heavenly power by these women. Hence, they may be regarded as theiai gynaikes or "divine women."[36] Sometimes, like Thecla in the Acts of (Paul and) Thecla (27–39) and Mygdonia in the Acts of Thomas (135–136), the woman converts other women; on other occasions, as for the unnamed virgin in the Coptic Acts of Andrew[37] and Drusiana in the Acts of John (81–83), she rescues or resurrects men who have fallen into the grip of demonic powers, usually the power of lust. In almost every case, the women are given divine power to resist men who have socially sanctioned sexual authority over them. To cite only one example, the concubines Agrippina, Nicaria, Euphemia, and Doris in the Acts of Peter (Actus Vercellenses 9) have the "power of Jesus" to resist the prefect Agrippa.

The divine power possessed by these women also gives them a place in the line of apostolic authority, which they often exercise even after the male apostles have left the scene. Thecla baptizes herself (Acts of [Paul and] Thecla 34); Mygdonia anoints other women as Thomas anoints the male Vazan (Acts of Thomas 157). Maximilla in the Acts of Andrew continues her apostolic ministry even after Andrew's martyrdom and her husband Aegeates' suicide.[38] Thecla (Acts of [Paul and] Thecla 42–43) acts as a missionary and is unaccompanied by a male apostle. After reuniting with Paul, Thecla leaves him, returns to Iconium, and converts her mother, Theocleia; she is then off to Seleucia, where she "enlightens many with the word of God" before her peaceful death.

Do these literary heroines represent actual Christian women and their concerns? May such stories have arisen in communities of celibate women who claimed Thecla and others as their models?[39] It is impossible to answer either question for certain. Thecla's tomb and shrine at Seleucia was known as the site of numerous miracles and visions and was visited by the traveler Egeria on her tour of the holy places of the East (Pilgrimage 22.2–23.6). Gregory of Nyssa says that, at the birth of his sister, Macrina, their mother, Emmelia, had a vision of Thecla from which Macrina received the "secret name" of Thecla (Life of Saint Macrina 2.10). The elder Melania (342–410), founder with Rufinus of the double monastery in Jerusalem, was also praised as the "second Thecla" (Rufinus, Apology 2.26). In the Symposium written by Methodius of Olympus in the late third century, Thecla leads the discourse of the virgin participants. John Chrysostom is also supposed to have written a panegyric in praise of her. Nevertheless, it is less often as the bold, self-baptized heroine of the Acts of (Paul and) Thecla that she is so honored, but rather as the model and protector of virgin purity. The Christian writer Tertullian (ca. 160–220), in fact, inveighs against women who use the example of Thecla to justify their own authority to baptize or to assume "men's offices" (On Baptism 17.5). His critique suggests that, in early third-century Carthage at least, there were women who knew this version of the story and considered it an empowering one.

Domesticated Asceticism

Against the example of Thecla as authorizing women to perform a function that ought to be reserved for men, Tertullian cites 1 Tim 2:12 (which he attributes to "the apostle," Paul) to the effect that women are not permitted to teach or hold any form of authority over men in the Christian churches. He writes in the spirit of the polemic against ascetic women's authority that appears in 1 Tim 4:1–7, which attacks as "the teachings of demons" an apparent asceticism that "forbids marriage" and is connected with the "godless tales of old women."[40] The author further urges that younger widows still of childbearing age should be confined to households lest they go about freely saying what they should not (1 Tim 5:13–14). That women freed from the restraints of spousal authority, childbearing, and confinement within a household embody a challenge to the second-century churches represented in the Pastoral Letters is also clear from 2 Tim 3:6–7 and Titus 2:3–5. The independent and celibate life is no option for women in these letters, unless they are widows well past their childbearing years, dedicated to piety, good works, and instructing younger women on how to be good wives and mothers.

   Yet there were male Christian writers who praised women who chose lifelong celibacy or adopted it after the death of a husband. This alternative gained strength in many Christian circles throughout the fourth century. Like pious and faithful widows dedicated to a nominally genderless and sexless deity, young women who refused to marry human husbands could dedicate their sexuality to Christ, the heavenly bridegroom. Groups of ascetic Christian women, often led by wealthy widows or by the virgin sisters or daughters of male clergy, gathered together in all-female households. Peter Brown notes that the female ascetic movement in fact grew out of Christian households, although not of the type praised in the Pastoral Letters.[41] Because of their containment within the traditional confines of the household and because even the redoubtable Paulas and Melanias never laid claim to be "charismatic spiritual guides" or "representatives of the [male] clergy," they were praised rather than condemned by the male episcopal hierarchy.[42] The *Canons of Athanasius*, for example, wax fulsome over the redemptive and protective power of such chaste women: "In every house of Christians, it is needful that there be a virgin, for the salvation of that whole house is that one virgin. And when wrath comes upon the whole city, it shall not come upon the house wherein a virgin is" (98.62–63).

Mary of Nazareth: Redemptive Virgin

In support of a virginal lifestyle that was honored as holy, yet not remote, capable of being practiced by women within households and not claiming apostolic freedom or the authority reserved for male clergy, Christian writers praised Mary of Nazareth as the model virgin. Her two greatest Latin-speaking exponents, Irenaeus of Lyons in the second century and Ambrose of Milan in the late fourth century, were eloquent in their praise of her as a woman who had "redeemed" the sin of the disobedient Eve by her obedient virginity (Irenaeus) and had achieved the state of total and original purity intended for humankind (Ambrose). Irenaeus went so far as to state that Mary had become "the cause of salvation, both to herself and the whole human race" (*Against Heresies* 3.21–22). For Ambrose, as for Irenaeus, this sinless "mother of virgins" has "worked the salvation of the world . . . the redemption of all" (*Letter* 49.2). Even Epiphanius of Salamis, who condemns the worship of Mary by certain Christian women, declares that she is the "virginal woman" who remedies the "defect" of Eve (*Medicine Box* 79.2–3, 9). For Syriac-speaking writers, Mary is also a savior figure, the one who redeems the sin of Eve, the fallen nature of womankind. Ephrem the Syrian (306–373) compares Mary's "conception by the Word" to Eve's deception "through hearing" the word of the serpent (*Hymns on the Church* 35.17; *Hymn to the Virgin* 23.5). She is the "cup of salvation" (*Hymn on the Crucifixion* 3.9) that is symbolized in the Eucharist. In other words, for male clerical authorities and writers, Mary had become the model of the obedient virgin, whose submissiveness to the divine will no less than her sexual purity singled her out from all other women. It is for this reason that, in their eyes, she is the cause of salvation, just as pious Christian women who led ascetic or celibate lives, yet were obedient to clerical male authority, were held up as examples of feminine virtue.

These Christian bishops and writers, like others before and after, may also have been influenced by a more popular version of the "life" of Mary, the second-century *Protevangelium Jacobi* (*Protogospel of James*). In it, Mary herself is shown to be conceived miraculously. Her virginity is perpetual, with miraculous proofs supporting it. In other noncanonical texts and legends, like the Syriac *History of the Blessed Virgin* and *The Miracles of Mary*, Mary is the source of miraculous healings, including the resurrection of the infant, Thomas Didymos. Certain Arabian

Christian women and their counterparts in Thrace and Scythia functioned as priestesses of Mary and offered cakes to her as a redeemer. For this, they are vilified by Epiphanius as vessels for the devil's "vomit" (*Medicine Box* 70.1) and as typical of the sex that is "easily mistaken, fallible and poor in intelligence," allied with the kind of "mania" that infected the teachings of the New Prophets Quintilla, Maximilla, and Priscilla.

What conclusions can we derive from these sources? First, female virginity was both praised and condemned by male ecclesial authorities that belonged to those circles of Christianity later known as orthodoxy. It was praised, as in the case of Mary, the model virgin, as long as it did not lay claim to male clerical privilege. It was condemned, as in the case of Thecla, when it symbolized both apostolic freedom and apostolic authority. Women themselves seem to have followed both models and to have revered both Mary and Thecla as sources of redemption. Whether they did so under male guidance or in defiance of it is difficult to tell from the male-authored texts.

Redemption through the Body: The Martyrs

The ambivalence shown toward celibate women as examples of authority and power within certain Christian circles of the first four centuries continues in the case of women who are martyrs. The same Tertullian who disparaged Thecla as an example for women seeking authority within the church makes the grandiose claim that "the blood of the martyrs is the seed [of the church]" (*Apology* 50). Martyrdom remains the ideal Christian witness until the legalization of Christianity in the early fourth century CE, when its themes of physical suffering, endurance, and struggle carry over into descriptions of the ideal ascetic life. Further, martyrdom was an "equal opportunity employer" for women and men, slave and free, and guaranteed immediate entrance to the kingdom of heaven. Martyrs, moreover, could safely be used as models of encouragement and edification by ecclesiastical authorities without being a source of trouble or challenge to earthly power. In fact, martyrologies often pointed to the ability of women to transcend the limits of their supposed weaker nature and bodies through the superhuman strength granted them by God because of their fidelity to him.

Martyrdom is "bearing witness" (*martyria*) to one's faith by exemplary suffering. The martyr is one who achieves not only his or her own redemption, but also that of others. As a Christian ideal, martyrdom's immediate antecedent is the passion of Jesus, but its earlier roots are in Jewish writings of the Maccabean period. 2 Maccabees, which purports to be an abridgment of the history of the Greek domination of Judea from 180 to 161 BCE by one Jason of Cyrene (2 Macc 2:19–32), includes stories of the death by torture of the aged Eleazar, the scribe, and of a mother, who first encourages her seven sons to undergo torture and death for the faith before she herself dies also. Their deaths avert God's punishment of the whole sinful nation (2 Macc 7:37–38) and bring the martyrs eternal life (2 Macc 7:36). 4 Maccabees, probably dating from the first century, expands the martyrology in 2 Macc 6:12–7:42 and even more clearly reflects immediate immortality as a reward for righteous endurance (4 Macc 7: 19; 16:25). It also reiterates the ideal of martyrdom as atonement for the sins of the nation (4 Macc 17:10–12). In 4 Maccabees, moreover, the mother of the seven sons is given a more prominent role. She is praised above her sons because her maternal emotion, belonging to the "weaker sex," is overcome by her fidelity to God. When she herself is about to be put to death, she throws herself into the flames to preserve her body from an unholy stranger's touch (4 Macc 17: 1). Because of her masculine courage (*andreia*), she is hailed as "mother of the nation, . . . more noble than males in steadfastness, and more courageous than men in endurance!" (4 Macc 15:29–30; NRSV). She is compared to Noah's ark, which saved the world (4 Macc 15:31–32), and to "the moon in heaven" since she has lighted the way for her sons and stands with them before God (4 Macc 17:5). Like the deity of a mystery, she "gives rebirth for immortality" to her sons (4 Macc 16:13). By encouraging them to die for the faith, she has given them eternal life.

Jesus and Martyrdom

The Maccabean martyrs were celebrated in later Christian, as well as Jewish, devotion, but for Christians, the prime exemplar of redemptive suffering was Jesus. All four New Testament gospels recount his torture, his death, his burial, and his resurrection. Luke's account of the death by stoning of Stephen in Acts 7:54–60 has distinct, and probably deliberate, parallels to the death of Jesus, including Stephen's forgiveness of his killers (Acts 8:60; cf. Luke 23:34). As he is dying, Stephen has a vision in which he sees Jesus standing at God's right hand in heaven, perhaps an indication that, for Stephen, the final judgment has already come. In the late first-century New Testament Book of Revelation, John's visions of heaven include the sight of "the souls of those who had been slain for the word of God and for the testimony [*martyria*]" (Rev 5:9). Paul's defense of his apostolic authority often included recounting the many physical afflictions he suffered (2 Cor 4:8–9, 6:4–5, 11:23–27; 1 Cor 4:9–13), speaking of himself as "a spectacle to the world, to angels and to mortals" (1 Cor 4:9) and of "carrying in the body the death of Jesus, so that the life of Jesus may also be made visible in our bodies" (2 Cor 4:10; NRSV).

Redeemed and Redemptive: Women Martyrs

Martyrdom is thus envisioned as an incarnation of Christ and his redemptive death in one's own body. Women's bodies are also transformed. Writing about the terrible tortures and death of the slave, Blandina, with her fellow martyrs in 177–178 CE, Irenaeus of Lyons says that witnesses "saw with their outward eyes in the person of their sister, the One who was crucified for them" (*Against Heresies* 8.1). The *Martyrdom of Perpetua and Felicitas*, dating from the early third century, contains an account, possibly her own, of four visions received in prison by the young Roman matron, Vibia Perpetua. The narrative of her imprisonment, her final vision, and the editor's account of her death and that of the slave woman, Felicitas, paradoxically reinforce and also undercut their embodiment as women who "carry in the body" the death of Christ along with the image of women. On the one hand, they seem, because of their imprisonment for Christ, to be set apart from typical social limits imposed on women. Perpetua's husband is not named, nor is the father of Felicitas' child. Perpetua deliberately severs ties with her family, especially her father, who is unable to shake her resolve. Her infant son is taken from her, her anxiety for him ceases, and her breast milk dries up. In her last vision, she is stripped of her clothes, and perhaps her identity as a woman, and becomes a man, a gladiator who wins the fight with a "vicious" Egyptian.

On the other hand, as Perpetua enters the arena, the narrator celebrates her as "beloved of God, a wife of Christ" (18). In the arena, both Perpetua and Felicitas are at first exposed naked, so that the crowd can see the delicate body of the young matron and the "dripping breasts" of the mother who has just given birth. Both are tossed by a mad heifer, "suitable to their sex." Perpetua, in an ecstatic state, seems more concerned for a modest matronly appearance; she fastens up her hair and pulls down her ripped tunic. In the end, however, Perpetua proves to have more manly courage than her male executioner. She guides the trembling gladiator's hand to cut her throat: "It was as though so great a woman, feared as she was by the unclean spirit, could not be dispatched unless she herself were willing" (21). The womanhood of Felicitas is also emphasized, along with her ability to transcend its supposed limitations through the ecstasy of martyrdom. Pregnant when she enters the prison, she and her companions pray for the child to be born early so that Felicitas may suffer martyrdom with the others. Taunted by a guard because of the pains of a premature labor, Felicitas replies that she is suffering now by herself, but in the martyrdom "another will be inside me who will suffer for me, just as I shall be suffering for him" (15). Felicitas rejoices as she enters the arena, "going from one bloodbath to another, . . . ready to wash after childbirth in a second baptism" (18). She gives birth to her own eternal life.

The trials and tortures of these heroic women emphasize their possession of heavenly power within female bodies, which are no obstacle to their strength. Indeed, their strength may be represented, as in Perpetua's vision, by having a male body or, as in Felicitas' case, by having a male within a female body. Perpetua, in particular, possesses extraordinary power. When asked by one of the "brothers" in prison to request a vision so that they may know their fate, it is granted in answer to her prayer. Again through her intercessory prayer, she delivers her dead brother Dinocrates from tormenting thirst in a dark and dirty hole. As Perpetua's dreams about Dinocrates show, martyrs have the power through prayer to redeem others. By virtue of their fidelity, the martyrs enter heaven as redeemed souls and do not have to wait for the universal judgment (Tertullian, On the Soul 55). But martyrdom results in the casting aside of the earthly body and with it earthly concerns. By their deaths, martyrs may transform the "suffering of the flesh" into redemptive suffering, but they are examples of how to die, not how to live. Their authority is in heaven, not on earth.

In summary, we may see that there were four general types of women acknowledged as sources of salvation, either for themselves or for others, within
emergent Christianity. Patrons and benefactors continued the example of pagan
and Jewish women, in the spirit of those women cited by Luke in Luke 8:1–3
and by Paul in his letters, using their own often considerable means as preservers
(*sospitatrices*) of congregations, clergy, and monastic foundations. Second, there
were the wise women and prophets, those like Mary of Magdala and Mary and
Martha of Bethany in the New Testament, who knew the "mysteries" of the
kingdom of God and communicated them to others, who were explicit models
for gnostic teachers like Marcellina. Prophets like Quintilla, Priscilla, and Maximilla exemplified the tradition of ecstatic prophecy that they found in the examples of Miriam and the daughters of Philip. These did not fare as well in the
history and canon written by the champions of "right belief" (Greek: orthodoxy). Instead, their inspiration was attributed to madness, unchastity, and possession by demonic spirits. Third were the ascetic and celibate women, praised
by both the "right believers" and those who opposed them, but for different
reasons. Those who called themselves orthodox praised the celibate virgins and
widows for their dedication to Christ and to doing good in order to benefit
congregations that were ruled by men. For them, the ideal woman was the
obedient virgin Mary, whose unquestioning submission to the will of God redeemed the sin of the disobedient Eve. Those who were called "heterodox" by
the self-designated "orthodox" looked to examples of rebellious virgins like
Thecla and disobedient wives like Mygdonia in the *Acts of Thomas* and Maximilla
in the *Acts of Andrew* as models not only of spiritual freedom, but also of an
earthly authority that was the equivalent to that of other, male apostles. Finally,
there were the female martyrs, whose courageous affirmation of Christ and reso-
lute endurance of suffering at the hands of the pagan authorities helped them
to transcend the limitations of their gendered bodies, to redeem the sins of
others by their fidelity, and to challenge both men and women to emulate their
struggle and their victory.

NOTES

1. Mircea Eliade, *History of Religious Ideas* (Chicago: University of Chicago Press, 1982)
2: 277.

2. For a fuller discussion of the meanings and nuances of salvation and redemption
in formative Christianity, see Gail Paterson Corrington, *Her Image of Salvation: Female Saviors
and Formative Christianity* (Louisville, KY: Westminster/John Knox, 1992) 43–80.

3. Luther H. Martin, *Hellenistic Religions* (New York: Oxford University Press, 1988)
24.

4. Susan Ashbrook Harvey, "Women in Early Syriac Christianity," in *Images of Women
in Antiquity*, ed. Averil Cameron and Amélie Kuhrt (Detroit, MI: Wayne State University
Press, 1983) 290.

5. Elaine Pagels, *The Gnostic Gospels* (New York: Random House, 1989; first edition,
New York: Random House, 1979) 60.

6. Ross S. Kraemer, *Her Share of the Blessings: Women's Religion among Pagans, Jews and Christians*

in the *Greco-Roman World* (New York: Oxford University Press, 1992) 71. See also Martin, "The Mysteries and the Sovereignty of the Feminine" 58–89.

7. Corrington, *Her Image* 81–102.

8. See esp. the Greek philosopher and moralist Plutarch's approving account of the Isis myth in his *On Isis and Osiris*.

9. For the English translation of this text, see Ross S. Kraemer, ed., *Maenads, Martyrs, Matrons, Monastics: A Sourcebook on Women's Religions in the Greco-Roman World* (Philadelphia: Fortress, 1988) 368–70.

10. See Corrington, *Her Image* 96, 102 n.44, for references to this stele.

11. Maria Dzielska, *Hypatia of Alexandria*, trans. F. Lyra (Cambridge, MA: Harvard University Press, 1995) 104.

12. Victor Tran Tam Tinh, *Isis Lactans*. EPRO 26 (Leiden: E. J. Brill, 1973) 29–30, 45; Gail Paterson Corrington, "The Milk of Salvation: Redemption by the Mother in Late Antiquity and Early Christianity," HTR 82/4 (July 1989) 393–420; Corrington, *Her Image* 188–89.

13. Mary R. Lefkowitz and Maureen B. Fant, *Women's Life in Greece and Rome. A Sourcebook in Translation*, 2nd ed. (Baltimore, MD: Johns Hopkins University Press, 1992) no. 162.

14. Peter Brown, *The Body and Society: Men, Women and Sexual Renunciation in Early Christianity* (New York: Columbia University Press, 1988) 144–45.

15. Silvia Schroer, "The Book of Sophia," in *Searching the Scriptures: Volume 2, A Feminist Commentary*, ed. Elisabeth Schüssler Fiorenza (New York: Crossroad, 1994) 17–18.

16. Claudia V. Camp, *Wisdom and the Feminine in the Book of Proverbs* (Sheffield: JSOT/ Almond, 1985).

17. Carole R. Fontaine, "Proverbs," in *The Women's Bible Commentary*, ed. Carol A. Newsom and Sharon H. Ringe (Louisville, KY: Westminster/John Knox, 1992) 151.

18. Ross S. Kraemer, "The Book of Aseneth," in Schüssler Fiorenza, *Searching the Scriptures* 861.

19. Ibid. 885.

20. Rebecca Lesses, "The Daughters of Job," in Schüssler Fiorenza, *Searching the Scriptures* 146–47.

21. Jacob Neusner, *The Incarnation of God: The Character of Diversity in Formative Judaism* (Philadelphia: Fortress, 1988) 202.

22. Amy-Jill Levine, "The Sibylline Oracles," in Schüssler Fiorenza, *Searching the Scriptures* 101.

23. Gail P. Corrington-Streete, "Sex, Spirit, and Control: Paul and the Corinthian Women," in *Ritual, Power, and the Body: Historical Perspectives on the Representation of Greek Women*, ed. C. Nadia Seremetakis (New York: Pella, 1993) 110–11.

24. Levine, "The Sibylline Oracles" 100–101.

25. Ibid. 108.

26. See Ross S. Kraemer, "Ecstasy and Possession: The Attraction of Women to the Cult of Dionysus," HTR 72 (1979) 55–80.

27. English translations of the *Testament of Job* (as well as those of the other patriarchs) and the *Sibylline Oracles* (Jewish Sibyllines with Christian editing) can be found in *The Old Testament Pseudepigrapha*, ed. James H. Charlesworth (Garden City, NY: Doubleday, 1983–1985).

28. For the relationship between Jesus and Wisdom in the community that produced Q, see esp. Burton Mack, *The Lost Gospel: The Book of Q and Christian Origins* (San Francisco: HarperSanFrancisco, 1993); Luise Schottroff, "The Sayings Source Q," *Searching the Scriptures* 510–34.

29. Anne McGuire, "Thunder, Perfect Mind," in Schüssler Fiorenza, *Searching the Scriptures* 48.

30. *Gospel of Mary* 9.12–24; 10.1–3; 18.14–15; *Gospel of Philip* 28(59.6–10); 48(63.30–64.10); *Gospel of Thomas* 114.

31. English translation from Kraemer, *Maenads* no. 78.

32. Corrington-Streete, "Sex, Spirit and Control"; Dale B. Martin, *The Corinthian Body* (New Haven, CT: Yale University Press, 1995) 229–49.

33. For a fuller discussion of the divine man in Greco-Roman antiquity and the relationship of this figure to New Testament Christology, see Gail Paterson Corrington, *The "Divine Man": His Origin and Function in Hellenistic Popular Religion* (Bern: Peter Lang, 1986).

34. Acts 1:8; 3:1–11; 5:12–16; 8:13; 9:36–42; 12:1–11; 13:1–12; 14:8–18; 16:25–34; 19:11–20, 27; 28:1–10.

35. Peter Brown, *Society and the Holy in Late Antiquity* (Berkeley, CA: University of California Press, 1981) 131–32.

36. For fuller exploration of this literary model, see Gail Paterson Corrington, "The 'Divine Woman'? Propaganda and the Power of Chastity in the New Testament Apocrypha," in *Rescuing Creusa: New Methodological Approaches to Women in Antiquity*, ed. Marilyn B. Skinner (*Helios* 13/2 [1986]) 151–62: Corrington, "The Divine Woman: A Reconsideration," *ATR* 70/3 (1988) 207–19.

37. Papyrus Coptic Utrecht, Wilhelm Schneemelcher, ed., *New Testament Apocrypha, Volume 2: Writings Relating to the Apostles, Apocalypses and Related Subjects*, rev. ed. of the collection initiated by Edgar Hennecke, English trans. ed. R. McL. Wilson. (Louisville, KY: Westminster/John Knox, 1992) 127.

38. Schneemelcher, volume 2, 151.

39. See, for example, Dennis R. MacDonald, "The Role of Women in the Production of the Apocryphal Acts of the Apostles," *Iliff Review* 41/4 (1984) 21–38; Sheila E. McGinn, "The Acts of Thecla," in Schüssler Fiorenza, *Searching the Scriptures* 800–28; Stevan L. Davies, *The Revolt of the Widows: The Social World of the Apocryphal Acts* (New York: Winston/Seabury, 1980); Virginia Burrus, *Chastity as Autonomy: Women in the Stories of the Apocryphal Acts* (Lewiston, NY: Edwin Mellen, 1987). For a counterargument, see Jean-Daniel Kaestli's critique of Burrus in "Response," *Semeia* 38 (1986) 119–31. McGinn also points out that even noncanonical documents like the Apocryphal Acts were "affected by the redactional interests of an institutional and patriarchal church" (801).

40. Translation by Joanna Dewey, "1 Timothy," in Newsom and Ringe, *Women's Bible Commentary* 354.

41. Brown, *Body and Society* 263.

42. Ibid. 265.

ABBREVIATIONS

1QSa	Rule of the Community of Qumran, Appendix A
1QM	War Scroll
4Q502	Ritual of Marriage from Qumran Cave 4
ABD	*Anchor Bible Dictionary* (David Noel Freedman, ed., New York: Double-day and Co., 1992)
AJPhil	*American Journal of Philology*
ANRW	*Aufstieg und Niedergang der römischen Welt* (H. Temporini and W. Haase, ed., Berlin, 1972)
ATR	*Anglican Theological Review*
b. Avodah Zarah	Tractate Avodah Zarah of the Babylonian Talmud
b. Erub	Tractate Erubin of the Babylonian Talmud
b. Git.	Tractate Gittin Zarah of the Babylonian Talmud
b. Meg.	Tractate Megillah of the Babylonian Talmud
b. Ned	Tractate Nedarim of the Babylonian Talmud
b. Pesah.	Tractate Pesahim of the Babylonian Talmud
b. Sanh.	Tractate Sanhedrin of the Babylonian Talmud
CD	Damascus Document
CIJ	*Corpus Inscriptionum Judaicarum*, (J.-B. Frey, ed., Vatican City, 1936–52)
CPJ	*Corpus papyrorum Judaicarum*, (A. Tcherikover et al., ed., 3 vols. Cambridge, MA, 1957–64)
EPRO	*Études préliminaires aux religions orientales dans l'Empire romain*
GCS	*Die griechische christliche Schriftsteller der ersten drei Jahrhund erte* (Leipzig, 1897–1941; Berlin and Leipzig, 1953; Berlin, 1954–)
HTR	*Harvard Theological Review*
HWW	*A History of Women in the West* (Pauline Schmitt Pantel, ed.; Arthur Goldhammer, trans.; Cambridge, MA: Belknap Press of Harvard University Press, 1992)

ISBE	International Standard Bible Encyclopedia (2d ed., G. W. Bromiley, ed.)
JANES	Journal of Ancient Near Eastern Studies
JBL	Journal of Biblical Literature
JECS	Journal of Early Christian Studies
JFSR	Journal of Feminist Studies in Religion
JSNT	Journal for the Study of the New Testament
JSNTS	Journal for the Study of the New Testament Supplements
JSOT	Journal for the Study of the Old Testament
JTS	Journal of Theological Studies
LCL	Loeb Classical Library
m. Soṭa	Tractate Soṭa of the Mishnah
NHC	Nag Hammadi Codex
NovT	Novum Testamentum
NRSV	New Revised Standard Version
NTS	New Testament Studies
P. Cowley	Papyrus Cowley
PGM	Papyri graecae magicae (3 vols, K. Priesendanz, ed., Leipzig, 1928–41)
P. Oxy	Papyrus Oxyrhynchus
P. Yadin	Papyrus Yadin
RSV	Revised Standard Version
SBL	Society of Biblical Literature
T. Job	Testament of Job
T. Reuben	Testament of Reuben
VigChr	Vigiliae Christianae
WUNT	Wissenschaftliche Untersuchungen zum Neuen Testament
ZTK	Zeitschrift für Theologie und Kirche

COMPREHENSIVE BIBLIOGRAPHY

TEXTS AND TRANSLATIONS FOR THE ANCIENT SOURCES

Many of the sources cited in this text are available in:

Kraemer, Ross S., ed. *Maenads, Martyrs, Matrons, Monastics: A Sourcebook on Women's Religions in the Greco-Roman World.* Philadelphia: Fortress, 1988.

Complete English translations of the Qumran (Dead Sea) scrolls can be found in:
Garcia-Martinez, Florentino. *The Dead Sea Scrolls Translated. The Qumran Texts in English.* 2nd ed. Trans. Wilfred G. E. Watson. Leiden: E. J. Brill, 1994.

Other early Jewish texts are available in:
Charlesworth, James H. *The Old Testament Pseudepigrapha in English.* 2 vols. Garden City, NY: Doubleday, 1985.

The gnostic texts are available in the following:
Layton, Bentley. *The Gnostic Scriptures.* Garden City, NY: Doubleday, 1988.
Robinson, James M., ed. *The Nag Hammadi Library in English.* 3rd rev. ed. San Francisco: HarperSanFrancisco, 1988; 4th rev. ed. Leiden: E. J. Brill, 1996.

Most early Christian texts are available in a number of standard series; the most comprehensive is Roberts, Alexander, and Donaldson, James, eds. *The Ante-Nicene Fathers: Translations of the Fathers down to A.D. 325.* 10 vols. Grand Rapids, MI: W. B. Eerdmanns, 1950–53; Schaff, Philip, ed. *A Select Library of the Nicene and Post-Nicene Fathers of the Christian Church.* 14 vols. Grand Rapids, MI: W. B. Eerdmanns, 1978–79. Others are easiest to find in the following:

Bright, William. *The Canons of the First Four General Councils.* Oxford: Clarendon, 1892.

Chadwick, Henry, ed. *Origen, Contra Celsum.* Cambridge: Cambridge University Press, 1980.

Dix, Gregory, and Henry Chadwick, eds. *The Treatise on the Apostolic Tradition of St. Hippolytus of Rome.* 2nd rev. ed., reissued with additional corrections. London: Alban, 1992.

Hefele, Charles Joseph. *A History of the Councils of the Church.* 5 vols. Edinburgh: T&T Clark, 1883–96.

Schneemelcher, Wilhelm, ed. *New Testament Apocrypha.* 2 vols. Rev. ed. English translation by Robert McL. Wilson. Louisville, KY: Westminster/John Knox, 1991–92.

Most Greek and Roman authors (including some early Christian authors) cited in this volume are available in the Loeb Classical Library, which provides both an original language text and facing English translation. Others can be found in the following:

Minucius Felix, Marcus. *The Octavius of Marcus Minucius Felix,* trans. G. Clarke. New York: Newman, 1974.

Soranus, *Gynecology.* Trans. Owsei Temkin. Baltimore, MD: Johns Hopkins University Press, 1956.

Stern, Menahem. *Greek and Latin Authors on Jews and Judaism.* 3 vols. Jerusalem: Israel Academy of Sciences and Humanities, 1976–84.

Walzer, Richard. *Galen on Jews and Christians.* London: Oxford University Press, 1949.

STUDIES

Abrahamsen, Valerie. "Women at Philippi: The Pagan and the Christian Evidence." *JFSR* 3 (1987) 17–30.

Achtemeier, Paul J. "Mark, Gospel of," *ABD* 4:541–57.

Alexandre, Monique. "Early Christian Women." In *A History of Women in the West: Volume 1: From Ancient Goddesses to Christian Saints,* ed. Pauline Schmitt Pantel, trans. Arthur Goldhammer. Cambridge, MA: Belknap Press of Harvard University Press, 1992, 407–44.

Allen, Charlotte. "The Search for a No-Frills Jesus." *Atlantic Monthly* (December 1996), 5/ff.

Allison, Dale C., Jr. *The Jesus Tradition in Q.* Harrisburg, PA: Trinity Press International, 1997.

The American Heritage Dictionary of the English Language. 3rd ed. Boston: Houghton Mifflin, 1992.

Arnal, William E. "Gendered Couplets in Q and Legal Formulations: From Rhetoric to Social History." *JBL* 116 (1997) 75–94.

———. "Reconstruction of Q 7:29–30." Paper presented to the International Q Project, Claremont CA, May 1994.

———. "The Rhetoric of Marginality: Apocalypticism, Gnosticism, and Sayings Gospels." *HTR* 88/4 (1995) 471–94.

Arthur, Rose H. *The Wisdom Goddess: Feminine Motifs in Eight Nag Hammadi Documents.* Lanham, MD: University Press of America, 1984.

Atkinson, Clarissa W., Constance H. Buchanan, and Margaret R. Miles, eds. *Immaculate and Powerful: The Female in Sacred Image and Social Reality.* Boston: Beacon, 1985.

Atwood, Margaret. *The Robber Bride.* New York: Doubleday, 1994.

Aune, David E., ed. *Greco-Roman Literature and the New Testament: Selected Forms of Genres.* Atlanta, GA: Scholars Press, 1988.

Balch, David L. "Household Codes." In *Greco-Roman Literature and the New Testament: Selected Forms and Genres,* ed. David E. Aune. Atlanta, GA: Scholars Press, 1988, 25–50.

Balsdon, J. V. P. D. *Roman Women, Their History and Habits.* London: Bodley Head, 1962; New York: Barnes and Noble, 1983.

Bassler, Jouette. *1 Timothy, 2 Timothy, Titus.* Abingdon New Testament Commentaries. Nashville, KY: Abingdon, 1996.

———. "The Widows' Tale: A Fresh Look at 1 Tim 5:3–16." *JBL* 103 (1984) 23–41.

Batten, Alicia. "More Queries for Q: Women and Christian Origins." *Biblical Theology Bulletin* 24/2 (Summer 1994) 44–51.

Bauer, Walter, William F. Arndt, F. Wilbur Gingrich, and Frederick Danker. *A Greek-English Lexicon of the New Testament and Other Early Christian Literature.* Chicago: University of Chicago Press, 1979.

Baumgarten, Joseph M. "4Q502, Marriage or Golden-Age Ritual?" *Journal of Jewish Studies* 34 (1983) 125–35.

Beard, Mary, and John North, eds. *Pagan Priests: Religion and Power in the Ancient World.* Ithaca, NY: Cornell University Press, 1990.

Beckwith, John. *Early Christian and Byzantine Art.* 2nd ed. The Pelican History of Art. Harmondsworth, UK: Penguin Books, 1979.

Benko, Stephen. "The Libertine Gnostic Sect of the Phibionites According to Epiphanius." *VigChr* 21 (1967) 103–19.

———. "Pagan Criticism of Christianity During the First Two Centuries AD." In *ANRW* 2.23.2, 1054–1118.

Betz, Hans Dieter, ed. *The Greek Magical Papyri in Translation, Including the Demotic Spells.* 2nd ed. Chicago: University of Chicago Press, 1992.

Betzig, Laura. "Roman Polygyny." *Ethnology and Sociobiology* 13 (1992) 309–49.

Bianchi, Ugo, ed. *Le origini dello gnosticismo: Colloquio di Messina, 13–18 Aprile 1966.* Studies in the History of Religions 12. Leiden: E. J. Brill, 1967.

Blackman, Philip. *Mishnayoth.* New York: Judaica, 1963; reprint 1990.

Bloom, Harold. "'Whoever Discovers the Interpretation of These Sayings . . . ': A Reading." In *The Gospel of Thomas: The Hidden Sayings of Jesus*, ed. Marvin Meyer. San Francisco: HarperSanFrancisco, 1992, 111–21.

Boswell, John. *Christianity, Homosexuality, and Social Tolerance: Gay People in Western Europe from the Beginning of the Christian Era to the Fourteenth Century.* Chicago: University of Chicago Press, 1980.

Bowman, Alan K., and J. David Thomas. "New Texts from Vindolanda." *Britannia* 18 (1987) 135–42.

Boyarin, Daniel. *Carnal Israel. Reading Sex in Talmudic Culture.* Berkeley, CA: University of California Press, 1993.

———. *Intertextuality and the Reading of Midrash.* Bloomington, IN: Indiana University Press, 1990.

Bradshaw, Paul F. "Redating the *Apostolic Tradition*: Some Preliminary Steps." In *Rule of Prayer, Rule of Faith: Essays in Honor of Aidan Kavanagh, O.S.B.*, ed. Nathan Mitchell and John F. Baldovin. Collegeville, MN: Liturgical Press, 1996, 3–17.

———. *The Search for the Origins of Christian Worship.* New York: Oxford University Press, 1992.

Briggs, Sheila. "Galatians." In *Searching the Scriptures: Volume 2, A Feminist Commentary*, ed. Elisabeth Schüssler Fiorenza. New York: Crossroad, 1994, 218–36.

Brock, Sebastian, and Susan Ashbrook Harvey, eds. *Holy Women of the Syrian Orient.* Berkeley, CA: University of California Press, 1987.

Broek, R. van den. "The Present State of Gnostic Studies." *VigChr* 37 (1983) 41–71.

Brooks, Roger. "Mishnah." *ABD* 4:871–73.

Brooten, Bernadette. "Early Christian Women and Their Cultural Context: Issues of Method in Historical Reconstruction." In *Feminist Perspectives on Biblical Scholarship*, ed. Adela Yarbro Collins. Biblical Scholarship in North America 10; Chico, CA: Scholars Press, 1985, 65–91.

———. "Inscriptional Evidence for Women as Leaders in the Ancient Synagogue." *SBL Seminar Papers* 20. Chico, CA: Scholars Press, 1981, 1–17.

———. "Jewish Women's History in the Roman Period, A Task for Christian Theology." In *Christians among Jews and Gentiles. Essays in Honor of Krister Stendahl on His Sixty-Fifth Birthday*, ed. G. W. E. Nickelsburg and George W. MacRae. Philadelphia: Fortress, 1986, 22–30 (also published in HTR 79 [1986]:3–4).

———. "Junia . . . Outstanding among the Apostles (Rom 16:7)." In *Women Priests: A Catholic Commentary on the Vatican Declaration*, ed. Leonard and Arlene Swidler. New York: Paulist, 1977, 141–44.

———. "Könnten Frauen in Alten Judentum die Scheidung betrieben? Überlegung zu Mk 10, 11–12 und 1 Kor 7, 10–11." *Evangelische Theologie* 42 (1982) 66–80.

———. *Love Between Women: Early Christian Responses to Female Homoeroticism*. Chicago: University of Chicago Press, 1996.

———. "Paul's Views on the Nature of Women and Female Homoeroticism." In *Immaculate and Powerful: The Female in Sacred Image and Social Reality*, ed. Clarissa W. Atkinson, Constance H. Buchanan, and Margaret R. Miles. Boston: Beacon, 1985, 61–87.

———. *Women Leaders in the Ancient Synagogue*. Brown Judaic Studies 36. Chico, CA: Scholars Press, 1982.

Brown, Cheryl Anne. *No Longer Be Silent. First Century Jewish Portraits of Biblical Women*. Gender and the Biblical Tradition. Louisville, KY: Westminster Press, 1992.

Brown, Peter. *The Body and Society: Men, Women and Sexual Renunciation in Early Christianity*. New York: Columbia University Press, 1988.

———. "Late Antiquity: The 'Wellborn' Few." In *A History of Private Life: volume 1: from Pagan Rome to Byzantium*, ed. Paul S. Veyne. Cambridge, MA: Belknap, 1987, 239–97.

———. *Society and the Holy in Late Antiquity*. Berkeley, CA: University of California Press, 1981.

Brown, Raymond E. *The Churches the Apostles Left Behind*. New York: Paulist, 1984.

———. *The Gospel According to John volume 1*. Anchor Bible Commentary volume 29. Garden City, NY: Doubleday, 1966.

———. "Roles of Women in the Gospel of John," *Theological Studies* 36 (1975) 688–699. Reprinted in Brown, *The Community of the Beloved Disciple: The Life, Loves and Hates of an Individual Church in New Testament Times*. New York: Paulist, 1979, 183–89.

Brown, Raymond E., J. Fitzmyer, and R. Murphy, eds. *The New Jerome Biblical Commentary*. Englewood Cliffs, NJ: Prentice-Hall, 1990.

Buckley, Jorunn Jacobsen. "A Cult-Mystery in the Gospel of Philip." *JBL* 99 (1980) 569–581.

———. *Female Fault and Fulfillment in Gnosticism*. Chapel Hill, NC: University of North Carolina Press, 1986.

———. "An Interpretation of Logion 114 in the Gospel of Thomas." *NovT* 27 (1985) 245–72.

———. "Libertines or Not: Fruit, Bread, Semen and Other Body Fluids in Gnosticism." *JECS* 2 (1994) 15–31.

———. "Two Female Gnostic Revealers." *History of Religions* 19 (1980) 259–69.

Budge, E. A. W., trans. *The History of the Blessed Virgin*. London: Luzac and Co., 1899.

Bultmann, Rudolf. *The Gospel of John: A Commentary*, trans. G. R. Beasley-Murray. Philadelphia: Westminster, 1971.

————. *The Johannine Epistles*, trans. R. Philip O'Hara with Lance C. McGaughy and Robert W. Funk. Hermeneia—A Critical and Historical Commentary on the Bible. Philadelphia: Fortress, 1973.

Burridge, Kenelm. *New Heaven, New Earth. A Study in Millenarian Activities*. New York: Schocken, 1969.

Burrus, Virginia. *Chastity as Autonomy: Women in the Stories of the Apocryphal Acts*. Lewiston, NY: Edwin Mellen, 1987.

————. "The Heretical Woman as Symbol in Alexander, Athanasius, Epiphanius, and Jerome." HTR 84 (1991) 229–48.

Butrica, James. "Lygdamus, Nephew of Messalla?" *Liverpool Classical Monthly* 18/4 (1993) 51–53.

Bynum, Caroline. "Introduction: The Complexity of Symbols." In *Gender and Religion: On the Complexity of Symbols*, ed. Stevan Harrell, Caroline Bynum, and Paula Richman. Boston: Beacon, 1986, 1–20.

Cameron, Averil, and Amélie Kuhrt, eds. *Images of Women in Antiquity*. Detroit, MI: Wayne State Press, 1983.

Cameron, Ron. "The Gospel of Thomas: A Forschungsbericht and Analysis." ANRW 2.25.6, 4195–4251.

Camp, Claudia V. *Wisdom and the Feminine in the Book of Proverbs*. Sheffield, UK: JSOT/Almond, 1985.

Cardman, Francine. "Acts of the Women Martyrs." *Anglican Theological Review* 70 (1988) 144–50.

Carpenter, Thomas H., and Christopher Faraone, eds. *Masks of Dionysos*. Ithaca, NY: Cornell University Press, 1993.

Casey, Robert P. *The Excerpta ex Theodoto of Clement of Alexandria*. London: Christophers, 1934.

Castelli, Elizabeth A. "Allegories of Hagar: Reading Galatians 4.21–31 with Postmodern Feminist Eyes." In *The New Literary Criticism and the New Testament*, ed. Edgar V. McKnight and Elizabeth Struthers Malbon. JSNTS 109. Sheffield, UK: Sheffield Academic Press, 1994, 228–50.

————. "Heteroglossia, Hermeneutics, and History: A Review Essay of Recent Feminist Studies of Early Christianity." JFSR 10/2 (1994) 73–98.

————. "'I Will Make Mary Male': Pieties of the Body and Gender Transformation of Christian Women in Late Antiquity." In *Body Guards: The Cultural Politics of Gender Ambiguity*, ed. Julia Epstein and Kristina Straub. London: Routledge, 1991, 29–49.

————. "Romans." In *Searching the Scriptures: Volume 2, A Feminist Commentary*, ed. Elisabeth Schüssler Fiorenza. New York: Crossroad, 1994, 272–300.

————. "Virginity and Its Meaning for Women's Sexuality in Early Christianity." JFSR 2 (1986) 62–85.

Castelli, Elizabeth A., and James McBride. "Beyond the Language and Memory of the Fathers: Feminist Perspectives in Religious Studies." In *Transcending Boundaries: Multi-Disciplinary Approaches to the Study of Gender*, ed. Pamela R. Frese and John M. Coggeshall. New York: Bergin & Garvey, 1991, 113–50.

Catchpole, David. *The Quest for Q*. Edinburgh: T&T Clark, 1993.

Chadwick, Henry. *The Early Church*. The Pelican History of the Church, Vol. 1. Harmondsworth: Penguin Books, 1967.

Charlesworth, James H., ed. *The Old Testament Pseudepigrapha*. 2 vols. Garden City, NY: Doubleday, 1983–85.

Clark, Elizabeth A. "Ascetic Renunciation and Feminine Advancement: A Paradox of Late Antique Christianity." ATR 63 (1981) 240–57.

————. "Friendship between the Sexes: Classical Theory and Christian Practice." In

Jerome, Chrysostom, and Friends: Essays and Translations. Lewiston, NY: Edwin Mellen, 1979, 35–106.

———. "Ideology, History, and the Construction of 'Woman' in Late Ancient Christianity." *JECS* 2 (1994) 155–84.

———. "Theory and Practice in Late Ancient Asceticism: Jerome, Chrysostom, and Augustine." *JFSR* 5/2 (1989) 25–46.

Cockerill, Gareth Lee. "Joses." *ABD* 3:998.

Cohen, Shaye J. D. "Menstruants and the Sacred in Judaism and Christianity." In *Women's History and Ancient History,* ed. Sarah B. Pomeroy. Chapel Hill, NC: University of North Carolina Press, 1991, 271–99.

Cole, Susan Guettel. "Could Greek Women Read and Write?" *Women's Studies* 8 (1981) 129–55. Reprinted in Helene P. Foley, ed. *Reflections of Women in Antiquity.* New York: Gordon & Breach, 1981, 219–45.

Collins, Adela Yarbro. *The Beginning of the Gospel: Probings of Mark in Context.* Minneapolis, MN: Fortress, 1992.

———, ed. *Feminist Perspectives on Biblical Scholarship.* Chico, CA: Scholars Press, 1985.

Conzelmann, Hans. *Acts of the Apostles: A Commentary on the Acts of the Apostles.* trans. James Limburg, A. Thomas Kraabel, and Donald H. Juel, ed. Eldon Jay Epp with Christopher R. Matthews, Hermeneia—A Critical and Historical Commentary on the Bible. Philadelphia: Fortress, 1987.

———. *The Theology of St. Luke.* Trans. Geoffrey Buswell. New York: Harper and Row, 1961.

Cooper, Kate. *The Virgin and the Bride: Idealized Womanhood in Late Antiquity.* Cambridge, MA: Harvard University Press, 1996.

Corley, Kathleen E. "Feminist Myths of Christian Origins." In *Reimagining Christian Origins. A Colloquium Honoring Burton L. Mack,* ed. Elizabeth A. Castelli and Hal Taussig. Valley Forge, PA: Trinity Press International, 1996, 51–67.

———. "Jesus, Mary Magdalene and Salome." *The Fourth R* (January–February 1996) 12–16.

———. *Private Women, Public Meals: Social Conflict in the Synoptic Tradition.* Peabody, MA: Hendrickson, 1993.

Corrington, Gail Paterson. *The "Divine Man": His Origin and Function in Hellenistic Popular Religion.* New York: Peter Lang, 1986.

———. "The 'Divine Woman'? Propaganda and the Power of Chastity in the New Testament Apocrypha." In *Rescuing Creusa: New Methodological Approaches to Women in Antiquity.* ed. Marilyn B. Skinner. *Helios* 13/2 (1986) 151–62.

———. "The Divine Woman: A Reconsideration." *ATR* 70:3 (1988) 207–19.

———. *Her Image of Salvation: Female Saviors and Formative Christianity.* Louisville, KY: Westminster/John Knox, 1992.

———. "The Milk of Salvation: Redemption by the Mother in Late Antiquity and Early Christianity." *HTR* 82/4 (July 1989) 393–420.

Corrington-Streete, Gail P. "Sex, Spirit, and Control: Paul and the Corinthian Women." In *Ritual, Power, and the Body: Historical Perspectives on the Representation of Greek Women.* ed. C. Nadia Seremetakis. New York: Pella, 1993, 95–117.

Cotter, Wendy J. "Prestige, Protection and Promise: A Proposal for the Apologetics of Q2." In *The Gospel Behind the Gospels: Current Studies in Q.* NovTSup 75, ed. Ronald A. Piper. Leiden: E. J. Brill, 1995, 117–38.

———. "Women's Authority Roles in Paul's Churches: Counter-cultural or Conventional?" *NovT* 36 (1994) 350–72.

Couliano, Ioan P. "Feminine versus Masculine: The Sophia Myth and the Origins of Feminism." In *Struggles of Gods,* ed. H. G. Kippenberg. Berlin: Mouton, 1984, 65–98.

Crossan, John Dominic. *The Historical Jesus: The Life of a Mediterranean Jewish Peasant.* San Francisco: HarperSanFrancisco, 1991.

———. *Jesus, A Revolutionary Biography.* San Francisco: HarperSanFrancisco, 1994.

———. *In Parables: The Challenge of the Historical Jesus.* San Francisco: Harper and Row, 1973, 1985.

Cuffari, Katie. "Confrontation of Cosmic and Social Systems of Authority: The Female Character as Textual Tool." Term paper, Haverford College, Haverford, PA, December 1996.

Dahl, Nils A. "The Arrogant Archon and the Lewd Sophia: Jewish Tradition in Gnostic Revolt." In *The Rediscovery of Gnosticism,* Vol. 2, ed. Bentley Layton. Leiden: E. J. Brill, 1981, 659–712.

Danby, Herbert. *The Mishnah.* Oxford: Oxford University Press, 1933.

D'Angelo, Mary Rose. "*Abba* and 'Father': Imperial Theology and the Jesus Traditions." *JBL* 111 (1992) 611–30.

———. "Beyond Father and Son." In *Justice as Mission: An Agenda for the Church,* ed. T. Brown and C. Lind. Burlington, Ontario, Canada: Trinity Press, 1985, 107–18.

———. "Blessed the One Who Reads and Those Who Hear: The Beatitudes in Their Biblical Contexts." In *New Perspectives on the Beatitudes,* ed. Francis A. Eigo. Proceedings of the Theology Institute of Villanova University; Villanova, PA: Villanova University Press, 1995, 45–92.

———. "Colossians." In *Searching the Scriptures: Volume 2, A Feminist Commentary,* ed. Elisabeth Schüssler Fiorenza. New York: Crossroad, 1994, 313–24.

———. "The Concrete Foundation of Christianity: Re-membering Jesus." In *Proceedings of the Catholic Theological Society of America.* Volume 49, ed. Paul Crowley, 13–146.

———. "A Critical Note: John 20:17 and Apocalypse of Moses 31." *JTS* n.s. 41 (1990) 529–36.

———. "Diakonia." In *Dictionary of Feminist Theologies,* ed. Letty M. Russell and Shannon Clarkson. Louisville, KY: Westminster/John Knox, 1996, 66–67.

———. "Gender and Power in the Gospel of Mark: The Daughter of Jairus and the Woman with the Flow of Blood." In *Aspects of the Miraculous in Ancient Judaism and Christianity,* ed. John C. Cavadini. Notre Dame, IN: University of Notre Dame Press, forthcoming.

———. "Remarriage and the Divorce Sayings Attributed to Jesus." In *Divorce and Remarriage: Religious and Psychological Perspectives,* ed. William P. Roberts. Kansas City, MO: Sheed and Ward, 1990, 78–106.

———. "Re-Membering Jesus: Women, Prophecy and Resistance in the Beginnings of Christianity." *Horizons* 19 (1992) 198–218.

———. "A Response to 'Pursuing the Spiritual Eve' by Elaine Pagels." In *Images of the Feminine in Gnosticism,* ed. Karen L. King. Philadelphia: Fortress, 1988, 207–10.

———. "Theology in Mark and Q: Abba and 'Father' in Context." *HTR* 85 (1992) 149–74.

———. "Veils, Virgins and the Tongues of Men and Angels: Women's Heads as Sexual Members in Ancient Christianity." In *Off with Her Head! The Denial of Women's Identity in Myth, Religion and Culture,* ed. Howard Eilberg Schwartz and Wendy Doniger. Berkeley, CA: University of California Press, 1995, 131–64.

———. "Women in Luke-Acts: A Redactional View." *JBL* 109 (1990) 441–61.

———. "Women Partners in the New Testament." *JFSR* 6 (1990) 65–86.

Dash, Julie. *Daughters of the Dust.* American Playhouse Theatrical Films in Association with WMG. New York: Kino Video, 1992.

Davies, J. G. "Deacons, Deaconesses and the Minor Orders in the Patristic Period." *Journal of Ecclesiastical History* 14 (1963) 1–15.

Davies, Margaret. "New Testament Ethics and Ours: Homosexuality and Sexuality in Romans 1.26–27." *Biblical Interpretation* 3 (1995) 315–31.

Davies, Stephen. *The Gospel of Thomas and Christian Wisdom.* New York: Seabury Press, 1983.

Davies, Stevan L. *The Revolt of the Widows: The Social World of the Apocryphal Acts.* Carbondale, IL: Southern Illinois University Press, 1980.

———. "Women, Tertullian and the Acts of Paul." In *Semeia* 38 (1986) 139–43.

Davies, W. D. *The Setting of the Sermon on the Mount.* Cambridge: Cambridge University Press, 1966.

DeConick, A. D., and Jarl Fossum. "Stripped Before God: A New Interpretation of Logion 37 in the Gospel of Thomas." *VigChr* 45 (1991) 123–50.

DeConick, April D. *Seek to See Him: Ascent and Vision Mysticism in the Gospel of Thomas.* Leiden: E. J. Brill, 1996.

Deen, Edith. *All the Women of the Bible.* New York: Harper and Row, 1955; reprint San Francisco: HarperSanFrancisco, 1988.

Deutsch, Celia. *Hidden Wisdom and the Easy Yoke: Wisdom, Torah and Discipleship in Matthew 11.25–30.* Sheffield, UK: JSOT, 1987.

———. *Lady Wisdom, Jesus and the Sages: Metaphor and Social Context in Matthew's Gospel.* Valley Forge, PA: Trinity Press International, 1996.

———. "Wisdom in Matthew: Transformation of a Symbol." *NovT* 32 (1990) 13–47.

de Vaux, Roland. *Archaeology and the Dead Sea Scrolls.* London: British Academy, by Oxford University Press, 1973.

Dewey, Joanna. "The Gospel of Mark." In *Searching the Scriptures: Volume 2, A Feminist Commentary,* ed. Elisabeth Schüssler Fiorenza. New York: Crossroad, 1994, 470–509.

———. "Jesus' Healings of Women: Conformity and Non-conformity to Dominant Cultural Values as Historical Reconstruction." In *SBL Seminar Papers* 32. Atlanta, GA: Scholars Press, 1993, 178–93.

———. "1 Timothy." In *The Women's Bible Commentary,* ed. Carol A. Newsom and Sharon H. Ringe. Louisville, KY: Westminster/John Knox, 1992, 351–58.

Dibelius, Martin, and Conzelmann, Hans. *The Pastoral Epistles.* Hermeneia—A Critical and Historical Commentary on the Bible. Philadelphia: Fortress, 1972.

Diotima: Materials for the Study of Women and Gender in the Ancient World. http://www.uky.edu/ArtsSciences/Classics/gender.html.

Dixon, Suzanne. *The Roman Mother.* Norman, OK: University of Oklahoma Press, 1988.

Donahue, John. "Mark." In *Harper's Bible Commentary,* ed. James L. Mays. San Francisco: Harper & Row, 1988, 983–1009.

Douglas, R. Conrad. "'Love Your Enemies.' Rhetoric, Tradents, and Ethos." In *Conflict and Invention: Literary, Rhetorical, and Social Studies on the Sayings Gospel Q,* ed. J. Kloppenborg. Valley Forge, PA: Trinity Press International, 1995, 116–31.

Dowd, Sharyn Echols. *Prayer, Power, and the Problem of Suffering: Mark 11:22–25 in the Context of Markan Theology.* Atlanta, GA: Scholars Press, 1988.

Dubisch, Jill. "Culture Enters through the Kitchen: Woman, Culture and Social Boundaries in Rural Greece." In *Gender and Power in Rural Greece,* ed. Jill Dubisch. Princeton, NJ: Princeton University Press, 1986, 195–214.

———, ed. *Gender and Power in Rural Greece.* Princeton, NJ: Princeton University Press, 1986.

Dzielska, Maria. *Hypatia of Alexandria,* trans. F. Lyra. Cambridge, Mass.: Harvard University Press, 1995.

Edelstein, Emma and Ludwig Edelstein. *Asclepius: A Collection and Interpretation of the Testimonies.* 2 vols. Baltimore, MD: Johns Hopkins University Press, 1945.

Edwards, R. B. "Woman." In *ISBE*. Grand Rapids, MI: Eerdmans, 1988.

Ehrman, Bart D. "Cephas and Peter." *JBL* 109 (1990) 463–74.

Eilberg-Schwartz, Howard. *God's Phallus: And Other Problems for Men and Monotheism*. Boston: Beacon, 1994.

Elaw, Zilpha. *Memoirs of the Life, Religious Experience, Ministerial Travels and Labours of Mrs. Zilpha Elaw, an American Female of Color; Together with Some Account of the Great Religious Revivals in America (Written by Herself)*. In William L. Andrews, ed. *Sisters of the Spirit: Three Black Women's Autobiographies of the Late Nineteenth Century*. Bloomington, IN: Indiana University Press, 1986.

Elder, Linda Bennet. "The Woman Question and Female Ascetics Among Essenes." *Biblical Archaeologist* 57/4 (1994) 220–34.

Eliade, Mircea. *History of Religious Ideas*. 3 Vols. Chicago: University of Chicago Press, 1978–1985.

Fallon, Francis. *The Enthronement of Sabaoth: Jewish Elements in Gnostic Creations Myths*, NHS 10. Leiden: E. J. Brill, 1978.

Faraone, Christopher, and Dirk Obbink, eds. *Magika Hiera: Ancient Greek Magic and Religion*. New York: Oxford University Press, 1991.

Farmer, William R. *The Gospel of Jesus: The Pastoral Relevance of the Synoptic Problem*. Louisville, KY: Westminster/John Knox, 1994.

———. *The Synoptic Problem: A Critical Analysis*. New York: Macmillan, 1964.

Fatum, Lone. "1 Thessalonians." In *Searching the Scriptures: Volume 2, A Feminist Commentary*, ed. Elisabeth Schüssler Fiorenza. New York: Crossroad, 1994, 250–62.

Ferrua, Antonio. "Questioni di Epigrafia Eretica Romana." *Rivista di archeologia cristiana* 21 (1944–45) 165–221.

Filoramo, Giovanni. *A History of Gnosticism*, trans. Anthony Alcock. Oxford: Basil Blackwell, 1990.

Fischer-Mueller, E. A. "Yaldabaoth: The Gnostic Female Principle in Its Fallenness." *NovT* 32 (1990) 79–95.

Foley, Helene P., ed. *The Homeric Hymn to Demeter: Translation, Commentary, and Interpretive Essays*. Princeton, NJ: Princeton University Press, 1994.

Fontaine, Carole R. "Proverbs." In *The Women's Bible Commentary*, ed. Carol A. Newsom and Sharon H. Ringe. Louisville, KY: Westminster/John Knox, 1992, 145–52.

Förster, Werner. *Gnosis: A Selection of Gnostic Texts*. Volume 1, trans. R. McL. Wilson. Oxford: Oxford University Press, 1972.

Fox, Robin Lane. *Pagans and Christians*. New York: Alfred A. Knopf, 1986.

Fredriksen, Paula. "Did Jesus Oppose the Purity Laws?" *Bible Review* (June 1995) 18–25, 42–47.

———. "Hysteria and the Gnostic Myths of Creation." *VigChr* 33 (1979) 287–290.

Friesen, Steven J. *Twice Neokoros: Ephesus, Asia and the Cult of the Flavian Imperial Family*. Leiden: E. J. Brill, 1991.

Funk, Robert W., Roy W. Hoover, and the Jesus Seminar. *The Five Gospels: The Search for the Authentic Words of Jesus*. New York: Macmillan, 1993.

Gager, John G. *Curse Tablets and Binding Spells from the Ancient World*. New York: Oxford University Press, 1992.

———. *Kingdom and Community. The Social World of Early Christianity*. Englewood Cliffs, NJ: Prentice-Hall, 1975.

Galinsky, Karl. *Augustan Culture: An Interpretive Introduction*. Princeton, NJ: Princeton University Press, 1996.

Gardner, Jane F. *Women in Roman Law and Society*. Bloomington, IN: Indiana University Press, 1986.

Gilhus, Ingvild. "Gnosticism—A Study in Liminal Symbolism." Numen 31 (1984) 106–28.

———. "Male and Female Symbolism in the Gnostic Apocryphon of John." Temenos 19 (1983) 33–43.

———. The Nature of the Archons: A Study in the Soteriology of a Gnostic Treatise from Nag Hammadi (CGII, 4). Studies in Oriental Religions 12. Wiesbaden, Germany: Otto Harrassowitz, 1985.

———. "The Tree of Life and the Tree of Death: A Study of Gnostic Symbols." Religion 17 (1987) 337–353.

Glazer, B. "The Goddess with a Fiery Breath: The Egyptian Derivation of a Gnostic Mythologoumenon." NovT 33 (1991) 92–94.

Goehring, James E. "Libertine or Liberated: Women in the So-Called Libertine Gnostic Communities." In Images of the Feminine in Gnosticism, ed. Karen L. King. Philadelphia: Fortress, 1988, 329–44.

———. "A Classical Influence on the Gnostic Sophia Myth." VigChr 35 (1981) 16–23.

Gonzalez, Justo. Faith and Wealth: A History of Early Christian Ideas on the Origin, Significance and Use of Money. San Francisco: Harper and Row, 1990.

Good, Deirdre J. "Pistis Sophia." In Searching the Scriptures: Volume 2, A Feminist Commentary, ed. Elisabeth Schüssler Fiorenza. New York: Crossroad, 1994, 678–707.

———. Reconstructing the Tradition of Sophia. Atlanta, GA: Scholars Press, 1987.

Goss, Robert. Jesus Acted Up: A Gay and Lesbian Manifesto. San Francisco: HarperSanFrancisco, 1993.

Grabar, André. The Beginnings of Christian Art: 200–395. London: Thames and Hudson, 1967.

Grabbe, Lester. Judaism from Cyrus to Hadrian. Volume 2: The Roman Period. Minneapolis, MN: Fortress, 1992.

Grant, Robert M. "Marcion, Gospel of." ABD 4:516–20.

———. "The Mystery of Marriage in the Gospel of Philip." VigChr 15 (1961) 129–40.

Green, Henry A. "Power and Knowledge: A Study in the Social Development of Early Christianity." Studies in Religion/Sciences Religieuses 20 (1991) 217–31.

Greenblatt, Michael. "Mary Magdalen: Gnostic Icon of Salvation." Term paper, Haverford College, Haverford, PA, December 1996.

Greenfield, Jonas. " 'Because He/She Did Not Know Letters': Remarks on a First Millennium CE Legal Expression." JANES 22 (1993) 39–43.

Grossman, Susan. "Women and the Jerusalem Temple." In Daughters of the King: Women and the Synagogue, A Survey of History, Halachah and Contemporary Realities, ed. Susan Grossman and Rivka Haut. Philadelphia: Jewish Publication Society, 1992, 15–37.

Gryson, Roger. The Ministry of Women in the Early Church. Collegeville, MN: Liturgical Press, 1976.

Guarducci, M. "Valentiniani a Roma." Deutsches Archäologisches Institut. Römische Abteilung. Mitteilungen 80 (1973) 169–86.

Guenther, Heinz O. "The Sayings Gospel Q and the Quest for Aramaic Sources: Rethinking Christian Origins." Semeia 55 (1992) 41–75.

Hagner, David. "James." ABD 3:616–618.

Hallett, Judith P. Fathers and Daughters in Roman Society: Women and the Elite Family. Princeton, NJ: Princeton University Press, 1984.

———. "Feminist Theory, Historical Periods, Literary Canons, and the Study of Greco-Roman Antiquity." In Feminist Theory and the Classics, ed. Nancy Sorkin Rabinowitz and Amy Richlin. New York: Routledge, 1993, 44–72.

———. "Women as 'Same' and 'Other' in the Classical Roman Elite." Helios 16/1 (1989) 59–78.

———. "Martial's Sulpicia and Propertius' Cynthia." Classical World 88/2 (1992) 99–123.

Harrington, Daniel. "The Gospel According to Mark." In *New Jerome Biblical Commentary*, ed. Raymond E. Brown, J. Fitzmyer, and R. Murphy. Englewood Cliffs, NJ: Prentice-Hall, 1988, 596–629.

Hartin, Patrick J. "'Yet Wisdom Is Justified by Her Children' (Q7:35): A Rhetorical and Compositional Analysis of Divine Sophia in Q." In *Conflict and Invention: Literary, Rhetorical and Social Studies on the Sayings Gospel Q*, ed. John S. Kloppenborg. Valley Forge, PA: Trinity Press International, 1995, 151–64.

Harvey, Susan Ashbrook. "Women in Early Syriac Christianity." In *Images of Women in Antiquity*, ed. Averil Cameron and Amélie Kuhrt. Detroit, MI: Wayne State University Press, 1983.

Hayne, Léonie. "Thecla and the Church Fathers." *VigChr* 48 (1994) 209–18.

Hedrick, Charles W., and Robert Hodgson, Jr., eds. *Nag Hammadi, Gnosticism, and Early Christianity*. Peabody, MA: Hendrickson, 1986.

Herford, Robert Travers. *Pirke Aboth: The Ethics of the Talmud: Sayings of the Fathers*. New York: Jewish Institute of Religion, 1945; reprint, New York: Schocken, 1962.

Heyob, Sharon Kelly. *The Cult of Isis among Women in the Graeco-Roman World*. EPRO 51. Leiden: E. J. Brill, 1975.

Hoffman, Daniel L. *The Status of Women and Gnosticism in Irenaeus and Tertullian*. Studies in Women and Religion 36. Lewiston, NY: Edwin Mellen, 1995.

Hoffman, R. Joseph. "De Statu Feminarum: The Correlation between Gnostic Theory and Social Practice." *Église et Théologie* 14 (1983) 293–304.

Horbury, William, and David Noy. *Jewish Inscriptions of Greco-Roman Egypt*. Cambridge: Cambridge University Press, 1992.

Hull, John. *Hellenistic Magic and the Synoptic Tradition*. Studies in Biblical Theology, Second Series, 28. London: SCM, 1974.

Ilan, Tal. "The Attraction of Aristocratic Women to Pharisaic Judaism during the Second Temple Period." *HTR* 88 (1995) 1–33.

———. *Jewish Women in Greco-Roman Palestine, An Inquiry into Image and Status*. Texte und Studien zum Antiken Judentum 44. Tübingen: J. C. B. Mohr (Paul Siebeck), 1995.

———. "Josephus and Nicolaus on Women," in *Geschichte-Tradition-Reflexion: Festschrift für Martin Hengel zum 70. Geburtstag, Band I: Judentum*. ed. Peter Schäfer; Tübingen: J.C.B. Mohr (Paul Siebeck), 1996, 221–62.

———. "Julia Crispina, Daughter of Berenicianus, a Herodian Princess in the Babatha Archive: A Case Study in Historical Identification." *Jewish Quarterly Review* 82/3–4 (1992) 361–81.

———. "Notes and Observations from a Newly Published Divorce Bill from the Judean Desert," *HTR* 89/2 (1996) 195–202.

Irvin, Dorothy. "Archaeology Supports Women's Ordination." *The Witness* 63 (1980) 4–8.

———. "The Ministry of Women in the Early Church: The Archaeological Evidence." *Duke Divinity School Review* 45 (1980) 76–86.

Irwin, K. M. "Archaeology Does Not Support Women's Ordination; A Response to Dorothy Irvin." *Journal of Women and Religion* 3 (1984) 32–42.

Jacobson, Arland Dean. "Divided Families and Christian Origins." In *The Gospel Behind the Gospels: Current Studies in Q*. NovTSup 75, ed. Ronald A. Piper. Leiden: E. J. Brill, 1995, 361–80.

———. *The First Gospel: An Introduction to Q*. Sonoma, CA: Polebridge, 1992.

Jay, Eric G. "From Presbyter-Bishops to Bishops and Presbyters: Christian Ministry in the Second Century: A Survey." *The Second Century* 1 (1981) 125–62.

Jeremias, Joachim. *Jerusalem in the Time of Jesus*. Philadelphia: Fortress, 1969.

Jewett, Robert. "Paul, Phoebe and the Spanish Mission." In *The Social World of Formative Christianity and Judaism: Essays in Tribute to Howard Clark Kee*, ed. J. Neusner et al. Philadelphia: Fortress, 1988, 142–61.

Johnson, E. Elizabeth. "Ephesians." In *The Women's Bible Commentary*, ed. Carol A. Newsom and Sharon H. Ringe. Louisville, KY: Westminster/John Knox, 1992, 338–42.

Joshel, Sandra. *Work, Identity, and Legal Status at Rome. A Study of the Occupational Inscriptions.* Norman, OK: Oklahoma University Press, 1991.

Kaestli, Jean-Daniel. "Response." *Semeia* 38 (1986) 119–31.

Katz, Marilyn Arthur. "Patriarchy, Ideology and the Epikleros." *Studi italiani di filologia classica* 10 (1992) 693–708.

Kelly, Joan. "The Social Relation of the Sexes: Methodological Implications of Women's History." In *Women, History, and Theory: The Essays of Joan Kelly.* Chicago: University of Chicago Press, 1984.

Keuls, Eva C. *The Reign of the Phallus: Sexual Politics in Ancient Athens.* Berkeley, CA: University of California Press, 1985.

King, Karen L. "The Book of Norea, Daughter of Eve." In *Searching the Scriptures: Volume 2, A Feminist Commentary*, ed. Elisabeth Schüssler Fiorenza. New York: Crossroad, 1994, 66–85.

———. "The Gospel of Mary." In *The Complete Gospels: Annotated Scholars Version*, ed. Robert J. Miller. Sonoma, CA: Polebridge, 1992, 357–66.

———. "The Gospel of Mary Magdalene." In *Searching the Scriptures: Volume 2, A Feminist Commentary*, ed. Elisabeth Schüssler Fiorenza. New York: Crossroad, 1994, 357–66.

———. "Is There Such a Thing as Gnosticism?" Unpublished paper presented at the annual meeting of the SBL, Nag Hammadi and Gnosticism Section, Washington, DC, November 1993.

———. *The Origins of Gnosticism.* Princeton, NJ: Princeton University Press, forthcoming.

———. "Prophetic Power and Women's Authority: The Case of the Gospel of Mary (Magdalen)." In *Women Preachers and Prophets through Two Millenia of Christianity*, ed. Beverly Mayne Kienzle and Pamela Walker. Berkeley, CA: University of California Press, 1998, 21–41.

———. "Ridicule and Rape, Rule and Rebellion: Images of Gender in the Hypostasis of the Archons." In *Gnosticism and the Early Christian World: Festschrift for J. M. Robinson*, ed. J. A. Sanders and C. Hedrick. Sonoma, CA: Polebridge, 1990, 1–35.

———. "Sophia and Christ in the Apocryphon of John." In *Images of the Feminine in Gnosticism*, ed. Karen L. King. Philadelphia: Fortress, 1988, 158–76.

———, ed. *Images of the Feminine in Gnosticism.* Studies in Antiquity and Christianity. Philadelphia: Fortress, 1988.

Kingsbury, Jack Dean. "Matthew, Gospel According to." *HarperCollins Bible Dictionary*, ed. Paul J. Achtemeier. San Francisco: HarperSanFrancisco, 1996, 661–63.

Kinukawa, Hisako. *Women and Jesus in Mark.* Maryknoll, NY: Orbis, 1994.

Kloppenborg, John S. *The Formation of Q: Trajectories in Ancient Wisdom Collections.* Philadelphia: Fortress, 1987.

———. "Jesus and the Parables of Jesus in Q." In *The Gospel Behind the Gospels: Current Studies in Q*, ed. Ronald A. Piper. NovTSup 75. Leiden: E. J. Brill, 1995, 275–319.

———. "Literary Convention, Self-Evidence and the Social History of the Q People." *Semeia* 55 (1991) 77–102.

———. "Symbolic Eschatology and the Apocalypticism of Q." *HTR* 80 (1987) 287–306.

———, ed. *Conflict and Invention: Literary, Rhetorical and Social Studies on the Sayings Gospel Q.* Valley Forge, PA: Trinity Press International, 1995.

————, ed. *The Shape of Q: Signal Essays on the Sayings Gospel*. Minneapolis, MN: Augsburg Fortress, 1994.

———— and M. Meyer, S. J. Patterson, and M. G. Steinhauser, eds. *The Q-Thomas Reader*. Sonoma, CA: Polebridge, 1990.

Kobelski, Paul J. "The Letter to the Ephesians." In *The New Jerome Biblical Commentary*, ed. Raymond E. Brown, J. Fitzmyer, and R. Murphy. Englewood Cliffs, NJ: Prentice-Hall, 1990, 883–90.

Koester, Helmut. *Ancient Christian Gospels*. Philadelphia: Trinity Press International, 1990.

————. *Introduction to the New Testament I: History, Culture and Religion of the Hellenistic Age*. Philadelphia: Fortress, 1982.

Kraemer, Ross S. "The Book of Aseneth." In *Searching the Scriptures: Volume 2, A Feminist Commentary*, ed. Elisabeth Schüssler Fiorenza. New York: Crossroad, 1994, 859–88.

————. "The Conversion of Women to Ascetic Forms of Christianity." *Signs: Journal of Women in Culture and Society* 6 (1980) 298–307.

————. "Ecstasy and Possession: The Attraction of Women to the Cult of Dionysus." HTR 72 (1979) 55–80.

————. *Ecstatics and Ascetics: Studies in the Functions of Religious Activities for Women in the Greco-Roman World*. Ph.D. dissertation, Princeton University, Princeton, NJ, 1976.

————. *Her Share of the Blessings: Women's Religions among Pagans, Jews and Christians in the Greco-Roman World*. New York: Oxford University Press, 1992.

————. "Jewish Women in the Diaspora World of Late Antiquity." In *Jewish Women in Historical Perspective*, ed. Judith Baskin. Detroit, MI: Wayne State University Press, 1991, 43–67.

————. "Monastic Jewish Women in Greco-Roman Egypt: Philo and the Therapeutrides." *Signs. Journal of Women in Culture and Society* 14/2 (1989) 342–70.

————. "Response to 'Virginity and Subversion: Norea against the Powers in the Hypostasis of the Archons' by Anne McGuire." In *Images of the Feminine in Gnosticism*, ed. Karen L. King. Philadelphia: Fortress, 1988, 259–64.

————. *When Aseneth Met Joseph: A Late Antique Tale of the Biblical Patriarch and his Egyptian Wife Revisited*. New York: Oxford University Press, 1998.

————. "Women's Authorship of Jewish and Christian Literature in the Greco-Roman Period." In *"Women Like This": New Perspectives on Jewish Women in the Greco-Roman Period*. Early Judaism and its Literature 1, ed. Amy-Jill Levine. Atlanta, GA: Scholars Press, 1991, 221–42.

————, ed. *Maenads, Martyrs, Matrons, Monastics: A Sourcebook on Women's Religions in the Greco-Roman World*. Philadelphia: Fortress, 1988.

Krautheimer, Richard. *Rome: Profile of a City, 312–1308*. Princeton, NJ: Princeton University Press, 1980.

Kümmel, W. G. *Introduction to the New Testament*. London: SCM, 1975.

Kysar, Robert. "John, The Gospel of." *ABD* 3:912–31.

Lampe, Peter. "Mary 7." *ABD* 4:582–83.

Layton, Bentley. "The Hypostasis of the Archons." In *Nag Hammadi Codex II,2–7, together with XIII,2, Brit. Lib. Or. 4926(1), and P. Oxy. 1,654, 655*, ed. Bentley Layton. Leiden: E. J. Brill, 1989.

————. "Prolegomena to the Study of Ancient Gnosticism." In *The Social World of the First Christians: Essays in Honor of Wayne A. Meeks*, ed. L. Michael White and O. Larry Yarbrough. Minneapolis, MN: Augsburg Fortress, 1995, 334–50.

————. "The Riddle of the Thunder (NHC VI,2): The Function of Paradox in a Gnostic Text from Nag Hammadi." In *Nag Hammadi, Gnosticism, and Early Christianity*, ed. Charles W. Hedrick, and Robert Hodgson, Jr. Peabody, MA: Hendrickson, 1986, 37–54.

————, ed. *The Rediscovery of Gnosticism: Proceedings of the International Conference on Gnosticism at Yale, New Haven, Connecticut, March 28–31, 1978. Volume One: The School of Valentinus. Volume Two: Sethian Gnosticism.* Leiden: E. J. Brill, 1980.

————, ed. and trans. *The Gnostic Scriptures.* Garden City, NY: Doubleday, 1987.

Lefkowitz, Mary R. "Did Ancient Women Write Novels?" In *"Women Like This": New Perspectives on Jewish Women in the Greco-Roman World*, ed. Amy-Jill Levine. Early Judaism and its Literature 1. Atlanta, GA: Scholars Press, 1991, 199–219.

Lefkowitz, Mary R., and Maureen B. Fant. *Women's Life in Greece and Rome. A Source Book in Translation.* 2nd ed. Baltimore, MD: Johns Hopkins University Press, 1992.

Lesses, Rebecca. "The Daughters of Job." In *Searching the Scriptures: Volume 2, A Feminist Commentary*, ed. Elisabeth Schüssler Fiorenza. New York: Crossroad, 1994, 139–52.

Levine, Amy-Jill. "Discharging Responsibility: Matthean Jesus, Biblical Law and Hemorrhaging Women." In *Treasures New and Old: New Essays in Matthean Studies*, ed. Mark Allan Powell and David Bauer. Atlanta, GA: Scholars Press, 1996, 379–97.

————. "Second-Temple Judaism, Jesus and Women: Yeast of Eden." *Biblical Interpretation* 2 (1994) 1:8–33.

————. "The Sibylline Oracles." In *Searching the Scriptures: Volume 2, A Feminist Commentary*, ed. Elisabeth Schüssler Fiorenza. New York: Crossroad, 1994, 99–108.

————. "Who's Catering the Q Affair? Feminist Observations on Q Paraenesis." *Semeia* 50 (1990) 145–61.

————, ed. *"Women Like This": New Perspectives on Jewish Women in the Greco-Roman Period.* Early Judaism and its Literature 1. Atlanta, GA: Scholars Press, 1991.

Lewis, Naphtali, ed. *The Documents from the Bar Kochba Period in the Cave of Letters: Greek Papyri.* Judean Desert Studies. Jerusalem: Israel Exploration Society, Hebrew University, Shrine of the Book, 1989.

LiDonnici, Lynn. *The Epidaurian Miracle Inscriptions: Text, Translation and Commentary.* Atlanta, GA: Scholars Press, 1995.

Lipinski, E. "The Wife's Right to Divorce in the Light of an Ancient Near Eastern Tradition." *The Jewish Law Annual* 4 (1981) 9–27.

Loraux, Nicole. "Herakles: The Super-Male and the Feminine." In *Before Sexuality: The Construction of Erotic Experience in the Ancient Greek World*, ed. David Halperin et al. Princeton, NJ: Princeton University Press, 1990, 21–52.

————. "What is A Goddess?" In *A History of Women in the West 1: From Ancient Goddesses to Christian Saints*, ed. Pauline Schmitt Pantel. Trans. Arthur Goldhammer. Cambridge, MA: The Belknap Press of Harvard University Press, 1992, 11–45.

Luz, Ulrich. *Matthew in History: Interpretation, Influence and Effects.* Minneapolis, MN: Fortress, 1994.

MacDonald, Dennis R. *The Legend and the Apostle: The Battle for Paul in Story and Canon.* Philadelphia: Westminster, 1983.

————. "The Role of Women in the Production of the Apocryphal Acts of the Apostles." *Iliff Review* 41/4 (1984) 21–38.

————. *There Is No Male and Female: The Fate of a Dominical Saying in Paul and Gnosticism.* Harvard Dissertations in Religion 20. Philadelphia: Fortress, 1987.

MacDonald, Dennis R., and Andrew D. Scrimgeour. "Pseudo-Chrysostom's Panegyric to Thecla: The Heroine of the *Acts of Paul* in Homily and Art." *Semeia* 38 (1986) 151–59.

MacDonald, Margaret Y. *Early Christian Women and Pagan Opinion: The Power of the Hysterical Woman.* Cambridge: Cambridge University Press, 1996.

————. *The Pauline Churches: A Socio-historical Study of Institutionalization in the Pauline and Deutero-Pauline Writings.* Cambridge: Cambridge University Press, 1988.

————. "Women Holy in Body and Spirit: The Social Setting of 1 Corinthians 7." NTS 36 (1990) 161–81.

Mack, Burton L. The Lost Gospel: The Book of Q and Christian Origins. San Francisco: HarperSan-Francisco, 1993.

————. A Myth of Innocence: Mark and Christian Origins. Philadelphia: Fortress, 1988.

MacRae, George W. "The Jewish Background of the Gnostic Sophia Myth." NovT 12 (1970) 86–101.

Macurdy, Grace H. "Julia Berenice." AJPhil 56 (1935) 246–53.

————. Vassal Queens and Some Contemporary Women in the Roman Empire. The Johns Hopkins University Studies in Archaeology 22. Baltimore, MD: Johns Hopkins University Press, 1937.

Majercik, Ruth. "Dialogue." ABD 2:185–88.

Malbon, Elisabeth Struthers. "Fallible Followers: Women and Men in the Gospel of Mark." Semeia 28 (1983) 29–48.

Maly, Eugene H. "Women and the Gospel of Luke." Biblical Theology Bulletin 10 (1980) 99–104.

Marjanen, Antti. "Mary Magdalene in the Dialogue of the Savior." In Abstracts, 1996 Annual Meeting, Society of Biblical Literature. Atlanta, GA: Scholars Press, 1996.

————. The Woman Jesus Loved: Mary Magdalene in the Nag Hammadi Library and Related Documents. NHMS 40. Leiden: E. J. Brill, 1996.

————. "The Woman Jesus Loved: Mary Magdalene in the Nag Hammadi Library and Related Documents." Ph.D. dissertation, University of Helsinki, Finland, 1995.

Martimort, Aimé Georges. Deaconesses: An Historical Study. San Francisco: Ignatius, 1986.

Martin, Clarice J. "The Acts of the Apostles." In Searching the Scriptures: Volume 2, A Feminist Commentary, ed. Elisabeth Schüssler Fiorenza. New York: Crossroad, 1994, 763–99.

Martin, Dale B. The Corinthian Body. New Haven, CT: Yale University Press, 1995.

————. "Heterosexism and the Interpretation of Romans 1:18–32." Biblical Interpretation 3 (1995) 332–55.

————. "Slavery and the Ancient Jewish Family." In The Jewish Family in Antiquity. Brown Judaic Studies 289, ed. Shaye J. D. Cohen. Atlanta, GA: Scholars Press, 1993, 113–29.

Martin, Luther H. Hellenistic Religions. New York: Oxford University Press, 1988.

Marxsen, Willi. Mark the Evangelist, trans. James Boyce, Donald Juel, and William Poehlmann with Roy A. Harrisville. Nashville, TN: Abingdon, 1969.

————. The Resurrection of Jesus of Nazareth, trans. Margaret Kohl. Philadelphia: Fortress, 1970.

Mastin, B. A. "Scaeva the High Priest." JTS 27 (1976) 405–12.

Matthews, Shelly. "2 Corinthians." In Searching the Scriptures: Volume 2, A Feminist Commentary, ed. Elisabeth Schüssler Fiorenza. New York: Crossroad, 1994, 196–217.

McGinn, Sheila E. "The Acts of Thecla." In Searching the Scriptures: Volume 2, A Feminist Commentary, ed. Elisabeth Schüssler Fiorenza. New York: Crossroad, 1994, 800–28.

McGuire, Anne. "Conversion and Gnosis in the Gospel of Truth." NovT 28 (1986) 338–55.

————. "Thunder, Perfect Mind." In Searching the Scriptures: Volume 2, A Feminist Commentary, ed. Elisabeth Schüssler Fiorenza. New York: Crossroad, 1994, 39–54.

————. "Thunder, Perfect Mind (NHC VI,2)." In Nag Hammadi Reader's Guide, ed. Karen L. King and Charles Hedrick. Sonoma, CA: Polebridge, forthcoming.

————. "Virginity and Subversion: Norea against the Powers in the Hypostasis of the Archons." In Images of the Feminine in Gnosticism, ed. Karen L. King. Philadelphia: Fortress, 1988, 239–58.

Meadors, Edward P. Jesus: The Messianic Herald of Salvation. WUNT 2.72. Tübingen: J. C. B. Mohr (Paul Siebeck), 1995.

Meeks, Wayne. *The First Urban Christians: The Social World of the Apostle Paul*. New Haven, CT: Yale University Press, 1983.

―――. "The Image of the Androgyne: Some Uses of a Symbol in Earliest Christianity." *History of Religions* 13 (1974) 165–208.

―――. *The Moral World of the First Christians*. Library of Early Christianity 6; Philadelphia: Westminster, 1986.

Meier, John. "Matthew, Gospel of." *ABD* 4:624–25.

Methuen, Charlotte. "Widows, Bishops and the Struggle for Authority in the *Didascalia Apostolorum*." *Journal of Ecclesiastical History* 46 (1995) 197–213.

Meyer, Marvin. "Making Mary Male: The Categories of 'Male' and 'Female' in the Gospel of Thomas." *NTS* 31 (1985) 554–70.

―――, ed. *The Gospel of Thomas: The Hidden Sayings of Jesus*. San Francisco: HarperSanFrancisco, 1992.

Meyers, Carol, Toni Craven, and Ross S. Kraemer, eds. *Dictionary of Women in Scripture*. Boston: Houghton Mifflin, forthcoming.

Milik, J. T. "Le travail d'édition des manuscrits du Désert de Juda." *Volume du congrès Strasbourg 1956*, Supplements to Vetus Testamentum 4. Leiden: E. J. Brill, 1956, 17–26.

Miller, Patricia Cox. "In Praise of Nonsense." In *Classical Mediterranean Spirituality*, ed. A. H. Armstrong. New York: Crossroad, 1986, 481–505.

Miller, Robert J., ed. *The Complete Gospels: Annotated Scholars Version*. Sonoma, CA: Polebridge, 1992.

Moltmann-Wendel, Elisabeth. *Liberty, Equality, Sisterhood: On the Emancipation of Women in Church and Society*. Philadelphia: Fortress, 1978.

Morrison, Toni. *Jazz*. New York: Knopf, 1992.

Mortley, Raoul. *Womanhood: The Feminine in Ancient Hellenism, Gnosticism, Christianity, and Islam*. Sydney: Delacroix, 1981.

Neirynck, Franz. "Synoptic Problem." In *New Jerome Biblical Commentary* ed. Raymond E. Brown, J. Fitzmyer, and R. Murphy. Englewood Cliffs, NJ: Prentice-Hall, 1988, 587–95.

Neusner, Jacob. *The Incarnation of God: The Character of Diversity in Formative Judaism*. Philadelphia: Fortress, 1988.

―――. *The Mishnah, a New Translation*. New Haven, CT: Yale University Press, 1988.

Neusner, Jacob, et al., eds. *The Social World of Formative Christianity*. Philadelphia: Fortress, 1988.

Newsom, Carol A., and Sharon H. Ringe, eds. *The Women's Bible Commentary*. Louisville, KY: Westminster/John Knox, 1992.

O'Day, Gail R. "Acts." In *The Women's Bible Commentary*, ed. Carol A Newsom and Sharon H. Ringe. Louisville, KY: Westminster/John Knox, 1992, 305–12.

―――. "John." In *The Women's Bible Commentary*, ed. Carol A Newsom and Sharon H. Ringe. Louisville, KY: Westminster/John Knox, 1992, 294–304.

Olds, L. Calista. In Emil Schürer. *The History of the Jews in the Age of Jesus Christ*. Rev. ed. 3 vols. in 4. G. Vermes, F. Millar, and M. Goodman, eds. Edinburgh: T&T Clark, Ltd., 1986.

Osiek, Carolyn. "Philippians." In *Searching the Scriptures: Volume 2, A Feminist Commentary*, ed. Elisabeth Schüssler Fiorenza. New York: Crossroad, 1994, 237–49.

―――. "The Widow as Altar: The Rise and Fall of a Symbol." *The Second Century* 3 (1983) 159–69.

Oster, Richard E. "Ephesus as a Religious Center under the Principate I: Paganism before Constantine." In *ANRW* 2.18.3: 1661–1728.

Otranto, Giorgio. "Notes on the Female Priesthood in Antiquity." Translated in Mary Ann Rossi, "Priesthood, Precedent, and Prejudice: On Recovering the Women Priests of Early Christianity." *JFSR* 7 (1991) 80–84.

Pagels, Elaine. "Adam and Eve and the Serpent in Genesis 1–3." In *Images of the Feminine in Gnosticism*, ed. Karen L. King. Philadelphia: Fortress, 1988, 412–23.

————. *The Gnostic Gospels.* New York: Random House, 1979; Vintage Books, 1989.

————. "The 'Mystery of Marriage' in the Gospel of Philip Revisited." In *The Future of Early Christianity: Essays in Honor of Helmut Koester*, ed. Birger A. Pearson. Minneapolis, MN: Fortress, 1991, 442–54.

————. "Pursuing the Spiritual Eve: Imagery and Hermeneutics in the *Hypostasis of the Archons* and the *Gospel of Philip*." In *Images of the Feminine in Gnosticism*, ed. Karen L. King. Philadelphia: Fortress, 1988, 187–206.

Painchaud, Louis, and A. Pasquier, eds. *Les Textes de Nag Hammadi et le Problème de leur Classification. Actes du Colloque tenu à Québec du 15 au 19 septembre 1993.* BCNH, Section "Études" 3. Québec: Les Presses de l'Université Laval; Louvain: Éditions Peeters, 1995.

Pantel, Pauline Schmitt, ed. *A History of Women in the West 1: From Ancient Goddesses to Christian Saints.* Cambridge, MA: The Belknap Press of Harvard University Press, 1992.

Parvey, Constance F. "The Theology and Leadership of Women in the New Testament." In *Religion and Sexism*, ed. Rosemary Radford Ruether. New York: Simon and Schuster, 1974, 139–46.

Patterson, Stephen J. *The Gospel of Thomas and Jesus.* Foundations and Facets Reference Series. Sonoma, CA: Polebridge, 1993.

Pearson, Birger A. "Revisiting Norea." In *Images of the Feminine in Gnosticism*, ed. Karen L. King. Philadelphia: Fortress, 1988, 265–75.

Perkins, Judith. *The Suffering Self: Pain and Narrative Representation in the Early Christian Era.* New York: Routledge, 1995.

Perkins, Pheme. *The Gnostic Dialogue: The Early Church and the Crisis of Gnosticism.* New York: Paulist, 1980.

————. "Gospel of Thomas." In *Searching the Scriptures: Volume 2, A Feminist Commentary*, ed. Elisabeth Schüssler Fiorenza. New York: Crossroad, 1994, 534–60.

————. "Philemon." In *The Women's Bible Commentary*, ed. Carol A. Newsom and Sharon H. Ringe. Louisville, KY: Westminster/John Knox, 1992, 362–63.

————. "Pronouncement Stories in the Gospel of Thomas," *Semeia* 20 (1981).

————. "Sophia as Goddess in the Nag Hammadi Codices." In *Images of the Feminine in Gnosticism*, ed. Karen L. King. Philadelphia: Fortress, 1988, 96–112.

Pervo, Richard, and Mikael Parson. *Rethinking the Unity of Luke and Acts.* Minneapolis, MN: Fortress, 1993.

Piper, Ronald A. "In Quest of Q: The Direction of Q Studies." In *The Gospel Behind the Gospels: Current Studies in Q*, ed. Ronald A. Piper. NovTSup 75. Leiden: E. J. Brill, 1995, 1–18.

Pleket, H. W. *Epigraphica. Vol. 2. Texts on the Social History of the Greek World.* Leiden: E. J. Brill, 1969.

Poirier, Paul-Hubert. *Le Tonnerre, Intellect Parfait (NH VI,2).* BCNH, Section "Textes" 22. Québec: Les Presses de l'Université Laval; Louvain: Peeters, 1995.

Pomeroy, Sarah. *Goddesses, Whores, Wives and Slaves: Women in Classical Antiquity.* New York: Schocken, 1975.

Portefaix, Lilian. *Sisters Rejoice: Paul's Letter to the Philippians and Luke-Acts as Received by First-Century Philippian Women.* Stockholm: Almqvist & Wiksell International, 1988.

Porter, Stanley E. "Joseph." *ABD* 3:968–69.

Porton, Gary. "Talmud." *ABD* 6:310–15.

Price, Simon R. F. *Rituals and Power: The Roman Imperial Cult in Asia Minor.* Cambridge: Cambridge University Press, 1984.

Quesnell, Quentin. "The Women at Luke's Supper." In *Political Issues in Luke-Acts*, ed. R. J. Cassidy and P. J. Scharper. Maryknoll, NY: Orbis, 1983, 59–79.

Quispel, Gilles. "L'Inscription de Flavia Sophē." *Gnostic Studies*. Vol. 1. Istanbul: Nederlands Historisch-Archaeologisch Instituut in het Nabije Oosten, 1974, 58 ff.

————. *Ptolémée. Lettre à Flora*. Paris: Les Éditions du Cerf, 1966.

Reimer, Ivoni Richter. *Women in the Acts of the Apostles: A Feminist Liberation Perspective*. Minneapolis, MN: Fortress, 1995.

Reinhartz, Adele. "From Narrative to History: The Resurrection of Mary and Martha." In *"Women Like This": New Perspectives on Jewish Women in the Greco-Roman World, Early Judaism and its Literature* 1, ed. Amy-Jill Levine. Atlanta, GA: Scholars Press, 1991, 161–84.

————. "The Gospel of John." In *Searching the Scriptures: Volume 2, A Feminist Commentary*, ed. Elisabeth Schüssler Fiorenza. New York: Crossroad, 1994, 580–82.

Ricci, Carla. *Mary Magdalene and Many Others: Women Who Followed Jesus*. Minneapolis, MN: Fortress, 1994.

Richlin, Amy. "Approaches to the Study of Adultery at Rome." In *Reflections of Women in Antiquity*, ed. Helene P. Foley. New York: Gordon and Breach, 1981, 379–404.

————. "The Ethnographer's Dilemma and the Dream of a Lost Golden Age." In *Feminist Theory and the Classics*, ed. Nancy Sorkin Rabinowitz and Amy Richlin. New York: Routledge, 1993, 273–303.

Riley, Gregory. *Resurrection Reconsidered: Thomas and John in Conflict*. Minneapolis, MN: Fortress, 1995.

Roberts, William P., ed. *Divorce and Remarriage: Religious and Psychological Perspectives*. Kansas City, MO: Sheed and Ward, 1990.

Robinson, James M. "The Jesus of Q as a Liberation Theologian." In *The Gospel Behind the Gospels: Current Studies in Q. NovTSup* 75, ed. Ronald A. Piper. Leiden: E. J. Brill, 1995, 259–74.

————. "International Q Project Work Session, 17 November 1989." *JBL* 109 (1990) 501.

————, ed. *The Nag Hammadi Library in English*, 3rd edition. San Francisco: Harper and Row, 1988.

Rogers, Guy MacLean. *The Sacred Identity of Ephesos: Foundation Myths of a Roman City*. New York: Routledge, 1991.

Rordorf, Willy. "Tradition and Composition in the *Acts of Thecla*: The State of the Question." *Semeia* 38 (1986) 43–52.

Rossi, Mary Ann. "Priesthood, Precedent, and Prejudice: On Recovering the Women Priests of Early Christianity." *Journal of Feminist Studies in Religion* 7 (1991) 73–93.

Rossmiller, Celeste J. "Prophets and Disciples in Luke's Infancy Narrative." *Bible Today* 22/6 (1984) 361–65.

Rousseau, A. H., and L. Doutreleau, eds. *Irénée de Lyons, Contre les Hérésies, livre* 1. Paris: Les Éditions du Cerf, 1979.

Rudolph, Kurt. *Gnosis: The Nature and History of Gnosticism*. San Francisco: Harper and Row, 1983.

Ruether, Rosemary R. "Misogynism and Virginal Feminism in the Fathers of the Church." In *Religion and Sexism*, ed. Rosemary R. Ruether. New York: Simon and Schuster, 1974, 150–83.

————. *Sexism and God-Talk: Toward a Feminist Theology*. Boston: Beacon, 1983.

Ruether, Rosemary R., and Eleanor McLaughlin, eds. *Women of Spirit: Female Leadership in the Jewish and Christian Traditions*. New York: Simon and Schuster, 1979.

Ryan, Rosalie. "The Women from Galilee and Discipleship in Luke." *Biblical Theology Bulletin* 15 (1985) 56–59.

Saldarini, Anthony. "The Gospel of Matthew and Jewish-Christian Conflict." In *Social His-*

tory of the Matthean Community: Cross Disciplinary Approaches, ed. David L. Balch. Minneapolis, MN: Fortress, 1991, 38–61.

———. Matthew's Jewish Christian Community. Chicago: University of Chicago Press, 1994.

Sanders, E. P., and Margaret Davies. Studying the Synoptic Gospels. Philadelphia: Trinity Press International, 1989.

Santirocco, Matthew. "Sulpicia Reconsidered." Classical Journal 74/3 (1979) 229–39.

Satlow, Michael L. "'Try to be a Man': The Rabbinic Construction of Masculinity," HTR 89/1 (1996) 19–40.

Schaberg, Jane C. The Illegitimacy of Jesus: A Feminist Theological Interpretation of the Infancy Narrative. San Francisco: Harper and Row, 1987.

———. "Luke." In The Women's Bible Commentary, ed. Carol A. Newsom and Sharon H. Ringe. Louisville, KY: Westminster/John Knox, 1992, 275–92.

———. "Thinking Back through the Magdalene." Continuum 1 (1991) 71–90.

Schiffman, Lawrence. "Women in the Scrolls," Reclaiming the Dead Sea Scrolls: The History of Judaism, The Background of Christianity, The Lost Library of Qumran. Philadelphia: The Jewish Publication Society, 1994, 127–43.

Schneemelcher, Wilhelm. New Testament Apocrypha. 2 Vols. Rev. ed., English trans. ed. R. McL Wilson. Louisville, KY: Westminster/John Knox, 1991–92.

Schottroff, Luise. "Itinerant Prophetesses: A Feminist Analysis of the Sayings Source Q." In The Gospel Behind the Gospels: Current Studies in Q, ed. Ronald A. Piper. NovTSup 75. Leiden: E. J. Brill, 1995, 347–60.

———. Lydia's Impatient Sisters: A Feminist Social History of Early Christianity, trans. Barbara and Martin Rumscheidt. Louisville, KY: Louisville, KY: Westminster/John Knox, 1995.

———. "The Sayings Source Q." In Searching the Scriptures: Volume 2, A Feminist Commentary, ed. Elisabeth Schüssler Fiorenza. New York: Crossroad, 1994, 510–34.

Schroer, Silvia. "The Book of Sophia." In Searching the Scriptures: Volume 2, A Feminist Commentary, ed. Elisabeth Schüssler Fiorenza. New York: Crossroad, 1994, 17–38.

Schuller, Eileen M. "Women in the Dead Sea Scrolls." In Methods of Investigation of the Dead Sea Scrolls and the Khirbet Qumran Site: Present Realities and Future Prospects, ed. Michael O. Wise et al. New York: New York Academy of Sciences, 1994, 115–31.

Schüssler Fiorenza, Elisabeth. "The Apostleship of Women in Early Christianity." In Women Priests: A Catholic Commentary on the Vatican Declaration, ed. Leonard Swidler and Arlene Swidler. New York: Paulist, 1977, 135–40.

———. But She Said: Feminist Practices of Biblical Interpretation. Boston: Beacon, 1992.

———. "A Feminist Critical Interpretation for Liberation: Martha and Mary: Luke 10: 38–42." Religion and Intellectual Life 3 (1986) 21–35.

———. Jesus: Miriam's Child, Sophia's Prophet: Critical Issues in Feminist Christology. New York: Continuum, 1994.

———. In Memory of Her: A Feminist Theological Reconstruction of Christian Origins. New York: Crossroad, 1983.

———. "Missionaries, Apostles, Coworkers: Romans 16 and the Reconstruction of Women's Early Christian History." Word and World 6 (1986) 420–33.

———. "The 'Quilting' of Women's History: Phoebe of Cenchreae." In Embodied Love: Sensuality and Relationship as Feminist Values, ed. Paula M. Cooey, Sharon A. Farmer, and Mary Ellen Ross. San Francisco: Harper and Row, 1987, 35–49.

———. "Word, Spirit and Power: Women in Early Christian Communities." In Women of Spirit: Female Leadership in the Jewish and Christian Traditions, ed. Rosemary Radford Ruether and Eleanor McLaughlin. New York: Simon and Schuster, 1979, 29–70.

———, ed. Searching the Scriptures: Volume 2, A Feminist Commentary. New York: Crossroad, 1994.

Scopello, Madeleine. "Jewish and Greek Heroines in the Nag Hammadi Library." In *Images of the Feminine in Gnosticism*, ed. Karen L. King. Philadelphia: Fortress, 1988, 71–90.

Scroggs, Robin. "Woman in the New Testament." In *Interpreter's Dictionary of the Bible*. Suppl. vol., ed. Keith Crim. Nashville, TN: Abingdon, 1976, 966–68.

Scullard, H. H. *Festivals and Ceremonies of the Roman Republic*. Ithaca, NY: Cornell University Press, 1981.

Segal, Alan. "Matthew's Jewish Voice." In *Social History of the Matthean Community: Cross Disciplinary Approaches*, ed. David L. Balch. Minneapolis, MN: Fortress, 1991, 3–37.

———. *Rebecca's Children: Judaism and Christianity in the Roman World*. Cambridge, MA: Harvard University Press, 1986.

Seim, Turid Karlsen. *The Double Message: Patterns of Gender in Luke-Acts*. Nashville, TN: Abingdon, 1994.

———. "The Gospel of Luke." In *Searching the Scriptures: Volume 2, A Feminist Commentary*, ed. Elisabeth Schüssler Fiorenza. New York: Crossroad, 1994, 728–62.

Selvidge, Marla J. "Mark 5:25–34 and Leviticus 15:19–20: A Reaction to Restrictive Purity Regulations." *JBL* 103 (1984) 619–23.

———. *Woman, Cult and Miracle Recital: A Redactional Critical Investigation on Mark 5:24–34*. Lewisburg, PA: Bucknell University Press, 1990.

Setzer, Claudia. "Excellent Women: Female Witness to the Resurrection." *JBL* 116 (1997) 259–72.

Siker, Jefferey S. "Gnostic Views on Jews and Christians in the Gospel of Philip." *NovT* 31 (1989) 275–88.

Smith, Jonathan Z. "The Bare Facts of Ritual." In *Imagining Religion: From Babylon to Jonestown*. Chicago: University of Chicago Press, 1982, 53–65.

Smith, Morton. "The History of the Term Gnostikos." In *The Rediscovery of Gnosticism*, Vol. 2: *Sethian Gnosticism*, ed. B. Layton. Leiden: E. J. Brill, 1980, 796–807.

Smith, Richard. "Sex Education in Gnostic Schools." In *Images of the Feminine in Gnosticism*, ed. Karen L. King. Philadelphia: Fortress, 1988, 345–60.

Stead, G. C. "The Valentinian Myth of Sophia." *JTS* 20 (1969) 75–104.

Stendahl, Krister. *Paul among Jews and Gentiles*. Philadelphia: Fortress, 1976.

Stern, Menahem. *Greek and Latin Authors on Jews and Judaism*. Jerusalem: Israel Academy of Science and Humanities, 1980.

Strack, H. L., and G. Stemberger. *Introduction to the Talmud and Midrash*, trans. Markus Bockmuehl. London: T&T Clark, 1991; Minneapolis, MN: Fortress, 1992.

Strange, James F. "Magdala." *ABD* 4:463–64.

Stroumsa, Gedaliahu, A. G. *Another Seed: Studies in Gnostic Mythology*, Nag Hammadi Studies 25. Leiden: E. J. Brill, 1984.

Swidler, Leonard. *Women in Judaism. The Status of Women in Formative Judaism*. Metuchen, NJ: Scarecrow Press, 1976.

Swidler, Leonard, and Arlene Swidler, eds. *Women Priests: A Catholic Commentary on the Vatican Declaration*. New York: Paulist, 1977.

Syme, Ronald. "A Great Orator Mislaid." *Classical Quarterly* 31 (1981) 421–27.

Takács, Sarolta A. *Isis and Sarapis in the Roman World*. Religions in the Graeco-Roman World (formerly EPRO) 124. Leiden: E. J. Brill, 1995.

Talbert, Charles. *Literary Patterns, Theological Themes and the Genre of Luke-Acts*. Missoula, MT: SBL and Scholars Press, 1974.

Tanzer, Sarah J. "Ephesians." In *Searching the Scriptures: Volume 2, A Feminist Commentary*, ed. Elisabeth Schüssler Fiorenza. New York: Crossroad, 1994, 325–48.

Taylor, Walter F., and John H. P. Reumann. *Ephesians, Colossians*. Minneapolis, MN: Augsburg, 1985.

Tetlow, Elizabeth. *Women and Ministry in the New Testament.* New York: Paulist, 1980.

Theissen, Gerd. *The Miracle Stories of the Early Christian Tradition*, trans. Francis McDonagh. Philadelphia: Fortress, 1983.

————. "Social Stratification in the Corinthian Community." In *The Social Setting of Pauline Christianity.* Philadelphia: Fortress, 1982, 92–94.

————. *Sociology of Early Palestinian Christianity.* Philadelphia: Fortress, 1978.

————. Wanderradikalismus: Literatur-soziologische Aspekte der Überlieferung von Worten Jesu in Urchristentum," *ZTK* 70 (1973).

Thomassen, Einar. "The Structure of the Transcendent World in the Tripartite Tractate (NHC I,5)." *VigChr* 34 (1980) 358–75.

Thurston, B. Bowman. *The Widows: A Women's Ministry in the Early Church.* Minneapolis, MN: Fortress, 1989.

Tolbert, Mary Ann. "Mark." In *The Women's Bible Commentary*, ed. Carol A. Newsom and Sharon H. Ringe. Louisville, KY: Westminster/John Knox, 1992, 263–74.

Torjesen, Karen Jo. *When Women Were Priests.* San Francisco: HarperSanFrancisco, 993.

Tran Tam Tinh, Victor. *Isis Lactans.* EPRO 26. Leiden: E. J. Brill, 1973.

Treggiari, Susan. *Roman Marriage: Iusti Coniuges from the Time of Cicero to the Time of Ulpian.* Oxford: Clarendon, 1991.

Trible, Phyllis. "Bringing Miriam out of the Shadows." *Bible Review* 5 (1989) 14–25, 34.

Tuckett, Christopher M. "Feminine Wisdom in Q?" In *Women in the Biblical Tradition*, ed. George J. Brooke. Studies in Women and Religion 31. Lewiston, NY: Edwin Mellen, 1992, 112–28.

————. "Q." *ABD* 5:567–72.

Turner, John D. "The Gnostic Threefold Path to Enlightenment: The Ascent of Mind and the Descent of Wisdom." *NovT* 22 (1980) 324–51.

Turner, John D., and Anne McGuire, eds. *The Nag Hammadi Library after Fifty Years: Proceedings of the 1995 Society of Biblical Literature Commemoration.* NHMS 44. Leiden: E. J. Brill, 1997.

Unger, Dominic J., ed. *St. Irenaeus of Lyons. Against the Heresies.* Ancient Christian Writers, 55. Mahwah, NJ: Paulist, 1992.

Uro, Risto. *Sheep among the Wolves: A Study of the Mission Instructions of Q.* Helsinki: Suomalainen Tiedeakatemia, 1987.

Vaage, Leif E. *Galilean Upstarts: Jesus' First Followers According to Q.* Valley Forge, PA: Trinity Press International, 1994.

Valantasis, Richard, and Vincent L. Wimbush, eds. *Asceticism.* New York: Oxford University Press, 1995.

van der Horst, Pieter. "Portraits of Biblical Women in Pseudo-Philo's Liber Antiquitatum Biblicarum." In *Essays on the Jewish World of Early Christianity.* Göttingen, Germany: Vandenhoeck and Ruprecht, 1990, 111–22.

Via, E. Jane. "Women, the Discipleship of Service and the Early Christian Ritual Meal in the Gospel of Luke." *St. Luke's Journal of Theology* 29 (1985) 37–60.

————. "Women in the Gospel of Luke." In *Women in the World's Religions: Past and Present*, ed. Ursula King. New York: Paragon House, 198.

Walzer, Richard. *Galen on Jews and Christians.* London: Oxford University Press, 1949.

Ward, Benedicta. *Harlots of the Desert: A Study of Repentance in Early Monastic Sources.* Kalamazoo, MI: Cistercian Publications, 1987.

Ward-Perkins, John. *Pompeii A.D. 79: Essay and Catalogue.* New York: Knopf, 1978.

Webster's New International Dictionary. 2nd ed. Unabridged. Springfield, MA: G&C Merriam Company, 1959.

Wegner, Judith. *Chattel or Person: The Status of Women in the Mishnah.* New York: Oxford University Press, 1988.

Whelan, Caroline F. "Amica Pauli: The Role of Phoebe in the Early Church." JSNT 49 (1993) 67–85.

Whelan-Donaghey, Caroline F. "A Rhetorical Analysis of Philippians 4.2–3: Euodia and Syntyche Reconsidered." Paper presented at annual meeting of the Canadian Society of Biblical Studies, University of Quebec at Montreal, 31 May–2 June 1995.

Wilken, Robert L. *The Christians as the Romans Saw Them.* New Haven, CT: Yale University Press, 1984.

Williams, Frank. *The Panarion of Epiphanius of Salamis, Book I (Sects 1–46).* NHMS 35. Leiden: E. J. Brill, 1987.

Williams, Michael A. "The Demonizing of the Demiurge: The Innovation of Gnostic Myth." In *Innovation in Religious Traditions,* ed. Michael A. Williams, Collett Cox, and Martin S. Jaffee. Berlin: Mouton de Gruyter, 1992, 73–107.

———. *The Immovable Race: A Gnostic Designation and the Theme of Stability in Late Antiquity,* Nag Hammadi Studies 29. Leiden: E. J. Brill, 1978.

———. *Rethinking "Gnosticism": An Argument for Dismantling a Dubious Category.* Princeton, NJ: Princeton University Press, 1996.

———. "Uses of Gender Imagery in Ancient Gnostic Texts." In *Gender and Religion: On the Complexity of Symbols,* ed. Caroline W. Bynum, Stevan Harrell, and Paula Richman. Boston: Beacon, 1986, 196–227.

———. "Variety in Gnostic Perspectives on Gender." In *Images of the Feminine in Gnosticism,* ed. Karen L. King. Philadelphia: Fortress, 1988, 2–22.

Wills, Larry. *The Jewish Novel in the Ancient World.* Ithaca, NY: Cornell University Press, 1995.

Wimbush, Vincent L., ed. *Ascetic Behavior in Greco-Roman Antiquity: A Sourcebook.* Minneapolis, MN: Fortress, 1990.

Winter, Sarah C. "Philemon." In *Searching the Scriptures: Volume 2, A Feminist Commentary,* ed. Elisabeth Schüssler Fiorenza. New York: Crossroad, 1994, 301–12.

Wire, Antoinette Clark. *The Corinthian Women Prophets: A Reconstruction through Paul's Rhetoric.* Minneapolis, MN: Augsburg Fortress, 1990.

———. "1 Corinthians." In *Searching the Scriptures: Volume 2, A Feminist Commentary,* ed. Elisabeth Schüssler Fiorenza. New York: Crossroad, 1994, 153–95.

———. "Gender Roles in a Scribal Community." In *Social History of the Matthean Community: Cross Disciplinary Approaches,* ed. David L. Balch. Minneapolis, MN: Fortress, 1991, 87–121.

———. "The Gospel Miracle Stories and Their Tellers." *Semeia* 11 (1978) 83–113.

Wisse, Frederik. "Flee Femininity: Antifeminity in Gnostic Texts and the Question of Social Milieu." In *Images of the Feminine in Gnosticism,* ed. Karen L. King. Philadelphia: Fortress, 1988, 297–307.

Witherington, Ben, III. *Women in the Ministry of Jesus.* Cambridge: Cambridge University Press, 1984.

———. "Women, in the New Testament." *ABD* 6:957–61.

Woolf, Virginia. *Three Guineas.* New York: Harcourt, Brace and World, 1938.

Yadin, Yigal. *Bar Kokhba. The Rediscovery of the Legendary Hero of the Second Jewish Revolt Against Rome.* New York: Random House, 1971.

Yardeni, Ada. *Nahal Se'elim Documents.* Jerusalem: Israel Exploration Society and Ben Gurion University in the Negev Press, 1995.

Young, Frances M. "On EPISKOPOS and PRESBYTEROS." *JTS* n.s. 45 (1994) 142–48.

Young, Steve. "'Being a Man': The Pursuit of Manliness in the *Shepherd of Hermas.*" *JECS* 2/3 (1994) 237–55.

Zaidman, Louise Bruit. "Pandora's Daughters and Rituals in Greek Cities." In *A History of*

Women in the West 1: *From Ancient Goddesses to Christian Saints,* ed. Pauline Schmitt Pantel. Trans. Arthur Goldhammer. Cambridge, MA: The Belknap Press of Harvard University Press, 1992, 338–76.

Zeller, Dieter. "Redactional Processes and Changing Settings in the Q-Material." In *The Shape of Q: Signal Essays on the Sayings Gospel,* ed. John S. Kloppenborg. Minneapolis, MN: Augsburg Fortress, 1994.

INDEX OF ANCIENT
SOURCES CITED

Sources, including biblical books, are arranged alphabetically by author, or by title for anonymous or pseudonymous works. Inscriptions, papyri, and Dead Sea Scrolls are listed separately at the end.

INDEX OF NAMES